Books are to be returned on or before
the last date below.

D1765731

LIBREX—

LIVERPOOL JMU LIBRARY

3 1111 01178 4665

ATTITUDE
STRUCTURE
and FUNCTION _____

The Third Ohio State University
Volume on Attitudes and Persuasion
_____

Edited by
Anthony R. Pratkanis
Steven J. Breckler
Anthony G. Greenwald

1989

LAWRENCE ERLBAUM ASSOCIATES, PUBLISHERS
Hillsdale, New Jersey   Hove and London

Copyright © 1989 by Lawrence Erlbaum Associates, Inc.
All rights reserved. No part of this book may be reproduced in
any form, by photostat, microform, retrieval system, or any other
means, with the prior written permission of the publisher.

Lawrence Erlbaum Associates, Inc., Publishers
365 Broadway
Hillsdale, New Jersey 07642

Library of Congress Cataloging in Publication Data

Attitude structure and function / edited by Anthony R. Pratkanis,
   Steven J. Breckler, Anthony G. Greenwald.
      p. cm.
   Includes index.
   ISBN 0-89859-991-1. ISBN 0-8058-0323-8 (pbk.)
    1. Attitude (Psychology). I. Pratkanis, Anthony R. II. Breckler,
Steven James. III. Greenwald, Anthony G.
BF327.A88 1989
152.4'52—dc 19

88-11142
CIP

PRINTED IN THE UNITED STATES OF AMERICA
10 9 8 7 6 5 4 3 2

CONTENTS

v

Foreword

Daniel Katz
University of Michigan

This volume returns to a central problem of social psychology but not in the sense of Schlesinger's cycles of history. It is not just a revival of the issues of yesteryear, though they are part of the story, as it is a new attack upon the structure and function of attitudes. It reformulates old concepts, explores new angles, seeks relationships among research findings from various sub-areas, digs deeper into the meaning of relevant psychological processes, and shows progress in the sophistication of research design and the specification of the variables concerned.

The concept of attitude has an interesting history as a broadly defined construct combining affect, conation, and belief intervening between stimulus and response. It was incorporated into social psychology by early writers including McDougall in his notion of sentiments and by Floyd Allport in his idea of predispositional sets to respond. In fact John B. Watson defined social psychology as the study of attitudes. The ambiguity of definition gave behaviorists a theoretical back door to admit mental processes and social meaning, on the one hand, and field theorists like Krech and Crutchfield to deal with relatively stable substructures in a dynamic field on the other. Thus attitude research burgeoned during the 1920s and 1930s and Murphy, Murphy, and Newcomb in their *Experimental Social Psychology* (1937) devoted some 157 pages and over 100 references to attitudes and their measurement. But attitude research did not maintain its momentum for two reasons. First, the many investigations produced few generalizable principles. Second, there was little to distinguish attitude from other concepts such as social conformity, stereotypes, habit strength, personality characteristics, schemata, sentiments, or values. There was no set of propositions or systematic hypotheses to guide the researcher and bring clarification to the field.

A push toward unification came with the functional approach. It tried to combine beliefs and motives and to take account of the diversity of motivational patterns. Attitudes were seen as a means for meeting some need of the individual including personal value systems. It called for analysis of the reasons for attitude formation, maintenance, and change. It assumed that change attempts, if they were to be successful, had to be directed at the specific conditions related to the causal basis of the attitude in question. There was some recognition of the plausibility of such theorizing in the early 1950s and some research was generated. But functionalism declined as an area of interest long before it matured and developed as a significant movement.

Four related reasons account for the failure of functionalism to take hold the first time around. First, it lacked a ready and rigorous methodology for the complexity of the problems attacked. Second, it called for a large scale research program of resources and personnel rather than a single experiment—one more readily publishable. Third, it ran counter to the search for a single explanatory concept. Psychologists were essentially monistic in their thinking and had difficulty with a two-factor theory of learning let alone a four-factor theory of attitude formation. And finally, consistency theory with its emphasis on cognitive processes was sweeping everything before it. Field theory replaced behaviorism and Freudian doctrines in social psychology. The concepts of balance, congruity, and dissonance were implemented by ingenious and well-controlled experiments. The swing was back to the rational man.

The impact of consistency theory was great and it made useful contributions—some of lasting importance. The present volume employs some of these findings and theorizing of the consistency literature. The concern with the psychological field of the individual corrected a prior neglect of human being as an active perceiver, interpreter, and thinking creature. People structure and restructure their changing world in ways that make sense to them.

A dilemma arose, however, with respect to objective logic and psychologic. Questions were raised about the predictability and permanence of the changes induced by the experimental setting, often highly contrived and gamelike in character. In more natural settings would individuals be as constrained by logical consistency or would they turn to a psycho-logic that allowed for selectivity, rationalization, and even distortion and denial? With a multitude of experiences and beliefs and conflicting demands, could wish thinking and the will to believe be ignored. When inconsistencies appeared in behavior, why not go beyond some idiosyncratic psycho-logic of an individual to look at the motivational patterns involved? How otherwise could one account for differences produced by the social setting as in the simple case of private and public attitudes? Why exclude studies dealing with the needs, the drives, and the desires of people emphasized by theories of social motivation, reinforcement and reward and the nature of personality determinants? Consistency of cognitive processes was only one chapter in attitude formation and change. A functional approach provided a broader framework and basically this is what the present volume is all about.

Attitude Structure and Function brings together the advances made by linking older functionalism with related bodies of research utilizing more sophisticated methodology and more precision in the definition of concepts. Its chapters examine the relationships between levels of cognitive structure, motives, and behavior in various social settings. It is both more inclusive of psychological findings and digs deeper into the specifics of structure and change. It embraces, as most earlier functional work did not, such important topics as level of representational structure, cognitive style, the relationship of attitudes to other systems, types of value conflict, the salvaging of ideology, the need for structure, the biological homeostatic model, intra-individual relationships of beliefs, behavioral habits and attitudes, the imitation and persistence of attitude change, beliefs as possessions, objective constraints and social settings on attitude formation and change, and the basis for individual differences in functional needs.

The shift toward functionalism came, however, in good part from the impingement of societal forces, often mediated by the other social sciences, upon the narrow scientism of the laboratory and its heavy concern with cognitive processes. The social disciplines bordering and interrelated with social psychology were increasingly under pressure to move from an armchair approach to empirical research to help in the solution of problems in the health field to issues of intergroup relations. Their studies of the dilemmas of racism, discrimination, the institutionalization of social inequities, group conflict, and individual and group adjustment reinstated the interests of the early realistic social psychology concerned with significant social issues. In fact SPSSI has been founded in 1938 for this purpose. Though SPSSI's influence declined after the depression and war years the objects of its concerns have become more salient in public thinking in recent years and once again a functional framework has gained adherents as motivational patterns in all their complexities call for increased study.

The use of a functional approach aids and abets the trend of psychologists to join social scientists to deal more broadly with social issues as the present work attests. The influence of system thinking from biology and sociology is evidenced in a number of chapters. The growth of political psychology is explicitly recognized in discussing the rise and fall of political movements, ther relationship between attitudes and larger belief structures, and the role of elite opinion and political leadership.

LIVERPOOL JOHN MOORES UNIVERSITY
LEARNING SERVICES

Central questions still remain in the development of a functional approach. The core issue is whether some types of attitudes serve different functions and require different conditions and procedures if they are to be changed. Increasing information, for example, about ethnic groups may not affect prejudices whose basis is ego defensive. We need much more experimentation that varies the influence attempts, to see if we can predict specific changes in attitudes. This was the point of departure of the functional approach of the 1950s with a bold and direct attack upon the problem of experimenting with various change procedures directed at different types of attitudes. These experiments were properly criticized for lacking a rigorous methodology. But the objective was lost sight of and the critics did not try to develop operational definitions of the independent and dependent variables that were not confounded. The assessment of motivational patterns and the conditions for changing them or making them salient called for improvements in measurement to provide specifications for the independent variables. Was such assessment always an empirical matter to be explored in every instance in advance of anticipated outcomes or could some generalization derive from experiments that could narrow prior assessment? Are the conditions for attitude formation and change basically external constraints or internal personality characteristics or some combination of the two, and what kinds of combinations or relationships between the two are critical? More attention could have been given in this volume to central questions of operationalization in change experiments. Fortunately some authors did not by-pass the problem and it is highlighted by a chapter dealing with object variation and situation variation.

An underlying rationale for this volume, moreover, is dissatisfaction with the fragmented character of the field with its unrelated pockets of knowledge. Our problem is still one of integrating bits and pieces of validated information into a systematic and adequate set of general principles. *Attitude Structure and Function* with its many excellent chapters, representing diverse interests, will not satisfy those seeking a grand theory in the old style. But it is more than the typical handbook with a compilation of findings. It does move us ahead toward the desired goal. It provides a framework for further unification and brings together authors who emphasize the relationships within and across sub-areas of our discipline. Its forward thrust has a definite answer to the cyclical theory: "No, this is not where we came in."

1

Why Are Attitudes Important?

Anthony G. Greenwald
University of Washington

Before reading beyond this paragraph, the reader might try to answer the question stated as the title of this chapter. Some relevant background starts with Allport's (1935) declaration that attitude is "social psychology's most indispensable concept." Allport apparently regarded the importance of attitudes as being so evident that it was not necessary to detail the basis for his assertion of its importance. Subsequent reviewers have often followed Allport's lead, resting the case for importance of the attitude construct chiefly on its great popularity (e.g., DeFleur & Westie, 1963; Doob, 1947; Fishbein & Ajzen, 1975; McGuire, 1969). However, if the construct of attitude is indeed of major importance, then there must be some important phenomena of social behavior that cannot be explained (or, at least, cannot easily be explained) without appealing to attitudes. But what are the phenomena that would be difficult to explain if *attitude* were stricken from the psychologist's vocabulary? (Here is where the reader can try to answer the question, before reading further.)

WHAT ANSWERS HAVE BEEN OFFERED?

An explanation of the importance of attitudes is not readily found in scholarly reviews or texts. More accurately, the four types of answers that one finds in the literature turn out to be unsatisfying. These are:

Attitudes Are Pervasive

This observation is accurate, as can be verified by noticing (a) the ease with which people report evaluative reactions to a wide variety of objects, (b) the difficulty of identifying categories of objects within which evaluative distinctions are not made, and (c) the pervasiveness of an evaluative component in judgments of meaning (Osgood, Suci, & Tannenbaum, 1957). Nevertheless, the pervasiveness of attitudes is itself not a reason for concluding that attitudes are important in explaining social behavior. As Bem (1967) suggested, attitudes might be cognitive illusions that are constructed after the fact of behavior.

Attitudes Predict Behavior Toward Their Objects

An important, early critique of the usefulness of attitudes in predicting behavior was given by LaPiere (1934). (Problems with LaPiere's critique are reviewed later in this chapter.) Thirty years later, Festinger (1964) critically noted the lack of published support for the reasonable expectation that changes in attitudes should lead to changes in behavior toward their objects. Subsequently, Wicker (1969) reviewed a body of research that revealed only weak correlations between measures of attitudes and measures of behavior toward their objects.

In the 1970s and 1980s two major programs of research succeeded in clarifying attitude-behavior relations. The first of these, directed by Martin Fishbein and Icek Ajzen (e.g., 1974; see chap. 10 in this volume), demonstrated that attitude and behavior are correlated (a) when the observed behavior is judged to be relevant to the attitude, (b) when attitude and behavior are observed at comparable levels of specificity, and (c) when mediation of the attitude-behavior relation by behavioral intentions is taken into account. The second major program, directed by Russell Fazio (e.g., 1986; see chap. 7 in this volume), showed that attitude and behavior, and changes therein, are correlated (a) when the attitude is based on direct experience with the attitude object, and (b) to the extent that the attitude is cognitively accessible.

Although the successful Fishbein–Ajzen and Fazio research programs have established that attitudes can and do predict behavior toward their objects, these programs have also placed important qualifying conditions on the attitude-behavior relationship. Attitude-behavior relations do not appear to be sufficiently powerful or robust to establish the importance of attitude as a theoretical construct. (Further discussion of attitude-behavior relations is found in chap. 3, 7, and 9 of this volume.)

Attitudes Are a Selective Force in Perception and Memory

It has long been supposed that perceptual and cognitive processes are guided by attitudes. The two most-often-stated principles regarding attitude-guided information processing are that persons selectively (a) seek information that agrees with their attitudes while avoiding disagreeing information (e.g., Festinger, 1957), and (b) remember attitude-agreeable information in preference to disagreeable information (e.g., Levine & Murphy, 1943). However, the empirical basis for both of these hypothesized distortions of perception and memory was sharply questioned in the 1960s (e.g., Freedman & Sears, 1965; Greenwald & Sakumura, 1967; Waly & Cook, 1966). It now appears that these selective effects on information seeking and memory occur only under rather limited circumstances (see Wicklund & Brehm, 1976). Consequently, these phenomena do not establish the importance of attitude as a theoretical construct. (Chap. 4 in this volume gives a more detailed review of the role of attitudes in cognitive processes, including evidence for substantial effects on cognitive processes more complex than the seeking and remembering of agreeable information.)

Attitudes Serve Various Psychic Functions

The most direct attention to the importance of attitudes was given in the *functional* analyses of Smith, Bruner, and White (1956) and Katz (1960); they proposed that attitudes serve functions designated by labels such as utilitarian, social adjustment, object appraisal, knowledge, value expression, and ego-defense. Because these functional theories generated little research, claims for functions of attitudes remain largely unsubstantiated. (The poverty of empirical support for attitude functions is only recently beginning to be addressed, with the initiation of research programs such as those described in chap. 4, 6, 12, 13, 14, and 15 in this volume.)

WHY HAS IT BEEN SO DIFFICULT TO DEMONSTRATE THE IMPORTANCE OF ATTITUDES?

Answering this question depends on understanding the relation of attitudes to behavior. Of the three answers to be suggested here, only the first encourages satisfaction with the current understanding of attitudes in relation to behavior.

Difficulty 1: Ordinary Situations Are Attitudinally Complex

In expecting attitudes to predict behavior toward their objects, researchers have often assumed that only a single attitude should be operative in the situation on which their research focused. This assumption is often implausible. LaPiere's (1934) research, which played an important role in criticism of the attitude construct, is used here to illustrate a setting complicated not only by uncertain identification of the focal attitude object, but also by multiple attitude objects beyond the one focal for the researcher.

Uncertain Identification of the Focal Object

In LaPiere's study, he and a young Chinese couple traveled widely in the United States, seeking accommodation at many hotels and restaurants while observing the hotel and restaurant proprietors' attitudes toward Chinese (assessed with a mailed questionnaire) and their behavior of providing accommodations or service to the Chinese couple. LaPiere assumed that the salient attitude object was "members of the Chinese race." However, the couple (who were described as "personable" and "charming") could also have been identified as *customers,* as *middle-class persons,* as *a young married couple,* and so forth. There is little justification for assuming that the only (or even the most) salient attitude-object identification was "members of the Chinese race."

Multiple Attitude Objects

A restaurant proprietor might be concerned that an unpleasant scene with the young Chinese couple could intrude on the meals of *other patrons* or harm the reputation of *the restaurant.* The proprietor's behavior toward the Chinese couple might therefore be as much (or more) influenced by attitudes toward those other objects (i.e., other patrons, the restaurant) as by attitudes toward the young couple. When, as in this situation, additional objects are important, attitude toward the presumably focal object should not dominate the prediction of behavior.

LaPiere's research is not an isolated example of the problems that (a) objects of behavior are difficult to identify in compact verbal labels, and (b) multiple attitude objects are potentially salient.[1] When these problems

---

[1] As Dillehay (1973) and others observed, the interpretation of LaPiere's research in terms of attitude-behavior relations was problematic in other respects. His study compared, not statements of attitude, but predictions of behavior ("Will you accept members of the Chinese race as guests in your establishment?") with actual behavior of hotel and restaurant proprietors toward the Chinese couple. Furthermore, the predictions and actual behavior must often have been assessed for different persons, because of the low likelihood that the person who answered each establishment's mail was also the person who greeted potential patrons.

characterize a research situation, the attitude measured by the researcher should predict behavior only weakly, if at all. Some solutions are to limit research on attitude-behavior relations to objects that are easily identifiable verbally, and to use behavior assessments that lack multiple potential attitude objects. The research successes of Fazio (1986) and of Fishbein and Ajzen (1974) were achieved in large part through such limitations.

Importance of a Phenomenon in Relation to the Difficulty of Demonstrating It

Because strong attitude-behavior correlations are difficult to produce, it may appear that attitudes are only weakly connected to behavior. On the contrary, however, the need for well-controlled research settings to demonstrate strong attitude-behavior relations may mean only that the influence of attitudes on behavior is so pervasive that it is difficult to observe the isolated effect of a single attitude. (An example of a parallel point is the difficulty of observing a classically conditioned response in isolation; in ordinary situations, such as eating a meal, classically conditioned responses are certainly important but are not easily observed due to masking by multiple other conditioned responses.) In general, the difficulty of demonstrating a phenomenon in research is irrelevant to a conclusion about its importance; the difficulty may mean only that the phenomenon is typically embedded in an obscuring degree of complexity.

Difficulty 2: The Concept of Attitude Needs to Be Refined

The Conception of "Attitude Object"

Collectively, and for the most part also individually, attitude researchers have treated virtually any nameable or describable entity as an attitude object. One can find studies of attitudes toward (a) sensory qualities (colors, odors, textures), (b) concrete objects (animals, persons, places, foods), (c) abstract concepts (personality traits, subjects of academic study), (d) verbal statements (beliefs, opinions, policies), (e) systems of thought (aesthetic styles, ideologies), (f) actions (e.g., drinking alcohol, sexual behavior), and even (g) attitudes (e.g., an attitude toward prejudice). The conceptual tolerance represented by this breadth is surely to be encouraged in the early stages of a concept's development. However, the present breadth of the attitude concept may now be an obstacle to theoretical development. That is, the cost that is exchanged for this benefit of breadth may be a lack of precision.

The Three-Component Definition

In noting the variety of definitions that have been offered for *attitude,* previous reviewers have often been reluctant to suggest that one definition is superior to others. Accordingly, many reviewers have supported definitions that (a) permit a broad array of research operations for attitude measurement, and (b) put no apparent boundaries on the sort of entity that can be regarded as the object of an attitude (e.g., Allport, 1935; DeFleur & Westie, 1963; Greenwald, 1968b). The definition that has been most attractive to social psychologists, perhaps because of both its breadth and its ancient philosophical roots, conceives attitude as having three components—*affective, cognitive, and conative* (or behavioral).

> We here indicate that attitudes are predispositions to respond to some class of stimuli with certain classes of responses and designate the three major types of response as cognitive, affective, and behavioral. (Rosenberg & Hovland, 1960, p. 3)

> . . . attitudes [are] enduring systems of positive or negative evaluations, emotional feelings, and pro or con action tendencies with respect to social objects. (Krech, Crutchfield, & Ballachey, 1962, p. 139)

The three-component definition has achieved widespread adoption and almost no criticism. The one active line of criticism has questioned the nature of relationships among the three hypothesized components (cf. Breckler, 1984; Kothandapani, 1971; Ostrom, 1969). This gentle treatment notwithstanding, a harsh evaluation of the three-component definition may be warranted—it appears to have bred confusions that have weakened the attitude construct. Chief among these confusions is that associated with investigations of attitude-behavior relationships. (See Zanna & Rempel, in press, for a similar conclusion about the three-component definition.)

Consider that the following four types of operations involving action in relation to an attitude object can serve equally *either* to measure the conative (behavioral) component of an attitude *or* to measure behavior that is presumably under the control of that attitude component: (a) observations of overt action, (b) verbal self-report of past action, (c) self-report of intentions regarding action, and (d) endorsement of statements about hypothetical actions. With this range of operations, a single research investigation can serve to test (a) the attitude-behavior relationship, (b) relations of the conative to other attitude components, or (c) the relation between behavior and the conative component of attitude. By affording this multiplicity of interpretations, the three-component definition appears to permit too broad an array of interpretations for a given set of data. Additionally, the three-component definition implicitly promotes the (below questioned) supposition that the chief behavioral impact of an attitude should be on behavior *toward* the attitude's object. (Further discussion and critique of the three-component definition is found in chap. 11 and 17 in this volume. Alternative definitions of attitude are suggested in several of this volume's chapters, including the present author's in chap. 17.)

Difficulty 3: The Understanding of Attitude Functions Is Underdeveloped

Through more than 50 years of social psychological study of attitudes, it has been implicitly assumed that the behavioral consequences of an attitude should be most apparent on measures of behavior *toward* the attitude's object. This assumption may be most apparent in critiques of the attitude concept (especially that of Wicker, 1969) that have been based on the empirical weakness of relationships between measured attitude and observed behavior toward the object. However, *there is no compelling theoretical reason to choose behavior toward the attitude object as the only, or even the most important, type of action that should be related to an attitude*. Furthermore, although it has not commonly been taken to the credit of the attitude construct, it is well established that attitudes are powerfully related to behavior that does *not* directly involve the attitude object.

As noted by McGuire (see chap. 3 in this volume), in well-done studies of relations between general measures of attitude and measures of behavior *toward* the attitude object, the proportion of behavior variance predicted by attitude measures is only about 10%. In striking contrast, attitude measures are capable of predicting nearer to 50% of the variance in selected behaviors that do not directly involve the attitude's object. For example, attitude predicts approximately 50% of the variance in the agreement–disagreement dimension of responses to attitude-related persuasive communications (e.g., Greenwald, 1968a; Petty, Ostrom, & Brock, 1981); and the similarity of attitudes between a person and a stranger predicts about 40% of the variance in interpersonal attraction toward the stranger (e.g., Byrne, 1969; Clore & Baldridge, 1968).

Behavior Toward One Object Can Be Controlled by Attitude Toward Another—Illustration

Consider the attitude of one member of a family toward another. Observing just the regular interaction between spouses, or between parents and their children, one might find little in the daily routine to indicate the expected highly positive attitude. Instead, one might observe criticisms, protests, and arguments. However, the spouse/parent's spending 8 or more hours per day at a disliked job may be explainable only in terms of the positive attitudes toward the family members who are supported by the resulting income. Similarly, if one considers the behavior at the disliked job only in terms of the attitude toward the job, again it would appear that attitude and behavior are inconsistent. This is a situation in which the attitude toward each object is *in*consistent with the behavior toward that object, but nevertheless the attitude toward one object (family) fully explains the behavior toward another (job).

A negative attitude toward members of a racial group (prejudice) may explain little in the way of behavior toward persons of that race—with whom the prejudiced person may have little or no contact. However, it can explain much behavior that occurs within groups of persons who share the prejudice or who perceive themselves collectively to be targets of the prejudice.

An attitude against nuclear power may be most apparent in conversations (with friends or acquaintances) that touch on nuclear power, in protest directed against persons who advocate nuclear power or corporations that use nuclear power, or in contributions to organizations that oppose nuclear power. Here the significant behavior is toward some object other than the attitude object (which in this case is an abstract concept).

These examples stand as thought experiments in support of the proposition that an attitude toward one object is often more significant in controlling behavior toward other objects than toward its own object. This major point has not yet been incorporated into theoretical analyses of attitude functions.

CONCLUSION: IMPLICATIONS FOR THE CONCEPT OF ATTITUDE

The first answer to the question, "Why has it been so difficult to demonstrate the importance of attitudes?" attributed the difficulty to the attitudinal complexity of ordinary situations, justifying a business-as-usual approach to attitude research. In contrast, the second and third answers identified conceptual problems that encourage efforts to strengthen theoretical analyses of attitude structure and function. Each of the chapters in this volume presents current programs by researchers who have not been content with the business-as-usual approach. Their research constitutes the leading wave of a revolution in attitude theory. This revolution can be expected to complete the already-begun overthrow of the three-component definition, and to establish effective methods for investigating attitude functions. The concluding chapter of this volume continues the present discussion and attempts to anticipate the next generation of conceptions of attitude structure and function.

REFERENCES

Allport, G. W. (1935). Attitudes. In C. Murchison (Ed.), *A handbook of social psychology* (pp. 798–844). Worcester, MA: Clark University Press.

Bem, D. J. (1967). Self-perception: An alternative interpretation of cognitive dissonance phenomena. *Psychological Review, 74,* 183–200.

Breckler, S. J. (1984). Empirical validation of affect, behavior, and cognition as distinct components of attitude. *Journal of Personality and Social Psychology, 47,* 1191–1205.

Byrne, D. (1969). Attitudes and attraction. In L. Berkowitz (Ed.), *Advances in experimental social psychology* (Vol. 4, pp. 36–89). New York: Academic Press.

Clore, G. L., & Baldridge, B. (1968). Interpersonal attraction: The role of agreement and topic interest. *Journal of Personality and Social Psychology, 9,* 340–346.

DeFleur, M. L., & Westie, F. R. (1963). Attitude as a scientic concept. *Social Forces, 42,* 17–31.

Dillehay, R. C. (1973). On the irrelevance of the classical negative evidence concerning the effect of attitudes on behavior. *American Psychologist, 28,* 887–891.

Doob, L. W. (1947). The behavior of attitudes. *Psychological Review, 54,* 135–156.

Fazio, R. H. (1986). How do attitudes guide behavior? In R. M. Sorrentino & E. T. Higgins (Eds.), *Handbook of motivation and cognition* (pp. 204–243). New York, Guilford Press.

Festinger, L. (1957). *Theory of cognitive dissonance.* Stanford, CA: Stanford University Press.

Festinger, L. (1964). Behavioral support for opinion change. *Public Opinion Quarterly, 28,* 404–417.

Fishbein, M., & Ajzen, I. (1974). Attitudes toward objects as predictors of single and multiple behavioral criteria. *Psychological Review, 81,* 59–74.

Fishbein, M., & Ajzen, I. (1975). *Belief, attitude, intention and behavior: An introduction to theory and research.* Reading, MA: Addison-Wesley.

Freedman, J. L., & Sears, D. O. (1965). Selective exposure. In L. Berkowitz (Ed.), *Advances in experimental social psychology* (Vol. 1, pp. 57–97). New York: Academic Press

Greenwald, A. G. (1968a). Cognitive learning, cognitive responses to persuasion, and attitude change. In A. G. Greenwald, T. C. Brock, & T. M. Ostrom (Eds.), *Psychological foundations of attitudes* (pp. 147–170). New York: Academic Press.

Greenwald, A. G. (1968b). On defining attitude and attitude theory. In A. G. Greenwald, T. C. Brock, & T. M. Ostrom (Eds.), *Psychological foundations of attitudes* (pp. 361–388). New York: Academic Press.

Greenwald, A. G., & Sakumura, J. S. (1967). Attitude and selective learning: Where are the phenomena of yesteryear? *Journal of Personality and Social Psychology, 7,* 387–397.

Katz, D. (1960). The functional approach to the study of attitudes. *Public Opinion Quarterly, 24,* 163–204.

Kothandapani, V. (1971). Validation of feeling, belief, and intention to act as three components of attitude and their contribution to the prediction of contraceptive behavior. *Journal of Personality and Social Psychology, 19,* 321–333.

Krech, D., Crutchfield, R. S., & Ballachey, E. L. (1962). *Individual in society.* New York: McGraw-Hill.

LaPiere, R. T. (1934). Attitudes versus actions. *Social Forces, 13,* 230–237.

Levine, J. M., & Murphy, G. (1943). The learning and forgetting of controversial material. *Journal of Abnormal and Social Psychology, 38,* 507–517.

McGuire, W. J. (1969). The nature of attitudes and attitude change. In G. Lindzey, & E. Aronson (Eds.). *Handbook of social psychology* (2nd ed., Vol. 3, pp. 136–314). Reading, MA: Addison-Wesley.

Osgood, C. E., Suci, G. J., & Tannenbaum, P. H. (1957). *The measurement of meaning.* Urbana, IL: University of Illinois Press.

Ostrom, T. M. (1969). The relationship between the affective, behavioral, and cognitive components of attitude. *Journal of Experimental Social Psychology, 5,* 12–30.

Petty, R. E., Ostrom, T. M., & Brock, T. C. (Eds.). (1981). *Cognitive responses to persuasion.* Hillsdale, NJ: Lawrence Erlbaum Associates.

Rosenberg, M. J., & Hovland, C. I. (1960). Cognitive, affective, and behavioral components of attitudes. In C. I. Hovland & M. J. Rosenberg (Eds.), *Attitude organization and change* (pp. 1–14). New Haven, CT: Yale University Press.

Smith, M. B., Bruner, J. S., & White, R. W. (1956). *Opinions and personality.* New York: Wiley.

Waly, P., & Cook, S. W. (1966). Attitude as a determinant of learning and memory: A failure to confirm. *Journal of Personality and Social Psychology, 4,* 280–288.

Wicker, A. W. (1969). Attitudes versus actions: The relation of verbal and overt behavioral responses to attitude objects. *Journal of Social Issues, 25,* 41–78.

Wicklund, R. A., & Brehm, J. W. (1976). *Perspectives on cognitive dissonance.* Hillsdale, NJ: Lawrence Erlbaum Associates.

Zanna, M. P., & Rempel, J. K. (in press). Attitudes: A new look at an old concept. In D. Bar-Tal & A. Kruglanski (Eds.), *The social psychology of knowledge.* New York: Cambridge University Press.

2

Interdependence of Attitude Theory and Measurement

Thomas M. Ostrom
Ohio State University

Theory contributes to understanding in a variety of ways. Not only should an attitude theory provide a conceptual vocabulary to help organize empirical observations, but it should also identify both the determinants of attitude and the consequences of attitude for thought and behavior. To say that a theory should deal with consequences is to say that it should directly address issues of measurement. Attitude theory and measurement are completely intertwined, and advances in one contribute to (and benefit from) advances in the other.

Explicit attempts to link measurement and theory were absent in a great deal of past attitude research. For example, the problem of cognitive consistency dominated attitude research throughout the 1960s (e.g., Abelson, Aronson, McGuire, Newcomb, Rosenberg, & Tannenbaum, 1968). Yet, nearly all the empirical work in this area ignored issues of measurement. Similarly, research that focused strictly on empirical problems such as communicator credibility and communication discrepancy rarely, if ever, provided a conceptual basis for their measurement operations. These researchers selected their measurement procedures more on the basis of face validity and convenience than on the basis of the measure's relation to theory.

The purpose of this chapter is to illustrate the codevelopment of measurement and theory. It is an expansion on issues first raised in an earlier chapter (Ostrom, 1980). In courses on test construction and philosophy of science students are taught that theory and measurement go hand in hand. Yet, no concrete illustrations of this process are provided. The field of attitudes provides an excellent arena in which to explore this in-

11

terdependence. There has been a considerable amount of empirical work conducted in the area, there have been a large number of theories proposed, and there have been a wide variety of measures developed.

This chapter is not intended as a review of existing methods of measurement. Coverage of the most prominent measurement techniques can be found in other sources such as Dawes and Smith (1985), Mueller (1986), and Ostrom, Bond, Krosnick, and Sedikides (in press).

A listing of attitude theorists who have explicitly addressed the codevelopment of theory and measurement would include Anderson (1981, 1982), Fishbein and Ajzen (1975), Osgood, Suci, and Tannenbaum (1957), Ostrom and Upshaw (1968), Rosenberg (1956), Smith, Bruner, and White (1956), Thurstone (1931), Weiss (1968), and Wyer (1974). This list is not very long considering that attitudes have been under study for over 80 years. Of these theorists, Thurstone was the earliest to explicitly address issues of interdependence between attitude theory and measurement. His work still provides one of the best examples of this interdependence.

THURSTONE: A CASE STUDY OF THEORY AND MEASUREMENT

Social Psychology owes an enormous debt to L. L. Thurstone for his insights regarding the study of attitudes. Although he is often thought of as contributing only to measurement (for his method of equal-appearing intervals), he was actually one of the first to realize that theory and measurement go hand in hand. The development of knowledge about constructs such as attitude, constructs that are hypothetical and thus not amenable to direct observation, demand that equal attention be paid to both theory and measurement.

Thurstone grappled with three different theoretical concerns. One had to do with the nature of the construct of attitude. A second had to do with the nature of the continuum on which attitudes (and attitude statements) were located. The third had to do with the correspondence between person's subjective attitudinal responses and their overt responses.

Thurstone viewed an attitude as a complex psychological entity. By identifying attitudes as complex, he meant that they, like other objects such as chairs or food markets, have a large number of elements and attributes. By recognizing that fact, he dispelled any hope of developing a single quantitative index that would measure all the properties of the wholistic concept *attitude.* He believed that it was as futile to ask a social scientist to measure an attitude as it would be to ask a furniture maker to measure a chair or a business person to measure a food market. Yet in all three instances one can identify one or more features of interest. Just as a business person is usually most interested in a profit–loss analysis of the food market's financial structure, the social psychologist has shown the greatest interest in the positive-to-negative affective character of an attitude.

To have measurement implications, an attitude theory must specify what observables should reflect the construct. Thurstone's conception of attitude focused on subjective attitudinal responses. These responses consist of person's beliefs and thoughts about the attitude object, their affective feelings about the object, and their past actions and future intentions toward the object (Ostrom, 1969). These covert responses could be linguistically represented in the form of opinion statements.

Each attitudinal response (or its corresponding opinion statement) could be located on the evaluative (or positive-to-negative) dimension. Because a person's attitudinal responses would almost certainly differ from one another in their location (or scale value) on the evaluative dimension, a person's attitude under the Thurstone approach was most properly thought of as being a distribution of values rather than a single point on the measurement continuum. A measure of central tendency of the distribution of attitudinal responses (usually the median) provided a best estimate of where the person's overall attitude was located on the continuum.

This overall index, although not inconsistent with the underlying evaluative heterogenity, enabled researchers to systematically study the determinants and correlates of an attitude's evaluative property. It allowed an analysis of individual differences, as well as the differences between groups, in terms of assessing who was generally more pro and who was more anti. Although ignored by most investigators, Thurstone's approach also allowed the testing of hypotheses regarding changes in the shape of the distribution of attitudinal responses. For example, factors producing greater ambivalence should be reflected through an increase in variance of the distribution of attitudinal responses (e.g., Edwards & Ostrom, 1971).

The second use of theory by Thurstone was to devise a way to locate opinion statements on an interval scale (as opposed to nominal or ordinal scales; see Stevens, 1951). If opinion statements could be given interval scale values, then an overall attitude score based on a distribution of those opinions would have interval properties. Interval scales are important because they give meaning to the concept of attitude change. That is, it is important to be assured that one unit of change for a person on the pro side of the continuum is equivalent to one unit of change for a person on the anti side of the continuum.

Thurstone's solution to this problem was to devise a theory of human judgment that would enable him to actually reconstruct the subjective continuum people used when making attitudinal judgments. He developed the "law of comparative judgment" (Thurstone, 1927). Using the principle that "equally often noticed differences are equal," he devised a method of scaling stimuli (opinion items) on interval scales based on persons making pair comparison judgments. The basic notion can be simply illustrated. If attitude statement B is seen as more favorable than attitude statement A by 80% of the subjects, and if attitude statement C is seen as more favorable than attitude statement B by 80% of the subjects, then the attitudinal distance between A and B should be identical to that between B and C.

This theory of human judgment had the additional attractive feature of being capable of disconfirmation through an internal consistency test. If the distance between attitude statements A and C cannot be computed by adding the difference between A and B to the difference between B and C then the theory is disconfirmed. If the internal consistency test fails, then the item scale values do not fall on an interval scale. Fortunately, most applications of the theory have produced item values that are internally consistent.

The main point to be made here is that a theory must be available to validate whether or not the value assigned to opinion items fall on an interval scale. Other theoretical approaches could easily be substituted for this task. For example, Thurstone proposed a "law of categorical judgment," that also provided interval scale values for attitude items. But the values were based on categorical judgment data rather than pair comparison data. More recently developed theoretical models that can be used to obtain interval scale values are the direct magnitude estimation approach of Stevens (1968, 1975) and the functional measurement approach to Anderson (1976, 1982).

It should be noted that in most of the scale construction efforts of Thurstone and his students, the atheoretical methodology of equal-appearing intervals was used most often. In this approach, item scale values were simply the average rating given the item by a group of subjects on a pro-to-anti rating scale. No theory of human judgment suggested that these scale values fell on an interval scale nor were they validated by tests of internal consistency. Instead, this approach was validated empirically. It was thought of as a rough-and-ready approximation to the theoretically more exacting (but far more time consuming) methods of pair comparisons and successive intervals. Early research validated its use by showing that a linear relationship exists between equal-appearing interval scale values and the values obtained through the application of the law of comparative judgment and the law of categorical judgment (e.g., Saffir, 1937).

Thurstone's third major theoretical concern had to do with whether or not subjects' overt responses to the opinion items on the attitude questionnaire provided an adequate estimate of the subjects' distribution of subjective attitudinal responses. Unlike the other two theoretical concerns, he did not have a well-developed theory for this problem area. Instead, he chose to make several assumptions that, unfortunately, have yet to be adequately evaluated.

Because the objective of the measurement task is to provide an estimate of the subjects' distribution of attitudinal responses, it is crucial that the questionnaire contain a representative sample of opinion items. Thurstone's item selection procedure insured that all points along the attitude continuum were equally represented, but it did not insure that all possible content themes would be represented in the set of selected items. The diversity of item content was necessarily restricted by the practical need to limit the total number of items to 20 or 25 and to exclude items that were ambiguously located on the continuum (i.e., items with high variance or Q-values). No procedure was developed to maximize the heterogeneity of the selected items.

There is a second possible source of discrepancy between subjective attitudinal responses and the overt responses given to the opinion items. Subjects may not endorse all of the opinion statements they actually agree with or reject all the items they privately disagree with. They may, for example, be embarrassed to indicate agreement with socially undesirable opinions. Also, for reasons of social desirability they may choose to indicate agreement with statements with which they actually disagree.

This problem of nonrepresentative (or inaccurate) endorsements may not arise only from social desirability concerns. The psychoanalytic tradition speculates that many beliefs are hidden in the subconscious, especially those that are heavily emotion-laden. This suggests that people may just be unaware of some of their subjective attitudinal responses. Indeed, people may actually deny or distort some of their deeply held feelings.

The seriousness of distortions introduced by such biases has yet to be thoroughly explored in attitude measurement, although some work using the "bogus pipeline" has undertaken to examine the contribution of social desirability to these biases (Jones & Sigall, 1971; Ostrom, 1973). Most researchers have assumed that unless subjects are given an explicit incentive to behave in a socially desirable way, their pattern of endorsements are subject to only minimal distortion. This is especially likely to be the case under conditions of anonymous responding, conditions that are common research practice in this area.

As mentioned previously, Thurstone did not provide any explicit theory on the problems of establishing the correspondence between overt and covert attitudinal responses. However, his careful theoretical work in the other two areas make the problems of correspondence more easily recognizable and specifiable.

Thurstone's contributions offer a nice illustration of the codevelopment of theory and measurement. However, theoretical conceptions and measurement methods are interdependent in other ways. In fact, each has had a profound influence on the other. Two major points are developed in the remainder of this chapter. It shows how the easy availability and common usage of certain methods has influenced the conceptual and empirical problems studied. Conversely, it also describes how specific conceptions of attitude have guided researchers in their selection of measurement techniques. These issues are explored in the next two sections.

THE INFLUENCE OF METHOD
ON UNDERSTANDING ATTITUDES

Method has affected the study of attitudes in at least two general ways. The very definition of attitude has shifted over the last 40 years, due in large measure to wide-spread adoption of particular methodologies. Second, the techniques themselves have prompted researchers to explore new empirical phenomena.

Conceptual Status of Attitude

Thurstone's conception of attitude stood in distinct contrast to the definition that was more popularly accepted during the 1920s and 1930s (Allport, 1935; Merton, 1940). The most influential analysis of attitudes in that era was offered by Gordon Allport (1935). Although his definition of attitude is still widely cited in modern texts, it is probably the least well-understood by contemporary students in the field of attitude change. Indeed, since 1935, an enormous shift has taken place in how the construct of attitude is used in social psychology.

The central idea of Allport's definition was that an attitude is a state of readiness that exerts a dynamic influence upon an individual's responses. Allport used the term *attitude* to cover nearly all psychological states in which a person has some readiness to respond. These circumstances range from a momentary mental or motor set (as when a footracer awaits the starting gun) to comprehensive and stable dispositions (as with a system of values or a philosophy of life). With such a spectrum of dispositions included under the concept of attitude, at the time, it was impossible for Allport and other workers to view attitudes in Thurstone's terms. They felt his emphasis on the evaluative dimension misrepresented and trivialized the construct.

Allport agreed that many attitudes do have an evaluative dimension. In reading his chapter one gets the impression that he feels this evaluative feature is primarily characteristic of more primitive and childish attitudes. In adult life we develop many more complicated and subtle "readinesses." Although Allport (1935) acknowledged that many attitudes show a positive or negative character, he also noted that:

And yet attitudes are not readily classified (as positive or negative). What shall one do, for example, with a detached, impersonal, or judicial attitude, or with an attitude of neutrality? Complacency, amusement, tolerance, and open-mindedness are not easily reduced to "affect for or against" an object . . . Is the degree of positive or negative affect aroused by the concept of "God" as significant as the *qualitative* distinctions involved in theistic, diestic, pantheistic, agnostic, intellectualistic, or emotional attitudes? When one speaks of attitudes toward sex, it is obviously only the qualitative distinctions that have any intelligible meaning. What is a "serene and benevolent mind?" Certainly not one devoid of attitudes, nor yet one that is a battleground of tendencies "for" and tendencies "against." All of these objections to the unidimensional view argue strongly for the recognition of the *qualitative* nature of attitudes. (pp. 819–820)

This passage not only illustrates Allport's opposition to a unidimensional view of attitudes, but it provides an abundant sampling of the different kinds of attitudes (or "readinesses") that he felt could be fit under one theoretical term.

Allport's broad conception of attitudes also led him to overlook any necessity of endowing all attitudes with an object. Whereas Thurstone's unidimensional view demanded that the pro or con disposition be directed toward a specific attitude object, Allport chose not to incorporate the concept of an attitude object into his definition. Indeed, it would seem impossible to designate a specific object for Allport's impersonal attitudes, complacent attitudes, or emotional attitudes.

One should not get the impression that Allport was alone in his conception of attitudes. He lists 16 definitions of attitude in his chapter, and only two argue that attitudes should be viewed as falling on an evaluative continuum and directed toward a specific object. The remainder, in some form or another, endorse the broader "readiness to respond" conception of attitude.

A silent revolution has occurred over the 5 decades since Allport's chapter appeared. One can examine the attitude chapters in many introductory social psychology texts, as well as in many text books on theories of attitudes, and not find one study dealing with the broad Allport conception of "readiness." Nearly all the research deals with the evaluative dimension of attitudes.

This is not to say that social psychologists have ignored the other kinds of dispositions that Allport addressed in his chapter. What has happened instead, is that those dispositions are no longer called attitudes. Problems of aggression, affiliation, conformity, altruism, values, and stereotyping all appear relevant to Allport's conception, but are omitted from attitude chapters. Instead they have their own separate chapters in contemporary introductory textbooks.

An entirely different set of Allport "readinesses" consists of constructs like need for achievement, need for affiliation, social desirability tendencies, internal–external locus of control, and authoritarian attitudes. These are usually not covered at all in social psychology textbooks. Instead, they are discussed in books dealing with theories of personality.

How did method contribute to this conceptual revolution? The shift was primarily due to the character of the dominant research methodologies in use during the 1930s, 1940s, and 1950s. Empirical advances could only be made if some way was found to quantify the concept of attitudes. Allport's diffuse conception did not point the way to any rigorous quantification. Alternatively, Thurstone's view of attitude allowed one to preserve the potential richness desired by Allport (by agreeing that attitude is a complex psychological entity), while permitting empirical advances to be made in understanding the evaluative dimensions of attitude.

Although they adopted somewhat different views about the nature of attitudes, the measurement procedures of Thurstone and his contemporaries (Guttman, 1944; Likert, 1932/1933) all preserved the unidimensional logic of attitude measurement. The few studies that tried to examine the qualitative features of attitude (see the classic work by Smith, Bruner, & White, 1956) proved to be enormously cumbersome and time-consuming to conduct. The later development of multidimensional techniques (e.g., factor analysis, latent structure analysis, and multidimensional scaling) only reinforced this tendency. They allowed the examination of more than one dimension of attitude, and, at the same time, preserved the basic logic of Thurstone that the several dimensions of attitude were isolatable.

Two other methodological forces contributed to this conceptual shift. One was the discovery of statistical hypothesis testing procedures. Not long after Thurstone's unidimensional measures became available, R. A. Fisher's (1938) analysis of variance approach for the statistical analysis of research data was gaining acceptance. It was ideally suited for the analysis of dimensional measures. And by the 1960s, almost all published attitude studies employed his analytic approach.

Even if Allport had been able to develop measures that could make the qualitative aspects of an attitude available for empirical examination, he would have found it difficult to quantify them in a way that would allow the use of analysis of variance designs for data analysis. The qualitative features of attitude that interested Allport could not be captured on an interval scale, which is a prerequisite for using analysis of variance.

The technique of analysis of variance also encouraged the use of laboratory experiments in which subjects are randomly assigned to conditions. This advance in experimental design allowed, for the first time, causal predictions generated from attitude theory to be tested. It was difficult to predict causal relationships on the basis of Allport's qualitative view of attitude. It was just too complex (and amorphous) a construct. Most theorists adopted the more manageable approach of theorizing about the evaluative component exclusively. Advances in experimental design and methods of data analysis contributed substantially to the widespread adoption of the unidimensional view of attitude.

New Attitudinal Phenomena

It is easy to underestimate how much the field of social psychology has learned about attitudes in the last 50 years. Findings that appear obvious today were often surprising to the early workers. With their qualitative view of attitude as a readiness to respond, it was easy for these workers to be overwhelmed by the complexities of an attitude. Through introspection or through interviewing another person, they would encounter a wide variety of beliefs, feelings, remembrances, and policy stands toward the attitude object.

These qualitative differences between persons' attitudes must have seemed incredibly complex and diffuse. To these workers, it was nearly an impossible task to scientifically capture any differences between the attitudinal responses of any two persons or any two groups of persons. How could the researcher ever hope to measure the many ways a nun and a prostitute differed in their attitude toward sex? Yet, with the advent of unidimensional measurement techniques, such questions could be and were answered.

Much of the early research with the Thurstone technique was directed toward discovering that stable individual and group differences existed for a variety of attitudes. It was an open question as to whether attitudes were stable over time, that the attitude expressed today can be predicted from the attitude expressed last month. This early work established that across a variety of attitude objects, attitudes were stable, that the attitude scales showed high test-retest reliability.

It was a separate issue to show that each person had different attitudes toward different objects. It was necessary to establish that attitudes were not just an extension of a general disposition to be positive or negative toward objects in general. The methods developed by Bogardus (1925) and Remmers and Silance (1934), along with the later semantic differential procedures of Osgood, Suci, and Tannenbaum (1957), had the capacity to measure attitudes toward a variety of objects on a common scale. This work clearly showed that people commonly hold widely different attitudes toward different objects.

It may even have been surprising to find that people agreed with one another in their ratings of opinion items on the evaluative dimension, a task that was required of Thurstone's subjects in the equal-appearing intervals

item sorting task. It was impressive to show that considerable social consensus existed in the ordering of statements of attitude on a pro-to-anti
continuum (Thurstone & Chave, 1929). Similarities in judgment were even
found between groups that come from such different backgrounds as Blacks
and Whites (Hinckley, 1932).

No one would be surprised today to find high intercorrelations among
opinion items that all relate to the same attitude object. We take it for
granted that if a man agrees with one pro democracy item he is likely to
agree with other pro democracy items. This, however, was not the case
when Likert (1932/1933) conducted his original scaling studies. He reported that he originally expected to find that there was little or no
correlation among items of attitude toward the Blacks. This was because for
the items he used, there was no logical requirement that agreement with
one item demanded either agreement or disagreement with any other item.
For example, the belief that all Blacks are lazy does not compel the belief
that it would be undesirable to have a Black live in one's neighborhood.
Likert reported that because of the high intercorrelations, the data forced
him to conclude that there must be a single pro or anti attitude underlying
subjects' responses to all items in the set. In a real sense, the Likert
technique led to the discovery that belief homogeneity (now referred to as
internal consistency) underlies all attitudes.

Not Until the work of Guttman and Suchman (1947) was attention given
to the concept of a zero point. Guttman's (1944) theory of scalogram
analysis for attitude measurement does not allow direct identification of a
zero point, rather it simply orders items (and people) on the attitude
continuum. Yet, for the purpose of predicting positive (approach) or negative (avoidant) response tendencies it is necesary to identify a neutral point.

Guttman and Suchman reasoned that the midpoint should coincide with
the region of the scale where people held their beliefs with the least
intensity (as measured by strength of agreement). Over a variety of attitude
issues they found a U-shaped relation between attitude and intensity, in
which people in the mid-region of the scale held the least intense attitudes.
Here again we see that a measurement concern (locating the zero point) led
to the discovery of a curvilinear relation between attitude extremity and
intensity.

As new measurement techniques emerge, new questions about the nature of attitudes arise. Each method embodies its own view of attitude and
alerts the researcher to phenomena that emerge within the context of that
view. But as mentioned previously, it is not a one-way process. Just as the
development of a method may alter our conception of attitude and alert us
to new relationships, concerns of a strictly conceptual nature can guide us
in the construction of new methods.

THE INFLUENCE OF THEORY
ON ATTITUDE MEASUREMENT

Even though contemporary conceptions of attitude are much more restricted (and specific) than those offered by Allport, they remain ambiguous in several respects. The theorist is obligated to be specific about both the property of attitude and the hypotheses being tested, because each have implications for how the dependent measure is constructed. This section outlines three different ways in which methodological decisions are determined by the nature of the researcher's theoretical objectives.

Specifying a Property of Attitude

The researcher must always keep in mind that an attitude, like a food store, is a very complicated entity. It is an entity composed of a heterogeneous array of thoughts and other responses relevant to the attitude object. As such, it has the potential of being analyzed along a large number of dimensions. The first task of the theorist, then, is to designate what features of attitude his or her research is directed toward.

Which Conceptual Property of Attitude?

The evaluative dimension has been the focus of most past attitude research. It is viewed as being bipolar, running from positive (or pro, favorable, likes, supports) to negative (or anti, unfavorable, dislikes, opposes). The continuum has a zero point where the valence shifts from one pole to the other. Attitudes also vary in extremity within each pole. For example, people can have positive attitudes ranging from slightly pro to extremely pro.

The popularity of the evaluative dimension is due in part to its intuitive appeal. When we speak with others about our attitude toward a specific object, we most often seem to convey overall likes and dislikes. Consider your own response to questions like "What is your attitude toward turnips?," "What do you think about abortion?," "What are your feelings toward the president?," and "What is your attitude toward communism?" In all cases, your first subjective reactions probably reflected one or the other evaluative pole.

A second reason for focusing on the evaluative dimension is that it holds the most promise for predicting behavioral reactions toward the attitude object. Evaluative bipolarity relates directly to approach/supportive behaviors on the one hand and avoidant/antagonistic behaviors on the other. Although other dimensions may bear on the likelihood of action, it is primarily the evaluative dimension that reflects the direction of the behavioral act.

Theorists have shown interest in many properties other than the evaluative dimension. A reasonably comprehensive summary of these other properties was provided by Scott (1968); intensity, ambivalence, salience, affective salience, cognitive complexity, overtness, flexibility, and consciousness. An even more extensive array of attitudinal properties have been catalogued by Pratkanis (chap. 4 in this volume).

Recall that Thurstone viewed attitude as a set of subjective responses toward the attitude object. These responses do not stand in cognitive isolation from one another, but can be interconnected in a variety of ways. Some researchers have examined the structure of those responses. For example, Zajonc (1960) developed a procedure that not only assessed the dimensionality of attitudinal beliefs, but allowed an identification of which beliefs were most central to the entire attitude structure. Scott, Osgood, and Peterson (1979) extensively studied a large number of different measures of structure. Fazio (chap. 7 in this volume) studies the accessibility of the attitude and Pratkanis (chap. 4 in this volume) investigates the dimensionality and organization of attitudinal knowledge structures.

The semantic differential (Osgood, Suci, & Tannenbaum, 1957) provides one popular way of assessing the dimensional character of responses to an attitude object. This approach starts with the view that all objects have a connotative (as distinct from denotative) meaning. The structure of this connotative meaning can be retrieved by having people rate the object on a variety of bipolar scales. A factor analysis of those ratings typically reveals three dimensions: evaluative (e.g., good/bad), potency (e.g., strong/weak), and activity (e.g., fast/slow). A nice feature of this approach is that it provides information about the traditional evaluative dimension along with the two other dimensions. It illustrates better than most other methods Thurstone's point that the evaluative dimension is only one of many dimensions that can characterize a set of attitudinal responses.

In addition to such structural concerns, one can also study the emotional aspects of an attitude. These include motivational and arousal features such as the degree of confidence or level of certainty people have in their attitude, how intensely it is held, how important or salient it is to them, and the extent of their ego involvement. Of this list, only importance and ego involvement have received any extensive theoretical attention (e.g., Judd & Krosnick, chap. 5 in this volume; Ostrom & Brock, 1968; Sherif, Sherif, & Nebergall, 1965).

Investigators do, on some occasions, assess more than one facet of the attitude. In the outstanding book by Smith, Bruner, and White (1956), an impressive attempt was made to comprehensively assess the attitudes of ten different American men toward Russia. Not only did they assess the evaluative dimension (which they termed *object value*), they also measured the degree of differentiation, the salience of the attitude, its time perspective (or temporal frame of reference), the extensiveness of the person's informational support, and the action tendencies and policy stands that characterized the attitude. Seven different methods were used to assess these attitudinal features. Each subject was given an open-ended interview on Russia, a polling interview, an information test, a conformity interview, an information apperception test, a cartoon stereotype test, and a stress interview. These were embedded amidst 28 measurement procedures that took 15 weekly 2-hour sessions to complete.

This study provides one of the best illustrations of research in which the investigators clearly specified the theoretically relevant properties of attitude and then devised corresponding measurement procedures. But given the amount of work required for such a comprehensive assessment of the multiple properties of an attitude, it is not surprising that few researchers have emulated this excellent example of scholarship. Thankfully, researchers persevere in the difficult task of measuring attitude functions. Chapters 12, 13, and 14 in this volume all describe advances that have been made in this area.

Central Tendency or Variance?

Most unidimensional measures yield a single numerical value to index the person's location on the dimension. These measures make the tacit assumption that attitude can be represented as a single point on the continuum. But one need not view attitude as a single point. As previously mentioned, Thurstone's measures also allow for the computation of the variance of the distribution of opinions.

Thurstone's assumption that each person's attitudinal responses are distributed across the continuum led Edwards and Ostrom (1971) to argue that people differ in the extent to which their beliefs cluster closely (or are widely dispersed) around the point on the continuum representing their overall attitude. They showed that whereas people can have equivalent neutral attitudes as assessed by a single index of central tendency, the dispersion of their beliefs can vary widely. They found that dispersion was a function of the range of information people received at the time they formed their attitude. Subjects receiving evaluatively heterogeneous information showed an ambivalent distribution of beliefs, whereas subjects receiving homogeneously neutral information showed a more assertively neutral array of beliefs.

In a similar vein, Sherif (e.g., Sherif, Sherif, & Nebergall, 1965) argued that attitude ought to be represented as a set of regions on the continuum. That is, an attitude leads one to accept a certain range of beliefs or policies, reject another range, and be indifferent to the remainder. Their latitude of acceptance then, refers to the evaluative range of attitude-relevant beliefs or policy stands that one endorses.

Need for More Diverse and Comprehensive Theory

Most attitude theories (c.f. Abelson et al., 1968; Fishbein & Azjen, 1975; Greenwald, Brock, & Ostrom, 1968; Kiesler, Collins, & Miller, 1969; Petty & Cacioppo, 1986; Petty, Ostrom, & Brock, 1981) focus exclusively on the evaluative continuum. Although it may be that this is the most pervasive feature of attitude, it is time that researchers begin devising theories and methods to advance understanding of the other dimensions. To the extent that we are ever to acquire a comprehensive body of knowledge, multivariate approaches (Smith, Bruner, & White, 1956) to theory and method must also be developed.

We are now beginning to see clear progress on this problem. Lingle and Ostrom (1981) showed that the information processing approach to cognition provides one useful approach to understanding how attitudinal information is stored in memory. The present volume is primarily devoted to improving our understanding of the structure and functions of attitude. The evaluative property is regarded as only one constituent of a more elaborate psychological system.

What Responses Should Be Measured?

A second role of theory is to guide the researcher in selecting responses for observation. Once a dimension (or dimensions) is selected for study, the researcher must decide what responses to observe for empirical investigation. A theory offers guidance in determining what responses are relevant to attitude processes and what responses are irrelevant. There is almost an infinite number of behavioral characteristics one could potentially choose to record when observing another. Theory offers a spotlight that allows us to identify the responses that are conceptually germane. Different theories, even about the same dimension, guide the researcher to measure different responses.

Problems of response selection have been most explicitly addressed by the cognitive theories of attitude, and those theories are used to illustrate the main issues presented in this section. The cognitive view of attitude requires one to sample thoughts or beliefs the person holds about the attitude object. Four different concerns arise when attempting to sample a person's attitude-relevant thoughts. The investigator must decide what the content of the thoughts is, what their subjective properties are, what aggregation rule to use, and what the domain of response generalization is.

Content

Thurstone was not very specific about the content of attitude-relevant thoughts. He advocated simply looking at any and all opinion statements that were relevant to the attitude object. Such opinion statements could contain a wide variety of content themes. This view is also consistent with more recent work on the *cognitive response* approach toward attitudes (Greenwald, 1968; Petty & Cacioppo, 1986; Petty, Ostrom, & Brock, 1981). In this latter approach, persons are invited to list all of the thoughts they have about the attitude object after they (the persons) were exposed to a persuasive communication. No constraints are placed on the number or relevance of these thoughts. The index of overall attitude is derived from persons' own judgments of how positive or how negative each of the thoughts is.

Other theories have been more restrictive in the content of attitudinal responses they consider relevant to their theory. Rather than sampling from all attitudinal beliefs, Rosenberg (1956) chose to focus on how the attitude object was related to the person's important values. His model was derived from the view that attitudes perform a value-maintenance function for the individual (Katz, 1960), so it was theoretically important to employ personal values in the measurement instrument. Other functions of attitude, such as those explored by Shavitt (chap. 12 in this volume), guide the researcher to focus on different subcategories of content.

The semantic differential approach to measurement (Osgood, Suci, & Tannenbaum, 1957) evolved from a learning theory analysis of attitudes. Connotative meaning is acquired through repeated pairing of the attitude object with experiences that are either positive or negative, powerful or weak, and active or passive. It followed, therefore, that the underlying evaluative reaction (along with the other connotative reactions) evoked by an attitude object should be assessed by having persons rate the object on bipolar trait scales that reflect these dimensions.

In general, theory has not provided much guidance to the researcher in identifying the proper content for opinion items to be used on scales of measurement. And perhaps this is proper for studies that focus only on the overall evaluative disposition. However, the chapters in this volume make evident that, as our conceptions of structure and function become more refined, the importance of specifying content becomes a more important constituent of the research process.

Properties of the Response

Theory must also relate properties of the overt reponse to the conceptual dimension of interest. As Fishbein and Azjen (1975) argued, cognitive theories focus on two different properties of thought (and of the overt

expression of thought in the form of opinion items). First, people differ in
the extent to which they *believe* the attitude object possesses any given
characteristic. Second, people differ in whether or not they believe each
characteristic is *desirable* or *undesirable.*

One approach to measuring these two subjective properties requires the
subject to personally estimate both properties for every belief they hold
(e.g., Fishbein, 1967). Other approaches (e.g., Thurstone, 1931) obtain
normative scale values for the evaluative character of each belief and ask the
subject to provide only the belief response (i.e., agree vs. disagree) for each
attitude item. Other theories (e.g., Wyer, 1974) require not only simple
judgments of belief strength (in the form of subjective probabilities), but
also judgments of conditional probabilities (the probability of one belief
being true, given that another is true).

Other subjective properties of overt responses need to be assessed if one
is measuring features of attitude other than the evaluative dimension (see
Pratkanis, chap. 4 in this volume). For example, Zajonc's (1960) approach
requires people to make dependency judgments in order to measure
structural characteristics. After listing their beliefs about the attitude object,
subjects are asked to esimate how much they would revise their agreement
with each belief, given they had changed their minds about each of the
other beliefs in turn. As another example, structural measures that employ
multidimensional scaling are often based on judgments of similarity (Rosenberg & Sedlak, 1972). Here the respondent is required to indicate for all
pairs of beliefs, how similar or dissimilar one belief is to the other belief in
the pair.

All the properties reviewed refer to the subjective perceptions a person
has regarding the attitude object and its constituent elements. The focus has
been on whether the rating was high or low on the scale. But another
property of theoretical interest is the speed of response. Working from a
Hullian learning theory approach, Weiss (1968) asked subjects to agree or
disagree with opinion statements and measured the response latency. This
provided an index of excitatory potential as required by the theory, and
allowed a comparison of persuasion effects in humans with learning theory
principles that had been tested across a variety of tasks and species. Response time has also come into use more recently as information processing
constructs have been brought to bear on the analysis of attitudes (e.g.,
Lingle & Ostrom, 1981; Fazio, chap. 7 in this volume).

Aggregation Rule

A theory should specify the aggregation rule used to combine the
obtained properties into a single attitude score. In his method of equal-
appearing intervals, Thurstone advocated the use of the median to estimate
the overall attitude from the distribution of scale values of the endorsed

attitude items. Any measure of central tendency would have been theoretically appropriate, but because only a small sample of beliefs were obtained for each object, he believed the median would be the most stable estimate.

Other theorists (e.g., Fishbein, 1967; Rosenberg, 1956) adopted a *sums-of-products* aggregation rule. This procedure involves obtaining the product of the belief and evaluative judgments for each attitude statement. The use of multiplication insures that a strongly held belief (whether positive or negative) is weighed more heavily than a weakly held belief. Also, because beliefs can have a negative sign (that is, be a disbelief), a positive attitude is implied by disbelief toward a negatively valued characteristic of the attitude object. For example, it is attitudinally positive to reject the belief that nuclear power is dangerous.

The *sums* part of this rule requires that the *product* obtained for each attitude item be summed over all items. Because the sign of the product is retained, this aggregation rule yields an index ranging from positive to negative. Summation carries with it the presumption that the more beliefs one has, the more extreme one's attitude may become.

An alternative aggregation rule was explored in an extensive program of research by Anderson (1981). He showed that in first impression settings (i.e., the initial formation of interpersonal attitudes), people aggregate information on the basis of a weighted averaging rule rather than a sums-of-products rule. The basic difference is that people average the products rather than sum them. Although the averaging rule appears correct for describing how people integrate information in first impression settings, it has not yet been shown that this rule applies to the spontaneous sampling of thoughts people have at the time they are asked to express an attitude.

It is possible, of course, that people do not aggregate their thoughts at all when expressing or acting on attitudes in everyday settings. Instead they may just sample one or two of their thoughts and base their overt attitudinal responses on that sample. People may select the most salient, the most important, the most extreme, the most representative, or the most bland thought they have about the attitude object and base their response on that one thought alone. As shown by Ebbesen (1981) and Lingle and Ostrom (1981), knowledge about this problem is best advanced by borrowing methodologies from the field of cognitive psychology.

Domain of Response Generalization

When designing an attitude measure, investigators must consider the domain of attitudinal responses to which they wish to generalize. It is probably true that many beginning investigators come to grief in their research because of lack of attention to this problem. If a study is designed to influence one set of attitudinal responses, but a different set is being measured, it is unlikely that supportive results would be obtained. Two general areas of concern have been identified by Ostrom (1972).

The first problem has to do with whether the investigators' predictions relate to specific or to generalized attitudinal responses. If a persuasive communication focuses on a specific subset of arguments (e.g., the economic, rather than social or political consequences of a government policy) than the strongest experimental effects should be on just that one belief or subset of beliefs. When studying an independent variable (such as communicator credibility), the effects of that manipulation should appear most clearly on an attitude instrument designed to tap the specific beliefs presented in the communication. The general rule is that the attitude instrument should be most sensitive to the specific arguments contained in the message.

There are some circumstances under which investigators are interested in studying the remote effects of a communication. One important research problem is to find out whether a persuasive attack on specific beliefs will have indirect effects on other beliefs and attitudes (e.g., McGuire, 1960, 1981; Steele & Ostrom, 1974; Tannenbaum, 1967; Wyer, 1974). For example, McGuire's work on syllogistic reasoning examined the conditions under which a persuasive message that influenced the strength of belief in the premise of an argument would have detectable remote effects on a conclusion.

Attitude items can be clustered into different qualitative categories. For example, attitudinal responses can be categorized as affective, conative, or cognitive (c.f. Breckler, 1984; Ostrom, 1969; Upshaw, 1968). An investigator may have different predictions for how a given experimental treatment might influence each of the different item subsets. Research on the relationship between attitude and behavior deals with this problem. This research could benefit by employing an approach that measured the behavioral and affective components on the same evaluative continuum. This would allow any discrepancies to be measured on a common scale. Just such a procedure was devised by Ostrom (1969). These general issues are addressed more extensively in several other chapters in this volume.

The second major concern regarding response generalization has to do with whether the research focuses on a specific attitude dimension or whether it concerns the general *yielding response.* In the former case, both the persuasive communication and measurement instrument pertain solely to a single attitude object. The question is whether the communication moves the attitude in the pro or anti direction on the evaluative continuum. All the opinion items should be relevant to the single attitude object addressed in the communication.

Different considerations arise when the focus is on the yielding response. In these studies, subjects are asked to indicate the extent to which they agree or disagree with the several stands advocated by the communicator. In this case, both the communication and the response measure could include beliefs about a variety of different attitude objects. The focus of a yielding study is on the extent to which a person will agree with a communicator, regardless of the specific nature of the arguments made in the message. Indeed, one may have greater confidence in the conclusion of a yielding study if the attitude objects and beliefs that were attacked in the persuasive message are highly heterogeneous.

Yielding studies present the scale constructor with an interesting situation. It is the one case in which a test need not be internally consistent. If a message involves a variety of attitude topics that are not related to one another, then there is no reason to find a homogenous pattern of intercorrelations among the subjects' postcommunication responses. The evaluative disposition toward the several objects may be entirely uncorrelated. Yielding an equivalent amount on each dimension will have no effect on the pattern of intercorrelations. On the other hand, internal consistency should be obtained among the pre–post change scores obtained separately for the several different agree–disagree scales in the attitude test.

Metric Properties of the Scale

The preceding subsections of this chapter addressed two general ways in which theory influences measurement. One was through specifying the relevant properties of attitude and the other was through identifying what responses need to be observed. This third subsection describes the metric requirements of the research.

The evaluative dimension of attitude is viewed by most researchers as being a continuum that has the properties of an interval scale. An issue arises of whether investigators need the power of an interval scale for their research hypotheses. Even though the evaluative dimension is assumed to have interval properties in theory, often that interval character is irrelevant to the specific hypothesis being tested.

Nominal scales are often sufficient for descriptive purposes. For predicting what percentage of the vote a political candidate will receive, the pollster simply asks the respondents to name their first choice. This is clearly a nominal task. When assessing public attitudes toward some new government policy, it is often sufficient to obtain a simple two category nominal response such as "support" or "oppose."

The vast majority of modern attitude research is done in laboratory settings. Very often the predictions under examination are of a simple *ordinal* character. For example, high credibility communicators are predicted to produce more attitude change than low credibility communicators. The test of this hypothesis requires only an ordinal scale. It would be pointless for an experimenter to devote any extra effort or time to produce an interval scale. On the other hand, it is technically inappropriate to use means and variances as measures of central tendency and dispersion with an ordinal scale. Medians and interquartile ranges are more appropriate.

There are a great many research purposes for which an *interval* scale is required. For example, to accurately describe the relationship between communication discrepancy and attitude change, it is necessary to employ a scale with interval properties. Otherwise, one wouldn't know whether an obtained nonlinear (e.g., negatively accelerated) function was due to some distortion in the underlying metric of the scale or due to the discrepancy phenomenon itself. An interval scale is also required for the tests between averaging and summation aggregation rules using Anderson's (1981, 1982) functional measurement approach.

Finally, there are some theoretical objectives that require the utilization of a *ratio* scale. Because the evaluative dimension is two-valued (positive vs. negative), the zero point is located in the middle of that scale. The ratio property allows the experimenter to measure attitude extremity within each pole in the same way a meter stick is used to measure length. Person A can be described as being twice as pro as person B, when dealing with two persons on the positive side of the zero point. Such metric comparisons also apply across the zero point. For example, person C may be half as negative as person D is positive.

Some quantitative theories of attitude assume that their measurement instruments possess a ratio property. For example, in obtaining a sums-of-products index, the Fishbein model (Fishbein & Ajzen, 1975) tacitly assumes that people rate both the belief strength and the desirability of their beliefs on ratio scales. A ratio scale must also be available to the investigator who wishes to test congruity theory (Osgood & Tannenbaum, 1955). It makes the prediction that the impact of discrepant information on attitude increases as a function of the square of the information's distance from the scale midpoint. Any test of this prediction must involve locating items of information in terms of their distance from the midpoint of the attitude continuum. In general, predictions that take the form of a multiplicative function require the use of a ratio scale.

SOCIAL COGNITION AND ATTITUDES

Social cognition is offering a new conceptual orientation to the investigation of attitudes. At the heart of the social cognition approach is the conviction that the principles and methods of information processing, as currently being studied in cognitive psychology, are essential for a complete explanation of complex social behavior. The application of these principles to attitudes is a fairly recent enterprise. The earliest papers that advanced this orientation did not appear until around 1980 (e.g., Lingle & Ostrom, 1981). The present volume illustrates that the field is still in transition. Some chapters do draw in crucial ways upon principles of cognitive psychology (e.g., chap. 5, 7, and 8 in this volume), but most do not. Many of the ideas expressed in the other chapters reflect an awareness of general cognitive principles, but those ideas are not an explicit part of the theoretical presentation.

Because the social cognition approach is so new, it is impossible to fully anticipate the different theoretical issues and methodological procedures that will be part of the study of attitudes in the future. And certainly we do not yet have a vantage point from which to evaluate the interdependence between the two. Some changes, however, are inevitable.

Thurstone correctly identified an attitude as a collection of implicit responses linked to the attitude object, and he asserted that this collection could have many properties. He showed how one of those properties, the evaluative character of attitude, could be measured on a continuum. The social cognition approach would think of Thurstone's "implicit responses" as being cognitive elements. The evaluative character of attitudes derives from the assumption that many of those elements have positive or negative valences attached to them.

The parallels just described suggest there is a close isomorphism between the Thurstone and the social cognition conceptions of attitudes. But, in fact, they differ fundamentally in at least three ways. First, Thurstone was led by his analysis to assume that the evaluative property is best regarded as a *unidimensional continuum.* He believed that the measurement task was one of locating persons as points on a bipolar evaluative dimension. However, the information processing approach makes this assumption a matter of dispute.

As argued elsewhere (e.g., Devine & Ostrom, 1988; Ostrom, 1981; Ostrom, 1987), the information processing approach invites more of a categorical than a dimensional analysis of subjective judgments. The cognitions linked to the attitude object have evaluative tags indicating whether they are favorable or unfavorable. There is no reason to believe that these tags do anything more than convey valence, that they are either positive or negative. Consequently, in terms of the cognitive system, there may well be no evaluative continuum.

The evaluative tags on each element need not vary in extremity or intensity of evaluation. If indeed the tags do not vary in extremity, then it is conceptually inappropriate to locate a cognition (or its corresponding opinion item) on an evaluative continuum for purposes of measurement.

Yet this item scaling stage is at the heart of Thurstone's equal-appearing intervals measurement technique. Opinion items may be positive or negative, but their evaluative tags would not vary in intensity.

The social cognition approach differs in a second way from the traditional approach. Another objection to viewing evaluation as a continuum is that it suggests that self ratings of attitude derive from an implicit self-judgment of own attitude. This is a process whereby people locate their own attitude as a point on a subjective continuum, and simply interpolate that subjective response onto the overt rating scale.

As described elsewhere (Ostrom, 1987), people may not access such a subjective continuum when making ratings on a continuous rating scale. Instead, they may decompose the rating language into a small number of meaningful response categories, categories that may be as primitive as "favorable toward the object," "unfavorable toward the object," and "undecided." People may select the category that most accurately describes their current thoughts, and then mark the corresponding portion of the continuous scale. They may be indifferent as to which specific point they check, as long as it is in the part of the scale that coincides with their self-assigned category.

Social cognition is changing the study of attitudes in a third way. Thurstone clearly encouraged the view that attitudes, like supermarkets, have many properties. But his clear preference was to view these other properties as being dimensions of the attitude. In fact, many of the efforts to assess multiple properties of an attitude used a factor analysis approach to dimensionalize the belief structure. This equating of properties with dimensions led to a neglect of research on the qualitative structures that interlink the individual cognitions. For years the field learned almost nothing about the schematic structure of different attitudes. In contrast, issues of information and belief representation are at the heart of the information processing approach. For example, Pratkanis (chap. 4 in this volume) argues that some belief clusters have a bipolar structure and others have a unipolar structure. Such questions would not even be asked within the unidimensional framework of theory and method.

CONCLUDING COMMENTS

Method and theory can never be widely separated. Intelligent tests of theories require the investigator to carefully consider what measurement operations are most pertinent. Likewise, the ready availability of unidimensional measurement procedures has strongly influenced the conception of attitude in research practice. Fortunately, there is a distinct trend in current attitude research to move away from the simple unidimensional view of attitude and to examine the more heterogenous set of cognitive reactions evoked in persuasion settings (c.f. Petty & Cacioppo, 1986; Petty, Ostrom, & Brock, 1981; this entire volume).

There are four challenges to the development of theory and method in the study of attitudes. Traditionally, most attitude measures have presented subjects with a set of fixed opinion statements. However, in naturalistic persuasion settings, most attitudinal responses are *spontaneously evoked.* We need to determine what thoughts are activated in those settings and how they compare to the thoughts elicited just prior to initiation of behavioral acts. We need to avoid the limitations of structured instruments and devise ways of examining attitudinal thoughts in the settings in which they naturally occur.

Second, in the past our theories and measures have both been primarily univariate in nature. It is time to begin examining *multivariate conceptions* of attitudes. Researchers may well have reached the point of diminishing returns in understanding the evaluative dimension of attitude. Once investigators become accustomed to their strengths and weaknesses, the techniques of multivariate analysis of variance and path analysis should provide useful approaches for understanding the simultaneous effects of several independent variables on the multiple aspects of an attitude.

Researchers need to become more concerned about the *qualitative characteristics* of attitudes. There may be general categories of attitude objects that are organized in qualitatively different ways. For example, are person attitudes different in any general sense than political attitudes, racial attitudes, or attitudes toward different food products? Sherif's concern of whether there are qualitative differences between the organization of a highly ego-involved attitude and a more dispassionate attitude has never been adequately answered. These kinds of questions return us to some of the concerns raised by Allport in his insistence that we study all different types of attitudes.

A final issue has to do with the need to study newly formed attitudes as distinct from attitudes that have been held over a long period of time. Attitudes that have a history for the person are more *based on memory* and less dependent on recently acquired information. Unfortunately, most past attitude research, especially laboratory research, has avoided using attitudes with a long personal history. But it is likely that the mechanisms of change (and especially resistance to change) would differ for the two types of attitudes.

These are all areas in which investigators are currently showing interest and concern, as the present volume ably demonstrates. However, for such advancement to continue, the improvement of both theory and method must go hand in hand.

ACKNOWLEDGMENTS

This chapter benefited substantially from the comments of Deborah Davis, Anthony Pratkanis, and Harry Upshaw.

REFERENCES

Abelson, R. P., Aronson, E., McGuire, W. J., Newcomb, T. M., Rosenberg, M. J., & Tannenbaum, P. H. (1968). *Theories of cognitive consistency: A sourcebook.* Chicago: Rand McNally.
Allport, G. W. (1935). Attitudes. In C. Murchinson (Ed.), *A handbook of social psychology,* (Vol. 2, pp. 798–844). Worcester, MA: Clark University Press.
Anderson, N. H. (1976). How functional measurement can yield validated scales of mental quantities. *Journal of Applied Psychology, 61,* 677–692.
Anderson, N. H. (1981). *Foundations of information integration theory.* New York: Academic Press.
Anderson, N. H. (1982). *Methods of information integration theory.* New York: Academic Press.
Bogardus, E. S. (1925). Measuring social distances. *Journal of Applied Sociology, 9,* 299–308.
Breckler, S. J. (1984). Empirical validation of affect, behavior, and cognition as distinct components of attitude. *Journal of Personality and Social Psychology, 47,* 1191–1205.
Dawes, R. M., & Smith, T. L. (1985). Attitude and opinion measurement. In G. Lindzey & E. Aronson (Eds.), *Handbook of social psychology* (3rd ed., Vol. 1, pp. 509–566). New York: Random House.
Devine, P. G., & Ostrom, T. M. (1988). Dimensional vs information processing approaches to social knowledge: The case of inconsistency management. In D. Bar-Tal & A. Kruglanski (Eds.), *The social psychology of knowledge.* Cambridge, MA: Cambridge University Press.
Ebbesen, E. B. (1981). Cognitive processes in inferences about a person's personality. In E. Higgins, C. Herman, & M. Zanna (Eds.), *Social cognition: The Ontario symposium* (Vol. 1, pp. 247–276). Hillsdale, NJ: Lawrence Erlbaum Associates.
Edwards, J. D., & Ostrom, T. M. (1971). Cognitive structure of neutral attitudes. *Journal of Experimental Social Psychology, 7,* 36–47.
Fishbein, M. (1967). A consideration of beliefs and their role in attitude measurement. In M. Fishbein (Ed.), *Readings in attitude theory and measurement* (pp. 257–266). New York: Wiley.
Fishbein, M., & Ajzen, I. (1975). *Belief, attitude, intention and behavior: An introduction to theory and research.* Reading, MA: Addison-Wesley.
Fisher, R. A. (1938). *Statistical methods for research workers.* Edinburgh, England: Oliver & Boyd.
Greenwald, A. G. (1968). Cognitive learning, cognitive response to persuasion, and attitude change. In A. Greenwald, T. Brock, & T. Ostrom (Eds.), *Psychological foundations of attitudes* (pp. 147–170). New York: Academic Press.
Greenwald, A. G., Brock, T. C., & Ostrom, T. M. (1968). *Psychological foundations of attitudes.* New York: Academic Press.
Guttman, L. (1944). A basis for scaling qualitative data. *American Sociological Review, 9,* 139–150.
Guttman, L., & Suchman, E. A. (1947). Intensity and a zero-point for attitude analysis. *American Sociological Review, 12,* 55–67.
Hinckley, E. D. (1932). The influence of individual opinion on construction of an attitude scale. *Journal of Social Psychology, 3,* 283–296.

Jones, E. E., & Sigall, H. (1971). The bogus pipeline: A new paradigm for measuring affect and attitude. *Psychological Bulletin, 76*, 349–364.

Katz, D. (1960). The functional approach to the study of attitudes. *Public Opinion Quarterly, 24*, 163–204.

Kiesler, C. A., Collins, B. E., & Miller, N. (1969). *Attitude change.* New York: Wiley.

Likert, R. (1932/1933). A technique for the measurement of attitudes. *Archives of Psychology, 22* (140).

Lingle, J. H., & Ostrom, T. M. (1981). Principles of memory and cognition in attitude formation. In R. Petty, T. Ostrom, & T. Brock (Eds.), *Cognitive responses in persuasion.* Hillsdale, NJ: Lawrence Erlbaum Associates.

McGuire, W. J. (1960). Cognitive consistency and attitude change. *Journal of Abnormal and Social Psychology, 60*, 345–353.

McGuire, W. J. (1981). The probabilogical model of cognitive structure and attitude change. In R. E. Petty, T. M. Ostrom, & T. C. Brock (Eds.). *Cognitive responses in persuasion* (pp. 291–307). Hillsdale. NJ: Lawrence Erlbaum Associates.

Merton, R. K. (1940). Facts and facetiousness in ethnic opinionnaires. *American Sociological Review, 5*, 13–28.

Mueller, D. J. (1986). *Measuring social attitudes: A handbook for researchers and practitioners.* New York: Teacher's College Press.

Osgood, C. E., Suci, G. J., & Tannenbaum, P. H. (1957). *The measurement of meaning.* Urbana, IL: University of Illinois Press.

Osgood, C. E., & Tannenbaum, P. H. (1955). The principle of congruity in the prediction of attitude change. *Psychological Review, 62*, 42–55.

Ostrom, T. M. (1969). The relationship between the affective, behavioral, and cognitive components of attitude. *Journal of Experimental Social Psychology, 5*, 12–30.

Ostrom, T. M. (1972). Item construction in attitude measurement. *Public Opinion Quarterly, 35*, 593–600.

Ostrom, T. M. (1973). The bogus pipeline: A new *Ignis Fatuus? Psychological Bulletin, 79*, 252–259.

Ostrom, T. M. (1980). Wechselseitige Beeinflussung von Einstellungstheorie und Einstellungsmessung [Interdependence of attitude theory and attitude measurement]. In F. Petermann (Ed.), *Einstellungsmessung* (pp. 37–54). Gottingen, West Germany: Verlag Fur Psychologie.

Ostrom, T. M. (1981). *Attribution theory: Whence and whither?* In J. Harvey, W. Ickes, & R. Kidd (Eds.), *New directions in attribution theory,* (Vol. 3). Hillsdale, NJ: Lawrence Erlbaum Associates.

Ostrom, T. M. (1987). Bipolar survey items: An information processing perspective. In H. Hippler, N. Schwarz, & S. Sudman (Eds.), *Social information processing and survey methodology* (pp. 71–85). New York: Springer-Verlag.

Ostrom, T. M., Bond, C., Krosnick, J., & Sedikides, C. (in press). How we measure attitudes. In S. Shavitt & T. Brock (Eds.). *Psychology of persuasion.* New York: Freeman.

Ostrom, T. M., & Brock, T. C. (1968). A cognitive model of attitudinal involvement. In R. Abelson, E. Aronson, W. McGuire, T. Newcomb, M. Rosenberg, & P. Tannenbaum (Eds.), *Theories of cognitive consistency: A sourcebook* (pp. 373–383). Chicago: Rand McNally.

Ostrom, T. M., & Upshaw, H. S. (1968). Pychological perspective and attitude change. In A. Greenwald, T. Brock, & T. Ostrom (Eds.), *Psychological foundations of attitudes* (pp. 217–242). New York: Academic Press.

Petty, R. E., & Cacioppo, J. T. (1986). *Communication and persuasion: Central and peripheral routes to attitude change.* New York: Springer-Verlag.

Petty, R. E., Ostrom, T. M., & Brock, T. C. (1981). *Cognitive responses in persuasion.* Hillsdale, NJ: Lawrence Erlbaum Associates.

Remmers, H. H., & Silance, E. B. (1934). Generalized attitude scales. *Journal of Social Psychology, 5*, 298–312.

Rosenberg, M. J. (1956). Cognitive structure and attitudinal affect. *Journal of Abnormal and Social Psychology, 53,* 367–372.

Rosenberg, S., & Sedlak, A. (1972). Structural representations of implicit personality theory. In L. Berkowitz (Ed.), *Advances in experimental social psychology* (Vol. 6). New York: Academic Press.

Saffir, M. A. (1937). A comparative study of scales constructed by three psychophysical methods. *Psychometrika, 2,* 179–198.

Scott, W. A. (1968). Attitude measurement. In G. Lindzey and E. Aronson (Eds.). *The handbook of social psychology* (2nd ed., Vol. 2 pp. 204–273). Reading, MA: Addison-Wesley.

Scott, W. A., Osgood, D. W., & Peterson, C. (1979). *Cognitive structure: Theory and measurement of individual differences.* Washington, DC: Winston.

Sherif, C. W., Sherif, M., & Nebergall, R. E. (1965). *Attitude and attitude change: The social judgment-involvement approach.* Philadelphia, PA: Saunders.

Smith, M. B., Bruner, J., & White, R. (1956). *Opinions and personality.* New York: Wiley.

Steele, C. M., & Ostrom, T. M. (1974). Perspective-mediated attitude change: When is indirect persuasion more effective than direct persuasion? *Journal of Personality and Social Psychology, 29,* 737–741.

Stevens, S. S. (1951). Mathematics, measurement, and psychophysics. In S. S. Stevens (Ed.), *Handbook of experimental psychology* (pp. 1–49). New York: Wiley.

Stevens, S. S. (1968). Ratio scales of opinion. In D. K. Whitla (Eds.), *Handbook of measurement and assessment in behavioral sciences.* Reading, MA: Addison-Wesley.

Stevens, S. S. (1975). *Psychophysics: Introduction to its perceptual, neural, and social prospects.* New York: Wiley.

Tannenbaum, P. H. (1967). The congruity principle revisited: Studies in the reduction, induction, and generalization of persuasion. In L. Berkowitz (Ed.), *Advances in experimental social psychology.* (Vol. 3, pp. 217–320). New York: Academic Press.

Thurstone, L. L. (1927). A law of comparative judgment. *Psychological Review, 34,* 273–286.

Thurstone, L. L. (1931). The measurement of attitudes. *Journal of Abnormal and Social Psychology, 26,* 249–269.

Thurstone, L. L., & Chave, E. J. (1929). *The measurement of attitude.* Chicago: University of Chicago Press.

Upshaw, H. S. (1968). Attitude measurement. In H. Blalock, Jr. & A. Blalock (Eds.), *Methodology in social research* (pp. 60–111). New York: McGraw-Hill.

Weiss, R. F. (1968). An extension of Hullian learning theory to persuasive communication. In A. Greenwaid, T. Brock, & T. Ostrom (Eds.). *Psychological foundations of attitudes* (pp. 109–145). New York: Academic Press.

Wyer, R. S., Jr. (1974). *Cognitive organization and change: An information processing approach.* Hillsdale, NJ: Lawrence Erlbaum Associates.

Zajonc, R. B. (1960). The process of cognitive tuning in communication. *Journal of Abnormal and Social Psychology, 61,* 159–164.

3

The Structure of Individual Attitudes and Attitude Systems

William J. McGuire
Yale University

Attitude structure is a timely topic because social psychology is moving into a 1980s and 1990s systems era in which it will be a central concern (McGuire, 1986a). This systems preoccupation will be the third time that attitudes has become social psychology's central focus since the discipline emerged as a respected field of psychology in the 1920s. The first flourishing of social psychology in the 1920s and 1930s was focused on attitude measurement with psychologists like Bogardus, Thurstone, and Likert bequeathing a legacy of still-popular scaling procedures. Interest in attitudes declined during the 1935 to 1955 group dynamics era of social psychology but reemerged in the 1950s and 1960s attitude-change flourishing. Now, after the recent 1965 to 1985 social cognition era, we are witnessing the emergence of a third attitude flourishing, likely to dominate in the 1980s and 1990s, focused on attitude systems—their content, structure, and functioning.

The progress of a discipline by such faddish swings of fashion is an embarrassing but basically healthy form of evolution. Each fad still leaves other topics root-room even while it congregates trendy researchers on the fashionable quays and so provides a critical mass for the mutual stimulation that some researchers need. Each successive enthusiasm inevitably declines due to excesses of virtue such as overelaborate conceptualization, excessive quantification and premature application, as we have described elsewhere (McGuire, 1985, 1986a). This dampening of each fad lets its topic lie fallow for some years so that when interest revives after a period of benign neglect, the topic is viewed from new perspectives on a more complex level. This

37

evolution can be noted in the increasing complexity of the three attitude flourishing. The first and second dealt with attitudes in isolation, but evolved from the static topic of attitude measurement to the more dynamic topic of attitude change; and now the new, third flourishing deals with the still more complex issues of multiple attitudes organized into systems.

Topics as central to social psychology as attitudes, groups, or social perceptions are never completely ignored, even when out of fashion. Prior to the 1920s and 1930s attitude measurement era, interesting work had been done on the measurement of subjective states and further advances have occurred on the topic in every decade since then (McGuire, 1985). Similarly, there was some good work done on attitude change before and after its ascendancy in the 1950s and 1960s, and some respectable work on attitude systems long antedates the currently developing enthusiasm. The dominance of an era by a topic is a matter of degree rather than an exclusive preoccupation.

The coming attitude-systems' flourishing will include advances on three levels of structural complexity, the simplest involving the structure of individual attitudes, a more complex level involving systems of attitudes, and the most complex level involving systems of attitudes in relation to other systems within the person. The next three sections of this chapter deal with these three progressively more complicated types of attitude structure. The content, structure, and functioning of systems are intricately intertwined so that, although structure is emphasized here, it is also necessary in places to discuss attitudinal content and functioning.

We use *attitudes* throughout this chapter in a broad sense, so that what we say here is generally relevant to what are also called by such terms as cognitions, values, thoughts, beliefs, and opinions. The clearest terminology would use a generic noun, such as "attitude" (or "thought" or "experience") for any mental act, plus a distinctive adjective when specific reference is being made only to a subtype involving some special dimension, for example, "an evaluation attitude," or "an expectation attitude," when we wish to discuss specifically attitudes about the desirability or the likelihood, of the topic of the attitude.

THE STRUCTURE OF INDIVIDUAL ATTITUDES

We shall describe seven alternative models of the structure of individual attitudes (or "thoughts"), some overused and some neglected in past work. We shall indicate which of the models we regard as the most promising for study in the coming systems era.

Subjects-on-Dimensions Models
of Attitude Structure

Our own preferred model (McGuire, 1960, 1968, 1981) for the structure of individual thoughts, including attitudes or other mental operations, is a points-on-line one which assumes that the cognitive arena is made up of topics of meaning in multidimensional mental space. Attitudes (or indeed any thoughts) are covert acts that project some topic of meaning to a position on some dimension of judgment. (Some use the term *attitudes* solely for thoughts projecting topics on the evaluative dimension.)

Topics of meaning are any mental content (foci of attention) about which the person can make a judgment on at least one dimension or can distinguish from at least one other topic. Some are relatively concrete (such as self, mother, astronaut, or Mars). Some are more complex in being aggregates (such as humankind or a football game), or abstractions (such as peace or justice), or involve complex syntactical relationships (such as William of Occam's position regarding Duns Scotus's theory of individuation).

Dimensions of judgment, the second primitive term in this analysis of attitudes, include any respect in which two or more topics of meaning are distinguished. Some dimensions are transcendental in that all topics can be projected on them, such as goodness, truth, beauty, complexity, and importance. Other dimensions of judgment are more restricted in being relevant only to certain subdomains of topics of thought. For example, color or mass are dimensions that apply only to physical objects, while loyalty and intelligence apply only to humans and perhaps to some higher domestic mammals, although these restricted dimensions can be extended metaphorically. This subjects-on-dimensions analysis is, in my judgment, the richest structural model for providing comprehension and heuristic provocativeness. It is discussed further in the later section of this chapter that deals with the structure of systems of attitudes.

Subject-Verb-Object Models of Attitude Structure

The syntactical approach of analyzing attitudes and communication units into a subject-verb-object structure has had some popularity ever since the measurement of meaning work by Osgood, Suci, and Tannenbaum (1957). It treats attitudes as expressions whose verb specifies a relationship (usually evaluative) between a subject and an object. This model has received its most elegant statement in Gollob's (1974) analysis of the variance in such triadic structures into three main and four interactional components, which has given rise to fruitful controversy (Anderson, 1979; Rossman & Gollob, 1976; Wyer & Carlston, 1979, pp. 314–333).

Too often psychologists reduce the information in the verb simply to its evaluation component, as if people think of topics solely in terms of how good or bad they are. However, when one asks people to describe themselves and other familiar topics, fewer than 10% of their thought segments are explicitly evaluative (McGuire, 1984; McGuire & Padawer-Singer, 1976). Evaluation may be the single most important dimension, but not to an extent that justifies the present neglect of other dimensions of meaning. Midcentury uses of the subject-verb-object analysis were less restrictive in this regard than are current usages. Heider's (1958) seminal balance theory distinguished verbs into several categories (of which evaluation and unit-formation have received most attention); and Osgood's meaning theory, although it emphasized the evaluation dimension, did identify activity and potency as two additional dimensions.

The richest promise for developing this subject-verb-object model resides in the middle term because several lines of research suggest that verbs carry the most meaning in utterances. Verbs are most determining of the judged completeness (Healy & Miller, 1971) and similarity (Healy & Miller, 1970) of thoughts and to the drawing of inferences (Kanouse & Abelson, 1967). Also, verbs are most resistant to errors such as slips of the tongue and the pen (Hotopf, 1980; Meringer, 1908), systematic distortion (Semin & Greenslade, 1985), and the effects of purpose (Sandell, 1977, pp. 110–127). Several alternative verb classifications are available for developing this model (Brown & Fisk, 1983; Gilson & Abelson, 1965; McGuire & McGuire, 1986; Schank & Riesbeck, 1981).

Cognitive-Affective-Conative Models of Attitude Structure

The trichotomy of human experience into thought, feeling, and action, although not logically compelling, is so pervasive in Indo-European thought (being found in Hellenic, Zoroastrian, and Hindu philosophy) as to suggest that it corresponds to something basic in our way of conceptualization, perhaps (Sagan, 1977) reflecting the three evolutionary layers of the brain, cerebral cortex, limbic system, and old brain. The trichotomy is reflected in Locke's analyzing knowledge into semeiotika, practica, and physica in his *Essay Concerning Human Understanding* and was explicitly revived as a basic classification by von Wolff in his 18th-century reprofessionalization and systematization of philosophy, whence it provided the basis of division for Kant's three *Critiques* of pure reason, judgment, and practical reason.

This tripartite division has been used pervasively in psychology (Hilgard, 1980), nowhere more than in attitude research (e.g., Campbell, 1947; Krech & Crutchfield, 1948), as when a person's attitude toward a given ethnic group is analyzed into cognitive components in the form of stereotypes or beliefs about characteristics of the group (Karlins, Coffman, & Walters, 1969), affective components in the form of liking for the group as measured by Likert or Osgood, evaluative scales or occasionally by physiological indices of sympathetic autonomic arousal or incipient movements of facial muscles (Cacioppo & Petty, 1983), and conative components in the form of behavioral proclivity regarding the group as measured by a social distance (Bogardus, 1925; Triandis, 1977) or a behavioral intention scale (Ajzen & Fishbein, 1980; Saltzer, 1981).

Although psychodynamic approaches (Adorno, Frenkel-Brunswick, Levinson, & Sanford, 1950; Katz, 1960; Rosenberg, 1960) focus on imbalanced attitudes in which these three components are out of line, empirical work (Campbell, 1947) has long revealed the opposite embarrassment of a high redundancy among the three components such that their correlations with one another are as large as their own internal reliabilities (Ostrom, 1969; but see Breckler, 1984).

This tricomponential analysis is a tired approach, but its pervasive use in the past makes its future popularity likely. Its yield may increase if the usually overlooked nonevaluative information in the cognitive and conative components is more adequately investigated, perhaps by allowing open-ended responses (McGuire, 1984). Also likely to maintain interest in this model is the confusion as to whether thought, feeling, and action are to be considered as three aspects of a single attitude or whether attitude is to be equated with the affective component, so that its relation to thought and action involves a higher molecular structure among three different systems within the person as discussed in a later section of this chapter.

Attributes × Evaluation Models of Attitude Structure

Ever since midcentury (Cartwright, 1949; Smith, 1949), the most popular depiction of attitude structure has been the attributes × instrumentality model, also called by other names such as the values × instrumentality, ends × means, expected value, and subjective utility. It depicts a person's attitude toward a topic of thought as composed of his or her subjective probability that the topic has a certain attribute multiplied by his or her evaluation of the attribute, these products being summed or averaged across attributes to yield a bottom-line evaluation of the topic. A needs version of this model uses a list of human needs or values (e.g., Murray, 1938; Rokeach, 1960) and asks the person how conducive the topic is to the satisfaction of each need and how highly he or she evaluates each need. An alternative properties version asks the person to judge the extent to which the topic of thought possesses each of a set of properties and the desirability of each property (McGuire, 1985).

There are many reasons for the perennial popularity of this attributes ×
evaluation model of attitude structure. Its commonsensicality makes it
easily understood, a characteristic welcome to the masses of psychologists;
also, it is easily quantified (Anderson, 1981; Edwards, 1954; Savage, 1954), a
feature as welcome to the classes as simplicity is to the masses. Another
attraction is that the model's explicitness brings out issues such as whether
cognitive algebra follows a summation or an averaging rule in combining
the attributes × evaluation products (Anderson, 1981; Fishbein, 1980).
Also, the model is easily elaborated by additional factors (Bagozzi, 1982;
Fishbein, 1980; Sheth, 1974; Triandis, 1980), and is easily applied to practical situations.

With all these popular features the attributes × evaluation model deserves to be true, but sadly it is not. It typically accounts for a proportion of
the variance that is statistically significant, but is paradoxically small in view
of its a priori obviousness. If humans were designed to function solely as
decision-making machines, the attributes × evaluation operation would be
an efficient way of maximizing subjective utility. However, the human need
to perform many additional functions is unlikely to leave sufficient capacity
available for the onerous operations required by the attributes × evaluation
model. It would require the supermarket shopper to decide among alternative breakfast cereals by an implausibly complicated procedure of constructing a matrix whose columns are alternative cereals (Cheerios, Wheat-
ies, Sugar Pops) and whose rows are characteristics affecting purchase of
the product (taste, price, healthfulness, etc.), then filling in each cell with a
score for how well the column cereal satisfies the row characteristic, then
multiplying this matrix by a matrix that scores each characteristic for
desirability, then summing (or averaging) the products to arrive at a desirability ordering of the brands. This procedure seems implausibly ponderous even for a peculiarly deliberative person forming attitudes regarding a
particularly vital domain of life space.

Serial Sufficing-Selections Models
of Attitude Structure

Considering shoppers' glazed-eye passage through supermarket aisles, it is
unlikely that they use the ponderous attributes × evaluation model to
choose attitudes among breakfast cereals or among most other alternatives
in their lives. A more plausible, simpler approximation would be a serial
sufficing-selection such that the cereal shopper first takes into account just
one salient characteristic and selects all cereals that meet a sufficing value
on it; for example, he or she may use price for making his or her first cut,
selecting for further consideration only cereals that cost less than a dollar.
To this surviving subset of reasonably cheap cereals the shopper then

applies his or her next most salient characteristic, perhaps a nutritional one with the cutoff criterion being that the cereal has added vitamins sufficient to meet a person's daily nutritional requirements. To the small subset of cereals that survive both the price and the nutritional cutoffs, additional criteria can be applied until the shopper is left with just one preferred cereal, together with a short fallback list (Tversky, 1972).

This procedure would typically yield an attitudinal preference ordering similar to that yielded by the classic attributes × evaluation model with much less cognitive work. Peculiar associations among characteristics may occasionally obtain (and can easily be rigged in laboratory experiments) such that this procedure will yield nonoptimal attitude orderings (optimal being defined by the attributes × evaluation model because it takes most information into account), but that will be rare. Some evidence that people use the simpler model is provided by findings that people make decisions on the basis of fewer criteria than they report using and actually give characteristics more steeply declining weights than they think they do.

Basal-Peripheral Models of Attitude Structure

A number of theorists have distinguished between an underlying stable component of attitudes and a superficial, easily changed penumbra (Anderson, 1959; Kelman, 1980; Lazarsfeld, 1959), using concepts such as loose-linkage (McGuire, 1968), latitude of acceptance (Sherif & Hovland, 1961), and oscillation (Kaplowitz, Fink, & Bauer, 1983). They depict an attitude as the end link of a chain secured at the other end, which can be pulled by a relatively small force for the short distance until the slack is taken up, but once the chain becomes taut further change can be produced only by a qualitatively greater force.

The stable basal component not only limits the range of easily induced attitude change but also has an anchoring effect in pulling the easily-changed superficial component back to its original position once the social influence pressure is removed. Some support for this conceptualization comes from the finding that such slight attitudinal changes induced by mass media material tend to be short-lived (DeBock & Van Lil, 1981; Diem, 1980; McGuire, 1986b) and by the snap-back finding that anticipatory belief change induced by forewarning of persuasive attack (McGuire & Millman, 1965) quickly dissipates if the attack is not forthcoming (Cialdini, Levy, Herman, Kozlowski, & Petty, 1976; Hass & Mann, 1976; Nuttin, 1975).

Dimensional Models of Attitude Structure

A final approach to attitude structure is to identify dimensions on which attitudes differ in psychologically important ways, although it is often unclear how different a newly suggested dimension is from older dimensions or how important it is in the sense of affecting how the attitudes are related to other interesting variables.

Such attitude dimensions can distinguish either the topics of meaning or the dimensions of judgment. As regards topics of meaning, Katz (1960) distinguished among attitudes on the basis of their topics' generality, differentiation, and unity; Harvey, Hunt, and Schroder (1961) suggested inclusiveness, amount of internal structure, and degree of relatedness to other topics of thought; Rokeach (1960), centrality and permeability; and Zajonc (1960), differentiation, complexity, unity, and organization. After this flurry of classification work around 1960, the approach has lain relatively dormant (but see Scott, Osgood, & Peterson, 1979).

Alternatively, attitudes can be classified in terms of their dimensions of judgment. One favorite distinction is into expectation (likelihood of occurrence, truth) versus evaluation (desirability of occurrence, goodness) dimensions (Hastie & Park, 1986; McGuire, 1960). Analysis into evaluation, activity, and potency has been popular since Osgood, Suci, and Tannenbaum (1957). Attempts have also been made to divide the cognitive, affective, and conative compnents into subdimensions, the cognitive component by Transgaard (1973), Funk, Horowitz, Lipshitz, and Young (1976), Davis and O'Neill (1977), Taylor (1980), Bobo (1983), Toglia and Battig (1978), and Kreitler and Kreitler (1982), the affective by Marascuilo and Zwick (1983), and the conative by Triandis (1977) and Breler (1984). Such distinctions are useful only to the extent that the attitudes that they distinguish relate differently to other variables of interest.

This most basic, individual-attitude, level of structure deserves further research attention in the 1980s and 1990s systems era, even by researchers primarily interested in higher levels of structure, because how one analyzes structure at higher levels tends to be affected by one's assumptions regarding the structure of individual attitudes. In the final section of this chapter, particularly promising lines of work on the structure of individual attitudes are identified.

STRUCTURE OF ATTITUDE SYSTEMS

At this point we turn the discussion from structures on the elemental level of individual attitudes to more complex structures within systems of attitudes, leaving to a later section discussion of the still more complicated structures involving systems of attitudes in relation to other systems within the person. It is on the intermediate level of complexity that the most exciting advances will occur during the coming systems era.

The topics-on-dimensions model of individual attitudes provides a framework for discussing structures within systems of attitudes. Defining an individual attitude as a topic of thought projected on a dimension of judgment suggests that structures can arise within systems of attitudes on any of three bases: when multiple topics of thought are projected on a single dimension of judgment, when a single topic is projected on multiple dimensions, and when multiple topics of thought are projected on multiple dimensions. These three types will be discussed in turn.

Attitude Systems 1: Multiple Topics Projected on a Single Dimension

Attitudinal structures of this type, involving several interrelated topics of thought projected on a common dimension of judgment, are typically studied in social inference research (Hastie, 1983).

The Probabilogical Postulates

General models for this type of attitude systems were developed by Wyer (Wyer & Goldberg, 1970; Wyer & Carlston, 1979) and McGuire (1960, 1968, 1981). They have dealt mainly with propositional topics of thought projected on a common dimension of judgment, usually the expectancy (truth or likelihood of occurrence) dimension but the desirability and other dimensions are potentially as appropriate. Structural constraints can arise within such a system from the axioms of logic if the propositions are logically related, and from the axioms of probability theory if the propositions' locations on the dimension of judgment are measured on a probability scale. An example would be a syllogistically-related triad of propositions such as the two premises, (a) "A US President has performed well in office if the country does not become involved in a war during his/her term," and (b) "The US has not become involved in a war during Ronald Reagan's presidency," and their valid conclusion, (c) "Ronald Reagan has performed well as president of the US." If a person's expectancy attitudes are measured on propositions a, b, and c by asking him or her to estimate the probability that each is true, and if we theorize that the believer operates on the basis of the axioms of logic and probability theory, then we can predict that this system of attitudes at a given time will be interrelated according to the following equation:

$$p(c) = p[c/(a \ \& \ b)] \times p(a \ \& \ b) + p[c/\sim(a \ \& \ b)] \times p\sim(a \ \& \ b) \ \text{[Equation 1]}$$

It can be specified further that if the person's belief on premise a is changed by an amount $\Delta p(a)$ (for example, by a persuasive message arguing that avoidance of war during a president's administration is a noteworthy achievement) then our probabilogical model predicts that the amount of attitude change, $\Delta p(c)$ on the conclusion c (that Reagan has done a good job as president) will be defined by the following equation:

$$\Delta p(c) = \Delta p(a) \times p(b) \times \{p[c/(a \ \& \ b)] - p[c/\sim(a \ \& \ b)]\} \quad [\text{Equation 2}]$$

Alogical Functioning Postulates

Few spectators of the human comedy would seriously theorize that people's attitude systems operate strictly by these axioms of probability theory and logic. We have postulated that attitude systems operate also by a series of arational processes (McGuire, 1960, 1981) such as wishful thinking whereby the person's attitude regarding the truth of the conclusion, $p(c)$ in Equation 1, is affected by his or her desire on the conclusion c (the subjective probability that c is desirable), as well as by logical thinking (that is, by his or her expectation that premises a and b are true). Other arational processes postulated to operate within attitude systems include rationalization, spatial and temporal inertia, threshold, etc., as discussed in McGuire (1981). Some of these arational processes, like wishful thinking, serve to provide autistic gratification; others serve as simplifying heuristics that yield approximations of more adequate but vastly more onerous processes. It is currently fashionable to emphasize how shortcut heuristics cause errors under rigged laboratory conditions; but such widely diffused approximations have probably been phylogenetically and ontogenetically acquired because they are generally adaptive in the usual human environment.

Empirical Implications

The probabilogical and arational postulates in combination yield four classes of empirical predictions. First it is predicted and found that the initial relationships among attitudes in multiple-topic, single-dimension systems do approximate the probabilogical requirements in Equation 1 and are even more fully accounted for by also taking into account the corresponding desirability ratings as required by the wishful thinking postulate (Dillehay, Insko, & Smith, 1966; McGuire, 1960; Watts & Holt, 1970).

A second class of predictions is that attitudes can be changed, not only by presenting new information from outside sources, but also by self-persuasion procedures that enhance the salience of related attitudes already accepted by the person. We have called this procedure the *Socratic method* (McGuire, 1960) because, like Socrates' questioning of Meno's slave, attitudes on a given issue are changed by asking people questions about their related attitudes, their answers sensitizing them to the inconsistencies (as defined by the probabilogical model) among the related attitudes and thus cause adjustments. Several variants of this Socratic method have since proved effective (Ball-Rokeach & Grube, 1983; Millar & Tesser, 1986; Tesser, 1978). The predicted change toward mutual consistency occurs even if the issue of consistency is not explicitly raised during the elicitation, and even if the interrelated attitudes are scattered among other issues, over a variety of time intervals, and among people of modest as well as high intelligence (Henninger & Wyer, 1976; McGuire, 1960; O'Malley & Thistlethwaite, 1980; Watts & Holt, 1970). More work is needed on what determines which attitudes within a system are most likely to be changed to restore consistency.

A third class of predictions from this theory is that an attitude's resistance to persuasion will be increased by making salient its relationships to other attitudes as this makes the person more aware that any change on the given attitude would pull it out of alignment with the others in the system. Empirical evidence demonstrates this enhanced resistance (Watts & Holt, 1970), especially when the communication argues in an inconsistency-increasing direction (McGuire, 1960) or when the person anticipates receiving further information (Holt & Watts, 1969), or actively participates (Holt, 1970; Nelson, 1968).

The richest class of predictions from this attitude-system model concerns how a change induced on one attitude spreads to others in the system. Equation 2 provides a precise formula for how a change induced on one attitude should affect related but unmentioned attitudes in the system if the person operates strictly in accord with the axioms of logic and probability theory. To a surprising extent the remote ramifications do approximate those predicted by the simple probabilogical Equation 2 (Wyer & Carlston, 1979), with "wishful thinking" being one arational postulate that adds substantially to predictive power (McGuire, 1960). Evidence is mixed on the spatial attenuation postulate that the indirect impact on remote issues falls short of the Equation 2 specification and on the temporal inertia postulate that remote effects seep down to other attitudes only gradually (Dillehay, Insko, & Smith, 1966; McFarland & Thistlethwaite, 1970; McGuire, 1960; Watts & Holt, 1970). An obtained asymmetry deserving of more study is that remote effects flow vertically but not horizontally, that is, to antecedents and consequences but not to coordinate premises that logically would serve as well (Holt & Watts, 1969; McFarland & Thistlethwaite, 1970; McGuire, 1960).

Attitude Systems 2: Single Topics Projected on Multiple Dimensions

The minisystems just considered, made up of multiple topics projected on a single dimension, allow study of divergent processes by introducing a focused change on one target attitude and then tracing how it spreads divergently through the system, as in social inference research. The minisystems to which we now turn, made up of multiple topics on a single dimension, allow study of convergent processes by presenting multiple pieces of information and tracing how they are combined to yield a bottom-line attitude, as in person-perception research. Good examples of this second type of attitude-systems research are the programs of Norman Anderson on information integration in social judgment and of Martin Fishbein on his theory of reasoned action.

Anderson's Information-Integration Model of Judgmental Systems

As elegant a program of research as any within recent social psychology has been the social-judgment investigations by Norman Anderson (1981, 1982) involving functional measurement, information integration, and cognitive algebra. A person's new attitude (his or her perception of where a topic of thought falls on a dimension of judgment after receiving some new pieces of information) is defined as his or her prior attitude plus where each new piece of information places that topic on some other dimension, multiplied by the perceived relevance of the new to the original dimension, the products summed across all new pieces of information, divided by the sum of the cross-dimensional relevances.

This weighted-averaging model of attitudinal structure has been studied over a wide range of materials and by an elegant methodology using functional measurement whereby orthogonal designs allow simultaneous scaling of the variables and testing of the relationship between them. Although most of this research has been done on an averaging model of attitudinal structure that calls for a parallelism postulate, Anderson has also described a fan model for handling multiplicative attitude structures with similar methodological elegance. This research program provides a standard to be emulated in its explicit theory of cognitive algebra, its wide range of empirical applications, its refined scaling that uses anchors and meets interval scale assumptions, its determining weights for individual respondents rather than using weights obscured by aggregation across individuals, and its use of goodness-of-fit tests rather than usual but potentially misleading correlation-with-criterion tests.

Fishbein's Theory of Reasoned Action

Although the Anderson model has usually been applied to person perception and social judgment, Fishbein's (1980) model has typically been applied to attitudes and behaviors (although Fishbein uses "attitude" more narrowly than our usage in this chapter). Fishbein's model of attitude structure is more inclusive than Anderson's by taking into account, not only a summation version of Anderson's weighted-averaging, attribution × evaluation structure, but also a "normative" structure based on where the person projects his or her reference group's placement of each topic on the dimension, multiplied by the reference group's importance to the person, with these normative products being summed across reference groups.

Other researchers propose adding still more terms to take into account additional information, but most of these additions do not substantially improve predictions (Sheth, 1974; Triandis, 1980). A promising route for research on this type of model is to record natural covariation over time in these variables and then to use structural-equation models to trace multiple causal paths (Bagozzi, 1982) and to redefine the variables (Bentler & Speckart, 1979; Songer-Nocks, 1976).

The rationalization/wishful-thinking work stemming from McGuire's (1960, 1968) theory of the structure of thought is also relevant to these single ministructures involving one topic of thought on multiple dimensions. A high across-dimensional correlation is typically found between people's judgment of desirabilities and likelihoods of events when measured at a static point in time (Granberg & Brent, 1983; McGuire, 1960; Sjöberg, 1982), although more research is needed to explain why inducing a change on one dimension, either likelihood or desirability, has so little effect on the other (McGuire, 1960; Holt, 1970).

Attitude Systems 3: Multiple Topics Projected on Multiple Dimensions

More elaborate systems of attitudes, made up of multiple subjects projected on multiple dimensions, can range from inclusive ideologies down to circumscribed schemata.

The Savaging of Ideology

Informal and, more recently, systematic observation have led scholars to question the prevalence of well-organized, inclusive ideologies in the general public (Bell, 1960; Converse, 1964, 1980; but see Judd, Krosnick, & Milburn, 1981). Among many lines of evidence (McGuire, 1985) questioning the existence of organized ideologies is that a shocking proportion of people are ignorant of, or hold erroneous beliefs about important matters widely discussed in the mass media. Also, people often have no stand on matters of vital interest; indeed, some languages even lack simple terms for what we call attitudes. Again, people's attitudes fluctuate so capriciously over time as to suggest that their stands are superficial and unconnected (Converse, 1970; Jennings & Niemi, 1981). Another worrisome phenomenon is context effects, such that trivial changes in the wording (Turner & Krauss, 1978) or the sequencing (Suchman & Presser, 1981) of questions sizably affect attitudes expressed on issues. In addition, the person's information about an issue often has little relationship to his or her evaluative stand on it. Also, the person often shows low correlations among attitudes on closely related issues, and his or her stand on a general issue often conflicts with his or her stand on the underlying specifics, as when the

LIVERPOOL JOHN MOORES UNIVERSITY
LEARNING SERVICES

public favors the death penalty in general but opposes it in the case of each individual criminal (Ellsworth, 1982).

The Salvaging of Ideology

Despite these reasons for doubt, one is reluctant to conclude that people's attitudes have no more internal coherence than a bowl of cornflakes (Axelrod, 1976; Graber, 1984). A dozen excuses can be put forward to salvage faith in the prevalence of ideological coherence, despite these nonsupportive appearances. Some excuses blame failures to detect organized ideology on poor methodology, such as unreliable measures of individual attitudes, faulty mathematical models for identifying associations among related attitudes, or lumping together the attitudes of involved people with those of uninterested people who state attitudes on public opinion polls simply to be courteous to the interviewer.

Seven other "fall-back" positions grant that people do not have overall ideologies but defend the existence of circumscribed types of ideological coherence. It can be argued that, although ideological coherence is lacking in the masses, it shows up in the more sophisticated thinking of the classes; or that although coherence is lacking in unpolarized societies like the US, it exists in the public opinion of more doctrinaire societies; or that although people had been nonideological in the old days, they have been ideological ever since Goldwater, or since L. B. Johnson, or Ronald Reagan, or Millard Fillmore. Another fall-back defense is that ideological coherence cannot be found across all persons and on all issues, but it can be found in certain personality types (the philosophically inclined, the one-issue types, or whatever); or that people are not consistent in all attitude domains, but they are in domains that are particularly meaningful to them. Alternatively, it is possible that people's personal ideological coherence is obscured because they feel obliged to express attitudes that reflect, not only their personal ideology, but also that of their reference groups and of their prescribed roles. Much of the salvaging work stemming from such excuses promises, at most, to yield picayune methodological improvements such as how better to handle the "don't know" responders or to tease out some Gideon's army of coherent ideologues.

A more promising, twelfth line of inquiry looks for new dimensions of ideological structure that would replace the traditional but disappointing polarities like liberalism-conservatism with novel deep structural dimensions such as nature-nurture, raw-cooked, masculine-feminine, or solar-lunar, or Jungian individuating polarities (Levinson, 1978) such as animus-anima, puersenex, and so forth, or content-general dimensions such as symbolic racism (Bobo, 1983; Kinder & Sears, 1981), general trust in people (Schuman & Presser, 1981), or various meaning-assignment propensities (Kreitler & Kreitler, 1982).

One can also attempt to salvage ideology by proposing alternatives to the classical bipolar dimensions, as in Kerlinger's (1984) contention that liberalism and conservatism are not so much polar opposites as two mutually orthogonal dimensions, representing interest in different issues, so that extreme liberals are not so much opposed to positions espoused by extreme conservatives as simply not interested in them.

Miniature Tacit Theories

A particularly popular fall-back position among researchers who have concluded that people lack general ideologies is to postulate that people do at least have miniature attitudinal systems. Like internally structured galaxies scattered over empty or disorganized ideological space, each of these locally organized systems functions in a key area of thought and behavior with little relation to one another. Precursors of this approach include Helmholtz's (1866/1962; Hochberg, 1981) theory of unconscious inference, Bartlett's (1932) schemata notion, and Michotte's (1946/1963) implicit physics work on the perception of causality.

Some of these miniature ideologies are attributed to a parallel organization and others to a serial organization. Theorists who conceptualize these attitudinal minisystems as being intake-organizing structures that give meaning to experience usually assume parallel organization under such terms as *scheme theory* (Eckblad, 1981), *experimental Gestalts* (Lakoff & Johnson, 1980), *representations* (Durkheim, 1898; Moscovici, 1984; Rummelhart & Ortony, 1977), *mental models* (Gentner & Stevens, 1983; Johnson-Laird, 1983), *prototypes* (Cantor & Mischel, 1977; Posner & Keele, 1970), etc. Theorists who conceptualize the minisystems in their mediating or output functions of processing information or guiding behavior usually assume a serial structure under names such as *plans* (Miller, Galanter, & Pribram, 1960), *frames* (Goffman, 1974; Tversky & Kahneman, 1980) *agenda* (Plott & Levine, 1978), *scripts* (Abelson, 1981; Tomkins, 1979), *stories* (Pennington & Hastie, 1986), *templates* (Powers, 1978), *storage and processing models* (Wyer & Srull, 1986), etc. Miniature attitude structures of this serial type seem especially likely to receive research attention during the coming decade.

ATTITUDE SYSTEMS IN RELATION
TO OTHER SYSTEMS WITHIN THE PERSON

A third, still more complex level on which attitude structure may be studied is that involving correspondences between attitude systems and other systems within the person. The earlier interest was in attitudes' correspondences with action, how the person's pattern of feelings within some conceptual domain corresponds to his or her pattern of actions in that domain. The low correspondence between attitudes and actions has been the scandal of social psychology since the 1930s (LaPiere, 1934). Lately interest has shifted to attitudes' correspondences to information because computer-simulated advances in cognitive science has advanced knowledge of and interest in information systems (e.g., Hintzman, 1986; Holyoak & Gordon, 1984).

The complex intersystemic level we are discussing here should not be confused with the similar-sounding but much simpler structure of the cognitive/affective/conative components of individual attitudes, discussed earlier in this chapter, which deals with a single subject of thought projected on the three interrelated mental dimensions. In contrast, here we turn to a much more complicated level of structure between systems, each involving multiple subjects of thought projected on multiple dimensions of judgment.

Coordination between two such systems is usually sought in terms of a molecular one-to-one correspondence between the elements of each system, which generally yields low correlations. Consideration should be given to the possibility of molar coordination involving nonisomorphic ways of slicing up reality space within the two systems. To investigate molar correspondence it is necessary to discover separately the structure of attitudinal systems as discussed in previous sections and also of informational (or action) systems which may be analyzed into different subjects and dimensions.

Molecular Correspondence Between Informational and Attitudinal Systems

Most of the empirical work on intersystemic structures focuses on low level, one-to-one molecular correspondence, which we discuss first, but only briefly because other aspects of molecular correspondence are covered in chapters 7, 9, and 10.

Theoretical Explanations

Most common sense theories assume a high one-to-one correspondence between information about and liking for a topic of thought, that is, between how favorable is the salient information that the person has about a topic and how much the person likes the topic. The learning theory approach to attitude change (Hovland, Lumsdaine, & Sheffield, 1949; Hovland, Janis, & Kelley, 1953) postulated that acquiring new valenced information about a topic is what changes evaluation of that topic. The attribution × evaluation approaches (Cartwright, 1949; Smith, 1949) also assume close information-evaluation correspondence, though later uses of the model have added other determinants as well (Fishbein, 1980; Triandis, 1980). Dissonance theory (Festinger, 1957; Irle & Katz, 1982; Wicklund & Brehm, 1976) also assumes this correspondence, though reversing the learning theory emphasis on the information-to-evaluation direction of causal flow by stressing the flow in the evaluation-to-information direction. The cognitive-response approach (McGuire, 1960, 1964; Petty, Ostrom, & Brock, 1981; Petty & Cacioppo, 1986) also implies high information-evaluation correspondence, though with a stress on information actively generated by the believer more than for information absorbed from an outside source.

Empirical Weakness

In contrast to this plethora of theoretical explanations for why informational-attitudinal correspondence should be high, empirical support has been surprisingly weak. Six lines of empirical research on the topic, using progressively more complex designs, are mentioned only briefly here, fuller summaries being available in other chapters of this volume and elsewhere (McGuire, 1985). The simplest approach, investigating static correspondence between information favorability and positivity of attitudes toward topics at a given time, generally reveals a significant correlation but of a surprisingly modest magnitude relative to its obviousness.

Five lines of dynamic work yield predominantly positive correlations, sometimes significant but of a lower magnitude than in the static case—as might be expected considering that extraneous factors produce uncorrelated fluctuations in each variable. The simplest dynamic approach is to communicate a persuasive message and then correlate the amount of favorable attitude change with the net increase of favorable over unfavorable information acquired or self-generated. A second dynamic approach is to measure how the comprehensibility of a persuasive message (presumably related to the amount of information acquired) is related to the amount of attitude change it induces; careful design (Chaiken & Eagly, 1976) suggests that the modest positive relationship obtained derives in part from the clearer message's yielding more information, although also from its inducing a more favorable source impression and a more positive hedonic state. Another approach is to investigate how third variables that affect how much information is acquired from persuasive messages also affect their persuasive impact, but both derivations and results tend to be ambiguous (McGuire, 1985). A fourth dynamic approach is illustrated by the Socratic-effect and other self-persuasion studies (McGuire, 1960, 1981) already mentioned which indicate that changing the salience of already-possessed subsets of information about the topic of thought changes the person's evaluation of it.

A still more complicated dynamic strategy is to compare the retention of new information acquired from a persuasive message with the persistence of the message-induced attitude change. Close theoretical and empirical analysis suggest that the obtained relationship is affected by the type of information measured, the time parameters, and the operation of relative or absolute delayed action "sleeper" effects, and so forth (Cook & Flay, 1978; Hastie & Park, 1986; Pratkanis, Greenwald, Leippe, & Baumgardner, 1988; Watts & McGuire, 1964). Future work on this topic should vary the time parameter, as short-term relationships are likely to be different from those that obtain in the long run.

Molecular Correspondence Between Attitudinal and Action Systems

Although empirical support for one-to-one molecular correspondence between information and attitudes is sad, that for correspondence between action and attitude is tragic. Its elusiveness has continued to surprise and dismay researchers (or be ignored by them) for the half-century since LaPiere (1934). In the 1960s, the correspondence was taken for granted to the extent that the main debate between dissonance and reinforcement theories was over which causal direction accounted for the assumed close relationship. By the 1970s, psychologists had come to feel that seldom had so much explanation been offered for so little relationship (McGuire, 1966); it was even suggested (Abelson, 1972; Wicker, 1969), that attitudes had so little relation to the action payoff that the attitudinal concept may be an unnecessary one, leaving dispositionalists having to argue for the worth of attitude research (Dillehay, 1973; Kelman, 1974). These swings of fashion reflect a generational phenomenon, whether one has been socialized into psychology at a time when beliefs and behavior are thought to be unrelated, so that one is impressed on finding the correlation is as high as .30; or whether one has entered the field at a period when it was assumed that beliefs and behaviors are closely related, and so it is disappointing to find that the relationship is as low as .30.

Theoretical Explanations

Most interviewees questioned in surveys are willing to express an opinion on almost any issue, even though the high metabolic cost of human brain activity suggests that having attitudes is an effort-intensive activity. Considering that humans have been a fairly successful species, there must be some counterbalancing survival function of attitudes, most likely adjusting the person's behavior to the momentary state of the environment, which would seem to require a close correspondence between attitudinal and action systems. Indeed, even if attitudes do not have direct causal impacts on behavior but are only epiphenomena of actions, or if both attitudes and actions are merely coeffects of some more basic process, the attitude-action correspondence should be close.

These commonsensical assumptions have given rise to a variety of theories that account for the purported agreement between attitudes and actions, even though the empirically demonstrable correspondence turns out to be surprisingly weak. Three theories predict a positive and a fourth predicts a negative relationship between attitudes and actions. The most obvious theory gives causal priority to thought, depicting attitudes as determining actions. Then in the 1960s dissonance reaction an opposite causality was assumed such that attitudes are generated to justify (or in the 1970s attribution era, to explain) the action. Two other theories account for the purported attitude-action interrelation by third factors. One conjecture is the notion that attitude and action agree because both reflect some third factor, such as deep unconscious needs or physiological states. A less familiar fourth explanation is that attitudes and actions are in a hydraulic relationship as alternative outlets for a third underlying force such that the more the person expresses this force attitudinally the less is the need to express it in action. The first three theories would predict a positive relationship between attitudes and action; the fourth theory, a negative relationship. Inclusive designs and analyses (Bagozzi, 1982; Fredericks & Dossett, 1983) suggest that multiple causal paths may indeed be involved.

Empirical Weakness

Compared to its ad hoc plausibility and these multiple theories to account for relationships between attitudes and action, the size of the empirically established correspondence has been surprisingly slight. Dynamic designs have been less used in attitude-action than in information-attitude molecular research, but in compensation there has been particularly thorough investigation of static attitude-action correspondences in which the favorableness of one's attitude toward a topic of thought is related to the favorableness of one's behavior toward it at a given point in time. The general finding is of a positive relationship but of a surprisingly small magnitude, the attitude-action covariance seldom exceeding 10%. When more sizable correlations are reported, it is typically between the attitude and the behavioral intention rather than the behavior itself; that is, between the affective and conative aspects of verbalized attitudes, rather than between attitudes and behavior. More work is needed on attitude-action correspondence in each of the five dynamic designs described for information-attitude correspondence.

The size of the obtained static molecular attitudinal-action correspondence is affected by both method and substance. Among methodological factors that increase the correlation are use of more sensitive and similar measures of attitudes and actions, of within-participant rather than among-participant designs, and of laboratory rather than field studies. Substantive factors that increase the size of the attitude-action relationship include both dispositional and situational characteristics. Dispositional variables include the participants' self-monitoring, maturity, and felt responsibility for their own actions. Situational variables include the topics' being more salient, central, personally involving, confidently held, within a more familiar domain, typical of their class, and free from conflicting forces such as opposing attitudes, moral obligations, expectations of significant others, and fear of consequences. Such factors are discussed further in chapters 7, 9, and 10 in this volume and in McGuire (1985).

Molar versus Molecular Inter-Systemic Correspondence

A possible explanation for why the obtained information-attitude and attitude-action correlations are so modest relative to their intuitive obviousness and functional necessity is that their coordination is typically sought in terms of molecular one-to-one relationships between elements in the two systems when actually it may take place on a more molar level. To investigate this possibility one should determine the organization of each system separately, as previously discussed for describing attitude systems in terms of their atomistic components, their operating principles, and the compounds that result; that is, the words of which they are composed and the syntactical and semantic rules by which these words are related and the compound meaningful expressions that result.

The separate systems may be organized on quite different bases, slicing reality space in different planes and reassembling it into quite different compounds. Correspondence between the attitudinal and the action (or the information) systems may obtain only on a molar level without involving direct word-by-word connections between attitudes and actions in terms of the same topics projected in the same dimensions. The two systems may be coping with the same set of underlying needs, but each system may represent these needs and options in accord with its own distinctive idiom so that the correspondence is achieved only on a molar level.

This distinction between molar and molecular coordination of systems is sufficiently novel and subtle so that it might be clarified by the use of analogy. In the biological domain, a bee community and a flower community may be coordinated on a molar level without there being any molecular one-to-one correspondence pairing individual bees with individual flowers, or pairing the parts of bees with the parts of flowers. Or the weather and the economy may be coordinated without there being any molecular correspondence between the elements of the two. The economic system may have elements such as money supply, consumer demand, business investment, and employment; the weather system may involve quite different elements like solar radiation, jet stream activity, and reflectivity of cover; there may not be any one-to-one correspondence between their two sets of elements and yet the economic and the weather systems might be coordinated. Similarly, a person's systems of attitudes and of behaviors may be coordinated without being in one-to-one molecular correspondence. The topics with which one's attitudes are concerned may be quite different from those at which one's behaviors are directed; the dimensions that affect the operations of the two systems may also be different, attitudes perhaps concerned with the truth, attractiveness, or interestingness of their topics, and actions with their topics' threat, onerousness, or satisfyingness. Hence, the low molecular correlation found when both systems are analyzed in terms of the same set of topics on the same dimensions may be missing a molar coordination that obtains between the attitudinal and action systems.

To identify such molar correspondences between the systems, students of each must separately discover the structure of that system, proceeding as described in the middle section of this chapter. Work on the structure of information systems is currently in advance of that on action systems because cognitive scientists, inspired by the digital-computer metaphor, have made progress in describing the storage and retrieval of information. Less progress has been made in describing the structure of action, but some advances have been made in analyzing some circumscribed action domains in terms of either simple movements or purposive acts. Analyses in terms of basic movements are available for recording dance movements, time and motion studies of industrial workers, and in robotry work. Analyses in terms of purposive acts are illustrated by systems for encoding social communication (Bales, 1950), family interaction, and behavior of animals in the field. The movement approach is more operational and general but the act approach, by incorporating goal inferences, promises easier tie-ins with attitudinal constructs (although at the risk of premature assimilation of the action system to the attitudinal). At least some researchers on intersystemic structure should make the radical shift from the currently overemphasized molecular approach to the study of this molar type of correspondence.

INDICATIONS FOR FUTURE WORK

In this final section we recommend promising issues on which to focus the 1990s research on each of the three levels of structural complexity—the individual attitude, systems of attitudes, and relations between attitudinal systems and other systems within the person. Additional research priorities were mentioned in context in the preceding sections.

Needed Work on the Structure
of Individual Attitudes

As regards the structure of individual attitudes, it seems likely that basic researchers will continue to focus considerable effort on the already over-worked attribution × evaluation model and that it will continue to dominate application to marketing and public health. If so, some tactical improvements would include better lists of values and properties, preferably elicited from the participant population or even tailored to the individual, and taking salience into account. Better cognitive-algebra models that incorporate both summation and averaging processes and better weighting procedures should develop as the power and manageability of the functional measurement approach (Anderson, 1981) become better appreciated. The models should be put into more meaningful contexts by allowing the components to covary naturally over time, so that alternative causal paths can be explored by the use of structural-equation models (Bagozzi, 1982).

It would be better still to rechannel to other models of attitude structure much of the effort currently overconcentrated on the attribution × evaluation model, a peculiar combination of the trivially obvious and the absurdly implausible. The model is a common sense depiction of how attitudes might rationally be formed by an idiot-savant machine for maximizing subjective utility but it becomes wildly unlikely when one considers how demanding it would be on the human's limited cognitive capacities. More attention should be given to quick and dirty alternatives, such as the serial sufficing-selections model and other models that take into account salience (Fazio & Williams, 1986; Millar & Tesser, 1986) and heuristic shortcuts that in usual environments would yield attitudes approximating those yielded by the full attribution × evaluation model but with much less effort.

The other overpopular model of individual-attitude structure, analyzing it into cognitive, affective, and conative components, is also likely to continue to receive disproportionate attention, in part because it is mistakenly thought to investigate the most complex level of structure, that between attitude systems and information or action systems. Also likely to keep some attention focused on this tricomponential model is the revival of interest in the relation between affect and cognition (Zajonc, 1980). As regards the subject-verb-object model, work might best be focused on developing psychologically meaningful classifications of verbs (McGuire & McGuire, 1986).

The topics-on-dimensions model is particularly promising because it not only clarifies individual attitudes but also provides a basis for describing structure on the more complex systemic level, as illustrated in preceding sections of this chapter. Work is needed on both the topics of meaning and the dimensions of judgment. There is a need for developmental studies on such issues as whether topics of meaning arise in Saussurian pairs of opposites. Work is also needed on the partition of topics of meaning into subsets within which different functioning rules obtain.

As regards dimensions of judgment, work is needed on identifying the commonly-used dimensions of meaning space and how they originate; for example, does the person develop a dimension of female beauty whose orientation is determined by imprinting during infancy on his or her mother's features? How major meaning dimensions are oriented to one another deserves study by multivariate analysis but with awareness that the dimensions may have nonparsimonious oblique orientations to one another or may constitute a tree structure rather than being factors that radiate from a central focus. Investigations of transcendental dimensions of meaning should be extended beyond the present overconcentration on the evaluation dimension to cognitive and conative dimensions. As regards more restricted dimensions of meaning space, on which only a subset of topics of thought are properly projected, work is needed on how less appropriate topics are projected metaphorically or by other rhetorical devices, as in "a cruel winter" or a "weighty problem."

Needed Work on the Structure of Systems of Attitudes

Studies of intermediate levels of complexity, involving the structure of systems of attitudes, are particularly promising during the next 10 years. The most complex of these will involve attitude systems in the form of general ideologies made up of many topics of thought projected on multiple dimensions. The current lively controversy in survey research regarding the extent to which organized ideology exists has provoked several lines of work, as reviewed earlier, but these have dealt mainly with methodological or tactical issues and have focused on the conceptually sparse issue of the extent to which ideology is organized. Until attention is focused on more richly textured issues regarding the substance of ideology, especially its deep-structural dimensions, progress will be confined to the technical level.

For the immediate future, advances are more promising in understanding the three more circumscribed types of attitudinal subsystems, those involving multiple topics of thought on a single dimension, those involving a single topic on multiple dimensions, and implicit minitheories involving small subsets of topics on a few dimensions. Study of these should use more permissive approaches to data collection and stimulus construction that allow participants to generate their own belief systems in their own terms as regard content, salience, and connections. Also, this research should switch from the current overconcentration on studies of the static structure of attitude systems at a given time, toward study of dynamic functioning when attitude changes are induced on target attitudes in the system and remote ramifications on other attitudes are traced over space and time. The work should give more attention to the person's need, not only to maintain logical connectedness and coherence, but also to cope with information-processing limitations and hedonic demands that call for alogical operations. Higher levels of systemic organization may be described by combining several of these substructures at critical interfaces. For example, after some better grasp is achieved of subsystems composed of multiple topics of thought projected separately on the evaluation and on the expectation dimension the two can be fused into a broader system.

Most work on attitudinal subsystems is undertaken to investigate processes but the content should be studied in humanly important minisystems, such as the person as an implicit moralist (Fincham & Jaspers, 1980; Lerner & Lerner, 1981; Ryan, 1971; Semin & Manstead, 1983; Siegal, 1982), or implicit personality theorist (Borkenau, 1986; Bromley, 1977; Powell & Juhnke, 1983; Schneider, 1973). Three content areas likely to be of growing applied interest during the next decade are: (a) health psychologists' growing interest in the person as implicit biologist (Andreoli, 1981; Bishop & Converse, 1986; Burbach & Peterson, 1986; Herzlich, 1969/1973; Lau & Hartman, 1983; Leventhal, Meyer, & Nerenz, 1980; Pennebaker, 1982; Viney, 1983); (b) the financial community's desperate need for understanding the public's implicit theories of economics (Douglas & Isherwood, 1979; Hirschman, 1982; Lichtman, 1982; Maital, 1982; Stroebe & Meyer, 1982); and (c) developing the incipient interest in the person as implicit physicist (deKleer & Brown, 1985; Gentner & Stevens, 1983; Jones, 1986; Kaiser, Jonides, & Alexander, 1986; McCloskey, 1983; Michotte, 1946/1963).

Needed Work on Structures Relating Attitudinal with Other Systems

Researchers on the most complex structural level, studying the coordination of attitude systems with other systems within the person, are likely to shy away from the demanding molar conceptualization prescribed earlier. They are likely instead to continue focusing on a simplistic one-to-one molecular correspondence of a single topic of thought as regards its projections on an attitudinal and on an informational or action dimension. At most, this approach is likely to yield minor measurement refinements or banal and weak interaction effects, as in the past.

Still, one can have hope against hope for some 1990s advance in understanding intersystemic coordination on the molar level. Effort should focus on the relationships of attitudinal systems to informational systems rather than to action systems because current cognitive science work has made some progress in describing systems of information storage and retrieval (Wyer & Srull, 1986), while work on action systems remains elementary. The freer notion of molar correspondence suggests the utility of looking for translation rules between attitudinal and informational or action systems, each having its own distinctive syntax. Coordination may be achieved via an underlying third system, such as those conceptualized in neuroscience, though it should be recognized that premature physiologizing has in the past been detrimental to psychological advance.

The past is likely to be prologue, alas. Students of structure in the 1990s can be expected to expend excessive effort in rounding up the usual suspects. Still, we keep the faith that in the midst of this banal busy-ness some unusual ideas will be conceived, their hour come at last, and slouch toward Bethlehem to be born. At first they may seem of no more use than a baby but their development in the long run will justify the background of fussy trivia that constitutes the medium in which their birth becomes possible. Here we have been suggesting some localized opportunities for conceiving a great idea or at least for making the growth medium a little more fertile.

ACKNOWLEDGMENT

The writing of this chapter was much facilitated by grant number MH 32588, awarded by the International Processes and Problems Section, Behavioral Sciences Research Branch, National Institute of Mental Health, U.S. Department of Health and Human Services.

REFERENCES

Abelson, R. P. (1972). Are attitudes necessary? In B. T. King & E. McGinnies (Eds.), *Attitudes, conflicts, and social change* (pp. 19–32). New York: Academic Press.

Abelson, R. P. (1981). The psychological status of the script concept. *American Psychologist, 36,* 715–729.

Adorno, T. W., Frenkel-Brunswick, E., Levinson, D. J., & Sanford, R. N. (1950). *The authoritarian personality.* New York: Harper.

Ajzen, I., & Fishbein, M. (1980). *Understanding attitudes and predicting social behavior.* Englewood Cliffs, NJ: Prentice-Hall.

Anderson, N. H. (1959). Test of a model of opinion change. *Journal of Abnormal and Social Psychology, 59,* 371–381.

Anderson, N. H. (1979). Indeterminate theory: Reply to Gollob. *Journal of Personality and Social Psychology, 37,* 950–952.

Anderson, N. H. (1981). *Foundations of information integration theory.* New York: Academic Press.

Anderson, N. H. (1982). *Methods of information integration theory.* New York: Academic Press.

Andreoli, K. G. (1981). Self-concept and health beliefs in compliant and noncompliant hypertensive patients. *Nursing Research, 30,* 323–328.

Axelrod, R. M. (1976). *Structure of decision: The cognitive maps of political elites.* Princeton, NJ: Princeton University Press.

Bagozzi, R. P. (1982). A field investigation of causal relations among cognitions, affect, intentions, and behavior. *Journal of Marketing Research, 19,* 562–584.

Bales, R. F. (1950). *Interaction process analysis: A method for the study of small groups.* Reading, MA: Addison-Wesley.

Ball-Rokeach, S. J., & Grube, J. W. (1983). *The great American values test: Influencing behavior and belief through television.* New York: Free Press.

Bartlett, F. C. (1932). *Remembering.* Cambridge, England: Cambridge University Press.

Bell, D. (1960). *The end of ideology.* Glencoe, IL: Free Press.

Bentler, P. M., & Speckart, G. (1979). Models of attitude-behavior relations. *Psychological Review, 86,* 452–464.

Bishop, G. D., & Converse, S. A. (1986). Illness representations: A prototype approach. *Health Psychology, 5,* 94–114.

Bobo, L. (1983). Whites' opposition to busing: Symbolic racism or realistic group conflict. *Journal of Personality and Social Psychology, 45,* 1196–1210.

Bogardus, E. S. (1925). Measuring social distance. *Journal of Applied Sociology, 9,* 299–303.

Borkenau, P. (1986). Toward an understanding of trait interrelations: Acts as instances of several traits. *Journal of Personality and Social Psychology, 51,* 371–381.

Breckler, S. J. (1984). Empirical validation of affect, behavior, and cognition as distinct components of attitude. *Journal of Personality and Social Psychology, 47,* 1191–1205.

Bromley, D. B. (1977). *Personality description in ordinary language.* New York: Wiley.

Brown, R., & Fisk, D. (1983). The psychological causality implicit in language. *Cognition, 14,* 237–273.

Burbach, D. J., & Peterson, L. (1986). Children's concepts of physical illness: A review and critique of the cognitive-developmental literature. *Health Psychology, 5,* 307–325.

Cacioppo, J. T., & Petty, R. E. (Eds.). (1983). *Social psychophysiology: A sourcebook.* New York: Guilford Press.

Campbell, D. T. (1947). *The generality of social attitudes.* Unpublished doctoral dissertation, University of California, Berkeley.

Cantor, N., & Mischel, W. (1977). Traits as prototypes: Effects on recognition memory. *Journal of Personality and Social Psychology, 35,* 38–48.

Cartwright, D. (1949). Some principles of mass persuasion. *Human Relations, 2,* 253–267.

Chaiken, S., & Eagly, A. H. (1976). Communication modality as a determinant of message persuasiveness and message comprehensibility. *Journal of Personality and Social Psychology, 34,* 605–614.

Cialdini, R. B., Levy, A., Herman, C. P., Kozlowski, L. T., & Petty, R. E. (1976). Elastic shifts of opinion: Determinants of direction and durability. *Journal of Personality and Social Psychology, 34,* 663–672.

Converse, P. E. (1964). The nature of belief systems in mass publics. In D. E. Apter (Ed.), *Ideology and discontent* (pp. 206–261). New York: Free Press.

Converse, P. E. (1970). Attitudes and non-attitudes: continuation of a dialogue. In E. R. Tufte (Ed.), *The quantitative analysis of social problems* (pp. 168–189). Reading, MA: Addison-Wesley.

Converse, P. E. (1980). Rejoinder to Judd and Milburn. *American Sociological Review, 45,* 644–646.

Cook, T. D., & Flay, B. R. (1978). The persistence of experimentally induced attitude change. In L. Berkowitz (Ed.), *Advances in experimental social psychology* (Vol. 11, pp. 1–57). New York: Academic Press.

Davis, E. E., & O'Neill, M. (1977). *An Irish personality differential: A technique for measuring affective and cognitive dimensions of attitudes toward persons.* Dublin: Economic and Social Research Institute, No. 88.

DeBock, H., & Van Lil, J. (1981). "Holocaust" in the Netherlands. In G. C. Wilhoit & H. DeBock (Eds.), *Mass Communication Review Yearbook-2* (pp. 639–647). Beverly Hills, CA: Sage.

deKleer, J. & Brown, J. S. (1985). A quantitative physics based on confluences. In D. G. Bobrow (Ed.), *Qualitative reasoning about physical systems.* Cambridge, MA: MIT Press.

Diem, P. (1980). "Holocaust" and the Austrian viewer. *EBU-Review, 31,* 35–40.

Dillehay, R. C. (1973). On the irrelevance of the classic negative evidence concerning the effects of attitudes on behavior. *American Psychologist, 28,* 887–891.

Dillehay, R. C., Insko, C. A. & Smith, M. B. (1966). Logical consistency and attitude change. *Journal of Personality and Social Psychology, 3,* 646–654.

Douglas, M., & Isherwood, B. (1979). *The world of goods: An anthropologist's perspective.* New York: Basic Books.

Durkheim, E. (1898). Représentations individuelle et représentations collectives [Individual representations and collective representations]. *Revue de Metaphysique et de Morale, 6,* 272–302.

Eckblad, G. (1981). *Scheme theory: A conceptual framework for cognitive-motivational processes.* New York: Academic Press.

Edwards, W. (1954). The theory of decision making. *Psychological Bulletin, 51,* 80–417.

Ellsworth, P. C. (1982). *Public attitudes to capital punishment in general and in specific cases.* Personal communication.

Fazio, R. H., & Williams, C. J. (1986). Attitude accessibility as a moderator of the attitude-perception of attitude-behavior relations: an investigation of the 1984 presidential election. *Journal of Personality and Social Psychology, 51,* 3, 505–514.

Festinger, L. (1957). *A theory of cognitive dissonance.* Stanford: Stanford University Press.

Fincham, F. D., & Jaspars, J. M. (1980). Attribution of responsibility: From man as scientist to man as lawyer. In L. Berkowitz (Ed.), *Advances in experimental social psychology, 13,* (pp. 81–138). New York: Academic Press.

Fishbein, M. (1980). A theory of reasoned action: Some applications and implications. In H. Howe & M. Page (Eds.), *Nebraska symposium on motivation, 1979* (Vol. 27, pp. 65–116). Lincoln, NE: University of Nebraska Press.

Fredricks, A. J., & Dossett, D. L. (1983). Attitude-behavior relations: A comparison of the Fishbein–Ajzen and the Bentler–Speckart models. *Journal of Personality and Social Psychology, 45,* 501–512.

Funk, S., Horowitz, A. D., Lipshitz, R., & Young, F. W. (1976). The perceived structure of American ethnic groups: The use of multidimensional scaling in stereotype research. *Sociometry, 39,* 116–130.

Gentner, D., & Stevens, A. L. (1983). *Mental models.* Hillsdale, NJ: Lawrence Erlbaum Associates.

Gilson, C. & Abelson, R. P. (1965). The subjective use of inductive evidence. *Journal of Personality and Social Psychology, 2,* 301–310.

Goffman, E. (1974). *Frame analysis.* New York: Harper & Row.

Gollob, H. F. (1974). The subject-object-verb approach to social cognition. *Psychological Review, 81,* 286–321.

Graber, D. (1984). *Processing the news.* New York: Longmans.

Granberg, D., & Brent, E. (1983). When prophecy bends: The preference-expectation link in U.S. presidential elections, 1952–1980. *Journal of Personality and Social Psychology, 45,* 477–491.

Harvey, O. J., Hunt, D. E., & Schroder, H. M. (1961). *Conceptual systems and personality organization.* New York: Wiley.

Hass, R. G., & Mann, R. W. (1976). Anticipatory belief change: Persuasion or impression management? *Journal of Personality and Social Psychology, 34,* 105–111.

Hastie, R. (1983). Social inference. *Annual Review of Psychology, 34,* 511–542.

Hastie, R., & Park, B. (1986). The relationship between memory and judgment depends on whether the judgment task is memory-based or on-line. *Psychological Review, 93,* 258–268.

Healy, A. F., & Miller, G. A. (1970). The verb as the main determinant of sentence meaning. *Psychonomic Science, 20,* 372.

Healy, A. F., & Miller, G. A. (1971). The relative contribution of nouns and verbs to sentence acceptability and comprehensibility. *Psychonomic Science, 24,* 94–96.

Heider, F. (1958). *The psychology of interpersonal relations.* New York: Wiley.

Helmholtz, H. L. F. von. (1962). *Treatise on physiological optics [Handbuch der physiologischen Optik* (Vol. 3)].* New York: Dover. (Original work published in 1866)

Henninger, M., & Wyer, R. S., Jr. (1976). The recognition and elimination of inconsistencies among syllogistically related beliefs: Some new light on the "Socratic effect." *Journal of Personality and Social Psychology, 34,* 680–693.

Herzlich, C. (1973). *Health and illness: A social psychological study.* London: Academic Press. (Original work published in 1969).

Hilgard, E. R. (1980). The trilogy of mind: Cognition, affection, and conation. *Journal of the History of the Behavioral Sciences, 16,* 107–117.

Hintzman, D. L. (1986). "Schema abstraction" in a multiple-trace memory model. *Psychological Review, 93,* 411–428.

Hirschman, A. O. (1982). *Shifting involvements: Private interest and public action.* Princeton, NJ: Princeton University Press.

Hochberg, J. (1981). On cognition in perception: Perceptual coupling and unconscious inference. *Cognition, 10,* 127–134.

Holt, L. E. (1970). Resistance to persuasion on explicit beliefs as a function of commitment to and desirability of logically related beliefs. *Journal of Personality and Social Psychology, 16,* 583–591.

Holt, L. E., & Watts, W. A. (1969). Salience of logical relationships among beliefs as a factor in persuasion. *Journal of Personality and Social Psychology, 11,* 193–203.

Holyoak, K. J., & Gordon, P. C. (1984). Information processing and social cognition. In R. S. Wyer & T. K. Srull (Eds.), *Handbook of Social Cognition* (Vol. 1, pp. 39–70). Hillsdale, NJ: Lawrence Erlbaum Associates.

Hotopf, N. (1980). Lexical slips of the pen and the tongue: What they may tell us about language production. In B. Butterworth (Ed.), *Language production: Vol. 2. Development, writing, and other language processes* (pp. 147–199). London: Academic Press.

Hovland, C. I., Janis, I. L., & Kelley, H. H. (1953). *Communication and persuasion.* New Haven, CT: Yale University Press.

Hovland, C. I., Lumsdaine, A. A., & Sheffield, F. D. (1949). *Studies in social psychology in World War II. Volume 3: Experiments on mass communication.* Princeton, NJ: Princeton University Press.

Irle, M., & Katz, L. B. (Eds.). (1982). *Studies in decision making: Social psychological and socio-economic analyses.* Berlin: Walter de Gruyter.

Jennings, M. K., & Niemi, R. G. (1981). *Generations and politics: A panel study of young adults and their parents.* Princeton, NJ: Princeton University Press.

Johnson-Laird, P. N. (1983). *Mental models: Towards a cognitive science of language, inference, and consciousness.* Cambridge, MA: Harvard University Press.

Jones, L. A. (1986). Perception of force and weight: Theory and research. *Psychological Bulletin, 100,* 1, 29–42.

Judd, C. M., Krosnick, J. A., & Milburn, M. A. (1981). Political involvement and attitude structure in the general public. *American Sociological Review, 46,* 660–669.

Kaiser, M. K., Jonides, J., & Alexander, J. (1986). Intuitive reasoning about abstract and familiar physics problems. *Memory & Cognition, 14*(4), 308–312.

Kanouse, D. E., & Abelson, R. P. (1967). Language variables affecting the persuasiveness of simple communications. *Journal of Personality and Social Psychology, 7,* 156–163.

Kaplowitz, S. A., Fink, E. L., & Bauer, C. L. (1983). A dynamic model of the effect of discrepant information on unidimensional attitude change. *Behavioral Science, 28,* 233–250.

Karlins, M., Coffman, T. L., & Walters, G. (1969). On the fading of social stereotypes: Studies in three generations of college students. *Journal of Personality and Social Psychology, 13,* 1–16.

Katz, D. (1960). The functional approach to the study of attitudes. *Public Opinion Quarterly, 24,* 163–204.

Kelman, H. C. (1974). Attitudes are alive and well and gainfully employed in the sphere of action. *American Psychologist, 29,* 310–324.

Kelman, H. C. (1980). The role of action in attitude change. In H. E. Howe, Jr. & M. M. Page (Eds.), *Nebraska symposium on motivation: Beliefs, attitudes and values, 1979* (Vol. 27, pp. 117–194). Lincoln, NE: University of Nebraska Press.

Kerlinger, F. N. (1984). *Liberalism, conservatism, and the structure of social attitudes.* Hillsdale, NJ: Lawrence Erlbaum Associates.

Kinder, D. R., & Sears, D. O. (1981). Prejudice and politics: Symbolic racism versus racial threats to the good life. *Journal of Personality and Social Psychology, 40,* 414–431.

Krech, D., & Crutchfield, R. S. (1948). *Theory and problems in social psychology.* New York: McGraw-Hill.

Kreitler, H., & Kreitler, S. (1982). The theory of cognitive orientation: Widening the scope of behavior prediction. In B. A. Maher & W. B. Maher (Eds.), *Progress in Experimental Personality Research* (Vol. 11, pp. 102–169). New York: Academic Press.

Lakoff, G., & Johnson, M. (1980). *Metaphors we live by.* Chicago: University of Chicago Press.

LaPiere, R. T. (1934). Attitudes versus action. *Social Forces, 13,* 230–237.

Lau, R. R., & Hartman, K. A. (1983). Common sense representations of common illnesses. *Health Psychology, 2,* 167–185.

Lazarsfeld, P. F. (1959). Latent structure analysis. In S. Koch (Ed.), *Psychology: a study of a science* (Vol. 3, pp. 476–543). New York: McGraw-Hill.

Lerner, M. J., & Lerner, S. C. (Eds.). (1981). *The justice motive in social behavior: Adapting to times of scarcity and change.* New York: Plenum.

Leventhal, H., Meyer, D., & Nerenz, D. (1980). The common sense representation of illness danger. In S. Rachman (Ed.), *Medical Psychology* (Vol. 2, pp. 7–30). New York: Pergamon.

Levinson, D. J. (1978). *The seasons of a man's life.* New York: Knopf.

Lichtman, R. (1982). *The production of desire: The integration of psychoanalysis into Marxist theory.* New York: Free Press.

Maital, S. (1982). *Minds, markets, and money.* New York: Basic Books.

Marascuilo, L. A., & Zwick, R. (1983). Comment on Barnard: Another look at strength and direction of attitude using contrasts. *Psychological Bulletin, 94,* 534–539.

McCloskey, M. (1983). Naive theories of motion. In D. Gentner & A. L. Stevens (Eds.), *Mental Models.* Hillsdale, NJ: Lawrence Erlbaum Associates.

McFarland, S. G., & Thistlethwaite, D. L. (1970). An analysis of a logical consistency model of belief change. *Journal of Personality and Social Psychology, 15,* 133–143.

McGuire, W. J. (1960). A syllogistic analysis of cognitive relationships. In M. J. Rosenberg & C. I. Hovland (Eds.), *Attitude organization and change* (pp. 65–111). New Haven, CT: Yale University Press.

McGuire, W. J. (1964). Inducing resistance to persuasion. In L. Berkowitz (Ed.), *Advances in experimental social psychology* (Vol. 1, pp. 191–229). New York: Academic Press.

McGuire, W. J. (1966). Attitudes and opinions. In P. R. Farmsworth, O. McNemar, & Q. McNemar (Eds.), *Annual Review of Psychology, 17,* 475–514. Palo Alto, CA: Annual Reviews Press.

McGuire, W. J. (1968). Theory of the structure of human thought. In R. P. Abelson, E. Aronson, W. J. McGuire, T. M. Newcomb, M. J. Rosenberg, & P. H. Tannenbaum (Eds.), *Theories of cognitive consistency: A sourcebook* (pp. 140–162). Chicago: Rand McNally.

McGuire, W. J. (1981). The probabilogical model of cognitive structure and attitude change. In R. E. Petty, T. M. Ostrom, & T. C. Brock (Eds.), *Cognitive responses in persuasion* (pp. 291–307). Hillsdale, NJ: Lawrence Erlbaum Associates.

McGuire, W. J. (1984). Search for the self: Going beyond self-esteem and the reactive self. In R. A. Zucker, J. Aronoff, & A. I. Rabin (Eds.), *Personality and the prediction of behavior* (pp. 73–120). New York: Academic Press.

McGuire, W. J. (1985). Attitudes and attitude change. In G. Lindzey & E. Aronson (Eds.), *The handbook of social psychology* (3rd ed., Vol. 2, pp. 233–346). New York: Random House.

McGuire, W. J. (1986a). The vicissitudes of attitudes and similar representational constructs in twentieth century psychology. *European Journal of Social Psychology, 16,* 89–130.

McGuire, W. J. (1986b). The myth of massive media impact: Savaging and salvagings. In G. Comstock (Ed.), *Public communication and behavior* (Vol. 1, pp. 173–257). Orlando, FL: Academic Press.

McGuire, W. J., & McGuire, C. V. (1986). Differences in conceptualizing self versus conceptualizing other people as manifested in contrasting verb types used in natural speech. *Journal of Personality and Social Psychology, 51,* 1135–1143.

McGuire, W. J., & Millman, S. (1965). Anticipatory belief lowering following forewarning of a persuasive attack. *Journal of Personality and Social Psychology, 2,* 471–479.

McGuire, W. J., & Padawer-Singer, A. (1976). Trait salience in the spontaneous self-concept. *Journal of Personality and Social Psychology, 33,* 743–754.

Meringer, R. (1908). *Aus dem Leben der Sprache: Versprechen, Kindersprache Nachahmungstrich.* [On natural language: Speech errors, children's language, mispronunciations, omissions.] Berlin: Behr's Verlag.

Michotte, A. E. (1963). *The perception of causality* (T. R. & E. Miles, Trans.) New York: Basic Books. (Original work published 1946)

Millar, M. G., & Tesser, A. (1986). Effects of affective and cognitive focus on the attitude-behavior relation. *Journal of Personality and Social Psychology, 51,* 270–276.

Miller, G. A., Galanter, E., & Pribram, K. H. (1960). *Plans and the structure of behavior.* New York: Holt.

Moscovici, S. (1984). The phenomenon of social representation. In R. Farr and S. Moscovici, *Social representation* (pp. 3–69). Cambridge, England: Cambridge University Press.

Murray, H. A. (1938). *Explorations in personality.* New York: Oxford.

Nelson, C. E. (1968). Anchoring to accepted values as a technique for immunizing beliefs against persuasion. *Journal of Personality and Social Psychology, 9,* 329–334.

Nuttin, J. M., Jr. (1975). *The illusion of attitude change.* London: Academic Press.

O'Malley, M., & Thistlethwaite, D. L. (1980). Inference in inconsistency reduction: new evidence on the 'Socratic effect.' *Journal of Personality and Social Psychology, 39,* 1064–1071.

Osgood, C. E., Suci, G. J., & Tannenbaum, P. H. (1957). *The measurement of meaning.* Urbana, IL: University of Illinois Press.

Ostrom, T. M. (1969). The relationship between the affective, behavioral and cognitive components of attitude. *Journal of Experimental Social Psychology, 5,* 12–30.

Pennebaker, J. W. (1982). *The psychology of physical symptoms.* New York: Springer-Verlag.
Pennington, N., & Hastie, R. (1986). Evidence evaluation in complex decision making. *Journal of Personality and Social Psychology, 51,* 242–258.
Petty, R. E., & Cacioppo, J. T. (1986). The elaboration likelihood model of persuasion. In L. Berkowitz (Ed.), *Advances in experimental social psychology,* (Vol. 19, pp. 123–205). New York: Academic Press.
Petty, R. E., Ostrom, T. M., & Brock, T. C. (Eds.). (1981). *Cognitive responses in persuasion.* Hillsdale, NJ: Lawrence Erlbaum Associates.
Plott, C. R., & Levine, M. E. (1978). A model of agenda influence on committee decisions. *The American Economic Review, 68,* 146–160.
Posner, M. I., & Keele, S. W. (1970). Retention of abstract ideas. *Journal of Experimental Psychology, 83,* 304–308.
Powell, R. S., & Juhnke, R. G. (1983). Statistical models of implicit personality theory: A comparison. *Journal of Personality and Social Psychology, 44,* 911–922.
Powers, W. T. (1978). Quantitative analysis of purposive systems: Some spadework at the foundation of scientific psychology. *Psychological Review, 85,* 417–435.
Pratkanis, A. R., Greenwald, A. G., Leippe, M. R., & Baumgardner, M. H. (1988). In search of reliable persuasion effects: III. The sleeper effect is dead. Long live the sleeper effect. *Journal of Personality and Social Psychology, 54,* 203–218.
Rokeach, M. (1960). *The open and closed mind.* New York: Basic Books.
Rosenberg, M. J. (1960). An analysis of affective-cognitive consistency. In M. J. Rosenberg & C. I. Hovland (Eds.), *Attitude organization and change* (pp. 15–64). New Haven, CT: Yale University Press.
Rossman, B. B., & Gollob, H. F. (1976). Social inference and pleasantness judgments involving people and issues. *Journal of Experimental Social Psychology, 12,* 374–391.
Rummelhart, D. E., & Ortony, A. (1977). The representation of knowledge in memory. In R. C. Anderson, R. J. Spiro, & W. E. Montague (Eds.), *Schooling and the acquisition of knowledge.* Hillsdale, NJ: Lawrence Erlbaum Associates.
Ryan, W. (1971). *Blaming the victim.* New York: Pantheon.
Sagan, K. (1977). *Dragons of Eden: speculations on the evolution of human intelligence.* New York: Random House.
Saltzer, E. B. (1981). Cognitive moderators of the relationship between behavioral intention and behavior. *Journal of Personality and Social Psychology, 41,* 260–271.
Sandell, R. G. (1977). *Linguistic style and persuasion.* London: Academic Press.
Savage, L. J. (1954). *The foundations of statistics.* New York: Wiley.
Schank, R. C., & Riesbeck, C. K. (1981). Inside computer understanding: Five programs plus miniatures. Hillsdale, NJ: Lawrence Erlbaum Associates.
Schneider, D. J. (1973). Implicit personality theory: A review. *Psychological Bulletin, 79,* 294–309.
Schuman, H., & Presser, S. (1981). *Questions and answers in attitude surveys: Experiments on question form wording and context.* New York: Academic Press.
Scott, W. A., Osgood, D. W., & Peterson, C. (1979). *Cognitive structure: Theory and measurement of individual differences.* New York: Halsted Press.
Semin, G. R., & Greenslade, L. (1985). Differential contributions of linguistic factors to memory-based ratings: Systematizing the systematic distortion hypothesis. *Journal of Personality and Social Psychology, 49,* 1713–1723.
Semin, G. R., & Manstead, S. R. (1983). *The accountability of conduct: A social psychological analysis.* New York: Academic Press.
Sherif, M., & Hovland, C. I. (1961). *Social judgment: assimilation and contrast effects in communication and attitude change.* New Haven, CT: Yale University Press.

Sheth, J. N. (1974). A field study of attitude-structure and attitude-behavior relationship. In J. N. Sheth (Ed.), *Models for buyer behavior: Conceptual, quantitative and empirical.* New York: Harper & Row.

Siegal, M. (1982). *Fairness in children: A social-cognitive approach to the study of moral development.* London: Academic Press.

Sjöberg, L. (1982). Beliefs and values as attitude components. In B. Wegener (Ed.), *Social attitudes and psychophysical measurement* (pp. 199–217). Hillsdale, NJ: Lawrence Erlbaum Associates.

Smith, M. B. (1949). Personal values as determinants of a political attitude. *Journal of Psychology, 28,* 477–486.

Songer-Nocks, E. (1976). Situational factors affecting the weighting of predictor components in the Fishbein model. *Journal of Experimental Social Psychology, 12,* 56–69.

Stroebe, W., & Meyer, W. (Eds.). (1982). Social psychology and economics [Special issue]. *British Journal of Social Psychology, 21* Part 2, 79–183. .

Suchman, H., & Presser, S. (1981). *Questions and answers in attitude surveys: Experiments on question form, wording, and contexts.* New York: Academic Press.

Taylor, J. (1980). Dimensionalizations of racialism and the black experience: The Pittsburgh project. In R. L. Jones (Ed.), *Black psychology* (2nd ed., pp. 384–397). New York: Harper & Row.

Tesser, A. (1978). Self-generated attitude change. In L. Berkowitz (Ed.), *Advances in experimental social psychology,* (Vol. 11, pp. 289–338). New York: Academic Press.

Toglia, M. P. & Battig, W. F. (1978). *Handbook of semantic word norms.* Hillsdale, NJ: Lawrence, Erlbaum Associates.

Tomkins, S. (1979). Script theory: Differential magnification of affects. In H. E. Howe, Jr. (Ed.), *Nebraska symposium on motivation, 1978* (Vol. 26, pp. 201–236). Lincoln, NE: University of Nebraska Press.

Transgaard, H. (1973). *The cognitive components of attitudes and beliefs: Structure and empirical methods.* Kobenhavn: Teknisk Forlag.

Triandis, H. C. (1977). *Interpersonal behavior.* Monterey, CA: Brooks/Cole.

Triandis, H. C. (1980). Values, attitudes and interpersonal behavior. In H. E. Howe, Jr. (Ed.), *Nebraska symposium on motivation: 1979* (Vol. 27, pp. 195–259). Lincoln, NE: University of Nebraska Press.

Turner, C. F., & Krauss, E. (1978). Fallible indicators of the subjective state of the nation. *American Psychologist, 33,* 456–470.

Tversky, A. (1972). Elimination by aspects: A theory of choice. *Psychological Review, 79,* 281–299.

Tversky, A., & Kahneman, D. (1980). Causal schemas in judgments under uncertainty. In M. Fishbein (Ed.), *Progress in social psychology, 1* (pp. 49–72). Hillsdale, NJ: Lawrence Erlbaum Associates.

Viney, L. L. (1983). *Images of illness.* Melbourne, FL: Krieger.

Watts, W. A., & Holt, L. E. (1970). Logical relationships among beliefs and timing as factors in persuasion. *Journal of Personality and Social Psychology, 16,* 571–582.

Watts, W. A., & McGuire, W. J. (1964). Persistence of induced opinion change and retention of inducing message content. *Journal of Abnormal and Social Psychology, 68,* 233–241.

Wicker, A. W. (1969). Attitudes versus actions: The relationship of verbal and overt behavioral responses to attitude objects. *Journal of Social Issues, 25* (4), 41–78.

Wicklund, R. A., & Brehm, J. W. (1976). *Perspectives on cognitive dissonance.* Hillsdale, NJ: Lawrence Erlbaum Associates.

Wyer, R. S., Jr., & Carlston, D. E. (1979). *Social cognition, inference, and attribution.* Hillsdale, NJ: Lawrence Erlbaum Associates.

Wyer, R. S., Jr., & Goldberg, L. (1970). A probabilistic analysis of the relationships between beliefs and attitudes. *Psychological Review, 77,* 100–120.

Wyer, R. S., Jr., & Srull, T. K. (1986). Human cognition in its social context. *Psychological Review, 93,* 322–359.

Zajonc, R. B. (1960). The process of cognitive tuning in communication. *Journal of Abnormal and Social Psychology, 61,* 159–167.

Zajonc, R. B. (1980). Feeling and thinking: Preferences need no inferences. *American Psychologist, 35,* 151–175.

4

The Cognitive Representation of Attitudes

Anthony R. Pratkanis
University of California, Santa Cruz

The history of research on attitudes is marked by two characteristics. First, the concept of attitude is popular and widely accepted. It is a textbook staple and a useful theoretical construct for behavioral, mathematical, field-theoretical, and cognitive approaches. Second, the concept of attitude has been associated with a number of unreliable effects such as selective exposure, the sleeper effect in persuasion, behavior prediction, and selective learning. These null and contradictory findings have encouraged some to question the utility of the attitude concept (cf. Abelson, 1972; Wicker, 1969).

Perhaps these two characteristics of attitude research are related. The widespread acceptance of the concept of attitude has resulted in a watered-down construct that, as Blumer (1955) noted, "fails miserably to meet the requirements of a scientific concept" (p. 59; see also Bain, 1928; Symonds, 1927). Although attitude is a concept for all seasons, there appears to be little agreement on the question: "What is an attitude and how does it influence social processes?" and therefore, there is little reason to expect reliable attitude findings.

The goal of the present chapter is twofold. First, it summarizes the effects of attitudes on various cognitive processes to determine if (and when) the pessimism concerning the predictive validity of attitudes is warranted. Second, the results of this review are used to develop a sociocognitive model of the representation of attitudes—an effort that should be viewed as a continuation of the work of Katz and Stotland (1959) and of Lingle and

71

Ostrom (1981). In this model, an attitude is represented by a simple evaluative cue (or strategy), which serves a heuristic function and by a complex knowledge structure that serves a schematic function. We begin by looking at previous attempts at specifying the representation of attitude structure (see also McGuire, chap. 3 in this volume).

PREVIOUS CONCEPTUALIZATIONS
OF ATTITUDE STRUCTURE

Structure by Definition

One approach to specifying attitude structure is definitional, as exemplified in Allport's (1935) review of the attitude concept. Early usage of the term *attitude* was diverse (see Fleming, 1967) and included such concepts as adaptedness (by evolutionary biologists such as Spencer), muscular preparedness (by Lange and Baldwin), cognitive set (by the Wurzburg school), dynamic motivation (by Freud), and mental processes that determine response (by sociologists such as Thomas and Znaniecki). Allport's (1935) definition was a skillful integration of these varying usages: "An attitude is a mental and neural state of readiness, organized through experience, exerting a directive or dynamic influence upon the individual's response to all objects and situations with which it is related" (p. 810).

Although integrative, Allport's definition also included the theoretical assumptions of the various approaches popular at the time. For example, attitudes were assumed to drive behavior either through a mental or neural state of readiness. By including behavior prediction as a component of the definition of an attitude, the concept is reasonably declared useless if, as shown by Wicker (1969), there is a weak verbal attitude/overt behavior correlation (or if any other implicit component of the definition is not demonstrated).

Given that definitions may often imply undesired theoretical assumptions, I prefer a definition of attitude as a *person's evaluation of an object of thought*. This definition has two benefits. First, it is minimally endowed with excess meaning. That is, the definition is not bound to any given theory or model of attitude. Thus, the internal representation and the expression of an attitude (i.e., a model of attitude structure and function) is an empirical and theoretical concern. Second, it emphasizes the evaluative nature of attitude as did early attitude measurement researchers such as Thurstone (1928) and Edwards (1957). Thus, their techniques of scaling responses along an evaluative continuum can be used to operationalize the concept of attitude.

The Tripartite Model

One of the most widely assumed and least understood models of attitude structure is the tripartite model (Breckler, 1984; Rosenberg & Hovland, 1960). According to this perspective, an attitude consists of affective, behavioral, and cognitive components. Although frequently appearing in textbooks, the tripartite model has not inspired much research. One major obstacle to research is the lack of widespread agreement on the meaning of its terms. For example, affect has been variously described as an evaluation, as subjective feelings, and as physiological correlates. Thus, most of the research on the tripartite model has been directed towards validation (i.e., demonstrating that attitudes consist of three components [cf. Breckler, 1984; Kothandapani, 1971; Ostrom, 1969]). Only a few studies have investigated the implications of the model for such topics as attitude change and behavior prediction (see Ajzen, chap. 10 in this volume), and thus the tripartite model has *not* been demonstrated to have strong predictive or explanatory power.

Behavioral Perspectives

Behaviorists such as Thorndike (1935), Doob (1947), and Rhine (1958) described attitude structure in terms of an intervening response in an S → R connection. According to Doob (1947), an attitude is an anticipatory and mediating response (i.e., an implicit response preceding other, typically overt, behavior). Learned through contingencies of reward and punishment, an attitude is evoked by a variety of stimulus patterns determined by the principles of generalization and discrimination. Attitudes can vary on three properties (or strengths):

1. afferent-habit strength (the strength of the bond between the stimulus pattern and the internal response called attitude)
2. efferent-habit strength (the strength of the bond between attitude as stimulus and a response), and
3. drive strength (tension produced by an attitude that needs to be reduced by subsequent behavior).

During the 1950s and 1960s, the behavioral approach to attitudes stimulated much research, addressing such issues as attitude acquisition and development (Rhine, 1958), persuasion (Weiss, 1968), attitudes and interpersonal attraction (Lott & Lott, 1968), the role of attitudes in human motivation (Staats, 1968), and the reinforcing property of attitudes (Byrne, 1971). With the rise of more cognitive approaches, this research has not received much attention, perhaps due to the perceived animosity between cognitive and behavioral perspectives. In regards to the attitude construct, this assumption of antagonism may not be warranted. Doob's view of attitude can be translated into cognitive terms by substituting *implicit response* with *an evaluation stored in memory.* Afferent-habit strength then becomes construct accessibility. Efferent-habit strength is, in cognitive terms, a well-learned behavioral plan invoked by an attitude.

Expectancy-Value Perspectives

Expectancy-value theorists such as Fishbein and Ajzen (1975) and Rosenberg (1956) attempted to describe attitudes in terms of a multi-attribute structure. This structure is typically described by an equation relating beliefs to attitudes. The most popular form of this equation is given by Fishbein and Ajzen (1975, p. 29):

$$A_o = \sum_{i=1}^{n} b_i e_i$$

where A_o is the attitude toward some object, O; b_i is the belief i about O, (i.e. the subjective probability that O is related to attribute i); e_i is the evaluation of attribute i; and n is the number of beliefs. In other words, attitude structure consists of a collection of subjective beliefs about an object. Typically, expectancy-value researchers have placed little explicit organization on this collection of beliefs. However, attitude structure could be specified in multi-attribute terms by means of correlated attributes and clusters of beliefs. For example, attributes such as repair costs, frequency of repair, and amount of time in shop may all be related in the person's knowledge of cars and form a "reliability" script, schema, or prototype as part of the multi-attribute structure (see Yi, 1987).

Cognitive Perspectives

Whereas the behaviorist uses terms such as S—R, the cognitivist uses constructs such as proposition, knowledge structure, image, set of beliefs, and schema to describe the mental representation or cognitive structure of an attitude. The result has been a list of dimensions and properties on which attitudes are assumed to differ. Some of the more popular distinctions include: intensity, salience, differentiation, integration, centrality, and symbolic (see Katz & Stotland, 1959; Newcomb, Turner, & Converse, 1965; Raden, 1985; Scott, 1968; Scott, Osgood, & Peterson, 1979 for list of dimensions). Although the specification of these properties is a logical first step for distinguishing various types of attitudes, there has been far too little empirical work to indicate which properties are useful for predicting attitude effects. Scott et al. (1979) provided preliminary measures of many of these attitude properties. However without further empirical work, overlap in meaning among the terms and a lack of understanding about the relationship between the various properties will continue.

ATTITUDES AND CONCEPTUAL COGNITIVE PROCESSES

For the most part, the previously described approaches are logical and theoretical analyses of attitude structure. An alternative approach is to specify the representational format of an attitude by inferring structure from known, reliable (and expected, but frequently unobtained) effects of attitudes on cognition.

Most researchers who use the concept of attitude believe that attitudes induce a consistency or correspondence of response. *Positive* attitudes result in *positive* feelings, thoughts, and behaviors toward an object whereas *negative* attitudes engender the opposite, *negative* response. Attitude effects are assumed to follow the rules of balance theory (Heider, 1958; Zajonc & Burnstein, 1965), resulting in a consistency between the valence of evaluation of an object and response towards that object. The evidence indicates that attitudes reliably produce correspondence effects for at least one class of cognitive processes—those dealing with conceptual or semantic memory.

Conceptual and Episodic Memories

Tulving (1983) argued that human propositional memory can be divided into conceptual (semantic) and episodic memories. Conceptual memory is knowledge of the world, consisting of facts, ideas, and concepts. According to Tulving, "It is a mental thesaurus, organized knowledge a person possesses about words and other verbal symbols, their meaning and referents, about relationships among them, and about rules, formulas, and algorithms for the manipulation of symbols, concepts, and relations" (p. 21). The contents of conceptual memory are relatively permanent, are accessed automatically, and are context-free (i.e., not linked to a temporal event).

On the other hand, episodic memory is "a system that receives and stores information about temporally dated episodes or events, and temporal-spatial relations among them" (Tulving, 1983, p. 21). It consists of events and episodes (personal experiences) organized in a temporal sequence. The contents of episodic memory are prone to forgetting, are accessed deliberately, and are context-dependent.

Conceptual and episodic memories are each involved in different types of mental tasks. As Tulving stated, "Episodic tasks are those for which the learning of the material in a particular episode is *necessary,* whereas semantic [conceptual] tasks are those for which general pre-experimental knowledge of the world is *sufficient*" (p. 77). Conceptual memory tasks include the processes of comprehension, categorization, inference, judgment, and reasoning. Episodic memory is involved when an individual attempts to recall yesterday's happenings, a list of experimental nonsense syllables, or a persuasive message presented in a laboratory setting. However, conceptual memory may also be involved in the recall of an episode when that episode can be (more or less correctly) inferred and reconstructed from information stored in conceptual memory.

The Attitude Heuristic

Attitudes frequently guide conceptual cognitive processes by determining the strategy to be taken in regards to an object. In other words, attitudes serve as *heuristics*—positive attitudes invoke a favoring strategy whereas negative attitudes result in the opposite.

A heuristic is a simple strategy for solving a problem. Some examples include, "If the job applicant has a long vita, then interview" and "If the experimental results are positive, then publish." A heuristic can be contrasted with a more detailed set of procedures or an algorithm for solving a problem (see Sherman & Corty, 1984). Tversky and Kahneman (1974) demonstrated how such heuristics as representativeness and availability (accessibility) can influence judgments and decisions.

An *attitudinal heuristic* is a heuristic that uses the evaluative relationship as a cue in the problem-solving strategy. Attitudes are used to assign objects to a favorable class (for which strategies of favoring, approaching, and protecting are appropriate) or to an unfavorable class (for which strategies of disfavoring, avoiding, neglecting, and harming are used).

Examples of the Use of an Attitude as a Heuristic

At least 11 examples of classes of reliable attitude-correspondence effects on conceptual processes can be identified.

Interpretation and Explanation. Attitudes can be used to selectively interpret and explain social events. For example, Smith (1947) found that pro- and anti-Soviet individuals rated the credibility of Soviet news items consistent with their attitudes (see also Waly & Cook, 1965). Cooper and Jahoda (1947) and Kendall and Wolf (1949) demonstrated that prejudiced individuals misunderstood cartoons presenting a bigoted person in an unfavorable manner. Hastorf and Cantril (1954) found that interpretations of a Princeton versus Dartmouth football game varied as a function of support for the two opponents. Manis (1961) showed that attitudes affected the interpretation of a message such that subjects misattributed an attitude-consistent position on the issue of college fraternities to a prestigious individual. Regan, Straus, and Fazio (1974) found that subjects make internal attributions when an actor behaves consistently with attitudinal expectations (i.e., liked actors perform positive behaviors and disliked actors perform negative behaviors), but provided external attributions when an actor behaved inconsistently with the subject's attitude toward the actor.

Halo Effects: Expectations and Inferences.   The use of an attitude as a heuristic can result in halo effects: An overall favorable or unfavorable impression can selectively bias expectations and inferences. For example, much research shows that people who are evaluated as attractive are expected to be "better" than those not so evaluated (Hatfield & Sprecher, 1986) and that liked individuals are expected to possess positive traits whereas disliked individuals are assumed to possess negative traits (see Lott & Lott, 1972; Lott, Lott, Reed, & Crow 1970). Similarly, in surveys of economic expectations, Katona (1975) noted that good events such as the end of World War II and the end of the Cuban missile crisis are typically associated with optimistic expectations concerning the economy whereas negative events such as the U-2 incident and the Berlin crisis induce economic pessimism. As Katona stated, "What is considered to be good is seen as having good effects, and what is considered bad is seen as having bad effects" (p. 199).

Syllogistic Reasoning.   Attitudes towards the conclusion of a syllogism can influence the ability to determine if the syllogism is logically valid (cf. Evans, Barston, & Pollard, 1983; Feather, 1964; Gordon, 1953; Janis & Frick, 1943; Lefford, 1946; Morgan, 1945; Morgan & Morton, 1943, 1944). For example, Thistlethwaite (1950) asked respondents to state whether syllogisms such as the following were valid:

> Given: If production is important, then peaceful industrial relations are desirable. If production is important then it is a mistake to have Negroes for foreman and leaders over Whites.
> Therefore: If peaceful industrial relations are desirable, then it is a mistake to have Negroes for foreman and leaders over Whites.

For this syllogism, prejudiced individuals (who agree with the conclusion) are more likely to indicate (incorrectly) that the logic is valid compared to less prejudiced individuals.

Responses to Persuasive Communications. Greenwald (1968) found that individuals with an unfavorable attitude toward the topic of a persuasive communication are more likely to counterargue a message, whereas those with a favorable attitude are more likely to provide consonant cognitive responses. This pattern of results has been frequently obtained in studies of persuasion (see Petty, Ostrom, & Brock, 1981). Similarly, Waly and Cook (1965) discovered that an argument was considered more effective and plausible by those who agreed (as opposed to disagreed) with the position expressed in the argument (see Lord, Lepper, & Ross, 1979 for a recent replication of the Waly & Cook, 1965 finding).

Interpersonal Attraction. Byrne (1971) repeatedly found that individuals with attitudes similar to one's own are viewed as attractive. In a typical experiment, subjects receive information about others' attitudes. Attitude similarity is manipulated by varying the proportion of shared attitudes between the subject and a stimulus person. The more shared attitudes, the more attractive the subject rates the stimulus person. (See Rosenbaum, 1986 for an alternative repulsion interpretation of these findings).

Judgment of Social Stimuli. One's own attitude provides a reference point for the judgment of social stimuli. For example, Edwards (1941) discovered that an ambiguous message on the New Deal was interpreted as favorable to the New Deal by those supporting Roosevelt's plan and as anti-New Deal by those opposing this policy. Vroom (1960) found that individuals with a positive attitude toward an organization viewed that organization's goals as similar to their own. Granberg and Jenks (1977) found that survey respondents perceived the position of their preferred candidate in the 1972 presidential election (McGovern or Nixon) on nine sociopolitical issues to be highly similar to their own position on these issues. Sherif and Hovland (1961) presented additional evidence that attitudes bias social judgments.

False Consensus of Opinion. Wallen (1943) observed that subjects believe their attitude position to be more popular than it actually is. In this first "false-consensus" study, students were asked to give both their opinions on, and their estimate of, the percentage of students who supported the Selective Service, the St. Lawrence Seaway Project and war with Germany. The results showed that the respondents estimated the attitudes of others so that their own opinion coincided with that of the estimated majority. The false-consensus effect has been replicated often (cf. Fields & Schuman, 1976; Granberg, Jefferson, Brent, & King, 1981; Ross, Greene, & House, 1977; Sherman, Chassin, Presson, & Agostinelli, 1984).

Fact Identification. The use of an attitude can lead to the selective reconstruction of past events. For example, 2½ years after the event, Eberhart and Bauer (1941) assessed memory for a riot involving the Chicago police and a crowd of striking employees of the Republic Steel Company. Eberhart and Bauer noted that subjects with a pro-labor attitude were more likely to remember that the crowd was unarmed and that the police brutally shot peaceful citizens whereas anti-labor subjects recalled the opposite. Similarly, Pratkanis (in press) observed that subjects misidentified facts consistent with their attitudes. Given pairs of statements such as (a) Ronald Reagan maintained an 'A' average at Eureka college and (b) Ronald Reagan never achieved above a 'C' average at Eureka college (a fact), subjects were most likely to identify as true those statements that agreed with their attitudes (see also Smith, 1968).

Estimates of Personal Behavior. Past personal behavior is often revised to be consistent with current attitudes. For example, Bem and McConnell (1970) changed attitudes via a counterattitudinal essay procedure on the issue of student control of their university. The results showed that subjects erred by overestimating the extent to which their premanipulation attitudes (as assessed earlier by Bem and McConnell) were similar to their current attitudes. Although there is disagreement over the psychological mechanisms involved, this finding has often been replicated (cf. Aderman & Brehm, 1976; Goethals & Reckman, 1973; Ross & Shulman, 1973; and Shaffer, 1975a; 1975b). Recently, Markus (1985), in a national survey of teenagers and parents in 1965 with follow-up collections in 1973 and 1982, found that current attitudes on policy issues such as legalized marijuana, woman's roles, and rights of the accused biased the recall of past attitudes on these issues.

Ross, McFarland, and Fletcher (1981) provided another example of the use of attitudes in the selective estimation of the frequency of past personal behavior. In their studies, subjects received persuasive messages that either derogated or promoted daily toothbrushing and frequent bathing. Those who heard the anti-toothbrushing and anti-bathing messages estimated that they toothbrushed and bathed less often than those who heard the pro messages. Ross, McFarland, Conway, and Zanna (1983) replicated this effect, but found that it was less likely to occur when the domain of recall was objective, as opposed to ambiguous (i.e., recall of the frequency of one's exercise versus how vigorous one's exercise was perceived to be).

Information Error Technique. The fact that attitudes produce errors in judgments led Hammond (1948) to suggest an *information error technique* as an indirect measure of attitudes (see Kreman, 1949; Kubany, 1953;

Parrish, 1948; Weschler 1950a, 1950b). In this technique, respondents are asked, under the guise of an information survey, to select which of two statements is true. In reality both responses are incorrect—for example, (taken from Weschler, 1950a): "During the strike wave of April 1948, the percentage of estimated working time lost was (1) 1.1% or (2) 2.2%?" (The correct answer is 1.6%). Respondents frequently chose the error that is most consistent with their attitudes. Given that lost working time is viewed as negative, individuals with a pro-business attitude indicate that the strike produced considerable downtime, whereas the pro-labor supporter attributes less lost time to the strike.

Prediction of Future Events.   Hadley Cantril (1940) once observed, "What people want to happen, they tend to think will happen" (p. 406). The Gallup (1972) poll asked the following question of nationally representative samples before the presidential elections of 1944, 1948, 1952, 1960 and 1968: "If you were to guess at this time, who do you think will win the next presidency, a Republican or Democrat?" The results, averaged across the years, indicate that 63.3% of the Democrats believe that a Democrat will win the next election (versus 19.5% predicting a Republican victory and the rest undecided), whereas 57.0% of the Republicans believe a Republican will win (versus 26.3% predicting a Democratic win and the rest undecided). This partisan attitude effect held for all elections except the Truman/Dewey presidential election of 1948 (see also Granberg & Brent, 1983).

Previous Descriptions of the Attitude Heuristic

This review of 11 classes of effects of attitude on conceptual cognitive processes indicates that the general pessimism over the predictive value of the concept of attitude is unfounded. This perspective is shared by attitude theorists who have long noted that attitudes serve a cognitive function. For example, Lippmann (1922) viewed public opinion as an economical simplifier of a complex world. Smith, Bruner, and White (1957) posited that opinions serve an object appraisal function: "An attitude provides a ready aid in 'sizing up' objects and events in the environment" (p. 41). Katz (1960) suggested that attitudes satisfy a knowledge function, providing adequate structure to the social world. McGuire (1969) noted that attitudes serve as "a simplified and practical manual of appropriate behavior toward specific objects" (p. 158). Katona (1975) specified a principle of affect generalization—good things produce good consequences and bad things produce bad consequences. Pettigrew (1979) concluded that past research on prejudice indicates that people often commit an ultimate attribution error—that is, the attribution of good and bad qualities to liked and disliked groups of people (respectively).

Factors Influencing the Use of an Attitude as a Heuristic

Given the ubiquity of attitudinal influences on conceptual cognitive processes, a valuable question is: "What conditions increase (and decrease) the probability of using an attitude as a heuristic?" Six factors can be identified.

First, an attitude must be stored in memory. Converse (1970) noted that survey respondents often do not possess an attitude toward a given issue, but respond to a survey question anyway (i.e., the attitude is created only when the respondent is asked about an issue). In cases of nonattitudes, responses will be highly variable and correspondence effects should be less likely to occur.

Second, the attitude must represent the best (or only) strategy for solving a problem (i.e., there are no available competing strategies or theories). For example, Granberg (1985), analyzing survey responses to the question, "What is Ted Kennedy's position on abortion?" found that respondents' answers varied as a function of their own attitude toward abortion plus their perception of Democrats' position on abortion, their perception of Kennedy as a liberal, and as a member of the Catholic church. Attitude toward abortion was one of a number of strategies for answering the Kennedy on abortion question.

A third factor determining attitude heuristic usage is the accessibility and strength of the attitude. Fazio (chap. 7 in this volume) has marshalled impressive evidence that highly accessible attitudes are more likely to influence cognitive processes and behavior. In the Pratkanis (in press) fact identification study, subjects with extreme (strong) attitudes were more likely to identify attitude-consistent facts as true. In the Ted Kennedy/ abortion study, Granberg (1985) also found that manipulating the salience of the various competing cues systematically influenced Kennedy's perceived position on abortion.

A fourth factor, identified by Jamieson and Zanna (chap. 15 in this volume), is time pressure. In a series of studies, Jamieson and Zanna found that attitudes are more likely to be used to solve a problem if subjects are placed under time constraints. Similarly, variables such as information overload and a message-dense environment should also lead to the increased use of heuristic strategies.

Fifth, there must be a problem to solve (i.e., the answer to a problem is not objective and clear). Ross et al. (1983) noted that subjects used their attitudes to estimate past behavior in domains where the answer was ambiguous, but not in domains where the answer was clear and objective.

Finally, there is preliminary evidence that awareness of an attitude bias may eliminate the bias or induce an individual to compensate for the effect. For example, Galanis and Jones (1986) found that Black individuals negatively stereotyped a mentally ill patient (as did Whites). However, when black subjects were reminded of the role of victimization in the mental health commitment process, Black subjects (but not White subjects) ceased to respond consistent with their stereotypes (see Darley & Gross, 1983 and Devine, chap. 8 in this volume for other examples). In cases such as this, the automatic effects of attitudes appear to be replaced by controlled processes.

ATTITUDES AND EPISODIC MEMORY

In contrast to the influence of attitudes on conceptual processes, the effects of attitudes on episodic memory (the recall of temporally dated materials) are not very well-understood. A plausible expectation is that individuals will demonstrate superior learning and recall of information that agrees with the direction of their attitude (an attitude and selective learning effect). Previous research on the attitude and selective learning effect is, to quote one reviewer (Greaves, 1972), "unambiguously inconclusive." Some studies have revealed that agreeable information is learned best; others have demonstrated no attitude and learning relationship; still others have found better recall of attitudinally extreme information; and at least one study has yielded a negative attitude and learning correlation (see Pratkanis, 1984 and Roberts, 1985 for reviews). Similarly, research on attitude change and the recall of a persuasive message has also failed to obtain consistent correlations between message agreeableness and recall of message content (Greenwald, 1968).

A Brief History of Attitude and Learning Research

In 1943, Levine and Murphy provided one of the best demonstrations of the attitude and selective learning effect. In their study, five pro-communist and five anti-communist students attempted to learn and recall two persuasive communications—one supporting and one denouncing communism. The results indicated that the pro-communist students learned the supporting communication better than the anti-communists and the anti-communist students learned the denouncing message better than the pro-communists. Additional research claimed support for this effect (cf. Edwards, 1941; Jones & Kohler, 1958; Weldon & Malpass, 1981) and the attitude and selective learning effect took its place in social psychology textbooks (cf. Krech & Crutchfield, 1948, p. 191) as one of the core findings of the discipline.

In 1966, Waly and Cook presented two experiments that failed to find an attitude and selective learning effect. In their studies, which used procedures similar to those of Jones and Kohler (1958), pro-, neutral, and anti-segregation students attempted to learn plausible pro-segregation, implausible pro-segregation, plausible anti-segregation, and implausible anti-segregation statements. The results from both studies failed to replicate the Jones and Kohler results and provided little consistent evidence for an attitude and selective learning effect. Other researchers have also failed to obtain this learning effect (cf. Brigham & Cook, 1969; Greenwald & Sakumara, 1967; Smith & Jamieson, 1972).

In 1980, Judd and Kulik demonstrated another attitude effect— information rated at the extremes of an agreement scale are recalled best. In their study, college students were presented with 54 Thurstone-scaled attitude statements on the topics of women's rights, capital punishment, and majority rule in South Africa. Subjects stated their agreement with each statement and then rated each statement for the degree it reflected an extremely pro or extremely anti position. After a 1-day delay, subjects attempted to recall the statements. Judd and Kulik found that items rated at the extremes of either the agree/disagree or the pro/anti continuum were recalled the best. Judd and Kulik also found that subjects were fastest in providing their opinion for items at the extremes of the attitude continuum. Although they have not received as much attention as the attitude and selective learning effect, attitude-extremity effects have been obtained in the past by Doob (1953) and by Postman and Murphy (1943).

The inconclusive history of research on attitudes and episodic memory suggests that multiple processes may be involved in the learning of any attitude relevant communication. For example, an attitude can be used as a heuristic to selectively bias the interpretation, encoding, retrieval and recognition of to-be-learned materials and thus affect episodic recall (cf. Edwards, 1941; Pratkanis, in press; Read & Rosson, 1982). In addition, an attitude can serve to motivate the processing of a communication (i.e., inducing message scrutiny, uncritical acceptance, counterarguing and so on). The differential elaboration of a message as a function of attitude can result in variable effects of attitude on recall (cf. Cacioppo & Petty, 1979).

Nevertheless, it appears from the complexity of the pattern of attitude and memory findings, that a simple evaluation of an object stored in memory does not provide the requisite structure necessary for encoding and reproducing a complex communication. Recent research is demonstrating the importance of the pre-existing knowledge structures or schemas supporting an attitude for determining learning and memory within attitude domains.

The Schematic Function of Attitudes

A schema is an organization of a subset of pre-existing knowledge relevant to a limited domain. It consists of both *content* (information in the schema and its organization) and *procedure* (the usage of this information in knowing). The dual role of a schema as content and procedure is similar to that of the heuristic as cue (an evaluation stored in memory) and strategy (the use of this cue in problem-solving). A schema differs from a heuristic in its complexity. A heuristic is one simple rule, whereas a schema is an organization of many rules and pieces of data within a domain.

A frequent finding in learning and memory research is that individuals with well-developed knowledge structures within an area demonstrate superior episodic memory for terms and information related to that domain. (As just one example, see the research of Voss and his colleagues on expertise and memory [Chiesi, Spilich, & Voss, 1979; Spilich, Vesonder, Chiesi, & Voss, 1979; Voss, Vesonder, & Spilich, 1980].) The facilitation of learning and memory by a schema is most likely a multiple-determined effect, as a schema is used at encoding (to aid in comprehension, interpretation, and elaboration of to-be-learned materials) and at retrieval (to provide internal cues that serve as covert mnemonics for recall and reconstruction of an event).

Bipolar Attitude Structure

The Judd and Kulik attitude-extremity results suggest an interesting hypothesis about the schema supporting an attitude. As Judd and Kulik (1980) stated: "Attitudes thus may act as bipolar schemas that contain representations or expectations of very agreeable and disagreeable points of view. Information that closely matches these expectations is more easily judged and recalled than is information that, although relevant, does not match as well" (p. 570). In other words, the knowledge structure supporting an attitude (evaluation) contains not only arguments, beliefs, and expectations supporting one position, but also opposing information (and perhaps counterarguments refuting this opposing material).

Figure 4.1 presents a hypothetical bipolar structure for the topic of nuclear power. This knowledge structure (i.e., information about the domain of nuclear power) is similar regardless of one's own position on the issue. An individual with the knowledge structure of Fig. 4.1 should demonstrate superior learning and faster encoding for information that fits the knowledge frame—that is, information that is consistent with either a pro- or anti-position as opposed to just materials that the individual finds agreeable.

Support for the bipolar hypothesis comes from a variety of sources. Hymes (1986) reasoned that subjects who are neutral on abortion are likely

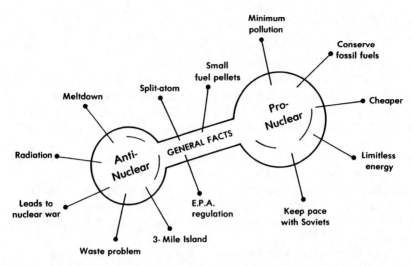

FIG. 4.1. A hypothetical bipolar knowledge structure for the topic of nuclear power.

to be aschematic on this issue (i.e., lacking well-defined knowledge), where-as pro- and anti-abortionists should possess a bipolar schema for abortion. Those individuals with a bipolar schema should use the category labels of "pro-" and "anti-abortion" to organize and better recall abortion-related information. Hymes found that subjects possessing a bipolar schema (pro- and anti-abortionists) were better at recognizing favorable and unfavorable information (as opposed to information congruent with their attitude) than did neutral subjects (assumed to be aschematic).

Pratkanis (1984) also provided date in support of the bipolar hypothesis for some attitude domains. In one study, college students were asked to list arguments for and against 1 of 10 controversial social issues (i.e., nuclear power, gun control, abortion, draft registration, death penalty). The results revealed that 82.7% of the subjects could generate at least one argument on both sides of an issue. (However, subjects typically listed more arguments agreeing with their own position, consistent with the findings of Feather [1969].)

In two additional experiments, Pratkanis (1984) obtained recall, recogni-tion, and reaction time data consistent with the bipolar pattern of results. In these two studies, subjects first stated their agreement with pro, neutral, and anti-statements on the issues of nuclear power, defense spending, and welfare. After a filler task, subjects attempted a free recall and a recognition of the statements. The results revealed no attitude and selective learning effect—the correlation between recall and statement agreement was −.04 in Experiment 1 and .02 in Experiment 2. However, subjects tend to recall better, evaluate faster, and recognize more quickly those items rated at the extremes of the agreement scale.

Unipolar Attitude Structure

Pratkanis (1984) reasoned that some attitudes may be supported by a unipolar knowledge structure such as that depicted in Fig. 4.2. A unipolar knowledge structure contains information on only one side of an issue. For example, a sports fan typically possesses an elaborate knowledge structure containing technical and esoteric information relative to those with less favorable attitudes. Unlike bipolar attitudes, knowledge covaries with uni-polar attitudes such that persons with positive attitudes have a vast amount of knowledge whereas those with less favorable (or neutral) attitudes do not. For uni-polar attitudes, an attitude and selective learning effect is expected to occur. The individual with a positive attitude possesses knowledge structures useful for encoding and recalling domain-related information whereas the individual with a neutral attitude does not possess such knowledge and skills.

Three criteria have been preliminarily identified to distinguish domains for which individuals are likely to possess unipolar versus bipolar knowledge structures. First, bipolar topics tend to be controversial with arguments for and against a given issue readily available in the social environment. For example, there are many lobbyists, PACs, and advocacy groups on both sides of the nuclear power and abortion issues whereas there are only support groups for sports (i.e., little leagues, NFL, NCAA, Olympic com-

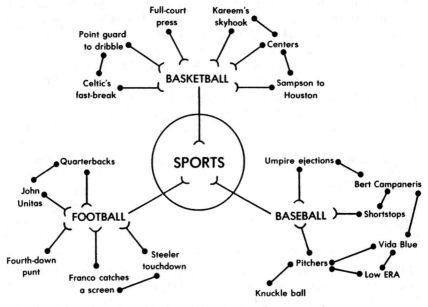

FIG. 4.2.   A hypothetical unipolar knowledge structure for a sports fan.

mittees). Second, the attitude scale for a bipolar topic ranges from anti to neutral to pro (with attitudes distributed across the range), whereas the scale for unipolar topics ranges from neutral to pro (or anti). Finally, there is a simple linear correlation between domain knowledge and attitude for unipolar topics (i.e., the more positive the attitudes, the more knowledge of the issue). A frequent finding for bipolar topics is that individuals with extreme attitudes are more knowledgeable (see Hymes, 1986), although other distributions of knowledge in the population can be expected for bipolar topics (i.e., all members of a society may have equal knowledge concerning widely discussed issues). A fruitful area for further research is to further refine these three criteria and to identify propositions for relating attitude structure to individual differences, the function of the attitude, and environmental activities.

Three studies have demonstrated the role of unipolar versus bipolar knowledge structures for determining learning of attitude related materials. Pratkanis (1984) asked subjects to complete a relationship judgment task similar to the one used in self-reference research (see Rogers, Kuiper, & Kirker, 1977). In this task, subjects answered questions with the stem, "Is this word or phrase related to" with one of these six topics completing the question: welfare, defense spending, nuclear power, sports, music and religion. Subjects answered questions for 72 words, 12 of which were related to each topic. For example, words related to defense spending included pentagon, freeze, and domino and words related to sports included screen, touchdown, and forward. After a filler task, subjects attempted a free recall of the words and completed a survey to assess attitudes and knowledge concerning the various domains.

The results revealed that the topics of sports and music were unipolar in nature. Few subjects endorsed negative statements concerning these activities and the correlation between attitude and knowledge measures was linear and positive. In contrast, the topics of welfare, nuclear power, and defense spending showed the bipolar pattern. Attitudes were distributed across the full range of the scale and subjects with extreme attitudes professed to know slightly more about the issue. Knowledge structures supporting religion were found to be quite complex and did not fit either the unipolar or bipolar pattern. The recall results showed that subjects with more knowledge of bipolar and unipolar topics demonstrated superior free recall of topic-related terms (an *attitude-reference* effect). This effect translated into an attitude and selective learning effect for unipolar topics, that is, a positive attitude/recall correlation. However, for bipolar topics, subjects at the extremes of the attitude scale demonstrated a tendency for better recall.

Pratkanis (1987) replicated the unipolar–bipolar results using persuasive communications (as opposed to words and terms). In this study, subjects completed an attitude/knowledge survey and then attempted to learn and recall messages that were anti-nuclear power, pro-defense spending, pro-music, and pro-sports. Each message consisted of a series of arguments in support of the message conclusion (i.e., Nuclear power plants have a high risk of accidental meltdown; The simple Bach chorale moves the soul).

The results showed the expected unipolar and bipolar patterns. For sports and music, few subjects endorsed the negative end of the attitude continuum and there was a positive correlation between attitudes and knowledge. For the issues of defense spending and nuclear power, subjects were distributed along the attitude continuum and subjects with attitudes at the extremes of the continuum professed the most knowledge about the domain. For the two unipolar messages, there was an attitude and selective learning effect—subjects who held positive attitudes towards sports and music showed superior learning of the message. These subjects also professed more knowledge about the domains. For the bipolar messages, there was a tendency for those with extreme attitudes to better recall the information.

Pratkanis, Syak, and Gamble (1987) investigated the relationship between attitude toward social drinking and recall of persuasive communications concerning drinking. The domain of social drinking is interesting because for sociopolitical arguments it tends to be bipolar in nature (i.e., individuals can list reasons for and against drinking). However, in regards to performing drinking activities, knowledge may be distributed in a unipolar manner. Individuals with positive attitudes are more likely to know technical details such as how to fix exotic drinks, the number of gallons in a keg of beer, and the names of various liquors. Pratkanis, Syak, and Gamble asked subjects to learn three communications: a pro-social drinking message, an anti-social drinking message, and a technical message (containing esoteric details about alcohol) on how to make a Pousse-cafe (an exotic liqueur). The results showed that attitudes were not related to the learning of the pro- or anti-social drinking message. However, subjects with positive drinking attitudes demonstrated superior learning of the technical Pousse- cafe message. Subjects with positive attitudes also possessed greater technical knowledge concerning drinking (as assessed by an objective test) and this greater knowledge moderated the attitude/learning results.

There are other domains (in addition to those described) that have evidenced the unipolar pattern. For example, Greenwald and Pratkanis (1984) reviewed evidence that judgments about the *self* are made faster and self-relevant information (which is usually positive) is recalled better. Gustafson (1957) found that members of various *ethnic* groups were better at learning the accomplishments of in-group members in American history. Liben and Signorella (1980) and others noted that children with traditional *gender role* attitudes (compared to those who have not as yet developed these attitudes) demonstrate superior memory for materials that portray traditional sex roles. Becker and Byrne (1985) reviewed research on *sexual attitudes* and present a pattern of memory results that are similar to those obtained with attitudes toward social drinking—erotophiles obtain higher test scores in a college sexuality course, retained more information from a birth-control lecture, and were better at recalling erotica than erotophobes.

A SOCIOCOGNITIVE MODEL OF ATTITUDE STRUCTURE

In the previous two sections, the distinction between conceptual and episodic memory was used to classify and interpret the effects of attitude on cognitive processes. In this section, attitude structure is inferred from the cognitive functioning of attitudes to answer the question posed at the beginning of the chapter, "How are attitudes represented in memory?" Our answer is sociocognitive in nature. The terminology of *cognitive* psychology is used to describe attitude structure. The form, content, and organization of this attitude structure is determined by an individual in interaction with the *social* environment. In this model, the cognitive representation of a fully developed attitude consists of three parts: an object-category, an evaluative summary of the object, and a supporting knowledge structure.

Object Categorization

Attitude researchers and theorists implicitly assume that an attitude object is represented as a category in semantic memory. In other words, individuals identify the attitude object as a member of a set or class of objects (see Smith & Medin, 1981). Attitude researchers have paid little attention to categorization processes. Some exceptions include: Newcomb, Turner, and Converse's (1965) discussion of dimensionality and inclusiveness as properties of attitude objects; Fishbein and Ajzen's (1975) treatment of level of specificity in attitude measurement and prediction; and Greenwald's (Chap. 1 in this volume) proposal for characterizing the level of representation of an attitude object.

Nevertheless, categorization processes may be important for understanding attitudinal effects. For example, Lord, Lepper, and Mackie (1984) obtained stronger attitude-behavior relationships when an attitude object was prototypical of a class. Survey researchers such as Payne (1952) frequently find that the wording of a question (definition of an issue category) can influence agreement. Reis and Trout (1981) argued that much effective advertising is what can be called a prepersuasion process of successfully creating product categories in which a sponsor's brand is, by default, the best.

The Evaluative Summary

The essential characteristic of an attitude is its evaluation component—a simple evaluative cue or summary statistic stored in memory. It is the storage of an evaluation in memory that distinguishes an attitude from other cognitive structures such as categories and schema. In regards to conceptual processes, attitudes often serve a heuristic function. The stored evaluation of an object is used as part of the strategy for sizing up an object, for classifying a thing as good or bad, and for determining whether a favoring or disfavoring approach is to be adopted toward the object. This evaluative cue and strategy influences conceptual cognitive processes such as reasoning, decision-making, interpretation, inference, attribution, and, in some cases, recall of past events.

Many terms and properties such as intensity, strength, and salience have been proposed to describe the nature of an evaluation of an object (see Raden, 1985). Two important properties of a stored evaluation for determining the effects of attitudes on conceptual processes are direction and accessibility (Fazio, chap. 7 in this volume) or afferent-habit strength (Doob, 1947). Direction refers to the valence of an attitude as either positive/negative, agree/disagree, or favor/oppose and determines the overall strategy to be taken toward an object. The formation and change of the direction of an attitude has been the focus of much research on persuasion and influence.

Accessibility refers to the strength of the association between an evaluation and an object category. The degree of accessibility of an evaluation determines the likelihood that an attitude will be spontaneously used (or used in relationship to other competing heuristics) to determine the overall strategy toward an object. The construct of accessibility is useful for describing the conditions under which an attitude will more likely serve a heuristic function (Fazio, chap. 7 this volume). Fazio and his colleagues identify repeat expression, direct experience, and recency of use as factors that increase accessibility.

Attitudinal Knowledge Structure

Attitudes may sometimes consist of nothing more than an evaluation of an object stored in memory, as in the case of McGuire's (1964) cultural truisms. However, as demonstrated in research on attitudes and memory for a persuasive communication, attitudes are often associated with elaborate knowledge structures about a domain. This attitudinal schema or organization of knowledge may contain arguments for and against a given proposition, esoteric and technical knowledge about the domain, subjective beliefs, information on how to behave toward the object, goals and wishes about the object, the social meaning of adopting a certain attitude position, personal episodes and events, and other pieces of information. The organization of attitude-related knowledge can serve a schematic function useful for understanding and interpreting complex information and for learning and recalling of a persuasive communication. An attitudinal schema is not synonymous with a belief structure. A belief about an object is a proposition that is endorsed and accepted as true, and is thus a subset of information an individual possesses about an object. (See Devine, chap. 8 in this volume and Goldberg, Gottesdiener, & Abramson, 1975 for examples of when beliefs and knowledge about an attitude domain are in conflict.)

The content and organization of attitudinal knowledge can take a variety of formats. A reasonable hypothesis is that attitude structure is shaped by the requirements of the social environment or, in other words, the function of the attitude in relating an individual to the social world (see Tetlock, chap. 6 in this volume for a similar proposal). Three possible functions of attitude structure include: (a) assessing and evaluating the *utility* of an object, (b) guiding *usage* of (or complex behavior towards) an object, and (c) *arguing* the merits of a proposal. The consistent use of attitude structure to serve one (or multiple) of these functions can result in the development of the types of structures identified in attitude and memory research. For example, some functions and resulting organizational formats include: (a) utility: The benefits and drawbacks of using a given object are listed in a structure similar to that proposed by expectancy-value theorists; (b) usage: Technical and action-oriented information is organized in a linear manner such as a script (Abelson, 1976; see also Doob's, 1947 efferent-habit strength) or around natural groups of people or categories of things as in sports teams and different types of music; and (c) argumentation: Reasons for and against an issue are sorted along an evaluative continuum resulting in a bipolar structure (see also McGuire's, 1964 innoculation procedure as an experimental analog of the development of a bipolar attitude).

Comparison of the Sociocognitive Model with Other Approaches

The sociocognitive model of attitude can be seen as an integration and extension of some previous models of attitude. For example, Smith, Bruner, and White (1956) distinguished between the affective tone (evaluative summary) and the information support (knowledge structure) of an attitude. More recently, Schlegel and DiTecco (1982) suggested that attitudes consist of evaluations and knowledge structures. In the area of person memory, researchers frequently find evidence for the independence of a general impression (evaluation) and more specific facts and information about a person (see Anderson & Hubert, 1963; Carlston, 1980; Dreben, Fiske, & Hastie, 1979; Hastie & Park, 1986). Finally, the sociocognitive model of attitude is similar to Fiske and Pavelchak's (1986) model of person perception where an individual is represented by a category label, an affective (evaluative) tag, and a schema (knowledge of person attributes).

Prospectus: The Attitude Construct

Given past pessimism concerning attitudes, it is reasonable to ask: "What is the prospect for the attitude concept in social psychology?" Two observations concerning recent attitude research indicate that the attitude construct is an important and much needed one. First, despite all the pessimism, the concept of attitude has performed yeoman service for the field of social psychology. Attitudes are excellent predictors of conceptual cognitive processes, reliably determining how individuals make sense of their social world. Second, as witnessed by the chapters in this volume, unruly attitude effects are increasingly being brought under experimental control by specifying the nature and structure of an attitude. As this research continues, the next few years will see the attitude concept evolve to become a more powerful predictive construct, thus reinforcing Allport's now 50-plus-year-old belief that "attitudes are the most distinctive and indispensable concept" in social psychology.

ACKNOWLEDGMENTS

Marlene E. Turner provided helpful comments on a preliminary version.

REFERENCES

Abelson, R. P. (1972). Are attitudes necessary? In B. T. King & E. McGinnies (Eds.), *Attitudes, conflict, and social change* (pp. 19–32). New York: Academic Press.

Abelson, R. P. (1976). Script processing in attitude formation and decision-making. In J. S. Carroll & J. W. Payne (Eds.), *Cognition and social behavior* (pp. 33–45). Hillsdale, NJ: Lawrence Erlbaum Associates.

Aderman, D., & Brehm, S. S. (1976). On the recall of initial attitudes following counterattitudinal advocacy: An experimental reexamination. *Personality and Social Psychology Bulletin, 2,* 59–62.

Allport, G. W. (1935). Attitudes. In C. Murchison (Ed.), *The handbook of social psychology* (pp. 798–844). Worchester, MA: Clark University Press.

Anderson, N. H., & Hubert, S. (1963). Effects of concomitant verbal recall on order effects in personality impression formation. *Journal of Verbal Learning and Verbal Behavior, 2,* 379–391.

Bain, R. (1928). An attitude on attitude research. *American Journal of Sociology, 33,* 940–957.

Becker, M. A., & Byrne, D. (1985). Self-regulated exposure to erotica, recall errors, and subjective reactions as a function of erotophobia and Type A coronary-prone behavior. *Journal of Personality and Social Psychology, 48,* 760–767.

Bem, D. J., & McConnell, H. K. (1970). Testing the self-perception of dissonance phenomena: On the salience of premanipulation attitudes. *Journal of Personality and Social Psychology, 14,* 23–31.

Blumer, H. (1955). Attitudes and the social act. *Social Problems, 3,* 59–65.

Breckler, S. J. (1984). Empirical validation of affect, behavior, and cognition as distinct components of attitude. *Journal of Personality and Social Psychology, 47,* 1191–1205.

Brigham, J. C., & Cook, S. W. (1969). The influence of attitude on the recall of controversial materials: A failure to confirm. *Journal of Experimental Social Psychology, 5,* 24–243.

Byrne, D. (1971). *The attraction paradigm.* New York: Academic Press.

Cacioppo, J. T., & Petty, R. E. (1979). Effects of message repetition and position on cognitive response, recall, and persuasion. *Journal of Personality and Social Psychology, 37,* 97–109.

Cantril, H. (1940). America faces the war: A study in public opinion. *Public Opinion Quarterly, 4,* 387–407.

Carlston, D. E. (1980). Events, inferences, and impression formation. In R. Hastie, T. M. Ostrom, E. B. Ebbesen, R. S. Wyer, D. L. Hamilton, & D. E. Carlston (Eds.), *Person memory: The cognitive basis of social perception* (pp. 89–119). Hillsdale, NJ: Lawrence Erlbaum Associates.

Chiesi, H. L., Spilich, G. J., & Voss, J. F. (1979). Acquisition of domain-related information in relation to high and low domain knowledge. *Journal of Verbal Learning and Verbal Behavior, 18,* 257–273.

Converse, P. E. (1970). Attitudes and non-attitudes: Continuation of a dialogue. In E. R. Tufte (Ed.), *The quantitative analysis of social problems* (pp. 168–189). Reading, MA: Addison-Wesley.

Cooper, E., & Jahoda, M. (1947). The evasion of propaganda: How prejudiced people respond to anti-prejudice propaganda. *Journal of Social Psychology, 23,* 15–25.

Darley, J., & Gross, P. (1983). A hypothesis-confirming bias in labelling effects. *Journal of Personality and Social Psychology, 44,* 20–33.

Doob, L. W. (1947). The behavior of attitudes. *Psychological Review, 54,* 135–156.

Doob, L. W. (1953). Effects of initial serial position and attitude upon recall under conditions of low motivation. *Journal of Abnormal and Social Psychology, 48,* 199–205.

Dreben, E. K., Fiske, S. T., & Hastie, R. (1979). The independence of evaluative and item information: Impression and recall order effects in behavior-based impression formation. *Journal of Personality and Social Psychology, 37,* 1758–1768.

Eberhart, J. C., & Bauer, R. A. (1941). An analysis of the influences on recall of a controversial event: The *Chicago Tribune* and the Republic Steel strike. *Journal of Social Psychology, S.P.S.S.I. Bulletin, 14,* 211–228.

Edwards, A. L. (1941). Political frames of reference as a factor influencing recognition. *Journal of Abnormal and Social Psychology, 36,* 34–50.

Edwards, A. L. (1957). *Techniques of attitude scale construction.* New York: Appleton-Century-Croft.

Evans, J. St., B. T., Barston, J. L., & Pollard, P. (1983). On the conflict between logic and belief in syllogistic reasoning. *Memory and Cognition, 11,* 295–306.

Feather, N. T. (1964). Acceptance and rejection of arguments in relation to attitude strength, critical ability, and intolerance of inconsistency. *Journal of Abnormal and Social Psychology, 69,* 127–136.

Feather, N. T. (1969). Attitude and selective recall. *Journal of Personality and Social Psychology, 12,* 310–319.

Fields, J. M., & Schuman, H. (1976). Public beliefs about the beliefs of the public. *Public Opinion Quarterly, 40,* 427–448.

Fishbein, M., & Ajzen, I. (1975). *Belief, attitude, intention and behavior: An introduction to theory and research.* Reading, MA: Addison-Wesley.

Fiske, S. T., & Pavelchak, M. A. (1986). Category-based versus piecemeal-based affective responses: Developments in schema-triggered affect. In R. M. Sorrentino & E. T. Higgins (Eds.), *Handbook of motivation and cognition: Foundations of social behavior* (pp. 167–203). New York: Guilford Press.

Fleming, D. (1967). Attitude: The history of a concept. *Perspectives in American History, 1,* 287–365.

Galanis, C. M. B., & Jones, E. E. (1986). When stigma confronts stigma: Some conditions enhancing a victim's tolerance of other victims. *Personality and Social Psychology Bulletin, 12,* 169–177.

Gallup, G. H. (1972). *The Gallup Poll: Public opinion 1935–1971.* New York: Random House.

Goethals, G. R., & Reckman, R. F. (1973). The perception of consistency in attitudes. *Journal of Experimental Social Psychology, 9,* 491–501.

Goldberg, P. A., Gottesdiener, M., & Abramson, P. R. (1975). Another put-down of women? Perceived attractiveness as a function of support for the feminist movement. *Journal of Personality and Social Psychology, 32,* 113–115.

Gordon, R. L. (1953). The effect of attitude toward Russia on logical reasoning. *Journal of Social Psychology, 37,* 103–111.

Granberg, D. (1985). An anomaly in political perception. *Public Opinion Quarterly, 49,* 504–516.

Granberg, D., & Brent, E. (1983). When prophecy bends: The preference-expectation link in U.S. Presidential elections, 1952–1980. *Journal of Personality and Social Psychology, 45,* 477–491.

Granberg, D., Jefferson, N. L., Brent, E. E., & King, M. (1981). Membership group, reference group, and the attribution of attitudes to groups. *Journal of Personality and Social Psychology, 40,* 833–842.

Granberg, D., & Jenks, R. (1977). Assimilation and contrast effects in the 1972 election. *Human Relations, 30,* 623–640.

Greaves, G. (1972). Conceptual system functioning and selective recall of information. *Journal of Personality and Social Psychology, 3,* 327–332.

Greenwald, A. G. (1968). Cognitive learning, cognitive response to persuasion, and attitude change. In A. G. Greenwald, T. C. Brock, & T. M. Ostrom (Eds.), *Psychological foundations of attitudes* (pp. 147–170). New York: Academic Press.

Greenwald, A. G. & Pratkanis, A. R. (1984). The self. In R. S. Wyer & T. K. Srull (Eds.), *Handbook of social cognition* (Vol. 3, pp 129–178). Hillsdale, NJ: Lawrence Erlbaum Associates.

Greenwald, A. G., & Sakumara, J. S. (1967). Attitude and selective learning: Where are the phenomena of yesteryear? *Journal of Personality and Social Psychology, 7,* 387–397.

Gustafson, L. (1957). Relationship between ethnic group membership and the retention of selected facts pertaining to American history and culture. *Journal of Educational Sociology, 31,* 49–56.

Hammond, K. B. (1948). Measuring attitudes by error-choice: An indirect method. *Journal of Abnormal and Social Psychology, 43,* 38–48.

Hastie, R., & Park, B. (1986). The relationship between memory and judgment depends on whether the judgment task is memory-based or on-line. *Psychological Review, 93,* 258–268.

Hastorf, A. H., & Cantril, H. (1954). They saw a game. *Journal of Abnormal and Social Psychology, 49,* 129–134.

Hatfield, E., & Sprecher, S. (1986). *Mirror, mirror: The importance of looks in everyday life.* Albany, NY: State University of New York Press.

Heider, F. (1958). *The psychology of interpersonal relations.* New York: Wiley.

Hymes, R. W. (1986). Political attitudes as social categories: A new look at selective memory. *Journal of Personality and Social Psychology, 51,* 233–241.

Janis, I. L., & Frick, F. (1943). The relationship between attitudes toward conclusions and errors in judging the logical validity of syllogisms. *Journal of Experimental Psychology, 33,* 73–77.

Jones, E. E., & Kohler, R. (1958). The effects of plausibility on the learning of controversial statements. *Journal of Abnormal and Social Psychology, 53,* 27–33.

Judd, C. M., & Kulik, J. A. (1980). Schematic effects of social attitudes on information processing and recall. *Journal of Personality and Social Psychology, 38,* 569–578.

Katona, G. (1975). *Psychological economics.* New York: Elsevier.

Katz, D. (1960). The functional approach to the study of attitudes. *Public Opinion Quarterly, 24,* 163–204.

Katz, D., & Stotland, E. (1959). A preliminary statement to a theory of attitude structure and change. In S. Kock (Ed.), *Psychology: A study of a science* (Vol. 3, pp. 423–475). New York: McGraw-Hill.

Kendall, P. L. & Wolf, F. M. (1949). The analysis of deviant cases in communications research. In P. F. Lazarsfeld & F. N. Stanton (Eds.), *Communications Research 1948–49* (pp 152–179). New York: Harper & Brothers.

Kothandapani, V. (1971). Validation of feeling, belief, and intention to act as three components of attitude and their contribution to prediction of contraceptive behavior. *Journal of Personality and Social Psychology, 19,* 321–333.

Krech, D., & Crutchfield, R. S. (1948). *Theories and problems of social psychology.* New York: McGraw-Hill.

Kreman, E. O. (1949). *An attempt to ameliorate hostility towards the Negro through role playing.* Unpublished master's thesis, Ohio State University, Columbus, OH.

Kubany, A. J. (1953). A validation study of the error-choice technique using attitudes on national health insurance. *Educational and Psychological Measurement, 13,* 157–163.

Lefford, A. (1946). The influence of emotional subject matter on logical reasoning. *Journal of General Psychology, 34,* 127–151.

Levine, J. M., & Murphy, G. (1943). The learning and retention of controversial statements. *Journal of Abnormal and Social Psychology, 38,* 507–517.

Liben, L. S., & Signorella, M. L. (1980). Gender-related schemata and constructive memory in children. *Child Development, 51,* 11–18.

Lingle, J. H., & Ostrom, T. M. (1981). Principle of memory and cognition in attitude formation. In R. E. Petty, T. M. Ostrom, & T. C. Brock (Eds.), *Cognitive responses in persuasion* (pp. 399–420). Hillsdale, NJ: Lawrence Erlbaum Associates.

Lippmann, W. (1922). *Public Opinion.* New York: Harcourt, Brace & Co.

Lord, C. G., Lepper, M. R., & Mackie, D. (1984). Attitude prototypes as determinants of attitude-behavior consistency. *Journal of Personality and Social Psychology, 46,* 1254–1266.

Lord, C. G., & Lepper, M. R., & Ross, L. (1979). Biased assimilation and attitude polarization: The effects of prior theories on subsequently considered evidence. *Journal of Personality and Social Psychology, 37,* 2098–2109.

Lott, A. J., & Lott, B. E. (1968). A learning theory approach to interpersonal attitudes. In A. G. Greenwald, T. C. Brock, & T. M. Ostrom (Eds.), *Psychological foundations of attitudes* (pp. 67–88). New York: Academic Press.

Lott, A. J., & Lott, B. E. (1972). The power of liking: Consequences of interpersonal attitudes derived from a liberalized view of secondary reinforcement. In L. Berkowitz (Ed.), *Advances in experimental social psychology* (Vol. 6, pp. 109–148). New York: Academic.

Lott, A. J., Lott, B. E., Reed, T., & Crow, T. (1970). Personality-trait descriptions of differentially liked persons. *Journal of Personality and Social Psychology, 16,* 284–290.

Manis, M. (1961). The interpretation of opinion statements as a function of message ambiguity and recipient attitudes. *Journal of Abnormal and Social Psychology, 63,* 76–81.

Markus, G. B. (1985). *Stability and change in political attitudes: Observed, recalled, and explained.* Unpublished manuscript. University of Michigan.

McGuire, W. J. (1964). Inducing resistance to persuasion. In L. Berkowitz (Ed.), *Advances in experimental social psychology* (Vol. 1, pp. 191–229). New York: Academic Press.

McGuire, W. J. (1969). The nature of attitudes and attitude change. In G. Lindzey & E. Aronson (Eds.), *The handbook of social psychology* (Vol. 3, pp. 136–314). Reading, MA: Addison-Wesley.

Morgan, J. J. B. (1945). Attitudes of students toward the Japanese. *Journal of Social Psychology, 21,* 219–227.

Morgan, J. J. B., & Morton, J. T. (1943). Distorted reasoning as an index of public opinion. *School and Society, 57,* 333–335.

Morgan, J. J. B., & Morton, J. T. (1944). The distortion of syllogistic reasoning produced by personal convictions. *Journal of Social Psychology, 20,* 39–59.

Newcomb, T. M., Turner, R. H., & Converse, P. E. (1965). *Social psychology: A study of human interaction.* London: Routledge & Kegan.

Ostrom, T. M. (1969). The relationship between the affective, behavioral, and cognitive components of attitude. *Journal of Experimental Social Psychology, 5,* 12–30.

Parrish, J. A. (1948). *The direct and indirect assessment of attitudes as influenced by propagandized radio transcripts.* Unpublished master's thesis, Ohio State University, Columbus, OH.

Payne, S. L. (1952). *The art of asking questions.* Princeton, NJ: Princeton University Press.

Pettigrew, T. F. (1979). The ultimate attribution error: Extending Allport's cognitive analysis of prejudice. *Personality and Social Psychology Bulletin, 5,* 461–476.

Petty, R. E., Ostrom, T. M., & Brock, T. C. (1981). *Cognitive responses in persuasion.* Hillsdale, NJ: Lawrence Erlbaum Associates.

Postman, L., & Murphy, G. (1943). The factor of attitude in associative memory. *Journal of Experimental Psychology, 33,* 228–238.

Pratkanis, A. R. (1984). *Attitudes and memory: The heuristic and schematic functions of attitudes.* Unpublished doctoral dissertation, Ohio State University, Columbus, OH.

Pratkanis, A. R. (1987). [Unipolar and bipolar attitudes in learning persuasive communications]. Unpublished data. Carnegie-Mellon University, Pittsburgh, PA.

Pratkanis, A. R., Syak, P., & Gamble, E. (1987). *The role of technical knowledge in attitudinal learning.* Paper presented at Midwestern Psychological Association, Chicago, IL.

Pratkanis, A. R. (In Press). The attitude heuristic and selective fact identification. *British Journal of Social Psychology.*

Raden, D. (1985). Strength-related attitude dimensions. *Social Psychology Quarterly, 48,* 312–330.

Read, S. J., & Rosson, M. B. (1982). Rewriting history: The biasing effects of attitudes on memory. *Social Cognition, 1,* 240–255.

Regan, D. T., Straus, E., & Fazio, R. (1974). Liking and the attribution process. *Journal of Experimental Social Psychology, 10,* 385–397.

Reis, A., & Trout, J. (1981). *Positioning: The battle for your mind.* New York: Warner.

Rhine, R. J. (1958). A concept-formation approach to attitude acquisition. *Psychological Review, 65,* 362–370.

Roberts, J. V. (1985). The attitude-memory relationship after 40 years: A meta-analysis of the literature. *Basic and Applied Social Psychology, 6,* 221–241.

Rogers, T. B., Kuiper, N. A., & Kirker, W. S. (1977). Self-reference and the encoding of personal information. *Journal of Personality and Social Psychology, 35,* 677–688.

Rosenbaum, M. E. (1986). The repulsion hypothesis: On the nondevelopment of relationships. *Journal of Personality and Social Psychology, 51,* 1156–1166.

Rosenberg, M. J. (1956). Cognitive structure and attitudinal affect. *Journal of Abnormal and Social Psychology, 53,* 367–372.

Rosenberg, M. J., & Hovland, C. I. (1960). Cognitive, affective, and behavioral components of attitudes. In C. I. Hovland & M. J. Rosenberg (Eds.), *Attitude organization and change* (pp. 1–14). New Haven, CT: Yale University Press.

Ross, L., Greene, D., & House, P. (1977). The "false-consensus effect": An egocentric bias in social perception and attribution process. *Journal of Experimental Social Psychology, 13,* 279–301.

Ross, M., McFarland, C., Conway, M., & Zanna, M. P. (1983). Reciprocal relation between attitudes and behavior recall: Committing people to newly formed attitudes. *Journal of Personality and Social Psychology, 45,* 257–267.

Ross, M., McFarland, C., & Fletcher, G. J. O. (1981). The effect of attitude on the recall of personal history. *Journal of Personality and Social Psychology, 40,* 627–634.

Ross, M., & Shulman, R. F. (1973). Increasing the salience of initial attitudes: Dissonance versus self-perception theory. *Journal of Personality and Social Psychology, 28,* 138–144.

Schlegel, R. P., & DiTecco, D. (1982). Attitudinal structures and the attitude-behavior relation. In M. P. Zanna, E. T. Higgins, & C. P. Herman (Eds.), *Consistency in social behavior* (pp. 17–49). Hillsdale, NJ: Lawrence Erlbaum Associates.

Scott, W. A. (1968). Attitude measurement. In G. Lindzey & E. Aronson (Eds.), *The handbook of social psychology* (Vol. 2, pp. 204–273). Reading, MA: Addison-Wesley.

Scott, W. A., Osgood, D. W., & Peterson, C. (1979). *Cognitive structure: Theory and measurement of individual differences.* Washington, DC: V. H. Winston & Sons.

Shaffer, D. R. (1975a). Some effects of consonant and dissonant attitudinal advocacy on initial attitude saliency and attitude change. *Journal of Personality and Social Psychology, 32,* 160–168.

Shaffer, D. R. (1975b). Another look at the phenomenological equivalence on pre- and post-manipulation attitudes in the forced compliance experiment. *Personality and Social Psychology Bulletin, 1,* 497–500.

Sherif, M., & Hovland, C. I. (1961). *Social judgment.* New Haven, CT: Yale University Press.

Sherman, S. J., Chassin, L., Presson, C. C., & Agostinelli, G. (1984). The role of evaluation and similarity principles in the false consensus effect. *Journal of Personality and Social Psychology, 47,* 1244–1262.

Sherman, S. J., & Corty, E. (1984). Cognitive heuristics. In R. S. Wyer & T. K. Srull (Eds.), *The handbook of social cognition* (Vol. 1 pp. 189–286). Hillsdale, NJ: Lawrence Erlbaum Associates.

Smith, D. D. (1968). Cognitive consistency and the perception of others' opinions. *Public Opinion Quarterly, 32,* 1–15.

Smith, E. E., & Medin, D. L. (1981). *Categories and concepts.* Cambridge, MA: Harvard University Press.

Smith, G. H. (1947). Beliefs in statements labelled fact and rumor. *Journal of Abnormal and Social Psychology, 42,* 80–90.

Smith, M. B., Bruner, J. S., & White, R. W. (1957). *Opinions and personality.* New York: Wiley.

Smith, S. S., & Jamieson, B. D. (1972). Effects of attitude and ego-involvement on the learning and retention of controversial material. *Journal of Personality and Social Psychology, 22,* 303–310.

Spilich, G. J., Vesonder, G. T., and Chiesi, H. L., & Voss, J. F. (1979). Text processing of domain-related information for individuals with high and low domain knowledge. *Journal of Verbal Learning and Verbal Behavior, 18,* 275–290.

Staats, A. W. (1968). Social behaviorism and human motivation: Principles of the attitude-reinforcer-discriminative system. In A. G. Greenwald, T. C. Brock, & T. M. Ostrom (Eds.), *Psychological foundations of attitudes* (pp. 33–66). New York: Academic Press.

Symonds, P. M. (1927). What is an attitude? *Psychological Bulletin, 24,* 200–201.

Thistlethwaite, D. (1950). Attitude and structure as factors in the distortion of reasoning. *Journal of Abnormal and Social Psychology, 45,* 442–458.

Thorndike, E. L. (1935). *The psychology of wants, interests and attitudes.* New York: Apple-ton-Century Co.

Thurstone, L. L. (1928). Attitudes can be measured. *American Journal of Sociology, 33,* 529–554.

Tulving, E. (1983). *Elements of episodic memory.* New York: Oxford.

Tversky, A., & Kahneman, D. (1974). Judgments under uncertainty: Heuristics and biases. *Science, 185,* 1124–1131.

Voss, J. F., Vesonder, G. T., & Spilich, G. J. (1980). Text generation and recall by high-knowledge and low-knowledge individuals. *Journal of Verbal Learning and Verbal Behavior, 19,* 651–667.

Vroom, V. H. (1960). The effects of attitudes on perception of organizational goals. *Human Relations, 13,* 229–240.

Wallen, R. (1943). Individuals' estimates of group opinion. *Journal of Social Psychology, 17,* 269–274.

Waly, P., & Cook, S. W. (1965). Effects of attitude on judgment of plausibility. *Journal of Personality and Social Psychology, 2,* 745–749.

Waly, P., & Cook, S. W. (1966). Attitude as a determinant of learning and memory: A failure to confirm. *Journal of Personality and Social Psychology, 4,* 280–288.

Weiss, F. W. (1968). An extension of Hullian learning theory to persuasive communication. In A. G. Greenwald, T. C. Brock, & T. M. Ostrom (Eds.), *Psychological foundations of attitudes* (pp. 109–145). New York: Academic Press.

Weldon, D. E., & Malpass, R. S. (1981). Effects of attitudinal, cognitive and situational variables on recall of biased communications. *Journal of Personality and Social Psychology, 40,* 39–52.

Weschler, I. R. (1950a). An investigation of attitudes toward labor and management by means of the error-choice method: I. *Journal of Social Psychology, 32,* 51–62.

Weschler, I. R. (1950b). A follow-up on the measurement of attitudes toward labor and management by means of the error-choice method: II. *Journal of Social Psychology, 32,* 63–69.

Wicker, A. W. (1969). Attitudes versus actions: The relationship of verbal and overt behavioral responses to attitude objects. *Journal of Social Issues, 25,* 41–78.

Yi, Y. (1987). *Inter-dependence EV model and chain-reaction model of advertising effects.* Unpublished doctoral dissertation, Stanford University.

Zajonc, R. B., & Burnstein, E. (1965). The learning of balanced and unbalanced social structures. *Journal of Personality, 33,* 153–163.

5

The Structural Bases of Consistency Among Political Attitudes: *Effects of Political Expertise and Attitude Importance*

Charles M. Judd
University of Colorado

Jon A. Krosnick
Ohio State University

A great deal of research in social psychology and in related disciplines has examined ways in which attitudes are organized or structured. This work has defined attitude structure in a variety of different ways. Some researchers have looked at the structure of single attitudes, hypothesizing three structural components: cognitive, affective, and conative (Breckler, 1984; Insko & Schopler, 1967; Kothandapani, 1971; Ostrom, 1969; Rosenberg, 1960; Rosenberg & Hovland, 1960). Assessments of individual differences in attitude structure in this tradition have focused on differences between individuals or differences within individuals between attitudes in the consistency of these three attitude components (e.g., Chaiken & Baldwin, 1981; Chaiken & Yates, 1985; Millar & Tesser, 1986). Another approach to attitude structure has focused on relationships between attitudes toward different attitude objects, focusing on the degree to which these attitudes are consistent with each other (e.g., Abelson & Rosenberg, 1958; Festinger, 1957; Heider, 1958; Newcomb, 1968; Osgood & Tannenbaum, 1955). Thus, in this second case, attitude structure has been defined by reference to constellations of attitudes rather than by reference to components of a single attitude.

Our purpose in this chapter is to explore factors responsible for differences in attitude structure in the second sense previously defined. That is, we intend to explore the bases of structural consistency between attitudes and factors responsible for differences in such consistency. In particular, we are concerned with the effects of two different factors on consistency between attitudes: expertise in the attitude domain and the importance or centrality of the attitudes.[1] For the sake of simplicity, we define an attitude as an evaluation of an attitude object that is stored in memory.

Although the theoretical speculations offered have relatively broad implications, our discussion is focused on political attitudes. In particular, we concern ourselves with the structure of attitudes toward government policies. These attitudes were chosen because structural relationships among them are thought to reveal important aspects of political cognition, because they are assumed to be especially consequential determinants of political behavior, and because a large body of research has examined structural consistency among them. In the course of analyzing relationships among attitudes toward government policies, we consider their relationships with basic values, attitudes toward political reference groups, and attitudes toward political actors and candidates.

The chapter is divided into three sections. In the first, we review past research on consistency between attitudes in psychology and political science, focusing on factors presumed to be responsible for differences in attitude consistency. Social psychologists have argued that the importance of an attitude should be positively related to the consistency of that attitude with others. Political scientists have argued that an individual's degree of political expertise should be positively related to the degree of consistency among political attitudes. In reviewing both literatures, we identify the typical procedures used to assess attitude consistency and discuss problems with such assessment procedures. We conclude this section by arguing that nearly all prior work on the assessment of between-attitude consistency has inappropriately assumed that the ability to predict one attitude from another across individuals necessarily reflects consistency between attitudes within a given individual.

Given this problem, we attempt in the second section of the chapter to develop a model for the representation of attitudes or evaluations, defining between-attitude consistency within the context of this representational model. We then attempt to specify the structural effects of attitude importance and political expertise, showing how each may lead to increases in consistency of attitudes within a given individual. The final step in this section is to attempt to identify the conditions that are necessary for this within-individual definition of attitude consistency to translate into be-

---

[1]Attitude researchers have used a number of different terms to refer to the subjective importance of an attitude. The most frequently used are *importance, centrality,* and *ego-involvement.* Although a variety of different definitions of these terms have been offered, we think the theoretical distinctions among them are relatively small. We use the term *importance* throughout this chapter, giving it a very precise definition in the second section of the chapter. Our choice to use this term was, however, somewhat arbitrary. We mean to subsume by it the notions of centrality and ego-involvement.

tween-individual correlations between attitudes. Finally, in the third section of the chapter, we derive a set of predictions from the model and test them with national survey data.

ATTITUDE CONSISTENCY: THEORY AND RESEARCH

Within social psychology, attitude organization has been addressed most extensively by the cognitive consistency theorists. Balance theory (Heider, 1958; Newcomb, 1968), congruity theory (Osgood & Tannenbaum, 1955), and dissonance theory (Festinger, 1957) all presume that people prefer consistency among their attitudes to inconsistency and tinker with them whenever necessary in order to maintain consistency. According to these perspectives, attitude consistency is driven by a system of syllogistic logic (Abelson & Rosenberg, 1958). Similar attitudes (i.e., both positive or both negative) toward two objects are defined as consistent if the objects both constitute instances of the same category or are positively linked to each other through some sort of association. Contrasting attitudes (i.e., one positive and one negative) toward two objects are consistent if the objects are negatively linked to one another.

Consistency theorists asserted that a variety of factors determine whether two linked attitudes are consistent with one another. Probably the factor most often discussed is the importance of the attitudes involved (Festinger, 1957; Newcomb, 1956, 1961; Singer, 1968). For example, according to Festinger (1957), the intensity of discomfort associated with inconsistency between two attitudes is a joint function of (a) the average importance of the two attitudes, and (b) the discrepancy between their importances. Discomfort is presumed to be greatest when two equally and highly important attitudes are inconsistent, and it presumably decreases as the discrepancy increases and as the average falls. This suggests that inconsistency between attitudes may be tolerated if one or both of the attitudes involved are unimportant. If both attitudes are highly important, the inconsistency would presumably be resolved, perhaps by either changing the less important of the two or lowering its importance. As a consequence, an individual's important attitudes tend to be relatively consistent with one another.

Within political science, the origins of attitude consistency and the factors that enhance it have been viewed quite differently. Political scientists' concerns with these questions were motivated initially by an interest in the degree to which citizens' attitudes toward public policies are derived from or *constrained* by ideologies (Converse, 1964). Because the political environment in many countries is structured largely by two political parties, each on one side of a liberal–conservative ideological continuum, political scientists have focused primarily on liberalism and conservatism as ideological bases for policy attitudes. Campbell, Converse, Miller, & Stokes (1960), Converse (1964, 1970), and others did not argue that most people generally prefer consistency among their policy attitudes to inconsistency. Rather, they claimed, some people derive their attitudes toward policies from ideologies, and others form each attitude on the basis of considerations specifically relevant to it. Presumably, individuals who employ the first approach evidence attitude consistency and structure across a wide array of policy attitudes; those who employ the second approach do not. The difference here is one of style.

Political scientists think of style of policy attitude formation as a relatively stable individual difference variable and assume that domain-specific expertise is a prerequisite for ideologically consistent political attitudes (e.g., Converse, 1964, 1970, 1975, 1980). The confluence of knowledge about past political events and practice at thinking about them presumably helps some individuals to derive policy attitudes from general principles. Political experts are assumed to be best able to (a) manipulate abstract concepts such as political ideologies, (b) recognize the applicability of ideologies to particular policy issues, and (c) derive attitudes toward specific policies from those general principles. Therefore, political experts' policy attitudes are especially likely to evidence consistency among themselves because they are all derived from a single ideological principle.

Because political experts presumably think often about political events and issues and have strong feelings on such matters, these individuals may be likely to consider relevant attitudes to be personally important. If this is so, then the literatures in political science and social psychology can be seen as making complementary, although distinct, predictions about the determinants of attitude consistency. Notice, however, that the focus in the two literatures is rather different. In the psychological literature, importance is seen as a characteristic of an individual attitude, increasing the probability that that attitude will be consistent with other attitudes. The literature in political science has focused on the way in which expertise in a given domain increases consistency. Expertise is a characteristic of a domain of knowledge rather than a characteristic of an individual attitude. The two factors may work in tandem to produce particularly high levels of consistency among attitudes that are important to political experts.

Surprisingly, given the theoretical predictions made by psychological theories of attitude consistency, few studies in the psychological literature have compared the level of consistency among attitudes differing in importance. Not a single study within the dissonance literature on forced compliance or voluntary exposure to information measured or manipulated attitude or belief importance, and studies of postdecision dissonance reduction examined the importance of the decision, not of the attitudes or beliefs involved (e.g., Converse & Cooper, 1979). Newcomb (1961) and Osgood (Osgood & Tannenbaum, 1955; Tannenbaum, 1967, 1968) incorporated attitude importance into their analyses but did not compare important attitudes to unimportant ones. Some empirical support for the claim that more important attitudes evidence greater consistency comes from studies of interpersonal attraction. Liking of a stranger or a presidential candidate is more consistent with agreement on important attitudes than with agreement on unimportant ones (Byrne, London, & Griffitt, 1968; Clore & Baldridge, 1968; Krosnick, 1986). More direct evidence for the association between attitude consistency and importance comes from studies showing higher correlations between attitudes toward government policies among those who say those attitudes are personally important than among those who say they are less important (Jackman, 1977; Judd & Krosnick, 1982; Schuman & Presser, 1981, pp. 264–266; Smith, 1982).

The hypothesis that political experts should evidence greater policy attitude consistency has been tested more extensively. Support for this notion comes from studies showing that political expertise (as measured directly by political knowledge or indirectly via interest in politics, exposure to political news, or educational attainment) is associated with larger correlations among policy attitudes (Axelrod, 1967–1968; Bishop, 1976–1977; Bishop, Hamilton, & McConahay, 1980; Converse, 1964; Hagner & Pierce, 1983; Judd & Milburn, 1980; Judd, Krosnick, & Milburn, 1981; Kritzer, 1978; Nie & Anderson, 1974; Nie, Verba, & Petrocik, 1979; Pierce & Hagner, 1980). These correlations consistently indicate that people who adopt a liberal position on one policy question tend to adopt a liberal position on others as well, and this tendency is stronger among political experts.

In sum, there is evidence in both the psychological and political science literatures suggesting that attitude importance and political expertise are related to differences in between-attitude consistency. Correlations between different attitudes seem to be generally higher among experts and among those who regard those attitudes as more personally important.

Problems in the Assessment of Consistency

The available literature supports the conclusion that political expertise and attitude importance are both related to larger attitude-attitude correlations. There are, however, a number of problems in using such correlations to assess differences between groups in attitude consistency. In this section, we discuss three particular difficulties:

1. distortions in between-group comparisons due to differences in measurement error,
2. distortions in between-group comparisons due to differences in response variance, and
3. distortions in between-group comparisons due to differences in within-individual structural relations between attitudes.

Measurement Error

The first problem derives from the well-known fact that random errors of measurement attenuate correlation coefficients (Judd & Kenny, 1981). The more random error is present in attitude reports, the lower attitude-attitude correlations will be, assuming all else equal. If political experts and novices differ in the amount of random measurement error in their attitude reports, comparisons of correlations across levels of political expertise may be misleading.

In fact, policy attitude reports by political experts are likely to contain less random error for two reasons. First, these individuals are likely to answer survey questions more easily and precisely because they are likely to have had practice at expressing their policy opinions. Second, because these individuals are generally well-educated, they are likely to be adept at handling testlike survey questions. Consequently, stronger between-attitude correlations among political experts may simply reflect less random measurement error in their attitude reports. Similarly, it seems reasonable to suppose that personally important attitudes might be reported with less random error (Schuman & Presser, 1981). If this is the case, then comparisons of correlations between attitudes differing in importance might erroneously conclude that there is greater consistency between important attitudes when the difference in correlations may simply be due to a difference in measurement error.

Norpoth and Lodge (1985) recognized this problem and estimated attitude intercorrelations after correction for attenuation due to measurement error. They found that political experts did in fact report their attitudes with less random error. However, even after correction for attenuation, these attitudes were still more strongly intercorrelated than were those of novices.

Similarly, Judd and Krosnick (1982) recognized that differences in attitude-attitude correlations as a function of attitude importance may reflect differences in random errors of measurement. However, they found that reports of important attitudes do not contain any more random measurement error than do reports of less important attitudes (see also Krosnick,

1986). Furthermore, they found higher correlations among more important attitudes even after correcting for attenuation due to random errors of measurement.

Response Variance

A second problem with past studies involves the relationship between response variance and the magnitude of correlation coefficients. It is well-known that between-group differences in the variance of attitudes will lead to differences in the size of attitude-attitude correlations even when unstandardized measures of association, such as unstandardized regression coefficients, are equivalent between groups (Barton & Parsons, 1977; Balch, 1979; Blalock, 1967; Weissberg, 1976). Groups displaying more variance in their responses will generally evidence higher correlations. Tesser (1978; Tesser & Leone, 1977) repeatedly showed that merely thinking about an attitude object increases the extremity of one's evaluation of that object. Certainly one might expect those who regard an attitude toward a policy option as important to think about that option more frequently. Similarly, we would expect political experts to think about political and policy options more frequently. As a result, we might expect important attitudes and the attitudes of political experts to be more polarized or variable. Differences in attitude-attitude correlations as a function of attitude importance may then simply reflect differences in variability.

Barton and Parsons (1977) and Hagner and Pierce (1983) recognized this problem and compared policy attitude consistency among political experts and novices using a method unbiased by variance differences. Consistent with theory-based expectations, they found experts' attitudes to be more consistent with one another. However, these investigators failed to take between-group differences in measurement error into account in their analyses, rendering their findings inconclusive.

Judd and Krosnick (1982) used a second-order confirmatory factor analysis procedure to examine differences in consistency as a function of attitude importance while allowing for between group differences in measurement error and variability. They built a model in which attitudes toward five different policy issues were presumed to load on a single latent factor. By the use of multiple measures of each of these attitudes, they were able to examine separately differences between high and low importance groups in attitude variability, measurement error, and second-order factor loadings of the attitudes on the single higher-order latent variable. These second-order factor loadings were presumed to reflect the degree of attitude consistency between different attitudes unbiased by differences in variability and random errors of measurement. Although they found evidence for differences in variability, they failed to uncover any differences in the second-order factor loadings, thus calling into question the assertion that more important attitudes are more highly correlated.[2]

Unit of Analysis

The methodological problems of differences in variability and measurement error certainly complicate the assessment of consistency differences between groups of subjects who differ in attitude importance and political expertise. In addition, however, there is another more fundamental problem with the standard approach to this issue, a problem that pervades all of the research that we have mentioned. In this research, consistency has been assessed by examining correlations, covariances, and factor loadings based on variability in attitude responses across individuals. That is, one typically examines consistency between two attitudes by looking at whether between-subject differences in evaluations of one attitude object are predictive of between-subject differences in evaluations of another attitude object. Yet, conceptually, the notion of consistency is defined by reference to the structural relationships between attitudes *within* individuals rather than *between* them. Our definition of consistency, and the one used most frequently in both the psychological and political research we have reviewed, focuses on the extent to which an individual's attitudes are derived from or are connected to the other attitudes and values of that individual. Thus, consistency refers fundamentally to a structural connectedness between attitudes within any given individual. Individuals with more consistent attitudes should have a tighter attitude structure, with stronger links between different attitudes and between attitudes and underlying values and ideological preferences than individuals whose attitudes are less consistent with each other. If we define consistency in this way, it is not at all clear that consistency differences can be appropriately examined by looking at correlations between attitudes computed across individuals. The structure of such between-subject correlations may or may not reflect internal structural differences in the representation of political attitudes that we think of as attitude consistency. (For similar arguments, see Bennett, 1975; Brown, 1980; and Lane, 1973.)

To illustrate the potential problem here, consider the four hypothetical individuals whose attitudes are described in Fig. 1. Two attitudes have been assessed for each individual: attitude toward Ronald Reagan and

---

[2]Bielby (1986) subsequently showed that such factor loadings in the unstandardized case may not be an appropriate statistic for examining differences between samples. Although the ratio of loadings is informative, it is probably not the case that individual loadings are informative about the level of consistency within any one sample.

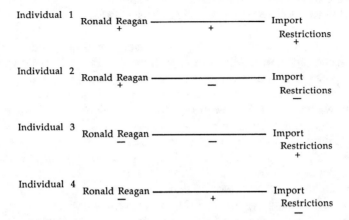

FIG. 5.1.   Consistency relations between two attitudes for four individuals.

attitude toward the government policy of import restrictions. For each individual, the valence of each attitude is indicated by the sign associated with the attitude object. Thus, two individuals favor each object and two oppose each one. In addition, individuals have indicated whether or not the two objects go together or imply one another. More concretely, the sign attached to the link between the two objects indicates each individual's belief about whether Reagan favors or opposes import restrictions.

According to syllogistic models of what it means for two attitudes to be consistent with each other (e.g., Abelson & Rosenberg, 1958; Heider, 1958), each of these four individuals displays consistent evaluations of the two attitude objects. Individual 1 likes both objects and believes that Reagan likes restrictions. Individual 2 likes Reagan, dislikes restrictions, and consistently believes that Reagan dislikes restrictions. Likewise individuals 3 and 4 display consistent evaluations. Yet, if we were to compute a correlation between the two attitudes across the four individuals, we would find a correlation of zero! Thus, correlations computed between attitudes across individuals do not necessarily reflect within-individual attitude consistency.

In order to assess attitude consistency and differences in consistency as a function of political expertise and attitude importance, we need to think about the way in which individuals represent political attitudes in memory and then derive within-individual consistency measures. We need to think about the representational structure of political attitudes within individuals rather than examining the structure of correlations computed across individuals. A preliminary version of such a representational structure is offered in the next section.

A REPRESENTATIONAL MODEL FOR THE
EVALUATION OF POLITICAL ATTITUDE OBJECTS

Our representational model draws on semantic network models in cognitive psychology (Anderson, 1983; Anderson & Bower, 1973; Collins & Quillian, 1969). Few of these semantic models, however, include provisions for the representation of evaluation. We incorporate evaluation in these models by attaching a positive or negative sign to each node in the network, consistent with the few others who have thought about the representation of evaluation (Bower, 1981; Fiske & Pavelchak, 1986; Sears, Huddy, & Schaffer, 1986). This sign indicates an individual's attitude toward the object represented by the node.

We can think of a variety of politically relevant attitude objects that might be represented in memory. Most abstractly, fundamental or underlying values, such as Rokeach's (1973) terminal values, or abstract ideological principles might be represented. Somewhat less abstractly, political and government policies, such as affirmative action, unilateral nuclear disarmament, and abortion on demand are likely to be represented. Another category of represented attitude objects includes political reference groups such as Democrats, Right to Lifers, and Black Militants. Finally, individual political actors and candidates, such as Ronald Reagan, Jesse Jackson, and Edward Kennedy might be represented.

Represented object nodes have two characteristics. They have associated strengths and they have associated evaluations (or attitudes). The strength of a node is presumed to be a function of prior activation of the node, as in Anderson's (1983) ACT* model. The more one has thought about an object in the past, the greater the strength of its node. Consistent with Anderson's (1983) model, these node strengths affect the probability that an object will come into awareness, along the lines to be discussed. The evaluation associated with a node can be either positive or negative and they also vary in strength. We represent these associated evaluations by a positive or negative sign attached to each node. The relative sizes of the signs indicate the strength or intensity of the associated evaluations. Consistent with Fazio's notions (Fazio, Powell, & Herr, 1983; Fazio, Sanbonmatsu, Powell, & Kardes, 1986), the strength of an object evaluation derives from prior thought about that evaluation and affects, in turn, the probability that the object evaluation will come into awareness whenever the object itself does.

We suspect that there is a relationship in the political domain between the strength of the object node and the strength of the associated evaluation, such that the greater the probability that an object comes to mind, the greater the probability that the associated evaluation comes to mind. We also suspect that the strength of the associated evaluation is highly related to the extremity of that evaluation, consistent with the work of Tesser

(1978), such that object evaluations that have been thought about previously have a greater probability of coming into awareness in the future and are also relatively more extreme.

The representational structure becomes a network under the assumption that nodes may be linked to one another. These links are similar to Heider's (1958) notions of sentiment and unit relations between attitude objects. Links may be between object nodes within a given category of political objects or between different categories. Thus, for instance, the policy of affirmative action may be linked to the policy of school integration. At the same time, the policy of affirmative action is also likely to be linked to more abstract value nodes, such as freedom or equality, as well as to object nodes representing political reference groups (e.g., Blacks) and candidates. It is beyond the scope of this chapter to specify the origins of these links in detail. Briefly, we assume that two nodes become linked when they are thought about simultaneously. This is likely to occur whenever the individual comes to believe that one object implies, favors, contradicts, or opposes the other object.

Links can also be thought of as having two characteristics. Information about the implicational relation between the linked nodes is stored along with each link. Implicational relations, like node evaluations, are either positive or negative. A positive implicational relation means that one represented object is seen as implying the other linked object. A negative implicational relation means that one represented object is seen as implying the converse of the linked object. These implicational relations subsume both unit and liking relations from Heider's balance theory (1958), indicating the perceived relation between two represented political objects.

Consider the following examples that illustrate the meaning of these implicational relations. The policy of affirmative action might have a positive implicational relation with the value of equality and a negative one with the value of freedom. That is, one might believe that affirmative action increases the likelihood of achieving the value of equality while decreasing the likelihood of achieving the value of freedom. The political actor node representing Ronald Reagan might share a link with the node representing "abortion on demand." In all probability, the implicational relation between these linked nodes would be a negative one, because we might expect the individual to believe that Reagan espouses the converse of abortion on demand. A node representing Edward Kennedy as a political actor might be linked to organized labor as a reference group node, and the implicational relation between them would probably be positive.

The second characteristic of a link is its strength, indicating the probability that one node will be activated given activation of the linked node. Following Anderson (1983), we assume that the strength of a link is completely determined by the strength of the two nodes that it connects.

Accordingly, this characteristic of links is actually subsumed by the strength of nodes. Nevertheless, it is heuristically useful to think of link strengths. The probability that the ith node will be activated, assuming activation in the jth linked node, is assumed to equal the strength of the ith node divided by the sum of the strengths of all nodes, including i, with which the jth node is linked. Thus, as the ith node increases in strength, the probability of its activation from any other linked node increases. Heuristically, then, we can think of the strength of links to a node as being a function of the strength of that node. Under this formulation, the strength of the link from the jth node to the ith does not necessarily equal the strength of the link from the ith node to the jth. The strength of the destination node determines the strength of links to that node.

As in semantic network models, link strength derives from prior simultaneous activation of linked nodes. Thus, if in the past one has thought about the Defense Budget whenever Ronald Reagan came to mind, the link from Reagan to Defense Budget nodes would be relatively strong. As a result, activation of Reagan in the future would, with high probability, also activate the Defense Budget node. Activation of a node increases the probability that the represented object will be brought into awareness. Furthermore, as we said earlier, activation of a represented object may also activate the associated object evaluation, depending on the strength of that evaluation.

A simple example of the sort of representational structure we are defining is presented in Fig. 5.2. At the top of the figure the abstract value of equality, with an associated positive evaluation, is represented. Two policy issues, affirmative action and defense spending are represented, with only the former being linked with the Equality value. Affirmative action is positively evaluated, whereas the defense spending attitude is negative. Two political candidates, Jackson and Reagan, are also represented. Finally, Blacks as a political reference group are also represented. In this example, we have indicated evaluation strength by the relative size of the evaluation sign attached to each node. Thus, for instance, the evaluation of affirmative action is strongly positive and likely to be quite accessible. Link strength is indicated crudely by the presence or absence of links between pairs of nodes. The lack of a link between pairs of nodes is as informative as the presence of one. Thus, this individual would rarely think about the two policy issues of affirmative action and defense spending simultaneously, and strictly speaking, given the sparse example we are using, would do so only if the political candidate Jesse Jackson was also considered.

The Definition of Attitude Consistency

Given this set of assumptions about a representational model for the evaluation of political objects, we can specify what it means for different attitudes or evaluations to be consistent with each other. We define two attitudes as

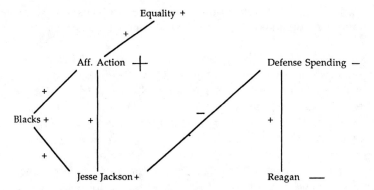

FIG. 5.2.   A simple attitude representation structure.

being consistent in this representational model when the product of the
signs of the evaluations of the two objects times the sign of the implicational
relation between them is positive. When the product of these three is
negative, evaluative inconsistency is indicated. Thus, two positively evaluated objects that share a positive implicational link are evaluatively consistent. Similarly, two negatively evaluated objects sharing a positive
implicational relation are evaluatively consistent. When the two object
evaluations are of opposite sign, evaluative consistency is produced by a
negative implicational relation between them. Evaluative inconsistency results when only one of the three signs is negative or when they are all
negative. Of course, this specification is completely consistent with earlier
specifications from the cognitive consistency literature that we have reviewed (e.g., Abelson & Rosenberg, 1958; Heider, 1958).

Our specification differs from earlier ones, however, in specifying that
the strength of the link between two represented objects directly affects the
probability that the two associated evaluations will be consistent with each
other. We assume that attitude consistency is enhanced as a result of
simultaneous activation of the two linked objects. Because the strength of
the link indicates the probability that one node will be activated given
activation in the linked one, we are thus assuming that the probability of
evaluative consistency between two objects will be a positive function of
the probability that the two objects are brought into awareness simultaneously. To be more precise, because links do not have strengths in our
model and nodes do, we are assuming that the evaluation of any given
object will be more likely to be consistent with the evaluation of another
linked object the greater the combined strengths of the two object nodes.
On average, the greater the strength of any given node, the greater the
probability that its evaluation will be consistent with the nodes to which it
is linked. In addition, the evaluation of any given node is more likely to be
consistent with the evaluation of other linked nodes that are strong than

with the evaluation of other linked nodes that are relatively weak. When two nodes are unlinked, evaluative consistency between the two is undefined.

An interesting case arises when a strong node is linked to two other strong nodes that are each positively valued. When the two implicational relations are both positive or both negative, consistency of evaluation of the focal node is easily accomplished. However, when the focal node shares a positive implicational relation with one linked node and a negative one with the other linked node, evaluative consistency is hard to achieve.

Consider, for instance, the individual who values both freedom and equality and for whom both of these value nodes have considerable strength. This individual may see school busing as enhancing equality and limiting freedom. In this case, if the school busing node is also strong, evaluative consistency may be difficult to achieve. The evaluation of busing that is most consistent is perhaps a moderate one. Such an outcome represents an exception to our earlier hypothesis that nodes with greater strength ought to have more intense evaluations. More generally, when a given node shares a positive implicational relation with another strong node that is positively evaluated, and a negative implicational relation with another strong node that it also positively evaluated, the press toward evaluative consistency implies that the greater the strength of the focal node, the more likely it is that that node will have a moderate evaluation. This hypothesis is consistent with Tetlock's (1983, 1984) value pluralism model, though it does not contradict the hypothesis that, *on average,* objects towards which more thought is devoted (i.e., nodes with greater strength) are associated with more intense or extreme evaluations (Tesser, 1978). Node strength is not isomorphic with evaluative intensity.

Once the consistency between two political attitudes is defined in this way, it is possible to talk about system-wide or domain-wide attitude consistency. The degree of attitude consistency of a domain of attitude objects is defined as the probability that evaluative consistency will hold for any randomly selected pair of objects in that domain. This implies that domain-wide evaluative consistency varies positively with the number of links between pairs of nodes in the domain and with the average node strength in the domain. This definition of domain-wide consistency is quite different from those offered by Cartwright and Harary (1956; Harary, Norman, & Cartwright, 1965).

The consistency between attitudes toward two government policies can be assessed at a global level within a given individual by examining the perceived implicational relations between each of the policies and various candidates and reference groups. If a person's evaluation of one policy is consistent with his or her evaluation of a second policy, then he or she should perceive political candidates and reference groups to take consistent stands toward the two policies. Suppose, for instance, that one has a positive evaluation of policy 1 and a negative evaluation of policy 2. If there is a relatively high degree of domain-wide consistency relative to these two issues, then candidates who are seen as liking policy 1 (positive implicational relation) should be seen as disliking policy 2 (negative implicational relation). Conversely, candidates seen as disliking policy 1 should be seen as liking policy 2. Hence, within an individual, the consistency between two policy attitudes can be assessed by correlating the individual's judgments of where many candidates stand on each of the two policies.

The Structural Definition of Attitude Importance and Domain Expertise

Given this representational model, we can now define attitude importance and political expertise in structural terms. Our goal in these definitions is to see how they might each be responsible for greater evaluative consistency between attitudes.

Attitude importance has been defined in numerous ways in the attitude literature (see Krosnick, 1986, for a comprehensive review). Two defining characteristics have been used repeatedly. First, important or central attitudes are those that are extensively linked to other attitudes, beliefs, or values (Bem, 1970; Krech & Crutchfield, 1948; Lewin, 1951; Ostrom & Brock, 1969; Sherif & Cantril, 1947). Second, important attitudes are those that the individual thinks about frequently and that are therefore the focus of personal interest or subjective importance (Converse, 1970; Freedman, 1964; Smith, Bruner, & White, 1956). To quote Converse (1970), the centrality or importance of an attitude is reflected by "the proportion of 'mental time' which is occupied by attention to the attitude object over substantial periods" (p. 182).

In order to capture both of these defining characteristics of importance, we define the importance of an attitude in our representational model as the strength of the node representing the attitude object. Because the strength of a node derives from past activation of the node and is a determinant of the strength of the links from other nodes to the focal one, this definition is consistent with both defining characteristics of attitude importance. First, more important attitudes are those that are more potently linked to other political attitudes. Second, important attitudes are thought about more frequently and should therefore be judged to be of greater interest. Note that this definition differentiates between attitude importance and the intensity or extremity of the evaluation of the attitude object. Importance is defined by the strength of the node representing the attitude object, and strong nodes may be associated with moderate evaluations.

In defining evaluative consistency between two attitudes, we suggested that the probability of consistency ought to be a direct function of the combined strengths of the two nodes. Accordingly, nodes with greater strength ought to be, on average, more evaluatively consistent with other nodes to which they are linked. It follows that more important attitudes ought to be more consistent with other attitudes.

Political expertise is assumed to have structural correlates similar to correlates of expertise suggested in other domains (e.g., Chase & Simon, 1973; Chi & Koeske, 1983; Fiske & Kinder, 1981; Larkin, McDermott, Simon, & Simon, 1980; McKeithen, Reitman, Rueter, & Hirtle, 1981). Specifically, political experts are presumed to know of many more political attitude objects than those who have little expertise. They should know of more policy options, political actors, and reference groups than those who are less expert. Within our representational model, this implies that there ought to be more nodes in experts' representational networks. In addition, experts are presumed to see connections among diverse policy options, political actors, and reference groups that may not be apparent to those who have less expertise. Thus, for instance, the political expert may realize that a restrictive trade policy has implications for affirmative action policies: A tighter job market makes affirmative action goals harder to achieve. The less expert individual may simply not represent these policy options in memory and, if they are represented, may fail to see the connection between them. Similarly, the political expert is more likely to recognize that policy options have implications for values and reference groups. Finally, political experts are more likely to know what policies various political actors endorse and thus see links between policies and actors that the less expert individual is unlikely to see. All this suggests that the political expert will have more nodes represented in memory and will have more links per node. Each node can be activated by a larger number of other nodes than is likely to be the case in the representational network of a less expert individual.

These two structural effects of expertise, more nodes and more links per node, should lead to greater evaluative consistency throughout the political domain. Given more links per node, the average strength of nodes for experts should be higher than that for the nonexpert. As a result, the average degree of evaluative consistency throughout the domain ought to be higher. In addition, when the expert sees a link between two represented objects that the nonexpert fails to see, there is some pressure toward consistency in the evaluations of the linked nodes, whereas the nonexpert feels no such pressure.

These structural differences between the expert and nonexpert do not suggest that we would *always* find greater evaluative consistency between pairs of attitudes with the expert. Even for the most expert person, we would hardly expect all possible pairs to be linked. Furthermore, the expert may feel conflicting claims of diverse implicational relations with other valued objects that make evaluative consistency with the set of other linked objects difficult. The nonexpert, who perhaps sees only consistent implicational relations, may actually have less difficulty achieving consistency. The notion of *value pluralism* (Tetlock, 1983, 1984) suggests that experts may have a harder time achieving evaluative consistency between specific political attitudes than the less expert individual.

Given this view of political expertise, it is interesting to consider the often-heard claim that political experts' attitudes are more likely to evidence ideological organization. This organization may simply result from greater pressure toward evaluative consistency in diverse political attitudes. Alternatively, it may be that the political expert is more likely to have an explicit ideological node at the highest level of the representational hierarchy than the nonexpert, and nearly all represented policy options and candidates are linked to this ideological node. These two specifications of the structural bases of ideology, although conceptually distinct, may be very hard to distinguish empirically.

Assessing Attitude Consistency

These structural definitions of how attitude consistency derives from attitude importance and political expertise have no necessary implications for covariances or correlations between attitudes computed across individuals. Rather, we simply maintain that more important evaluations ought to be more predictable from an individual's evaluation of other objects given that we know how that individual perceives the implicational relationships between the objects. An important positive evaluation predicts positive evaluations of other linked objects when one object implies the others. When one object imples the *converse* of the others, then a more important positive evaluation predicts more strongly negative evaluations of linked objects than does a less important positive evaluation. Similarly, the political evaluations of the political expert ought to be more evaluatively consistent on average across the domain of political attitudes.

If two individuals perceive different implicational relations between objects, enhanced within-individual consistency will not result in enhanced predictability of one attitude from another across individuals. In order for enhanced within-individual consistency for more important attitudes and for the political expert to translate into greater predictability of one attitude from another across individuals, individuals' perceived implicational relationships between attitude objects must be constant across levels of importance or expertise. If individuals agree on the implicative relationships among policy options, values, and candidates, then structural consistency within an individual will result in between-individual predictability of attitudes. If two people disagree in their evaluations of one object, they should disagree on the evaluation of another object only if they agree on the implicational relationship between the two objects.

This suggests that if attitude consistency is assessed by examining covariances or correlations computed across individuals, attitude importance ought to be associated with larger attitude-attitude correlations only if there is agreement across individuals in the implicational relationship between the two attitude objects. Furthermore, the absence of a between-individual correlation between two attitudes does not necesssarily imply the absence of within-individual attitude consistency. A low correlation computed across individuals can result from disagreements in the perceived implicational relationship between the two attitude objects, even though the links between the two objects may be quite strong within individuals.

Interestingly, attitude importance and political expertise may enhance the probability that individuals will agree on the implicational relationships between diverse political issues and policy options (see, e.g., Krosnick, 1986). Whereas two experts may disagree on their evaluations of two attitude objects, they seem more likely than nonexperts to agree about the implication of one object for the other. As a result, higher associations between attitudes computed across individuals may be found for experts than for nonexperts partly because of enhanced agreement on the implicational relations between different policy options. This may also be the case with attitude importance. Those who regard a particular attitude as important may show greater agreement in the implicational relations between that attitude object and other represented objects. This would produce larger correlations between them when the correlation is computed across individuals.

In sum, when we assess attitude consistency by examining associations between two different attitudes computed across individuals, we need to be sure that those individuals agree on the implicational relation between the attitude objects. If groups differ in their agreement about the implicational relation, differences between groups in between-attitude correlations will be uninformative about between-group differences in attitude consistency.

SOME EMPIRICAL SUPPORT
FOR THESE SPECULATIONS

In this section, we report a preliminary evaluation of our speculations regarding the relation of attitude consistency to attitude importance and political expertise. In particular, we test the claims that (a) highly important attitudes evidence greater consistency with other attitudes than do less important attitudes, and (b) attitudes held by experts evidence greater consistency than those held by novices. In the process, we illustrate how traditional approaches to testing these hypotheses lead to inaccurate estimates.

Our model argues that an individual's attitude toward a particular policy should be more consistent with that person's attitude toward a particular presidential candidate or political party to the extent that the policy attitude is important to him or her and to the extent that he or she is a political expert. We evaluate this claim while attempting to control not only for differences in variability and measurement error, but also for differences in agreement on the implicational relations between the attitude objects.

The data we use come from the 1980 National Election Study (NES), conducted by the Center for Political Studies (CPS) at the University of Michigan. Every 2 years since the early 1950s, CPS has interviewed large, representative national samples of American adults both before and after the presidential and midterm elections. In 1980, the study design was somewhat more complex than usual, because it involved interviews with three distinct samples, two of which we made use of in the present analysis. The first sample we examined consisted of 1614 individuals who were interviewed in September and October of 1980. During these interviews, respondents were asked to report their attitudes toward a number of government policies, political candidates, and the major political parties. The policy attitude measure we focus on was phrased as follows:

> Some people think the government should provide fewer services, even in areas such as health and education, in order to reduce spending. Other people feel it is important for the government to continue the services it now provides even if it means no reduction in spending. Where would you place yourself on this scale, or haven't you thought much about this?

Answers to this question were collected on a 7-point scale with the end points labeled "Government should provide many fewer services, reduce spending a lot" and "Government should continue to provide services, no reduction in spending." Respondents reported their perceptions of the stands taken on this social welfare issue by the major presidential candidates, Jimmy Carter and Ronald Reagan, and by the Democratic and Republican parties, and reported their attitudes toward the candidates and parties on 100-point feeling thermometers. For the analyses reported below, all attitude measures were recoded to range from zero to one in order to facilitate interpretation of unstandardized regression coefficients.

This survey also included measures of the importance of attitudes toward government spending on social welfare programs. Consistent with our definition of importance, this construct has usually been measured by asking individuals how much they think about a particular policy or how important it is to them personally (e.g., Judd & Krosnick, 1982; Schuman & Presser, 1981). Because the policy attitude measures in the 1980 NES all addressed potential government actions, the measures in that survey were geared accordingly. The policy attitude measures asked respondents what they thought the federal government should do on various issues, and the importance measures asked respondents how important it was to them that the government do what they thought was best on each issue. Ratings of importance were made on 10-point scales.

Political expertise was measured by an extensive battery of questions tapping four constructs. Exposure to political information was measured by nine items asking respondents how often they talk with others about politics and how much political information they are exposed to through various media. Interest in politics was measured by four questions asking about interest in the presidential campaign and its outcome. Political participation was assessed by 10 items asking whether the respondent had voted in recent elections and whether he or she had performed various political behaviors, such as attending political meetings or contacting a congressman. Finally, political knowledge was measured by two items, one asking whether the respondent knew which presidential candidate was ahead in the public opinion polls at the moment, and the other asking respondents to recall the names of their congressmen. Four indicies, constructed by averaging these groups of items, were strongly correlated with each other and were therefore averaged to produce an overall measure of political expertise. Political expertise, as measured in this way, was only very weakly correlated with the importance of attitudes toward social welfare spending ($r=.10$, $n=1162$, $p<.01$).[3]

The traditional method of assessing consistency between two attitudes is to regress one on the other. The larger the correlation or standardized regression coefficient, the more consistent the two attitudes are thought to be. As we argued earlier, however, these are three problems in using this approach. First, differences in standardized regression coefficients or correlations between groups that differ in expertise or attitude importance may emerge because of differences in response variance. To solve this problem, we should examine unstandardized regression coefficients rather than standardized ones. Second, differences in error variance between groups may differentially bias or attenuate regression coefficients. To solve this problem, we should estimate the reliabilities of the variables in each group and

---

[3]In our model, political expertise increases the number of nodes and the number of links between nodes. In contrast, importance affects the strength of a particular node. The small observed correlation between political expertise and the importance of social welfare attitudes suggests that system-wide attributes, such as the number of nodes and links, cannot be used to predict the strength of any particular node, although on average stronger nodes are those having more links.

disattentuate the unstandardized regression coefficients. Finally, disagreement about implicational relations between the two attitudes may lead to relatively small regression coefficients even when attitude consistency within individuals may be quite large. Furthermore, it is likely that experts and people for whom an attitude is important should show more agreement on implicational relations than those who are less expert or for whom the attitude is relatively unimportant. Accordingly, between-group differences in regression coefficients should be examined only among individuals who agree on the implicational relation between the attitude objects.

In Table 5.1, we report the unstandardized regression coefficients that result if we simply regress respondent's social welfare attitudes on their evaluations of the candidates and parties. This regression was done separately for samples differing in attitude importance and political expertise. By examining unstandardized coefficients, we alleviate the problem of differences in response variance, although the problems of measurement error and lack of agreement on implicational relations persist. The coefficients in this table show a clear trend for both attitude importance and political expertise: The coefficients have larger absolute values among samples high in political expertise or attitude importance.

TABLE 5.1
Effects of Attitudes Toward Candidates and Parties on Attitudes Toward
Spending for Social Welfare Programs

| Predictor | Importance of Attitudes Toward Social Welfare Spending | | | Political Expertise | | |
	Low	Medium	High	Low	Medium	High
Attitude Toward Carter	.12*	.34**	.57**	.19**	.29**	.43**
	(407)	(420)	(301)	(368)	(446)	(453)
Attitude Toward Reagan	−.15**	−.28**	−.50**	−.01	−.25**	−.50**
	(406)	(416)	(297)	(357)	(445)	(452)
Attitude Toward Democrats	.26**	.56**	.66**	.32**	.41**	.63**
	(405)	(419)	(307)	(359)	(441)	(458)
Attitude Toward Republicans	−.20**	−.30**	−.38**	.05	−.19**	−.51**
	(407)	(419)	(307)	(359)	(443)	(459)

Note. Entries are unstandardized regression coefficients. Ns are shown in parentheses.
*$p < .05$.
**$p < .01$

In order to assess these relationships more formally, we conducted four regressions across the entire sample. Each utilized just one predictor attitude (toward a candidate or a party) and regressed attitudes toward social welfare spending on the predictor attitude, importance, political expertise, the interaction between the predictor attitude and importance, and the interaction between the predictor attitude and political expertise. The 2 two-way interactions were both large and statistically significant in all four regressions, thus indicating that attitude importance and expertise both enhance the size of the association between the attitudes and do so independently of each other.

To eliminate the problem caused by lack of agreement on implication relations, we selected individuals in each of the importance and expertise groups who correctly identified Carter and the Democrats as being relatively liberal on the issue of social welfare and Reagan and the Republicans as being relatively conservative on the issue. Note that this is a very crude operationalization of agreement on implicational relations. Accordingly, two individuals are said to agree if they place the respective candidates and parties on the same side of the issue, even though they may disagree about exactly where the candidates and parties stand on the issue. Although we selected individuals who agree on the "correct" implicational relation between this issue and the candidates or parties, our argument about the need for agreement on implicational relations does not necessitate the selection of individuals who agree on the correct implicational relations. We could have selected only those individuals who agreed that Reagan and the Republicans were relatively liberal on the issue. We simply need to compute the regressions coefficients using samples that agree on implicational relations.

In Table 5.2 we report the proportions of each sample who correctly identified the candidates' or parties' position on the issue of social welfare. The high importance and expertise groups are more likely than the low importance and expertise groups to place Carter and the Democrats on the liberal side of the issue and to place Reagan and the Republicans on the conservative side of the issue. Therefore, some of the apparent effects of expertise and importance in Table 5.1 may be due to greater agreement among the high importance and expertise groups than among the low ones.

To control for agreement on implicational relations, we selected only those individuals who correctly identified Carter and the Democrats as liberal on the issue and Reagan and the Republicans as conservative. We then regressed respondents' social welfare attitudes on their attitudes toward each candidate and each party, separately for samples differing in attitude importance and political expertise. The resulting unstandardized regression coefficients are presented in Table 5.3. Consistent with our expectations, these coefficients are all greater for individuals who agree on

TABLE 5.2
Proportions of Respondents Who Perceive the Candidate's or Party's
Stand on the Issue of Social Welfare Spending Correctly

Political Actor	Importance of Attitudes Toward Social Welfare Spending			Political Expertise		
	Low	Medium	High	Low	Medium	High
Carter	65.2%	68.7%	72.3%	56.5%	66.7%	77.6%
	(397)	(409)	(292)	(315)	(418)	(437)
Reagan	50.4%	52.5%	63.4%	43.4%	50.4%	64.2%
	(357)	(379)	(254)	(251)	(375)	(419)
Democrats	67.7%	77.1%	76.0%	59.0%	72.0%	82.5%
	(356)	(375)	(267)	(249)	(368)	(424)
Republicans	45.9%	52.4%	57.2%	41.8%	45.9%	60.8%
	(353)	(359)	(257)	(237)	(355)	(418)

Note. Ns are shown in parentheses.

implications than they were for the full samples. Each coefficient in Table 5.3 is larger in absolute value than the corresponding one in Table 5.1. However, the associations between importance and expertise on the one hand and attitude consistency on the other remain strong in Table 5.3. The strength of the attitude association is greater for the high importance and expertise groups than it is for the low importance and expertise groups in all cases but one. Therefore, this evidence supports the assertion that attitude consistency is greater among political experts and among people for whom an attitude is important.

There is one remaining problem with the figures in Table 5.3. These regression coefficients are attenuated due to random measurement error in the assessments of the party and candidate attitudes. In order to handle this problem, it is necessary to estimate the reliability of the candidate and party attitude measures for each importance and expertise group and to disattenuate the coefficients accordingly.

To estimate these reliabilities, we used data collected from a second sample as a part of the 1980 NES. A representative national cross-section of 769 American adults was interviewed on three occasions during the 1980 presidential election campaign, first in January and February, then again in June, and finally in September and October. During each of these interviews, respondents were asked to report their attitudes toward Jimmy Carter, Ronald Reagan, the Democratic party, and the Republican party on the 100-point feeling thermometers. During the third wave, respondents reported their attitudes on the issue of social welfare spending and reported

TABLE 5.3

Effects of Attitudes Toward Candidates and Parties on Attitudes Toward
Spending for Social Welfare Programs: Respondents Who Perceive
Implicational Relationship Correctly

Predictor	Importance of Attitudes Toward Social Welfare Spending			Political Expertise		
	Low	Medium	High	Low	Medium	High
Attitude Toward Carter	.33**	.45**	.79**	.52**	.51**	.52**
	(251)	(273)	(200)	(170)	(270)	(329)
Attitude Toward Reagan	−.31*	−.67**	−.77**	−.31*	−.52**	−.69**
	(172)	(192)	(153)	(100)	(184)	(259)
Attitude Toward Democrats	.35**	.73**	.85**	.55**	.62**	.72**
	(239)	(282)	(200)	(140)	(262)	(347)
Attitude Toward Republicans	−.50**	−.62**	−.70**	−.12	−.50**	−.75**
	(161)	(184)	(146)	(96)	(162)	(251)

Note. Entries are unstandardized regression coefficients. Ns are shown in parentheses.
 *$p<.05$.
 **$p<.01$

the personal importance of those attitudes. Finally, during the third interview and during a fourth one conducted shortly after the election in
November, respondents were asked almost all of the items that compose the
political expertise index described.

Given three waves of data from this panel of respondents, it is possible to
estimate the reliability of each candidate and party attitude measure within
each importance and expertise group. To do so, we estimated the parameters of a three-wave latent variable model first proposed by Heise (1969)
and later refined by Wiley and Wiley (1970). This model assumes that
attitude change is a first-order autoregressive process and that the amount
of random error variance in responses remains constant across waves. Given
these assumptions, it is possible to estimate the reliability of the attitude
measure at each wave.

For the present analysis, we used only the reliability of the attitude
measures at the first wave, because our primary analyses were based upon
data from the first interview with respondents. Using these reliability estimates, we disattenuated the unstandardized regression coefficients shown
in Table 5.3. As expected, the resulting coefficients (shown in Table 5.4) are

TABLE 5.4

Effects (Corrected for Unreliability) of Attitudes Toward Candidates and
Parties on Attitudes Toward Spending for Social Welfare Programs:
Respondents Who Perceive Implicational Relationship Correctly

Predictor	Importance of Attitudes Toward Social Welfare Spending			Political Expertise		
	Low	Medium	High	Low	Medium	High
Attitude Toward Carter	.43	.51	.86	.64	.56	.69
Attitude Toward Reagan	−.38	−.88	−.93	−.46	−.63	−.77
Attitude Toward Democrats	.50	.84	1.06	.82	.70	.92
Attitude Toward Republicans	−.71	−.76	−.93	−.20	−.75	−.90

Note. Entries are unstandardized regression coefficients. Ns and significance levels are the same as shown in Table 5.3.

larger than the attenuated ones. And consistent with our theoretical arguments, the coefficients are still generally larger for the high importance and
expertise groups than they are for the low importance and expertise groups.
The relationship between attitude importance and attitude consistency is
particularly clear across all of the candidate and party attitudes. The
relationship between expertise and consistency is clearly apparent in the
case of attitudes toward Reagan and the Republicans, but it is less clear in
the case of Carter and the Democrats. For these two attitudes, the low
expertise group's coefficient is smaller than the high expertise group's, but
the medium group falls below both. Probably the most appropriate conclusion to reach from these numbers is that expertise does not vary with
consistency in these cases.

CONCLUSION

In this chapter we have argued that there are serious problems in assessing
attitude consistency by examining between-subject correlations between
different attitudes. We discussed the problems of heterogeneity of variance

and measurement error, and claimed that between-subject associations may not indicate within-subject attitude structure. To solve this latter problem, we suggested a model for the representation of political attitudes and defined attitude consistency in terms of this model. We then explored some possible structural effects of attitude importance and political expertise, showing how differences in attitude consistency may result from the structural differences imputted to attitude importance and expertise. This representational analysis suggested that attitude consistency is properly examined when looking at between-subject associations only if subjects agree on the implications between the attitude objects in question. If experts and those whose attitudes are important show greater agreement in those implications, differences in associations between attitudes may reflect these agreement differences in addition to or instead of differences in attitude consistency.

To evaluate these hypotheses, in the third section of the chapter we assessed attitude consistency in groups differing in political expertise and attitude importance while controlling for differences in agreement on implicational relations between the attitude objects. Consistent with our expectations, those who are more expert and those whose attitudes are important show more implicational agreement. Furthermore, predicted differences in attitude consistency are found even when controlling for these differences in implicational agreement.

The analyses we reported are only preliminary attempts to validate the model of attitude representation developed here. We view the model as a heuristic tool that is suggestive of further empirical work on attitude consistency. Because the model is a representational one, making assumptions about the activation of attitude objects from memory, it seems appropriate to examine attitude consistency within individuals as well as by examining between-individual associations. We suggested, for instance, that one might examine attitude consistency within an individual by asking the individual to indicate the implicational relations between each issue and a set of political candidates (i.e., "Where do you think this candiate stands on this issue?") and then correlating within each individual the two issues across candidates. Other procedures could be used as well to assess attitude consistency at the individual level. For instance, our model suggests that activation of a given attitude ought to increase the activation of another linked attitude, particularly for individuals who regard the second attitude as important. Consistency, then, might be examined by using priming and response latency procedures, much like they have been fruitfully used in cognitive psychology.

Regardless of the empirical issues raised by this analysis, we hope that the present analysis prompts others to explore representational issues in the attitude domain more than has been done in the past. The development of representational models has been a fruitful endeavor in cognitive psychology, but such models have rarely addressed the issue of how evaluations or attitudes are represented in memory. Attitude researchers are perhaps uniquely situated to rectify this omission.

REFERENCES

Abelson, R. P., & Rosenberg, M. J. (1958). Symbolic psychologic: A model of attitudinal cognition. *Behavioral Science, 3,* 1–8.

Anderson, J. R. (1983). *The architecture of cognition.* Cambridge, MA: Harvard University Press.

Anderson, J. R., & Bower, G. H. (1973). A propositional theory of recognition memory. *Memory and Cognition, 2,* 406–412.

Axelrod, R. (1967–1968). The structure of public opinion on policy issues. *Public Opinion Quarterly, 31,* 51–60.

Balch, G. I. (1979). Statistical manipulation in the study of issue consistency: The gamma coefficient. *Political Behavior, 1,* 217–241.

Barton, A. H., & Parsons, R. W. (1977). Measuring belief system structure. *Public Opinion Quarterly, 41,* 159–180.

Bem, D. J. (1970). *Beliefs, attitudes, and human affiars.* Belmont, CA: Brooks/Cole.

Bennett, W. L. (1975). *The political mind and the political environment.* Lexington, MA: Heath.

Bielby, W. T. (1986). Arbitrary metrics in multiple indicator models of latent variables. *Sociological Methods and Research, 15,* 3–23.

Bishop, G. F. (1976–1977). The effect of education on ideological consistency. *Public Opinion Quarterly, 40,* 337–359.

Bishop, G. D., Hamilton, D. L., & McConahay, J. B. (1980). Attitudes and non-attitudes in the belief systems of mass publics: A field study. *Journal of Social Psychology, 110,* 53–64.

Blalock, H. M. (1967). Causal inferences, closed populations, and measures of association. *American Sociological Review, 61,* 130–136.

Bower, G. H. (1981). Mood and memory. *American Psychologist, 36,* 129–148.

Breckler, S. J. (1984). Empirical validation of affect, behavior, and cognition as distinct components of attitude. *Journal of Personality and Social Psychology, 47,* 1191–1205.

Brown, S. R. (1980). *Political subjectivity.* New Haven, CT: Yale University Press.

Byrne, D., London, O., & Griffitt, W. (1968). The effect of topic importance and attitude similarity-dissimilarity on attraction in an intrastranger design. *Psychonomic Science, 11,* 303–304.

Campbell, A., Converse, P. E., Miller, W. A., & Stokes, D. E. (1960). *The American voter.* Chicago: University of Chicago Press.

Cartwright, D., & Harary, F. (1956). Structural balance: A generalization of Heider's theory. *Psychological Review, 63,* 277–293.

Chaiken, S., & Baldwin, M. W. (1981). Affective-cognitive consistency and the effect of salient behavioral information on the self-perception of attitudes. *Journal of Personality and Social Psychology, 41,* 1–12.

Chaiken, S., & Yates, S. (1985). Affective-cognitive consistency and thought-induced attitude polarization. *Journal of Personality and Social Psychology, 49,* 1470–1481.

Chase, W. G., & Simon, H. A. (1973). The mind's eye in chess. In W. G. Chase (Ed.), *Visual information processing.* New York: Academic Press.

Chi, M. T. H., & Koeske, R. (1983). Network representation of a child's dinosaur knowledge. *Developmental Psychology, 19,* 29–39.

Clore, G. L., & Baldridge, B. (1968). Interpersonal attraction: The role of agreement and topic interest. *Journal of Personality and Social Psychology, 9,* 340–346.

Collins, A. M., & Quillian, M. R. (1969). Retrieval time from semantic memory. *Journal of Verbal Learning and Verbal Behavior, 8,*240–247.

Converse, P. E. (1964). The nature of belief systems in the mass public. In D. E. Apter (Ed.), *Ideology and discontent.* New York: Free Press.

Converse, P. E. (1970). Attitudes and non-attitudes: Continuation of a dialogue. In E. R. Tufte (Ed.), *The quantitative analysis of social problems.* Reading, MA: Addison-Wesley.

Converse, P. E. (1975). Public opinion and voting behavior. In F. Greenstein and N. Polsby (Ed.), *Handbook of political science* (Vol. 4). Reading, MA: Addison-Wesley.

Converse, J., & Cooper, J. (1979). The importance of decisions and free-choice attitude change: A curvilinear finding. *Journal of Experimental Social Psychology, 15,* 48–61.

Converse, P. E. (1980). Comment: Rejoinder to Judd and Milburn. *American Sociological Review, 45,* 644–646.

Fazio, R. H., Powell, M. C., & Herr, P. M. (1983). Toward a process model of the attitude-behavior relation: Accessing one's attitude upon mere observation of the attitude object. *Journal of Personality and Social Psychology, 44,* 723–735.

Fazio, R. H., Sanbonmatsu, D. M., Powell, M. C., & Kardes, F. R. (1986). On the automatic activation of attitudes. *Journal of Personality and Social Psychology, 50,* 229–238.

Festinger, L. (1957). *A theory of cognitive dissonance.* Stanford, CA: Stanford University Press.

Fiske, S. T., & Kinder, D. R. (1981). Involvement, expertise, and schema use: Evidence from political cognition. In N. Cantor & J. Kihlstrom (Eds.), *Personality, cognition, and social interaction.* Hillsdale, NJ: Lawrence Erlbaum Associates.

Fiske, S. T., & Pavelchak, M. A. (1986). Category-based versus piecemeal-based affective responses: Developments in schema-triggered affect. In R. M. Sorrentino & E. T. Higgins (Eds.), *Handbook of motivation and cognition: Foundations of social behavior.* New York: Guilford Press.

Freedman, J. L. (1964). Involvement, discrepancy, and change. *Journal of Abnormal and Social Psychology, 69,* 290–295.

Hagner, P. R., & Pierce, J. C. (1983). Levels of conceptualization and political belief consistency. *Micropolitics, 2,* 311–349.

Harary, F., Norman, R. Z., & Cartwright, D. (1965). *Structural models: An introduction to the theory of directed graphs.* New York: Wiley.

Heider, F. (1958). *The psychology of interpersonal relations.* New York: Wiley.

Heise, D. R. (1969). Separating reliability and instability in test-retest correlations. *American Sociological Review, 34,* 93–101.

Insko, C. A., & Schopler, J. (1967). Triadic consistency: A statement of affective-cognitive-conative consistency. *Psychological Review, 74,* 361–376.

Jackman, M. R. (1977). Prejudice, tolerance, and attitudes toward ethnic groups. *Social Science Research, 6,* 145–169.

Judd, C. M., & Kenny, D. A. (1981). *Estimating the effects of social interventions.* New York: Cambridge University Press.

Judd, C. M., & Krosnick, J. A. (1982). Attitude centrality, organization, and measurement. *Journal of Personality and Social Psychology, 42,* 436–447.

Judd, C. M., Krosnick, J. A., & Milburn, M. A. (1981). Political involvement and attitude structure in the general public. *American Sociological Review, 46,* 660–669.

Judd, C. M., & Milburn, M. A. (1980). The structure of attitude systems in the general public: Comparison of a structural equation model. *American Sociological Review, 45,* 627–643.

Kothandapani, V. (1971). Validation of feeling, belief, and intention to act as three components of attitude and their contribution to prediction of contraceptive behavior. *Journal of Personality and Social Psychology, 19,* 321–333.

Kretch, D., & Crutchfield, R. S. (1948). *Theory and problems of social psychology.* New York: McGraw-Hill.

Kritzer, H. M. (1978). Ideology and American political elites. *Public Opinion Quarterly, 42,* 484–502.

Krosnick, J. A. (1986). *Policy voting in American presidential elections: An application of psychological theory to American politics.* Unpublished doctoral dissertation, University of Michigan, Ann Arbor, MI.

Lane, R. E. (1973). Patterns of political belief. In J. Knutson (Ed.), *Handbook of political psychology.* San Francisco, CA: Jossey-Bass.

Larkin, J. H., McDermott, J., Simon, D. P., & Simon, H. A. (1980). Expert and novice performance in solving physics problems. *Science, 200,* 1335–1342.

Lewin, K. (1951). *Field theory in social science.* New York: Harper & Row.

McKeithen, K. B., Reitman, J. S., Rueter, H. H., & Hirtle, S. C. (1981). Knowledge organization and skill differences in computer programmers. *Cognitive Psychology, 13,* 307–325.

Millar, M. G., & Tesser, A. (1986). Effects of affective and cognitive focus on the attitude-behavior relation. *Journal of Personality and Social Psychology, 51,* 270–276.

Newcomb, T. M. (1956). Prediction of interpersonal attraction. *American Psychologist, 11,* 575–586.

Newcomb, T. M. (1961). *The acquaintance process.* New York: Holt, Rinehart & Winston.

Newcomb, T. M. (1968). Interpersonal balance. In R. P. Abelson, W. J. McGuire, T. M. Newcomb, M. J. Rosenberg, and P. A. Tannenbaum (Eds.), *Theories of cognitive consistency: A sourcebook.* New York: Rand McNally.

Nie, N. H., & Anderson, K. (1974). Mass belief systems revisited: Political change and attitude structure. *Journal of Politics, 36,* 540–587.

Nie, N. H., Verba, S., & Petrocik, J. R. (1979). *The changing American voter.* Cambridge, MA: Harvard University Press.

Norpoth, H., & Lodge, M. (1985). The difference between attitudes and nonattitudes in the mass public: Just measurements. *American Journal of Political Science, 29*(2), 291–307.

Osgood, C. E., & Tannenbaum, P. A. (1955). The principle of congruity in the prediction of attitude change. *Psychological Review, 62,* 42–55.

Ostrom, T. M. (1969). The relationship between the affective, behavioral, and cognitive components of attitude. *Journal of Experimental Social Psychology, 5,* 12–30.

Ostrom, T. M., & Brock, T. C. (1969). Cognitive bonding to central values and resistance to a communicating change in policy orientation. *Journal of Experimental Research in Personality, 4,* 42–50.

Pierce, J. C., & Hagner, P. R. (1980). Changes in the public's political thinking: The watershed years, 1956–1968. In J. C. Pierce & J. L. Sullivan (Eds.), *The electorate reconsidered.* Beverly Hills, CA: Sage.

Rokeach, M. (1973). *The nature of human values.* New York: Free Press.

Rosenberg, M. J. (1960). An analysis of affective-cognitive consistency. In M. J. Rosenberg, C. I. Hovland, W. J. McGuire, R. P. Abelson, & J. W. Brehm, (Eds.), *Attitude organization and change.* New Haven, CT: Yale University Press.

Rosenberg, M. J., & Hovland, C. I. (1960). Cognitive, affective, and behavioral components of attitudes. In M. J. Rosenberg, et al. (Eds.), *Attitude organization and change.* New Haven, CT: Yale University Press.

Schuman, H., & Presser, S. (1981). *Questions and answers: Experiments on question form, wording, and context in attitude surveys.* New York: Academic Press.

Sears, D. O., Huddy, L., & Schaffer, L. G. (1986). A schematic variant of symbolic politics theory, as applied to racial and gender equality. In R. R. Lau & D. O. Sears (Eds.), *Political cognition*. Hillsdale, NJ: Lawrence Erlbaum Associates.

Sherif, M., & Cantril, H. (1947). *The psychology of ego-involvements*. New York: Wiley.

Singer, J. E. (1968). The bothersomeness of inconsistency. In R. P. Abelson, et al. (Eds.). *Theories of cognitive consistency: A sourcebook*. Chicago: Rand McNally.

Smith, T. W. (1982). *Attitude constraint as a function of non-affective dimensions* (General Social Survey Tech. Rep. No. 39). Chicago: National Opinion Research Center.

Smith, M. B., Bruner, J. S., & White, R. W. (1956). *Opinions and personality*. New York: Wiley.

Tannenbaum, P. A. (1967). The congruity principle revisited: Studies in the reduction, induction, and serialization of persuasion. In L. Berkowitz (Ed.). *Advances in experimental social psychology* (Vol. 3). New York: Academic Press.

Tannenbaum, P. A. (1968). The congruity principle: Retrospect in reflection and recent research. In R. P. Abelson, et al. (Eds.), *Theories of cognitive consistency: A sourcebook*. Chicago: Rand McNally.

Tesser, A. (1978). Self-generated attitude change. In L. Berkowitz (Ed.), *Advances in experimental social psychology* (Vol. 11). New York: Academic Press.

Tesser, A., & Leone, C. (1977). Cognitive schemas and thought as determinations of attitude change. *Journal of Experimental Social Psychology, 13*, 340–356.

Tetlock, P. E. (1983). Accountability and complexity of thought. *Journal of Personality and Social Psychology, 45*, 74–83.

Tetlock, P. E. (1984). Cognitive style and political belief systems in the British House of Commons. *Journal of Personality and Social Psychology, 46*, 365–375.

Weissberg, R. (1976). Consensual attitudes and attitude structure. *Public Opinion Quarterly, 40*, 349–359.

Wiley, D. E., & Wiley, J. A. (1970). The estimation of measurement error in panel data. *American Sociological Review, 35*, 112–117.

6

Structure and Function in Political Belief Systems

Philip E. Tetlock
University of California, Berkeley

Different methods of studying attitudes can be likened to looking through a microscope at different levels of magnification. At the most intense levels of magnification—such as provided by highly controlled experimental studies of the information integration rules underlying attitude formation—one can observe the phenomenon in detail. The price of ability to see detail is, however, the inability to see the phenomenon in a broader systems context. At intermediate levels of magnification—such as those provided by laboratory work on cognitive responses to persuasion (Petty, Ostrom, & Brock, 1981) or on defensive avoidance responses to fear appeals (Janis & Mann, 1977)—one gains the ability to monitor complex, naturally occurring psychological processes, but at some cost in experimental control and precision of measurement. Finally, at the least intense levels of magnification—such as provided by archival and interview studies of political belief systems—one can explore context in great detail, but at a very substantial cost in internal validity and ability to observe subsystem detail.

Not surprisingly perhaps, communication across levels of analysis tends to be both difficult and rare. What excites the attention of investigators at one level of analysis may well be invisible at other levels. One can study attitudes at a fundamental information processing level of analysis (e.g., spreading activation networks in memory) without ever referring to work on social or personality functions of attitudes. Conversely, one can study linkages among personality, institutional, and ideological variables without ever referring to the elementary information processing operations that underlie these phenomena.

My most general goal in this chapter is to encourage communication across these traditionally compartmentalized levels of analysis. My research program on the cognitive structure of policy reasoning illustrates some of the ways in which such communication can be encouraged. The research originally focused on a long-standing issue in political psychology: the nature of the relationship between political ideology and cognitive style. Are some political groups predisposed to reason in more one-dimensional, dogmatic, and absolutist ways than other political groups? And, if so, why do such relationships exist? In the course of investigating this issue, it was necessary to reformulate the question several times (for the relationships between the content and structure of political thought depend on a variety of contextual variables). It was also necessary to draw on a combination of research methods (including content analysis of archival documents and laboratory experimentation) in studying these complex relationships. Finally, the task would have been hopeless if we had restricted the range of theory-derived hypotheses to only one major intellectual tradition. A comprehensive account of the data needs to take into account an awkward set of findings—some of which indicate the existence of fairly stable individual differences in styles of political reasoning, others of which indicate the capacity of many people to shift their styles of political reasoning in response to different issues and features of the social-political situation confronting them.

This chapter sketches the evolution of my work on the linkages between cognitive style and political ideology. It begins by describing the traditional personality perspectives on this issue: the *rigidity-of-the-right* and *ideologue* hypotheses. Although each perspective illuminates important aspects of the relationship between cognitive style and political ideology (*main effect* relationships), each blinds us to other equally important facets of the relationship between these two classes of variables (in particular, the existence of ideology-by-issue and ideology-by-political-context interactions in styles of reasoning). The chapter reviews recent archival and laboratory research and advances a functionalist framework for organizing the findings that have emerged from these studies. From this functionalist perspective, how people think about political issues is only in part the product of reasonably stable (cross-issue, cross-context) personality dispositions. How people think about political issues is also powerfully shaped by the fundamental values they are trying to advance in particular policy domains, by the degree of conflict or tension among those values, and by the role and accountability relationships within which they must work.

EARLY PERSONALITY RESEARCH ON COGNITIVE
STYLE AND POLITICAL IDEOLOGY

People obviously vary widely in the political views that they endorse. Less obviously people also vary widely in their styles of thinking about political issues. For instance, some people rely on a few broad principles or generalizations in interpreting events, reject inconsistent evidence, and have little tolerance for alternative viewpoints. Others interpret events in more flexible, multidimensional ways, actively seek out novel or counterattitudinal evidence, and attempt to develop perspectives on policy problems that integrate a wide range of considerations and values (cg. Lasswell, 1948; Putnam, 1971; Rokeach, 1960; Suedfeld & Rank, 1976; Taylor, 1960; Tetlock, 1984).

Psychologists and political scientists alike have shown a great deal of interest in the interrelations between content and stylistic dimensions of political thought. Most of this work has been dominated by a "trait" conception of cognitive style. People, it is assumed, have relatively characteristic modes of processing political information. The major research task has been to clarify the relationships between these stable cognitive stylistic attributes of individuals and the political views that they endorse.

Two points of view have dominated psychological speculation on this topic: the rigidity-of-the-right and ideologue hypotheses. Both hypotheses are grounded in functionalist assumptions concerning the usefulness of particular styles of political reasoning for achieving individual or group goals.

The rigidity of the right hypothesis derives largely from the path-breaking work on the authoritarian personality (Adorno, Frenkel-Brunswick, Levinson, & Sanford, 1950). According to authoritarian personality theory, people often develop extremely conservative political–economic opinions as means of coping with deep-rooted psychodynamic conflicts. It is posited, for instance, that ambivalence toward authority figures motivates people to project their unacceptable hostile impulses onto out-groups toward whom they then adopt punitive stances. In this view conservative attitudes frequently serve ego-defensive functions. Individuals who identify with the sociopolitical right are more likely than their centrist and left-wing counterparts to feel threatened by ambiguous or counterattitudinal information that challenges their political worldviews (information that, by implication, also challenges the elaborate network of defense mechanisms they have evolved to cope with unconscious needs and conflicts).

Advocates of the ideologue hypothesis were quick, however, to note the insensitivity of this analysis to "authoritarianism of the left" (Rokeach, 1960;

Shils, 1956; Taylor, 1960). Differences in the content of left-wing and right-wing belief systems should not be allowed to obscure fundamental similarities in how ideologues organize and process political information. True believers of the left and right are more likely to view issues in rigid, dichotomous terms than are individuals who take less extreme or polarized political positions. In part, this relationship emerges because persons with simple, dogmatic cognitive styles are naturally drawn to belief systems that offer clear-cut causal analyses of what is wrong with society and clear-cut solutions to those problems. There is a special affinity between the cognitive structure of the individual and the cognitive structure of the political ideology. And, in part, this relationship emerges because extremist groups—in order to maintain in-group cohesion and identity in a hostile world—need to draw sharp ideological and group boundaries. In short, extremist groups need enemies.

Until recently, empirical work on this topic has been limited to the mass administration of personality and attitude scales to survey respondents or college students. Stone (1980) concluded in his review of the literature that the preponderance of the evidence is consistent with the rigidity-of-the-right hypothesis and inconsistent with the ideologue hypothesis. He noted that across a variety of measurement instruments and subject populations, right-wing respondents appear more dogmatic, intolerant of ambiguity, and conceptually undifferentiated that their left-wing and moderate counterparts (e.g., Barker, 1963; McClosky, 1967; Neuman, 1981, Wilson, 1973). These findings do not, of course, indicate that there is no authoritarianism of the left (Eysenck, 1981). They indicate only that in 20th-century Western democracies (e.g., Britain, United States, Sweden) certain cognitive stylistic traits occur more frequently among members of the public conventionally classified as being on the sociopolitical right.

Many of these studies suffered from serious methodological problems. One recurring problem is potential ideological or content bias in self-report measures of cognitive style. A strong case could be made that conservative answers to scales designed to measure dogmatism, moral development, and tolerance of ambiguity lead by definition to lower scores than do liberal answers (e.g., Johnson & Hogan, 1981). The relation between cognitive style and political ideology, from this standpoint, may be a tautology. A second objection concerns the range of political positions represented in most of the samples studied. The far right has typically included advocates of racial segregation, supporters of major restrictions on civil liberties, and radical militarists. By contrast, the far left has rarely included Marxists or doctrinaire socialists. Indeed, the far left has often not extended beyond advocates of welfare state liberalism and social democracy. Finally, a third objection concerns the seriousness of respondents' commitment to the political views that they endorse. Are respondents in mass samples express-ing more than vague sympathies or antipathies toward groups and causes? Disconcerting doubts on this score are raised by the substantial impact of question-wording manipulations (Schuman & Presser, 1981) and of re-sponse sets (acquiescence and social desirability) on the political positions that people stake out for themselves.

Over the last 10 years, my research group has carried out a series of content analysis studies of the policy statements of political elites—United States Senators, Supreme Court Justices, British parliamentarians, Soviet Politburo members, among others. This line of work avoids many of the methodological objections raised to the personality-and-politics literature. The data analysis techniques employed—integrative complexity coding (Schroder, Driver, & Streufert, 1967) and evaluative assertion analysis (Osgood, Saporta, & Nunnally, 1956)—allow one to derive cognitive structural indices that are, by definition, independent of the content of the arguments analyzed. It is possible to advance conceptually differentiated or undifferentiated claims in support of polar opposite positions on the politi-cal spectrum (cf. Suedfeld & Rank, 1976; Tetlock, 1983a, 1984, 1985b). And it is relatively easy for archival investigators to obtain access to articulate and influential advocates of a broad range of political positions. Moreover, the individuals under study are clearly not just expressing top-of-the-head questionnaire opinions; they have made major personal and professional commitments to particular ideological stands.

Before describing the results of these archival studies, it is appropriate to describe the content analysis technique most frequently used in the studies: the integrative complexity coding system. This coding system was originally developed for analyzing response to a semiprojective test designed to measure individual differences in cognitive style (Schroder, Driver, & Streufert, 1967; Streufert & Streufert, 1978). The coding system is, however, a flexible one that can be applied to a wide range of archival documents, including policy statements, judicial opinions, speeches, and letters (Tet-lock & Suedfeld, 1988). The coding rules define integrative complexity in terms of two cognitive structural variables: conceptual *differentiation* and *integration.* Differentiation refers to the number of evaluatively distinct characteristics or dimensions of a problem that are taken into account in decision making. For instance, a decision maker might analyze policy issues in an undifferentiated way by placing options into one of two value-laden categories: the "good socialist policies," which promote redistribution of wealth, and the "bad capitalist policies," which preserve or exacerbate inequality. A highly differentiated approach would recognize that different policies can have many, sometimes contradictory, effects that cannot be readily classified on a single evaluative dimension of judgment—for ex-

LIVERPOOL JOHN MOORES UNIVERSITY
LEARNING SERVICES

ample, effects on the size of the government deficit, interest rates, inflation, unemployment, the balance of trade, and a host of other economic and political variables.

Integration refers to the development of complex connections among differentiated characteristics. (Differentiation is thus a prerequisite for integration.) The complexity of integration depends on whether the decision maker perceives the differentiated characteristics as operating in isolation (low integration), in first-order or simple interactions (the effects of A on B depend on levels of C, moderate integration), or in multiple, contingent patterns (high integration). Common examples of integration include references to value trade-offs (e.g., how much unemployment are we willing to endure as a society in order to bring inflation under control?), attempts to explain why "reasonable people" view the same problem in different ways (e.g., which position you take on the abortion debate depends on the stands you take on a mixture of constitutional and medical issues), and recognition of the need to take into account the joint—not just the separate—impact of causal variables on an outcome (e.g., The Federal Reserve Board will be willing to risk recession and raise interest rates only if several unlikely contingencies simultaneously arise: continuing deterioration in the trade deficit combined with new signs of weakness in the dollar and the re-emergence of inflation in the domestic economy. And even then, the Federal Board may not act if it is an election year.).

Integrative complexity is measured on a 7-point scale, with scores of 1 representing low differentiation and low integration, scores of 3 representing moderate differentiation and low integration, scores of 5 representing moderate differentiation and integration, and scores of 7 representing high differentiation and integration. Scores of 2, 4, and 6 represent transition points between adjacent levels (e.g., implicit differentiation through use of qualifiers, implicit integration through allusions to interactive causation or value trade-offs).[1]

I summarize the major findings that have emerged from applying the integrative complexity coding system to the policy statements of a number of elite political groups. The first two studies yielded results highly consistent with the rigidity-of-the-right hypothesis; the third study yielded results consistent with a modified version of the ideologue hypothesis. The remaining studies yielded results that are difficult to assimilate into either

---

[1]Training coders to assess the integrative complexity of texts reliably is a fairly time-consuming process. Coders typically reach adequate levels of inter-rater agreement ($r = .85$) only after participating in a two to three week training workshop. Integrative complexity coding is, however, considerably less time-consuming than such content analysis systems as cognitive mapping (Axelrod, 1976) and evaluative assertion analysis (Osgood, Saporta, & Nunnally, 1956). And integrative complexity scores are quite highly correlated with relevant cognitive structural indices derived from these other techniques (e.g., Levi & Tetlock, 1980; Tetlock, 1979, 1981b).

framework—results that reveal the relationship between cognitive struc-ture and political ideology to depend on the social context (political role and accountability demands) and issue context (the types of values brought into conflict by a given policy problem).[2]

EARLY SUPPORT FOR
THE RIGIDITY-OF-THE-RIGHT HYPOTHESIS

Tetlock (1981b) reported the first of a series of studies of individual differences among United States senators in the integrative complexity of their policy statements. The primary goal of the study was to test hypoth-eses derived from McClosky's (1967) influential study of personality corre-lates of isolationist foreign policy sentiment in the American public. On the basis of three national surveys in the 1950s, in which a large battery of personality and attitude scales were administered, McClosky concluded that isolationists differed from nonisolationists on a variety of dimensions. Isola-tionists—particularly "jingoistic" ones who sought to insulate the United States from the rest of the world by overwhelming superiority of force—were more intolerant of ambiguity, closed to new experiences, prone to dichotomous (good-bad) forms of thinking, and likely to possess strong positive affect toward in-groups (patriotic Americans) and strong negative affect toward out-groups (foreigners, Communists). McClosky argued that psychodynamic processes similar to those hypothesized to underlie the authoritarian personality (Adorno et al., 1950) shaped the content and structure of isolationist belief systems. For instance, he proposed that the rigidly chauvinistic overtones in isolationism represented means of coping with severe inner conflicts and feelings of inferiority.

Tetlock (1981b) tested the generalizability of McClosky's psychological

---

[2]A number of methodological precautions need to be taken in this type of archival research—precautions taken in all of the major studies discussed in this chapter. Perhaps the most obvious and elementary precaution is the employment of double-blind coding pro-cedures. Coders should be unaware of the hypotheses being tested, and, to the extent possible, the sources of the materials coded. In scoring controversial material, it is also helpful to include coders in the research team from diverse political viewpoints and to check on potential ideological contamination of coding judgments by planting "test paragraphs" (simple and complex arguments in support of a broad range of political positions). It is useful to remind coders repeatedly that there is no necessary relationship between the structural complexity of an argument and their judgments of its moral or political appropriateness (a key theme of the complexity coding manual). It is not hard to find integratively complex advocacies of posi-tions, that, given contemporary political norms, are widely viewed as immoral (e.g., the complex arguments of antiabolitionists in pre–Civil War America or complex arguments of classical economic theorists in the early 19th century in opposition to aid for starving children). Nor is it hard to find examples of integratively simple statements that now provoke wide moral approval (e.g., simple arguments of those who opposed the appeasement of Nazi Germany in the 1930s or de jure segregation in the American South in the 1950's).

portrait of the isolationist to senators who held office in the 82nd Congress (1951–1952). Speeches of senators were subjected to both integrative complexity coding and a complementary coding technique—evaluative assertion analysis—for measuring the intensity of speakers' attitudes toward ingroup and outgroup symbols (see Osgood, Saporta, & Nunnally, 1956). Tetlock used the coding techniques to analyze randomly selected passages from foreign policy speeches of senators who had been classified, on the basis of Guttman scaling of their foreign policy voting patterns, as isolationist, ambivalent isolationist, and internationalist. The results strongly supported McClosky's analysis. Isolationists were much less integratively complex than nonisolationists. Relative to nonisolationists, isolationists also evaluated outgroups more negatively and in-groups more positively. Ambivalent isolationists fell between these two groups. Discriminant analysis indicated that the content analytic indicators were powerful joint predictors of isolationist orientation. One highly discriminant function emerged that accounted for 41% of the total variation and permitted correct classification of 66% of the senators in the isolationist, ambivalent, and nonisolationist categories, against a chance accuracy of 37%.

McClosky thus appears to have been correct: Isolationist sentiment in the early post–World War II period—among both elites and followers—seems to have been a posture of belligerency in international affairs, one that had "more to do with hostility against foreign nations and disavowal for the well-being of others than with the considered assessment of risks arising from foreign entanglements" (McClosky, 1967; p. 104). The isolationist relies heavily upon "dichotomous thought processes, that lack breadth of perspective and that seek to exclude whatever is different, distant, or unfamiliar" (p. 107).

A second study of senatorial rhetoric (Tetlock, 1983b) explored the relationship between integrative complexity and the overall liberalism-conservatism of senatorial voting records in the 94th Congress (1975–1976). The results were, once again, highly consistent with both the rigidity-of-the-right hypothesis and previous work on personality correlates of conservatism. Senators with conservative voting records in the 94th Congress made less integratively complex policy statements ($\bar{X}=1.79$) than their moderate ($\bar{X}=2.51$) and liberal ($\bar{X}=2.38$) colleagues. This finding, moreover, remained highly significant after controlling for a host of potential confounding variables, including political party affiliation, education, years of service in the Senate, and types of issues discussed.

These results converge impressively with personality research that indicates right-wing members of the general public score higher than their moderate and left-wing counterparts on self-report measures of dogmatism, intolerance of ambiguity, and cognitive simplicity. Nonetheless, two problems complicate interpretation of the results. The first problem stems from the potential confounding effects of political role and the reliance on public policy statements. Conservatives were an out-of-power minority in both the 82nd and 94th Congresses. The lower integrative complexity of conservative policy statements may reflect a rhetorical strategy that legislative minorities use to rally opposition to governing factions (sharp, unqualified criticism—a "give 'em hell" approach). The greater integrative complexity of liberals and moderates may reflect a rhetorical strategy that dominant legislative coalitions use to justify the policies that they are enacting (complex rhetoric that weighs the pros and cons of competing proposals in order to take into account the interests of diverse constituencies).

The second problem stems from the limited ideological range of positions represented in the United States Senate. A defender of the ideologue hypothesis could argue that there were simply not enough representatives of the ideological left to provide a fair test of the hypothesis. In contrast to most advanced industrial societies, there is no influential socialist or communist party in the United States.

Some Support for the Ideologue Hypothesis

Tetlock (1984) conducted a study that provided a stronger test of the integrative complexity/political ideology relationship than the earlier work on senators. The raw data consisted of confidential, in-depth interviews that the political scientist Robert Putnam (1971) conducted with 93 members of the British House of Commons. There is good reason to believe that strategic political motives exerted much less influence on what the politicians said in this setting than in more public settings such as press conferences or in parliament (see Putnam, 1971, for relevant evidence). The politicians interviewed were willing on numerous occasions to criticize their own party and even themselves in the course of the discussions. In addition, the politicians examined in this study represented a wider variety of ideological positions than exists in the United States Senate. The parliamentarians included extreme socialists (who favored nationalization of all major industries), moderate socialists (who favored limited public control of major industries), moderate conservatives (who favored limited denationalization of industry), and extreme conservatives (who opposed any government intervention in the economy).

Coders rated the integrative complexity of statements randomly drawn from the interviews with the parliamentarians (Tetlock, 1984). The results revealed highly significant differences among the four ideological groups. Moderate socialists ($M = 3.07$) discussed issues in more integratively complex terms than extreme socialists ($M = 2.17$), moderate conservatives ($M = 2.65$), and extreme conservatives ($M = 1.97$). Moderate conservatives were more complex than extreme conservatives and extreme socialists. Extreme conservatives and socialists, the two groups most dissimilar in the content of their political beliefs, had the most similar levels of integrative complexity. These relationships between political ideology and integrative complexity remained highly significant after controlling for a variety of background variables as well as belief and attitudinal variables assessed in the Putnam research.

In addition to its relationship to political ideology, integrative complexity was correlated with a host of overlapping cognitive stylistic variables assessed in the original Putnam (1971) research. From these correlations emerges a more detailed portrait of the integratively complex politician. The more integratively complex the politician, the more likely he or she was to: (a) deemphasize the differences between the major political parties, (b) be tolerant of opposing viewpoints, (c) think about issues in relatively nonideological terms, and (d) be unconcerned with assigning blame for societal problems. In short, integrative complexity was associated with a pragmatic, open-minded and nonpartisan world view.

These results appear at first glance to vindicate advocates of the ideologue hypothesis. When the confidential statements of politicians from a broad spectrum of ideological positions were analyzed, we found that extremists of the left and right were very similar to each other in their styles of reasoning, but very different from individuals closer to the center of the political spectrum. The ideologue hypothesis still, however, leaves important questions unanswered. Why is the point of maximum integrative complexity consistently displaced to the left of center? Why are liberals generally more integratively complex than conservatives in the United States Senate? Why are moderate socialists more integratively complex than moderate conservatives in the British House of Commons? The ideologue hypothesis is not explanatory, but rather descriptive. It simply asserts that as one departs from an ill-defined political center of gravity, one is increasingly prone to view issues in simple, dichotomous terms. What determines where this mysterious midpoint lies? Why are liberals and moderate socialists apparently closer to it than conservatives? Why was it necessary to go as far out to the political left as radical socialists to observe a marked decline in the integrative complexity of thought?

A VALUE PLURALISM MODEL
OF IDEOLOGICAL REASONING

Both the rigidity-of-the-right and ideologue hypotheses assume that it is possible to map multidimensional political belief systems onto a unidimensional left–right measurement scale. Such mapping exercises can, of course, be done, but the price in loss of knowledge is substantial. People try to achieve a wide range of objectives through political action—objectives that often do not correlate nearly as highly as one would expect if one assumed that people structure their thought along conventional ideological lines (cf. Converse, 1964; Lane, 1973). It is not hard, for example, to identify people (including policy elites) who are liberal on social welfare policy but conservative on defense, conservative on social welfare policy but liberal on defense, or liberal or conservative across the board except, say, on environmental protection and civil liberties issues. Researchers ignore this multidimensional variation at their peril. As we shall see in a later section on ideology-by-issue interactions, the relationships between integrative complexity and political ideology take quite different forms in different issue domains.

Equally problematic, it is often unclear how to define the left–right continuum in non-Western political systems. For instance, Tetlock and Boettger (in press) have noted the enormous problems that arise in applying the rigidity-of-the-right and ideologue hypotheses to the Soviet Union. They found that reformist Soviet politicians (advocates of at least limited political liberalization and economic decentralization) tended to be more integratively complex than traditionalists (opponents of these measures). This finding could be construed as support for the ideologue hypothesis. Traditionalists, it could be argued, represent the extreme left, which resists the introduction of market mechanisms and individual incentives into the centrally planned Soviet economy; reformers, it could be argued, represent the right, which is willing to compromise orthodox Marxist-Leninist principles in order to stimulate economic efficiency, entrepreneurial initiative and individual creativity (an effort to achieve some form of mixed economy). As one moves toward the center from the far (rigid-state-control) left, one discovers greater integrative complexity. Alternatively however, this same finding could be construed as support for the rigidity-of-the-right hypothesis. It could just as plausibly be argued that Soviet traditionalists, like American conservatives, are more likely to be authoritarian personalities who are deeply committed to traditional in-group symbols and to resent attempts to tamper with fundamental systemic values (e.g., the Protestant or socialist work ethic, law and order, free enterprise or central planning, support for free world or progressive regimes abroad). As one moves from the center toward the right (more ethnocentric, nationalistic, forms of ideology), one discovers less integrative complexity.

To avoid conceptual conundra of this sort, we need a theoretical model that satisfies three key requirements. First, the model should not force political belief systems into a simple, one-dimensional classification scheme. The model should allow for the possibility that advocates of different viewpoints reason in more or less complex patterns in different issue domains. Second the model should also not be limited to descriptive correlational hypotheses (e.g., as one moves in this or that direction on an attitude continuum, integrative complexity of reasoning rises or falls). The model should focus on the underlying social-cognitive processes that shape the complexity of political thought. Third, the model should yield reasonably specific predictions concerning the forms complexity-ideology relationships will take in different issue domains and political systems. The model should, in brief, be simultaneously subtle and falsifiable.

The *value pluralism model* of ideological reasoning is an attempt to fill this theoretical void. The model can be summarized in the following two general sets of propositions: (a) Underlying all political ideologies are core or *terminal* values (Lane, 1973; Rokeach, 1973, 1979) that specify what the ultimate goals of public policy should be (e.g., economic efficiency, social equality, individual freedom, crime control, national security). Ideologies vary not only in the types of values to which they assign high priority (Rokeach, 1973), but also in the degree to which high priority values are acknowledged to be in some degree of tension or conflict with each other. In monistic ideologies high priority is attached to only one value or set of values that, it is claimed, are highly consistent with each other. In pluralistic ideologies high priority is attached to values that are acknowledged to be in frequent, even intense, conflict with each other. Important values often point in opposite policy directions (e.g., "I value social equality, but dislike paying for it through taxes," "I want to protect the environment, but don't want to slow economic growth."). (b) Advocates of the more pluralistic ideologies should exhibit more integratively complex styles of reasoning. This prediction is based on Abelson's (1959, 1968) influential work on the strategies people use for resolving cognitive inconsistency in belief systems. Abelson maintained that, *whenever feasible,* people prefer modes of resolving cognitive inconsistency that are simple and require minimal effort. (People, in this view, are "cognitive misers"; Fiske & Taylor, 1984). Simple modes of resolving inconsistency are feasible when the conflicting values activated by a policy choice are of very unequal strength. It is then easy to deny the less important value and to bolster the more important one, a process that cognitive dissonance theorists have described as "spreading of alternatives."

By contrast, simple modes of inconsistency reduction are much less practical for advocates of pluralistic ideologies. Whe conflicting values are of approximately equal strength, denial of one value and bolstering of the other are much less plausible coping strategies (Abelson, 1959, 1968). People must turn to more effort-demanding strategies such as differentiation (e.g., distinguishing the impact of policies on conflicting values) and integration (developing rules or schemata for coping with trade-offs between important values). For instance, in domestic policy debates, liberals and social democrats are most committed to the often conflicting values of social equality and economic freedom (see Rokeach, 1973, 1979). They are therefore under the greatest psychological pressure to take into account the effects of policy proposals on both values as well as to develop guidelines or criteria for finding appropriate compromises between the two values (compromises that may, of course, have to take different forms in different economic and political circumstances).

To summarize, the value pluralism of an ideology determines both the frequency with which people experience cognitive inconsistency and the complexity of the strategies they rely upon to cope with inconsistency. A value pluralism analysis of the complexity-ideology relationship has several noteworthy advantages. It not only helps to explain existing data; it leads to a variety of novel and testable theoretical predictions—a number of which have subsequently been supported.

With respect to existing data, the value pluralism model is well positioned to explain why several studies have found that advocates of centrist and moderate left-wing causes tend to interpret issues in more integratively complex ways than do advocates of conservative causes. Evidence from survey studies of the general public and from content analyses of political writings suggests that advocates of centrist and moderate left-wing causes are more likely to attach high importance rankings to values that often come into conflict in public policy debates. They are likely to value both social equality and economic freedom, economic growth and environmental protection, crime control and civil liberties, and deterring "Soviet expansion" and maintaining good working relations with that country. From this standpoint, the point of maximum integrative complexity is often displaced to the left of center because that is the point of maximum value conflict, at least on many issues.

The value pluralism model also clarifies how far to the sociopolitical left or right one must go for integrative complexity to decline: to the point where conflict between core values begins to diminish sharply. For instance, in domestic policy debates, one would expect to—and actually does—find a sharp reduction in integrative complexity as one moves from moderate socialists (who, according to Rokeach, 1973, place nearly equal importance on freedom and equality) to extreme socialists (for whom concern for equality seems to dominate concern for individual economic rights). Similarly, one would expect to—and one does—find a reduction in integrative complexity as one moves from moderate socialists to moderate conservatives (for whom economic freedom is a dominant value) to extreme conservatives (for whom economic freedom is the overwhelmingly dominant value).

Although the value pluralism model can account for existing data on ideological "main effects" in integrative complexity, the model strongly implies that traditional trait analyses of the complexity-ideology relationship are of only limited usefulness. We should not assume that certain ideological groups will always be more integratively complex than other groups; rather, we should expect ideology-by-issue and ideology-by-situation interactions in the integrative complexity of styles of reasoning.

IDEOLOGY-BY-ISSUE INTERACTIONS IN INTEGRATIVE COMPLEXITY

One key determinant of the feasibility of simple modes of resolving value conflict is the degree to which the policy domain under discussion activates conflicting values of approximately equal strength. And value conflict may well be most intense in different issue domains for different ideological groups. For instance, in the 1980s, American conservatives may experience their most intense value conflicts over such issues as defense spending (e.g., national security vs. fiscal restraint) or compulsory military service (e.g., national security vs. individual liberty). Liberals may experience their most intense value conflicts over such issues as redistributive income policies (e.g., equality vs. economic efficiency).

Two studies have revealed support for ideology-by-issue interaction predictions of the value pluralism model. In one study, Tetlock, Bernzweig, and Gallant (1985) examined the relations between integrative complexity and political ideology among United States Supreme Court justices who served on the Court between 1946 and 1978. The study assessed the integrative complexity of opinions that each of 25 justices authored (or at least put their names on) as well as the liberalism-conservatism of each justice's voting record on civil liberties and economic cases (Tate, 1981). Consistent with past work on senators, justices with liberal and moderate voting records exhibited more integratively complex styles of reasoning than did justices with conservative voting records. However, these relationships between integrative complexity and political ideology were more powerful on cases involving economic conflicts of interest (e.g., labor versus management, business versus government) than on cases involving civil liberties issues (e.g., due process and First Amendment questions). Tetlock et al (1985) argue that civil liberties issues were more likely to activate shared elite values—common to both liberals and conservatives—such as constitutional protections for freedom of speech and press and due process of law (see McClosky and Brill, 1983 for supporting evidence). The competing ideological groups were less likely, therefore, to experience differential value conflict on these issues. By contrast, much less value consensus existed on the economic conflict of interest cases (see Chong, McClosky, & Zaller, 1983). Good reasons exist, moreover, for suspecting value conflict in this policy domain to be more intense for liberals than for conservatives (a policy domain that frequently activates conflicts between private economic interests and redistributive ones).

In a second study, Tetlock (1986) obtained much more direct experimental evidence for the hypothesized role of value conflict in promoting integratively complex thought. Two types of information were collected from a nonelite (college student) sample: (a) subjects' rank order evaluations of the importance of each of 18 terminal values from the Rokeach Value Survey (values included national security, natural beauty, economic prosperity, equality, and freedom); (b) subjects' support for six public policy positions and their thoughts on each issue (e.g., redistributive income policies, domestic CIA activities, defense spending). Each of the public policy issues had been selected on the basis of pretest scaling data indicating that the issue clearly brought two values from the Rokeach Value Survey into conflict (e.g., the defense spending question was phrased in such a way as to activate tension between the values of national security and economic prosperity). On five of six issues, a significant trend was found for people to report more integratively complex thoughts to the degree the issue domain activated conflicting values that people held to be: (a) important in their value hierarchy; (b) close to equally important. This study reveals that issue-to-issue variation in integrative complexity is not random, but a lawful function of the intensity of value conflict activated by the issue domain.

POLITICAL ROLES
AND INTEGRATIVE COMPLEXITY

Intensity of value conflict is a major, but not the only determinant of the integrative complexity of people's reasoning about a policy domain. For instance, political roles appear to exert an important influence. Some roles seem to encourage integrative complexity; others, integrative simplicity.

A particularly powerful variable in this regard is the distinction between being "in power" (the policymaking role) and "out of power" (the opposition role). Governing a country—developing policies one actually expects to implement—is generally a more integratively complex task than opposing the government. The policymaking role inevitably requires making unpopular trade-off decisions (Katz & Kahn, 1978; Thurow, 1980) that, in most societies, must be justified to skeptical constituencies motivated to argue against the positions one has taken (e.g., explaining to various interest groups why it was not possible to satisfy all of their conflicting demands). Integrative complexity is needed both at the level of private thought (to work out viable compromise policies that at least partly satisfy major constituencies) and at the level of public rhetoric (to develop cogent two-sided appeals that sensitize antagonized constituencies to the complexity of the policymaking role) (see Tetlock, 1983a).

Far fewer pressures exist on opposition politicians to think or speak in integratively complex terms. The mass electorate possesses little knowledge of major policy issues and little motivation to think carefully about political messages or to defend the government (see Kinder & Sears, 1985; Sniderman & Tetlock, 1986). The essence of the opposition role is to rally antigovernment sentiment—a goal that is most effectively achieved not by evenhanded "on the one hand" and "on the other" rhetoric, but rather by constructing easily understood (integratively simple) and memorable attacks on the government. In the opposition role, one is free to find fault, to focus selectively on the shortcomings of proposals advanced by those in power and on the advantages of one's own proposals.

Several studies support the claim that the policymaking role encourages integrative complexity. Suedfeld and Rank (1976), for instance, observed that revolutionary leaders (from several nations) made more integratively complex statements after coming to power than before coming to power. Perhaps even more telling, Suedfeld and Rank (1976) also found that revolutionary leaders who retained power in the postrevolutionary period were much more likely to display such upward shifts in integrative complexity than were leaders who failed to retain power. Tetlock (1981a) observed a similar upward shift in the integrative complexity of policy statements that American presidents issued during election campaigns and immediately after coming to power (postinauguration). Most 20th-century presidents apparently have believed that, although integratively simple rhetoric is useful for rallying popular support during elections, it is politically prudent to present issues in more integratively complex terms once they have assumed office. Tetlock, Bernzweig, and Gallant (1985) found evidence for the "in-power"/"out of power" complexity shift among (life-tenured) justices of the United States Supreme Court. Judicial opinions for the majority (which thus have the force of law) tended to be more integratively complex than dissenting or minority opinions. And Tetlock and Boettger (in press) have recently reported that reformist Soviet politicians have become more integratively complex since Gorbachev and his political allies gained working control of the Politburo and Central Committee of the Communist Party—an event marked by Gorbachev's appointment as First Party Secretary (see also Tetlock, 1988).

Transitions in political roles do not, however, affect all ideological groups equally. Tetlock, Hannum, and Micheletti (1984) examined the integrative complexity of liberal, moderate and conservative senators in five Congresses, three dominated by liberals and moderates (the 82nd, 94th, and 96th Congresses) and two dominated by conservatives (the 83rd and 97th Congresses). Tetlock and his colleagues found that liberals and moderates were more integratively complex than conservatives in the Democrat-controlled 82nd, 94th, and 96th Congresses, replicating the earlier Tetlock (1983b) findings. However, when the political balance of power shifted in favor of conservatives (e.g., in 1953 and 1981 with Republicans gaining control of both the Senate and the presidency), the complexity-ideology relationship disappeared. No significant differences existed in integrative complexity as a function of political ideology. Interestingly, this pattern was due to *sharp declines* in the integrative complexity of liberals and moderates in the Republican-dominated Congresses, not to an increase in the integrative complexity of conservatives. Conservatives displayed much more traitlike stability in integrative complexity both within and across Congresses.

In a similar vein, Tetlock and Boettger (in press) found that whereas reformist Soviet politicians increased the integrative complexity of their policy statements upon coming to power, traditionalist Soviet politicians were relatively unaffected by the power transition. Soviet traditionalists, like American conservatives, displayed more traitlike stability in their levels of integrative complexity across time.

These findings suggest an important qualification to the value pluralism model's prediction of greater integrative complexity among advocates of pluralistic as opposed to monistic belief systems. Advocates of pluralistic belief systems may present issues in more integratively complex terms only when they are forced, so to speak, by their political role to confront the tensions between basic values inherent in their ideological outlooks. Advocates of monistic belief systems, with their more internally consistent value systems, are relatively unaffected by shifts in political role. There is less potential value conflict that they can be forced to confront.

It should also be noted that the archival evidence on links between political roles and integrative complexity is highly consistent with recent experimental evidence on the effects of accountability on complexity of reasoning. The policymaking role is a high-accountability role. One can be called upon to justify what one has done by a variety of constituencies. One is, moreover, potentially accountable not only for the short-term consequences of one's policies, but for the (more unpredictable) long-term consequences as well. The opposition role is a low-accountability role. One has the rhetorical freedom to focus single-mindedly on the flaws in the position of the other side. Experimental data suggest that the types of accountability created in policymaking roles are indeed likely to promote integratively complex reasoning by subjects on policy issues (see Carnevale, 1985; Tetlock, 1983a, 1983c, 1985d; Tetlock & Kim, 1987). Accountability, especially to unknown or multiple constituencies, encourages subjects to engage in "preemptive self-criticism" in which they try to anticipate objections to the policy stands they have taken. This flexible cognitive response can be viewed as an adaptive strategy to protect one's self or social image as a competent, thoughtful being ("I'm no fool. I may believe this, but I'm aware of these counterarguments"). By contrast, subjects in low accountability roles tend to rely on integratively simple processing rules that permit them to make up their minds quickly, confidently and with relatively little mental effort. The price of cognitive economy can, however, be steep. Subjects in low accountability roles are much more susceptible to judgmental bias. They are too quick to make personality attributions on the basis of fragmentary and inconclusive evidence (Tetlock, 1985d), too slow to revise their opinions in response to new evidence (Tetlock, 1983c), and excessively confident in the correctness of their factual judgments and predictions (Tetlock & Kim, 1987).

CONCLUDING REMARKS: THE NEED FOR
A FLEXIBLE FUNCTIONALIST FRAMEWORK

The data reviewed in this chapter can be viewed from a wide range of theoretical perspectives. There is something for almost everybody. Advocates of authoritarian personality theory can point to the frequently replicated and powerful relationship between integrative simplicity and political conservatism. They can also point to the greater traitlike consistency of conservative thought. Advocates of the ideologue hypothesis can note the cognitive stylistic similarities between extreme conservatives and socialists in the British House of Commons. Role theorists and symbolic interactionists can note that how people think about political issues depends on the institutional role they occupy and the political balance of power. Advocates of the value pluralism model can note that how people think about political issues depends on the degree to which issues bring important values into clear conflict with each other.

Given the range of findings reported here, it is tempting to agree with McGuire's (1983) radically contextualist perspective on theory-testing in social psychology. All hypotheses, he argues, are under some conditions true. Research is a "discovery process to make clear the meaning of the hypothesis, disclosing its hidden assumptions and thus clarifying the circumstances under which it is false" (McGuire, 1983, p. 7). From this standpoint, work on the links between cognitive style and political ideology has been successful in illuminating boundary conditions for the applicability of the rigidity-of-the-right and ideologue hypotheses. Both hypotheses highlight certain interesting empirical regularities but blind us to others—in particular, to the impact of value conflict, political role, and accountability demands on political thought. Many people (although not all) display styles of political reasoning that are much more responsive to situational demands than these personality-trait perspectives led us to expect.

What kind of theory can explain all of the data? My current nomination would be for an updated version of the classic functionalist theories of Smith, Bruner, and White (1956) and Katz (1960). From a functionalist perspective, the key theoretical question is: Of what use to a person is a particular pattern or style of political reasoning? It is possible to organize existing research findings by invoking a fairly small number of functionalist postulates:

1. All other things being equal, people generally prefer integratively simple styles of political reasoning. Integratively simple reasoning requires relatively little mental effort (people are assumed to be "cognitive misers"), and makes few emotional demands (it does not require acknowledging painful value trade-offs). These straightforward assumptions help to explain why integrative complexity scores tend to be so positively skewed (it is not unusual for 50% or more of the assigned scores to be at the lowest scale value).

2. People can be motivated to think in integratively complex ways. Integratively complex reasoning is especially useful in coping with intrapsychic, interpersonal and political conflict. The value pluralism model, for example, suggests that complex reasoning is a quite common coping response to policy problems that clearly bring important values in conflict (e.g., lives vs. economic growth, liberty vs. crime control). Work on political roles and accountability suggests that complex reasoning is quite common when people expect to be held personally responsible for the consequences of their actions or when people need to justify their actions to constituencies with unknown or conflicting policy preferences.

3. Individual differences exist in thresholds for the activation of integratively complex coping responses. Some individuals—in both archival and experimental settings—show remarkably little variability in the integrative complexity of their political reasoning. These highly consistent individuals also tend to have low average scores on the complexity scale and to be extremely conservative. Other individuals show a great deal of variability in the integrative complexity of their reasoning. These individuals modify (whether consciously or not is unclear) the complexity of their reasoning in response to the value conflicts activated by the policy problems they confront and in response to the political demands of the roles they occupy.[3]

---

[3]These findings obviously raise as many questions as they answer. Do psychodynamic theories help to explain the apparent cognitive rigidity of extreme conservatives (e.g., insecure individuals feel particularly threatened by ambiguity and hence rely on integratively simple coping responses)? Or are more parsimonious sociocultural or information-processing explanations available? Do impression management theories (e.g., work on self-monitoring) help to explain the strategic ease with which many centrists and moderate reformers adjust the integrative complexity of their rhetoric? Or are these findings better explained by noting the complexity of the belief and value systems of such individuals and the often intense role conflicts with which they must cope? Much work clearly remains to be done.

The list of functionlist themes invoked here is by no means exhaustive. Other motives—for example, concern for cognitive mastery or for protecting one's self or social image—undoubtedly play important roles in shaping how people think (Tetlock, 1985a). The various functional goals also come into conflict with each other. Minimization of mental effort quickly collides with the goal of finding integratively complex solutions to policy problems that satisfy opposing internal values or external constituencies. Maintaining psychological equilibrium in an authoritarian personality may often make it difficult to accept the accommodations and trade-offs necessary to achieve other personal or social goals. It is certainly reasonable to expect a functionalist theory of political thought to be both more comprehensive in specifying motives and more precise in specifying interrelations among motives than I have been here. I have simply sketched the general form that a functionalist explanation of the data will probably have to take.

Finally, it is appropriate to close with a warning. McGuire's contextualist perspective reminds us not to grow too attached to our theories. The first-order interactions of today can easily become the second- or higher-order interactions of tomorrow. Research to date has revealed that the complexity-ideology relationship depends on the intensity of value conflict activated within an issue domain and on one's social–political role. Future research may well show that increased integrative complexity of thought is by no means the only possible coping response to intense value or political conflict. Some people may respond by rigid, defensive bolstering, denial or procrastination (Janis & Mann, 1977; Tetlock, 1985c). Future research may reveal that in some political contexts, extremism is associated with greater cognitive flexibility and multidimensionality than centrism. And future research may reveal that in some political contexts, opposition factions display more integratively complex patterns of reasoning than do ruling factions. The functionlaist perpective per se is not testable. It is possible to generate post hoc functionalist explanations for any finding. The functionalist perspective is, however, heuristically provocative—it leads to new ways of thinking about the content, structure, and adaptability of political thought. And, perhaps most important, the functionalist perspective is sufficiently flexible to accommodate the complex, context-dependent relationships that so frequently emerge in this line of inquiry.

ACKNOWLEDGMENTS

Preparation of this chapter was assisted by grants from the National Institute of Mental Health (RO1 MH39942A) and the MacArthur Foundation.

REFERENCES

Abelson, R. P. (1959). Modes of resolution of belief dilemmas. *Journal of Conflict Resolution, 3,* 343–352.

Abelson, R. P. (1968). Psychological implications. In R. P. Abelson, E. Aronson, W. McGuire, T. Newcomb, M. Rosenberg, & P. Tannebaum (Eds). *Theories of cognitive consistency: A sourcebook.* Chicago: Rand McNally.

Adorno, T., Frenkel-Brunswick, E., Levinson, D., & Sanford, N. (1950). *The authoritarian personality.* New York: Harper & Row.

Axelrod, R. (1976). *Structure of decision.* Princeton: Princeton University Press.

Barker, E. N. (1963). Authoritarianism of the political right, center and left. *Journal of Social Issues, 19,* 63–74.

Carnevale, P. (1985). Accountability of group representatives and intergroup relations. *Advances in group processes.* (Vol. 2) Pp. 227–248. Greenwich, CT: JAI Press.

Chong, G., McClosky, H., & Zaller, J. (1983). Patterns of support for democratic and capitalist values in the United States. *British Journal of Political Science, 13,* 401–440.

Converse, P. (1964). The nature of belief systems in mass publics. In D. Apter (ed.) *Ideology and discontent.* Pp. 235–294. New York: Free Press.

Eysenck, H. J. (1981). Left-wing authoritarianism: Myth or reality. *Political Psychology, 3,* 234–239.

Fiske, S. T., & Taylor, S. E. (1984). *Social cognition.* Reading, MA: Addison-Wesley.

Janis, I. L., & Mann, L. (1977). *Decision making.* New York: Free Press.

Johnson, J. A., & Hogan, R. (1981). Moral judgments as self-presentations. *Journal of Research in Personality, 15,* 57–83.

Katz, D. (1960). The functional approach to the study of attitudes. *Public Opinion Quarterly, 24,* 163–204.

Katz, D., & Kahn, R. (1978). *The social psychology of organizations.* New York: Wiley.

Kinder, D., & Sears, D. O. (1985). Public opinion and political behavior. In G. Lindzey & E. Aronson (Eds.), *Handbook of Social Psychology* (3rd ed.). Reading, MA: Addison-Wesley.

Lane, R. E. (1973). Patterns of political belief. In J. N. Knutson (Ed.), *Handbook of political psychology.* San Francisco, CA: Jossey-Bass.

Lasswell, H. (1948). *Power and personality.* New York: Norton.

Levi, A., & Tetlock, P. E. (1980). A cognitive analysis of the Japanese decision to go to war. *Journal of Conflict Resolution, 24,* 195–212.

McClosky, H. (1967). Personality and attitude correlates of foreign policy orientation. In J. M. Rossenau (Ed.), *Domestic sources of foreign policy.* New York: Free Press.

McClosky, H., & Brill, A. (1983). *Dimensions of tolerance: What Americans believe about civil liberties.* New York: Russell Sage.

McGuire, W. J. (1983).A contextualist theory of knowledge: Its implications for innovation and reform in psychological research. In L. Berkowitz (Ed.), *Advances in experimental social psychology* (Vol. 16). New York: Academic Press.

Neuman, W. R. (1981). Differentiation and integration in political thinking. *American Journal of Sociology. 86,* 1236–1268.

Osgood, C. E., Saporta, S., & Nunnally, J. C. (1956). Evaluative assertion analysis. *Litera, 3,* 47–102.

Petty, R. E., Ostrom, T. M., & Brock, T. C. (1981). *Cognitive responses in persuasion.* Hillsdale, NJ: Lawrence Erlbaum Associates.

Putnam, R. (1971). Studying elite culture: The case of ideology. *American Political Science Review, 65,* 651–681.

Rokeach, M. (1960). *The open and closed mind: Investigations into the nature of belief systems and personality systems.* New York: Basic Books.

Rokeach, M. (1973). *The nature of human values.* New York: Free Press.

Rokeach, M. (1979). *Understanding human values: Individual and Social.* New York: Free Press.

Schroder, H. M., Driver, M. J., & Streufert, S. (1967). *Human information processing.* New York: Holt, Rinehart & Winston.

Schuman, H., & Presser, S. (1981). *Questions and answers in attitude surveys: Experiments on question form, wording, and context.* New York: Academic Press.

Shils, E. E. (1956). Ideology and civility: On the politics of the intellectual. *Sewanee Review, 66,* 950–980.

Smith, M. B., Bruner, J., & White, R. (1956). *Opinions and personality.* New York: Wiley.

Sniderman, P. M., & Tetlock, P. E. (1986). Public opinion and political ideology. In M. G. Hermann (Ed.), *Handbook of political psychology* (Vol. 2). San Francisco, CA: Jossey-Bass.

Stone, W. F. (1980). The myth of left-wing authoritarianism. *Political Psychology, 2,* 3–20.

Streufert, S., & Streufert, S., (1978). *Behavior in the complex environment.* Washington, DC: V. H. Winston & Sons.

Suedfeld, P., & Rank, D. (1976). Revolutionary leaders: Long-term success as a function of changes in conceptual complexity. *Journal of Personality and Social Psychology, 34,* 169–178.

Tate, C. N. (1981). Personal attribute models of the voting behavior of U.S. Supreme Court justices: Liberalism in civil liberties and economics decisions, 1946–1978. *American Political Science Review, 75,* 355–367.

Taylor, I. A. (1960). Similarities in the structure of extreme attitudes. *Psychological Monographs, 74* (2, Whole No. 489).

Tetlock, P. E. (1979). Identifying victims of groupthink from public statements of decision-makers. *Journal of Personality and Social Psychology, 37,* 1314–1324.

Tetlock, P. E. (1981a). Pre- to post-election shifts in presidential rhetoric: Impression management or cognitive adjustment. *Journal of Personality and Social Psychology, 41,* 207–212.

Tetlock, P. E. (1981b). Personality and isolationism: Content analysis of senatorial speeches. *Journal of Personality and Social Psychology, 41,* 437–443.

Tetlock, P. E. (1983a). Accountability and complexity of thought. *Journal of Personality and Social Psychology, 45,* 74–83.

Tetlock, P. E. (1983b). Cognitive style and political ideology. *Journal of Personality and Social Psychology, 45,* 118–126.

Tetlock, P. E. (1983c). Accountability and the perseverance of first impressions. *Social Psychology Quarterly, 46,* 285–292.

Tetlock, P. E. (1984). Cognitive style and political belief systems in the British House of Commons. *Journal of Personality and Social Psychology, 46,* 365–375.

Tetlock, P. E. (1985a). Accountability: The neglected context of judgment and choice. In B. M. Staw & L. Cummings (Eds.), *Research in organizational behavior* (Vol. 1, pp. 297–332). Greenwich, CT: JAI Press.

Tetlock, P. E. (1985b). Integrative complexity of American and Soviet foreign policy statements: A time series analysis. *Journal of Personality and Sovial Psychology, 49,* 1565–1585.

Tetlock, P. E. (1985c). Integrative complexity of policy reasoning. In S. Kraus & R. M. Perloff (Eds.), *Mass media and political thought.* Beverly Hills, CA: Sage.

Tetlock, P. E. (1985d). Accountability: A social check on the fundamental attribution error. *Social Psychology Quarterly, 48,* 227–236.

Tetlock, P. E. (1986). A value pluralism model of ideological reasoning. *Journal of Personality and Social Psychology, 50,* 819–827.

Tetlock, P. E. (1988). Monitoring the integrative complexity of American and Soviet policy rhetoric: What can be learned. *Journal of Social Issues, 44,* 101–131.

Tetlock, P. E., & Boettger, R. (in press). Cognitive and rhetorical styles of reformist and traditionalist Soviet politicians: A content analysis study. *Political Psychology.*

Tetlock, P. E., Hannum, K., & Micheletti, P. (1984). Stability and change in senatorial debate: Testing the cognitive versus rhetorical style hypothesis. *Journal of Personality and Social Psychology, 46,* 979–990.

Tetlock, P. E., Bernzweig, J., & Gallant, J. L. (1985). Supreme Court decision making: Cognitive style as a predictor of ideological consistency of voting. *Journal of Personality and Social Psychology, 48,* 1227–1239.

Tetlock, P. E., & Kim, J. I. (1987). Accountability and judgment processes in a personality prediction task. *Journal of Personality and Social Psychology, 52,* 700–709.

Tetlock, P. E., & Suedfeld, P. (1988). Integrative complexity coding of verbal behavior. In C. Antaki (Ed.), Analyzing lay explanation: A casebook of methods (pp. 72–87). Beverly Hills, CA: Sage.

Thurow, L. C. (1980). *The zero sum society: Distribution and the possibilities for economic change.* New York: Basic Books.

Wilson, G. D. (1973). *The psychology of conservatism.* New York: Academic Press.

7

On the Power and Functionality of Attitudes:
The Role of Attitude Accessibility

Russell H. Fazio
Indiana University

> Without guiding attitudes the individual is confused and baffled. Some kind of
> preparation is essential before he can make a satisfactory observation, pass
> suitable judgment, or make any but the most primitive reflex type of response.
> Attitudes determine for each individual what he will see and hear, what he will
> think and what he will do. To borrow a phrase from William James, they
> "engender meaning upon the world"; they draw lines about and segregate an
> otherwise chaotic environment; they are our methods for finding our way
> about in an ambiguous universe. (Allport, 1935, p. 806)

Much power has been ascribed to attitudes. As evidenced by the preceding
quotation, attitudes are thought to accomplish a great deal for an individual;
they are highly functional. Attitudes guide perception, information processing, and behavior. They structure one's social universe and, in so doing, ease
decision-making. This presumed power of attitudes has contributed to the
position of attitudes historically as one of the most central concepts in the
field of social psychology (McGuire, 1985, 1986). Any construct that ac-
complishes so much for an individual obviously merits extensive theoretical
and empirical inquiry.

However, this ascription of power to the attitude construct has not gone
unchallenged. In the waxing and waning of interest in the attitude concept
that the field has exhibited over the last few decades, there have been
periods marked by considerable pessimism regarding the power and utility
of attitudes. Indeed, in the late 1960s and early 1970s, attitudes were
viewed by some as epiphenomenal explanations for past behavior (Bem,
1972) that had little or no influence upon subsequent behavior (Wicker,
1969). This pessimism led to discussion of whether the attitude concept
was necessary (Abelson, 1972) and to pleas that it be abandoned (Wicker,
1971).

The essence of the thesis to be presented in this chapter is that the optimistic and the pessimistic views of the power of attitudes each have some validity, but they do so for different kinds of attitudes. That is, the ascription of power to the attitude construct is appropriate, and justified by an accumulation of data, for certain kinds of attitudes. On the other hand, skepticism about the impact of other kinds of attitudes is warranted. A conceptualization of attitudes that permits one to specify the likelihood that a given attitude will be powerful, and that addresses the mechanisms by which this influence is exerted, is presented. In addition, recent research stemming from this conceptual model and illustrating the greater power and functionality of certain kinds of attitudes over other kinds is summarized.

CONCEPTUALIZING ATTITUDES AND ATTITUDE ACCESSIBILITY

The Importance of Attitude Accessibility

If an attitude is to exert any influence upon perceptions, judgments, or behavior, it must first be activated from memory. Unless the attitude comes to mind when the individual encounters the attitude object, the individual may never view the object in evaluative terms. Or, if the individual does consider the object evaluatively, he or she may do so on the basis of an on-the-spot appraisal of whatever features of the attitude object happen to be salient in the immediate situation. Such an on-the-spot appraisal may not be consistent with any previously constructed and stored attitude toward the object.

It is this proposition concerning attitude accessibility that forms the core of a model of the process by which attitudes guide behavior that has been the focus of my research over the last few years. The model is presented in detail in Fazio (1986). The model and an associated conceptualization of attitudes provide the basis for a more general discussion of the power and functionality of attitudes that constitutes the focus of this chapter. According to the model, an attitude must be accessible from memory in order to have any potential to serve as the sort of powerful force alluded to earlier. It is the chronic accessibility of an attitude from memory, i.e., the likelihood that the attitude will be activated from memory upon mere exposure to the attitude object, that determines the power and functionality of an attitude. It shall be argued that attitudes that are highly accessible from memory are much more likely to guide the processing of relevant information and behavior than attitudes that are less accessible from memory. In so doing, highly accessible attitudes also have much more functional value for the individual.

A Model of Attitudes as Object-Evaluation Associations

Given the importance of attitude accessibility, it is essential to discuss how attitudes and their accessibility from memory are conceptualized in the present framework. An attitude is viewed as an association between a given object and a given evaluation (Fazio, Chen, McDonel, & Sherman, 1982; Fazio, 1986). As is common in the attitude literature, the term *object* is used in a very broad sense. Individuals may hold evaluations of a wide variety of potential attitude objects, including social issues, categories of situations, categories of people, and specific individuals, as well as physical objects. However, the term *evaluation* is meant broadly as well. It may range in nature from a very "hot" affect (i.e., a strong emotional response to the attitude object) to "colder" judgment of one's feelings of favorability or unfavorability toward the object (Abelson, Kinder, Peters, & Fiske, 1982; Zanna & Rempel, in press). Furthermore, this evaluative summary may be based upon emotions that the attitude object produces for the individual (as in the case of a conditioned emotional response, e.g., Zanna, Kiesler, & Pilkonis, 1970), beliefs that the individual holds about the attitude object's instrumentality (e.g., Fishbein, 1963; Rosenberg, 1960), and/or previous behavioral experiences with the attitude object (e.g., Bem, 1972; Fazio, 1987). Regardless of the precise "hot vs. cold" nature of the evaluation and regardless of the basis for the evaluation, the attitude itself is viewed as an association between the attitude object and the evaluation.

Although very simple, this conceptualization of attitudes is quite powerful when one considers its implications for attitude accessibility. Viewing an attitude as an association, it becomes obvious that the strength of an attitude, like any construct based on associative learning, can vary. That is, the strength of the association between the object and the evaluation can vary. This associative strength is postulated to be the major determinant of the chronic accessibility of the attitude and, hence, the likelihood that the attitude will be activated from memory upon the individual's encountering the attitude object.

Empirical tests of this view of attitudes as object-evaluation associations have yielded confirming results. Subjects who had been induced to express their attitudes repeatedly, which should have the consequence of strengthening the object-evaluation association, have been found to be capable of responding relatively quickly to direct inquiries about their attitudes (Fazio et al., 1982; Powell & Fazio, 1984). For example, Powell and Fazio (1984) manipulated the number of times that an attitude was expressed by varying the number of semantic differential items that were listed relevant to a given attitude issue. In this way, subjects expressed their attitudes zero, one, three, or six times toward a given attitude object.[1] In a subsequent task, subjects were presented with each attitude issue and instructed to make a good–bad judgment about each object as quickly as possible. Response latency was found to relate to the number of previous attitudinal expressions. The greater the number of expressions, the faster the latency of response to an attitudinal inquiry.

These findings lend credence to the view of attitudes as object-evaluation associations and suggest that attitude accessibility depends on the strength of the object-evaluation association. However, in terms of the process by which attitudes exert their influence, the critical issue is whether individuals's attitudes are activated from memory upon mere observation of the attitude object. These findings concern accessing one's attitude from memory in response to a direct inquiry. Thus, these findings are not at all informative with respect to the issue of spontaneous activation. Responding quickly to a direct attitudinal inquiry may mean that the stored evaluation was activated spontaneously upon presentation of the attitude issue. Alternatively, it may mean that the evaluation was retrieved efficiently via an effortful process.

The distinction to be drawn at this point is one between automatic and controlled attitude activation. Automatic versus controlled processes have received considerable theoretical and empirical attention in cognitive psychology (e.g., Schneider & Shiffrin, 1977; Shiffrin & Schneider, 1977). Shiffrin and Dumais (1981) characterized any process that leads to the activation of some concept or response "whenever a given set of external initiating stimuli are presented, regardless of a subject's attempt to ignore or bypass the distraction" (p. 117) as automatic. The key feature of such automatic activation is its inescapability. In contrast, a controlled process requires the active attention of the individual. Thus, when an individual becomes aware of a situational cue that implies the importance of considering one's attitude toward an object, the individual might attempt to retrieve a previously stored evaluation of the attitude object or actively construct such an attitude on the spot. In either case, the process is reflective and effortful in nature.

According to the model, attitudes can be activated automatically and the likelihood of such activation depends on the strength of the object-evaluation association. This hypothesis was confirmed in a recent series of experiments conducted by Fazio, Sanbonmatsu, Powell, and Kardes (1986). These experiments involved a priming procedure that permitted the ex-

---

[1]Our use of this manipulation is not intended to imply that object-evaluation associations must necessarily be semantic in nature. Strong object-evaluation associations could result, for example, from a classical conditioning of emotional responses. Repeated attitudinal expression merely provides one convenient vehicle by which associative strength can be manipulated.

amination of the following hypothesis: The mere presentation of an attitude object toward which an individual possesses a strong evaluative association would automatically activate the evaluation. On each trial, the prime that was presented was the name of an attitude object. Its presentation was followed by the display of a positive or negative evaluative adjective. The subject's task was to press a key as quickly as possible to indicate whether the adjective had a positive or a negative connotation. The latency with which these judgments were made was examined.

To provide an example, assume that the attitude object "cockroach" is evaluated negatively by an individual and that this object-evaluation association is strong. Presentation of "cockroach" as the prime may automatically activate the negative evaluation. If the target adjective that is subsequently presented is also negative (e.g., disgusting), then the individual may be able to indicate relatively quickly that the target adjective has a negative connotation. That is, responding should be facilitated. Thus, the technique relies on the presence of facilitation as an indication that the evaluation associated with the primed attitude object has been activated upon its mere presentation.

Precisely such facilitation was observed on trials that involved evaluatively congruent primes (attitude objects) and target adjectives—provided that the attitude object possessed a strong evaluative association for the subject. In two of the experiments, preexperimentally strong and weak associations were identified via a measurement procedure. The measurement involved latency of response to an attitudinal inquiry—the same measure that had been shown in the research described earlier (e.g., Powell & Fazio, 1984) to reflect the strength of the object-evaluation association. Attitude objects for which the subject was able to respond relatively rapidly when faced with an attitudinal inquiry had served as the strong primes and those for which the subject responded relatively slowly as the weak primes. Only the former produced facilitation and, thus, showed any evidence of automatic attitude activation. In an additional experiment, strength of the object-evaluation association was manipulated rather than measured. Attitude objects for which subjects had been induced to express their attitudes repeatedly produced facilitation when the objects later served as primes in the adjective connotation task.

These findings provide corroboration for the hypothesis that the likelihood of automatic activation of an attitude upon mere observation of the attitude object depends on the strength of the object-evauation association in memory. The existence of facilitation suggests that the subject's attitude toward the object was activated automatically upon its mere presentation as the prime. Such a conclusion regarding automatism appears justifiable for two reasons. The first argument concerns the nature of the adjective connotation task. Subjects were merely exposed to the attitude object and were not asked to consider their attitudes toward the object. Nor was it to the subjects' advantage to do so, for the subjects' major task was simply to respond to the target adjective. Nevertheless, despite this irrelevance of attitudes to the immediate task concerns, exposure to objects for which subjects possessed strong affective associations appears to have prompted activation of the associated evaluation. Thus, the very nature of the task leads to the suggestion that the facilitation observed in the case of strong primes was a result of automatic, rather than controlled, processing.

A second basis for this conclusion stems from the fact that facilitation was observed only under conditions that involved a relatively short interval between onset of the attitude object presented as the prime and onset of the target adjective, commonly referred to as the stimulus onset asynchrony or SOA. Under conditions involving a longer SOA, no facilitation was observed. Yet, if the results had been due to a controlled, effortful process, one would have expected that allotting the subjects more time to actively retrieve their attitudes would have produced greater facilitation. Instead, the findings imply that the attitude was activated automatically upon presentation of the prime in the case of strong object-evaluation associations. The level of activation of the associated evaluation was apparently sufficient to facilitate responding to an evaluatively congruent target adjective if the adjective was presented very soon thereafter (SOA = 300 m/s). However, this level of activation apparently dissipated quickly (or was actively suppressed) due to the presumed irrelevance of the subject's attitudes to the major task of identifying the connotation of the target adjective. As a result, presentation of the target adjective 1,000 m/s after presentation of the attitude object appears to have been too late for the prime to facilitate responding to adjectives of congruent valence. Thus, the results of these experiments indicate that attitudes can be activated from memory automatically and that the strength of the object-evaluation association determines the likelihood of such automatic activation.

The findings from the Fazio et al. (1986) series of experiments have now been replicated a number of times. For example, Sanbonmatsu and Fazio (1986) employed the same adjective connotation task to examine the activation of attitudes toward brands of products. Brands toward which subjects possessed strongly associated evaluations (as indicated by fast latencies of response to direct attitudinal inquiries) produced facilitation on trials involving target adjectives of congruent valence. Brands involving weak object-evaluation associations did not.

The results have also been replicated in the context of a perceptual recognition task rather than the adjective connotation task (Sanbonmatsu, Osborne, & Fazio, 1986). This new task involved having the target adjective gradually become legible on the computer screen. Initially, the adjective was masked by a block of dots, which gradually faded away on a random basis until only the letters of the word were visible. The subject's task was to recognize the word as quickly as possible. The degree to which presentation of an attitude object immediately prior to presentation of the target adjective facilitated recognition of the adjective served as the dependent measure. Replicating the past research, the findings revealed that positively valued attitude objects facilitated the recognition of positive adjectives and negatively valued attitude objects facilitated the recognition of negative adjectives. Furthermore, these effects were particularly apparent for attitude objects involving strong object-evaluation associations, once again, as indicated by fast responding to a direct attitudinal inquiry.

The Attitude–Nonattitude Continuum

The findings from the research on attitude accessibility clearly indicate that not all attitudes are equal. Of course, social psychologists have long recognized that attitudes vary in their "strength." A variety of attempts have been made to assess the centrality or importance of an attitude issue for a given individual. Social judgment theory's focus upon ego-involvement serves as an illustration of such an approach (Hovland, Harvey, & Sherif, 1957; Sherif & Cantril, 1947). More recently, various indices of the "strength" of an attitude have been identified as moderators of the relation between attitudes and behavior, e.g., the confidence with which an attitude is held (Sample & Warland, 1973; Fazio & Zanna, 1978) and the consistency between affective and cognitive measures of the attitude (Norman, 1975).

Relevant to this idea of attitudes varying in strength is the so-called *attitude–nonattitude* distinction. A number of years ago, both Hovland (1959) and Converse (1970) attempted to reconcile differences that had been observed between laboratory and survey research on attitude change. In so doing, they each—but Converse in particular—focused on a distinction between attitudes and nonattitudes. The distinction centered on the observation that a person may respond to an item on an attitude survey, even though that particular attitude does not really exist in any a priori fashion for the individual. That is, the attitude object may be one that the individual has not even considered prior to the administration of the survey.

Converse (1970) discussed the attitude–nonattitude distinction in terms of measurement error. A nonattitude was characterized by unreliable measurement—virtually random responses—across the waves of a panel survey. The present conceptualization of attitudes suggests that it may be fruitful to view the attitude–nonattitude distinction, not as a dichotomy, but as a continuum—one that focuses upon the accessibility of the attitude from memory. At the lower end of the continuum is the nonattitude. No a priori evaluation of the attitude object exists in memory. As we move along the continuum, an evaluation does exist and the strength of the association between that evaluation and the object and, hence, the chronic accessibility of the attitude, increases. In the case of a weak association, the attitude can be retrieved via an effortful, reflective process but is not capable of automatic activation. At the upper end of the continuum is a well-learned, strong association that is likely to be activated automatically upon mere observation or mention of the attitude object.

The reader may be asking why the focus of the attitude–nonattitude continuum should be attitude accessibility as opposed to some other strength-related dimension of attitude. The advantage of doing so is the clear relevance of attitude accessibility to the issue of the *process* by which attitudes exert their influence. Unlike other indicants of the strength of an attitude (see Raden, 1985, for a recent review of such strength-related attitude dimensions), attitude accessibility operates at an information processing level of analysis and, hence, has implications for the mechanisms by which attitudes guide perceptions and behavior.

Furthermore, attitude accessibility may be related to other qualities of the attitude that are reflective of attitudinal strength. Precisely such covariation has been hypothesized (Fazio et al., 1982; Fazio, 1986). It has been suggested that attitudinal qualities that have been identified as moderators of the attitude-behavior relation all may do so because they reflect the strength of the object-evaluation association and, the chronic accessibility of the attitude. Thus, attitude accessibility may provide a means of conceptually integrating the catalog of attitudinal qualities known to determine attitude-behavior consistency, as well as explaining why such moderating variables exert their impact.

As an illustration, consider one such variable—the manner of attitude formation. Attitudes based upon direct, behavioral experience with the attitude object have been found to be stronger in many senses than attitudes based on indirect, nonbehavioral experience. Attitudes based on direct experience are more likely to influence later behavior (Fazio & Zanna, 1981), are held with greater confidence (Fazio & Zanna, 1978), and are more resistant to counterinfluence (Wu & Shaffer, 1987). Importantly, such attitudes also have been found to be more accessible from memory than attitudes based upon indirect experience—both in terms of latency of response to an attitudinal inquiry (Fazio et al., 1982; Fazio, Herr, & Olney, 1984) and in terms of the likelihood of activation upon mere presentation of the attitude object (Fazio, Powell, & Herr, 1983). It appears, then, that the differential power of direct vs. indirect experience attitudes is a reflection of their differential position along the attitude–nonattitude continuum.

This continuum provides an interesting means of conceptualizing the strength of an attitude. Position along the continuum determines the power and functionality of the attitude. The attitudes of two individuals with identical scores from some attitude measurement instrument may still differ markedly with regard to their strength, that is, their likelihood of activation upon the individual's encountering the attitude object. The attitude of one individual may be activated in such a situation whereas the attitude of the other may not be. As a result, the attitude of the former individual is in a better position to influence perceptions and behavior and to ease decision-making than the attitude of the latter individual. It is to the power of accessible attitudes that the discussion now turns.

ACCESSIBLE ATTITUDES GUIDE
INFORMATION PROCESSING

"Attitudes determine for each individual what he will see and hear, what he will think. . . ." (Allport, 1935, p. 806)

Presumably, one of the basic consequences of holding an attitude toward some object is that the attitude guides one's perceptions of the attitude object when it is encountered and the processing of information relevant to the attitude object. The present conceptualization of attitudes suggests that such selective processing is more likely for attitudes that are chronically accessible from memory. Such attitudes are apt to be activated automatically from memory upon observation or mention of the attitude object and, thus, are apt to serve as a filter through which available information is viewed. Without such activation of the attitude from memory, there can be no sense in which the attitude guides processing. A number of findings from our program of research on attitude accessibility converge on this notion that attitude accessibility governs the degree to which biased processing as a function of attitude occurs.

One of the first approaches that was pursued to examine this issue centered on the principle that, once a construct has been activated from memory, the accessibility of that construct is temporarily increased. Such enhancement of acute accessibility has been shown to increase the likelihood that the construct will be applied to the interpretation of subsequently presented, relevant information (e.g., Higgins, Rholes, & Jones, 1977; Srull & Wyer, 1979). That is, the primed and now highly accessible construct influences the interpretation of ambiguous information.

In light of this principle, Fazio, Powell, and Herr (1983) primed positive or negative evaluative categories by exposing subjects to evaluative adjectives in the context of a Stroop color-word task. Some subjects were primed with: pleasant, exciting, entertaining, and amusing. In contrast, those in the negative condition were primed with: frustrating, irritating, tiresome, and dull. Then, in the context of an ostensibly separate experiment concerning person perception, subjects were presented with an ambiguous description of a target person's behavior. Subjects for whom the accessibility of positive evaluations had been enhanced arrived at more positive interpretations of the target's behavior than did subjects for whom negative evaluations had been primed.

Thus, the accessibility of positive versus negative evaluations influenced subjects' processing of the information. The implication is that the activation of an attitude from memory would have similar effects upon subsequent processing. That is, the acute accessibility of any evaluation that is activated from memory upon an individual's encountering the attitude object would be temporarily enhanced by such activation and would affect subsequent processing.

Fazio, Powell, and Herr (1983) examined this hypothesis in a second experiment. The one difference between the two experiments was that the latter involved priming by exposure to an attitude object that was positively or negatively valued instead of direct exposure to positive or negative evaluative terms. In the relevant conditions, subjects were introduced to a set of five types of intellectual puzzles by being exposed to previously solved examples of each type while listening to an audio recording describing the puzzle type. Subjects then rated how interesting they found each type of puzzle. In order to enhance the strength of the object-evaluation associations, some subjects were induced to express these attitudes repeatedly. Recall that the research on attitude activation described earlier indicates that such repeated attitudinal expression increases the likelihood that the associated evaluation (i.e., the attitude) will be activated from memory upon later presentation of the attitude object (Fazio et al., 1986). Subjects in a control condition did not repeatedly express their attitudes. It was the puzzle type that each subject evaluated most positively or most negatively that later served as the prime.

As in the previous experiment, subjects' interpretations of a target person's behavior were examined. Among subjects in the control condition, interpretations did not vary significantly as a function of whether the subject's most positively or most negatively valued puzzle type had served as the prime. In contrast, a reliable difference was apparent among subjects in the repeated expression condition. Those primed with a positively valued puzzle type viewed the target's behavior more positively than did those primed with a negatively valued puzzle. Apparently, the object-evaluation associations among these repeated expression subjects were sufficiently strong that the mere presentation of the puzzle type during the color perception phase of the experiment led to activation of the associated evaluation. Having been activated, the accessibility of that positive or negative evaluation was temporarily increased and influenced subjects' processing of the subsequent information. That is, priming the evaluation indirectly by exposure to a puzzle type that was strongly associated with a positive or negative evaluation influenced interpretations, just as priming the evaluation directly had done in the first experiment. Among subjects in the control condition, for whom object-evaluation associations had not been strengthened, spontaneous attitude activation upon presentation of a puzzle type as a prime apparently did not occur. Consequently, no effects upon subsequent processing occurred.

The findings indicate that biased processing of information is likely following the activation of attitudes from memory. Without such activation, selective processing as a function of attitude does not occur. This conclusion is drawn from an experimental context in which the information being judged did not directly concern the attitude object itself. That is, subjects' attitudes toward puzzles were activated and the impact of enhancing the accessibility of positive or negative evaluations on interpretations of Ted's behavior was examined. Thus, in this context, the biased processing stems from the increased accessibility of an evaluation as a function of it having been recently activated.

In additional research, the focus has been on information that concerns the attitude object directly. In this case, biased processing may stem either from the mechanism previously discussed (i.e., the attitude having been activated and, as a result, increasing the accessibility of a positive or negative evaluation) or from the fact that the attitudinal evaluation is activated at the time that the information is being processed. Through whichever mechanism, greater selective processing as a function of attitude is expected in the case of attitudes that are likely to be activated automatically upon exposure to the attitude object than in the case of less accessible attitudes. That is, attitude accessibility is expected to moderate the extent of the relation between attitudes and perceptions of the attitude object in the immediate situation.

Fazio and Williams (1986) tested this hypothesis in an investigation concerning the 1984 presidential campaign. The portion of the study that is relevant to the present discussion involved respondents' perceptions of the candidates' performance during the nationally televised debates and how such judgments varied as a function of attitude toward Reagan and the accessibility of this attitude. Attitude accessibility was measured via latency of response to an attitudinal inquiry. The research described earlier on automatic attitude activation (Fazio, et al., 1986) indicates that such response latencies relate to the likelihood that the attitude will be activated from memory automatically upon mere exposure to the attitude object. Attitude objects for which an individual could indicate an attitude relatively quickly when faced with a direct inquiry were likely to activate the attitude automatically upon their presentation. In contrast, attitude objects for which response latencies to an inquiry were relatively slow were unlikely to produce automatic attitudinal activation upon their presentation.

A large sample of townspeople participated in the attitude assessment phase of this study at a local shopping mall. They responded to a number of attitude statements by pressing one of five buttons, labelled "Strongly Agree" to "Strongly Disagree." The participants were instructed to respond as quickly as possible while being sure that their response accurately reflected their opinion on each issue. The critical target statements were "A good president for the next four years would be Ronald Reagan" and a similarly worded statement concerning Walter Mondale. This phase of the investigation was conducted during June and July of 1984.

The next phase focused on the debates. Subjects were sent a letter from the "Political Behavior Research Laboratory" asking them to complete an enclosed, stamped postcard concerning the performance of the candidates in the first two of the series of three scheduled debates. The first debate in the series involved the presidential candidates and was held on October 7; the second involved the vice-presidential candidates and was held on October 11. It was judgments of these two debates that served as the perception measures. Subjects were asked to endorse one of five statements regarding the presidential debate: "Reagan was much more impressive," "Reagan was slightly more impressive," "The two candidates performed equally well," "Mondale was slightly more impressive," or "Mondale was much more impressive." A similarly worded question concerned the performance of the vice-presidential candidates George Bush and Geraldine Ferraro. We did not query subjects about the third debate in the series because we were concerned that they might not complete and return the questionnaire prior to their voting on election day.

Only the data concerning the Reagan attitude and its accessibility is summarized here. The interested reader is referred to the original report for a complete presentation. As expected, attitudes toward Reagan were predictive of respondents' judgments of the debates. The more positive the attitude toward Reagan, the better respondents judged his performance relative to Mondale's during the presidential debate (among those respondents who reported watching the debate on the postcard questionnaire, $r=.458$) and the better they judged Bush's performance relative to Ferraro's during the vice-presidential debate ($r=.538$).

However, further analyses indicated that these relations were stronger among subjects whose attitude toward Reagan was relatively accessible than among those whose attitude was less accessible. In order to classify subjects into high and low accessibility groups that were not confounded by differential attitude scores, division into high and low accessibility groups was accomplished by performing a median split on the latency of response to the statement concerning Reagan at *each and every* level of the response scale. For example, the latencies of all subjects who had responded "Strongly Agree" were examined. Those whose latency was faster than the median for this subsample were classified in the high accessibility group and those with latencies slower than the median to the low accessibility group. This same procedure was followed for each of the other response levels. As a result, attitude distributions in the two groups were perfectly equivalent. Such division into high and low accessibility groups was performed anew on the specific set of respondents who provided data on each perception measure.

Correlations between attitude toward Reagan and judgments of debate performance were higher among the high accessibility subjects than among the low accessibility subjects. Among respondents who reported having watched the presidential debate, the correlations were .529 and .394, respectively. Again, among those who watched, correlations between attitude toward Reagan and judgments of the outcome of the vice-presidential debate were .679 and .410 in the high and low accessibility groups respectively. Among those respondents who reported having viewed both debates, the correlation between attitude toward Reagan and the sum of the two perception measures was significantly higher in the high accessibility group than in the low (.738 vs. .404).

These findings suggest that accessible attitudes guide perception to a greater degree than do less accessible attitudes. That is, attitude accessibility appears to act as a determinant of the attitude-perception relation. Individuals in the high accessibility group apparently held attitudes that involved strong object-evaluation associations. Consequently, their attitudes were more likely to be activated while they were viewing the debates and, hence, were more likely to color their perceptions of the outcomes of the debates.

Although the findings are supportive of our conceptual framework, the correlational nature of the Fazio and Williams (1986) investigation should not be overlooked. As mentioned earlier, it appears that attitude accessibility is related to a number of other strength-related dimensions of attitude. Thus, as in any correlational study, a number of additional variables may be related to the classification of individuals as possessing attitudes of either high or low accessibility. Which single dimension or combination of dimension is causally responsible for the moderating effects that were observed cannot be discerned. Experimental work is necessary to isolate the causal influence of attitude accessibility.

Such an experimental approach was followed in a recent investigation conducted by Fazio and Houston (1986). This experiment involved a paradigm developed by Lord, Ross, and Lepper (1979), who demonstrated that individuals' attitudes toward a social policy issue affected their evaluations of relevant empirical evidence. Subjects were exposed to summaries of two studies; the results of one supported the notion that the death penalty had a deterrent effect and the results of the other questioned the deterrent efficacy of the death penalty. Subjects' attitudes were found to influence their evaluations of the studies. They viewed the study that confirmed their attitudes as better conducted and more convincing than the study that disconfirmed their attitudes.

In order to examine the causal influence of attitude accessibility on the attitude-perception relation, Fazio and Houston (1986) employed an experimental manipulation involving repeated attitudinal expression. The research described earlier indicates that this manipulation affects both the latency of response to an attitudinal inquiry (Fazio et al., 1982; Powell and Fazio, 1984) and the likelihood of automatic activation of the attitude from memory upon mere exposure to the attitude object (Fazio, et al., 1986). In the present experiment, as in Powell and Fazio (1984), all subjects completed a questionnaire in which a number of attitude issues appeared more than once. In the repeated expression condition, one such issue was the death penalty, which appeared a total of five times. Each appearance was followed by a differently labelled semantic differential scale (approve/disapprove, good/bad, necessary/unnecessary, foolish/wise, appropriate/inappropriate). In the single expression condition, the death penalty issue was replaced by another issue. All subjects then completed a second questionnaire concerning a number of issues. Each question, including one concerning the death penalty, was of the form "To what extent do you consider yourself to be in favor of, versus opposed to" X?

After completing this attitude measurement experiment, subjects participated in an ostensibly separate experiment conducted by a second experimenter. This experiment was presented as a study of people's ability to understand and criticize research. In this context, subjects were exposed to the same information that Lord and his colleagues had employed. They received a summary of a study that purported to support the death penalty, including a description of the methodology and a presentation of the data, along with a summary of a critique of the study and the authors' reply to the criticisms. Subjects were then asked to make judgments about the quality of the research study. An identical procedure was followed with respect to a study that purported to oppose the death penalty. The order of presentation was, of course, counterbalanced across subjects.

The degree to which attitudes were predictive of judgments of the quality of the research studies was examined as a function of repeated versus single attitude expression. As predicted, subjects in the repeated expression condition displayed greater biased processing as a function of attitude than did subjects in the single expression condition. For example, the correlation of the difference between subjects' judgments of how well conducted each study was, with their attitudes, was .503 in the repeated expression condition, as opposed to a correlation of $-.067$ in the single expression condition. Within the repeated expression condition, the more positive subjects' attitudes toward the death penalty, the better conducted they viewed the pro study relative to the con study. Thus, an experimental manipulation of attitude accessibility produced results that paralleled the earlier research in which attitude accessibility was measured.[2]

It is interesting to note that the subjects in the Lord et al. study all held extreme attitudes. The subjects were selected for participation in the study on the basis of their responses to an initial questionnaire administered in an earlier session. The pro and con death penalty subjects who participated in the actual study all had responded at or near the endpoints of the initial attitude scale. Attitude extremity has been found to relate to attitude accessibility. Although the relation is by no means perfect, extreme attitudes do tend to be more accessible from memory, as measured by latency of response to an attitudinal inquiry. Powell and Fazio (1984) observed an average correlation, across 12 contemporary social issues, of .30 between attitude extremity and response latency. In their investigation of the presidential election, Fazio and Williams (1986) observed a correlation of .53 between the extremity of attitudes toward Reagan and response latencies. (It was this observation that necessitated the classification of subjects into high and low accessibility groups by median splits at each level of the attitude response scale so as not to confound attitude accessibility with attitude extremity.) Thus, it appears likely that the successful demonstration of biased processing by Lord et al. was facilitated by the selection of individuals who possessed highly accessible attitudes as experimental subjects.

Taken as a whole, the set of investigations that have been summarized in this section clearly lead to the conclusion that attitudes do influence perceptions and judgments. However, this is particularly true of attitudes that are readily accessible from memory. Regardless of whether attitude accessibility was measured or manipulated, individuals with relatively accessible attitudes displayed greater selective processing of information than did individuals with less accessible attitudes.

ACCESSIBLE ATTITUDES GUIDE BEHAVIOR

"Attitudes determine for each individual what he will see and hear, what he will think and *what he will do* [italics added]. (Allport, 1935, p. 806)

---

[2]A similar study, which employed the same procedure of having subjects evaluate research relevant to the capital punishment issue, but which involved the measurement rather than the manipulation of attitude accessibility, leads to the same conclusion regarding the moderating role of attitude accessibility (Houston & Fazio, 1987). Subjects with attitudes that could be classified as highly accessible on the basis of relatively fast latencies of response to an attitudinal inquiry displayed greater biased processing than did subjects with less accessible attitudes.

Whether an attitude is accessible from memory is also expected to have an impact upon the degree to which the attitude guides behavior toward the attitude object. Once again, the attitude needs to be activated from memory if it is to influence an individual's behavior. This hypothesis about attitude accessibility as a moderator of the attitude-behavior relation was also examined in the Fazio and Williams (1986) investigation of the 1984 presidential election. Beginning the day after the election, the respondents were telephoned and asked whether they had voted and, if so, for whom. As with the debate data, the degree to which attitude toward Reagan predicted voting behavior was examined as a function of attitude accessibility. Once again, classification of respondents who had provided both attitude and voting data was done by a median split at each response level of the attitude scale.

Correlations between attitude and voting behavior were substantially higher among respondents whose attitudes were characterized by high accessibility than among those with attitudes of low accessibility. Within the high accessibility group, nearly 80% of the variance in voting behavior, as compared to 44% within the low accessibility group, was predicted by attitude toward Reagan. This finding is all the more striking when one keeps in mind that attitude was measured via a single item nearly 4 months prior to the election.

The influence of attitude accessibility upon the consistency between attitudes, as assessed months earlier, and voting behavior appears to have been a function of the stability of those attitudes. Initial attitudes characterized by high accessibility were likely to have biased people's interpretations of any information about the candidates that they received during the course of the campaign. The data concerning respondents' judgments of the debates indicate that such selective perception was less likely for individuals whose attitudes were relatively less accessible. Yet, the amount of selective processing is apt to have determined the persistence of the attitude over time. Thus, greater selective processing on the part of those individuals with highly accessible attitudes is likely to mean that their final voting decisions were affected by attitudinal positions more equivalent to the ones that they held months earlier than was the case of individuals with less accessible attitudes. Indeed, as suggested by this reasoning, the data from this study revealed a strong association between the extent of biased processing as a function of attitude and attitude-behavior correspondence. The less an individual's attitude promoted selective processing of the debates, the less likely the individual was to vote in a manner that was consistent with that initial attitude.

Confirming evidence regarding the moderating role of attitude accessibility also has been obtained in a context that did not involve a lengthy time interval between attitude assessment and behavior and, thus, was unlikely to have been mediated by attitude stability. Furthermore, the evidence to be described involved actual behavior, in contrast to the self-reports of behavior that were collected in the voting study. Fazio, Powell, and Williams (1986) examined the relation between attitudes and behavior toward a set of 10 products as a function of the accessibility of those attitudes from memory. Subjects responded to the names of 100 products, as they each appeared on a computer screen, by pressing either a key labelled "like" or a key labelled "dislike." The latency with which these responses were made was recorded by the microcomputer. Following this task, subjects completed a questionnaire on which they rated the extent of their liking or disliking for each product along a 7-point scale. These data constitute the attitude scores. In order to obtain behavioral data, subjects were shown a set of 10 of the 100 products and told that they could select 5 to take as "reimbursement" for having participated in the experiment. The 10 alternatives, which were roughly equivalent in value, were: a Snickers candy bar, a small bag of Fritos corn chips, two boxes of Sun-maid raisins, a small can of Star-kist tuna, a can of Dr. Pepper, a box of Cracker Jacks, a bag of Planters peanuts, two cans of V-8 juice, two five-stick packs of Dentyne gum, and a Mounds candy bar.

Subjects were classified into groups of high, moderate, and low attitude accessibility for *each* product. As in the Fazio and Williams (1986) study, this group assignment was performed at each and every level of the attitude scale so as to avoid confounding attitude scores with attitude accessibility. Unlike the Fazio and Williams investigation, however, attitude accessibility was not indexed simply by raw response latency. Instead, the accessibility measure employed for classification purposes was the z-score of the response latency for a given target product relative to the mean and standard deviation of the latencies for the 90 filler products. This change was necessitated by the fact that interitem correlations among the response latencies were substantial, whereas interitem correlations in the Fazio and Williams investigation were quite minimal.[3] The use of raw latency in the present case would have led to the consistent classification of individuals with tendencies to respond quickly to any inquiry as high accessibility subjects.

For each product, the correlation between attitude and the dichotomous

---

[3]Why the two studies differed in this regard is not clear. However, it is worth noting one difference in the attitude accessibility measurement procedures employed in the two studies. The Fazio and Williams (1986) investigation involved subjects responding to an audio-recorded statement, the end of which contained the electronic marker that initiated the timing. In contrast, the Fazio, Powell, and Williams (1986) study involved displaying the name of an attitude object on a computer screen, the onset of which initiated the timing. The time necessary to read the visual display may have enhanced the amount of covariation observed. Reading time may be a fairly constant individual difference that formed a component of each response latency.

behavior of having selected the product or not was computed within the high, moderate, and low accessibility groups. Averaged across the 10 products, the correlations displayed a significant linear trend as a function of level of attitude accessibility (.61, .59, and .51 for the high, moderate, and low attitude accessibility groups, respectively). Thus, the findings indicate that attitude accessibility moderated the attitude-behavior relation. The more accessible a subject's attitude toward a given product was, the more likely it was that product selection behavior was consistent with that attitude.

Fazio's (1986) model of the attitude-behavior process views behavior as a function of the individual's perceptions of the attitude object in the immediate situation. An attitude that is highly accessible from memory and, hence, likely to be activated automatically when the individual encounters the attitude object is apt to result in immediate perceptions that are congruent with the attitude. In contrast, when the attitude is not activated from memory, immediate perceptions are likely to be based on momentarily salient, and potentially unrepresentative, features of the attitude object that are not necessarily congruent with the attitude.

This greater influence of a momentarily salient dimension was apparent in a rather surprising and dramatic fashion in the product selection study. The 10 products had been arranged in two rows of 5 on a tabletop for the subjects' viewing and selection. On the assumption that the products positioned in the front row are more salient than those in the back row, we can offer the suggestion that the selection of a given product will be more influenced by row status if the attitude is low in accessibility than if its accessibility is high. The data revealed precisely this pattern. Among the products in the front row, the *lower* the accessibility of their attitudes, the *greater* the likelihood that subjects selected the product. For products in the back row, the reverse was true. The *lower* the accessibility of the attitude, the *less* likely subjects were to select the product. The strength of these "row effects" constituted a significant linear trend. Among subjects whose attitudes toward a given product were characterized by low accessibility, an average (across products) of 19% more selected the product if it was one that had been positioned in the front row than if it had been one from the back row. The comparable figures for moderate and high accessibility subjects were 13% and 5%, respectively. Thus, the lower the attitude accessibility, the more selection behavior was influenced by the relative salience afforded a product by its positioning. In contrast, the linear trend that was presented earlier with respect to attitude-behavior correlations suggests that the greater the attitude accessibility, the more selection behavior was influenced by the attitude.

The importance of attitude accessibility in determining the extent to which attitudes guide behavior has also been confirmed in experimental work involving the manipulation of accessibility (in contrast to the correlational work presented above involving the measurement of accessibility). The experiment (Fazio et al., 1982; Experiment 4) employed our now standard means of manipulating attitude accessibility via repeated attitudinal expression and involved attitudes and behavior toward types of intellectual puzzles. Indeed, these were the same set of puzzles whose mere presentation in the context of research described earlier was found to activate the associated attitude, provided that the strength of the object-evaluation association had been enhanced via repeated attitudinal expression (Fazio, Powell, & Herr, 1983). After being introduced to the puzzles and after expressing their attitudes either a single time or repeatedly, the subjects were given an opportunity to work with any of the types of puzzles in a free-play period. Attitude and behavior were much more consistent among subjects in the repeated expression condition than among those in the single expression condition. For example, the average within-subject correlation between attitude and the proportion of available problems of a given type that were attempted was .474 in the repeated expression condition, significantly greater than the average of .218 observed in the single expression condition.

In sum, both experimental and correlational investigations have yielded evidence of the moderating role of attitude accessibility. The more accessible an attitude is from memory, the greater the likelihood that the attitude will influence subsequent behavior.

ACCESSIBLE ATTITUDES ARE FUNCTIONAL

"Without guiding attitudes the individual is confused and baffled . . . they [attitudes] draw lines about and segregate an otherwise chaotic environment; they are our methods for finding our way about in an ambiguous universe" (Allport, 1935, p. 806)

Like Allport, numerous theorists have considered attitudes to be functional constructs that ease decision-making and facilitate the individual's "movement" through the diverse array of objects and people that are encountered daily. In delineating various functions that attitudes might serve, both Katz (1960) and Smith, Bruner, and White (1956) commented upon this knowledge or object appraisal function. For example, Smith and his colleagues argued that an attitude toward an object saves the person from "the energy-consuming and sometimes painful process of figuring out *de novo* how he shall relate himself to it" (p. 41). Having categorized the elements in one's social world into good and bad enables the individual to progress easily through daily life. What to approach and what to avoid is clear. In this way, the individual is also in a position to maximize the likelihood of having positive day-to-day life experiences and to minimize the occurrence of aversive experiences.

This object appraisal function can be considered the primary value of attitudes. In contrast to the many other functions that attitudes also can serve, this one is applicable to all attitudes. The other functions that theorists have discussed have more to do with the content or direction of attitudes than with the general utility of simply holding an attitude, regardless of its valence. For example, the utilitarian function that has been posited centers on the development of positive attitudes toward those objects that have previously produced satisfaction or reward and the development of negative attitudes toward objects that have thwarted needs or desires or that generally have produced some dissatisfaction. Similarly, in discussing an ego-defensive function that attitudes might serve, the functional theorists have noted that an attitude of a particular valence can help maintain or enhance an individual's self-esteem. For example, concerns about one's own self-esteem may be lessened by the development of a negative attitude toward some outgroup and the noting of one's superior relative standing.

In all of these cases, the resulting attitudes, regardless of whether they stem from the utilitarian value of the attitude object, the ego-protective benefits of the attitude, or whatever, serve an object appraisal function. When the attitude objects are encountered, the "holding of an attitude provides a ready aid in 'sizing up' objects and events in the environment" (Smith, Bruner, & White, 1956, p. 41). That is, regardless of why the individual's attitude took on a particular valence, the mere possession of any attitude is useful to the individual in terms of orienting him or her to the object in question.

The implications of the central thesis of the present chapter for this notion of functionality are obvious. The degree to which an attitude adequately fulfills this object appraisal function would appear to depend on the extent to which the attitude is capable of being automatically activated from memory when the individual observes the attitude object. The likelihood of such automatic activation depends on the strength of the object-evaluation association. Attitudes that involve a strong association are truly functional. By virtue of their accessibility from memory, such attitudes provide the individual with the "ready aid" mentioned earlier. They free the individual from the processing required for reflective thought about his or her evaluation of the object. Furthermore, by guiding the individual's perceptions of the object in the immediate situation in which the object is encountered and thus influencing the individual's definition of the event that is occurring (in the manner suggested by Fazio's (1986) model of the attitude-behavior process), such attitudes can guide the individual's behavior in a fairly automatic manner. Thus, the individual is freed from much of the effort of having to engage in deliberative reasoning processes before behaving toward the object in question.

The functionality of accessible attitudes is illustrated by an experiment conducted recently by Fazio and Driscoll (1986). The effect of accessible attitudes upon subjects' self-reports concerning the difficulty and stress involved in performing a task for which those attitudes were relevant was examined. The attitude objects were slides of abstract paintings. The critical task involved subjects' expression of a preference between the members of pairs of such slides. Forty-five pairs were presented and, on each trial, subjects indicated whether they preferred the one on the left or the one on the right. In the condition that is most relevant to the present concerns, the difficulty of this task was increased by forcing subjects through the series of trials at a fairly rapid pace. Only 4 seconds separated the onset of each trial.

Prior to engaging in this pairwise preference task, subjects underwent one of two procedures in which they were exposed to each abstract painting a total of four times. Subjects in the attitude rehearsal condition were instructed to indicate their liking for each slide by saying aloud either "like strongly," "like," "dislike," or "dislike strongly." Subjects in the control condition were asked to judge the apparent primary color in each slide and to estimate the percentage of the painting composed of that color. Thus, although all subjects were exposed to each slide an equivalent number of times, some subjects expressed their attitudes repeatedly and some did not.

The effect of this attitude rehearsal manipulation on subjects' judgments of the subsequent pairwise preference was examined. Subjects were asked to rate how difficult, hurried, and stressful they found the pairwise preference task. An overall index consisting of the sum of these three ratings revealed that subjects in the attitude rehearsal condition had found the task less problematic than did subjects in the control condition. Thus, it appears that one benefit of holding accessible attitudes is that such attitudes ease the stress that can sometimes accompany decision-making. Decisions can be made with less difficulty.

The "quality" of these decisions also seems to be affected. As the final task of the experiment, subjects were provided with prints of each painting and given unlimited time to rank-order the entire set in terms of their liking for each painting. The number of times that each subject's expressed pairwise preferences concurred with these rank-orderings was counted. On the average, such concurrences were significantly more numerous in the attitude rehearsal condition than in the control condition. This finding suggests that accessible attitudes guide decision-making in a relatively satsifying direction that one is less likely to regret or wish to modify at a later point in time.

Because an accessible attitude guides perceptions of the attitude object once it has been activated from memory, an individual who possesses such an attitude is much more likely to arrive at immediate perceptions of the object that concur with his or her affect than will an individual who holds a less accessible attitude. As illustrated earlier, the latter individual is more likely to be influenced by momentarily salient, potentially idiosyncratic, features of the object and, as a result, may make a decision that is not reflective of his or her attitude. It is as a consequence of such a mechanism that accessible attitudes may result in more satisfying decisions than in-accessible attitudes. By making less attitudinally based decisions, individuals with relatively inaccessible attitudes risk deciding on courses of action that they later come to regret. For example, such individuals may inadvertently choose to place themselves in situations that are potentially aversive.

Thus, not only do accessible attitudes ease the actual decision process, but they help the individual orient to the environment in such a way that rewards are maximized and negative outcomes minimized. One might even go so far as to speculate that individuals lacking accessible attitudes toward objects that they commonly encounter in their daily lives may be especially vulnerable to mental health difficulties. Needing to engage in more effort and deliberation to make mundane decisions, such individuals experience more stress during decision-making. They are also more likely to make decisions that, in the long run, prove dissatisfying. Thus, as a consequence of both the decision process and its outcomes, such individuals are apt to experience more stress in their daily lives.

In addition, because they have to deliberate about even routine de-cisions, such individuals may be in a less adequate position to concentrate on those stressors that really do require active coping. That is, individuals for whom much decision-making is relatively automatized, as a function of their holding accessible attitudes, may be able to devote more cognitive energy and resources to the more serious stressors that demand their attention. Thus, they may cope with such stressors better and experience debilitating effects of a lesser magnitude than do individuals who need to devote relatively greater conscious thought and reflection to less serious matters.

Whether any such relation exists between the possession of accessible attitudes and mental health remains to be empirically investigated. Never-theless, the possibility merits future research. Such research may be particu-larly enlightening with regard to the functionality of attitudes, especially accessible ones.

FURTHER IMPLICATIONS
OF ATTITUDE ACCESSIBILITY

Consideration of the role of attitude accessibility raises a number of addi-tional issues that merit some commentary. We have seen that the position of an attitude along the attitude–nonattitude continuum, and the corresponding accessibility of that attitude, determines the power and functionality of the attitude. Many of the consequences and benefits ascribed to attitudes appear to be limited to ones that are accessible from memory. It may be that many phenomena relevant to attitudes are similarly limited to a particular domain of the attitude–nonattitude continuum.

To provide an example, Fazio (1987) discussed precisely such a limitation with regard to the applicability of self-perception processes. Bem (1972) originally postulated that individuals infer attitudes from observation of their behavior "to the extent that internal cues are weak, ambiguous, or uninterpretable" (p. 2). Subsequent research has indicated that individuals are most likely to rely upon self-inference from behavior when their attitudes are weak, and presumably nonexistent or relatively inaccessible from memory (Chaiken & Baldwin, 1981; Fazio, 1981). An individual who possesses an accessible attitude does not need to rely upon an inferential process when faced with a request to indicate his or her attitude. Instead, the individual can access the attitude easily and directly from memory.

Other social influence strategies may be similarly limited. The research described earlier on the selective processing of information indicates that accessible attitudes are less susceptible to change as a function of new information that is received about the attitude object than are less accessible attitudes. For example, individuals with highly accessible attitudes toward Reagan displayed evidence of having selectively processed the debates, implying that only individuals with less accessible attitudes were in a position to have their attitudinal stances modified by the information that became available during the course of the debates. These data, along with the recent work of Wood and her colleagues (Wood, 1982; Wood, Kallgren, & Priesler, 1985) suggest that the more accessible an individual's attitude is from memory, the less susceptible the individual is to counterpersuasion.

Thus, the effectiveness of persuasion strategies may be limited to attitudes that occupy a relatively low position along the attitude–nonattitude continuum. Two implications arise from such an inference. The first concerns the implementation of persuasion campaigns. Such campaigns will be most effective and will make maximal use of available resources if they are targeted toward segments of the population that hold relatively inaccessible attitudes. Such targeting may be feasible in a case in which various demographic variables are found to be associated with the accessibility of the relevant attitude.

The second issue that arises concerns attitude change versus attitude formation. If only relatively inaccessible attitudes are modifiable via persuasion, then, as Converse (1970) noted, the findings from the multitude of persuasion studies that have been conducted may have more to say about attitude formation than about attitude change. This raises the question of what social influence strategies might be effective in terms of producing attitude *change,* i.e., modifying a highly accessible attitude. This is clearly an important concern that the field needs to address.

In addition to raising questions about the kinds of attitudes that are likely to be susceptible to persuasive attempts, consideration of the role of attitude accessibility highlights an important issue concerning the goal of social influence strategies. If the ultimate goal of such attempts is to influence individuals' behavior, then it is not sufficient to instill positive attitudes. The new attitudes must also be such that they involve a strong object-evaluation association and, hence, are highly accessible from memory. Only then can they be expected to affect behavior. Thus, just as the accessibility of the attitude prior to the social influence attempt is critical, so too is the accessibility of the resulting attitude important. Here, then, is yet another important issue for future research. How can persuasion attempts be designed so as to not only maximize the likelihood of producing the desired attitude but also to maximize the accessibility of this attitude?

It is toward such issues that consideration of the relevance of attitude accessibility forces attention. The bottom line is simply that not all attitudes are equal. Some attitudes—those that are highly accessible from memory—are more powerful in terms of the impact that they have on the individual's perceptions and behavior and are more functional for the individual than are other attitudes. Furthermore, recognition of this differential power and functionality calls attention to the need to be aware of the status of individuals' attitudes both prior to and following any social influence attempt.

ACKNOWLEDGMENTS

Preparation of this chapter and much of the research summarized herein was supported by Research Scientist Development Award MH00452 and by Grant MH38832 from the National Institute of Mental Health. Some of the research was supported by a grant from the Ogilvy Center for Research and Development. The author thanks Arie Kruglanski, Carol Williams, and Mark Zanna for their helpful comments on an earlier draft.

REFERENCES

Abelson, R. P. (1972). Are attitudes necessary? In B. T. King & E. McGinnies (Eds.), *Attitudes, conflict, and social change* (pp. 19–32). New York: Academic Press.

Abelson, R. P., Kinder, D. R., Peters, M. D., & Fiske, S. T. (1982). Affective and semantic components in political person perception. *Journal of Personality and Social Psychology, 42,* 619–630.

Allport, G. W. (1935). Attitudes. In C. Murchison (Ed.), *Handbook of social psychology* (pp. 798–844). Worcester, MA: Clark University Press.

Bem, D. J. (1972). Self-perception theory. In L. Berkowitz (Ed.), *Advances in experimental social psychology* (Vol. 6, pp. 1–62). New York: Academic Press.

Chaiken, S., & Baldwin, M. W. (1981). Affective-cognitive consistency and the effect of salient behavioral information on the self-perception of attitudes. *Journal of Personality and Social Psychology, 41,* 1–12.

Converse, P. E. (1970). Attitudes and non-attitudes: Continuation of a dialogue. In E. R. Tufte (Ed.), *The quantitative analysis of social problems* (pp. 168–189). Reading, MA: Addison-Wesley.

Fazio, R. H. (1981). On the self-perception explanation of the overjustification effect: The role of salience of initial attitude. *Journal of Experimental Social Psychology, 17,* 417–426.

Fazio, R. H. (1986). How do attitudes guide behavior? In R. M. Sorrentino & E. T. Higgins (Eds.), *The handbook of motivation and cognition: Foundations of social behavior* (pp. 204–243). New York: Guilford Press.

Fazio, R. H. (1987). Self-perception theory: A current perspective. In M. P. Zanna, J. M. Olson, & C. P. Herman (Eds.), *Social influence: The Ontario symposium* (Vol. 5, pp. 129–150). Hillsdale, NJ: Lawrence Erlbaum Associates.

Fazio, R. H., Chen, J., McDonel, E. C., & Sherman, S. J. (1982). Attitude accessibility, attitude-behavior consistency, and the strength of the object-evaluation association. *Journal of Experimental Social Psychology, 18,* 339–357.

Fazio, R. H., & Driscoll, D. M. (1986). [The role of attitude accessibility in easing decision-making]. Unpublished raw data.

Fazio, R. H., Herr, P. M., & Olney, T. J. (1984). Attitude accessibility following a self-perception process. *Journal of Personality and Social Psychology, 47,* 277–286.

Fazio, R. H., & Houston, D. A. (1986). [Biased processing as a function of attitude accessibility]. Unpublished raw data.

Fazio, R. H., Powell, M. C., & Williams, C. J. (1986). [Attitude accessibility as a moderator on the attitude-behavior relation]. Unpublished raw data.

Fazio, R. H., Powell, M. C., & Herr, P. M. (1983). Toward a process model of the attitude-behavior relation: Accessing one's attitude upon mere observation of the attitude object. *Journal of Personality and Social Psychology, 44,* 723–735.

Fazio, R. H., Sanbonmatsu, D. M., Powell, M. C., & Kardes, F. R. (1986). On the automatic activation of attitudes. *Journal of Personality and Social Psychology, 50,* 229–238.

Fazio, R. H., & Williams, C. J. (1986). Attitude accessibility as a moderator of the attitude-perception and attitude-behavior relations: An investigation of the 1984 presidential election. *Journal of Personality and Social Psychology, 51,* 505–514.

Fazio, R. H., & Zanna, M. P. (1978). Attitudinal qualities relating to the strength of the attitude-behavior relationship. *Journal of Experimental Social Psychology, 14,* 398–408.

Fazio, R. H., & Zanna, M. P. (1981). Direct experience and attitude-behavior consistency. In L. Berkowitz (Ed.), *Advances in experimental social psychology* (Vol. 14, pp. 162–202). New York: Academic Press.

Fishbein, M. (1963). An investigation of the relationships between beliefs about an object and attitude toward that object. *Human Relations, 16,* 233–240.

Higgins, E. T., Rholes, W. S., & Jones, C. R. (1977). Category accessibility and impression formation. *Journal of Experimental Psychology, 13,* 141–154.

Houston, D. A., & Fazio, R. H. (1987). *Biased processing as a function of attitude accessibility.* Paper presented at the annual meeting of the Midwestern Psychological Association, Chicago.

Hovland, C. I. (1959). Reconciling conflicting results derived from experimental and survey studies of attitude change. *American Psychologist, 14,* 8–17.

Hovland, C. I., Harvey, O. J., & Sherif, M. (1957). Assimilation and contrast effects in reactions to communication and attitude change. *Journal of Abnormal and Social Psychology, 55,* 244–252.

Katz, D. (1960). The functional approach to the study of attitudes. *Public Opinion Quarterly, 24,* 163–204.

Lord, C. G., Ross, L., & Lepper, M. R. (1979). Biased assimilation and attitude polarization: The effects of prior theories on subsequently considered evidence. *Journal of Personality and Social Psychology, 37,* 2098–2109.

McGuire, W. J. (1985). Attitudes and attitude change. In G. Lindzey & E. Aronson (Eds.), *The handbook of social psychology* (3rd ed., Vol. 2, pp. 233–346). New York: Random House.

McGuire, W. J. (1986). The vicissitudes of attitudes and similar representational constructs in twentieth century psychology. *European Journal of Social Psychology, 16,* 89–130.

Norman, R. (1975). Affective-cognitive consistency, attitudes, conformity, and behavior. *Journal of Personality and Social Psychology, 32,* 83–91.

Powell, M. C., & Fazio, R. H. (1984). Attitude accessibility as a function of repeated attitudinal expression. *Personality and Social Psychology Bulletin, 10,* 139–148.

Raden, D. (1985). Strength-related attitude dimensions. *Social Psychology Quarterly, 48,* 312–330.

Rosenberg, M. J. (1960). A structural theory of attitude dynamics. *Public Opinion Quarterly, 24,* 319–341.

Sample, J., & Warland, R. (1973). Attitude and prediction of behavior. *Social Forces, 51,* 292–304.

Sanbonmatsu, D. M., & Fazio, R. H. (1986). *The automatic activation of attitudes toward products.* Paper presented at the annual meeting of the Association for Consumer Research, Toronto, Canada.

Sanbonmatsu, D. M., Osborne, R. E., & Fazio, R. H. (1986). *The measurement of automatic attitude activation.* Paper presented at the annual meeting of the Midwestern Psychological Association, Chicago.

Schneider, W., & Shiffrin, R. M. (1977). Controlled and automatic human information processing: Detection, search, and attention. *Psychological Review, 84,* 1–66.

Sherif, M., & Cantril, H. (1947). *The psychology of ego involvement.* New York: Wiley.

Shiffrin, R. M., & Dumais, S. T. (1981). The development of automatism. In J. R. Anderson (Ed.), *Cognitive skills and their acquisition* (pp. 111–140). Hillsdale, NJ: Lawrence Erlbaum Associates.

Shiffrin, R. M., & Schneider, W. (1977). Controlled and automatic human information processing: II. Perceptual learning, automatic attending, and a general theory. *Psychological Review, 84,* 127–190.

Smith, M. B., Bruner, J. S., & White, R. W. (1956). *Opinions and personality.* New York: Wiley.

Srull, T. K., & Wyer, R. S., Jr. (1979). The role of category accessibility in the interpretation of information about persons: Some determinants of implications. *Journal of Personality and Social Psychology, 37,* 1660–1672.

Wicker, A. W. (1969). Attitudes versus actions: The relationship of verbal and overt behavioral responses to attitude objects. *Journal of Social Issues, 25,* 41–78.

Wicker, A. W. (1971). An examination of the "other variables" explanation of attitude-behavior inconsistency. *Journal of Personality and Social Psychology, 19,* 18–30.

Wood, W. (1982). Retrieval of attitude-relevant information from memory: Effects on susceptibility to persuasion and on intrinsic motivation. *Journal of Personality and Social Psychology, 42,* 798–810.

Wood, W., Kallgren, C. A., & Priesler, R. M. (1985). Access to attitude-relevant information in memory as a determinant of persuasion: The role of message attributes. *Journal of Experimental Social Psychology, 21,* 73–85.

Wu, C., & Shaffer, D. R. (1987). Susceptibility to persuasive appeals as a function of source credibility and prior experience with the attitude object. *Journal of Personality and Social Psychology, 52,* 677–688.

Zanna, M. P., Kielser, C. A., & Pilkonis, P. A. (1970). Positive and negative attitudinal affect established by classical conditioning. *Journal of Personality and Social Psychology, 14,* 321–328.

Zanna, M. P., & Rempel, J. K. (in press). Attitudes: A new look at an old concept. In D. Bar-Tal & A. Kruglanski (Eds.)., *The social psychology of knowledge.* New York: Cambridge University Press.

8

Automatic and Controlled Processes in Prejudice:
The Role of Stereotypes and Personal Beliefs

Patricia G. Devine
University of Wisconsin

The latter half of the 20th century has witnessed legislative changes that have made discrimination based on race illegal (e.g., the 1954 Supreme Court ruling on segregation, the Civil Rights Laws of the 1960s). The impact of such legislative changes has led many to question whether shifts in personal attitudes have kept pace with legal changes. This type of question is particularly interesting in light of the fact that nearly two-thirds of the current American population lived during a time when it was not just customary, but legal to discriminate against Blacks (Gaertner & Dovidio, 1986). Has racial prejudice been reduced in the United States? What evidence should be taken as an indication that prejudice has declined?

Recent attempts to explore the state of racial and ethnic attitudes in the United States have produced a conflicting set of findings. Some of the research suggests that prejudice is declining in the US (Greeley & Sheatsley, 1971; Taylor, Sheatsley & Greeley, 1978). For example, the survey literature on racial attitudes suggests that attitudes toward integration have become more positive and beliefs that Blacks are inferior to Whites have steadily declined (see Dovidio & Gaertner, 1986, for a recent summary of the survey data). Other studies, which do not rely on subjects' verbal reports of their attitudes, suggest that prejudice is still prevalent in the U. S. and continues to be a dominant (negative) force in intergroup contacts (see Crosby, Bromley, & Saxe, 1980, for a review).

It appears that the answer to the question of whether racial prejudice has declined in the US depends very importantly on the criteria that are used as evidence of prejudice or the lack of prejudice. For example, Crosby and her colleagues (1980; see also Gaertner, 1976) argued that the reactive nature of questionnaires undermines their utility as measures of prejudice. According to their analysis, nonprejudiced responses to survey questions reflect, at best, respondents' self-presentational efforts to create a socially desirable image. Crosby, Bromley, and Saxe (1980) suggested that although Whites *comply* with an egalitarian, nonracist ideology, they have not yet *internalized* these values. Based on a review of studies that use less reactive measures (e.g., nonverbal behaviors, nonconsciously monitored responses), Crosby and her colleagues (1980) concluded that "whites still discriminate against blacks in terms of behaviors that lie largely out of awareness" (p. 556). They suggested that overt expressions of prejudice have been replaced with more subtle, covert expressions of prejudice.

Which criteria for prejudice or the lack of prejudice should be trusted— the primarily nonconscious or the conscious responses? I would like to argue that an either/or answer to this question may not be the most productive approach to this question. A major goal of the present chapter is to develop a model that specifies the role of both the *more* and *less* conscious aspects of responses to ethnic group members. That is, it is likely that both types of responses to ethnic group members occur. If this is so, it becomes important to have a model that accounts for both types of responses and delineates the role of nonconscious and conscious processes in responses to ethnic group members. Before outlining the assumptions of the model, some of the factors that contribute to the development of stereotypes and prejudiced attitudes are considered.

SOCIALIZATION FACTORS: LEARNING STEREOTYPES AND PREJUDICE

> Ethnic attitudes are part of the social heritage of the developing child. They are transmitted across generations as a component of the accumulated knowledge of a society. No person can grow up in a society without learning the prevailing attitudes concerning major ethnic groups. Given the polarization of ethnic attitudes, we ought to consider the question of how some people escape prejudice. (Ehrlich, 1973, p. 110)

A tremendous amount of theoretical and empirical attention has been directed toward determining the nature of prejudice and discovering the factors that contribute to its formation and change. Implicit in such work was an assumption that if we understood the factors that contributed to prejudice we could design effective prejudice reduction techniques. One of the issues underscored by theorists in the prejudice literature is that negative intergroup attitudes are learned through a very subtle process early in the developmental experience[1] (Allport, 1954; Ashmore, 1970; Katz, 1976; Proshansky, 1966). Although many factors have been implicated in the development of negative ethnic and racial attitudes and stereotypes, the strongest or most important factors remain unknown.

Some theorists argue, for example, that the formation of ethnic attitudes is integrally related to the establishment of the child's self-identity. Attitudes toward other groups may be formed as the child begins to figure out to which group he or she belongs and the groups to which he or she does not belong. Children typically show evidence of racial awareness by age 3 or 4 and this awareness increases rapidly for the next few years. By the time children reach first grade racial awareness is very well-established (Katz, 1976; Proshansky, 1966). Soon thereafter, young children manifest negative attitudes and knowledge of the cultural stereotype commonly associated with Blacks (Ashmore, 1970; Proshansky, 1966).

Ashmore (1970) suggested that there are societal level and individual level theories of prejudice that implicate different factors in the development of prejudice. For example, Katz (1976), summarizing the developmental acquisition of racial attitudes, proposed that parents may play a role in learning of racial attitudes through direct instruction or observational modeling of such attitudes. Child-rearing techniques may also play a role. Indeed, Adorno, Frenkel-Brunswik, Levinson, and Sanford (1950) submitted that development of an authoritarian personality follows from parental harshness, dominance, and status consciousness.

It is likely that the development of racial and ethnic attitudes is a function of complex interrelationships among the various factors. Whatever the origin, it seems clear that negative racial attitudes and stereotypes are firmly in place early in the developmental sequence. Katz (1976) reported a telling example of the 3-year-old child, who upon seeing a Black infant says to her mother, "Look mom, a baby maid" (p. 147). By the age of three, this child had learned that Blacks assume a particular role in society—as though this was a foregone conclusion. It seems unlikely that the child could fully understand the implications of her statement, but this idea had become integrated into her conception of members of the Black racial group. Katz (1976) argued, for example, that the negative predispositions toward various ethnic groups acquired at such early developmental stages may form the irrational but potent foundation for racism.

---

[1]This analysis does not deal directly with negative attitudes that would serve the ego-defensive function of protecting one's self-esteem through derogating an ethnic group member. It is not claimed, for example, that the present theoretical framework can directly address scapegoat theory of prejudice or the authoritarian personality (Adorno, Frenkel-Brunswik, Levinson, & Sanford, 1950). However, the evidence for these approaches is, at best, mixed (see Ashmore, 1970, for a review).

It is important to note that the presence of these negative attitudes does not imply that the individual had previously made a decision to hold negative attitudes or endorse the stereotype. Allport (1954) suggested, for example, that in many circumstances ethnic attitudes are acquired through a process of learning and conformity to expected patterns of behavior during the child's socialization experiences. Conformity to cultural expectations leads to reward, whereas deviations lead to punishment or rejection.

The expected patterns of behavior are part of the social heritage described by Ehrlich (1973) and are often communicated to children in indirect ways (Allport, 1954; Ashmore, 1970; Trager & Yarrow, 1952). Although there have been changes over time and there are differences among different subgroups in America, a cultural pattern of prejudice still exists (Ashmore, 1970; Gaertner & Dovidio, 1986). Thus, racial attitudes are frequently acquired without individuals going through a rational analysis of the merits of the beliefs and attitudes. This process is not unlike the process by which children learn many of their social attitudes. Frequently, these negative attitudes are firmly in place prior to the development of cognitive skills that provide the ability or flexibility to make such a rational analysis that would allow one to decide whether negative attitudes and stereotypes were personally acceptable (Allport, 1954; Proshansky, 1966; Katz, 1976). The impetus for change arises only when one begins to question these previously learned attitudes (Katz, 1960).

An important question becomes whether there can be a meaningful distinction between knowledge of cultural prejudices and stereotypes and acceptance of them. The analysis described implies that to escape prejudice the individual must first decide that his or her prejudice is unwarranted and, second, he or she must replace the negative prejudice with a more acceptable attitude. It is through consideration of such escape efforts that we may gain some insights concerning structure and function issues associated with ethnic attitudes. In the next section, we attempt to explore the relationship between stereotypes and prejudice in efforts to understand the *more* and *less* conscious aspects of peoples' responses to members of a stereotyped group.

STEREOTYPES VERSUS PERSONAL BELIEFS: AN INTEGRATIVE MODEL

Inevitability of Prejudice

Crosby, Bromley, and Saxe's (1980) analysis in which they argue that nonconsciously monitored responses are the best indicators of prejudice is similar in many ways to arguments advanced by many classic and contemporary theorists that prejudice is an inevitable consequence of ordinary categorization processes (see Billig, 1985, for a review). Some theorists in the prejudice literature suggest that knowledge of stereotypes is integrally linked with and provides a basis for prejudice. The basic argument of this "inevitability of prejudice" approach is that so long as stereotypes exist prejudice will follow. This perspective could have serious implications because our socialization experiences seem to insure that we learn the stereotypes and attitudes associated with major ethnic groups (Ehrlich, 1973). Billig (1985), summarizing this perspective, suggested that "People will be prejudiced so long as they continue to think" (p. 81).

This pessimistic analysis overlooks a very important distinction between knowledge of a cultural stereotype and acceptance or endorsement of the stereotype. That is, although one can have *knowledge* of a stereotype, his or her *personal beliefs* may or may not be congruent with the stereotype. For example, people can know that the racial stereotypes of Blacks holds that Blacks are lazy. Belief in that stereotypic ascription is likely to vary across individuals. Even if one does believe that a stereotypic ascription is true, the *reasons* underlying that belief tend to differ across people. For example, statistics document that Blacks in our society are poorer than Whites. Those who believe that Blacks are poor because they are Black have belief structures that differ dramatically from those who believe that Blacks are poor because, historically, they have been systematically denied educational and occupational opportunities. Such differences may be revealing regarding our current understanding of racial attitudes in America.

Other models have also made the assumption that stereotypes and prejudice are inextricably intertwined. For example, the tripartite model of attitudes assumes that stereotypes are the cognitive component of prejudiced attitudes (Harding, Kunter, Proshansky, & Chein, 1954; Harding, Proshansky, Kunter, & Chein, 1969; Secord & Backman, 1964). Other theorists purport that stereotypes are functional for the individual because they allow him or her to rationalize his or her prejudice against the group (Allport, 1954; LaViolette & Silvert, 1951; Saenger, 1953; Simpson & Yinger, 1965).

However, there is no good evidence that knowlege of a stereotype about a group implies prejudice toward the group. For example, in an in-depth interview study of prejudice in war veterans, Bettleheim and Janowitz (1964) found no significant relationship between stereotypes reported about Blacks and Jews and the degree of hostility or prejudice the veterans displayed toward the groups. In other studies of stereotype assessment it has become clear that subjects' ability to report the content of the cultural stereotype of Blacks is not reliably related to their attitudes toward the ethnic groups (Brigham, 1972; Devine, in press; Karlins, Coffman, & Walters, 1969).

Although stereotypes and personal beliefs may have overlapping features, they are conceptually distinct cognitive structures (Ashmore & Del Boca, 1981; Billig, 1985; Devine, in press). Each structure represents only part of our entire knowledge base of a particular group. Current models of attitudes, such as that proposed by Pratkanis (chap. 4 in this volume) recognize that the attitudinal knowledge structures contain a variety of types of information about the attitude object. Pratkanis argues, for example, that "a *belief* is a proposition that is endorsed and accepted as true, and is thus a subset of information a person possesses about an object" (p. 33). Beliefs can differ from one's affective reaction to attitude object or one's knowledge about the object. To the extent that stereotypes and personal beliefs represent different (and only potentially overlapping) subsets of information about ethnic or racial groups, they may have different implications for evaluation of and behavior toward members of the ethnic and racial groups. Previous prejudice theorists have not adequately captured this distinction and explored its implications for responding to stereotyped group members. In what follows, we explore how stereotypes and personal beliefs are related to the more and less conscious components of responses to stereotyped groups.

Challenge to the Inevitability of Prejudice Perspective

Devine (in press) challenged the inevitability of prejudice perspective and argued that the failure to consider the distinction between stereotypes and prejudice may underlie the inevitability of prejudice arguments. Devine developed theoretical framework that (a) underscores the importance of the stereotype/personal belief distinction and (b) incorporates the more and less conscious components of responses to stereotyped groups. The framework draws upon recent theoretical models in information processing that distinguish between automatic (involuntary) and controlled (voluntary) processes (Posner & Snyder, 1975; Schneider & Shiffrin, 1977; Shiffrin & Schneider, 1977).

Automatic and Controlled Processes

Automatic processes involve the unintentional or spontaneous activation of some well-learned set of associations or responses that have been developed through repeated activation in memory. That is, automatic processes do not require conscious effort and appear to be initiated by the presence of stimulus cues in the environment (Shiffrin & Dumais, 1981). A crucial component of automatic processes is their inescapability; they occur despite deliberate attempts to bypass or ignore them (Shiffrin & Dumais, 1981; Neely, 1977). In contrast, controlled processes are intentional and require the active attention of the individual. Controlled processes, although limited by capacity, are more flexible than automatic processes. Their intentionality and flexibility makes them particularly valuable for decision-making, problem-solving, and the initiation of new behaviors.

Ronis, Yates, and Kirscht (chap. 9 in this volume) appeal to the auto-matic-controlled process distinction in their analysis of the development and persistence of repeated behaviors such as flossing one's teeth or wear-ing a seat belt. Ronis and his colleagues argue that initially such repeated behaviors are guided by conscious deliberate processes. One's attitude toward the behavior is central to the initiation or development of the response. Over time—with repetition of the response—persistence of the response may be determined more by habit (automatic processes) than by decisions to behave based on attitudinal variables (controlled processes). That is, after the habit has been established people don't need to think carefully about buckling the seat belt; the stimulus cues in the car cue the buckling response. One important consequence of this analysis is that over time there may be a tendency for responses to be less correlated with and poorly predicted by attitudes. The habit becomes autonomous from the attitudes and beliefs of the individual. Thus, changes in attitudes and beliefs may not be manifested in changes in responses when the responses have become habitual and this may produce the often observed attitude-behavior inconsistency. This analysis is very much related to processes involved in prejudice as is discussed later.

One of the implications of Ronis, Yates, and Kirscht's analysis is that automatic and controlled processes can operate independently of each other. This potential dissociation of automatic and controlled processes has been empirically supported (Logan & Cowan, 1984; Neely, 1977). For example, using a semantic priming task, Neely (1977) demonstrated that when automatic processes would produce a response that would conflict with conscious expectancies (induced through verbal instructions), sub-jects can inhibit the response based on automatic processes and in-tentionally replace it with one consistent with their conscious expectan-cies.

Neely used a lexical decision task (e.g., the subject's task is to decide if the target is a word?) in which primes were either semantically related to the target (e.g., BODY-hand) or were related to the target only through experimenter instructions (e.g., subjects were led to expect BODY would be followed by a bird name such as canary). In the latter situation, although subjects have a conscious expectancy for bird names, the prime should *also* activate its semantic category of body parts. Neely (1977) manipulated the interval between the prime and target. Following brief intervals (i.e., 250 m/s), the prime facilitated judgments about semantically related targets regardless of experimenter induced expectancies. At longer delays (i.e.,

2000 m/s), however, facilitation was observed for expected targets and inhibition for unexpected targets regardless of their semantic relationship of the targets to the prime. The key to inhibition of automatically activated responses is that there has got to be enough *time* and cognitive *capacity* available for the conscious expectancy to develop and inhibit the automatic processes.

Automatic and Controlled Processes in Prejudice

The automatic-controlled process distinction may provide similar theoretical leverage for understanding prejudiced and nonprejudiced responses to stereotyped group members (Devine, in press). The potential dissociation of automatic and controlled processes has been particularly useful in developing an analysis of the cognitive processes involved in responding to stereotyped group members. For example, there may be some important parallels to Ronis, Yates, and Kirscht's analysis of habit formation and change in the automatic-controlled analysis of prejudice. They argue that once habit is established, a decision to change the habit requires the use of the more flexible, intentional, attention demanding, limited capacity controlled processes. We argue that prejudice could be considered analogous to a bad habit. Breaking automatically instigated bad habits, according to Ronis and his colleagues, requires a decision that the habit is bad and conscious efforts to replace the bad habit with a new set of more acceptable responses. We argue that the low prejudice person has decided that prejudice and stereotypes are inappropriate bases for action and evaluation, has modified his or her beliefs, and has decided to initiate a new set of responses. This requires both inhibition of the automatic response and intentional activation of controlled responses. This process is likely to require a great deal of capacity and attention.

Devine's (in press) model interest centers on the conditions under which stereotypes versus personal beliefs are activated and the likelihood that beliefs (ideas endorsed) overlap with the cultural stereotype. Given that stereotypes are learned and firmly in place *before* an individual has the cognitive ability and flexibility to question or critically evaluate their validity, beliefs (decisions about the appropriateness of prejudice and stereotypic ascriptions) are necessarily newer cognitive structures; they do not have a long history of activation. To the extent that an individual *does not* accept or endorse stereotypic ascriptions or ideas, there exists a fundamental conflict between the already existing stereotype and the newly formed personal beliefs. Devine argued that the different structures hold different implications for evaluation of and behavior toward stereotyped group members and differentially involve automatic and controlled cognitive processes.

Devine argued that primarily due to common socialization experiences (Ehrlich, 1973; Brigham, 1972; Proshansky, 1966; Katz, 1976) high and low prejudice persons are equally knowledgeable of the cultural stereotype of Blacks. Second, because the stereotype has been frequently activated in the past, it is a well learned set of associations (Dovidio, Evans, & Tyler, 1986; Reeder & Brewer, 1979) that are *automatically* activated in the presence of Blacks (or some symbolic equivalent). The model holds that this un-intentional activation is equally strong and equally *inescapable* for high and low prejudice persons (it has become a habit of sorts).

A major assumption of the model is that high and low prejudice persons have different personal beliefs about Blacks. Whereas high prejudice persons are likely to have beliefs that overlap substantially with the cultural stereotype, low prejudice persons experience a conflict between the content of the automatically activated stereotype and their personal beliefs. The cultural stereotype, which denies individuality of Blacks by ascribing characteristics to the group and assumes their inferiority to Whites, conflicts with their nonprejudiced, egalitarian values. Because stereotypes have a longer history (and thus greater frequency) of activation than newly acquired personal beliefs (Higgins & King, 1981), overt nonprejudiced responses require the intentional inhibition of the automatically activated stereotype and therefore involve controlled processes.

This analysis suggests that whereas stereotypes are automatically activated, activation of personal beliefs requires conscious attention. In addition, nonprejudiced responses require both the inhibition of the automatic stereotype activation and the intentional activation of nonprejudiced ideas[2] (see Higgins & King for a similar analysis concerning gender stereotypes). This should not be surprising if an individual must overcome a lifetime of socialization experiences. This model implies, interestingly, that if a stereotype is automatically activated in the presence of Blacks and those who reject the cultural stereotype do not, or perhaps cannot, consciously monitor this activation, then information activated in the stereotype could influence subsequent processing. The implications of such processing may be serious particularly when the content of the stereotype is primarily negative, as is the case with the Black stereotype. A particular strength of the model, then, is that it suggests how knowledge of a stereotype can influence perception and behavior even for those who do not endorse the stereotype and/or have *changed* their beliefs about the stereotyped group.

---

[2]We make reference to nonprejudiced ideas here rather than beliefs because it is possible for both high and low prejudice persons to produce nonprejudiced responses. Both high and low prejudice persons are likely to have knowledge of nonprejudiced ideas, but they differ in their endorsement of those ideas and their willingness to act based on nonprejudiced ideas.

Automatic Stereotype Activation and Prejudice

The model suggests that "inevitability of prejudice" arguments may follow from tasks that are likely to engage automatic processes. According to the model, automatic processes are those on which high and low prejudice persons are presumed not to differ. Allport (1954) suggested, for example, that "an ethnic label arouses a stereotype which in turn leads to rejective behavior" (p. 333). His writing implied that activation of the stereotype was automatic and included no discussion of possible differences between those high and low in prejudice regarding stereotype activation.

Duncan (1976) provided indirect support for this analysis. Duncan had White subjects view a videotape of an ambiguously hostile exchange between a White actor and a Black actor and then asked subjects to evaluate the hostileness of the actor's behavior. Duncan found that White subjects interpreted the same ambiguous shove as hostile or violent when the actor was Black and as playing around or dramatizing when the actor was White. Duncan interpreted this stereotype congruent interpretation of the Black's ambiguous behavior as a reflection of Whites negative attitudes toward Blacks. He argued that the presence of the Black actor automatically primed the stereotypes of Blacks and because the stereotype associates Blacks with violence, the concept of violence was more accessible when viewing a Black compared to a White actor. Sager and Schofield (1980) replicated this finding with both Black and White children as subjects. In neither of these studies, however, was the prejudice level of subjects assessed.

Devine (in press, Study 2) provides more direct support for the automatic stereotype activation and examines these processes in both high and low prejudice persons. The study directly explored the possibility that stereotypes can be automatically activated in perceivers' memories and can affect subsequent information processing. Specifically, interest focused on the effects of automatic racial stereotype activation on the interpretation of ambiguous stereotype-related behaviors engaged in by a race-unspecified target person. The target person in this study engages in ambiguously hostile behaviors. Evaluation of ambiguously hostile behaviors was of interest because the assumption that Blacks are hostile is part of the racial stereotype (Brigham, 1971; Boyton, 1941; Devine, in press, Study 1) and has been assumed to play an important role in research on subjects' evaluations of and behaviors toward Blacks (Donnerstein & Donnerstein, 1972; Donnerstein, Donnerstein, Simon, & Ditrichs, 1972; Duncan, 1976; Sager & Schofield, 1980).

The study follows in the logic of several previous studies that have found that increasing the temporary accessibility of trait categories in memory (e.g., through priming) influences subsequent evaluations of target persons who perform ambiguous trait-relevant behaviors. These findings have been reported with conscious processing of the primes (Carver, Ganellin, Froming, & Chambers, 1983; Higgins, Rholes, & Jones, 1977; Srull & Wyer, 1979;

1980) and priming that is nonconscious (i.e., automatic or without aware-ness of the primes). For example, to prevent subjects from having conscious access to their priming stimuli, Bargh and Pietromonaco (1982) presented primes to subjects parafoveal visual field (i.e., outside the fovea). In addi-tion, the primes were presented very rapidly and were followed im-mediately by a mask (i.e., a series of jumbled letters). Using these automatic priming procedures, Bargh and Pietromonaco (1982) found that priming increased the likelihood that the primed category would be used to in-terpret the subsequently presented ambiguous information even though subjects were not consciously aware of the content of the primes. Subjects in this study could not recall or recognize the primes.

Using the automatic priming task developed by Bargh and Pietromonaco (1982), Devine (in press) presented both high and low prejudiced subjects with either a low level (20% of a 100 word list) or a high level (80% of a 100 word list) of stereotype priming. The primes were selected based on their degree of association with the racial stereotype and included labels for the racial category (e.g., Blacks, Negroes) and stereotypic associates (e.g., afro, lazy, musical, athletic, poor, etc.). Subjects then participated in an ostensibly unrelated impression formation task in which they read a 12-sentence paragraph describing a race-unspecified target person's ambigu-ously hostile behaviors.

The paragraph is the now familiar "Donald" paragraph developed by Srull and Wyer (1979; 1980; see also Bargh & Pietromonaco, 1982 and Carver et al., 1983). The paragraph portrays Donald engaging in a series of empirically established ambiguously hostile behaviors such as demanding his money back immediately after a purchase and refusing to pay his rent until his apartment is repainted. Subjects then evaluated Donald on a series of 11-point (not at all to extremely) trait dimensions related to hostility (e.g., hostile, dislikeable, kind, etc.) and a series of trait dimensions unrelated to hostility (e.g., boring, narrow-minded, intelligent, etc.). Positively valenced scales were reverse scored so that more extreme scores reflected more extreme hostility ratings.

Subjects were separated into high and low prejudice groups based on a median split of responses to McConahay, Hardee, and Batts' (1981) Modern Racism Scale.[3] The judgment data suggested that ratings of the target's

---

[3]The validity of the Modern Racism scale as a measure of prejudice is difficult to establish with automatic processing tasks on which high and low prejudice subjects are expected to perform similarly. However, McConahay and his colleagues (McConahay et al., 1981; McCona-hay, 1986; Sears & McConahay, 1973) and Sears and Kinder (1971; Kinder & Sears, 1981) found that scores o the Modern Racism Scale have been useful predictors of such things as respondents' voting patterns and their reactions to bussing. In addition, Devine (in press, Study 3), which is reviewed later in this chapter, found that different scores on the Modern Racism Scale were associated with types of thoughts subjects listed about Blacks. This thought listing task involves controlled processes.

hostility were more extreme (i.e., indicated more hostility) in the high (M = 7.52) than the low (M = 6.87) priming condition. The hostility-unrelated scales, however, were unaffected by priming (Ms = 6.00 and 5.89 in the high and low prime conditions respectively). This pattern of ratings suggested that, overall, the target person was not simply rated as more negative following high than low priming. In addition, and very importantly for the model, the prime X scale relatedness interaction was not affected by subjects' prejudice level. Thus, in line with the model, the findings of this study suggest that when subjects' ability to monitor consciously stereotyped activation was precluded, both high and low prejudice subjects produced stereotype-congruent or prejudice-like responses. The effects of automatic stereotype activation appeared to be equally strong and inescapable for high and low prejudice subjects.

Up to this point, emphasis was focused on activation of stereotype content and its implications for judgments. Recent research (Devine, 1987) has begun to explore the *automatic affective* processing effects associated with racial category priming. Attitudes toward Blacks have historically been characterized as involving intense negative affect in the form of dislike, hatred, or hostility (Ackerman & Jahoda, 1950; Allport, 1954; Ashmore, 1970; Kelman & Pettigrew, 1959). Allport (1954) suggested, for example, that a category such as a racial group category "saturates all that it contains with the same ideational and emotional flavor" (p. 21). If this is the case, priming of the racial category could likely prime negative affect that is associated with the category (see also Fiske & Pavelchak, 1986).

Fazio, Powell, and Herr (1983) demonstrated that increasing the accessibility of positive or negative evaluations associated with attitude objects influenced subjects' interpretations of a target person's ambiguous behaviors in a evaluatively congruent direction. Greenwald, Klinger, and Liu (in press) presented subjects with an evaluative priming task in which subjects were to judge whether target words were evaluatively positive or negative. Primes were evaluatively negative (e.g., evil), positive (e.g., candy), or neutral (e.g., house); targets were evaluatively positive or negative. Greenwald and his colleagues found that when there was evaluative congruence between the primes and targets (e.g., evil-dagger; candy-rainbow) judgments about the targets were facilitated (i.e., reaction times were faster compared to a neutral prime control). Evaluative incongruence between the primes and targets (e.g., evil-rainbow) inhibited judgments about the targets (i.e., reaction times were slower compared to a neutral prime controls). These studies suggest that increasing the accessibility of an evaluation associated with an attitude object or word can influence subsequent processing of information.

Devine (1987) reported preliminary support for the hypothesis that the racial category "Blacks" functions as an evaluatively negative prime for both high and low prejudice subjects. Using an evaluative priming similar to that used by Greenwald, Klinger, and Liu (in press), the racial category "Blacks" was presented as a prime and reaction times for judgments about evaluatively positive and negative targets were examined. The effectiveness of Blacks as a prime was compared to negative, positive, and neutral primes. The negative, positive, and neutral primes replicated the findings of Greenwald and his colleagues (in press). However, when the interval between the prime and the target was brief (i.e., 250 m/s), the prime "Blacks" produced facilitation for the evaluatively negative targets ($M = 627.33$) and inhibition for the evaluatively positive targets ($M = 667.30$). The pattern was identical to the negative prime condition and was observed for subjects who scored high and low on the Modern Racism Scale. When the duration between the prime and target was longer (i.e., 2000 m/s) the pattern replicated the brief interval condition for evaluatively negative (and positive) primes, but was reversed for when Blacks was the prime. That is, at the long duration, with Blacks as the prime subjects responded more quickly to positive ($M = 627.29$) than to negative ($M = 651.59$). This difference in response times was much greater for high prejudice subjects (M pos. targets $= 625.53$; M neg. targets $= 664.29$) than for low prejudice subjects (M pos. targets $= 629.04$; $M = 638.90$).

The findings at brief prime-target intervals suggest that there is evaluative congruence for Blacks as a prime and negative targets and incongruence for Blacks with positive targets. Increasing the temporary accessibility of the racial category activated negative affect that influenced speed of responding to subsequently presented evaluative words. At longer delays when conscious processes could be involved in judgments the evaluative congruence effect is eliminated. It may be that, for whatever reason, subjects hesitate when judging the negative words following Blacks as a prime. Examination of these reasons may provide some insight into the *strategies* subjects use in consciously controlled tasks.

The findings of the studies summarized suggests that both high and low prejudice subjects have cognitive structures that can support prejudiced responses (i.e., stereotypes and negative affect associated with the racial category). These automatic processing responses are in line with Crosby, Bromley, and Saxe's (1980) conclusions that we cannot escape prejudice. However, it may be inappropriate to interpret these findings as an indication that all people are prejudiced. In the next section, tasks that involve the more consciously directed, more flexible controlled processes are examined.

Controlled Processes and the Inhibition of Prejudice

It could be argued, for example, that automatic processing tasks do not allow for the possibility of nonprejudiced responses and that to examine nonprejudice one must consider responses at the level of intentional, controlled processes. That is, when the racial category is activated subjects' ability to consciously monitor this activation is bypassed, their responses reflect the activation of cognitive structures with a longer history (i.e., greater frequency) of activation. As previously summarized, it appears that these structures are the culturally defined stereotypes (Higgins & King, 1981) that are part of our social heritage rather than necessarily part of subjects' personal beliefs.

The knowledge/endorsement distinction takes on particular importance at this point. People have knowledge of a lot of information that they may not endorse. Feminists are likely to be knowledgeable of the stereotype of women. Likewise, Blacks, Jews, and Gays may have knowledge of the Black, Jewish, and Gay stereotypes. In none of these cases does knowledge of the stereotype imply endorsement or acceptance of it. Pratkanis' model (chap. 4 in this volume) suggests that these groups might have bipolar schematic representations of their own group. It is likely that members of these groups will be motivated to reject the stereotype corresponding to their group. In each of these cases, however, the present analysis suggests that it is likely that the stereotype can be intentionally or automatically activated in memory. The case of gender stereotypes is particularly interesting because, as with Blacks, views about women and their role in society has changed dramatically over the last 30 years. Although nonchauvinist values are endorsed by many, the traditional stereotype still exerts some influence on judgments and evaluations (Higgins & King, 1981; Smith & Branscombe, 1985).

It appears that changes at the conscious level do not easily overcome or replace our lifetime of socialization experiences. This point is well summarized in a recent quote by Thomas Pettigrew in the *New York Times* (May 12,1987): "Many southerners have confessed to me, for instance, that even though in their minds they no longer feel prejudice against blacks, they still feel squeamish when they shake hands with a black. These feelings are left over from what they learned in their families as children" (p. 20). The affect experienced is not something that we can necessarily prevent, but it is something that we can *decide* is an inappropriate basis for action. This would require controlled inhibition of such tendencies.

Devine (in press) suggested that one of the features that differentiates high from low prejudice persons is the effort they will put into such inhibition processes. That is, when their nonprejudiced identity is threatened, low prejudice persons are motivated to reaffirm their nonprejudiced self-concepts (Dutton, 1976; Dutton & Lake, 1973). When the conflict between their nonprejudiced personal beliefs and the stereotype of Blacks is made salient, low prejudiced persons are likely to resolve the conflict by denouncing the stereotype and expressing their egalitarian, nonprejudiced ideas. To express stereotype-congruent thoughts would be inconsistent with, and perhaps threaten, their nonprejudiced identities.

Devine (in press, Study 3) tested this hypothesis by asking high and low prejudice subjects to list their thoughts (any and all thoughts) about the racial group "Blacks" under anonymous conditions. This task, it was argued, was likely to make the stereotype/belief conflict salient for low prejudice subjects. Subjects were again assigned to the high prejudice and low prejudice conditions based on a median split of scores on the Modern Racism Scale. Consistent with expectations from the model, the data suggested that high and low prejudice subjects are willing to report very different thoughts about Blacks. Overall, low prejudiced subjects wrote very few pejorative thoughts. They appeared reluctant to ascribe stereotypic traits to the group as a whole. Interestingly, many of their thoughts reflected knowledge of the stereotype through negation of it. A predominant theme in low prejudice subjects' protocols was the equality of the races. In contrast, high prejudice subjects' protocols contained primarily negative thoughts and these subjects seemed to be quite willing to ascribe stereotypic traits (particularly negative traits) to the group. High prejudice subjects' thoughts were much more consistent with the cultural stereotype of Blacks.

Thus, even under anonymous conditions, low prejudice subjects apparently inhibited (Neely, 1977) negative stereotype congruent information (which was automatically activated) and deliberately reported thoughts that reflect their nonprejudiced values. These findings suggest that prejudice need not be an inevitable consequence of ordinary thought processes. That is, although stereotypes exist and can influence responses of both high and low prejudice subjects, particularly when those responses are not subject to close conscious scrutiny, there are individuals who actively reject the negative stereotype and make efforts to respond in nonprejudiced ways. And these efforts appear to be more than merely attempts at self-presentation. If impression management had been a primary concern for subjects in the thought listing task, then high prejudice subjects would also have been likely to inhibit stereotype-congruent thoughts. The present framework, with its emphasis on the possible dissociation of automatic and controlled processes, *allows for the possibility* that those who report being low in prejudice are actually low in prejudice (see Billig, 1985, for a relevant discussion).

Escaping Prejudice: Breaking a Bad Habit

The preceding analysis suggests that a change in one's beliefs or attitude toward a stereotyped group may or may not be reflected in change in corresponding evaluations of or behaviors toward members of that group. The automatically activated stereotype-congruent or prejudice-like responses have become autonomous of one's current attitudes or beliefs. Crosby, Bromley, & Saxe (1980) argued that the inconsistency sometimes observed between expressed attitudes and behaviors that are less consciously mediated is evidence that (all) White Americans are prejudiced against Blacks and that nonprejudiced responses are simply impression management effects (i.e., efforts to cover up truly believed but socially undesirable attitudes) (see also Baxter, 1973; Gaertner, 1976; Gaertner & Dovidio, 1977; Linn, 1965; Weitz, 1972). They argued that nonconsciously monitored responses are more trustworthy than are consciously mediated responses.

In the context of the dissociation model of prejudice, we disagree fundamentally with this premise. Such an argument denies the possibility for change in one's attitudes and beliefs and we view this as a severe limitation of the Crosby, Bromley, and Saxe analysis. Crosby and her colleagues seem to identify the flexibility of controlled processes as a limitation. In contrast, the present framework considers such processes as the key to escaping prejudice. This statement does not imply that change is likely to be easy or speedy (and it is certainly not all or nothing). Nonprejudiced responses are, according to the dissociation model, argued to be a function of intentional, controlled processes and require a conscious decision to behave in a nonprejudiced fashion. In addition, new responses must be learned and well practiced before they could serve as competitive responses to automatically activated stereotype-congruent response.

Thus, in contrast to Crosby, Bromley, and Saxe's pessimistic analysis, the present framework suggests that rather than all people being prejudiced, all are victims of being limited capacity processors. Perceivers cannot attend to all aspects of a situation or their behavior. In situations in which controlled processes are precluded or interfered with, automatic processing effects may exert the greatest influence on responses. In the context of racial stereotype and attitudes, automatic processing effects appear to have negative implications (Devine, in press, 1987).

We have likened behaving in nonprejudiced ways to the breaking of a bad habit. Automatic stereotype activation functions much like a bad habit. Its consequences are spontaneous and undesirable (at least for the low prejudice person). That is, for those who have integrated egalitarian ideals into their value system a conflict would exist between these ideals and expressions of racial prejudice. The conflict experienced is likely to be involved in the initiation of controlled stereotype inhibiting processes that are required to eliminate the habitual response (activation). Ronis, Yates, and Kirscht (chap. 9 in this volume) argue that elimination of a bad habit requires essentially the same steps as the formation of a habit. The individual must (a) initially decide to stop the old behavior, (b) must remember the resolution, and (c) must try repeatedly and decide repeatedly to eliminate the habit before the habit can be eliminated. In addition, the individual must develop a new cognitive (attitudinal and belief) structure that is consistent with the newly determined pattern of responses.

An important assumption to keep in mind in the change process, however, is that neither the formation of an attitude from beliefs nor the formation of a decision from attitudes or beliefs entails the elimination of earlier established attitudinal or stereotype representation. The dissociation model holds that although low prejudice persons have changed their beliefs concerning stereotyped group members, the stereotype has not been eliminated from the memory system. In fact, it remains a well-organized, frequently activated knowledge structure. During the change process the new pattern of ideas and behaviors must be consciously activated and serve as the basis for responses, or the individual is likely to "fall into old habits" (e.g., stereotype-congruent or prejudice-like responses).

We expect that the change process involves developing associations between the stereotype structure and the personal belief structure. For change to be successful, each time the stereotype is activated the person must activate and think about his or her personal beliefs. That is, the individual must increase the frequency with which the personal belief structure is activated when responding to members of the stereotyped group. To the extent that the personal belief structure becomes increasingly accessible, it will better provide a rival response to the responses that would likely follow from automatic stereotype activation. In cognitive terms, before the newer beliefs and attitudes can serve a knowledge function consistent with value expressive function of the recently adopted attitude, the strong association between the previously learned negative attitude and Blacks will have to be weakened and the association of Blacks to the new nonprejudiced attitudes and beliefs will have to be made stronger and conscious.

In summary, at minimum, the attitude and belief change process requires intention, attention, and time. During the change process an individual must not only inhibit automatically activated information, but also intentionally replace such activation with nonprejudiced ideas and responses. It is likely that these factors contribute to the difficulty of changing one's responses to members of stereotyped groups. In addition, these factors probably contribute to the often observed inconsistency between expressed attitudes and behavior. The nonprejudiced responses take time, attention, and effort. To the extent that any (or all) of these are limited, the outcome is likely to be stereotype-congruent or prejudice-like responses.

Other Contemporary Models of Prejudice

It is useful at this point to compare the present theoretical framework with other contemporary models of prejudice. All of the models suggest that the current state of attitudes toward Blacks in contemporary American society are complex and difficult to assess. However, whereas the present theoretical framework explores the cognitive and, to a minimal extent, motivational[4] processes involved in prejudice and nonprejudice, most of the other models place greatest emphasis on prejudice.

For example, Gaertner and Dovidio (1986) are primarily interested in exploring the dynamics of what they call the aversive racist (see also Gaertner, 1976; Kovel, 1970). Gaertner and Dovidio use the term *aversive racism* to characterize White Americans who possess strong egalitarian values but covert antiBlack attitudes and beliefs (e.g., the ambivalence of political liberals). Aversive racism is contrasted with the dominative or old-fashioned form of racism (Kovel, 1970). Dominative racists are characterized by red-neck bigotry. Gaertner and Dovidio (1986) suggested that aversive racists cling desperately to their egalitarian values and keep their negative feelings toward Blacks from awareness. They further suggested that aversive racists will repudiate their negative attitudes when they are made salient, but that these negative attitudes are expressed in subtle forms.

What is striking about Gaertner and Dovidio's (1986) analysis is that the focus of their analysis is on the *racist,* whether of the dominative or aversive variety. They suggest, however, that they do believe that White Americans are hypocritical as Crosby and her colleagues (1980) suggested, but rather that "they are victims of cultural forces and cognitive processes that continue to promote prejudice and racism" (Gaertner & Dovidio, 1986, p. 85). Although their analysis is not completely inconsistent with the present theoretical framework and the possibility of aversive racism is not disputed, Gaertner and Dovidio did not consider the possibility of escaping prejudice. Because aversive racists do not recognize their negative feelings, the presence of *racism* is simply relegated to a more subtle, and they argue a more, insidious form. However, there are those who recognize that they previously had negative beliefs and attitudes and have *decided* that those beliefs are no longer functional. There is no room for this type of person in the framework of aversive versus dominative racism.

This conception of the shift in attitudes from overt bigotry to more subtle forms of racism is similar to McConahay's (1986; Kinder & Sears, 1981; McConahay, Hardee, and Batts, 1981; McConahay & Hough, 1976; Sears & Kinder, 1971) concept of *Modern Racism*. McConahay suggested that, in contrast to old-fashioned racists, modern racists reject traditional racist beliefs and displace their antiBlack feelings onto more abstract social or political issues. AntiBlack reactions to issues such as bussing or affirmative action can easily be rationalized and therefore not considered to reflect prejudice. McConahay's *Modern Racism Scale* is intended to measure this

---

[4]When one considers the functions that different attitudes serve for the individual, motivations become very important. Exploring the motivational influences of prejudice reduction in the context of the dissociation model of prejudice is a high priority for future research.

more subtle form of racism. Scores on the *Modern Racism Scale,* however, correlate positively with scores on the *Old Fashioned Racism Scale* and thus its utility as a less reactive measure of racism has been called into question. It should be noted that whether or not the *Modern Racism Scale* serves as a nonreactive measure of prejudice, the scale has been useful in differentiating between high and low prejudice persons (see McConahay, 1986, for a review; Devine, in press). As was the case with aversive racism, the emphasis is on the *racist.* In addition, the research program focuses primarily on measurement issues.

Katz (1981; Katz & Glass, 1979; Katz, Hass, & Wackenhut, 1986) proposed that White Americans' ambivalence toward Blacks is a consequence of simultaneously possessing both positive and negative tendencies toward Blacks. That is, the ambivalent person possesses conflicting beliefs (i.e., endorsements) about Blacks. Ambivalence is "assumed to create in the person a high vulnerability to emotional tension in situations of contact with socially stigmatized individuals or cues associated with such persons" (Katz, Hass, & Wackenhut, 1986, p. 45). As a result, depending on the nature of the contact with stigmatized others, people who experience ambivalence have polarized or amplified positive or negative responses than those who do not experience ambivalence or have conflicting feelings. Thus, the responses of those experiencing ambivalence will likely be unstable. Katz and his colleagues (1986) summarized work directed at developing a scale to measure individual differences in ambivalence. In contrast to the approaches of Gaertner and Dovidio (1986) and McConahay (1986), Katz, Hass, and Wackenhut (1986) did not focus on racists, but on those who are truly conflicted about their feelings and beliefs toward Blacks.

The dissociation model makes some fundamentally different assumptions about the origins of prejudiced responses than the summarized models. For example, whereas the ambivalence-amplification model places emphasis on the conflict between beliefs, the dissociation model emphasized the distinction between stereotypes (knowledge) and beliefs (endorsement). The dissociation model also emphasized the importance of exploring the nature of nonprejudice and makes the study of nonprejudice possible. The specific strengths of the dissociation model are that (a) it is less value laden than the other models and (b) it specifies the cognitive underpinnings of previously observed prejudice findings. This latter point is especially important when one begins to design prejudice reduction techniques. Before successful change techniques can be devised, one must understand the cognitive mechanisms that may help to maintain prejudice.

None of the alternative models summarized deal adequately with the structure or functioning of attitudes toward racial groups. The process approach of the dissociation model (Devine, in press) considers aspects of structure and function to be crucial components of an analysis of prejudice and nonprejudice. The model's emphasis on process issues allows predictions to be made concerning the type of structure involved in responding to members of a stereotyped group and the conditions prejudiced and nonprejudiced responses are likely to be observed. The distinction between automatic and controlled processes involved in stereotypes and prejudice provides a framework for developing a model of nonprejudice. Prejudice reduction apparently requires a change in the functionality of prejudiced attitudes. When expressions of prejudice become dysfunctional, the individual becomes motivated to inhibit the expression of prejudice (break the bad habit) and respond in nonprejudiced ways.

Learning of prejudiced attitudes and negative stereotypes is assumed to have occurred through a long socialization process. It is not expected that changes in such well-learned responses will occur quickly and without effort. In fact, changing of prejudiced attitudes would apparently be a very difficult thing to do. There is a strong association between the racial category Blacks and the racial stereotype making the stereotype and its corresponding negative affect highly accessible in the presence of representatives of the racial group. Fazio (chap. 7 in this volume) suggests that modifying highly accessible attitudes is likely to be difficult. What is needed is an analysis of the conditions that make individuals want to change their attitudes. Successful prejudice reduction will depend on developing interventions that will weaken the association between the attitude object (i.e., the racial group and its members) and the cognitive structure that support prejudiced responses (i.e., stereotypes and negative affect) and strengthen the association between the attitude objects and cognitive structures that are inconsistent with prejudice (i.e., nonprejudiced personal beliefs).

BEYOND STEREOTYPES AND PERSONAL BELIEFS: THE ROLE OF SITUATIONAL FACTORS

Many theorists have been puzzled over the apparent shift in racial attitudes in a positive direction and continued manifestations of prejudice in some behaviors (e.g., Campbell, 1963; Poskocil, 1977; Crosby, Bromley, & Saxe, 1980; Katz & Glass, 1979; Gaertner & Dovidio, 1986). The present analysis suggests, however, that it is not sufficient to know whether a person views him or herself as prejudiced or nonprejudiced. Because automatic and controlled processes can be dissociated, and can operate independently of each other, it is argued that models of prejudice must include an analysis of the situations in which intergroup evaluations and behaviors are measured. That is, some situations may engage controlled processes, whereas others place demands on the individual's processing capacity and interfere with controlled, but not automatic, processing effects. According to the model, nonprejudiced responses follow from controlled, stereotype/negative affect inhibiting processes.

The theorists who prefer nonconsciously monitored behaviors as indicators of prejudice have not provided a rationale that is grounded in theory. Although such findings suggest that there is differential treatment based on group membership, the current model based on the cognitive structures and processes involved in responding to members of a stereotyped group, suggests that it may be misleading to characterize these responses as reflecting the hostility and hatred of Blacks that is so common in definitions of prejudice. To do so makes a conception of prejudice reduction exceedingly difficult. Allport (1954) wrote that "prejudgments become prejudices only if they are not reversible when exposed to new information" (p. 9). On tasks that involve controlled, consciously monitored processes, there are people who have reversed their previously held beliefs and are making efforts to behave in nonprejudiced ways. This should be viewed as an encouraging sign not one to be continuously held suspect as an impression formation tactic.

It should also be noted that factors other than the stereotype or personal beliefs could influence reactions to members of a stereotyped group. Fazio (1986) pointed out that situations often contain variables other than attitudes, such as normative expectations (Ajzen & Fishbein, 1980; Ajzen, 1982), that could compete with attitudes to influence behavior. The impact of such variables must be carefully considered if we are to understand the unique role of attitudes (or stereotypes) in behavior. To the extent that controlled processes are activated, the person can take into consideration all the situational and interpersonal factors that could influence behavior in addition to one's personal attitude. In fact, Ronis, Yates, and Kirscht (chap. 9 in this volume) argue that once behavior is in the controlled decision phase, the person may engage in a comparison process for all the alternative patterns of behavior available to him or her. A person may have a positive attitude toward a behavior but see negative consequences associated with it and therefore avoid the behavior. This situation would likely create a discrepancy between the person's expressed attitude toward the object and his or her behavior toward the object.

This type of situation is well exemplified in a study by Warner and DeFleur (1969). They suggested that "such interactional concepts such as norms roles, group memberships, reference groups, subcultures, etc., pose *contingent* conditions which can modify the relationship between attitudes and action" (p. 154, emphasis in the original). They examined a variable they called *social constraint.* Social contraint is introduced when the individual's behavior is likely to be known to others whose opinions and reactions are important to the individual. Social constraint can vary from high to low depending on who is likely to become privy to the individual's behavior. High social constraint imposed by the presence of important significant others "exerts pressure to act in accordance with what those others are perceived to feel as appropriate and desirable conduct" Warner & DeFleur, 1969, p. 155).

Subjects in Warner and DeFleur's study were identified as high or low in prejudice based on their responses to a 16-item Likert scale concerning their beliefs about and behaviors toward Blacks (e.g., Negroes do not make good workers because they are lazy; I would not be willing to invite Negroes to a dinner party at my home). In Warner and DeFleur's (1969) study the behaviors requested of subjects ranged from dating a Black student to making an anonymous contribution to a Black educational fund. At the time this study was done, Warner and DeFleur argued that the normative environment was hostile toward integration. Warner and De-Fleur suggested that under certain conditions norms can exert a more powerful influence on behavior than personal attitudes. They expected that favorable responses towards Blacks would be normatively disapproved of and therefore avoided under conditions of high social constraint. Their findings strongly confirmed their expectations.

Under conditions of low social constraint (e.g., responses were anonymous), there was a fair amount of correspondence between expressed attitudes and responses to the behavioral requests for the low prejudiced subjects. Under conditions of high social constraint (e.g., significant others were privy to subjects' responses), however, there was inconsistency between the attitudes and behaviors of the least prejudiced subjects. For the most prejudiced subjects, the greatest consistency between attitudes and behavior was observed in the high social constraint condition. In this condition, social constraint and the initial negative attitude combined to produce attitude-behavior consistency.

The power of normative influences should not be underestimated. Linn (1965) suggested that when two norms are in conflict, behavior will be determined by the stronger norm (the norm that is more accessible). In Linn's (1965) study, subjects were asked to pose with a Black person of the opposite sex for a photograph. Subjects' expressed degree of willingness to have the photograph taken did not correspond with overt behavior. Linn suggested that subjects' nonprejudiced attitudes conflicted with a stronger social norm of avoiding personal involvement with Blacks (see also DeFleur & Westie, 1958). Expected negative evaluation from reference groups was presumed to more strongly influence behavior than personal attitudes in these settings. Silverman (1974) found that subjects' perceptions of the reactions of reference groups affected their willingness to choose a Black person as a college roommate. Silverman measured subjects' attitudes toward Blacks and their perceptions of various significant others (e.g., parents, best friends, fellow students) reactions to their having a Black roommate. Silverman reported that subjects expected that these significant others would withhold rewards if they chose roommates in a nondiscriminatory manner. The findings of the study revealed that regardless of subjects' prejudice level, they chose White roommates.

Each of these studies suggested that there was considerable social pressure toward racial discrimination. The important point to note here is that behavior does not occur in a vacuum and that there are consequences associated with any path of action. Although one may harbor no specific prejudices against Blacks, if a behavior is likely to lead to social rejection in all (or many) other domains of social experience, he or she may not choose to behave in accordance with his or her attitudes. Interestingly, times have changed and current normative expectations favor racial equality and nondiscrimination. The individual can expect negative social sanctions for expression of prejudice or discrimination. In fact, these nondiscriminatory norms may work in the favor of nonprejudice. That is, because discriminatory behaviors are currently viewed as socially unacceptable, neither low nor high prejudice subjects are likely to behave in blatantly prejudiced ways when their behavior is public.

Furthermore, it has been demonstrated that perceived reference group support not only plays a role in determining one's attitudes (Allport, 1954; Fendrich, 1968), but also in the attitude change process (Eddy, 1964; Mann, 1960; Pearlin, 1954; Sims & Patrick, 1936; Watson, 1950). For example, Pearlin (1954) studied the attitudes of southern students attending a northern integrated university at which the prejudiced attitudes were not normative. Pearlin (1954) found that the change in environment (i.e., mere exposure to nonprejudiced values) was not enough to produce attitude change in the southern students. Change depended on students developing strong attachment to their new references groups (e.g., college professors, new friends) and decreasing their attachments to old reference groups (e.g., parents, high school friends). Those who did not change their reference groups did not change their attitudes. It is possible that the new reference group members served as reminders to subjects' newer attitudes—making these ideas consciously accessible and increasing subjects' efforts to inhibit the stereotype.

One of the things that these studies suggest is that attitude or belief change must be functional before it will occur. In the terminology of classical functional theories of attitudes, such attitude change serves a utilitarian (Katz, 1960) or social adjustment (Smith, Bruner, & White, 1956) function. Attitude change appeared to be primarily in the service of maximizing social reward and avoiding social rejection. It is possible, however, that such changes serve the value expressive function. That is, students may have come to believe that their previously held negative attitudes were inappropriate and integrated the nonprejudiced ideas and attitudes into their value system. There is no way to tell from these studies.

The research on normative prescriptions and their influence on behavior suggests that the model proposed by Devine (in press) needs to be expanded to include individuals' cognitive representation of cultural norms and expectations. Although, it is likely that the personal beliefs of low prejudice persons would show more overlap with current normative prescriptions than would the beliefs of high prejudice persons, both are likely to have the norms stored in memory. If these structures are differentially activated they could exert independent influences on behavior.

For example, creating conditions of private self-awareness should lead to behavior that reflects subjects' private belief systems (Froming, Walker, & Lopyan, 1982). Under conditions of private self-awareness, high prejudice subjects' behavior should manifest prejudice whereas low prejudice subjects' behavior should not. In contrast, under conditions that produce public self-awareness the behavior of both high and low prejudice subjects should be consistent with what subjects believe are society's expectations regarding the appropriateness of prejudiced behavior (Froming, Walker, & Lopyan, 1982). Because contemporary society tends to value egalitarian behavior (see Dovidio & Gaertner, 1986, for a review) and fair treatment regardless of race, all subjects should respond in nonprejudice ways. Interestingly, this is a situation in which high and low prejudice subjects would respond in similar ways, but, in contrast to the automatic processing effects, responses would reflect low rather than high prejudice.

CONCLUSIONS

The emphasis in this volume is on attitude structure and function. Prejudice is a domain rich for the study of structure and function. Structure in the area of prejudice has typically been conceptualized as the stereotype, whereas function has focused on the usefulness of prejudice (or the stereotype) for the individual. Much of the research on prejudice reduction has centered, for example, on strategies to change negative stereotypes (e.g., through education campaigns) or to make an individual's negative attitudes nonfunctional (Carlson, 1956; Culbertson, 1957; Peak & Morrison, 1958).

In the study of prejudice, there has been insufficient theoretical development to allow clear exposition of the structure and function issues nor the relations between stereotypes and prejudice. The dissociation model proposed allows for a blend of contemporary interest in cognitive processes involved in social behavior with classical issues in study of the functions of attitudes. This blend provided a particularly useful framework for exploring an issue that has always been of interest to social psychologists—the problem of racial prejudice. It is possible that a functional analysis (Katz, 1960; Smith, Bruner, & White, 1956) can aid in the understanding of the conflict low prejudice persons experience between stereotypes and personal beliefs.

The classic work on functional theories of attitudes suggests that attitudes can serve a number of different functions for the individual. For example, attitudes can serve a knowledge (Katz, 1960) or object appraisal (Smith, Bruner, & White, 1956) function. Attitudes that serve this knowledge or object appraisal function considerably reduce the complexity of one's social experience. Such attitudes provide quick guides concerning who and what to avoid or approach. Attitudes can also serve as a vehicle for expressing one's central values. These different functions of attitudes may map on directly to features of the dissociation model automatic-controlled process distinction.

Consider, for example, that Katz (1960) argued that for prejudice, stereotypes served the knowledge function because they "provided order and clarity for a bewildering set of complexities" (p. 175). The dissociation model holds that stereotypes are strongly associated with the racial group whether or not people endorse the stereotype. Fazio (chap. 7 in this volume) suggests that the extent to which an attitude fulfills this function depends on the likelihood that the attitude is activated automatically in memory in the presence of the attitude object. An advantage of accessible attitudes is that they free the individual from the processing demands of reflective thought concerning his or her evaluation of the attitude object. However, it is exactly the automaticity of this knowledge or object appraisal function that sets up the conflict for the low prejudice person. If the stereotype and negative affect are antomatically activated in the presence of Blacks as the attitude objects, it would appear that the strong association of stereotype and negative affect with Blacks would be dysfunctional for the low prejudice person.

When one has changed one's attitudes or decided that the stereotype provides an inappropriate basis for evaluation or action, the knowledge function of the stereotype is in direct conflict with the value expressive function of nonprejudiced attitudes and beliefs. Prejudiced responses would likely represent a threat to the person's integrity. It is this type of conflict that may propel the individual in his or her efforts to "break the habit" and initiate the development of nonprejudiced responses. Resolution of the conflict, according to the dissociation model, would require controlled, intentional stereotype inhibiting processes.

In the study of attitudes, prejudice has always been a topic of concern. Prejudice is interesting for a number of reasons. First, whereas attitudes are typically conceptualized as ranging on evaluative continuum from pro to anti, the emphasis in the study of prejudice is on the anti side of the continuum.[5] In addition, more than any other attitude studied, prejudice typically takes as its object other people based on their group membership. Finally, with its negative orientation (e.g., hatred, hostility) and focus on other people, prejudice has typically been conceptualized as a problem to be solved. This particular focus heightens interest on developing strategies for escaping prejudice.

The clearest previous statement on the factors involved in intergroup prejudice is Gordon Allport's (1954) *The Nature of Prejudice.* This classic book is remarkably comprehensive and contemporary. Allport considers various historical, cultural, economic, personality, and cognitive factors that jointly contribute to the development and maintenance of prejudice. One of Allport's major messages is that prejudice derives from multiple sources and that a narrow focus on any one determinant will necessarily lead to an incomplete understanding of the phenomenon. He further argues, however, that one must consider the implications of the various sources for the ideas and beliefs that become internalized by the individual for it is the individual who feels dislike and practices discrimination. However, it is also the individual that can behave in an egalitarian, nondiscriminatory fashion.

We argue that through exploring these various factors in terms of their implications for the cognitive processes involved in responding to stereotyped group members, we will be in the best position to understand what factors contribute to the development of prejudice, maintenance of prejudice, and (ultimately) reduction of prejudice (see also Stephan, 1985). Whereas previous theorists have placed emphasis primarily on understanding prejudice and racism, it is argued that it may be productive to entertain and systematically explore the possibility that people can escape prejudice. Rather than assuming that nonconsciously monitored responses reflect some more subtle form of racism, the present framework argues for a more neutral interpretation based on the logic that all people are limited capacity processors. That is, the automatic-controlled distinction suggests that when the racial category is automatically accessed from memory it may have effects that are inaccessible to the individual. Thus, even for people who honestly report having no negative prejudices against Blacks, activation of the racial category can have automatic effects that when not consciously monitored produce effects that look like prejudiced responses.

The real challenge at this point is to determine the conditions that lead to

---

[5]This does not suggest that there cannot be positive prejudices, but the empahsis has been on negative prejudices. That is, in the literature prejudice *against* some group is almost always implied. In the present chapter that focus is maintained.

efforts at prejudice reduction in the form of controlled processes. It would appear that change must first occur at that level before changes could occur in the form of automatic processing. We have been talking about prejudice and nonprejudice as though they reflect a simple dichotomy. It is unlikely that this is the case. In fact, many people may be in the *process* of changing their beliefs. Others may not have strong attitudes one way or the other concerning Blacks. In both of these cases, however, the stereotype is likely to be well-integrated into their cognitive systems and will likely influence perception of and behavior toward members of the racial group.

Because not all people are likely to behave in nonprejudiced ways for the same reasons, it might be useful to develop a taxonomy of reasons for nonprejudiced behavior. Exploring reasons for nonprejudice may provide some insight on strategies for reducing prejudice. Several reasons have already been identified. For example, one may behave in a nonprejudiced fashion merely for impression management purposes. It is out of fashion to overtly express prejudice in contemporary American society. No particular change in underlying attitude would be expected to follow from this perspective. Others may express nonprejudiced attitudes for value expressive purposes. That is, they may have truly integrated nonprejudiced attitudes into their value system. Still others may reject prejudice because society devalues prejudice and discrimination. These persons would denounce prejudice because society does. In the long run, both of these reasons could lead to a reduction in prejudice.

One difficulty in the study of prejudice, however, is that it has been variably defined and measured and, as a result, comparisons across studies are often very difficult. In future theoretical and empirical efforts, it will be essential to specifically detail all of the assumptions guiding the measurement of prejudice and what is taken as evidence of prejudice and nonprejudice. The goal of the dissociation model is to gain an understanding of the cognitive underpinnings of responses to stereotyped group members. The focus of the present chapter has been on racial prejudice. We believe that the model is much more general than simply a model of racial stereotypes and beliefs and can easily be applied to other stereotyped groups (e.g., homosexuals, women, Jews, etc). It would also be possible to apply the model to groups about which we might have positive prejudices. But historically, positive biases have not been viewed as *problems* that need attention and intervention.

It is hoped that the present model will challenge us to design effective prejudice reduction interventions. It is argued that a strict emphasis on the nature of prejudice, however will be limiting and that prejudice reduction efforts will be best facilitated by exploring the nature of nonprejudice and the strategies people use to intentionally control and inhibit prejudiced responses.

ACKNOWLEDGMENTS

Preparation of this chapter was supported by a University of Wisconsin Graduate School Grant. The author is grateful to Anthony Pratkanis and Steven Breckler for very useful comments on an earlier draft of this chapter.

REFERENCES

Ackerman, N. W., & Jahoda, M. (1950). *Anti-Semitism and emotional disorder.* New York: Harper & Row.

Adorno, T. W., Frenkel-Brunswik, E., Levinson, D. J., & Sanford, R. N. (1950). *The authoritarian personality.* New York: Harper & Row.

Allport, G. W. (1954). *The nature of prejudice.* Reading, MA: Addison-Wesley.

Ashmore, R. D. (1970). The problem of intergroup prejudice. In B. Collins (Ed.), *Social Psychology* (pp. 246–296). Reading, MA: Addison-Wesley.

Ashmore, R. D., & Del Boca, F. K. (1981). Conceptual approaches to stereotypes and stereotyping. In D. L. Hamilton (Ed.), *Cognitive processes in stereotyping and intergroup behavior.* (pp. 1–35). Hillsdale, NJ: Lawrence Erlbaum Associates.

Ajzen, I. (1982). On behaving in accordance with one's attitudes. In M. P. Zanna, E. T. Higgins, & C. P. Herman (Eds.), *Consistency in social behavior: The Ontario symposium* (Vol. 2, pp. 3–15). Hillsdale, NJ: Lawrence Erlbaum Associates.

Ajzen, I., & Fishbein, M. (1980). *Understanding attitudes and predicting behavior.* Englewood Cliffs, NJ: Prentice-Hall.

Bargh, J. A., & Pietromonaco, P. (1982). Automatic information processing and social perception: The influence of trait information presented outside of conscious awareness on impression formation. *Journal of Personality and Social Psychology, 43,* 437–449.

Baxter, G. W. (1973). Prejudiced liberals? Race and information effects in a two person game. *Journal of Conflict Resolution, 17,* 131–161.

Bettleheim, B., & Janowitz, M. (1964). *Social change and prejudice.* Glencoe, IL: Free Press.

Billig, M. (1985). Prejudice, categorization and particularization: From a perceptual to a rhetorical approach. *European Journal of Social Psychology, 15,* 79–103.

Boyton, J. A. (1941). The racial stereotype of Negro college students. *Journal of Abnormal and Social Psychology, 36,* 97–102.

Brigham, J. C. (1971). Ethnic stereotypes. *Psychological Bulletin, 76,* 15–33.

Brigham, J. C. (1972). Racial stereotypes: Measurement variables and the stereotype-attitude relationship. *Journal of Applied Social Psychology, 2,* 63–76.

Campbell, D. T. (1963). Social attitudes and other acquired behavioral dispositions. In S. Koch (Ed.), *Psychology: A study of a science. Investigations of man as socius: Their place in psychology and the social science* (Vol. 6). New York: McGraw-Hill.

Carlson, E. R. (1956). Attitude change through modification of attitude structure. *Journal of Abnormal and Social Psychology, 52,* 256–261.

Carver, C. S., Ganellin, R. J., Froming, W. J., & Chambers, W. (1983). Modeling: An analysis in terms of category accessibility. *Journal of Experimental Social Psychology, 19,* 403–421.

Crosby, F., Bromley, S., and Saxe, L. (1980). Recent unobtrusive studies of black and white discrimination and prejudice: A literature review. *Psychological Bulletin, 87,* 546–563.

Culbertson, F. M. (1957). Modification of an emotionally held attitude through role playing. *Journal of Abnormal and Social Psychology, 54,* 230–233.

DeFleur, M. L., & Westie, F. R. (1958). Verbal attitudes and overt acts: An experiment on the salience of attitudes. *American Sociological Review, 23,* 667–673.

Devine, P. G. (in press). Stereotypes and prejudice: Their automatic and controlled components. *Journal of Personality and Social Psychology.*

Devine, P. G. (1987). *Automatic affective evaluations in prejudice.* Unpublished manuscript, University of Wisconsin, Madison.

Donnerstein, E., & Donnerstein, M. (1972). White rewarding behavior as a function of the potential for black retaliation. *Journal of Personality and Social Psychology, 24,* 327–333.

Donnerstein, E., Donnerstein, M., Simon, S., & Ditrichs, R. (1972). Variables in interracial aggression: Anonymity, expected retaliation and a riot. *Journal of Personality and Social Psychology, 22,* 236–245.

Dovidio, J. F., Evans, N. E., & Tyler, R. B. (1986). Racial stereotypes: The contents of their cognitive representations. *Journal of Experimental Social Psychology, 22,* 22–37.

Dovidio, J. F., & Gaertner, S. L. (1986). Prejudice, discrimination, and racism: Historical trends and contemporary approaches. In J. F. Dovidio & S. L. Gaertner (Eds.), *Prejudice, discrimination, and racism* (pp. 1–34). New York: Academic Press.

Duncan, B. L. (1976). Differential social perception and attribution of intergroup violence: Testing the lower limits of stereotyping of blacks. *Journal of Personality and Social Psychology, 34,* 590–598.

Dutton, D. G. (1976). Tokenism, reverse discrimination, and egalitarianism in interracial behavior. *Journal of Social Issues, 32,* 93–107.

Dutton, D. G., & Lake, R. (1973). Threat of own prejudice and reverse discrimination in interracial behavior. *Journal of Personality and Social Psychology, 24,* 94–100.

Eddy, E. M. (1964). Attitudes towards desegregation among northern students on a northern campus. *Journal of Social Psychology, 62,* 285–301.

Ehrlich, H. J. (1973). *The Social psychology of prejudice.* New York: Wiley.

Fazio, R. H. (1986). How do attitudes guide behavior? In R. Sorrentino & E. T. Higgins (Eds.), *Handbook of motivation and cognition: Foundations of social behavior* (pp. 204–243). New York: Guilford Press.

Fazio, R. H., Powell, M. C., & Herr, P. M. (1983). Toward a process model of the attitude-behavior relation: Accessing one's attitude upon mere observation of the attitude object. *Journal of Personality and Social Psychology, 44,* 723–735.

Fendrich, J. M. (1968). Perceived reference group support: Racial attitudes and overt behavior. *American Sociological Review, 45,* 960–970.

Fiske, S. T., & Pavelchak, M. A. (1986). Category-based versus Piecemeal-based affective responses: Developments in schema triggered affect. In R. Sorrentino & E. T. Higgins (Eds.), *Handbook of motivation and cognition: Foundations of social behavior* (pp. 167–203). New York: Guilford Press.

Froming, W. J., Walker, R., & Lopyan, K. J. (1982). Public and private self-awareness: When personal attitudes conflict with societal expectation. *Journal of Experimental Social Psychology, 18,* 476–487.

Gaertner, S. L. (1976). Nonreactive measures in racial attitude research: A focus on liberals. In P. A. Katz (Ed.), *Toward the elimination of racism* (pp. 183–211). New York: Pergamon Press.

Gaertner, S. L., & Dovidio, J. F. (1977). The subtlety of white racism, arousal, and helping behavior. *Journal of Personality and Social Psychology, 35,* 691–707.

Gaertner, S. L., & Dovidio, J. F. (1986). The aversive form of racism. In J. F. Dovidio & S. L. Gaertner (Eds.), *Prejudice, discrimination, and racism* (pp. 61–90). New York: Academic Press.

Galanis, C. M. R., & Jones, E. E. (1986). When stigma confronts stigma: Some conditions enhancing a victims tolerance of other victims. *Personality and Social Psychology Bulletin, 12,* 169–177.

Greeley, A. M., & Sheatsley, P. B. (1971). Attitudes toward racial integration. *Scientific American, 222,* 13–19.

Greenwald, A. G., Klinger, M. R., & Liu, T. J. (in press). Unconscious processing of dichoptically masked words. *Memory and Cognition.*

Harding, J., Kutner, B., Proshansky, H., & Chein, I. (1954). Prejudice and ethnic relations. In G. Lindzey (Ed.), *Handbook of social psychology* (Vol. 2). Cambridge, MA: Addison-Wesley.

Harding, J., Proshansky, H., Kutner, B., & Chein, I. (1969). Prejudice and ethnic relations. In G. Lindzey & E. Aronson (Eds.), *Handbook of social psychology* (2nd ed., Vol. 5). Reading, MA: Addison-Wesley.

Higgins, E. T., & King, G. (1981). Accessibility of social constructs: Information-processing consequences of individual and contextual variability. In N. Cantor & J. F. Kihlstrom (Eds.), *Personality and Social Interaction* pp. 69–121. Hillsdale, NJ: Lawrence Erlbaum Associates.

Higgins, E. T., Rholes, W. S., & Jones, C. R. (1977). Category accessibility and impression formation. *Journal of Experimental and Social Psychology, 13,* 141–154.

Karlins, M., Coffman, T. L., & Walters, G. (1969). On the fading of social stereotypes: Studies in three generations of college students. *Journal of Personality and Social Psychology, 13,* 1–16.

Katz, D. (1960). The functional approach to the study of attitudes. *Public Opinion Quarterly, 24,* 163–204.

Katz, D., & Stotland, E. (1959). A preliminary statement of a theory of attitude structure and change. In S. Koch (Ed.), *Psychology: A study of science* (Vol. 3). New York: McGraw-Hill.

Katz, I. (1981). *Stigma: A social psychological analysis.* Hillsdale, NJ: Lawrence Erlbaum Associates.

Katz, I., Hass, R. G., & Wachenhut, J. (1986). Racial ambivalence, value duality, and behavior. In J. F. Dovidio & S. L. Gaertner (Eds.), *Prejudice, discrimination, and racism* (pp. 35–59). New York: Academic Press.

Katz, I., & Glass, D. C. (1979). An ambivalence-amplification theory of behavior toward the stigmatized. In W. Austin & S. Worchel (Eds.), *The social psychology of intergroup relations.* Monterey, CA: Brooks/Cole.

Katz, P. A. (1976). The acquisition of racial attitudes in children. In P. A. Katz (ed.), *Toward the elimination of racism* (pp. 125–154). New York: Pergamon.

Kelman, H. C. & Pettigrew, T. (1959). How to understand prejudice. *Commentary, 28,* 411–436.

Kinder, D. R., & Sears, D. O. (1981). Symbolic racism versus racial threats to "The Good Life." *Journal of Personality and Social Psychology, 40,* 414–431.

Kovel, J. (1970). *White racism: A psychohistory.* New York: Pantheon.

LaViolette, F., & Silvert, K. H. (1951). A theory of stereotypes. *Social Forces, 29,* 237–257.

Linn, L. S. (1965). Verbal attitudes and overt behavior: A study of racial discrimination. *Social Forces, 43,* 353–364.

Logan, G. D., & Cowan, W. B. (1984). On the ability to inhibit thought and action: A theory of an act of control. *Psychological Review, 91,* 295–327.

Mann, J. H. (1960). The differential nature of prejudice reduction. *Journal of Social Psychology, 52,* 339–343.

McConahay, J. B. (1986). Modern racism, ambivalence, and the modern racism scale. In J. F. Dovidio & S. L. Gaertner (Eds.), *Prejudice, discrimination and racism* (pp. 91–125). New York: Academic Press.

McConahay, J. B., Hardee, B. B., & Batts, V. (1981). Has racism declined? It depends upon who's asking and what is asked. *Journal of Conflict Resolution, 25,* 563–579.

McConahay, J. B., & Hough, J. C., Jr. (1976). Symbolic racism. *Journal of Social Issues, 32,* 23–45.

Neely, J. H. (1977). Semantic priming and retrieval from lexical memory: Roles of inhibition-less spreading activation and limited-capacity attention. *Journal of Experimental Psychology, 106,* 226–254.

Peak, H., & Morrison, H. W. (1958). The acceptance of information into attitude structure. *Journal of Abnormal and Social Psychology, 57,* 127–135.

Pearlin, L. I. (1954). Shifting group attachments and attitudes toward Negroes. *Social Forces, 33,* 47–50.

Pettigrew, T. (1987, May 12). "Useful" modes of thought contribute to prejudice. *The New York Times.*

Poskocil, A. (1977). Encounters between blacks and white liberals: The collision of stereotypes. *Social Forces, 55,* 715–727.

Posner, M. I., & Snyder, C. R. R. (1975). Attention and cognitive control. In R. L. Solso (Ed.), *Information processing and cognition: The Layola symposium.* Hillsdale, NJ: Lawrence Erlbaum Associates.

Proshansky, H. M. (1966). The development of intergroup attitudes. In L. W. Hoffman & M. L. Hoffman (Eds.), *Review of child development research.* (Vol. 2, pp. 311–371). New York: Russel Sage Foundation.

Reeder, G. D., & Brewer, M. B. (1979). A schematic model of dispositional attribution in interpersonal perception. *Psychological Review, 86,* 61–79.

Saenger, G. (1953). *The social psychology of prejudice.* New York: Harper & Row.

Sager, H. A., & Schofield, J. W. (1980). Racial and behavioral cues in black and white children's perceptions of ambiguously aggressive acts. *Journal of Personality and Social Psychology, 39,* 590–598.

Sears, D. O., & Kinder, D. R. (1971). Racial tensions and voting in Los Angeles. In W. Z. Hirsch (Ed.), *Los Angeles: Viability and prospects for metropolitan leadership.* New York: Prager.

Sears, D. O., & McConahay, J. B. (1973). *The politics of violence: The new urban blacks and the Watts riot.* Boston: Houghton Mifflin.

Secord, P. F., & Backman, C. W. (1964). *Social psychology.* New York: McGraw-Hill.

Schneider, W., & Shiffrin, R. M. (1977). Controlled and automatic human information processing: I. Detection, search, and attention. *Psychological Review, 84,* 1–66.

Silverman, B. I. (1974). Consequences, racial discrimination, and the principal of belief congruence. *Journal of Personality and Social Psychology, 29,* 497–508.

Shiffrin, R. M., & Dumais, S. T. (1981). The development of automatism. In J. R. Anderson (Ed.), *Cognitive skills and their acquisition* (pp. 111–140). Hillsdale, NJ: Lawrence Erlbaum Associates.

Shiffrin, R. M., & Schneider, W. (1977). Controlled and automatic human information processing: II. Perceptual learning, automatic attending, and a general theory. *Psychological Review, 84,* 127–190.

Simpson, G. E., & Yinger, J. M. (1965). *Racial and cultural minorities.* (rev. ed.) New York: Harper & Row.

Sims, V. M., & Patrick, J. R. (1936). Attitude toward the Negro of northern and southern college students. *Journal of Social Psychology, 7,* 192–204.

Smith, E. R., & Branscombe, N. R. (1985). *Stereotype traits can be processed automatically.* Unpublished manuscript, Purdue University.

Smith, M. B., Bruner, J. S., & White, R. W. (1956). *Opinions and personality.* New York: Wiley.

Srull, T. K., & Wyer, R. S. (1979). The role of category accessibility in the interpretation of information about persons: Some determinants and implications. *Journal of Personality and Social Psychology, 37,* 1660–1672.

Srull, T. K., & Wyer, R. S., Jr. (1980). Category accessibility and social perception: Some implications for the study of person memory and interpersonal judgments. *Journal of Personality and Social Psychology, 38,* 841–856.

Stephan, W. G. (1985). Intergroup relations. In G. Lindzey & E. Aronson (Eds.), *The handbook of social psychology* (3rd ed., Vol. 2). Hillsdale, NJ: Lawrence Erlbaum Associates.

Taylor, D. G., Sheatsley, P. G., & Greeley, A. M. (1978). Attitudes toward racial integration. *Scientific American, 238,* 42–49.

Trager, H. G., & Yarrow, M. R. (1952). *They learn what they live: Prejudice in young children.* New York: Harper & Row.

Warner, L. G., & DeFleur, M. L. (1969). Attitude as an interactional concept: Social constraint and social distance as intervening variables between attitudes and action. *American Sociological Review, 34,* 153–169.

Watson, J. (1950). Some social and psychological situations related to change in attitude. *Human Relations, 3,* 15–56.

Weitz, S. (1972). Attitude, voice, and behavior: A repressed affect model of interracial interaction. *Journal of Personality and Social Psychology, 24,* 14–21.

9

Attitudes, Decisions, and Habits as Determinants of Repeated Behavior

David L. Ronis
*University of Michigan**

J. Frank Yates
University of Michigan

John P. Kirscht
University of Michigan

A key function ascribed to attitudes has been the utilitarian one of guiding behavior in ways that are beneficial to the individual. The theoretical centrality of this function is clear from the myriad definitions that have been proposed for the term *attitude,* most of which either define attitude as a predisposition to behave in a certain way (Allport, 1935) or include behavior as one component of attitude itself (e.g., Rosenberg & Hovland, 1960). The utilitarian or behavior-guiding function of attitudes is especially important to practitioners and researchers who are attempting to apply attitude theory to real world problems, such as low worker productivity, health threatening behaviors, and discrimination against minorities.

The purpose of this chapter is to examine the functions or roles of attitudes and related constructs (e.g., beliefs, values, decisions) in guiding repeated behavior. This chapter sketches the outlines of a theory of repeated behavior and reviews relevant theory and research. By the term *repeated behavior,* we mean any action that is taken more than one time. Many of the special characteristics of repeated behaviors, however, appear only if the behavior has been repeated both frequently (at least twice a month) and extensively (at least 10 times). Our major thesis is that repeated behaviors may be largely determined by habits rather than by attitudinal variables, although attitudes are central to the formation and modification of habits. We focus on repeated health-related behaviors (i.e., repeated behaviors that have clear positive or negative effects on health) because such behaviors

*Now at Michigan Health Care Education and Research Foundation, Detroit, Michigan

are of great practical importance and because they have not previously been given much theoretical attention.

THE UTILITARIAN FUNCTION OF ATTITUDES AND ATTITUDE-BEHAVIOR CONSISTENCY

Almost all research on the utilitarian/behavior-guiding function of attitudes has examined the correlation between measures of attitude and of behavior. Early research on this topic made it clear that verbally expressed attitudes do not usually correlate highly with overt behavior. A review of the literature by Wicker in 1969, for example, reported that the typical attitude-behavior correlation was about .2. This weak relationship between attitudes and behavior poses a serious problem for theorists, researchers, and practitioners. Recent approaches to understanding and predicting behavior and understanding its relationship to attitudes fall into three main categories.

Methodological Approach

One approach to improved prediction and understanding focuses on methodological issues, identifying *problems of measurement* that lower the observed relationship between attitudes and behavior, and developing and applying improved methods. The work of Martin Fishbein and Icek Ajzen has emphasized this approach. One of their main findings is that attitude-behavior consistency is higher if the level of generality or specificity of the attitude measure corresponds to that of the behavior measure. Thus, to predict a broad cluster of behaviors, one should use a global measure of attitude, but to predict a specific behavior, one should use a very focused attitude measure (Ajzen & Fishbein, 1977; Davidson & Jaccard, 1979; Fishbein & Ajzen, 1975; see Ajzen's chapter 10 in this volume).

Research using recently developed structural modeling techniques such as LISREL (Analysis of Linear Structural Relationships) (Jöreskog & Sörbom, 1984) also fits into this category (Bagozzi, 1981; Bentler & Speckart, 1979, 1981; Fredricks & Dossett, 1983). These statistical programs simultaneously estimate errors of measurement and relations among theoretical constructs (e.g., behavior and its predictors). The estimates of these relations are not biased by the presence of random measurement error and are often substantially higher than the estimates from more traditional correlation and regression analyses.

Cognitive Process Approach

A second approach to attitude-behavior relations focuses on understanding the cognitive processes relating attitudes to behavior. One major program of research within this approach is that of Russell Fazio and his colleagues. They have predicted and observed that the attitude-behavior link is stronger if the attitude is cognitively accessible. Accessibility of an attitude is increased by personal experience with the attitude object and by repeated expression of the attitude. Thus, attitude-behavior consistency will be high if the attitude was developed from direct interaction with the attitude object or if the individual has repeatedly discussed his or her attitude. But attitude-behavior consistency will be low under other conditions. In chapter 7 in this volume, Fazio discusses this perspective in detail.

Multivariate or "Other Variable" Approach

A third approach to improved understanding and prediction of behavior and of attitude-behavior relations is to look for variables other than attitudes that also influence behavior. The operation of these other influences reduces the correlation between attitudes and behavior. (If attitude were the only determinant of a behavior, attitude and behavior could correlate perfectly. This is not possible if other factors affect the behavior.) Including measures of these other variables in studies improves the prediction and understanding of behavior. (If all of the determinants of an action are included as predictors in a multiple regression, the multiple correlation can be perfect.)

This other variable approach has been followed by a number of different researchers over the years. Fishbein and Ajzen (1975) emphasized norms and also discussed unforeseen obstacles and lack of ability as factors influencing behavior. Triandis (1980) suggested habits and the environment as additional determinants of behavior. Recently, Ajzen (1985) and Rogers (1983) emphasized perceived self-efficacy as an important additional influence on behavior. Perceived self-efficacy is the belief that one is able to carry out the action (Bandura, 1977). To the extent that perceived self-efficacy influences behavior independently of attitude (or that attitude and perceived self-efficacy interact), the attitude-behavior correlation will be reduced, and including perceived self-efficacy as a predictor variable will improve prediction and understanding. The present chapter falls mainly within this third multivariate or other variable approach to understanding behavior and its relationship with attitudes.

IMPORTANCE OF REPEATED BEHAVIORS

Practical Importance

Many repeated behaviors have strong effects on health. Cardiovascular fitness depends on consistent exercise (American College of Sports Medicine, 1978). Occasional exercise is ineffective. Similarly, adequate dental health depends on frequent brushing (Kelner, Wohl, Deasy, & Formicola, 1974; Lang, Cumming, & Loe, 1973). Brushing once a week is much less helpful. The benefits of many other healthful behaviors (e.g., wearing seatbelts, performing breast self-examination, taking prescribed medication, using contraceptives) are also increased by consistent performance. On the other hand, many of the greatest threats to health are the results of consistently repeated unhealthy behaviors, such as smoking, overeating, drinking, and using addictive drugs. Thus, it is obviously important on practical grounds that an understanding of repeated behaviors be achieved.

Theoretical Importance

By their very nature, repeated behaviors possess features and pose problems in addition to those of nonrepeated behaviors. Repeated behaviors are characterized by at least two stages: *initiation* and *persistence*. The factors that determine persistence may be different from those that determine the initiation of the behavior. Even if the same factors or variables affect behavior at both stages, their values may change. For example, beliefs about the difficulty of tooth flossing may affect both initiation and persistence, but those beliefs may change rapidly with experience. These characteristics of repeated behaviors suggest that explanations of repeated behaviors are likely to be different from and more complex than explanations of nonrepeated behaviors.

There is empirical evidence that the determinants of initiation and persistence do indeed differ. Dishman (1982) for example, noted that the last few years have seen an increase in the proportion of people who *start* exercise programs, but no increase in persistence in such programs. Also, the initiation of an exercise program is reliably predictable from attitudinal variables, whereas persistence is not. Similarly, dieters' success in losing weight is influenced by physiological factors, whereas their success in maintaining weight loss is influenced by their relations with their spouses (Dubbert & Wilson, 1984). Analogously, alcoholics' posttreatment alcohol consumption is influenced by a number of posttreatment experiences that could not possibly have affected their initiation of treatment or their initial success (Cronkite & Moos, 1980). A later section of this chapter discusses the differing factors that influence initiation and persistence in smoking.

Past research and theory have given little attention to the special characteristics of repeated health-related behaviors. The psychological theory that is most widely employed to explain health-related behavior is the health belief model. According to this theory, health-related actions are determined by (a) perceived susceptibility to a health threat, (b) perceived severity of the health threat, (c) perceived benefits of the actions, (d) perceived costs of the action, and (e) cues to action, such as symptoms (Janz & Becker, 1984). Statements of the health belief model have not distinguished between repeated behaviors (such as toothbrushing, wearing seatbelts, and smoking) and nonrepeated behaviors (such as having an influenza vaccination, having surgery, voting for fluoridation, or being screened for a genetic problem). Recent attempts to integrate theories of health-related behavior (Cummings, Becker, & Maile, 1980; Wallston & Wallston, 1984) have also not distinguished repeated from nonrepeated behaviors. Except for theories of addiction, no theories have been proposed specifically to explain repeated health-related behaviors.

The purpose of this chapter is to review past research and theory and organize it into a model of repeated health-related behaviors. A central proposition of this model is that the continued repetition of behaviors is often determined by habits rather than by attitudes or beliefs. On the other hand, attitudes, along with other considerations, are important in the initiation of such behaviors. Ideas for this model were drawn from diverse areas of theory and research, including cognitive psychology, applied behavior analysis, attitude theory, social learning theories, and behavioral decision theory, as well as from work focused specifically on health. Though we developed this model in order to explain health-related behaviors, and virtually all of the examples are drawn from that area, we see no reason why the ideas would not be applicable to other repeated behaviors.

Figure 9.1 presents a broad overview of our model of repeated behavior. In this figure we wish to emphasize two main points: First, there are three main categories of variables (unreasoned influences, resources or enabling variables, and reasoned influences) that function to directly guide behavior. Attitude is only one of the variables within one of the categories that influence behavior. Second, behavior itself influences many of the other variables. For example, repetition of the behavior strengthens the habit and increases the level of skill. Experience with the behavior also affects relevant attitudes and beliefs. The influences of behavior on the other variables are particularly important because the model concerns repeated behaviors.

The presentation of the model is organized as follows. First, the distinction between habits and decisions is presented and the relevance of habits for repeated behaviors is discussed. Second, the factors that determine whether a person will make a decision are discussed. Third, the processes of decision-making are presented, including factors that influence the depth or thoughtfulness of the decision process and factors that determine the outcome of the decision. Fourth, the sequence of events through which a decision may lead to repeated behavior and to the development of a habit are described. Obstacles and alternatives to habit development are briefly presented. Fifth, the process of intentionally eliminating a habit is discussed. Finally, some implications for future research are presented. Throughout

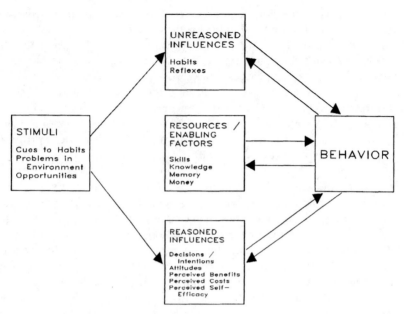

FIG. 9.1.   Overview of the theoretical model.

the presentation, factors that moderate or mediate the influence of attitudes on behavior are highlighted.

DECISIONS VERSUS HABITS

A critical distinction in this model is between behaviors that result from the implementation of conscious decisions and behaviors that result from habit. A habit is an action that has been done many times and has become automatic. That is, it is done without conscious thought. A decision to take or not to take an action, on the other hand, involves conscious thought and the consideration of at least one alternative to the selected course of action. The alternative may simply be inaction.

This distinction between habit and conscious decision is an old one. It was discussed extensively by William James in the *Principles of Psychology* (1890). James (1890) described the origins and consequences of habit as follows:

> Any sequence of mental action which has been frequently repeated tends to perpetuate itself; so that we find ourselves automatically prompted to *think, feel,* or *do* what we have been before accustomed to think, feel, or do, under like circumstances, without any consciously-formed *purpose,* or anticipation of results. (Vol. 1, p. 112)

Habit simplifies the movements required to achieve a given result, makes them more accurate and diminishes fatigue. (Vol. 1, p. 112)

Habit diminishes the conscious attention with which our acts are performed. (Vol. 1, p. 114)

Current conceptualizations of habit are very similar to those presented by James nearly a century ago, though they are now expressed in the language of cognitive psychology. Shiffrin and Schneider, for example, distinguished between *automatic* and *controlled* processes (Schneider & Shiffrin, 1977; Shiffrin, Dumais, & Schneider, 1981; Shiffrin & Schneider, 1977). Habits are the results of automatic cognitive processes. Such processes develop by extensive repetition. Automatic processes are so well-learned they do not require conscious effort. Automatic processes are unintentional. They are typically set in motion by stimulus cues. Automatic processes can go on simultaneously with other cognitive processes without any interference. We are often unaware of automatic cognitive processes. Habits and automatic processes are extremely useful for solving repetitive problems.

Controlled processes are the cognitive processes that require conscious effort. Controlled processes are intentional, and can be guided by verbal instructions. Two controlled processes cannot be carried out simultaneously—they interfere with each other. We are often conscious of the intermediate results of controlled cognitive processes. These characteristics of controlled processes are consistent with the postulate that controlled processes use the limited capacity of short-term memory. The advantage of controlled processes is their flexibility. Controlled cognitive processes allow us to deal with novel problems and to arrive at new solutions. They are the processes underlying decision-making.

Though the research directly inspired by Shiffrin and Schneider's theory has focused on microprocesses of perception, the general ideas are applicable to important overt behaviors. Consider, for example, two stages in the typical career of a smoker. It appears that some youngsters start to experiment with smoking in order to establish an image of toughness, maturity, and independence from authority. They make fully conscious and independent decisions to smoke. Other youngsters try cigarettes to comply with pressures from their friends (Leventhal & Cleary, 1980). Although they may have decided not to become smokers, they consciously decide to smoke in the social situation.

At a much later stage, continued smoking may be *partially* due to conscious decisions, but the reasons or perceived benefits have changed. Long-term smokers say they smoke *in order* to (a) produce positive sensations and emotions, (b) reduce anxiety, (c) reduce craving, or (d) have something to do with their hands (Ikard, Green, & Horn, 1969). Many smokers, however, are aware that they simply smoke by habit. They may notice, for example, that they are smoking, even though they do not recall having decided to smoke or having picked up or lit the cigarette (Ikard, Green, & Horn, 1969). This limited awareness is typical of an automatic process or habit, but not at all characteristic of a controlled process, or conscious decision-making. Smokers are more likely to see their smoking as habitual after a period of systematic self-monitoring (Leventhal & Avis, 1976). At least some of their smoking is due to an automatic habit, rather than to conscious decisions. This is one reason that people who have decided to stop often continue to smoke. They do not have conscious control of their behavior.

The initiation of a new pattern of behavior (whether it is an unhealthy one, like smoking or heavy drinking, or a healthy one, like wearing seatbelts, brushing and flossing one's teeth, exercising, or performing breast self-examination) generally requires conscious decision-making, guided by attitudes and beliefs. After the decision and the action are repeated many times, the action becomes habitual and repeated decision-making become unnecessary. The person will carry out the action when placed in the appropriate situation. Most adults, for example, brush their teeth at one or more specific times during the day, without a daily consideration of whether or when to do it.

THE UTILITARIAN FUNCTION (OR NONFUNCTION) OF ATTITUDES AMONG HABITUAL BEHAVIORS

The major implication of the habit-decision distinction for attitude-behavior relations is that habitual behaviors are not directly influenced by beliefs about the outcomes of the behavior, by conscious decisions to behave in one way or another, or by attitudes. These behaviors are not under volitional control. As a result, the correlation between habitual behavior and attitudes or beliefs may be extremely low.

Though we do propose that repeated health-related behaviors are originally initiated as the result of conscious decision-making based on relevant attitudes and beliefs, *attitudes and behavior can easily diverge after the behavior becomes habitual.* Once the behavior becomes a habit, it is relatively autonomous or independent of attitudes and beliefs. Thus, attitude change can occur without a corresponding change in behavior, leading to attitude-behavior inconsistency. There are innumerable ways by which attitudes can change (Insko, 1967; Kiesler, Collins, & Miller, 1969; Petty & Cacioppo, 1981). Perhaps the most common means by which attitudes are changed is exposure to communications, for example, (a) hearing about the surgeon general's report on smoking and health, (b) seeing advertisements for health-related products that you don't use, (c) having a doctor or someone else suggest that you should get more exercise or lose weight, (d) reading that it is not necessary to brush your teeth more than once a day, and (e) hearing that a friend of yours has stopped drinking coffee.

If the only process influencing the attitude-behavior correlation for repeated behaviors were the drifting of beliefs and attitudes away from the habitual behavior, a very clear prediction could be made: The longer the behavior has been repeated, the less it will be correlated with and predicted by attitude. Triandis (1977, 1980) made just this prediction and reviewed several studies that provided some support for the hypothesis. Specifically, in studies of extensively repeated behaviors—teachers' interpersonal behavior in the classroom (Landis, Triandis, & Adamopoulos, 1978) and productivity in well-learned factory jobs (Schachter, Festinger, Willerman, & Hyman, 1961)—behavior was not predictable from attitudinal variables. However, in studies of new behaviors e.g., productivity while learning a new factory job (Schachter et al., 1961), behavior was indeed predictable from attitudinal variables. As mentioned previously, Dishman (1982) also reported supportive results regarding exercise programs: initiation was predictable from attitudinal variables, but persistence was not.

A few studies have been conducted to assess the influences of attitudes and habits on repeated behaviors (Bagozzi, 1981; Bentler & Speckart, 1979, 1981; Fredricks & Dossett, 1983). These studies included a measure of past behavior as a predictor of future behavior and interpreted the relationship as being due to habit. Bagozzi (1981), for example, used actual blood donation behavior at two points in time as criteria, and used self-report measures of attitude, behavioral intention, and past blood donation behavior as predictors in a LISREL analysis. Results indicated that past blood donation behavior was a powerful predictor of future blood donation behavior even when the other predictors were statistically controlled. From this finding, Bagozzi (1981) concluded that habit influenced blood donation behavior. By this criterion, all the studies found evidence for the influence of habit on behavior. Because unmeasured factors other than habit may account for the relationship between past and future behavior, this evidence is rather weak.

In their study of seat belt use, Wittenbraker, Gibbs, and Kahle (1983) went beyond the previous approach by including a measure of habit. Multiple regression analyses indicated that habit contributed significantly (beyond behavioral intention) to the prediction of future seat belt utilization. Their measure of habit, however, consisted of only two questions, both of which asked how often the respondent wore seatbelts, "by force of habit" (p. 411). Thus, the measure (a) depended on respondents' interpretation of this phrase and (b) was confounded by past frequency of behavior.

Although this research provides some evidence that habit and attitudinal variables both influence behavior, a more precise determination of the importance of habits versus attitudes and decisions must await the development of more adequate measures of habit or automaticity.

Even though there is some evidence that attitude-behavior correlations are reduced as the behavior is repeated and becomes habitual, we are reluctant to accept the hypothesis that, other things being equal, it will always happen. Our reluctance to accept this hypothesis stems from our belief that there are other processes influencing attitude-behavior relations for repeated behaviors that may increase rather than reduce the correlation between attitude and behavior. In particular, the attitude-behavior correlation may be the result of the influence of behavior on attitude, rather than vice versa. There is ample evidence that inducing people to behave in a given manner leads them to develop positive attitudes related to the behavior (Wicklund & Brehm, 1976). This phenomenon was originally predicted from dissonance theory's postulated motive to reduce postdecisional dissonance due to the attractive features of the rejected alternatives and negative features of chosen ones (Festinger, 1957). It has also been explained on the basis of a process of self-perception, whereby people infer their attitudes from observations of their own behavior (Bem, 1967). According to self-perception theory and recent versions of dissonance theory, behavior will influence attitude only if people believe that they have freely chosen to take the action or that they are in some other way *responsible* for the action. Empirical evidence indicates that the effect of behavior on attitude is indeed much greater under these circumstances (Wicklund & Brehm, 1976).

There are also reasons to believe that repeatedly taking an action will improve attitude toward the action and associated stimuli, even if the action is not perceived as voluntary. There is a great deal of evidence that repeated exposure to stimuli—including nonsense words (Zajonc, 1968), people, abstract and representational visual images, and types of music—increases people's liking for the stimuli (Harrison, 1977). This phenomenon has also been demonstrated in other species besides humans (Cross, Halcomb, & Matter, 1967). There is nothing to suggest that this "mere exposure" effect should not affect people's attitudes toward their own repeated behavior.

Another reason that habitual behavior may be substantially correlated with attitudes and beliefs even though these variables are no longer directly determining the behavior is that the attitudes and beliefs may have been unchanged from the time—perhaps decades earlier—when the person consciously decided to start and to continue the repeated behavior. However, the longer the time since the original conscious decision was made, the less likely it is that the attitude would have remained the same.

WHEN DO PEOPLE MAKE DECISIONS?

Most repeated actions are habitual. When people are in situations they have encountered and acted in many times before, their actions will be automatic repetitions of their previously repeated behaviors. A commonly cited example of habitual behavior is driving to and from work (e.g., Lachman, Lachman, & Butterfield, 1979, p. 282). After a period of living and working in the same locations, people can make these trips while paying little attention to driving, even though the process requires using various landmarks to identify the locations of turns, and making thousands of adjustments to keep the car on the road and out of accidents.

Conscious decision-making occurs in novel situations and when new problems arise in old situations. Novelty is injected into our lives in many different ways. If drivers, in their habitual travel to or from work, for example, find that their usual route is closed due to construction, they face a novel problem and they switch from "automatic pilot" to conscious decision-making. Suddenly they need to know where they are, to consider alternative routes, and to make and implement a decision. One source of novelty that triggers health-related decisions is a noticeable change in one's body. Especially if the change is painful or disabling, it is likely to lead to a decision to seek medical help (Anderson & Aday, 1978; Sharp, Ross, & Cockerham, 1983). Interpersonal communications, whether face-to-face or presented through the media, are another source of novelty. Among these are (a) educational messages presented in schools, through the media, and in group settings, (b) face-to-face communications from health care personnel to individuals, either about a health-related behavior or about the individual's health, (c) news stories about the health problems of celebrities, about epidemics, about advances in health care, and about dramatic health threats (e.g., poisoned over-the-counter medications), (d) advertisements for health-related products and services, and (e) personal communications about the health and health-related behaviors of one's associates. These communications may stimulate the individual to think about a threat to his or her health and may suggest specific health-related behaviors. If the communications have sufficient personal relevance, they may lead to a decision to initiate, terminate, or modify some pattern of behavior.

Physical obstacles to performance often lead to decision-making. If, for example, a person who flosses his or her teeth daily runs out of dental floss, this will probably lead to a decision about whether (or when) to get some more. Other modifications of one's routine—whether due to major or minor life changes—alter the stimulus situations to which one is exposed and disrupt habitual behaviors. This may lead to conscious decision-making.

The role of external stimuli in triggering both habitual behavior and conscious decision-making is indicated in Fig. 9.1 by the two arrows coming
from the far left box.

In sum, people usually behave habitually, but will actively make a decision when they find themselves in new situations or facing new problems.
Because people usually behave habitually, there is ample opportunity for
attitude-behavior inconsistency. As discussed in the previous section of the
chapter, attitudes may simply have drifted away from the habits that are the
major determinants of behavior. Both the initiation of decision-making and
the depth or thoroughness of the decision process (to be discussed elsewhere) depend on the relevance of the problem to the individual. This
assumption is consistent with other contingency models of decision-making
(Beach & Mitchell, 1978; Janis & Mann, 1977). Stage 1 in Janis and Mann's
Model, for example, is deciding "whether the threat or opportunity is
important enough to warrant the effort of making an active decision about
it" (Janis, 1984, p. 334).

DECISION PROCESSES

Depth, Involvement, and Time Pressure

Decision processes begin when a person starts to think about a health threat
or about a health-related behavior. Recent theories of decision-making and
attitude change postulate that the depth and extent of the decision-making
processes will depend substantially on the importance of the problem to the
individual (Beach & Mitchell, 1978; Janis & Mann, 1977; Petty, Ostrom, &
Brock, 1981). The more impact the person believes the threat is likely to
have on him or her personally, the more extensively he or she will think
about it. A wide variety of studies support this generalization. Research on
cognitive responses to persuasive messages have repeatedly demonstrated
that increasing the personal relevance of a persuasive message increases the
thoroughness with which the recipient processes the arguments in the
message. Thorough processing of the message can either increase or decrease attitude change, depending on the quality of the arguments (Petty &
Cacioppo, 1979; Petty, Cacioppo, & Goldman, 1981). In one study demonstrating the impact of personal relevance, Chaiken (1980) manipulated
message-recipients' involvement with the topic of a persuasive message by
instructing them that they would (or would not) be discussing the subject
with another person. Both the likableness of the source of the message and
the quality (number of arguments) of the message were manipulated.
Opinion change among high-involvement subjects was affected by the

quality of the message, but not by source likableness. In contrast, opinion change among low-involvement subjects was affected by source likableness, but not by message quality. Thus, when the topic was unimportant (to the message recipient), a decision was based on a fairly superficial cue, but when a topic was important, the decision was based on a more extensive analysis. Langer, Blank, and Chanowitz (1978) reported similar results for reactions to a personal request.

A second factor that has a major impact on the thoroughness of the decision process is the availability of sufficient time to deliberate. Under high time pressure people tend to use simpler decision-making strategies than under low time pressure. This effect has been observed in studies where subjects reported the decision strategy they used or would use (Smith, Mitchell, & Beach, 1982), in studies where the process was inferred from the decision made (Wallsten & Barton, 1982; Wright, 1974), and in studies where the process was inferred from information-gathering be-havior (Ben Zur & Breznitz, 1981). Typically, the simplified decision pro-cess involves giving disproportionate weight to a small number of items of information, most commonly negative information about the alternatives (Payne, 1982). Distraction has been found to produce similar effects on the depth of cognitive processing (Petty, Wells, & Brock, 1976).

If the stimulus for thought was a health threat (without a suggested action) the first step in decision-making is searching for potential solutions and for information about the advantages and disadvantages of the alterna-tives. This is Stage 2 in Janis and Mann's (1977) model. The person will start by searching his or her memory. Depending on the personal importance of the problem and the apparent adequacy of remembered solutions, the individual may search for additional information—asking friends, reading books and magazines, conferring with health care personnel, and so forth (Beach & Mitchell, 1978; Janis & Mann, 1977). If the stimulus for thought included a suggested course of action, the individual will evaluate that possibility and may not search further—depending on the apparent ade-quacy of that course of action and on the perceived importance of the problem.

The next step in the decision process is that of evaluating the alternative courses of action and selecting one. This corresponds to Stage 3 in Janis and Mann's model. Because the information-gathering process varies in its thor-oughness, different decisions will be based on different *amounts of in-formation.* The *process* of combining the information will also vary in its complexity and thoroughness, depending on the same major factors: the importance of the decision to the individual and the amount of time available (Beach & Mitchell, 1978). When the decision is not very impor-tant or there is very little time for making the decision, decision makers may not use all the information they have. They may, for example, compare the alternatives on one attribute at a time while never considering all the attributes (Tversky, 1969; 1972) or they may consider the alternatives one at a time and select one they evaluate as adequate, without considering all of the available options (Simon, 1957).

If the decision is important to them and they have sufficient time, decision makers often employ more thorough evaluation techniques that use all of the information they have about every alternative. These evaluation processes may be conducted entirely within the heads of the decision makers (cf. Fishbein & Ajzen, 1975) or [if warranted by the importance of the decision and allowed by the time constraints,] they may include use of tools such as paper and pencil.

Whether the process of evaluating alternatives is simple and informal or complex and formal, two main factors determine the action that is chosen: (a) the decision maker's evaluation of the overall *desirability of the action,* and (b) the decision maker's *perceived self-efficacy,* i.e., confidence in his or her own ability to carry out the action. The judgment about the desirability of the action is generally based on (a) the perceived probabilities that the action will lead to various outcomes, including health-relevant outcomes, health-irrelevant outcomes, costs, rewards, direct outcomes of action, and socially mediated outcomes of action and (b) the decision maker's evaluations of those outcomes. In a fairly thoughtful decision, the decision maker will give greater weight to the evaluations of outcomes that are more likely to occur (Fishbein & Ajzen, 1975; Shanteau, 1974). If the decision maker has previously thought about these actions and their benefits and costs, the beliefs and values may already have been integrated into attitudes. In this case the decision maker may simply retrieve his or her previous evaluations/attitudes from memory, rather than reconsidering the advantages and disadvantages of the alternatives.

As previously mentioned, the decision is not only influenced by the decision maker's evaluation of the action and beliefs and values associated with the consequences of the action; it is also influenced by that individual's perceived self-efficacy with regard to the action. Empirical evidence for the importance of perceived self-efficacy (Bandura, 1982; Maddux & Rogers, 1983; Ronis & Kaiser, in press; Shifter & Ajzen, 1985) has been so compelling that at least two major attitude theorists have modified their models to include perceived self-efficacy along with attitudinal variables as an influence on behavior (Ajzen, 1985; Rogers, 1983). Even if the decision maker's evaluation of an alternative is extremely positive, that option is unlikely to be chosen unless the decision maker believes he or she can carry out the action (Bandura, 1977, 1982). Thus, each alternative action that is considered (including inaction) is evaluated in terms of the expected desirability of *trying* it. This requires considering both the outcomes of the action if it is successfully completed and the probability of successfully carrying out the action. If trying one course of action seems clearly more desirable than trying each of the other alternatives considered, the person will choose to attempt to follow that course of action.

Indecision

If no alternative seems desirable or clearly superior to the others, the person will not make a decision. The result of this will be inaction, or whatever action habitually occurs in the situation (Latané & Darley, 1970; Mischel, 1974, 1981; Yates & Revelle, 1979). It is important to note that indecision has practical consequences. In terms of behavioral outcomes, not deciding to take an action is effectively equivalent to deciding to take no action.

Research on bystander intervention in emergencies illustrates a possible negative consequence of indecision. Latané and Darley (1970) argued convincingly that one of the reasons people fail to help in an emergency is that they are undecided about whether to help or how to help. At the minimum, a protracted period of indecision delays the giving of help. Indecision may be an important element in delay in seeking health care (Antonovsky & Hartman, 1974; Green & Roberts, 1974; Safer, Tharps, Jackson, & Levanthal, 1979). Preventive health behaviors may be delayed indefinitely by indecision. Note that the failure to make a decision may result (a) from failure to notice a problem, (b) from an unsuccessful attempt to decide, or even (c) from intentional self-distraction from the decision.

Within the decision process described, there are at least three factors that lead to inconsistencies between decisions and attitudes or beliefs. Because the influence of attitudes and beliefs on behavior is largely mediated by decisions (Ajzen & Fishbein, 1980), these inconsistencies can be expected to result in attitude-behavior inconsistencies. The factors leading to decisions that are inconsistent with attitudes or beliefs are: (a) that decisions are strongly influenced by perceived self-efficacy, a variable that is not necessarily correlated with attitude, (b) that decisions are based on a comparison of alternative actions, and hence a person may have a very positive attitude toward some action but never decide to take the action because he or she has an even more positive attitude toward an alternative action, and (c) that hastily made decisions may often be based on only a fraction of the information (beliefs) that the person has about the alternatives.

FROM DECISIONS TO BEHAVIORS

Trying

Once an individual has decided on a new course of action, a period of trial begins for the person *and* for the action. The person tries to carry out the action and may succeed or fail. Thus, initial efforts at implementation provide a test of whether the individual's *resources* are adequate for carrying out the action (See Fig. 9.1). A wide variety of resources may be relevant to the action, including some that are cognitive, some that are physical, and some that are external to the individual. For example, dental flossing requires (a) a certain amount of time, (b) certain manipulative skills, and (c) possession of dental floss. If the person does not own dental floss, obtaining it requires money and transportation. Implementation of a regular program of tooth flossing requires memory—which may be facilitated by specific cognitive strategies or by the use of reminders, e.g., putting the dental floss container on the sink where it will be seen at the appropriate time. Memory is often a critical problem for repeated health-related behaviors. It may be particularly difficult to remember to perform novel behaviors in familiar settings because behavior in such settings is largely habitual and automatic. Thus, there are numerous ways that an individual's resources may be inadequate to carry out a selected course of action.

Unsuccessful efforts reduce the individual's confidence that he or she can carry out the action. As a result, when the person reconsiders the problem, the chance of deciding on the tried course of action is reduced. Repeated failures successively lower confidence and reduce the probability of choosing the action until it is not selected again (Abramson, Seligman, & Teasdale, 1978). Other possible consequences of failure include (a) trying new ways of carrying out the action, (b) reappraising previously rejected alternatives, and (c) considering completely new courses of action. These may eventually lead to successful resolution of the problem.

Initial implementation also provides the person with new information about the outcomes of the action. People who floss for the first time learn what it feels like and may learn that it makes their gums bleed. They may also learn that flossing removes substantial quantities of food debris from between their teeth. Thus, both favorable and unfavorable information may be gained in this way. The information gained through trial is *concrete* and *relevant* to the person. For these reasons, it is very likely that it will have more impact than the more abstract and general information that may have been the basis of the initial decision (Bar-Hillel, 1980). In addition, evaluations based on personal experience are more likely to carry over into action than are evaluations derived from other sources (Fazio & Zanna, 1981; see Fazio's chap. 7 in this volume). Thus, the experiences of the initial trial are likely to have a strong impact on future decisions. They may strongly reinforce the initial decision or may lead to a completely different decision when the problem is reconsidered. In addition, successful performance increases the person's confidence in his or her ability to carry out the action. The impact of experiences in trying a behavior on beliefs relevant to the behavior is indicated in Fig. 9.1 by the arrow from behavior to reasoned influences.

Deciding Again (And Again)

In many cases, early attempts to carry out a selected course of action become occasions for reconsidering the decision. Failure to carry out the desired action (except when the failure is due to forgetting) is likely to stimulate conscious problem-solving and decision-making. Because failure reduces the person's confidence in being able to carry out the action, a new course of action may often be selected after failure. Early tries may also stimulate decision-making when the personal experiences of the action provide information that is different from that previously possessed by the person. If the novel information is favorable to the behavior, the person is likely to reaffirm the decision. If the novel information is unfavorable, the person is likely to change his or her mind, deciding to do nothing new or to follow one of the alternative courses of action. Conscious decision-making may also be reinstituted by reexposure to the same kinds of novel stimuli that started decision-making for the first time. Each successive repetition of the same stimulus, however, is less likely to lead to attention and hence, less likely to lead to conscious decision-making (Harrison, 1977, p. 58). When decision-making occurs, it will be affected by the revisions in confidence and outcome expectancies resulting from the previous attempt(s). This discussion of the influence of decisions on repeated behavior has pointed out several factors that affect the consistency of repeated behaviors with decisions. Because the influence of attitudes on behaviors is largely mediated by decisions, these factors also affect attitude-behavior consistency. One factor reducing consistency is the influence of resources (including skill) on behavior. Obviously, people will not do things that they are unable to do. When people overestimate their own capabilities in relation to the task at hand, they often decide to do things that in fact they cannot do. This leads to behavior that is inconsistent with the person's decisions and attitudes. A second reason that decisions and attitudes may be inconsistent with later behavior is that the personal experiences that occur while trying to carry out the behavior often dramatically alter relevant decisions, attitudes, and beliefs. People may discover, for example, (a) that they cannot stand the taste of the healthy new food, (b) that their new medication has unpleasant side effects, (c) that they cannot get the floss to go where they want it, or (d) that performing breast self-examination leaves them confused and anxious rather than reassured. These new experience-based beliefs may easily reverse positive attitudes and decisions concerning the behaviors. This does not, however, reduce the consistency among these variables when they are measured simultaneously. In fact, these changes may increase the concurrent consistency among beliefs, attitudes, decisions, and behavior.

Development of a Habit: Trying Again (And Again)

People will not repeat an attempt to carry out an action if they have forgotten about it or if they have made a conscious decision and changed their minds. They will repeat an attempt if their most recent decision has been to try it. This could happen either because they haven't made a decision since the last time they attempted the behavior or because they have reconsidered the problem and have made the same decision again.

As people repeatedly try to carry out an action (with at least partial success), they get better at it. In flossing and smoking, for example, initial awkwardness is gradually replaced by skill, and initial discomfort is reduced. With extensive repetition, each step in flossing and smoking is done with less effort and less conscious awareness. The actions become automatic. Eventually, even the initiation of the behavior becomes automatic. It can be triggered by the stimulus cues that normally precede it. A habit has been formed. The effects of repetition on skill and habit are indicated in Fig. 9.1 by the arrows from behavior to unreasoned influences and to resources.

A Structural View of Beliefs, Attitudes, Decisions, and Habits

As previously noted in this chapter, the nature of habit or automaticity has been described by William James and by Shiffrin and Schneider. Both emphasized the need for extensive repetition for an action to become habitual. Anderson (1982) provided another analysis of this topic, which is quite detailed in describing the process of habit development—or as he labels it, acquisition of cognitive skill. In the first stage of habit development, the individual encodes information relevant to the behavior as a set of facts. Because of the nature of the internal representation of the information, this is referred to as the *declarative stage*. The facts are incapable of directly guiding behavior, but must be used by another set of cognitive elements—interpretive procedures—to generate behavior. People are consciously aware of the facts at this stage because the information has to be rehearsed in working memory to keep it available for the interpretive procedures (Anderson, 1982).

With practice, however, the information is converted into a procedural form in which it can directly guide behavior without the mediating action of the interpretive procedures. The gradual process by which the information is converted from declarative to procedural form is called *knowledge compilation*. During this phase, conscious attention to the information is gradually reduced. This is the process of habit formation. In the third, or *procedural stage*, the habit has been formed. However, even at this stage, further learning occurs. Specifically, there is additional tuning of the knowledge so that it will be applied more appropriately, and there is a gradual process of speedup.

One special merit of Anderson's (1982) analysis is that it explicitly indicates that the information guiding behavior is encoded or internally represented in at least two different forms. Throughout this chapter we have been referring to a number of different constructs relevant to behavior—beliefs, attitudes, decisions, and habits—without mentioning that they correspond to cognitive structures or elements, each of which is a (partially redundant) representation of the person's knowledge about the behavior. Beliefs, attitudes, and decisions are largely declarative representations of this information. The beliefs are the most detailed encoding of the information. The attitude toward the action is a separate structure representing the overall evaluation of the action. When freshly formed from beliefs, the attitude is entirely redundant with the beliefs. The person may hold attitudes toward each considered alternative action. The decision (or intention as it is called by most other attitude theorists) is a further integration of attitudes and beliefs. The habit is yet another representation of information about the behavior, this time encoded in procedural form, and including information about how to carry out the action.

Neither the formation of an attitude from beliefs, nor the formation of a decision from attitudes and beliefs, nor the formation of a habit entails the elimination of the earlier representations of the information. Rather, the different encodings coexist and may be retrieved and used at any time, as needed. If a person with a well-established seat belt habit rides in the back seat of someone else's car, where the seatbelt cannot be found, for example, he or she will switch out of the habitual mode of behavior to decide whether to dig between the seat and back to locate a seat belt. At this point, the person may decide not to bother with it—despite his or her beliefs, attitudes, past decisions, and habit, which may all favor the use of seat belts.

Obstacles to Habit Development

In the process just described, there are many obstacles to the formation of a healthy habit. First, the person may never think about the problem or the potential action. Second, the person may decide not to attempt the action, either because it seems too difficult or because it does not seem desirable.

Third, the person may forget to perform the new behavior. Fourth, after trying the behavior and finding out about its difficulty and/or its consequences, the person may decide against further efforts.

Because of these obstacles to developing a new habit, it is difficult to affect health by altering behavior. In light of this difficulty, one should consider the use of health-promotion techniques that do not require behavior change. Such techniques generally involve engineering the environment to be more conducive to health. Some techniques that have been implemented on a large scale are (a) fluoridation of water supplies, (b) addition of nutritional supplements to many foods (e.g., niacin in flour, iodine in salt), (c) safety features on cars, (d) childproof containers, (e) protective equipment in industry, and (f) removal of harmful substances such as asbestos, radium, and nitrates. In some cases, these techniques alter the outcomes of normal habits (eating baked goods, drinking water, and putting salt on food) so that the actions are more conducive to good health. Thus, it is not necessary to change the individual's attitudes, decisions, or habits.

ELIMINATION OF A BAD HABIT

Elimination of a habit requires the same steps as formation of a habit. The individual must initially decide to stop the behavior, must remember the resolution, must try repeatedly, and decide repeatedly before the habit can be eliminated. In both cases, one is trying to replace an habitual pattern of behavior with intentional behavior and eventually with a new pattern of habitual behavior. There is one difference between the formation and elimination of habits that has wide-ranging implications. Usually, when trying to develop a new health-related habit, the behavior is to be performed in specific settings and on specific occasions. For example, one may wish to brush one's teeth *after breakfast and before going to bed,* to take certain medication with meals, and to put on a seatbelt after getting into a car. Thus, it is usually possible for the behavior to become associated with (and be automatically set off by) a small number of specific cues. This facilitates memory for the action and development of a habit (Zifferblatt, 1975). In the case of a bad habit to be eliminated, one must abstain 24 hours a day in a wide variety of situations. In addition, the bad habit may be associated with (and automatically triggered by) a large number of different cues, to which the person may be exposed at any time. The more situations in which the undesired habit is performed, and the more cues with which it is associated, the more difficult the elimination of the habit. Eliminating a full-time habit may be a full-time job.

Attempts to eliminate bad habits often combine two different approaches. The *indirect approach* involves changing one's lifestyle to avoid the situations and cues that have been associated with the behavior. A booklet of tips on how to stop smoking recommends that the new ex-smoker temporarily avoid situations strongly associated with the pleasurable aspects of smoking, such as watching a favorite TV program, sitting in a favorite chair, or having a cocktail before dinner. It is suggested to people who smoked while driving that they take public transportation for a while. In tempting social situations, the new ex-smoker is advised to associate with the nonsmokers (Office of Cancer Communications, 1979). But, this indirect approach is not completely adequate for several reasons. First, it may require the person to change his or her whole lifestyle in order to eliminate one habit. Second, if the habit is associated with many situations and cues (as habits of heavy smoking and heavy drinking typically are), it is almost impossible to avoid all of the cues. For the individual trying to lose weight, cues to eating may be reduced but cannot be entirely eliminated. Third, if this were the only approach used, the individual would be helpless when (perhaps for some reason beyond his or her control) a dangerous situation cannot be avoided. Thus, a relapse is likely if someone offers the ex-smoker a cigarette. So, despite the power of the indirect approach, it is also necessary for the individual to take the *direct approach,* i.e., to suppress the behavior even in the contexts most strongly associated with it.

In attempting to reduce a behavior in its usual context, it is helpful to reduce the automaticity of the behavior. The person can make him or herself more aware of the behavior by systematic self-monitoring, e.g., by making a written note every time the behavior is performed. Self-monitoring of undesired behaviors produces a temporary reduction in the rate of the behavior (McFall, 1977). Another way to make the behavior less automatic is to change the physical steps used in carrying it out. The smoker trying to cut down on cigarettes may, for example, switch from carrying cigarettes in a shirt pocket to carrying them in a pants pocket, purse, or briefcase. These changes usually make a person more aware of his or her actions and turn each smoke into an opportunity for conscious decision-making.

A more extreme alteration in the behavior is appropriate for someone who wishes to eliminate it altogether. In such cases, it is appropriate to make the behavior much more difficult. The smoker who is trying to quit should stop carrying cigarettes and should make sure there are none at home. If possible, the person may find it useful not to carry money in a form that can conveniently be used to buy cigarettes. A person can make it harder to borrow or "bum" cigarettes by informing acquaintances that he or she is trying to stop. By all these techniques, the individual makes the action much slower, almost ensuring that the action must be preceded by substantial conscious decision-making. In addition, the increased difficulty of the action contributes to the disadvantages or "cost" side in such decision-making, increasing the likelihood that the person will decide repeatedly not to carry out the action.

Techniques to make the action more difficult are of no value for dealing with the social situation in which another person offers the ex-smoker (or ex-drinker) the substance he or she is trying to avoid. To deal with this situation, the individual must have the social skills necessary to refuse the offer. It may be helpful to many people who are eliminating bad habits to write and practice a routine for turning down such offers.

The individual stopping a habit, like the individual starting one, makes repeated decisions and repeated efforts. The experience of trying to quit alters his or her (a) expectancies about the costs and benefits of quitting, (b) confidence in his or her ability to quit, and (c) coping skills. These changes may lead to continuing effort and success or to a decision not to eliminate the habit.

It is quite common for people to successfully abstain from some undesirable action for several weeks or months and then to resume the bad habit. Typically, at least 50% of abstaining smokers, heroin addicts, and alcoholics resume their habits within 3 months of quitting (Hunt, Barnett, & Branch, 1971; Hunt, Matarazzo, Weiss, & Gentry, 1979). The first drink or smoke often happens in a high-risk situation (e.g., a bar) and is often a reaction to a negative emotional state. Very few smokers or drinkers return to abstinence after their initial slip. Marlatt and Gordon (1979, 1985) suggested that a major reason that slips lead to full relapse is that the individual loses confidence in his or her ability to control the behavior. This explanation is consistent with our view about the role of perceived self-efficacy in decision-making. The educational component of many treatment programs for alcoholism, smoking, and drug abuse leads participants to think that a slip will inevitably lead to total relapse. This is probably a self-fulfilling prophesy. We join Marlatt and Gordon (1979, 1985) in suggesting that treatment programs should avoid this prophesy and should put more emphasis on training in self-control and in the necessary social skills.

DIRECTIONS FOR RESEARCH

The current framework and the associated literature suggest a number of directions for future research. First, in correlational studies of repeated behaviors, it is important to determine how long a person has performed a particular action in addition to determining whether or not he or she is currently doing it. This will make it possible to look for different correlates of initiation and persistence. Similarly, it may be useful to identify respondents who have tried the behavior, but not persisted. It will also be useful to develop measures of habit that have discriminant validity with respect to past frequency of behavior. Instead of asking how often an action has been carried out, questions should ask about the central characteristics of habitual or automatic behaviors: the lack of conscious decision-making, the low level of awareness, and the ability to carry out the habitual behavior while doing something else. Survey questions about the habitual or nonhabitual nature of seat belt use or nonuse, for example, might ask, "When you get into a car, do you think about whether to put on a seat belt, or do you just do what you have done in the past," or, "Do you ever notice that you are wearing your seatbelt, but do not remember putting it on?"

Second, the current framework suggests that certain variables (skills, memory, obstacles) are likely to have stronger effects on persistence, whereas other variables (expectancies, values, attitudes) are likely to have stronger effects on initiation. Much past psychological research has emphasized the second group of variables while giving little attention to the first. Both sets of variables need to be studied.

Finally, the review of the literature revealed a dearth of studies specifically focused on relapse. Considering the great potential value of postponing or avoiding relapse, much more work should be done in this area. Marlatt and Gordon (1979, 1985) and Shiffman (1982) laid the groundwork with their studies of relapse episodes among smokers, alcoholics, and heroin users. It is hoped that similar approaches will be applied to discontinuations of healthful behaviors such as seatbelt wearing, exercise, medication compliance, and breast self-examination. Research designs including a longitudinal component will be most useful in such studies.

SUMMARY

In this chapter, we have drawn from a wide variety of sources to construct a description of the influences on repeated behaviors. The major premise of the chapter is that repeated behaviors are usually habitual and automatic rather than controlled by conscious decision-making. This raises the possibilities of (a) substantial attitude-behavior inconsistency due to attitude change occurring after the formation of the habit and (b) a very limited role for attitudes in guiding behavior. The processes through which habits are formed and eliminated were discussed. This discussion emphasized a variety of factors other than attitudes that influence behavior, among them (a) habits, (b) people's memory, skills, and other resources that are necessary to carry out the action, and (c) perceived self-efficacy or confidence that they can carry out the action. The influence of these factors on behavior reduces and masks the extent that attitudes function to guide behavior.

ACKNOWLEDGMENTS

Preparation of this chapter was supported by Grant CA31520 from the National Cancer Institute and by NIMH Grant T32MH16892.

REFERENCES

Abramson, L. Y., Seligman, M. E. P., & Teasdale, J. D. (1978). Learned helplessness in humans: Critique and reformulation. *Journal of Abnormal Psychology, 87,* 49–74.

Ajzen, I. (1985). From intentions to actions: A theory of planned behavior. In J. Kuhl. & J. Beckman (Eds.), *Action-control: From cognition to behavior.* Heidelberg: Springer.

Ajzen, I., & Fishbein, M. (1977). Attitude-behavior relations: A theoretical analysis and review of empirical research. *Psychological Bulletin, 84,* 888–918.

Ajzen, I., & Fishbein, M. (1980). *Understanding attitudes and predicting social behavior.* Englewood Cliffs, NJ: Prentice-Hall.

Allport, G. W. (1935) Attitudes. In C. Murchison (Ed.), *Handbook of social psychology* (pp. 798–844). Worchester, MA: Clark University Press.

American College of Sports Medicine (1978). Position statement on the recommended quantity of exercise for developing and maintaining fitness in healthy adults. *Medicine, Science and Sports, 10,* vii–x.

Anderson, J. R. (1982). Acquisition of cognitive skill. *Psychological Review, 89,* 369–406.

Anderson, R., & Aday, L. A. (1978). Access to medical care in the U.S.: Realized and potential. *Medical Care, 16,* 533–546.

Antonovsky, A., & Hartman, H. (1974). Delay in the detection of cancer: A review of the literature. *Health Education Monographs, 2,* 98–128.

Bagozzi, R. P. (1981). Attitudes, intentions and behavior: A test of some key hypotheses. *Journal of Personality and Social Psychology, 41,* 607–627.

Bandura, A. (1977). *Social learning theory.* Englewood Cliffs, NJ: Prentice-Hall.

Bandura, A. (1982). Self-efficacy mechanism in human agency. *American Psychologist, 37,* 122–147.

Bar-Hillel, M. (1980). The base-rate fallacy in probability judgments. *Acta Psychologica, 44,* 211–233.

Beach, L. R., & Mitchell, T. R. (1978). A contingency model for the selection of decision strategies. *Academy of Management Review, 3,* 439–448.

Bem, D. J. (1967). Self-perception: An alternative interpretation of cognitive dissonance phenomena. *Psychological Review, 74,* 183–200.

Bentler, P. M., & Speckart, G. (1979). Models of attitude-behavior relations. *Psychological Review, 86,* 452–464.

Bentler, P. M., & Speckart, G. (1981). Attitudes "cause" behavior: A structural equation analysis. *Journal of Personality and Social Psychology, 40,* 226–238.

Ben Zur, H., & Breznitz, S. J. (1981). The effect of time pressure on risky choice behavior. *Acta Psychologica, 47,* 89–104.

Chaiken, S. (1980). Heuristic versus systematic information processing and the use of source versus message cues in persuasion. *Journal of Personality and Social Psychology, 39,* 752–766.

Cronkite, R. C., & Moos, R. H. (1980). Determinants of the posttreatment functioning of alcoholic patients; A conceptual framework. *Journal of Consulting and Clinical Psychology, 48,* 305–316.

Cross, H. A., Halcomb, C. G., & Matter, W. W. (1967). Imprinting or exposure learning in rats given early auditory stimulation. *Psychonomic Science, 7,* 233–234.

Cummings, K. M., Becker, M. H., & Maile, M. C. (1980). Bringing the models together: An empirical approach to combining variables used to explain health actions. *Journal of Behavioral Medicine, 3,* 123–145.

Davidson, A. R., & Jaccard, J. (1979). Variables that moderate the attitude-behavior relation: Results of a longitudinal survey. *Journal of Personality and Social Psychology, 37,* 1364–1376.

Dishman, R. K. (1982). Compliance/adherence in health-related exercise. *Health Psychology, 3,* 237–267.

Dubbert, P. M., & Wilson, G. T. (1984). Goal setting and spouse involvement in the treatment of obesity. *Behavior Research and Therapy, 22,* 227–242.

Fazio, R. H., & Zanna, M. P. (1981). Direct experience and attitude-behavior consistency. In L. Berkowitz (Ed.), *Advances in experimental psychology* Vol. 14, (pp. 162–202). New York: Academic Press.

Festinger, L. (1957). *A theory of cognitive dissonance.* Stanford, CA: Stanford University Press.

Fishbein, M., & Ajzen, I. (1975). *Belief, attitude, intention, and behavior: An introduction to theory and research.* Reading, MA: Addison-Wesley.

Fredricks, A. J., & Dossett, K. L. (1983). Attitude-behavior relations: A comparison of the Fishbein–Ajzen and the Bentler–Speckart models. *Journal of Personality and Social Psychology, 45,* 501–512.

Green, L. W., & Roberts, B. J. (1974). The research literature on why women delay in seeking medical care for breast symptoms. *Health Education Monographs, 2,* 129–177.

Harrison, A. A. (1977). Mere exposure. In L. Berkowitz (Ed.), *Advances in experimental social psychology* (Vol. 10). New York: Academic Press.

Hunt, W. A., Barnett, L. W., & Branch, L. G. (1971). Relapse rates in addiction programs. *Journal of Clinical Psychology, 27,* 455–456.

Hunt, W. A., Matarazzo, J. D., Weiss, S. M., & Gentry, W. D. (1979). Associative learning, habit and health behavior. *Journal of Behavioral Medicine, 2,* 111–124.

Ikard, F. F., Green, D. E., & Horn, D. (1969). A scale to differentiate between types of smoking as related to the management of affect. *The International Journal of the Addictions, 4,* 649–659.

Insko, C. A. (1967). *Theories of attitude change.* New York: Appleton-Century-Crofts.

James, W. (1890). *The principles of psychology* (Vol. 1). New York: Holt.

Janis, I. L. (1984). The patient as decision maker. In W. D. Gentry (Ed.), *Handbook of behavioral medicine.* New York: Guilford Press.

Janis, I. L., & Mann, L. (1977). *Decision making: A psychological analysis of conflict, choice and commitment.* New York: Free Press.

Janz, N. K., & Becker, M. H. (1984). The health belief model: A decade later. *Health Education Quarterly, 11,* 1–47.

Jöreskog, J. G., & Sörbom, D. (1984). *LISREL VI Users guide.* Mooresville, IN: Scientific Software, Inc.

Kelner, R. M., Wohl, B. R., Deasy, M. J., & Formicola, A. J. (1974). Gingival inflammation as related to frequency of plaque removal. *Journal of Peridontology, 1974,* 303–307.

Kiesler, C. A., Collins, B. A., & Miller, N. (1969). *Attitude change.* New York: Wiley.

Lachman, R., Lachman, J. L., & Butterfield, E. C. (1979). *Cognitive psychology and information processing: An introduction.* Hillsdale, NJ: Lawrence Erlbaum Associates.

Landis, D., Triandis, H. C., & Adamopoulos, J. (1978). Habit and behavioral intentions as predictors of social behavior. *Journal of Social Psychology, 106,* 227–237.

Lang, N. P., Cumming, B. R., Loe, H., (1973). Toothbrushing frequency as it relates to plaque development and gingival health. *Journal of Peridontology, 44,* 396–405.

Langer, E., Blank, A., & Chanowitz, B. (1978). The mindlessness of ostensibly thoughtful actions: The role of "placebic" information in interpersonal interaction. *Journal of Personality and Social Psychology, 36,* 635–642.

Latané, B., & Darley, J. (1970). *The unresponsive bystander: Why doesn't he help?* Englewood Cliffs, NJ: Prentice-Hall.

Leventhal, H., & Avis, N. (1976). Pleasure, addiction, and habit: Factors in verbal report or factors in smoking behavior? *Journal of Abnormal Psychology, 85,* 478–488.

Leventhal, H., & Cleary, P. D. (1980). The smoking problem: A review of the research and theory in behavioral risk modification. *Psychological Bulletin, 88,* 370–405.

Maddux, J. E., & Rogers, R. W. (1983). Protection motivation and self-efficacy: A revised theory of fear appeals and attitude change. *Journal of Experimental Social Psychology, 19,* 469–479.

Marlatt, G. A., & Gordon, J. R. (1979). Determinants of relapse: Implications for the maintenance of behavior change. In P. Davidson (Ed.), *Behavioral medicine: Changing health lifestyles* (pp. 410–452). New York: Brunner/Mazel.

Marlatt, G. A., & Gordon, J. R. (Eds.). (1985). *Relapse prevention: Maintenance strategies in the treatment of addictive behaviors.* New York: Guilford Press.

McFall, R. M. (1977). Parameters of self-monitoring. In R. B. Stuart (Ed.), *Behavioral self-management: Strategies, techniques, and outcomes.* New York: Brunner/Mazel.

Mischel, W. (1974). Processes in delay of gratification. In L. Berkowitz (Ed.), *Advances in experimental social psychology* (Vol. 7, pp. 249–292). New York: Academic Press.

Mischel, W. (1981). Metacognition and the rules of delay. In J. H. Flavell & L. Ross (Eds.), *Social cognitive development: Frontiers and possible futures* (pp. 240–271). New York: Cambridge University Press.

Office of Cancer Communications (1979). *Clearing the air: A guide to quitting smoking.* NIH publication, 79–1647.

Payne, J. W. (1982). Contingent decision behavior. *Psychological Bulletin, 92,* 382–402.

Petty, R. E., & Cacioppo, J. T. (1979). Issue involvement can increase or decrease persuasion by enhancing message-relevant cognitive responses. *Journal of Personality and Social Psychology, 37,* 1915–1926.

Petty, R. E., & Cacioppo, J. T. (1981). *Attitudes and persuasion: Classic contemporary approaches.* Dubuque, IA: Wm. C. Brown.

Petty, R. E., Cacioppo, J. T., & Goldman, R. (1981). Personal involvement as a determinant of argument-based persuasion. *Journal of Personality and Psychology, 41,* 847–855.

Petty, R. E., Ostrom, T. M., & Brock, T. C. (1981). *Cognitive responses in persuasion.* Hillsdale, NJ: Lawrence Erlbaum Associates.

Petty, R. E., Wells, G. L., & Brock, T. C. (1976). Distraction can enhance or reduce yielding to propaganda: Thought disruption versus effort justification. *Journal of Personality and Social Psychology, 34,* 874–884.

Rogers, R. W. (1983). Cognitive and physiological processes in fear appeals and attitude change: A revised theory of protection motivation. In J. T. Cacioppo & R. E. Petty (Eds.), *Social psychophysiology: A sourcebook.* New York: Guilford.

Ronis, D. L., & Kaiser, M. K. (in press). Correlates of breast self-examination in a sample of college women: Analyses of linear structural relations. *Journal of Applied Social Psychology.*

Rosenberg, M. J., & Hovland, C. I. (1960). Cognitive, affective and behavioral components of attitudes. In C. I. Hovland, & M. J. Rosenberg (Eds.), *Attitude organization and change* (pp. 1–14). New Haven, CT: Yale University Press.

Safer, M., Tharps, Q., Jackson, T., & Leventhal, H. (1979). Determinants of three stages of delay in seeking care at a medical clinic. *Medical Care, 17,* 11–29.

Schachter, S., Festinger, L., Willerman, B., & Hyman, R. (1961). Emotional disruption and industrial productivity. *Journal of Applied Psychology, 45,* 201–213.

Schneider, W., & Shiffrin, R. M. (1977). Controlled and automatic human information processing: I. Detection, search, and attention. *Psychological Review, 84*, 1–66.

Shanteau, J. C. (1974). Component processes in risky decision-making. *Journal of Experimental Psychology, 103*, 680–691.

Sharp, K., Ross, C., & Cockerham, W. C. (1983). Symptoms, beliefs, and the use of physician services among the disadvantaged. *Journal of Health and Social Behavior, 24*, 255–263.

Shiffman, S. (1982). Relapse following smoking cessation: A situational analysis. *Journal of Consulting and Clinical Psychology, 50*, 71–86.

Shiffrin, R. M., Dumais, S. T., & Schneider, W. (1981). Characteristics of automatism. In J. Long & A. Baddeley (Eds.), *Attention and performance Vol. IX* (pp. 223–238). Hillsdale, NJ: Lawrence Erlbaum Associates.

Shiffrin, R. M., & Schneider, W. (1977). Controlled and automatic human information processing: II. Perceptual learning, automatic attending, and a general theory. *Psychological Review, 84*, 127–190.

Shifter, D. E., & Ajzen, I. (1985). Intention, perceived control, and weight loss: An application of the theory of planned behavior. *Journal of Personality and Social Psychology, 49*, 843–851.

Simon, H. A. (1957). *Models of man.* New York: Wiley.

Smith, J., Mitchell, T. R., & Beach, L. R. (1982). A cost-benefit mechanism for selecting problem-solving strategies: Some extensions and empirical tests. *Organizational Behavior and Human Performance, 29*, 370–396.

Triandis, H. C. (1977). *Interpersonal behavior.* Monterey, CA: Brooks/Cole

Triandis, H. C. (1980). Values, attitudes, and interpersonal behavior. In M. M. Page (Ed.), *Nebraska symposium on motivation, 1979* (pp. 195–259). Lincoln, NE: University of Nebraska Press.

Tversky, A. (1969). Intransitivity of preferences. *Psychological Review, 76*, 31–48.

Tversky, A. (1972). Elimination by aspects: A theory of choice. *Psychological Review, 79*, 281–299.

Wallsten, T. S., & Barton, C. (1982). Processing probabilistic multi-dimensional information for decisions. *Journal of Experimental Psychology: Learning, Memory, and Cognition, 8*, 361–384.

Wallston, B. S., & Wallston, K. A. (1984). Social psychological models of health behavior: An examination and integration. In A. Baum, S. Taylor, & J. Singer (Eds.), *Social psychological aspects of health* (pp. 25–53). Hillsdale, NJ: Lawrence Erlbaum Associates.

Wicker, A. W. (1969). Attitudes vs. actions: The relationship of verbal and overt behavioral responses to attitude objects. *Journal of Social Issues, 25*, 41–78.

Wicklund, R. A., & Brehm, J. W. (1976). *Perspectives on cognitive dissonance.* Hillsdale, NJ: Lawrence Erlbaum Associates.

Wittenbraker, J., Gibbs, B. L., & Kahle, L. R. (1983). Seatbelt attitudes, habits, and behaviors: An adaptive amendment of the Fishbein model. *Journal of Applied Social Psychology, 13*, 406–421.

Wright, P. (1974). The harassed decision maker: Time pressures, distractions, and the use of evidence. *Journal of Applied Psychology, 39*, 555–561.

Yates, J. F., & Revelle, G. L. (1974). Processes operative during delay of gratification. *Motivation and Emotion, 3*, 103–115.

Zajonc, R. B. (1968). The attitudinal effects of mere exposure. *Journal of Personality and Social Psychology, 9*, (Pt. 2), 1–27.

Zifferblatt, S. M. (1975). Increasing patient compliance through the applied analysis of behavior. *Preventive Medicine, 4*, 173–182.

10

Attitude Structure and Behavior

Icek Ajzen
University of Massachusetts at Amherst

Spurred largely by interest in the relation between attitudes and behavior, the attitude concept, following a period of relative neglect, has moved back into the focus of research in social psychology (Chaiken & Stangor, 1987). The general pessimism regarding our ability to predict behavior from attitudes that prevailed not too long ago has, in recent years, given way to the belief that strong attitude-behavior relations can be obtained under appropriate conditions. Most social psychologists now accept the proposition that the effect of attitude on behavior is contingent on the operation of other factors (e.g., Fazio & Zanna, 1981; Snyder, 1982; Warner & DeFleur, 1969). These moderating variables can be individual personality differences, circumstances surrounding performance of the behavior, the nature of the attitude, and so on (see Ajzen, 1987; Sherman & Fazio, 1983 for reviews). The present chapter focuses on attitude structure and the role it may play as a moderator of the attitude-behavior relation.

THE STRUCTURE OF ATTITUDES

An attitude is an individual's disposition to respond favorably or unfavorably to an object, person, institution, or event, or to any other discriminable aspect of the individual's world. Although formal definitions of attitude vary, most contemporary social psychologists seem to agree that the characteristic attribute of attitude is its evaluative (pro–con, positive–negative) dimension (see, e.g., Bem, 1970; Edwards, 1957; Fishbein & Ajzen, 1975; Hill, 1981; Osgood, Suci, & Tannenbaum, 1957; Oskamp, 1977). This view is strengthened by the fact that virtually all standard attitude scaling techniques result in a score that locates an individual on an evaluative continuum vis-à-vis the attitude object (cf. Fishbein & Ajzen, 1975; Green, 1954). It is possible, however, to go beyond attitude as a general evaluative disposition by considering the structure of the domain to which it applies. Two approaches to this issue are discussed, one focusing on relations among variables subsumed under the attitude construct, the other on an attitude's antecedents and consequences.

The Multicomponent View: Cognition, Affect, and Conation

It is generally acknowledged that attitude is a latent variable or hypothetical construct. Being inaccessible to direct observation, it must be inferred from measurable responses, and given the nature of the construct, these responses must reflect positive or negative evaluations of the attitude object. Beyond this requirement, however, virtually no limitations are placed on the kinds of responses that can be considered. To simplify matters it is possible to categorize attitude-relevant responses into various subgroups. Thus, we might distinguish between responses directed at others and responses directed at the self, between behaviors performed in public and behaviors performed in private, or between actions and reactions. However, the most popular classification system goes back at least to Plato and distinguishes between three categories of responses: cognition, affect, and conation (see Allport, 1954; Hilgard, 1980; and McGuire, 1985 for general discussions). Within each of these categories it is also useful to separate verbal from nonverbal responses. Based on Rosenberg and Hovland's (1960) analysis, Table 10.1 shows the different types of responses from which attitudes can thus be inferred.

TABLE 10.1
Responses Used to Infer Attitudes

Response Mode	Response Category		
	Cognition	Affect	Conation
Verbal	Expressions of beliefs about attitude object	Expressions of feelings toward attitude object	Expressions of behavioral intentions
Nonverbal	Perceptual reactions to attitude object	Physiological reactions to attitude object	Overt behaviors with respect to attitude object

Cognitive Responses

The cognitive category consists of responses that reflect perceptions of, and information about, the attitude object. Consider some of the responses we might use to infer attitudes toward the medical profession. Cognitive responses of a verbal nature are expressions of *beliefs* that link the medical profession with certain characteristics or attributes. Beliefs to the effect that physicians are mostly interested in money, that hospitals are overcrowded, that many health professionals are poorly qualified, or that most diseases cannot be cured by traditional methods, might be taken as evidence of a negative attitude toward the medical profession. By way of contrast, a favorable attitude would be implied by expressions of beliefs suggesting that nurses and doctors do their best to help patients, that medicine has made considerable progress over the years, that many physicians work long and inconvenient hours, and the like.

Cognitive responses of a nonverbal nature are more difficult to assess, and the information they provide about attitudes is usually more indirect. For example, we might argue that people with favorable attitudes toward the medical establishment have relatively low thresholds for the perception of attitude-relevant positive stimuli, whereas people with unfavorable attitudes have relatively low thresholds for negative stimuli. To infer attitude toward the medical profession, therefore, we might measure how long it takes a person to appreciate the significance of cartoons depicting doctors, nurses, and hospitals in either a favorable or an unfavorable light.

Affective Responses

The second category of responses from which attitudes can be inferred has to do with feelings toward the attitude object. Here again, we can distinguish between affective responses of a verbal and of a nonverbal kind. Verbal affective responses with respect to the medical profession, for example, can be expressions of admiration or disgust, appreciation or disdain. Thus, a person who claims to admire physicians or nurses, or to feel good about the available medical care, would seem to hold a favorable attitude toward the medical profession, but a person who indicates that the mere thought of doctors and hospitals is disgusting would seem to hold a negative attitude.

Facial expressions, as well as various physiological and other bodily reactions, are often assumed to reflect affect in a nonverbal fashion. Among the bodily reactions considered are the galvanic skin response, constriction and dilation of the pupil, heart rate, the reactions of facial muscles, and other reactions of the sympathetic nervous system. One of the difficulties inherent in methods that rely on responses of this kind is the problem of distinguishing between reactions that imply favorable attitudes and reactions that imply unfavorable attitudes, although recent research has reported some progress in this regard (see Cacioppo, Petty, Losch, & Kim, 1986).

Conative Responses

Responses of a conative nature are behavioral inclinations, intentions, commitments, and actions with respect to the attitude object. Starting again on the verbal side, we can consider what people say they do, plan to do, or would do under appropriate circumstances. Thus, people with negative attitudes toward the medical profession might indicate that they would refuse to be hospitalized, that they see a doctor only when absolutely necessary, or that they discourage their children from going to medical school. On the other hand, those with positive attitudes might express intentions to donate money to a fund for a new hospital wing, they might plan to encourage their children to go to medical school, they might indicate a readiness to read about advances in medicine, and so on.

Nonverbal responses indicating favorable or unfavorable attitudes toward the medical profession are also easily imagined. Thus, people who actually read books or articles about medicine, who encourage their children to go to medical school, or who accept and follow their physicans' advice would be classified as having positive attitudes, whereas people who refuse to donate money to a medical fund or who write letters to newspapers complaining about the medical profession would be said to have negative attitudes.

Attitudes Versus Behaviors

Before we continue our discussion, it is important to clarify what is meant when we examine the relation between attitude and behavior. We saw that an individual's favorable or unfavorable attitude toward a person, institution, or event can be inferred from verbal or nonverbal responses toward the object in question. These responses can be of a cognitive nature, reflecting perceptions of the object or beliefs concerning its likely characteristics; they can be of an affective nature, reflecting the person's feelings; and they can be of conative nature, indicating how a person does, would or plans to act with respect to the object.

When considering the relation between attitudes and behavior, the problem is typically defined as the degree of correspondence between evaluative responses of a verbal kind and evaluative responses of a nonverbal kind. It is a question of what we say versus what we do (Deutscher, 1966, 1973). The verbal and nonverbal responses could come from any one of the three response categories (cognition, affect, or conation), but the typical procedure is to use evaluative responses of a cognitive or affective nature on the verbal side and evaluative responses of a conative kind on the nonverbal side. Thus, religiousity, as assessed by means of a questionnaire that contains various statements of belief and feeling with respect to religion, the church, and so forth, might be correlated with observed church attendance. This way of approaching the issue has frequently led to misunderstandings. Consistent with the typical operationalization, many investigators have assumed that verbal responses reflect a person's attitude, whereas nonverbal (overt) actions are measures of behavior. In point of fact, however, both verbal and nonverbal responses are observable behaviors. Neither is more or less a measure of attitude than the other; both types of behavior can reflect the same underlying disposition (cf. Roth & Upmeyer, 1985; Upmeyer, 1981). Moreover, the validity of overt behaviors as indicators of a latent disposition cannot be taken for granted, any more so than can the validity of verbal responses to questionnaire items. Both types of behavior must be submitted to standard scaling procedures, and only some responses—whether verbal or nonverbal—will be found adequate for the assessment of a given attitude (cf. Ajzen & Fishbein, 1980; Jackson & Paunonen, 1985). Strictly speaking, therefore, most tests of the attitude-behavior relation are better conceptualized as tests of the relation between verbal and nonverbal indicators of the same evaluative attitude. However, for the sake of simplicity and in line with common practice, the present chapter continues to use the attitude-behavior terminology.

A Hierarchical Model of Attitude

Thus far we have assumed that an evaluative disposition is the same, whether it is inferred from responses of a cognitive, affective, or conative nature. Some theorists, however, would dispute this assumption. The multidimensional view of attitude holds that cognitive, affective, and conative response tendencies represent conceptually distinct components of attitude (see. e.g., Krech, Crutchfield, & Ballachey, 1962; McGuire, 1985). Specifically, the model offered by Rosenberg and Hovland (1960), which serves as the starting point of most contemporary analyses, is a hierarchical model that includes cognition, affect, and conation as first-order factors and attitude as a single second-order factor. In this model, the three components are defined independently and yet comprise, at a higher level of abstraction, the single construct of attitude. To extend this line of reasoning, recall that each component is made up of verbal and nonverbal response classes, and that each of these is further comprised of a large number of very specific response tendencies. Attitudes are thus always inferred from specific responses to the attitude object. We can classify these responses into broader categories and assign different labels to those categories, yet we are still dealing with the same evaluative disposition called attitude. The hierarchical three-component model of attitude is shown schematically in Fig. 10.1.

The shared evaluative character of the cognitive, affective, and conative attitudinal components has often been a source of confusion. This is especially apparent in attempts to distinguish empirically between cognition and affect. In fact, there is considerable disagreement as to the appropriate means of separating these two components. For example, some investigators (e.g., Norman, 1975) have employed the evaluative semantic differential as a measure of affect, whereas others (e.g., Breckler, 1984) have used it as a measure of cognition. Close examination of the semantic differential's evaluative factor (see Osgood, Suci, & Tannenbaum, 1957) actually reveals a mixture of what appear to be cognitive (e.g., useful–useless) and affective (e.g., pleasant–unpleasant) adjective scales. The two types of scales are often highly correlated and thus tend to load on the same factor, but at times they are found to tap two different underlying constructs (see Ajzen & Timko, 1986). It is thus possible, by carefully selecting appropriate scales, to use the semantic differential to assess an attitude's cognitive or affective component.

The empirical implications of the hierarchical attitude model can be stated as follows. Given that the three components reflect the same underlying attitude, they should correlate to some degree with each other. Yet, to the extent that the distinction between cognitive, affective, and conative response categories is of psychological significance, measures of the three components should not be completely redundant. In combination, these expectations imply correlations of moderate magnitude among measures of

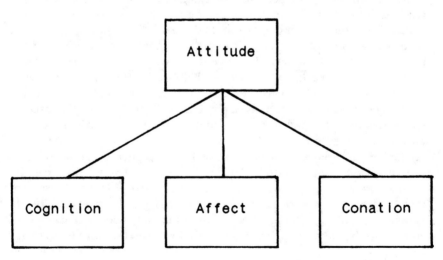

FIG. 10.1.   Hierarchical model of attitude.

the three components. A number of attempts have been made over the years to confirm the discriminant validity of measures designed to tap the different components, first with the aid of multitrait-multimethod matrices (Kothandapani, 1971; Ostrom, 1969) and, more recently, by means of confirmatory factor analyses (Bagozzi, 1978; Bagozzi & Burnkrant, 1979; Breckler, 1984; Widaman, 1985). Depending on the method used and the assumptions made, the data have variously been interpreted either as supporting a tripartite model or a single-factor model (see the exchange between Bagozzi & Burnkrant, 1985 and Dillon & Kumar, 1985). The major issue seems to revolve around whether differences between measures of the cognitive, affective, and conative components are to be interpreted as due to differences in the methods used to assess them (i.e., as theoretically uninteresting method variance) or as due to true differences between conceptually independent components. At a general level, however, most of the data reported in the literature is quite consistent with the hierarchical model in that a single factor is found to account for much of the variance in attitudinal responses, and the correlations among measures of the three components, although leaving room for some unique variance, are typically of considerable magnitude.

A CAUSAL CHAIN PERSPECTIVE: BELIEFS, ATTITUDES, INTENTIONS, AND BEHAVIOR

The hierarchical model of attitude, shown in Fig. 10.1, views cognition, affect, and conation as parallel first-order factors and overall evaluation or attitude as a general second-order factor. Fishbein and Ajzen (1975; Ajzen & Fishbein, 1980) proposed a theoretical framework that structures the attitudinal domain in a different way. Within this framework, the term *attitude* is reserved strictly for the overall evaluative response, whereas cognition, affect, and conation are treated as conceptually distinct antecedents or consequences of attitude.

As in other theories (e.g., Peak, 1955; Rosenberg, 1956), it is assumed that attitudes are consistent with cognitions, i.e., with beliefs about the attitude object. However, in the Fishbein–Ajzen framework, attitudes are not merely related to beliefs, they are actually a function of beliefs, i.e., beliefs are assumed to have *causal* effects on attitudes. An expectancy-value model is used to describe the effects of beliefs on attitudes. Each belief about an object links the object to a certain attribute (some other object, characteristic, outcome, or event). The attribute's subjective value contributes to the attitude in direct proportion to the strength of the belief, i.e., the subjective probability that the object has the attribute in question. To obtain an estimate of the resulting attitude, belief strength is multiplied by attribute evaluation, and these products are summed across all salient beliefs. It is important to note that, according to theory, attitude is a function of beliefs that are *salient* for the individual, and only of those beliefs. It is possible, as we saw, to infer attitudes from responses to various kinds of belief statements, but only beliefs that are salient in the individual's mind are assumed to have a causal impact on attitudes.

Attitudes, in turn, are assumed to exert a dynamic or directive influence on behavior. That is, the overall evaluation of an object predisposes the individual to perform generally favorable or unfavorable behaviors with respect to the object. Specifically, people are assumed to form intentions to behave in ways that are evaluatively consistent with their attitudes and, when appropriate opportunities arise, to act—or at least attempt to act—in accordance with those intentions (see Ajzen, 1985; Ajzen & Fishbein, 1980; Fishbein & Ajzen, 1975 for more detailed descriptions).

It can be seen that the Fishbein–Ajzen framework postulates a causal chain in which behavior is determined by intentions to perform the behavior, intentions follow from overall evaluations or attitudes, and these attitudes are a function of salient beliefs.[1] This is not to say that causal effects work only in one direction (see also Liska, 1984). Once established, attitudes may influence perception and interpretation of later events, thus determining in part the beliefs that are formed. Similarly, performance of behavior often provides new information that changes existing beliefs that, via attitudes and intentions, then have an impact on subsequent behavior. We are here, however, interested mainly in the causal links from beliefs to behavior, rather than vice versa.

The Principle of Compatibility

According to Fishbein and Ajzen's causal chain model, strong links from beliefs to attitudes, attitudes to intentions, and intentions to actions are expected only under certain conditions. These conditions have to do with the structural characteristics of the dispositional domain defined by the investigator. Any dispositional domain can be mapped along the dimension of generality, from the global to the specific. Thus, we may be concerned with the global evaluative disposition toward the medical profession or, at the other extreme, with the specific tendency to donate or not to donate blood at an upcoming blood drive. Or, to take another example, the domain

---

[1]The role of affect is not spelled out very clearly in the Ajzen-Fishbein framework. Affective reactions may depend at least in part on cognitions and, like cognitions, they may feed into the overall evaluative response to an attitude object. In addition, affect may be associated with the perceived attributes of an object and may thus be partly responsible for the evaluative direction and intensity of a person's beliefs.

may, at the global end of the spectrum, be defined as the disposition toward religiosity or, at the specific end, the disposition to attend Sunday worship services at one's church. And then, of course, there are various intermediate levels of generality at which a disposition can be approached. In the medical domain, for example, we might be concerned with the disposition to respond in a generally favorable or unfavorable manner toward a given hospital (rather than toward the medical establishment overall), with the disposition vis-à-vis a particular physician, and so forth.

It is important to realize that questions concerning level of generality can be raised with respect to all four concepts distinguished above: belief, attitude, intention, and behavior. We can assess beliefs about the medical establishment, about a particular physician, or about donating blood to the Red Cross at an upcoming blood drive. Similarly, we can measure evaluations of the medical establishment, of a particular physician, or of donating blood to the Red Cross at an upcoming blood drive. And we can assess various intentions and actions with respect to the medical establishment or with respect to a particular physician. As to the specific act of donating blood at an upcoming blood drive by the Red Cross this is, of course, a single behavior. At the most specific level of intention or action, therefore, we would simply assess whether or not a person intends to or actually does perform the behavior in question.

In a review of research on the attitude-behavior relation, Ajzen and Fishbein (1977) formulated a principle of compatibility that is closely related to the question of the generality or specificity of the dispositional domain. Any dispositional measure, whether verbal or nonverbal, can be defined in terms of four elements: the action involved, the target at which the action is directed, the context in which it occurs, and the time of its occurrence. Two indicators of a disposition are compatible with each other to the extent that their action, target, context, and time elements are assessed at identical levels of generality or specificity. The generality or specificity of each element depends on the measurement procedures employed. A single observation of an action is a highly specific behavioral indicator in that it involves a given response, directed at a particular target, and performed in a given context and at a given point in time. By aggregating actions across one or more elements, a behavioral indicator can be made arbitrarily general. In the same vein, belief, attitude, and intention measures can be analyzed according to the generality or specificity of the action, target, context, and time elements. For example, global attitudes toward objects specify no particular action, i.e., they are very broadly defined in terms of the action element; but attitudes toward such behaviors as donating blood or smoking cigarettes are much more specific. According to the compatibility principle, consistency between two indicators of a given disposition is a function of the degree to which the indicators assess the disposition at the same level of generality or specificity. Thus, the more similar the action, target, context, and time elements of a verbal response to an object (the attitude) to the elements of a nonverbal response (the behavior), the stronger should be the statistical relation between them.

The principle of compatibility can be viewed as a special case of the contiguity hypothesis in Guttman's (1955, 1957, 1959) facet theory. Guttman proposed that any variable can be analyzed in terms of an underlying facet structure. The action, target, context, and time elements of behavioral dispositions are examples of facets, and their levels of generality constitute facet elements. Like the principle of compatibility, "The contiguity hypothesis of facet theory states that the correlation between two variables increases with the similarity between the facet elements defining them" (Guttman, 1957, p. 130; see also Foa, 1958; Olweus, 1980).

The importance of compatibility for ensuring strong attitude-behavior correlations has been documented extensively (see Ajzen, 1982, 1987; Ajzen & Fishbein, 1977 for reviews) and is widely accepted among social psychologists (e.g., Hill, 1981; Liska, 1984; Petty & Cacioppo, 1981; Rajecki, 1982). Consistent with the principle of compatibility, research over the years has demonstrated three points quite conclusively. First, correlations tend to be low when verbal measures of global attitude are correlated with nonverbal measures of specific behaviors. Wicker's (1969) pessimistic conclusions concerning the attitude-behavior relation were based largely on research findings of this kind. Second, verbal measures of attitude toward a general target correlate well with equally general (aggregated) measures of behavior with respect to the same target (e.g., Bandura, Blanchard, & Ritter, 1969; Fishbein & Ajzen, 1974; Weigel & Newman, 1976). Third, attitudes toward a specific behavior tend to correlate quite well with performance of the behavior in question. Thus, by maintaining equivalent levels of generality in the dispositional domain defined by our verbal measures of attitude and our nonverbal measures of behavior, we can assure relatively strong attitude-behavior correlations.

A Theory of Planned Behavior

The logic of a causal chain from beliefs to behavior, together with the principle of compatibility, are embodied in Ajzen and Fishbein's (1980; Fishbein & Ajzen, 1975) theory of reasoned action and, more recently, in Ajzen's (1985; Ajzen & Madden, 1986) extension of that theory to the prediction of behavioral goals. As in the original model, a central factor in the theory of planned behavior is the individual's *intention* to perform a behavior. Intentions are assumed to capture the motivational factors that impact on a behavior; they are indications of how hard people are willing to try, of how much of an effort they are planning to exert, in order to perform the behavior.

The theory of planned behavior postulates three conceptually in-dependent determinants of intentions. The first is the *attitude* toward the behavior and refers to the degree to which the person has a favorable on unfavorable evaluation of the behavior in question. The second predictor is a social factor termed *subjective norm;* it refers to the perceived social pressure to perform or not to perform the behavior. The third and novel antecedent of intention, which was not part of the theory of reasoned action, is the degree of *perceived behavioral control.* This factor refers to the perceived ease or difficulty of performing the behavior and it is assumed to reflect past experience as well as anticipated impediments and obstacles. As a general rule, the more favorable the attitude and subjective norm with respect to a behavior, and the greater the perceived behavioral control, the stronger should be an individual's intention to perform the behavior under consideration.

Intention, in turn, is viewed as one immediate antecedent of actual behavior. That is, the stronger people's intentions to engage in a behavior or to achieve their behavioral goals, the more successful they are predicted to be. However, the degree of success will depend not only on one's desire or intention, but also on such partly nonmotivational factors as availability of requisite opportunities and resources (e.g., time, money, skills, cooperation of others, etc.; see Ajzen, 1985, for a review). Collectively, these factors represent people's *actual control* over the behavior. (See also the dis-cussions of "facilitating factors" by Triandis, 1977, "the context of opportu-nity" by Sarver, 1983, "resources" by Liska, 1984, and "action control" by Kuhl, 1985.) To the extent that a person has the required opportunities and resources, and intends to perform the behavior, to that extent he or she should succeed in doing so. A graphic representation of the theory is shown in Fig. 10.2.

Of course, in many situations perceived behavioral control may not be particularly realistic. This is likely to be the case when the individual has relatively little information about the behavior, when requirements or available resources have changed, or when new and unfamiliar elements have entered into the situation. Under those conditions, a measure of perceived behavioral control may add little to accuracy of behavioral pre-diction. The broken arrow in Fig. 10.2 indicates that the path from per-ceived behavioral control to behavior is expected to emerge only when there is some agreement between perceptions of control and the person's actual control over the behavior.

Finally, the theory deals with the antecedents of attitudes, subjective norms, and perceived behavioral control, antecedents that in the final analysis determine intentions and actions. At the most basic level of ex-planation, the theory postulates that behavior is a function of salient in-formation, or beliefs, relevant to the behavior. Three kinds of beliefs are distinguished: *behavioral beliefs,* which are assumed to influence attitudes

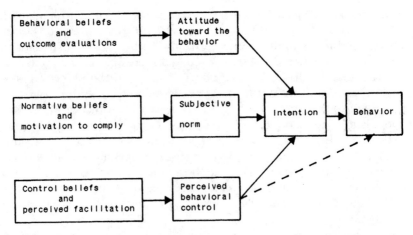

FIG. 10.2.   Theory of planned behavior.

toward the behavior; *normative beliefs,* which constitute the underlying determinants of subjective norms; and *control beliefs,* which provide the basis for perceptions of behavioral control. Each behavioral belief links the behavior to a certain outcome, or to some other attribute such as the cost incurred by performing the behavior. Based on the expectancy-value model of attitude described earlier, an estimate of attitude is obtained by multiply- ing belief strength with outcome evaluation and summing the resulting products across all salient behavioral beliefs. Normative beliefs, on the other hand, are concerned with the likelihood that important referent individuals or groups would approve or disapprove of performing the behavior. The strength of each normative belief is multiplied by the person's motivation to comply with the referent in question, and an estimate of subjective norm is obtained by summing the resulting products across all salient referents.

Finally, among the beliefs that ultimately determine intention and action there is, according to the theory of planned behavior, a set that deals with the presence or absence of requisite resources and opportunities. These control beliefs may be based in part on past experience with the behavior, but they will usually be influenced by secondhand information about the behavior, by the experiences of acquaintances and friends, and by other factors that increase or reduce the perceived difficulty of performing the behavior in question. The more resources and opportunities individuals think they possess, and the fewer obstacles or impediments they anticipate, the greater should be their perceived control over the behavior. Specifical- ly, each control belief is multiplied by the perceived facilitating (or inhibit- ing) effect of the resource or opportunity under consideration, and the resulting products are summed to obtain an estimate of perceived be- havioral control. Thus, just as beliefs concerning consequences of a behavior are viewed as determining attitudes, and normative beliefs are viewed as determining subject norms, so beliefs about resources and opportunities are viewed as underlying perceived behavioral control.

Empirical research over the past 15 years has provided evidence in support of the theory of reasoned action in a variety of experimental and naturalistic settings (see, e.g., Ajzen & Fishbein, 1980; Ajzen, Timko, & White, 1982; Bentler & Speckart, 1979, 1981; Fredricks & Dossett, 1983; Manstead, Proffitt, & Smart, 1983; Smetana & Adler, 1980). The behaviors involved have ranged from very simple strategy choices in laboratory games to actions of appreciable personal or social significance, such as having an abortion, smoking marijuana, and choosing among candidates in an election. Intentions to perform behaviors of this kind can be predicted from attitudes toward the behaviors and from subjective norms, and the intentions in turn correlate well with observed actions. For the most part, however, the behaviors investigated have been behaviors over which people tend to have considerable volitional control. Recent research on the theory of planned behavior has demonstrated that when volitional control is more problematic, the addition of perceived behavioral control significantly improves prediction of intentions as well as prediction of behavioral achievement (see Ajzen, 1988; Ajzen & Madden, 1986; Schifter & Ajzen, 1985).

ATTITUDE STRUCTURE AND THE PREDICTION OF BEHAVIOR

In the following pages we consider some of the implications of the two models of attitude, the hierarchical model and the causal chain model, especially in terms of the ways in which the specified attitude structure may moderate the relation between attitude and behavior. One case in point is the implication of the causal chain perspective that the intention to perform a particular behavior (in a given context) is the immediate antecedent of actual behavioral performance. Attitude toward the behavior, even though it is also compatible in its elements with the behavior, is assumed to exert its effect indirectly via intentions. It follows that behavioral intention should permit better prediction of the corresponding behavior than should attitude toward the behavior. Empirical evidence is generally supportive of this expectation.

Consider, for example, the study by Manstead, Proffitt, and Smart (1983) on prediction of breast-feeding versus bottle-feeding of newborn infants. Toward the end of their pregnancies, women completed a questionnaire that assessed, among other things, their attitudes and intentions with respect to breast-feeding and with respect to bottle-feeding their babies. Six weeks following delivery, a questionnaire sent to each women ascertained her actual feeding practices during the preceding 6 weeks. As expected, choice of feeding method was predicted with significantly greater accuracy from intentions ($r = .82$) than from attitudes toward the behavior ($r = .67$). Similar findings were reported with respect to cooperation and competition in prisoner's dilemma games (Ajzen, 1971; Ajzen & Fishbein, 1970) and with respect to use of marijuana by college students (Ajzen, Timko, & White, 1982).

The hierarchical three-component model of attitude may also have certain implications for the prediction of behavior, but these implications have not been clearly formulated. It could be argued that, to predict behavior, an appropriate measure of attitude must include all three components, i.e., that it must generalize across representative samples of cognitive, affective, and conative responses to the attitude object. In this view, more selective measures that rely, for example, on cognitive or affective responses only would not fully capture the attitudinal disposition and might exhibit a diminished relation to overt behavior. The best predictor of behavioral tendencies, therefore, should be a measure of attitudes that is broadly representative of the overall evaluative response.

It is, however, possible to look at this issue in a different way. An attitude's conative component, representing a global action tendency, seems closer to actual behavior than do the cognitive and affective components. It follows that a measure of the conative component, unconfounded by cognitive or affective responses, should be the best predictor of specific behaviors toward the attitude object.

Very few studies have examined this issue empirically, and those that have done so, have compared the predictive validities of the different components rather than the conative component versus an inclusive measure based on all three types of responses. Ostrom (1969) developed several scales designed to assess cognition, affect, and conation with respect to the church and examined the relations of the three components to various overt behaviors. The results revealed strong correlations among the three components, and little evidence for discriminant validity (see Widaman, 1985). Consequently, there were no major differences in the predictive powers of the cognitive, affective, and conative components.

In a conceptual replication of this study (Kothandapani, 1971), a sample of women completed various scales that were constructed to represent the cognitive, affective, and conative components of their attitudes toward personal use of birth control methods. A reanalysis of Kothandapani's data revealed strong evidence for convergent validity among the different types of scales, and for discriminant validity between measures of the three components (see Widaman, 1985). As to accuracy of behavioral prediction, it was found that the conative component correlated better with reported use of birth control methods than did either the cognitive or the affective component. The average component-behavior correlation was .81 for the conative component, .66 for the cognitive component, and .55 for the affective component.

Note that, overall, Kothandapani's study produced much stronger attitude-behavior correlations than those reported by Ostrom. One important difference between the two studies lies in the fact that Kothandapani assessed attitudes toward the particular behavior of interest. That is, he assessed attitudes toward personal use of birth control methods, which was also the behavioral criterion, rather than toward such concepts as birth control or family planning. In contrast, Ostrom attempted to predict specific behaviors involving the church from a measure of attitude toward the church in general. Of course, this pattern of results is quite consistent with the principle of compatibility, but it also raises an issue that will occupy us in the remainder of this chapter, namely, the relation between general attitudes and specific action tendencies.

Global Attitudes and Specific Behaviors

Although the principle of compatibility, and the theory of planned behavior, have helped shed light on the attitude-behavior problem, they have had little to say about the relation between global measures of attitude on one hand and, on the other hand, specific actions directed at the attitude object. As a general rule, and consistent with the principle of compatibility, broad attitude measures are found to be poor predictors of specific behaviors. This is perhaps the most important lesson to be learned from the prolonged controversy concerning the attitude-behavior relation, but also perhaps the most difficult to accept. It would indeed be very convenient if we could measure general attitudes and use the resulting scores to predict any behavior that appears relevant to the attitude in question. Unfortunately, both theory and empirical findings negate this possibility. Yet, by considering the structure of an attitudinal domain, it may be possible to identify conditions that are likely to facilitate strong relations between a general attitude measure and specific behaviors directed at the attitude object.

Internal Dynamics of Attitudes

In terms of the hierarchical model of attitude, attitude structure is mainly a question of the relations among elements within and between the cognitive, affective, and conative components. It has to do with the ways in which these components are organized and with the divergent attitudinal properties that emerge as a result of different organizational patterns.

Within-Component Structure

Many different lines of research are relevant for an understanding of the internal structure of an attitude's cognitive, affective, and conative components. Perhaps the most intensively studied aspect of attitude structure has to do with the dimensions and properties characterizing people's belief systems (see, e.g., Rokeach, 1968; Rosenberg & Sedlak, 1972; Schlegel & DiTecco, 1982; Scott, 1969; Tesser, 1978; Wish, Deutsch, & Biener, 1970). Much of this research has been descriptive in nature, because it has attempted to identify basic dimensions that underlie the great variety of beliefs people can hold. Work on the semantic differential (Osgood, Suci, & Tannenbaum, 1957; Snider & Osgood, 1969) is perhaps the best-known effort to identify belief dimensions at a very general level. The evaluation, potency, and activity factors that have consistently emerged in this research are found to be quite stable across concepts and cultures. (Recall, however, that the evaluative factor tends to contain not only cognitive scales but also scales of an affective nature.) Somewhat different and idiosyncratic factor structures tend to characterize belief systems in particular content domains. Thus, in the area of interpersonal perception, five major belief dimensions are generally identified: extraversion, agreeableness, conscientiousness, emotional stability, and culturedness (see Norman, 1963; Wiggins, 1973). These dimensions may be viewed as descriptive of people's "intuitive theories of personality" (Bruner & Tagiuri, 1954; Schneider, 1973). Or, to take another example, multidimensional scaling techniques revealed that beliefs about nations can be classified along the dimensions of political alignment, economic development, geography and population, and culture and race (Wish, Deutsch, & Biener, 1970).

Much less research has been devoted to affective and conative reactions, and the bulk of this research has again tended to be descriptive in nature. Investigations into affective reactions have been conducted primarily by personality psychologists interested in human emotions (e.g., Averill, 1975; Russell, 1978, 1983; Watson, Clark, & Tellegen, 1984). Multidimensional scaling as well as factor analyses of emotional terms have consistently found that affective structure can be defined in terms of two broad dimensions: pleasantness-unpleasantness (e.g., delighted, happy, glad vs. miserable, frustrated, sad) and arousal or activation (e.g., alarmed, tense, excited vs. tired, calm, relaxed). These dimensions, of course, parallel the evaluation and activity factors of the semantic differential.

Despite the recognized importance of behavioral taxonomies (e.g., Barker, 1963), relatively few empirical studies have been conducted to describe the structure of conation. Most prominent among these attempts is Triandis's (1964) work on the dimensions of interpersonal intentions. Factor analyses of expressed intentions to perform various behaviors with respect to a variety of stimulus persons have revealed five major underlying dimensions: admiration (admire the character of the stimulus person, praise his or her suggestions), subordination-superordination (be commanded by the person, elect him or her to political office), friendship (accept as an intimate friend, treat as an equal), social distance (invite the person to one's club, exclude from one's neighborhood), and marital acceptance (go on a date with the person, marry the person).

Cognitive Differentiation and Integration

Going beyond descriptive research, some investigators have attempted to identify and measure certain dynamic properties of attitude structure. Although properties of this kind could be defined with respect to each component of attitude, most efforts seem to have been directed at the cognitive component. Two characteristics of belief systems, *differentiation* and *evaluative consistency,* are of particular importance for our purposes. Differentiation refers to the number of belief dimensions used by an individual in thinking about an object or class of objects. This property is typically assessed by counting the number of beliefs listed by an individual in a free-response format or elicited in some other manner. Evaluative consistency is the extent to which the evaluative implications of different beliefs are consistent with each other. One way of measuring it is to average the (absolute) values of all pair-wise correlations among the beliefs. In a sense, then, evaluative consistency represents the extent to which the different belief dimensions are integrated with each other.

Because relatively differentiated belief systems have a greater potential for inconsistencies among the different kinds of beliefs, there is a tendency for evaluative consistency to be inversely related to differentiation (e.g., Schlegel & DiTecco, 1982; Scott, 1969). Nevertheless, there is reason to treat differentiation and evaluative consistency as two separate properties that may interact with each other. Thus, Schroder, Driver, and Streufert (1967) defined cognitive complexity to be a function of both, the number of different belief dimensions employed and their interrelations. A complex cognitive style is characterized by a relatively large number of different beliefs in a given domain and, at the same time, by the perception that these beliefs are not unrelated (see also Tetlock, 1983, 1984).

The complex interactions between cognitive differentiation and integration are illustrated in an investigation of the extremity of attitudinal judgments reported by Judd and Lusk (1984). In two different studies, these investigators manipulated or assessed the number of belief dimensions employed in a given cognitive domain and the relations among them. When the dimensions were highly correlated, judgmental extremity tended to increase with the number of dimensions. However, there was a tendency for extremity of judgments to decrease with differentiation when the dimensions were orthogonal or relatively uncorrelated.

Cognitive Structure and the Prediction of Behavior

Cognitive differentiation and integration can have important implications for the prediction of behavior from attitudes, but these implications have rarely been spelled out. Schlegel and DiTecco (1982) assumed that a relatively differentiated belief system would be poorly integrated. A single evaluative measure of attitude would be incapable of fully representing such a differentiated belief system, although it might be adequate in the case of a relatively integrated system. It follows that a general measure of attitude will predict behavior better when people's belief systems are relatively undifferentiated. The same hypothesis follows from Tesser's (1978) argument that attitudes can predict behavior effectively only when the attitude represents a well-articulated, evaluatively consistent cognitive schema. Various empirical implications of this hypothesis have been investigated over the years, with largely contradictory results.

Amount of Information and the Attitude-Behavior Relation.   It stands to reason that the number of belief dimensions employed by an individual will tend to increase as a function of the amount of information the individual has about the attitude object. Some evidence in support of this assumption can be found in Scott (1969). If this is the case, then, in light of the aforementioned considerations, we would expect that an increase in amount of information will tend to reduce the relations between attitude and behavior. Davidson, Yantis, Norwood, and Montano (1985), however, reported findings in the opposite direction. These investigators compared intention-behavior correlations among participants with varying amounts of information relevant to behaviors in the political domain and in the health domain. In each case, intention-behavior consistency was found to be significantly greater for respondents who were more informed about the issue involved, or who reported being more informed.

Davidson et al. (1985) interpreted their results without reference to the question of cognitive differentiation and integration. The measure of intention in their studies preceded assessment of the behavior by between several days and several months. With the passage of time, intentions may change, thus lowering the observed intention-behavior correlation. According to the investigators, however, changes in intentions are less likely to occur if the intentions are based on more rather than less information.

Direct Experience and the Attitude-Behavior Relation.   What effect should direct experience in the attitude domain have on the relation between a general measure of attitude and overt behavior? In terms of attitude structure, the answer to this question is not altogether clear. Direct experience may increase the amount of information a person has about the domain in question, and, as noted earlier, this could lower the attitude-behavior relation. On the other hand, depending on the kind of direct experience to which the person is exposed, it could also serve to increase evaluative consistency among beliefs, thus raising cognitive integration and, with it, the relation between attitude and behavior.

The effect of direct experience on the attitude-behavior relation has been studied extensively by Fazio and his associates (Fazio & Zanna, 1978a, 1978b; Regan & Fazio, 1977; see Fazio & Zanna, 1981, for a summary). These investigators have demonstrated that, as a general rule, direct experience tends to improve the prediction of behavior from attitudes. However, a discordant note can be found in a study by Schlegel and DiTecco (1982). In this study, nonusers or initial users of marijuana were shown to have less differentiated and more internally consistent attitudes toward marijuana than occasional or regular users. Attitudes toward smoking marijuana, assessed by means of an evaluative semantic differential, were employed to predict self-reports of actual marijuana use. These attitude-behavior correlations were found to be stronger among relatively inexperienced participants with undifferentiated belief systems (the average attitude-behavior correlation across different subpopulations was .36) than among participants with more experience whose attitude structure was relatively complex (mean correlation = .18).

Reflection and the Attitude-Behavior Relation.   It is usually assumed that people are more likely to act in accordance with their attitudes if they "think before they act" (Snyder, 1982). This idea is consistent with Tesser's (1978) argument that thoughtful reflection increases evaluative consistency among cognitions. Although it did not obtain a measure of overt behavior, Snyder and Swann's (1976) research on mock juror judgments in a sex discrimination court case provided some support for this hypothesis. A standard scale measuring attitudes toward affirmative action was administered and, 2 weeks later, participants were asked to reach a verdict in a mock court case involving alleged sex discrimination. Prior to delivering their verdicts, one-half of the participants were encouraged to reflect upon their attitudes toward affirmative action. In this condition, the correlation between general attitudes toward affirmative action and the specific verdict was .58, as opposed to a correlation of .07 in a control group without prior reflection.

Cacioppo, Petty, Kao, and Rodriguez (1986) argued that people high in need for cognition are more likely to process information carefully than are people with low standing on this dimension. In accordance with Petty and Cacioppo's (1986) elaboration likelihood model, high need for cognition individuals are therefore expected to exhibit stronger attitude-behavior correlations than are individuals low in need for cognition. A study designed to test this hypothesis assessed need for cognition by means of a personality scale and examined correlations between preferential attitudes toward candidates in a presidential election and voting choice. Consistent with the hypothesis, these correlations were found to be .86 versus .41 for people high and low in need for cognition, respectively. However, an analysis of responses obtained by means of thought elicitation provided little evidence that this effect was indeed due to differences in cognitive elaboration.

Although the research cited provided evidence suggesting that attitude-behavior consistency increases with reflection, a series of studies by Wilson, Dunn, Bybee, Hyman, and Rotondo (1984) arrived at contradictory conclusions. The first of three studies employed Regan and Fazio's (1977) intellectual puzzles task, the second dealt with vacation snapshots, and the third with the relationships of dating couples. One half of the participants in each study was asked to list reasons for their attitudes toward the behavioral target: why they found the different puzzles interesting or boring, why they enjoyed or did not enjoy watching the snapshots, and why the dating relationship was good or bad. The behavioral criteria in the three studies were amount of time spent working on each puzzle type, nonverbal expressions of enjoyment while watching the snapshots, and status of the dating relationship about 9 months later. In each case, the attitude-behavior correlation was stronger (ranging from .53 to .57 across studies) when repondents were *not* asked to list reasons for their attitudes than when they were asked to do so (range of correlations: −.05 to .17). Realizing that these findings are inconsistent with previous research, Wilson et al. (1984) argued that whereas other kinds of reflection may involve merely *observing* one's thoughts and feelings, i.e., focusing on them, participants in their studies were asked to *analyze* their thoughts and feelings, i.e., to find reasons for their attitudes. The investigators speculated that this difference may have been sufficient to produce the contradictory findings. In a follow-up study, Wilson and Dunn (1986) again demonstrated reduced attitude-behavior correlations when participants were asked to analyze their attitudes, but they failed to corroborate the finding that focusing on one's attitudes serves to improve behavioral prediction.

Conclusions.   Despite some contradictory findings, the research reviewed in the preceding sections suggests that the structure of cognitions may play an important role in the relation between general attitudes and specific behaviors. Unfortunately, most studies in this area have provided only indirect evidence concerning the moderating effects of cognitive differentiation and integration. Thus, amount of information about an attitude object, direct experience, and reflection may exert their effects on the attitude-behavior relation at least in part by increasing or diminishing cognitive differentiation, but few investigations have looked at cognitive structures directly. A notable exception is the study by Schlegel and Di-Tecco (1982), which showed that direct experience with an attitude object (marijuana smoking) was accompanied by greater differentiation and lower integration of people's belief systems. These effects were used to explain the decline in the attitude-behavior relation brought about by direct experience. Other studies (e.g., Fazio & Zanna, 1978a, 1978b), however, have shown direct experience to increase rather than reduce attitude-behavior relations. It is conceivable that in these instances, the nature of the direct experience was such as to create greater evaluative consistency among cognitions, as suggested by Tesser (1978). Such an effect would tend to increase the confidence with which the attitude is held and thus strengthen its relation to behavior (Fazio & Zanna, 1978a; Sample & Warland, 1973). Similar arguments could be made with respect to the conflicting findings concerning effects of reflection and amount of information on the attitude-behavior relation. However, without direct measures of the effects on cognitive structure exerted by variables of this kind in a given context, our post hoc interpretations must remain speculative.

Between-Component Structure

The discussion up to this point has focused on the internal structures of cognitive, affective, and conative response systems. We now turn to an examination of the relations between components, and how these relations may affect prediction of specific behavioral tendencies from measures of general attitudes.

Affective-Cognitive Consistency.   Dealing with such cognitive domains as nations, celebrities, and occupations, Scott (1962, 1969) defined on an a priori basis several structural properties of belief systems: dimensionality, centralization, image compatibility, affective-evaluative consistency, affective balance, and image ambivalence. Of greatest interest for our present purposes is affective-evaluative consistency, which is the extent to which overall liking for a given object corresponds to the evaluative implications of beliefs about the object. The index used by Scott (1969) to assess affective-evaluative consistency is the average correlation between expressed liking and the strength of each belief, disregarding the correlations' signs. It can be seen that this index is a measure of the consistency between affect (or overall evaluation) and the cognitive component of attitude.

Rosenberg (1968) proposed a different measure of affective-cognitive consistency based on his instrumentality-value model of attitude. According to Rosenberg (1956, 1960), people have a need to maintain consistency between the affective and cognitive components of their attitudes. Whereas the affective component is viewed as the overall positive or negative response to an object, the cognitive component of atitude is thought to be made up of beliefs about the potentialities of the attitude object for attaining or blocking the realization of valued states. In research on this model, the affective component of attitude is usually assessed in terms of expressed liking for the attitude object or by asking respondents to rate the object on an evaluative semantic differential. A measure of the cognitive component is obtained by assessing perceived instrumentality and subjective value of each potential goal, multiplying these two measures, and then summing across the resulting products. The assumption of affective-cognitive consistency implies that the more a given object is instrumental to obtaining positively valued goals and to blocking negatively valued goals, the more positive the person's affect toward the object. This model is quite similar to other expectancy-value models of attitude (e.g., Fishbein, 1963; see Fishbein & Ajzen, 1975), although not all theorists would assume a *need* for affective-cognitive consistency.

As an index of affective-cognitive consistency, Rosenberg (1968) proposed to rank-order measures of the affective and the cognitive components and then to compute the absolute difference between the two ranks (see also Norman, 1975). Inconsistency is observed when people with positive feelings toward the attitude object believe that it hinders attainment of valued goals and promotes attainment of negatively valued states; or when people with negative feelings toward the object expect it to help them attain positively valued goals and to prevent the occurrence of negatively valued events.

Affective-Cognitive Consistency and the Attitude-Behavior Relation.   Inconsistency between the cognitive and affective components of attitude implies that the attitude is poorly articulated or integrated. It follows that prediction of behavior from measures of either component should be impaired, relative to the predictive accuracy that can be expected when the two components are consistent with each other. Norman (1975) tested this hypothesis in a series of three experiments that attempted to predict participation in psychological research. The affective component of undergraduates' attitudes toward acting as subjects in psychological research was measured by means of a 9-point favorability scale and, in the third study, also by means of a 16-item evaluative semantic differential. The cognitive component was indexed by an expectancy-value scale based on 12 beliefs regarding the consequences of participating in psychological research. The results provided only partial support for the hypothesis. Across the three studies, the average correlation between behavior and the *affective* measure of attitude was .54 when affect was relatively consistent with cognition and significantly lower (mean $r = -.08$) when affect and cognition were relatively inconsistent with each other. With respect to the correlations between behavior and the *cognitive* measure of attitude, however, a significant difference between the high and low affective-cognitive consistency subgroups was obtained only in the third study (mean r = .47 and .28, respectively).

Moreover, Fazio and Zanna (1978a) failed to find any moderating effect of affective-cognitive consistency in a replication of Norman's experiments with only minor modifications. Their hierarchical regression analysis resulted in a significant main effect of attitude on behavior (r = .32), but the attitude by internal consistency interaction did not increase this correlation significantly.

Affective-Conative Consistency.   Several different theoretical orientations lead to the expectation that people's affective reactions will generally be consistent with their behaviors. In dissonance theory, this expectation follows from the assumption that people have a need to reduce dissonance (Festinger, 1957); in self-perception theory it follows from the assumption that people infer their feelings from their actions (Bem, 1972); and in impression management theory it follows from the assumption that people want to appear consistent in front of others (Tedeschi, Schlenker, & Bonoma, 1971). Much of the research generated by these theories has been concerned with the effect of behavior on attitudes rather than with the reverse causal relation. Whatever mechanism is assumed to be responsible for it, people have been shown to bring their feelings into line with their prior behavior. However, at least the theories of dissonance and impression management also imply that to maintain affective-conative consistency, people choose to behave in ways that are consistent with their affective tendencies.

Affective-Conative Consistency and the Attitude-Behavior Relation.   The question addressed in this section has to do with the factors that may foster more or less close links between affect and conation. If we consider dissonance theory first, the tendency to behave in accordance with one's overall evaluative response should be a function of the magnitude of dissonance that would be aroused if one acted in an inconsistent manner. One of the factors that, according to dissonance theory, should influence the magnitude of dissonance in this situation is the subjective importance of the attitude and behavior in question, i.e., the person's *involvement.* We would thus expect that the magnitude of the attitude-behavior relation will increase with involvement.

Several investigators have reported results in support of this proposition, although their hypotheses were not derived from dissonance theory. Fazio and Zanna (1978a) used latitude of rejection to operationalize involvement in the topic of psychological research. The number of positions college students judged as objectionable on a 7-point *boring–interesting* scale was taken as an index of latitude of rejection. The greater this latitude, the more involved a person is assumed to be (cf. Sherif & Hovland, 1961). Regan and Fazio (1977) took advantage of a housing shortage at Cornell University to study the moderating effect of involvement. Students assigned to temporary housing were more involved and had a greater vested interest in remedial action in comparison to students who had been assigned to permanent housing. Finally, Sivacek and Crano (1982) selected two topics that were more involving for younger than for older students: a referendum to raise the State's legal drinking age to 21 and instituting a senior comprehensive examination.

In each investigation, attitude-behavior correlations were found to be significantly stronger among respondents who were highly involved than among respondents with low involvement. Under conditions of high involvement, attitude-behavior correlations ranged from .30 to .82, whereas under low involvement they ranged from .04 to .53.

If involvement is a crucial factor from the point of view of dissonance theory, impression management theory would seem to suggest that behavior in accordance with attitudes should be more likely when the behavior is performed in public rather than in private (see also Salancik, 1982). At first glance, this prediction seems at variance with intuition. A public situation may be viewed as imposing constraints on people's behavior, thus making it more difficult for them to act in accordance with their private feelings (Warner & DeFleur, 1969). However, impression management theory suggests that pressures to create a favorable impression by appearing consistent are greatest when the behavior is public rather than private. In fact, the Warner and DeFleur (1969) study obtained findings in support of this expectation. A large sample of college students was divided at the median score on a Likert scale designed to assess attitudes toward Blacks. The measure of behavior was each participant's signed indication of willingness or refusal to perform one of eight behaviors, ranging from making a small donation to a charity for Black students to dating an attractive Black student. These commitments were elicited by means of a letter sent to each participant. For half the sample, the letter assured anonymity of response whereas for the other half it indicated that the participant's response would be made public in campus newspapers. Although the results of the study must be interpreted with caution because of a very low response rate, they showed the pattern predicted by impression management theory. The effect of attitude on signed approval or disapproval of the requested behavior was greater in the public condition (a difference of 77.8% between respondents with positive and negative attitudes toward Blacks) than in the private condition (a difference of 17.2%).

Finally, we turn to self-perception theory and its implications for the attitude-behavior relation. A broad attributional perspective would suggest that when internal cues are weak, people may infer their own attitudes from external events. Bem (1972) proposed that these external events are often an individual's own behavior. Based on this perspective, Fazio and Zanna (1981; Zanna, Olson, & Fazio, 1981) argued that attitude measures will be better predictors of subsequent behavior if the attitudes assessed were inferred from past behavior rather than from other kinds of cues. In other words, attitude-behavior consistency should increase with the *salience* of past behavior. The reason for this expectation is that behavior-based attitudes are likely to be more directly relevant for later behavior.

In the two studies conducted, attitudes toward religion, as assessed by means of a standard questionnaire, were correlated with intentions (see Fazio & Zanna, 1981) and self-reports of religious behavior (Zanna, Olson, & Fazio, 1981). Prior to the assessment of attitudes, participants in the experimental condition reviewed their past behaviors in the domain of religion whereas participants in the control condition did not. As expected, comparisons of the two conditions showed that attitudes assessed following review of past behavior correlated better with behavioral intentions ($r = .78$) and with behavioral self reports ($r = .39$ to $.59$) than did attitudes that were assessed without this review of past behavior ($r = .52$ for intentions and $r = .21$ to $.38$ for self reports of behavior).

In conclusion, theories dealing with consistency between the affective and conative components of attitude have interesting implications for the attitude-behavior relation. The variables suggested by the divergent theoretical frameworks are each found to moderate the magnitude of the attitude-behavior relation. The predictive accuracy of general attitudes is found to increase with involvement, publicity of the behavior to be predicted, and salience of past behavior.

Representativeness of Specific Behaviors

The causal chain perspective of attitudinal structure inherent in the work of Fishbein and Ajzen (1975; Ajzen & Fishbein, 1980) can also be used to suggest conditions under which a general attitude may be a reasonably good predictor of specific action tendencies. These conditions have to do with the extent to which the specific action tendency is representative of the dispositional domain tapped by the attitude. With respect to belief systems, Schlegel and DiTecco (1982) suggested that an overall evaluative response will be capable of capturing a *behavioral* domain only to the extent that the domain in question is well integrated rather than highly differentiated. The different response tendencies within a given domain can be indexed by measures of attitude toward the behaviors, by measures of intentions, or by observations of actual behaviors. Whichever measures are used, the proposition put forth can be investigated empirically by examining the factor structure of the behavioral dispositions. When a single factor is found to account for much of the nonrandom variance, the domain can be said to be well-integrated.

Unfortunately, no evidence with direct bearings on this hypothesis seems to be available, although it is possible to find some indirect support. Within a highly integrated dispositional domain, different behavioral tendencies should correlate reasonably well with each other and with the total score. That is, in a well-integrated domain, each individual behavioral tendency is to a considerable extent representative of the domain under investigation, and it is for this reason that the overall evaluative response tendency, i.e, the general attitude, is expected to correlate well with individual behaviors. However, this also implies that within *any* domain, the more that a given behavior is representative of the total domain, the stronger should be its correlation with a general attitude measure.

One possible way of testing this hypothesis is illustrated by Buss and Craik's (1980, 1981) work on the relation between personality traits and self-reports of behavior within the domain defined by the trait. These investigators examined the relevance to a given trait (e.g., dominance) of each of a set of behaviors by asking a sample of judges to rate how good an example of the trait it was. However, rather than looking at the correlations between a measure of the trait and individual behaviors in light of these ratings, Buss and Craik divided the total set of behaviors into four relevance categories (from low to high) and computed an aggregate measure of behavior for each category. The results showed that predictive validity increased with the rated relevance of the actions comprising a given category.

By way of contrast, Fishbein and Ajzen (1974) reported data on the prediction of individual behaviors varying in the rated relevance to a given attitude. In this study, attitudes toward religion were assessed by means of four standard scales and the college students who participated in the study indicated whether or not they had performed each of 100 behaviors related to matters of religion. An independent group of judges rated, for each behavior, the likelihood that it would be performed by individuals with positive attitudes toward religion and the likelihood that it would be performed by individuals with negative attitudes toward religion. The absolute difference between these two conditional probabilities was used as a measure of the behavior's relevance to the attitude. This measure of relevance was then correlated with the correlation between each behavior and the attitude score. The results thus show the extent to which the correlation between a general attitude and a specific action can be predicted from the action's judged relevance to the dispositional domain. These predictions ranged from .40 to .47 across the four measures of attitude toward religion.

Sjöberg (1982) replicated the Fishbein and Ajzen (1974) procedures in the domain of attitudes and behaviors with respect to aid to developing countries. The prediction of attitude-behavior correlations from the be-havior's judged relevance to the attitude was .28 and .36 for two measures of attitude. Sjöberg also demonstrated the utility of a somewhat simpler procedure to identify the relevance of a given behavior, namely, by using the correlation between the specific action and the total behavioral score. This index of a behavior's representativeness of the behavioral domain predicted attitude-behavior correlations at the level of .48 and .45 for the two measures of attitude.

In short, behavioral domains may often be highly differentiated and the multitude of behavioral tendencies they subsume cannot easily be captured by means of global attitude measures. When this is the case, any single action is generally unrepresentative of the domain at large, although some behaviors may be more representative than others. Tentative support for these ideas is provided by findings to the effect that prediction of specific behaviors from global measures of attitude improves as the behaviors be-come more representative of, or relevant to, the dispositional domain under study.

These findings, however, supply little information about the kinds of factors that make one behavior more relevant or prototypical than another. The specific action implications of a global attitude are likely to vary as a function of the person, the situation, and the behaviors considered. Thus, individuals who are equally religious may have learned to express their religiosity in different ways: one may regularly attend church services, another may meditate in private, and a third may donate money to religious institutions. Situational characteristics may render some behaviors more appropriate than others. Praying, for example, is more likely in the church and before or after meals than it is in a pub or while watching television. As to the behaviors themselves, some acts may be more salient or available than others. Fazio (1986; Fazio & Williams, 1986) showed that attitude-behavior correlations increase with the attitude's accessibility in memory, i.e., with its salience. By the same token it can be argued that increased salience of the specific behavior should improve predictive accuracy. For a general attitude to guide specific action it is necessary not only that the attitude be accessible but also that its behavioral implication be evident to the person.

SUMMARY AND CONCLUSIONS

This chapter has dealt with attitude structure from a multicomponent view of attitude and from a causal chain perspective. Despite the differences between these two approaches, both suggest that consideration of the structural characteristics of a disposition can contribute greatly to our understanding of the relation between attitude and behavior. The structural properties of greatest relevance in this context are differentiation and integration, where differentiation refers to the number of dimensions required to describe the dispositional domain and integration refers to the degree to which these dimensions are interconnected as opposed to independent. As a general rule, increased differentiation is accompanied by reduced integration.

Investigators who have adopted the view that attitudes are made up of cognitive, affective, and conative components have generally focused on two types of differentiation: that found within the cognitive component (i.e., differentiation and integration of belief systems), and integration of the cognitive and affective components (i.e., affective-cognitive consistency). When the dispositional domain is poorly integrated in either sense, it may be impossible to capture it fully by means of a unidimensional attitude measure that is represented by a single score. It follows that verbal attitude scores will tend to be poor predictors of specific nonverbal responses to the attitude object when people's belief systems are highly differentiated or when their affect is inconsistent with their cognitions. Prediction of specific behaviors from general verbal attitudes should improve as the dispositional domain becomes less differentiated and more integrated. The empirical evidence reviewed in this chapter provides qualified support for these expectations.

The causal chain perspective complements the multicomponent view by attending to a different aspect of dispositional structure. It directs attention to the fact that people not only have a multitude of beliefs about any attitude object but that they can also perform a variety of specific nonverbal behaviors with respect to it. The principle of compatibility suggests that these specific behaviors must be agggregated to yield a measure that is reflective of the global disposition, and that specific nonverbal responses can be predicted best from equally specific verbal responses. Empirical research has provided considerable support for these propositions.

The realization that dispositional domains are comprised of many specific behavioral tendencies also has implications for the relation between global attitude measures and specific actions. Just as the verbal belief system can vary in its degree of differentiation and integration, so too can the nonverbal response system. With a high degree of differentiation, and with low integration, specific behavioral tendencies may often be incompatible and the overall behavioral trend is not easily captured by a single score. Aggregating specific behaviors under these circumstances may thus be inappropriate, and a general attitude measure is unlikely to predict specific behavioral tendencies very well. On the other hand, single actions that correlate well with an aggregate measure of behavior, i.e., single actions that are representative of the domain under investigation, should correlate much better with general attitudes than single actions that are unrepresentative of the domain. Some evidence consistent with these ideas are also discussed.

Investigators interested in the attitude-behavior relation have paid relatively little attention to the role of attitude structure. Furthermore, most studies that have some bearing on the effect of attitude structure provide evidence of an indirect nature because the structural properties that would be expected to influence attitude-behavior relations are rarely assessed. The present chapter suggests that attitude structure is a potentially fruitful field for future research. Detailed examination of differentiation and integration of verbal and nonverbal response systems can contribute to our understanding of the attitude-behavior relation, and it may help explain some of the perplexing inconsistencies that have been reported in past research on conditions that moderate the strength of this relation.

REFERENCES

Ajzen, I. (1971). Attitudinal vs. normative messages: An investigation of the differential effects of persuasive communications on behavior. *Sociometry, 34,* 263–280.

Ajzen, I. (1982). On behaving in accordance with one's attitudes. In M. P. Zanna, E. T. Higgins, & C. P. Herman (Eds.), *Consistency in social behavior: The Ontario symposium* (Vol. 2, pp. 3–15). Hillsdale, NJ: Lawrence Erlbaum Associates.

Ajzen, I. (1985). From intentions to actions: A theory of planned behavior. In J. Kuhl & J. Beckman (Eds.), *Action-control: From cognition to behavior* (pp. 11–39). Heidelberg: Springer.

Ajzen, I. (1987). Attitudes, traits, and actions: Dispositional prediction of behavior in personality and social psychology. In L. Berkowitz (Ed.), *Advances in experimental social psychology* (Vol. 20, pp. 1–63). New York: Academic.

Ajzen, I. (1988). *Attitudes, personality, and behavior.* Milton Keynes, England: Open University Press.

Ajzen, I., & Fishbein, M. (1970). The prediction of behavior from attitudinal and normative variables. *Journal of Experimental Social Psychology, 6,* 466–487.

Ajzen, I., & Fishbein, M. (1977). Attitude-behavior relations: A theoretical analysis and review of empirical research. *Psychological Bulletin, 84,* 888–918.

Ajzen, I., & Fishbein, M. (1980). *Understanding attitudes and predicting social behavior.* Englewood Cliffs, NJ: Prentice-Hall.

Ajzen, I., & Madden, T. (1986). Prediction of goal-directed behavior: Attitudes, intentions, and perceived behavioral control. *Journal of Experimental Social Psychology, 22,* 453–474.

Ajzen, I., & Timko, C. (1986). Correspondence between health attitudes and behavior. *Journal of Basic and Applied Social Psychology, 7,* 259–276.

Ajzen, I., Timko, C., & White, J. B. (1982). Self-monitoring and the attitude-behavior relation. *Journal of Personality and Social Psychology, 42,* 426–435.

Allport, G. W. (1954). The historical background of modern social psychology. In G. Lindzey (Ed.), *Handbook of social psychology* (Vol. 1, pp. 3–56). Cambridge, MA: Addison-Wesley.

Averill, J. R. (1975). A semantic atlas of emotional concepts. JSAS *Catalogue of Selected Documents in Psychology, 5,* 330. (Ms. No. 421)

Bagozzi, R. P. (1978). The construct validity of the affective, behavioral, and cognitive components of attitude by analysis of covariance structures. *Multivariate Behavioral Research, 13,* 9–31.

Bagozzi, R. P., & Burnkrant, R. E. (1979). Attitude organization and the attitude-behavior relationship. *Journal of Personality and Social Psychology, 37,* 913–929.

Bagozzi, R. P., & Burnkrant, R. E. (1985). Attitude organization and the attitude-behavior relation: A reply to Dillon and Kumar. *Journal of Personality and Social Psychology, 49,* 47–57.

Bandura, A., Blanchard, E. B., & Ritter, B. (1969). Relative efficacy of desensitization and modeling approaches for inducing behavioral, affective, and attitudinal changes. *Journal of Personality and Social Psychology, 13,* 173–199.

Barker, R. G. (1963). The stream of behavior as an empirical problem. In R. G. Barker (Ed.), *The stream of behavior: Explorations of its structure and content.* New York: Appleton-Century-Crofts.

Bem, D. J. (1970). *Beliefs, attitudes and human affairs.* Belmont, CA: Brooks/Cole.

Bem, D. J. (1972). Self-perception theory. In L. Berkowitz (Ed.), *Advances in experimental social psychology* (Vol. 6, pp. 1–62). New York: Academic.

Bentler, P. M., & Speckart, G. (1979). Models of attitude-behavior relations. *Psychological Review, 86,* 452–464.

Bentler, P. M., & Speckart, G. (1981). Attitudes "cause" behavior: A structural equation analysis. *Journal of Personality and Social Psychology, 40,* 226–238.

Breckler, S. J. (1984). Empirical vallidation of affect, behavior, and cognition as distinct components of attitude. *Journal of Personality and Social Psychology, 47,* 1191–1205.

Bruner, J. S., & Tagiuri, R. (1954). The perception of people. In G. Lindzey (Ed.), *Handbook of social psychology* (Vol. 2, pp. 634–654). Reading, MA: Addison-Wesley.

Buss, D. M., & Craik, K. H. (1980). The frequency concept of disposition: Dominance and prototypically dominant acts. *Journal of Personality, 48,* 379–392.

Buss, D. M., & Craik, K. H. (1981). The act frequency analysis of interpersonal dispositions: Aloofness, gregariousness, dominance, and submissiveness. *Journal of Personality, 49,* 174–192.

Cacioppo, J. T., Petty, R. E., Kao, C. F., & Rodriguez, R. (1986). Central and peripheral routes to persuasion: An individual difference perspective. *Journal of Personality and Social Psychology, 51,* 1032–1043.

Cacioppo, J. T., Petty, R. E., Losch, M. E., & Kim, H. S. (1986). Electromyographic activity over facial muscle regions can differentiate valence and intensity of affective reactions. *Journal of Personality and Social Psychology, 50,* 260–268.

Chaiken, S., & Stangor, C. (1987). Attitudes and attitude change. *Annual Review of Psychology, 38,* 575–630.

Davidson, A. R., Yantis, S., Norwood, M., & Montano, D. E. (1985). Amount of information about the attitude object and attitude-behavior consistency: *Journal of Personality and Social Psychology, 49,* 1184–1198.

Deutscher, I. (1966). Words and deeds. *Social Problems, 13,* 235–254

Deutscher, I. (1973). *What we say/what we do: Sentiments and acts.* Glenview, IL: Scott, Foresman.

Dillon, W. R., & Kumar, A. (1985). Attitude organization and the attitude-behavior relation: A critique of Bagozzi and Burnkrant's reanalysis of Fishbein and Ajzen. *Journal of Personality and Social Psychology, 49,* 33–46.

Edwards, A. L. (1957). *The social desirability variable in personality assessment and research.* New York: Dryden.

Fazio, R. H. (1986). How do attitudes guide behavior? In R. M. Sorrentino, & E. T. Higgins (Eds.), *The handbook of motivation and cognition: Foundations of social behavior* (pp. 204–243). New York: Guilford Press.

Fazio, R. H., & Willaims, C. J. (1986). Attitude accessibility as a moderator of the attitude-perception and attitude-behavior relations: An investigation of the 1984 presidential election. *Journal of Personality and Social Psychology, 51,* 505–514.

Fazio, R. H., & Zanna, M. (1978a). Attitudinal qualities relating to the strength of the attitude-behavior relationship. *Journal of Experimental Social Psychology, 14,* 398–408.

Fazio, R. H., & Zanna, M. (1978b). On the predictive validity of attitudes: The roles of direct experience and confidence. *Journal of Personality, 46,* 228–243.

Fazio, R. H., & Zanna, M. P. (1981). Direct experience and attitude-behavior consistency. In L. Berkowitz (Ed.), *Advances in experimental social psychology* (Vol. 14, pp. 161–202). New York: Academic.

Festinger, L. (1957). *A theory of cognitive dissonance.* Evanston, IL: Row-Peterson.

Fishbein, M. (1963). An investigation of the relationships between beliefs about an object and the attitude toward that object. *Human Relations, 16,* 233–240.

Fishbein, M., & Ajzen, I. (1974). Attitudes toward objects as predictors of single and multiple behavioral criteria. *Psychological Review, 81,* 59–74.

Fishbein, M., & Ajzen, I. (1975). *Belief, attitude, intention, and behavior: An introduction to theory and research.* Reading, MA: Addison-Wesley.

Foa, U. G. (1958). The contiguity principle in the structure of interpersonal relations. *Human Relations, 11,* 229–238.

Fredricks, A. J., & Dossett, K. L. (1983). Attitude-behavior relations: A comparison of the Fishbein-Ajzen and the Bentler–Speckart models. *Journal of Personality and Social Psychology, 45,* 501–512.

Green, B. F. (1954). Attitude measurement. In G. Lindzey (Ed.), *Handbook of social psychology,* (Vol. 1, pp. 335–369). Reading, MA: Addison-Wesley.

Guttman, L. (1955). An outline of some new methodology for social research. *Public Opinion Quarterly, 18,* 395–404.

Guttman, L. (1957). Introduction to facet design and analysis. *Proceedings of the Fifteenth International Congress of Psychology, Brussels* (pp. 130–132). Amsterdam: North-Holland.

Guttman, L. (1959). A structural theory for intergroup beliefs and action. *American Sociological Review, 24,* 318–328.

Hilgard, E. R. (1980). The trilogy of mind: Cognition, affection, and conation. *Journal of the History of the Behavioral Sciences, 16,* 107–117.

Hill, R. J. (1981). Attitudes and behavior. In M. Rosenberg & R. H. Turner (Eds.), *Social psychology: Sociological perspectives* (pp. 347–377). New York: Basic.

Jackson, D. N., & Paunonen, S. V. (1985). Construct validity and the predictability of behavior. *Journal of Personality and Social Psychology, 49,* 554–570.

Judd, C. M., & Lusk, C. M. (1984). Knowledge structures and evaluative judgments: Effects of structural variables on judgmental extremity. *Journal of Personality and Social Psychology, 46,* 1193–1207.

Kothandapani, V. (1971). Validation of feeling, belief, and intention to act as three components of attitude and their contribution to prediction of contraceptive behavior. *Journal of Personality and Social Psychology, 19,* 321–333.

Kretch, D., Crutchfield, R. S., & Ballachey, E. L. (1962). *Individual in society.* New York: McGraw-Hill.

Kuhl, J. (1985). Volitional aspect of achievement motivation and learned helplessness: Toward a comprehensive theory of action control. In B. A. Maher (Ed.), *Progress in experimental personality research* (Vol. 13, pp. 99–171). New York: Academic.

Liska, A. E. (1984). A critical examination of the causal structure of the Fishbein/Ajzen attitude-behavior model. *Social Psychology Quarterly, 47,* 61–74.

Manstead, A. S. R., Proffitt, C., & Smart, J. L. (1983). Predicting and understanding mothers' infant-feeding intentions and behavior: Testing the theory of reasoned action. *Journal of Personality and Social Psychology, 44,* 657–671.

McGuire, W. J. (1985). Attitudes and attitude change. In G. Lindzey & E. Aronson (Eds.), *Handbook of social psychology*, (3rd ed., Vol. 2, pp. 233–346). New York: Random House.

Norman, R. (1975). Affective-cognitive consistency, attitudes, conformity, and behavior. *Journal of Personality and Social Psychology, 32,* 83–91.

Norman, W. T. (1963). Toward an adequate taxonomy of personality attributes: Replicated factor structure in peer nomination personality ratings. *Journal of Abnormal and Social Psychology, 66,* 574–583.

Olweus, D. (1980). The consistency issue in personality psychology revisited—with special reference to aggression. *British Journal of Social and Clinical Psychology, 19,* 377–390.

Osgood, C. E., Suci, G. J., & Tannenbaum, P. H. (1957). *The measurement of meaning.* Urbana, IL: University of Illinois Press.

Oskamp, S. (1977). *Attitudes and opinions.* Englewood Cliffs, NJ: Prentice-Hall.

Ostrom, T. M. (1969). The relationship between the affective, behavioral, and cognitive components of attitude. *Journal of Experimental Social Psychology, 5,* 12–30.

Peak, H. (1955). Attitude and motivation. In M. Jones (Ed.), *Nebraska symposium on motivation.* Lincoln, NE: University of Nebraska Press.

Petty, R. E., & Cacioppo, J. T. (1981). *Attitudes and persuasion: Classic and contemporary approaches.* Dubuque, IA: Wm. C. Brown.

Petty, R. E., & Cacioppo, J. T. (1986). The Elaboration Likelihood Model of persuasion. In L. Berkowitz (Ed.), *Advances in experimental social psychology* (Vol. 19, pp. 123–205). New York: Academic.

Rajecki, D. W. (1982). *Attitudes: Themes and advances.* Sunderland, MA: Sinauer.

Regan, D. T., & Fazio, R. H. (1977). On the consistency between attitudes and behavior: Look to the method of attitude formation. *Journal of Experimental Social Psychology, 13,* 38–45.

Rokeach, M. (1968). *Beliefs, attitudes, and values: A theory of organization and change.* San Francisco, CA: Jossey-Bass.

Rosenberg, M. J. (1956). Cognitive structure and attitudinal affect. *Journal of Abnormal and Social Psychology, 53,* 367–372.

Rosenberg, M. J. (1960). An analysis of affective-cognitive consistency. In C. I. Hovland & M. J. Rosenberg (Eds.), *Attitude organization and change* (pp. 15–64). New Haven, CT: Yale University Press.

Rosenberg, M. J. (1968). Hedonism, inauthenticity, and other goals toward expansion of a consistency theory. In R. P. Abelson, E. Aronson, W. J. McGuire, T. M. Newcomb, M. J. Rosenberg, & P. H. Tannenbaum (Eds.), *Theories of cognitive consistency: A sourcebook* (pp. 73–111). Chicago: Rand McNally.

Rosenberg, M. J., & Hovland, C. I. (1960). Cognitive, affective, and behavioral components of attitudes. In C. I. Hovland & M. J. Rosenberg (Eds.), *Attitude organization and change* (pp. 1–14). New Haven, CT: Yale University Press.

Rosenberg, S., & Sedlak, A. (1972). Structural representations of implicit personality theory. In L. Berkowitz (Ed.), *Advances in experimental social psychology* (Vol. 6, pp. 235–297). New York: Academic.

Roth, H. G., & Upmeyer, A. (1985). Matching attitudes towards cartoons across evaluative judgments and nonverbal evaluative behavior. *Psychological Research, 47,* 173–183.

Russell, J. A. (1978). Evidence of convergent validity on the dimensions of affect. *Journal of Personality and Social Psychology, 36,* 1152–1168.

Russell, J. A. (1983). Pancultural aspects of the human conceptual organization of emotions. *Journal of Personality and Social Psychology, 45,* 1281–1288.

Salancik, G. R. (1982). Attitude-behavior consistencies as social logics. In M. P. Zanna, E. T. Higgins, & C. P. Herman (Eds.), *Consistency in social behavior: The Ontario symposium* (Vol. 2, pp. 51–73). Hillsdale, NJ: Lawrence Erlbaum Associates.

Sample, J., & Warland, R. (1973). Attitude and prediction of behavior. *Social Forces, 51,* 292–303.

Sarver, V. T., Jr. (1983). Ajzen and Fishbein's "Theory of Reasoned Action": A critical assessment. *Journal for the Theory of Social Behavior, 13*, 155–163.

Schifter, D. B., & Ajzen, I. (1985). Intention, perceived control, and weight loss: An application of the theory of planned behavior. *Journal of Personality and Social Psychology, 49*, 843–851.

Schlegel, R. P., & DiTecco, D. (1982). Attitudinal structures and the attitude-behavior relation. In M. P. Zanna, E. T. Higgins, & C. P. Herman (Eds.), *Consistency in social behavior: The Ontario symposium* (Vol. 2, pp. 17–49). Hillsdale, NJ: Lawrence Erlbaum Associates.

Schneider, D. J. (1973). Implicit personality theory: A review. *Psychological Bulletin, 79*, 294–309.

Schroder, H. M., Driver, M., & Streufert, S. (1967). *Human information processing.* New York: Holt, Rinehart & Winston.

Scott, W. A. (1962). Cognitive complexity and cognitive flexibility. *Sociometry, 25*, 405–414.

Scott, W. A. (1969). Structure of natural cognitions. *Journal of Personality and Social Psychology, 12*, 261–278.

Sherif, M., & Hovland, C. I. (1961). *Social judgment: Assimilation and contrast effects in communication and attitude change.* New Haven, CT: Yale University Press.

Sherman, S. J., & Fazio, R. H. (1983). Parallels between attitudes and traits as predictors of behavior. *Journal of Personality, 51*, 308–345.

Sivacek, J., & Crano, W. D. (1982). Vested interest as a moderator of attitude-behavior consistency. *Journal of Personality and Social Psychology, 43*, 210–221.

Sjöberg, L. (1982). Attitude-behavior correlation, social desirability and perceived diagnostic value. *British Journal of Social Psychology, 21*, 283–292.

Smetana, J. G., & Adler, N. E. (1980). Fishbein's value x expectancy model: An examination of some assumptions. *Personality and Social Psychology Bulletin, 6*, 889–96.

Snider, R. J., & Osgood, C. E. (Eds.). (1969). *Semantic differential technique: A source book.* Chicago: Aldine.

Snyder, M. (1982). When believing means doing: Creating links between attitudes and behavior. In M. P. Zanna, E. T. Higgins, & C. P. Herman (Eds.), *Consistency in social behavior: The Ontario symposium* (Vol. 2, pp. 105–130). Hillsdale, NJ: Lawrence Erlbaum Associates.

Snyder, M., & Swann, W. B., Jr. (1976). When actions reflect attitudes: The politics of impression management. *Journal of Personality and Social Psychology, 34*, 1034–1042.

Tedeschi, J. T., Schlenker, B. R., & Bonoma, T. V. (1971). Cognitive dissonance: Private ratiocination or public spectacle. *American Psychologist, 26*, 685–695.

Tesser, A. (1978). Self-generated attitude change. In L. Berkowitz (Ed.), *Advances in experimental social psychology* (Vol. 11, pp. 289–338). New York: Academic.

Tetlock, P. E. (1983). Cognitive style and political ideology. *Journal of Personality and Social Psychology, 45*, 118–126.

Tetlock, P. E. (1984). Cognitive style and political belief systems in the British House of Commons. *Journal of Personality and Social Psychology, 46*, 265–375.

Triandis, H. C. (1964). Exploratory factor analysis of the behavioral component of social attitudes. *Journal of Abnormal and Social Psychology, 68*, 420–430.

Triandis, H. C. (1977). *Interpersonal behavior.* Monterey, CA: Brooks/Cole.

Upmeyer, A. (1981). Perceptual and judgmental processes in social contexts. In L. Berkowitz (Ed.), *Advances in experimental social psychology* (Vol. 14, pp. 257–308). New York: Academic.

Warner, L. G., & DeFleur, M. L. (1969). Attitude as an interactional concept: Social constraint and social distance as intervening variables between attitudes and action. *American Sociological Review, 34*, 153–169.

Watson, D., Clark, L. A., & Tellegen, A. (1984). Cross-cultural convergence in the structure of mood: A Japanese replication and a comparison with U.S. findings. *Journal of Personality and Social Psychology, 47*, 127–144.

Weigel, R. H., & Newman, L. S. (1976). Increasing attitude-behavior correspondence by broadening the scope of the behavioral measure. *Journal of Personality and Social Psychology, 33,* 793–802.

Wicker, A. W. (1969). Attitudes versus actions: The relationship of verbal and overt behavioral responses to attitude objects. *Journal of Social Issues, 25,* 41–78.

Widaman, K. F. (1985). Hierarchically nested covariance structure models for multitrait-multimethod data. *Applied Psychological Measurement, 9,* 1–26.

Wiggins, J. S. (1973). *Personality and prediction: Principles of personality assessment.* Reading, MA: Addison-Wesley.

Wilson, T. D., & Dunn, D. S. (1986). Effects of introspection on attitude-behavior consistency: Analyzing reason versus focusing on feelings. *Journal of Experimental Social Psychology, 22,* 249–263.

Wilson, T. D., Dunn, D. S., Bybee, J. A., Hyman, D. B., & Rotondo, J. A. (1984). Effects of analyzing reasons on attitude-behavior consistency. *Journal of Personality and Social Psychology, 47,* 5–16.

Wish, M., Deutsch, M., & Biener, L. (1970). Differences in conceptual structures of nations: An exploratory study. *Journal of Personality and Social Psychology, 16,* 361–373.

Zanna, M. P., Olson, J. M., & Fazio, R. H. (1980). Attitude-behavior consistency: An individual difference perspective. *Journal of Personality and Social Psychology, 38,* 432–440.

11

Attitude Structure and Function:
From the Tripartite to the
Homeostasis Model of Attitudes

John T. Cacioppo
Ohio State University

Richard E. Petty
Ohio State University

Thomas R. Geen
University of Iowa

Skin conductance lowers, as the small passageways to the skin out of which sweat comes close to minimize perspiration and the consequent loss of body heat. Peripheral vasoconstriction occurs, as the blood that had been shunted from the hot viscera and muscles to small blood vessels near the surface of the skin narrow and recede deeper into the underlying tissue where the heat of the little blood they carry is less easily dissipated. A pallor is observed as less and less heat-carrying blood flows near the surface of the skin. The raising of the individual's sparse body hair (and accompanying goosebumps) may also occur—a vestigial response which served our hairy ancestors effectively in all but the strongest of winds by forming an insulating sac of air, warmed by body heat, and maintained by the portruding and overlapping hair folicles. These events, which constitute the first line of defense against a lowering of the individual's body temperature (i.e., "cold"), go unnoticed, at least initially, by the individual.

These automated and unnoticed peripheral adjustments are often sufficient to maintain body temperature within the narrow range needed for orderly metabolic activity because processes such as the breaking down of food to composite packets and energy create heat in excess of 98.6 degrees Farenheit; hence, the first line of defense against cold is to turn-down the organism's own cooling operations. If the organism is exposed to yet more drain on its heat output, however, an involuntary tensing and relaxing of small muscles throughout the body (i.e., shivering) begins to occur. This second line of defense represents a turning-on of the body's heating operations. Each time a muscle fiber contracts, millions of ATP molecules (the body's major source of quick energy) are severed, creating some heat, and the friction produced as the muscle fibers slide across one another, produces yet additional heat. As the need for heat increases, more and larger muscles are recruited. In this way, heat production can increase five-fold for several critical minutes, although muscle coordination is lost in the process. If these defenses prove insufficient, body temperature falls, and extravagences of the organism such as coordinated movement, consciousness, and maintenance of appendiges are sacrificed, at least temporarily, while the remaining heated blood is shunted to the organs (e.g., brain, heart) that are absolutely vital to life in the short term.

Traditionally, social psychologists writing about the psychophysiological study of attitudes have trumpeted two major themes (e.g., Breckler, 1984; Mueller, 1986; Oskamp, 1977; Rosenberg & Hovland, 1960; Triandis, 1971): (a) Attitudes can be conceptualized as consisting of cognitive, affective, and behavioral components, and physiological measures are informative regarding the affective component of attitudes; and (b) physiological measures reflect the intensity but not the direction of people's affective reactions, and, consequently, arousal is the only process for which physiological analyses are of interest. Given this historical context, our opening description of the physiological events that occur when an individual is exposed to cold may seem out of place in a book on attitude structure and function. As should soon become clear, however, there has been a quiet revolution in thinking about the psychophysiological enterprise generally (e.g., see Cacioppo & Petty, 1986; Cacioppo, Petty, & Tassinary, in press; Coles, Gratton, & Gehring, in press; Donchin, 1981) and about the psychophysiological study of attitudes in particular (e.g., Cacioppo, Losch, Tassinary, & Petty, 1986; Cacioppo & Petty, 1985, 1987). Not only is there evidence that each of the two themes outlined is flawed, but also that the organismic-environmental transaction illustrated at the outset of this chapter embodies several important points regarding how one might think fruitfully about physiological responses and mechanisms to advance our understanding of attitude structure and function. These include the following:

1. peripheral physiological responses (e.g., changes in skin conductance) may be used to examine features of the organismic-environmental transaction (e.g., cold-challenges) even in instances in which verbal reports are insensitive or misleading;

2. because peripheral physiological responses have multiple causes, these responses are better conceived as episodic markers with limited ranges of validity rather than as correlates or invariants;

3. specific response patterns (e.g., decreased skin conductance, peripheral vasoconstriction, and the raising of body hair as markers of cold) have fewer antecedents, and hence can be used to mark particular events across a wider range, than do most single peripheral responses; and

4. understanding the physiological mechanism underlying the peripheral responses need not yield a reductionistic description of the organismic-environmental transaction, but rather can enrich psychological theorizing by contributing to the development of integrated and physiologically realistic conceptualizations.

In the present chapter, we review evidence regarding the flaws in the traditional views on the relationship between psychophysiology and attitudes, and we briefly introduce a more parsimonious and comprehensive conceptualization.

TRADITIONAL THEMES

The link between the attitude concept and bodily responses goes back, at least, to the 18th century, when the term *attitude* was used to refer to the posture or bodily orientation of a statue or figure in a painting (Fleming, 1967). Although remnants of this early formulation can still be found in statements such as "where do you stand on education" and "what is your position on nuclear disarmament," the definitional link between attitudes and bodily orientation no longer exists. Perusal of introductory social psychology textbooks, the third edition of the *Handbook of Social Psychology*, or various texts on attitudes reveal instead that bodily orientation has been replaced by the notion that general physiological arousal constitutes the most important bridge between people's attitude and physiological systems. We examine the evidence for this more recent conceptualization later in this chapter. We begin, however, by examining the first of the traditional themes already outlined.

Theme #1: The Attitude Tripartite

According to McGuire (1969), the trichotomy of feeling, knowing, and acting was first used by the early Greek philosophers as a way of conceptualizing general human experience rather than attitudes (see, also, McGuire, Chap. 3 in this volume). The influence of this trichotomy could be seen in the writings of the fathers of psychology as well as in those of early social psychologists (e.g., Bogardus, 1920; McDougall, 1908). It was not until Smith (1947), however, that the trichotomy was applied to attitudes. Not long afterwards, Rosenberg and Hovland (1960) proposed the model displayed in Fig. 11.1 wherein the first of the three traditional themes that still dominate this literature was clearly depicted: "Attitudes can be con-

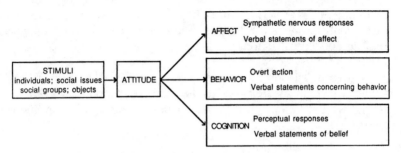

FIG. 1.   Schematic conception of attitudes from M. J. Rosenberg and C. I. Hovland (1960), "Cognitive, affective, and behavioral components of attitudes" (p. 3). From *Attitude Organization and Change: An Analysis of Consistency Among Attitude Components,* edited by M. E. Rosenberg, C. I. Hovland, W. J. McGuire, R. P. Abelson, and J. W. Brehm. Copyright © 1960 by Yale University Press, Inc. Reprinted by permission.

ceptualized as consisting of cognitive, affective, and behavioral components, and in this context physiological measures are viewed as being informative regarding the affective component of attitudes." More specifically, in Rosenberg and Hovland's (1960) conceptualization, responses reflecting the activation of the sympathetic nervous system, as well as verbal statements of affect, were said to be informative regarding the affective and only the affective component of attitudes.

It is apparent from the number of contemporary attitude texts that continue to promote this model that Rosenberg and Hovland's conceptualization continues to be influential. (e.g., see Eiser, 1986; Mueller, 1986; Oskamp, 1977; Rajecki, 1983; Zimbardo, Ebbesen, & Maslach, 1977). Moreover, the fact that verbal reports of affect were assigned the same status in the nomological net as more difficult to measure changes in sympathetic discharge justified: (a) the use of verbal reports and misattribution procedures in place of measures of bodily response; and (b) the simple dismissal of whichever measure proved unfriendly to the investigator's hypotheses (cf. Cacioppo, 1982). In perhaps the best study to date on the attitude tripartite, for instance, Breckler (1984) argued that studies of the attitude tripartite should measure responses from a variety of domains— such as the verbal, nonverbal, and physiological response domains when operationalizing the affective component of Rosenberg and Hovland's (1960) model. Accordingly, Breckler (1984) recorded heart rate in his first experiment to assess changes in sympathetic discharge and, hence, to gauge the affective component of the target attitude. Based on the Rosenberg and Hovland (1960) model, the results of this experiment, however, failed to confirm his expectations regarding the link between heart rate and the "affective component" of attitudes.

As Experiment 2, Breckler (1984) conducted a "verbal report anologue" (p. 1200) of his first experiment deleting all physiological measures in the replication. The deletion of physiological measures produced a pattern of data more friendly to the tripartite conceptualization. Specifically, evidence was obtained for convergent validity across the discriminant validity within the self-report measures of cognitive, affective, and behavioral response to the attitude object. No explanation was offered, however, for the failure of the model in terms of its psychophysiological predictions. Although the data from Breckler (1984, Experiment 1) might call into question at least one aspect of the model outlined by Rosenberg and Hovland (1960), there are several other reasons to question the model.

Response Fractionation Across
the Sympathetic Nervous and Verbal Systems is
the Rule Rather Than the Exception

An intense challenge or stimulus tends to bring about a convergence of verbal report and sympathetic nervous responses, but frationation of verbal and autonomic responses is the rule (e.g., Cacioppo, Tassinary, Stonebraker, & Petty, in press; Cantor, Bryant, & Zillmann, 1975; Mewborn & Rogers, 1979). The afferents from the viscera to the cortex are sparse and respond primarily to changes in activity rather than to absolute levels of activity; hence, changes in sympathetic tonus are difficult to detect and localize (Blascovich & Katkin, 1983), whereas the sentence of the newly achieved levels of visceral activity can quickly fade (Pennebaker, 1982; Zillmann, 1984). The anatomical architecture of visceral afferents, while minimizing the demands on the organism's limited cognitive resources to maintain the precious internal milieu, also provides the basis for striking disparities between actual sympathetic nervous response and verbal reports.

When a stimulus is sufficiently intense to provoke changes in both sympathetic and verbal responses, the dissipation of sympathetic excitation can be slowed by such sympathomimetic agents as circulating catechol-amines and corticosteroids excreted into the bloodstream as part of the organism's response to the stressor. Consequently, the diminution of interoceptive stimulation following the initial excitatory response to the stressor can result in a sharp reduction in or loss of the sentience of being aroused (see Zillmann, 1984).

Further evidence of fractionation between verbal and autonomic responses is apparent in recent studies by Wilson (1979) and Cacioppo, Petty, Losch, and Kim (1986), who demonstrated that reported changes in the likability of stimuli can occur in the absence of changes in visceral (e.g., cardiac, electrodermal) response. However, this is not to suggest that the response threshold for verbal reports is invariably lower than that for sympathetic responses. As exemplified in the opening description of the body's first line of defense against cold, changes in electrodermal and peripheral vascular status can be initiated before the individual is aware of being cold and, when the environmental challenge is mild, can actually abort the sensation of cold in the absence of changes in the individual's reported state.

Similarly, the simple anticipation of strenuous action (e.g., exercise, a vigorous retreat from an unpleasant stimulus) can lead to anticipatory compensatory physiological reactions (e.g., increased heart rate; cf. Berne & Levy, 1981). There is, of course, no metabolic utility in the verbal system being engaged in a parallel set of preparatory actions, as the peripheral physiological adjustments are designed to maintain homeostatic conditions in the organism and, thereby, provide the internal milieu required for sustaining thought, feeling, and coordinated behavior. The fractionation of verbal and physiological responses, therefore, can be viewed as a consequence of the body's eloquently orchestrated division of labor, an organization that provides the human organism with the capacity to adapt, aspire, and achieve more than other known species.

*Physiological Responses Are Not Limited to
the Affective Aspect of Human Experience but Can
Be Informative About the Cognitive and Behavioral
Aspects as Well*

It has long been known that emotionally evocative situations and stimuli can be autonomically arousing. Dating at least as far back as the third century BC, the Greek physician Erasistratos used this fact along with his observations of peripheral physiological responses such as the disruption of a regular heart beat in a young man when his stepmother visited, to isolate the individual's malady—"lovesickness" (Mesulam & Perry, 1972). The initial psychophysiological studies of attitudes also capitalized on this relationship. Smith (1936), for instance, studied social influence by monitoring the skin resistance responses (SRRs) of individuals as they were confronted by the information that their peers held attitudes that were discrepant from their own; Rankin and Campbell (1955) studied racial prejudice by monitoring the SRRs of individuals as they were exposed to White and Black experimenters; and Cooper (1959) studied prejudice generally by monitoring SRRs as individuals were exposed to complimentary comments about their most disliked ethnic group, derogatory comments about their most liked ethnic group, and complimentary or derogatory comments about ehtnic groups toward which the individuals felt neutrally. Affect, therefore, came to be viewed as the psychological antecedent for autonomic activation, and the emphasis was on identifying the "physiological correlates" of attitudes and attitude changes (cf. Cooper, 1959; Mueller, 1986; Summers, 1970).

Psychophysiological assessments are often viewed as being useful within social psychology, however, only to the extent that investigators can infer the presence or absence of a particular antecedent or process (e.g., affect) when a target physiological response (e.g., increased skin conductance) is observed. Yet evidence that an event or process leads to a particular physiological response is a necessary but not a sufficient condition to make such an inference. This is due to the fact that a statement and its converse are not logically equivalent. Thus, knowledge that a statement is true (i.e., A implies B) does not imply that the converse is true (i.e., B implies A). Hence, except in the rare circumstance in which one is dealing with an invariant (single cause, single effect) relationship, establishing that the manipulation of an event or process (A) leads to a particular physiological response or profile of responses (B) does *not* logically imply that "B predicts A." For example, increased electrodermal activity (EDA) is evoked by a variety of fractors, ranging from stress to novelty to arousal to significant events. To infer that a person was emotionally aroused based simply on increased EDA, therefore, is to commit the logical error of affirmation of the consequent (Runes, 1961). Evidence indicating that this conceptualization has not been fully appreciated by social psychologists using psychophysiological analyses is reviewed by Cacioppo, Petty, and Tassinary (in press).

Indeed, there is now considerable evidence that cognitive and behavioral processes also influence autonomic response. Even the actions of the heart, which was once thought to be the seat of all passions, are now known to be influenced by strong emotionally evocative stimuli (cf. Fowles, 1982), but also by cognitive activity (e.g., Lacey, Kagan, Lacey, & Moss, 1963) and overt behaviors and behavioral intentions (e.g., the anticipation and performance of strenuous movement; see Berne & Levy, 1981; Obrist, 1981). Bonvallet, Dell, and Hiebel (1954) and Bonvallet and Allen (1963) found that pressure-sensitive receptors (baroreceptors) in the arterial walls transmitted information regarding arterial pressure changes to the brainstem and thereby changed the excitability of the cortex. On the basis of these neurophysiological findings, the Laceys (Lacey & Lacey, 1974; Lacey, 1967; Lacey et al., 1963; Lacey & Lacey, 1970) speculated that accelerated heart rate was associated with mental concentration, whereas decelerated heart rate was associated with lowered sensorimotor thresholds.

Although the neurophysiological mechanism underlying these hypothesized relationships has been hotly debated (cf. Cacioppo & Petty, 1982b; Coles, Jennings, & Stern, 1984; Obrist, 1981), many studies using various kinds of stimuli have provided support for the notion that heart rate is influenced by information processing activity (e.g., Baker, Sandman, & Pepinsky, 1975; Blaylock, 1972; Cacioppo & Sandman, 1978; Tursky, Schwartz, & Crider, 1970). For instance, when persons engage in tasks such as spelling words backwards, mental arithmetic, and constructing multiple sentences (each beginning with the same first letter of the alphabet), heart rate increased from baseline levels. However, when persons performed tasks requiring attention and with minimal demands for cognitive manipulation, storage, and retrieval (e.g., watching lights flash), heart rate decreased from baseline levels (Lacey et al., 1963). Tursky, Schwartz, and Crider (1970) further demonstrated the time-locked nature of these psychophysiological relationships: when persons listened to a series of digits to be used later, their heart rates decelerated; when the digits were then reordered, their heart rates accelerated, particularly when the digit-transformation was difficult.

Moreover, autonomic activity such as pupillary responses has been found to reflect cognitive processes. Pupillary dilation, for instance, is under the control of the sympathetic nervous system, whereas pupillary constriction is under the control of the parasympathetic. In a widely cited paper, Hess (1965) equated the pupillary response with affective processes, claiming that pleasant stimuli led to pupillary dilation, whereas unpleasant stimuli led to pupillary constriction. A large number of attempts to validate Hess' hypothesis have produced generally negative results, with a few studies appearing confirmatory and a large number being highly contradictory. The most telling argument that Hess' findings are the result of methodological artifacts (e.g., resulting from inappropriate baselines, the wavelength of the visual stimuli on which subjects focused) is that the confirmatory evidence that does exist has only dealt with pictorial stimuli, where it is extremely difficult to control numerous light–reflex-related variables that can confound such studies (Goldwater, 1972; Janisse & Peavler, 1974; cf. Cacioppo & Sandman, 1981).

A second line of research has consistently demonstrated that the pupillary responses are influenced by cognitive processes such as attention (Libby, Lacey, & Lacey, 1973; Lynn, 1966) and cognitive effort (Beatty, 1982; Kahneman, 1973). Beatty (1986), for instance, reviewed evidence that the amplitude of pupillary dilations varies with the processing load or "mental effort" required by a task, regardless of the sensory modality in which the task is presented, and that these pupillary responses are sensitive to within-task, between-task, and between-individual factors that control task-processing demands.

In sum, cognitive and behavioral as well as affective antecedents for visceral responding have been identified. It is an error, therefore, to assume given the observation of an autonomic reaction that the affective substrates necessarily have been tapped. On the positive side, these observations mean that autonomic (or what Rosenberg and Hovland, 1960, presumably meant by "sympathetic nervous") responses can be used within limited ranges of validity to investigate cognitive and behavioral aspects of the organismic-environmental transaction as well as affective aspects.[1]

Responses from the Central and Somatic Nervous Systems as well as Those Mediated by the Autonomic Nervous System Can Be Informative Regarding Cognition, Emotion, and Behavior

A third misleading feature of Rosenberg and Hovland's (1960) attitude tripartite model is the implication that responses from the central and somatic nervous systems are not informative, at least within limited ranges of validity, about cognition, emotion, and behavior. Research on the messages carried by incipient (i.e., visually unobservable) facial actions illus-

---

[1]The notion of "limited ranges of validity" is perhaps foreign to investigators who still view the psychophysiological enterprise as the search for general mind-body correlates. Limited range of validity means that physiological measures have a particular "psychological meaning" only within conditions carefully prescribed theoretically and/or in a series of validation studies. That the search for general psychophysiological correlates is of limited use in psychophysiological research was illustrated in the opening example: (a) lowered skin conductance can be used unambiguously to mark an individual's exposure to cold only in some well specified circumstances, because lowered skin conductance can occur for other reasons, as well; and (b) describing the individual exposed to cold strictly in terms of the physiological reactions (e.g., in terms of afferent discharges rather than or to the exclusion of the resulting percepts) is as specious as expecting reaction time or verbal reports to capture the entire organismic–environmental transaction. The alternative to searching for physiological correlates of affect, cognition, or behavior is not dustbowl empiricism, just as the use of chronometric measures to study cognitive and emotional processes does not imply an atheoretical approach to these processes (see Cacioppo & Petty, 1986). Nor does it *preclude* investigators from capitalizing on knowledge about the mechanisms underlying physiological responses to generate theoretical statements about the functional significance of these responses (e.g., as illustrated in our opening example). As Coles et al. (in press) noted, however, the "ascription of psychological meaning to a physiological measure does not *depend*, logically, on knowledge of its physiological meaning." At the root of this alternative to the search for general correlates is the conceptualization of physiological measures as manifestations of processes invoked as part of an organismic–environmental interaction. Such processes may or may not be related to psychological activity, and may or may not be responsive to or influential in attitudinal processing. When measures within limited contexts are identified that are related to attitudinal processes or events, the nature of the relationship may or may not be monotonic. When the functional relationship is found, it is of use to the extent that it is possible to address issues of theoretical import by employing psychophysiological measures as a source of data about the social organism (Cacioppo & Petty, 1981a, 1985; Cacioppo, Petty, & Tassinary, in press; see, also, Coles et al., in press; Donchin, 1982).

trates the fallacy of this feature of the model. Before proceeding to this research, however, we need to say a bit more about the theoretical basis for the specific psychophysiological relationships with which we will be dealing.

The first century of research on the psychophysiology of behavioral processes dealt with perception, nocturnal dreams, imagination, learning, and problem-solving, most of which, at one time or another, were used to elicit responses in the skeletomotor, visceral, and central nervous systems. A characteristic finding, in part due to the intense nature of the independent variables and the insensitive nature of the dependent measures typically employed, was that physiological responding increased relative to baseline levels when people performed motor, emotional, and cognitive tasks. As a result, several elaborate theories regarding task performance and arousal (in one of its many forms) were developed (see review by Shapiro & Crider, 1969).

There were notable exceptions, however, to the focus on and evidence for the dominant notion of general physiological arousal. In 1929, for instance, Chester Darrow measured multiple physiological responses simultaneously while subjects performed a variety of tasks (e.g., mental arithmetic, being exposed to a sudden gun shot, attending to weak stimulation). Darrow observed that the notion of general arousal, though an evident consequence of some tasks, failed to account for much of the variance in physiological responding. As measurement procedures achieved greater sensitivity and standardization, a greater range of stimulus intensities was examined and the general finding was, in retrospect, all but surprising: The human organism responds to extremely intense stimuli in a fairly stereotyped fashion (e.g., Cannon, 1927; Selye, 1956), whereas it responds mildly to moderately intense stimuli in a more physiologically differentiated fashion (e.g., Ekman, Levenson, & Friesen, 1983; Lacey et al., 1963). Two early principles accounting for the differentiated patterns of physiological responding were: (a) *individual response stereotypy,* which refers to the tendency for the same individual to display the same profile of physiological response to all forms of stimulation; and (b) *stimulus response stereotypy,* which refers to the tendency for a situation or stimulus to elicit a common pattern or profile of response from people in general.

Model of Somatic Patterning. Additional principles were necessary, however, to account for the fact that particular elementary psychologic operators—such as attention, positive or negative affect, imagery, and interpreting and encoding incoming verbal information (which are induced by a wide variety of stimuli)—also tended to invoke distinctive patterns of somatovisceral activity. The notions of orienting, defensive, and startle responses were developed, and specifying the antecedents, parameters, and consequences of these response syndromes continues to be an active area of research (e.g., Jennings, 1986; Turpin, 1986). In addition, theoretical analyses of efferent activity during problem-solving, imagery, and emotion dating back to Charles Darwin and William James have shared assumptions regarding the specificity and adaptive utility of somatic responses (e.g., see McGuigan, 1978; Schwartz, 1975). To better specify these links, R. C. Davis (1939) postulated the principle of focus of muscular responses, which holds that each task a subject performs is accompanied by a focus of muscular activity. Davis' principle of focus of muscular response, however, does not predict *where* a focal point is located or *why*.

Several years ago, we proposed a descendent of Davis' postulate that possessed greater explanatory and predictive power to account for the fact that particular elementary psychologic operators tended to invoke distinctive patterns of somatic activity (Cacioppo & Petty, 1981a). The model consisted of a set of five principles, which both drew upon Davis' principle of focus of muscular response and extended Darwin's principles of serviceable associated habits and of antithesis to the level of unobservable muscle actions and patterns (e.g., see Cacioppo, Martzke, Petty, & Tassinary, 1988). The principles are as follows:

1. *There are foci of somatic activity in which changes mark particular psychological processes.* For instance, a student who closes her eyes and vividly imagines watching a professor pace back and forth across the room during a lecture might show localized electromyographic (EMG) activity over the orbicularis oculi (periocular) muscle region in a more rudimentary form but not unlike as if the student were actually visually scanning back and forth across the room to follow the pacing professor.

2. *Inhibitory as well as excitatory changes in somatic activity can mark a psychological process.* For instance, in the preceding example, the act of imagining that one was watching a professor pace back and forth across the room led to an increase in periocular EMG activity. However, if the student were to imagine that the professor stood motionless and speechless in the middle of the room, this stationary image could actually lead to a diminution of periocular activity.

3. *Changes in somatic activity are patterned temporally as well as spatially.* Thus, consider the case in which a professor was pacing back and forth during her lecture but who during the course of making a point slowed and then stopped; a student who is imagining this scenario should show predictable changes in EMG activity over the periocular muscle region across time (temporal specificity)—and these changes would be localized rather than expressed generally across somatic sites (spatial specificity).

4. *Changes in somatic activity become less evident as the distance of measurement from the focal point increases.* Thus, in the aforementioned example, any localized changes in EMG activity over the periocular region would be more measureable at sites proximal rather than distal to the source of the bioelectrical signals (e.g., near to rather than far from the orbicularis oculi muscle).

5. *Foci can be identified a priori by (a) analyzing the overt reactions that initially characterized the particular psychological process of interest but which appeared to drop out with practice, and (b) observing the somatic sites that are involved during the "acting out" of the particular psychological process of interest.* There are of course individual differences in the elementary psychologic operations initiated by a stimulus. For instance, most people who are asked to imagine a spiral respond by visualizing an exemplar, although some individuals (e.g., mathematicians) may respond by recalling the mathematical function for a spiral. This individual difference can be a source of error in a priori specifications of somatic foci. Hence, ideographic procedures can be useful to help ensure the particular psychological operation of interest was invoked in response to the experimental stimulus.

Consistent with this model, research using facial EMG recordings (see Fig. 11.2) has revealed that patterns of somatic activity can be as or more informative about cognitive, affective, and behavioral processes than can "sympathetic nervous responses."[2] In a study designed to examine the first

---

[2]Some social psychologists have tended to think of EMG as a measure of overt behavior rather than as a "physiological" measure. Two points are worth emphasizing, therefore. First, the term *physiological* refers to the functions of living organisms. The somatic nervous system, being the ultimate mechanism through which vertabrates interact with and modify their environments, clearly falls under the rubric of physiology (e.g., see Guyton, 1971; Mountcastle, 1980). The skeletomotor system is admittedly but a servant of the central nervous system, and this observation has led to instances in which it has been assigned a subservient role in psychophysiological investigations. It is, however, a loquacious servant. As Evarts (1973) noted: It seems possible that understanding the human nervous system, even its most complex intellectual functions, may be enriched if the operation of the brain is analyzed in terms of its output" (p. 103). Second, the levels of and changes in EMG activity with which we have been dealing are insufficient to evoke observable actions and, therefore, cannot be considered measures of overt behavior. Indeed, although similarities clearly exist, the facial EMG patterns we have been studying are not simply microvolt replicas of differentiated overt expressions of emotion, but rather are more rudimentary in form and locus. People appear less aware of, and less likely to monitor and control, incipient muscle action potentials than they are overt expressions of emotion. The leakage from incipient facial EMG patterns, therefore, may exceed that from overt expressions. Further discussion of these issues is, unfortunately, beyond the scope of the present chapter. Interested readers can consult Cacioppo, Petty, Losch, and Kim (1986) and Cacioppo, Martzke, Petty, and Tassinary (1988).

and fifth principles, for instance, subjects were led to believe they were participating in research on involuntary neural responses during "action and imagery" (Cacioppo, Petty, & Marshall-Goodell, 1984). Numerous dummy electrodes were placed on the subjects and a cover story was employed to deflect attention from the facial placements and the fact that the responses being monitored could be altered by the subject. Subjects on any given trial either: (a) lifted what was described as being a "light" (16g) or "heavy" (35g) weight (action); (b) imagined lifting the "light" or "heavy" weight (imagery); (c) silently read a neutral communication as if they agreed or disagreed with its thesis (action); or (d) imagined reading an editorial with which they agreed or disagreed (imagery). Based on the model previously outlined, we expected perioral (orbicularis oris) EMG activity would be greater during the communicative attitudinal tasks than during the physical tasks; and the affective processes invoked by the positive and negative attitudinal tasks would lead to distinguishable patterns of EMG activity over the brow (corrugator supercilii), cheek (zygomatic major), and possibly the nose (levator labii superioris—which is involved in expressions of disgust) regions, whereas the simple physical tasks would lead to distinguishable EMG activity over the superficial forearm flexors (whose actions control flexion about the wrist).

Imagining performing rather than actually performing the tasks was, of course, associated with lower mean levels of EMG activity, although multi-variate analyses revealed that the site and overall form of the task-evoked EMG responses were similar across the levels of this factor. More interestingly, results provided support for the suggestion that somatic responses are influenced by, and therefore in limited settings can be informative regarding, *cognition* (e.g., the load on the articulatory loop), *emotion* (e.g., affective valence), and *conation* (e.g., imagined action). Specifically, results revealed that:

1. Perioral EMG activity was higher during the silent language (attitudinal) than nonlanguage (physical) tasks.
2. EMG activity over the brow, cheek, and nose-wrinkler muscle regions in the face (muscles of mimicry) varied as a function of whether subjects thought about the topic in an agreeable or disagreeable manner.
3. EMG activity over the superficial forearm flexors was higher during the physical tasks than it was during the attitudinal tasks.

Perioral EMG Activity as a Function of Silent Language Processing. Although the relationship between cognition and perioral EMG activity illustrated in this study could conceivably be due to some other difference between the physical and attitudinal task (e.g., affectivity of the attitude tasks), a series of studies conducted in this area suggest otherwise.

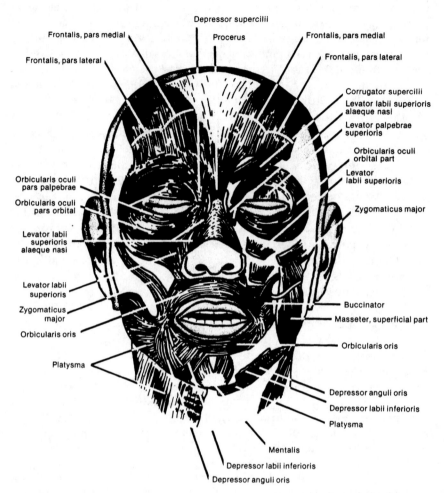

FIG. 11.2.   Schematic representation of selected facial muscles. Overt facial expressions of emotion are based on contractions of the underlying musculature that are sufficiently intense to result in visibly perceptible dislocations of the skin and landmarks. The more common visible effects of strong contractions of the depicted facial muscles include the following:

Muscles of the lower face: Depressor anguli oris—pulls the lip corners downward; *Depressor labii inferioris*—depresses the lower lip; *Orbicularis oris*—tightens, compresses, protrudes, and/or inverts the lips; *Mentalis*—raises the chin and protrudes the lower lip; *Platysma*—wrinkles the skin of the neck and may draw down both the lower lip and the lip corners.

Muscles of the mid-face: Buccinator—compresses and tightens the cheek, forming a "dimple"; *Levator labii superioris alaeque nasi*—raises the center of the upper lip and flares the nostrils; *Levator labii superioris*—raises the upper lip and flares the nostrils, exposing the canine teeth; *Masseter*—adducts the lower jaw; *Zygomaticus major*—pulls the lip corners up and back.

In one study, for instance, subjects received forewarnings of impending discrepant counterattitudinal appeals, and the level of communication discrepancy was varied (Cacioppo & Petty, 1979a, Experiment 1). Following each forewarning, subjects were asked to "collect their thoughts" about the proposal and, subsequently, to complete a thought-listing. Results replicated previous research (e.g., Brock, 1967) showing that counterargumentation increased as communication discrepancy increased. Analyses of perioral EMG activity, however, revealed it was insensitive to this change in the affectivity of the information processing; instead, and as would be expected if low-amplitude EMG activity over the perioral region was a consequence of short-term verbal processing rather than emotion per se, perioral EMG activity increased across all conditions (relative to prewarning baselines) during the period subjects were "collecting their thoughts" on the proposal.

In a second illustrative study, subjects were exposed to 60 trait adjectives spanning a range of likeability (Cacioppo & Petty, 1981b; also see Cacioppo & Petty, 1979b). Each trait adjective was preceded by one of five cue-questions, which defined the processing task. The cue questions were:

1. "Does the following word rhyme with————?" (Rhyme).
2. "Is the following word spoken louder than this question?" (Volume discrimination).
3. "Is the following word similar in meaning to————?" (Association).
4. "Is the following word good (bad)?" (Evaluation). and
5. "Is the following word self-descriptive?" (Self-reference).

Finally, as in all of our facial EMG research, subjects in this study knew bioelectrical activity was being recorded, but they did not realize that activity over which they had voluntary control was being monitored.

Results revealed that mean recognition confidence ratings were ordered as follows: self-reference, evaluation, association, rhyme, and volume discrimination. Importantly, all means except the last two differed significantly from one another. In addition we found that: (a) The mean amplitude of perioral (orbicularis oris) EMG activity was lowest for the nonsemantic

---

Muscles of the upper face: Corrugator supercilii—draws the brows together and downward, producing vertical furrows between the brows; *Depressor supercilii/procerus*—pulls the medial part of the brows downward and may wrinkle the skin over the bridge of the nose; *Frontalis, pars lateral*—raises the outer brows, producing horizontal furrows in the lateral regions of the forehead; *Frontalis, pars medial*—raises the inner brows, producing horizontal furrows in the medial region of the forehead; *Levator palpebrae superioris*—raises the upper eyelid; *Orbicularis oculi, pars orbital*—tightens the skin surrounding the eye causing "crowsfeet" wrinkles; *Orbicularis oculi, pars palpebrae*—tightens the skin surrounding the eye causing the lower eyelid to raise.

From Cacioppo, Martzke, Petty, & Tassinary (1988) by permission of the authors.

tasks of rhyme and volume discrimination, intermediate for the task of association, and equally high for the tasks of evaluation and self-reference (we subsequently found that these, too, could be differentiated using psychophysiological measures by analyzing the shape rather than simply the size of the EMG responses—Cacioppo, Petty, & Morris, 1985; cf. Cacioppo & Dorfman, 1987); (b) Cardiac activity and the mean amplitude of EMG activity over a peripheral muscle region (i.e., nonpreferred superficial forearm flexors region) did not vary as a function of the type of task performed; and (c) The association between task and perioral EMG activity was temporally specific, with task-discriminating EMG activity observed only while subjects analyzed the aurally presented trait adjectives and formulated their response. Finally, and consistent with the results of the previous studies, whether the trait-adjective being processed was positive, neutral, or negative had no impact on perioral EMG activity.

Facial EMG Activity as a Function of Affect-Laden Information Processing.   Given that perioral EMG activity varies as a function of short-term semantic processing, and that EMG activity over selected facial muscle regions (e.g., corrugator supercilii, zygomatic major) is influenced differentially by positive and negative affective states (e.g., recall the differences observed as a result of the affectivity of the attitudinal tasks outlined in our review of Cacioppo et al., 1984), we reasoned that facial EMG measures might prove informative regarding elementary processes evoked by the anticipation and presentation of personally involving persuasive communications. Elsewhere in our Elaboration Likelihood Model of persuasion we have outlined specific conditions under which recipients of persuasive communications "cognitively respond" to message arguments, generating new associations, linkes, and implications central to the merits of an advocacy rather than basing attiudes on reltively simple peripheral cues (e.g., see Petty & Cacioppo, 1981, 1986). Miller and Baron (1973), on the other hand, argued that these conditions did *not* elicit extensive cognitive activity (see, also, Langer, Blank, & Chanowitz, 1978; Miller, Maruyama, Beaber, & Valone, 1976). Experimental results based on subjects' reported attitudes and the thoughts and ideas they listed in retrospective verbal protocols ("thought listings") provided support for the former position (Petty & Cacioppo, 1977; cf. Cacioppo & Petty, 1981c; Cialdini & Petty, 1981), but others have expressed concerns that these data could reflect post hoc rationalizations produced in response to postexperimental questioning rather than processes evoked by the persuasive communication (e.g., Miller & Coleman, 1981).

We reasoned that if anticipating an involving, counterattitudinal appeal stimulated subjects to engage in anticipatory counterargumentation and, thereby, cognitively buttress their original position, then such a forewarning might lead spontaneously to detectable increases in levels of perioral

EMG activity (Cacioppo & Petty, 1979a, Experiment 2). Students were recruited for what they believed was an experiment on "biosensory processes," and as in the previous research, they were unaware that somatic responses were being monitored. After subjects adapted to the laboratory, we obtained recordings of basal EMG activity, forewarned subjects that in 60 seconds they would be hearing an editorial with which they agreed, an editorial with which they disagreed, or an unspecified meassage, obtained another 60 seconds of physiological recording while subjects sat quietly, and obtained yet another 120 seconds of data while subjects listened to a proattitudinal appeal, counterattitudinal appeal, and a news story about an archeological expedition. Subjects were not told to collect their thoughts in this study, but rather somatovisceral activity was simply monitored while subjects awaited and listened to the message presentation. This allowed us to assess the extent to which spontaneous perioral activity accompanied the anticipation of a persuasive communication.

As expected, subjects evaluated more positively and reported having more favorable thoughts and fewer counterarguments to the proattitudinal than to the counterattitudinal advocacy. Although unexpected, we also found that subjects reported enjoying the "neutral" newstory about an obscure archaeological expedition as much as they did the proattitudinal editorial. Analyses of perioral EMG indicated that perioral activity increased following the forewarning of an impending and personally involving counterattitudinal advocacy, and it increased for all conditions during the presentation of the message. This selective activation of perioral EMG activity during the postwarning–premessage period provided convergent evidence for the view that people engage in anticipatory cognitive activity to buttress their beliefs when they anticipate hearing a personally involving, counterattitudinal appeal. Moreover, the pattern of subtle facial EMG activity was found to reflect the positive/negative nature of the persuasive appeal before and during the message. Presentation of the proattitudinal and "neutral" messages was accompanied by a pattern of facial EMG activity similar to that found to accompany pleasant emotional imagery, whereas both the anticipation and presentation of the counterattitudinal message was associated with a pattern of EMG activity similar to that found to accompany unpleasant emotional imagery (see, also, reviews by Cacioppo & Petty, 1986; Fridlund & Izard, 1983; Lanzetta, Sullivan, Masters, & McHugo, 1985).

In sum, physiological responses in addition to those mediated by the sympathetic nervous system have been found to be influenced by cognitive, affective, and behavioral events. The surprising issue is not that these various relationships exist, but that attitude researchers have ignored these relationships so long. As noted, the somatic nervous system is the final pathway through which people respond to, interact with, and modify their physical and social environments. Efference has even been implicated in perception (Coren, 1986). That the pattern of efferent neural commands are not always as intended (e.g., as when one performs clumsily), not always a veridical reflection of goals (e.g., as when one deceives), and not always obvious (e.g., as when one hides feelings) is important to recognize when identifying the ranges of validity for the relationships outlined. But without efferent neural commands, individuals do not communicate, do not affiliate, do not proliferate, do not interact, and do not adapt. The theoretical basis for asserting that the subtle patterns of efferent commands can be used to study organismic-environmental transactions—including such abstract components of these transactions as the cognitive, affective, and behavioral processes activated by an attitude, appears solid.

The Notion of the Tripartite as a Parsimonious Heuristic for Thinking About Attitudes Can Be Questioned

Thurstone (1928), in his classic paper "Attitudes can be Measured," was sensitive to problems in attitude-behavior correspondence but used the terms *attitudes* and *affect* similarly. The tripartite model of attitudes served a valuable function in distinguishing not only between attitudes and behaviors, but between attitudes and cognitions, and between attitudes and affect. One possibly undesirable feature of the tripartite model, however, is the unparsimonious notion that affective, cognitive, and behavioral stimuli can influence affective, cognitive, and behavioral attitude-components, *each* of which in turn can mediate affective, cognitive, and behavioral responses.

Evidence for the Rosenberg and Hovland Tripartite Model of Attitudes Revisited

Is it necessary to internalize the trichotomy as part of the attitude construct?[3] Apparently some believe so. Breckler (1984) argued that "to say a researcher is measuring 'attitude' is ambiguous, because it does not specify which of the three components is being measured" (pp. 1203–1204). Such a position evokes images of "cognitive attitudes," "affective attitudes," and "behavioral attitudes," which are combined in some fashion to guide people's thoughts, feelings, and actions toward the attitude object (e.g., also see Batra & Ray, 1986). There is agreement across conceptualizations that

---

[3]As Cacioppo and Petty (1982a) noted, to ask this question does *not* imply that emotional and/or motivational processes are irrelevant to the formation or enduring modification of an attitude. Indeed, in reviewing the neuroanatomy of emotion, Mueller (1986) was moved to suggest: "It appears that sensory experience achieves meaning or attains permanence in memory only to the extent that it is paired, however indirectly, with the experience of pleasure or pain at a core-brain or 'visceral' level" (p. 99). The question addressed here is not whether emotional processes contribute to the formation or change of an attitude, but rather how should the consequent attitude be conceptualized.

attitudes have cognitive, affective, and behavioral antecedents and consequences (see Breckler, 1984, chap. 1). For instance, attitudes can be
based primarily on cognition, emotion, *or* behavior (Millar & Tesser, 1986).
There is also general agreement that evaluation is a critical attribute of the
concept of attitudes. Given all human experience can be partitioned into
categories of affect, cognition, and behavior (cf. McGuire, 1969, 1985, chap.
3 in this volume), one can clearly and usefully conceptualize the *knowledge
structure* for an attitude in terms of this age-old trichotomy as well. The
conceptualization of the *attitude* construct as a global and enduring evaluation is theoretically more parsimonious. However, if the data that are
thought to support the tripartite model of attitudes can be explained
equally well by the view that attitudes represent evaluative nodes connected by associative pointers to thoughts, images, actions, and emotions.
Before elaborating on this alternative conceptualization, however, two
aspects of the evidence purported to favor the tripartite model are noteworthy.

First, the evidence consists essentially of multitrait, multimethod studies
in which attitude measures based on verbal responses from the affective,
cognitive, and behavioral domains were found to exhibit convergent and
discriminant validity (e.g., see Ostrom, 1969). Second, in every study
supporting the attitude tripartite distinction, the indices of "cognition,"
"affect," and "behavior" have been scaled to reflect *evaluations* of the
attitude objects. For example, Breckler (1984) obtained thought listings
about an attitude object; however, rather than using the total number of
issue-relevant thoughts (or some other cognitive structure index) as a
measure of the cognitive component, he had the subjects rate each thought
along an evaluative dimension and used the ratio of the favorable to unfavorable thoughts about the attitude object as an index of the cognitive component. Indeed, in reviewing previous research in this area Breckler (1984)
found this feature of the experimental design to be so important that he
designated the requirement that "all dependent measures must be scaled on
a common evaluative continuum" (p. 1194) as one of the five essential
conditions for a strong test of the tripartite model's validity.[4]

---

[4]Although Breckler (1984) had subjects rate the cognitions in Experiment 1, he didn't
have subjects rate their behavioral responses (e.g., how closely subjects approached the
attitude object) along an evaluative continuum. This presumably was because the scaling of the
behaviors along an evaluative dimension was performed by the experimenter on intuitive
grounds in selecting the particular behaviors used in the study. (In Experiment 2, Breckler
(1984) *did* have subjects rate their behavioral reports along a good–bad dimension, but he did
not report the results of these data.) Other measures employed, such as the MACL used by
Breckler to assess affect, were scaled along the evaluative dimension by different individuals
during the development of the scales. Such diversity in the procedures used in scaling the
measures along the evaluative continuum contributes to method variance, which should work
against obtaining evidence for the unidimensional model of attitudes.

This raises an interesting question: Could the research purported to support the tripartite over the unidimensional model simply have resulted from the scaling of originally orthogonal, mutually exclusive, and exhaustive dimensions of experience along a common evaluative continuum? Consider, for instance, the following thought-experiment. Suppose one were to begin with two dimensions of meaning that were both theoretically and empirically independent—the dimensions of activity and potency (Osgood, Suci, & Tannenbaum, 1957). Furthermore, suppose it was confirmed that ratings of an attitude object along these two dimensions did indeed yield two orthogonal dimensions, but that scaling the dependent measures from these two theoretically and empirically orthogonal (activity and potency) dimensions along a common evaluative continuum eliminated the empirical independence between them (although not to such a degree that the dimensions became isomorphic). The result would be a pattern of data strikingly similar to that said to favor the tripartite over the unidimensional model of attitudes, because the (transformed) measures of the various components shared some common variance (i.e., convergent evidence would be said to exist) although the measures would not be reducible to a single factor (i.e., discriminant validity would be said to exist).

The results outlined in this thought-experiment seem reasonable because the dependent measures constituting originally independent semantic dimensions have been transformed, by the scaling process, to reflect in part the original dimension of meaning and in part a new and common dimension. Indeed, we have conducted such a study and confirmed the results derived from our thought experiment (Geen, 1987, see Table 1). It is worth reiterating, therefore, that this scaling process, such as the ordering beliefs about an attitude object along a common evaluative dimension when constructing a Thurstone scale, is essentially intrinsic to the measures used in previous research purported to support the attitude tripartite. We don't believe (nor would we advocate) anyone would accept the results illustrated in Table 11.1 as evidence that attitudes consisted of two components—activity and potency. If two theoretically and empirically orthogonal dimensions, such as activity and potency, that have little to do with attitudes per se can yield essentially the same pattern of results found in research purported to support the attitude tripartite once the activity and potency ratings of the stimulus have been rescaled in terms of a common evaluative stimulus, then: (a) we've learned something about *attitude measurement* (i.e., take a set of measures of any subjective stimulus dimension, scale them along an evaluative dimension, and the resulting measures will reflect albeit imperfectly the individual's attitude—i.e., evaluation—toward the stimulus); and (b) we've obtained further evidence that the central component of attitudes is evaluation; but (c) we've not obtained definitive support for the validity of the tripartite model of attitudes.[5]

The Homeostasis Model of Attitudes.   If the tripartite model is unsatisfactory, then how are attitudes best conceptualized? We have argued thus far that evaluation is a central and distinguishing feature of the concept of attitudes. Previous advocates of a unidimensional conceptualization of attitudes have acknowledged the importance of the positive–negative dimension but have equated attitudes with affect or have failed to distinguish affect from evaluation (e.g., Fishbein & Ajzen, 1975; Thurstone, 1928; but see Cacioppo & Petty, 1982a). These seem undesirable as well, as they blur the fact that some attitudes, such as those serving a consumatory function, can be evocative of a great deal of affect, whereas others, such as those serving an instrumental function, may evoke virtually no affect.[6] The stimulus category to which an attitude applies has a structure that includes beliefs about and attributes of the stimuli comprising the category; memories of prior behavioral, cognitive, and affective experiences; expectations and conations; and possible one or more affect nodes through which affective responses can be activated. However, accurate summaries of the merits or

---

[5]In terms of covariance structure analysis, the question posed here is to what extent is the covariance across the observed measures a reflection of common variance attributable to correlated errors and/or to the measurement instruments (e.g., a common evaluative continuum) rather than to a common underlying theoretical construct. For instance, LISREL analyses of the data summarized in the bottom panel of Table 11.1 replicated the results reported by Breckler (1984), although LISREL analyses of the ratings prior to their being scaled along a common evaluative dimension (top panel) revealed two independent factors.

[6]Affect is commonly used to refer to a mild emotional reaction which has a high probability of changes in awareness, expressive display, overt behavior, and physiological functioning (cf. Tomkins, 1981). The pleasantness–unpleasantness dimension of emotional experience is sometimes emphasized in conceptualizations of affect, whereas others have included dimensions such as activation and control (e.g., Osgood, 1966). Affect is used here as the superordinate construct which encompasses moods and emotions. Consistent with Bower (1981), each distinct affect state is conceptualized here as having a specific node in memory that is connected by associative pointers to other aspects of the emotion (some of which are not cortical). For instance, propositions describing issues, persons, and events from one's life during which a particular affect was activated all would be linked with varying associative strength to the corresponding functional affect-unit. When an affect-unit is activated, by whatever means (e.g., external stimuli, proprioceptive or interoceptive stimuli), excitation is transferred to nodes responsible for autonomic arousal, expressive behavior, socialized display rules governing emotional expressions and behavior, and associated memory structures. The effects of this excitation at each of these nodes can range from subthreshold to superthreshold activation. Hence, only a subset of the features that are thought to characterized intense emotional states (e.g., autonomic arousal, verbal report, expressive behavior, mood congruence effects) may be evident in any particular instance in which affect is evoked.

TABLE 11.1
Correlation Matrix for Ratings of the Concept, Bird

Measure	Original Ratings of Potency and Activity									
	1	2	3	4	5	6	7	8	9	10
Potency										
1. Large	—									
2. Strong	38***	—								
3. Thick	27**	33***	—							
4. Heavy	41***	27**	32***	—						
5. Rugged	36***	35***	22*	33***	—					
Activity										
6. Fast	−16*	01	01	−21*	−08	—				
7. Active	−18*	02	−06	−02	−19	12	—			
8. Excitable	−11	−19*	−24**	−17*	−13	20*	32***	—		
9. Sharp	04	13	15	−01	−02	08	19*	19*	24**	—
10. Angular	−04	−13	−23**	−17*	−05	06	19*	09	11	—

Measure	Ratings Scaled Along a Common Evaluative Continuum									
	1	2	3	4	5	6	7	8	9	10
Potency										
1. (Large)	—									
2. (Strong)	31***	—								
3. (Thick)	45***	40***	—							
4. (Heavy)	23**	22**	43***	—						
5. (Rugged)	46***	32***	27**	21*	—					
Activity										
6. (Fast)	48***	23**	27**	36***	30***	—				
7. (Active)	46***	29***	20*	14	31***	46***	—			
8. (Excitable)	28**	30***	18*	15	27**	28***	31***	—		
9. (Sharp)	37***	11	16	22**	20*	39***	28**	33***	—	
10. (Angular)	19*	28**	26**	37***	12	20*	18*	09	07	—

*$p < .05$. **$p < .01$. ***$p < .001$.
   Note. Decimal points are omitted.

demerits of the elements of stimulus categories (i.e., attitudes) are viewed as representing an important conceptual mechanism by which environmental demands are simplified, in much the same manner as homeostasis represents an important physiological mechanism by which organismic demands are simplified.

Specifically, homeostasis is used by physiologists to mean maintenance of constant conditions in the internal environment. As multicellular organisms developed and moved toward complexity, cell specialization and the isolation of interior cells from the external environment of the sea occurred. The latter required that the organism somehow bring the same nurturant environment previously provided by the sea to the interior cells. Claude Bernard was the first to enunciate that extracellular fluid constitutes the immediate environment—the internalized sea—for complex multicellular organisms. Homeostasis represents the dyanamic process by which constant conditions of life in the internal environment is achieved. It operates primarily through negative-feedback mechanism, whose actions are initiated or increased as the discrepancy between the present state and the organismic set-point increases. Individuals do not have to "do anything" to invoke homeostatic mechanisms, but rather they are said to be self-regulating. Individuals can, of course, engage in deliberate actions that alter homeostatic processes, as illustrated by dieting, but for organismic processes they need not be invoked to maintain a constancy of the internal milieu in the face of environmental stimulation. This facet of homeostasis led Claude Bernard (1878) to conclude that: "The constancy of the 'milieu interieur' is the condition of a free and independent existence" (p. 879).

An individual's system of attitudes functions in an analogous manner. Individuals do not have the time, energy, or ability to access and review all of the contents of the relevant representational structure(s) each time they are confronted by a stimulus. Attitudes, therefore, can be viewed as having evolved along with representational processes and structures to serve as rapid, cognitively inexpensive heuristics for deriving meaning from, imparting predictability to, and deriving behavioral guidelines for dealing with a complex, sometimes hostile world.

The homeostasis model of attitude structure and function also provides an interesting reversal in how thought and attitudes have been conceptualized previously. A prominent position among attitude theorists is that attitudes are based on knowledge about the attitude objects (e.g., Fishbein & Ajzen, 1975; Lingle & Ostrom 1981), and such a position implies that thought is primary—phylogenetically, ontogenetically, and formatively. According to the homeostasis model, attitudes might well function in the role of a summary statistic for people's beliefs about and experiences with an attitude object but—like the evolution of the physiological mechanisms underlying homeostasis—the need for more veridical, generalizable, and predictive evaluations of environmental events and challenges, through the forces of natural selection, favored the symbolic representation, manipulation, and organization of the external world. Consistent with this view, as one ascends the phylogenetic scale there remains the need for organisms to approach/prefer certain stimuli and avoid/disdain others to foster the continuation of their genetic code, but one finds organisms' evaluative responses guided by increasingly malleable mechanisms ranging from deterministic reflexes to fixed action patterns to learned (e.g., conditioned) emotional responses to hedonically biased combinative processes (e.g., wishful thinking) and relatively objective appraisals. Moreover, the contribution of heredity toward these ends moves from deterministic to propensities. One can find reflexes and fixed action patterns in humans, but the greater encephalization in humans places a greater emphasis on representational processes in the formation of global and enduring attitudes and systems of attitudes. For instance, research in ethology on the genetic determination of fixed action patterns to sign stimuli (e.g., see review by Kupfermann, 1985) and in classical conditioning regarding the increased likelihood of associations being formed between certain classes of stimuli and responses (including evaluative responses—e.g., see Ohman & Dimberg, 1984; Lanzetta & Orr, 1981; Seligman, 1970) suggest that biologic predispositions exist in humans as well as animals. Their influence, however, is limited greatly by symbolic representation (e.g., encoding), manipulation (e.g., cognitive responding), and organization (e.g., associative networks). In sum, the adaptive value of evaluative sensitivity and veracity within a generally stable and self-regulating system of attitudes can be conceptualized as the guiding force driving representational processes and structures rather than attitudes being conceptualized simply as having emerged subsequent to and serving as a convenient summary statistic for beliefs and knowledge about a stimulus.

Attitudes, like homeostasis, also tend to be maintained by the presence of negative-feedback mechanisms, whose actions are initiated or increased as the discrepancy between a set point (e.g., initial attitude) and an externally originated (e.g., recommended) position increases. The negative-feedback mechanisms governing an individual's attitude systems include biased information (e.g., top-down) processing, which serves to preserve existing beliefs and attitudes (e.g., Cacioppo, Petty, & Sidera, 1982; Lord, Ross, & Lepper, 1979), source derogation (Aronson, Turner, & Carlsmith, 1963), reactions of incredulity (Osgood & Tannenbaum, 1955), and a lighter scrutiny given to attitude-consistent than attitude-inconsistent information (Cacioppo & Petty, 1979a, 1979c). Second, individuals need not deliberately invoke these processes (e.g., see Petty & Cacioppo, 1986, chap. 5).

To summarize thus far, an individual's system of attitudes can be viewed as representing a dynamic process by which generally constant conditions of an individual's physical and social world are achieved. Although one can deliberately retrieve one's attitudes and think about issue-relevant information, attitudes can also be accessed automatically by the presentation of an exemplar (see Fazio, chap. 7 in this volume). Furthermore, individuals need neither review the various elements that make up the stimulus category nor deliberately think through the implications of the various attributes of a stimulus upon the presentation of an exemplar from a class of stimuli for an evaluative response to emerge (Zajonc, 1980). Consequently, an individual's system of attitudes can provide a guide for reacting to new exemplars from stimulus categories (e.g., environmental challenges) while minimizing the demands placed on one's limited processing resources. That is, an individual's system of attitudes contributes to a free and independent existence.

Once an attitude is activated, by whatever means (e.g., external stimuli, proprioceptive or interoceptive stimuli), excitation is transferred to nodes constituting the stimulus category, including attribute information, affect nodes controlling autonomic arousal, expressive behavior, socialized display rules governing emotional expressions and behavior, and so forth. The continuous flow model of human information processing (Coles, Gratton, Bashore, Erikson, & Donchin, 1985; Erikson & Schultz, 1979; cf. Cacioppo, Martzke, Petty, & Tassinary, 1988) provides a coherent account of this process within the framework of the homeostasis model of attitudes outlined. Information extracted in the processing of a stimulus is transferred in a continuous fashion to each of the nodes. The effects of the excitation at each of these nodes can range from subthreshold to superthreshold activation. The information extracted early in the processing of a stimulus is consistent with a range of nodes, and each node receives variable activation initially. As information continues to accumulate, activation continues to accumulate in nodes and, consequently, response channels that remain viable. These response channels may be verbal, visceral, expressive, and so forth. A given response is evoked when activation of its channel exceeds criterion. Although according to the present conceptualization there is no storage of attitude-relevant information at the peripheral physiological level, propositional representations of peripheral physiological events (e.g., memories of physical trauma associated with a class of stimuli) can be a component of the stimulus schema that, when accessed, can activate an organismic affect-unit. Clinical and animal studies further suggest that evaluations (attitudes) and related (e.g., affect) nodes can be activated and altered even when the normal links to verbal storage and/or verbal response channels are blocked or severed (e.g., Gazzaniga & LeDoux, 1978; Milner,

Corkin, & Teuber, 1968).[7] Thus, only a subset of the features that are thought to characterize attitudes (e.g., behavioral prediction, reported beliefs, affective arousal) may be evident in any particular instance in which an attitude is activated.

In sum, the homeostasis model of attitudes provides a coherent account for intriguing questions such as why attitudes serve at an abstract level as a functional summary statistic for knowledge about, reactions to, and experiences with a stimulus or category of stimuli; why attitudes evolved together with representational processes that internalized actual and anticipated environmental events; why stimulus categorization and evaluation have been found to occur at fairly rudimentary levels of information processing; why people want to hold correct attitudes, although the amount and nature of issue-relevant elaboration in which they are willing or able to engage to formulate or update their attitude varies with individual and situational factors; and why consequences such as the persistence, resistance, and behavioral significance of these structures vary despite what would appear to be equivalent attitudes.

Theme #2: Valence and Intensity of Affective Reactions

As noted, physiological measures have traditionally been viewed in social psychology as useful only in assessing general arousal and, therefore, that physiological measures reflect the intensity but not the direction of people's affective reactions and, consequently, that arousal is the only process for

---

[7]With provocation, individuals with hippocampal lesions show evidence of changing their emotional response to, and perhaps even their attitude toward, an individual even in circumstances where the provoker's name, attributes, and indeed previous exposure are not remembered (Zola-Morgan & Squire, 1986). Similarly, animals with hippocampal lesions exhibit impaired abilities to learn a maze even though their ability to learn to avoid shock may be enhanced. Although these data might invite the positing of emotional attitudes (Zajonc, 1980), scrutiny of additional data on hippocampal lesions favors the present argument that attitude nodes are represented propositionally (e.g., rather than verbally); and that cognitions, emotions, and behaviors can each influence (and be influenced by) an attitude without themselves being the attitude. Specifically, although humans with hippocampal lesions are greatly impaired at learning factual information (e.g., people's names, attributes), they do relatively well at learning skills such as learning to read material written in mirror fashion or learning to play a musical instrument (Cohen & Squire, 1980). Thus, the transfer of information from working to representational memory in humans with hippocampal lesions (e.g., the adoption of a new attitude based on some interaction, the facts of which might be forgotten) does not require that the transfer or the representational memory be emotional. The deficits in learning factual information are not entirely attributable to a consolidation deficit, either, but rather represent an inability to select the one appropriate memory among several competing ones (Weiskrantz, 1977). In this sense, the data from human and animal studies suggest even when factual information is learned it does not always appear so because of the organism's increased tendency to perseverate.

which physiological analyses are of interest in the field of attitudes. The psychophysiological studies reviewed in the preceding section, however, suggest that this theme is incorrect. Recall that we have found efferent commands to the muscles of facial expression (as measured by EMG activity) are influenced differentially by positive and negative affective states even in situations where there are no changes in overt facial action or in autonomic activity. Is it possible that gradients of EMG activity over the muscles of mimicry (i.e., those innervated by the 7th cranial nerve) are influenced by both the direction and intensity of affective reactions? If so, they would have the potential to serve as objective and continuous probes of the affective processes.

The finding by Cacioppo and Petty (1979a, Experiment 2) that facial EMG patterning tended to be more pronounced during the pro- and counterattitudinal message presentations than during the postwarning–premessage interval suggests a tentative yes to this question. Clearer evidence for an affirmative answer was provided, however, in two recent experiments (Cacioppo, Petty, Losch, & Kim 1986). Subjects were exposed to slides of moderately unpleasant, mildly unpleasant, mildly pleasant, and moderately pleasant scenes. Subjects viewed each slide for 5 seconds and rated how much they liked the scene that was depicted, how familiar the scene appeared, and how aroused it made them feel. Ratings of subjects' facial actions during the 5 seconds stimulus presentations by independent judges, who were blind to experimental conditions of the videorecordings, indicated that the scenes were sufficiently mild so that overt (e.g., socially perceptible) facial expressions were not evoked. Nevertheless, analyses revealed that EMG activity over the brow (corrugator supercilii) and periocular (orbicularis oculi) muscle regions differentiated the direction and intensity of people's affective reaction to the scenes: The more subjects liked the scene, the lower the level of EMG activity over the brow region. Moreover, EMG activity was higher over the periocular region when moderately pleasant than mildly pleasant or unpleasant stimuli were presented.

EMG recordings from the periocular (orbicularis oculi) muscle region have been shown to be heightened by expressions of pain, squinting, and so forth (e.g., see Fridlund & Izard, 1983). Activity over this region could, in some measurement settings, reflect variations in fixation rather than incipient facial actions associated with affect. EMG activity over this muscle region was greater when positive rather than negative stimuli were presented, however, even when subjects were given a point in the middle of the screen on which they focused during the prestimulus periods (see Cacioppo, Petty, Losch, & Kim, 1986, Pilot Study). Yet another interesting account for these data is based on Darwin's (1872) observations and Ekman and Frisen's (1982) research on "felt" smiles. Darwin suggested that people display a smile—whether happy or not—when they wish to present a happy image but that people display both a smile and crow's feet at the outer edges of their eyes when they *feel* happy. The common elements in the facial expressions of the person who actually experiences a positive emotion are the actions of two muscles: "the *zygomatic major* pulling the lip corners upwards towards the cheekbone; and the *orbicularis oculi* which raises the cheek and gathers skin inwards from around the eye socket" (Ekman & Friesen, 1982, p. 242, italics added). Because there was no reason in the experimental setting for subjects to feign positive affective reactions to the experimental stimuli, it was suggested that the heightened EMG activity over the orbicularis oculi region, which we found to differentiate the affective nature of the experimental stimuli, was related to the variations in the subjects' positive feelings regarding the stimuli.

Results also revealed that EMG activity over the cheek (zygomatic major) region also tended to be significantly greater for liked scenes than it was for disliked scenes. Importantly, these data are not attributable to the physiological arousal evoked by the stimulus: Neither EMG activity over the brow region nor EMG activity over the cheek region covaried with reported arousal, nor did autonomic activity, EMG activity over the perioral and forehead (control sites for facial tension) regions, or EMG activity over a peripheral muscle region (superficial forearm flexors—a control site for general somatic tension) vary as a function of stimulus likeability. These data, therefore, suggest that gradients of EMG activity over the muscles of mimicry are influenced by both the direction and intensity of affective reactions—reactions that visual analyses revealed were too subtle or fleeting to evoke expressions observable under normal conditions of social interaction.

Finally, it should be noted that Ekman, Friesen, and Ancoli (1980) presented evidence that *overt* facial expressions are also influenced by the direction and intensity of affective reactions; and Ekman, Levenson, and Friesen (1983) provided evidence that autonomic, as well as somatic responses can differentiate affective states. Hence, there is now clear evidence contradicting the longstanding belief that physiological measures reflect the intensity but not the direction of people's affective reactions.

CONCLUDING COMMENTS REGARDING ATTITUDE STRUCTURE AND FUNCTION

In this chapter we have focused primarily on the traditional themes linking psychophysiology and attitude structure and function, because these themes continue to dominate the literature (e.g., Lindsey & Aronson, 1985; Mueller, 1986). It is not difficult to understand why this simplistic approach has been and continues to be so attractive: It requires no knowledge of physiological mechanisms or systems, no technical knowledge regarding psychophysiological measurement (because verbal reports of affect are assigned equivalent status in the nomological net), and no basic research to establish psychophysiological links. Traditional thinking about the psychophysiology of attitudes has yielded little in the way of scientific knowledge, however, because these guiding themes are flawed in multiple ways; and we have outlined a new conceptualization of the psychophysiological enterprise that, although more complex, promises richer insights into attitude structure and function.

Moreover, a theme found throughout the chapters in this book is that similar verbal expressions of attitudes can fulfill distinct if sometimes idiosyncratic and situationally specific psychological needs and aspirations. Because somatovisceral responses can be used in carefully constructed contexts to gauge processes such as the extent to which the attitude stimulus evokes affect, conation, and cogitation, theoretically, they should also be helpful in identifying, at least in a general sense, the thoughts, ideas, images, affects, and habits that are activated by the attitude stimulus. As suggested by the homeostasis model of attitude structure and function previously outlined, the cognitive and affective processes underlying attitudes are dynamic, with the potential for spreading activation and structural modification as individuals struggle with or embrace an attitude stimulus. One nice feature of the homeostasis model is that it embraces the notion that the same attitude has the potential to serve multiple "apparent" functions for the same individual because the actual, more abstract function being served by the attitude is to maintain a constancy of the individual's evaluative representations of and modes of responding to a changing physical, social, and organismic (e.g., due to aging) environment. Thus, a student may value her academic scholarship because it provides the credentials needed to obtain a high-paying job (utilitarian function), it symbolizes her scholastic achievements and aspirations (value-expressive function), it helps deflect deep self-doubts about her innate intelligence (ego-defensive function), or it provides validation for her belief in a just world (knowledge function) depending on the psychological need that is the most salient when the attitude stimulus is presented. Attitudes serving particular functions may also manifest more frequently across individuals (e.g., see Shavitt, chapter 12 in this volume), and some individuals may tend to have attitudes that manifest as serving some chronically salient psychological needs (e.g., see Snyder & DeBono, chap. 13 in this volume). Such results are explicable in terms of these "apparent functions" manifesting as a consequence of the associative links between attitudes and elements (e.g., affect nodes) in the associated knowledge structures. At a higher level of abstraction, however, the function served in each of these instantiations is a constancy of the individual's system of attitudes. Finally, we have reviewed evidence showing that Rosenberg and Hovland's (1960) tripartite model of attitudes is flawed and is in need of revision. That is, although we believe the evidence does not favor Rosenberg and Hovland's model of attitudes, the homeostasis model of attitudes clearly embraces the notion that the tripartite of cognition, affect, and behavior is fundamental to the attitude concept. One clear possibility emanating from the present analysis is that the conative component reflects primitive reflexes and habits; the affective component, emotions; and the cognitive component, more cooly calculated appraisals. It should not be surprising, therefore, that the absolute persistence of attitude change is seldom achieved when a specific attitude is targeted using verbal persuasion alone, and that the shaping and changing of ideologies is a long and uphill struggle.

ACKNOWLEDGMENTS

Preparation of this chapter was supported by National Science Foundation Grant Nos. BNS-8444909 and BNS-8414853.

REFERENCES

Aronson, E., Turner, J. A., & Carlsmith, J. M. (1963). Communicator credibility and communication discrepancy as determinants of opinion change. *Journal of Abnormal and Social Psychology, 67,* 31–36.

Baker, W. M., Sandman, C. A., & Pepinsky, H. B. (1975). Affectivity of task, rehearsal time, and physiological response. *Journal of Abnormal Psychology, 84,* 539–544.

Batra, R., & Ray, M. (1986). Situational effects of advertising repetition: The moderating influence of motivation, ability, and opportunity to respond. *Journal of Consumer Research, 12,* 432–445.

Beatty, J. (1982). Task-evoked pupillary responses, processing load, and the structure of processing resources. *Psychological Bulletin, 91,* 276–292.

Beatty, J. (1986). The pupillary system. In M. G. H. Coles, E. Donchin, & S. W. Porges (Eds.), *Psychophysiology: Systems, processes, and applications* (pp. 43–50). New York: Guilford Press.

Bernard, C. (1878). *Les phenomenes de la vie* [The phenomena of life] (Vol. 1). Paris: Librarie J-B Bailliere et Fils.

Berne, R. M., & Levy, M. N. (1981). *Cardiovascular physiology.* St. Louis, MO: C. V. Mosby.

Blaskovich, J., & Katkin, E. S. (1983). Visceral perception and social behavior. In J. T. Cacioppo & R. E. Petty (Eds.), *Social psychophysiology: A sourcebook.* New York: Guilford Press.

Blaylock, B. (1972). Some antecedents of directional fractionation: Effects of "intake-rejection," verbalization requiremens, and threat of shock on heart rate and skin conductance. *Psychophysiology, 9,* 40–52.

Bogardus, E. S. (1920). *Essentials of social psychology.* Los Angeles: University of California Press.

Bonvallet, M., & Allen, M. B. (1963). Prolonged sponteaneous and evolved reticular activation following discrete bulbar lesions. *Electroencephalography and Clinical Neurophysiology, 15,* 969–988.

Bonvallet, M., Dell, P., & Hiebel, G. (1954). Tanus sympathique et activite electrique corticale [Sympathetic tonus and electracortical activation]. *Electroencephalography and Clinical Neurophysiology, 6,* 119–144.

Bower, G. H. (1981). Emotional mood and memory. *American Psychologist, 36,* 129–148.

Breckler, S. J. (1984). Empirical validation of affect, behavior, and cognition as distinct attitude components. *Journal of Personality and Social Psychology, 47,* 1191–1205.

Brock, T. C. (1967). Communication discrepancy and intent to persuade as determinants of counterargument production. *Journal of Experimental Social Psychology, 3,* 269–309.

Cacioppo, J. T. (1982). Social psychophysiology: A classic perspective and contemporary approach. *Psychophysiology, 19,* 241–251.

Cacioppo, J. T., & Dorfman, D. D. (1987). Waveform moment analysis in psychophysiological research. *Psychological Bulletin, 102,* 421–438.

Cacioppo, J. T., Losch, M. L., Tassinary, L. G., & Petty, R. E. (1986). Properties of affect and affect-laden information processing as viewed through the facial response system. In R. A. Peterson, W. D. Hoyer, & W. R. Wilson (Eds.), *The role of affect in consumer behavior: Emerging theories and applications* (pp. 87–118). Lexington, MA: D. C. Heath.

Cacioppo, J.T., Martzke, J. S., Petty, R. E., & Tassinary, L. G. (1988). Specific forms of facial EMG response index emotions during an interview: From Darwin to the continuous flow hypothesis of affect-laden information processing. *Journal of Personality and Social Psychology, 54,* 592–604.

Cacioppo, J. T., & Petty, R. E. (1979a). Attitudes and cognitive response: An electrophysiological approach. *Journal of Personality and Social Psychology, 37,* 2181–2199.

Cacioppo, J. T., & Petty, R. E. (1979b). Lip and nonpreferred forearm EMG activity as a function of orienting task. *Journal of Biological Psychology, 9,* 103–113.

Cacioppo, J. T., & Petty, R. E. (1979c). Effects of message repetition and position on cognitive response, recall, and persuasion. *Journal of Personality and Social Psychology, 37,* 97–109.

Cacioppo, J. T., & Petty, R. E. (1981a). Electromyograms as measures of extent and affectivity of informational processing. *American Psychologist, 36,* 441–456.

Cacioppo, J. T., & Petty, R. E. (1981b). Electromyographic specificity during covert information processing. *Psychophysiology, 18,* 518–523.

Cacioppo, J. T., & Petty, R. E. (1981c). Social psychological procedures for cognitive response assessment: The thought-listing technique. In T. V. Merluzzi, C. R. Glass, & M. Genest (Eds.), *Cognitive assessment* (pp. 309–342). New York: Guilford Press.

Cacioppo, J. T., & Petty, R. E. (1982a). A biosocial model of attitude change: Signs, symptoms, and undetected physiological responses. In J. T. Cacioppo & R. E. Petty (Eds.), *Perspectives in cardiovascular psychophysiology* (pp. 151–188). New York: Guilford Press.

Cacioppo, J. T., & Petty, R. E. (1982b). *Perspectives in cardiovascular psychology.* New York: Guilford Press.

Cacioppo, J. T., & Petty, R. E. (1985). Physiological responses and advertising effects: Is the cup half full or half empty? *Psychology and Marketing, 2,* 115–126.

Cacioppo, J. T., & Petty, R. E. (1986). Social processes. In M. G. H. Coles, E. Donchin, & S. Porges (Eds.), *Psychophysiology: Systems, processes, and applications* (pp. 646–679). New York: Guilford Press.

Cacioppo, J. T., & Petty, R. E. (1987). Stalking rudimentary processes of social influence: A psychophysiological approach. In M. P. Zanna, J. M. Olson, & C. P. Herman (Eds.), *Social influence: The Ontario symposium* (Vol. 5). Hillsdale, NJ: Lawrence Erlbaum Associates.

Cacioppo, J. T., Petty, R. E., Losch, M. E., & Kim, H. S. (1986). Electromyographic activity over facial muscle regions can differentiate the valence intensity of affective reactions. *Journal of Personality and Social Psychology, 50,* 260–268.

Cacioppo, J. T., Petty, R. E., & Marshall-Goodell, B. (1984). Electromyographic specificity during simple physical and attitudinal tasks: Location and topographical features of integrated EMG responses. *Biological Psychology, 18,* 85–121.

Cacioppo, J. T., Petty, R. E., & Morris, K. J. (1985). Semantic, evaluative, and self-referent processing: Memory, cognitive effort, and somatovisceral activity. *Psychophysiology, 22,* 371–384.

Cacioppo, J. T., Petty, R. E., & Sidera, J. A. (1982). The effects of a salient self-schema on the evaluation of proattitudinal editorials: Top-down versus bottom-up message processing. *Journal of Experimental Social Psychology, 18,* 324–338.

Cacioppo, J. T., Petty, R. E., & Tassinary, L. G. (in press). Social psychophysiology: A new look. *Advances in experimental social psychology,* (Vol. 22). New York: Academic Press.

Cacioppo, J. T., & Sandman, C. A. (1978). Physiological differentiation of sensory and cognitive tasks as a function of warning, processing demands, and reported unpleasantness. *Biological Psychology, 6,* 181–192.

Cacioppo, J. T., & Sandman, C. A. (1981). Psychophysiological functioning, cognitive responding, and attitudes. In R. E. Petty, T. M. Ostrom, & T. C. Brock (Eds.), *Cognitive responses in persuasion.* Hillsdale, NJ: Lawrence Erlbaum Associates.

Cacioppo, J. T., Tassinary, L. G., Stonebraker, T. B., & Petty, R. E. (in press). Self-report and cardiovascular measures of physiological arousal: Fractionation during residual arousal. *Biological Psychology.*

Cannon, W. B. (1927). The James-Lange theory of emotions: A critical examination and an alternative theory. *American Journal of Psychology, 39,* 106–124.

Cantor, J. R., Bryant, J., & Zillmann, D. (1975). Enhancement of humor appreciation by transferred excitation. *Journal of Personality and Social Psychology, 30,* 812–821.

Cialdini, R. B., & Petty, R. E. (1981). Anticipatory opinion effects. In R. E. Petty, T. M. Ostrom, & T. C. Brock (Eds.), *Cognitive responses in persuasion.* Hillsdale, NJ: Lawrence Erlbaum Associates.

Cohen, N. J., & Squire, L. R. (1980). Preserved learning and retention of pattern-analyzing skill in amnesia: Dissociation of knowing how and knowing that. *Science, 210,* 207–211.

Coles, M. G. H., Gratton, G., Bashore, T. R., Erikson, C. W., & Donchin, E. (1985). A psychophysiological investigation of the continuous flow model of human information processing. *Journal of Experimental Psychology: Human Perception and Performance, 11,* 529–553.

Coles, M. G. H., Gratton, G., & Gehring, W. J. (in press). Theory and cognition in psychophysiology. *Journal of Psychophysiology.*

Coles, M. G. H., Jennings, J. R., & Stern, J. A. (Eds.), (1984) *Psychophysiological perspectives: Festschrift for Beatrice and John Lacey.* New York: Van Nostrand Reinhold.

Cooper, J. D. (1959). Emotion and prejudice. *Science, 130,* 314–318.

Coren, S. (1986). An efferent component in the visual perception of direction and extent. *Psychological Review, 93,* 391–410.

Darrow, C. W. (1929). Electrical and circulatory responses to brief sensory and ideational stimuli. *Journal of Experimental Psychology, 12,* 267–300.

Darwin, C. (1965). *The expression of the emotions in man and animals.* Chicago: The University of Chicago Press. (Original work published 1872)

Davis, R. C. (1939). Patterns of muscular activity during "mental work" and their constancy. *Journal of Experimental Psychology, 24,* 451–465.

Donchin, E. (1981). Surprise! . . . surprise? *Psychophysiology, 18,* 493–513.

Donchin, E. (1982). The relevance of dissociations and the irrelevance of dissociationism: A reply to Schwartz and Pritchard. *Psychophysiology, 19,* 457–463.

Eiser, J. R. (1986). *Social psychology: Attitudes, cognition, and social behavior.* Cambridge, England: Cambridge University Press.

Ekman, P., & Friesen, W. V. (1982). Felt, false, and miserable smiles. *Journal of Nonverbal Behavior, 6,* 238–252.

Ekman, P., Friesen, W. V., & Ancoli, S. (1980). Facial signs of emotional experience. *Journal of Personality and Social Psychology, 39,* 1125–1135.

Ekman, P., Levenson, R. W., & Friesen, W. V. (1983). Autonomic nervous system activity distinguishes among emotions. *Science, 221,* 1208–1210.

Erikson, C. W., & Schultz, D. W. (1979). Information processing in visual search: A continuous flow conception and experimental results. *Perception and Psychophysics, 25,* 249–263.

Evarts, E. V. (1973). Motor cortex reflexes associated with learned movement. *Science, 179,* 501–503.

Fishbein, M. E., & Ajzen, I. (1975). *Belief, attitude, intention, and behavior: An introduction to theory and research.* Reading, MA: Addison-Wesley.

Fleming, D. (1967). Attitude: The History of a Concept. *Perspectives in American History, 1,* 287–365.

Fowles, D. C. (1982). Heart rate as an index of anxiety: Failure of a hypothesis. In J. Cacioppo & R. Petty (Eds.), *Perspectives in cardiovascular psychophysiology* (pp. 93–126). New York: Guilford Press.

Fridlund, A. J., & Izard, C. E. (1983). Electromyographic studies of facial expressions of emotions and patterns of emotion. In J. T. Cacioppo & R. E. Petty (Eds.), *Social psychophysiology: A sourcebook* (pp. 243–286). New York: Guilford Press.

Gazzaniga, M. S., & LeDoux, J. E. (1978). *The integrated brain.* New York: Plenum.

Geen, T. R. (1987). *A comparison of the tripartite and unidimensional conceptualizations of attitude structure.* Unpublished master's thesis, University of Iowa, Iowa City.

Goldwater, B. C. (1972). Psychological significance of pupillary movements. *Psychological Bulletin, 77,* 340–355.

Guyton, A. C. (1971). *Textbook of medical physiology* (4th ed.). Philadelphia: W. B. Saunders.

Hess, E. H. (1965). Attitude and pupil size. *Scientific American, 212,* 46–54.

Janisse, M. P., & Peavler, W. S. (1974). Pupillary research today: Emotion in the eye. *Psychology Today, 7,* 60–63.

Jennings, J. R. (1986). Memory, thought, and bodily response. In M. G. H. Coles, E. Donchin, & S. W. Porges (Eds.), *Psychophysiology: Systems, processes, and applications* (pp. 290–308). New York: Guilford.

Kahneman, D. (1973). *Attention and effort.* Englewood Cliffs, NJ: Prentice-Hall.

Kupfermann, I. (1985). Genetic determinants of behavior. In E. Kandel & J. M. Schwartz (Eds.), *Principles of neurological science* (2nd ed., pp. 795–804). New York: Elsever.

Lacey, J. I. (1967). Somatic response patterning and stress: Some revisions of activation theory. In M. H. Appley & R. Trumbull (Eds.), *Psychological stress: Issues in research.* New York: Appleton-Century-Crofts.

Lacey, J. I., Kagan, J., Lacey, B. C., & Moss, M. A. H. (1963). The visceral level: Situational determinants and behavioral correlates of autonomic response patterns. In P. N. Knapp (Ed.), *Expression of the emotions in man* (pp. 161–196). New York: International University Press.

Lacey, J. I., & Lacey, B. C. (1970). Some autonomic-central nervous system interrelationships. In P. Black (Ed.), *Physiological correlates of emotion* (pp. 205–227). New York: Academic Press.

Lacey, J. I., & Lacey, B. C. (1974). Studies of heart rate and other bodily processes in sensorimotor behavior. In P. Obrist, A. Black, J. Brener, & L. DiCara (Eds.), *Cardiovascular psychophysiology.* Chicago: Aldine.

Langer, E., Blank, A., & Chanowitz, B. (1978). The mindlessness of ostensibly thoughtful action: The role of "placebic" information in interpersonal intraction. *Journal of Personality and Social Psychology, 36,* 635–642.

Lanzetta, J. T., & Orr S. P. (1981). Stimulus properties of facial expressions and their influence on the classical conditioning of fear. *Motivation and Emotion, 5,* 225–234.

Lanzetta, J. T., Sullivan, D. G., Masters, R. D., & McHugo, G. J. (1985). Emotional and cognitive responses to televised images of political leaders. In S. Kraus & R. M. Perloff (Eds.), *Mass media and political thought: An information-processing approach.* Beverly Hills, CA: Sage.

Libby, W. L., Lacey, B. C., & Lacey, J. I. (1973). Pupillary and cardiac activity during visual attention. *Psychophysiology, 10,* 270–294.

Lindsey, G., & Aronson, E. (1985). *Handbook of social psychology* (3rd ed.). New York: Random House.

Lingle, J. H., & Ostrom, T. M. (1981). Principles of memory and cognition in attitude formation. In R. E. Petty, T. M. Ostrom, & T. C. Brock (Eds.), *Cognitive responses in persuasion.* Hillsdale, NJ: Lawrence Erlbaum Associates.

Lord, C. G., Ross, L., & Lepper, M. R. (1979). Biased assimilation and attitude polarization: The effects of prior theories on subsequently considered evidence. *Journal of Personality and Social Psychology, 37,* 2098–2109.

Lynn, R. (1966). *Attention, arousal, and the orientation reaction.* Oxford: Pergamon Press.

McDougall, W. (1908). *Introduction to social psychology.* London: Methuen.

McGuigan, F. J. (1978). *Cognitive psychophysiology: Principles of covert behavior.* Englewood Cliffs, NJ: Prentice-Hall.

McGuire, W. J. (1969). The nature of attitudes and attitude change. In G. Lindzey & E. Aronson (Eds.), *The handbook of social psychology* (2nd ed., Vol. 3). Reading, MA: Addison-Wesley.

McGuire, W. J. (1985). Attitudes and attitude change. In G. Lindzey & E. Aronson (Eds.). *Handbook of social psychology* (3rd ed., Vol. 2, pp. 233–346), New York: Random House.

Mesulam, M., & Perry, J. (1972). The diagnosis of lovesickness: Experimental psychophysiology without the polygraph. *Psychophysiology, 9,* 546–551.

Mewborn, C. R., & Rogers, R. W. (1979). Effects of threatening and reassuring components of fear appeals on physiological and verbal measures of emotion and attitudes. *Journal of Experimental Social Psychology, 15,* 242–300.

Millar, M. G., & Tesser, A. (1986). Effects of affective and cognitive focus on the attitude-behavior relation. *Journal of Personality and Social Psychology, 51,* 270–276.

Miller, N., & Baron, R. S. (1973). On measuring counterarguing. *Journal for the Theory of Social Behavior, 3,* 101–118.

Miller, N., & Colman, D. (1981). Methodological issues in analyzing the cognitive mediation of persuasion. In R. E. Petty, T. M. Ostrom, & T. C. Brock (Eds.), *Cognitive responses in persuasion.* Hillsdale, NJ: Lawrence Erlbaum Associates.

Miller, N., Maruyama, G., Beaber, R., & Valone, K. (1976). Speed of speech and persuasion. *Journal of Personality and Social Psychology, 34,* 615–625.

Milner, B., Corkin, S., & Teuber, H. L. (1968). Further analysis of the hippocampal amnesic syndrome: 14-year follow-up study of H. M. *Neuropsychologia, 6,* 215–234.

Mountcastle, V. B. (1980). *Medical physiology (14 e.).* St. Louis, MO: C. V. Mosby.

Mueller, D. J. (1986). *Measuring social attitudes: A handbook for researchers and practitioners.* New York: Teachers College Press.

Obrist, P. A. (1981). *Cardiovascular psychophysiology: A perspective.* New York: Plenum.

Ohman, A., & Dimberg, U. (1984). An evolutionary perspective on human social behavior. In W. Waid (Ed.), *Sociophysiology.* New York: Springer-Verlag.

Osgood, C. E. (1966). Dimensionality of the semantic space for communication via facial expressions. *Scandanavian Journal of Psychology, 7,* 1–30.

Osgood, C. E., & Tannenbaum, P. H. (1955). The principle of congruity in the prediction of attitude change. *Psychological Review, 62,* 42–55.

Osgood, C. E., Suci, G. J., & Tannenbaum, P. H. (1957). *The measurement of meaning.* Urbana, IL: University of Illinois Press.

Oskamp, S. (1977). *Attitudes and opinions.* Englewood Cliffs, NJ: Prentice-Hall.

Ostrom, T. M. (1969). The relationship between the affective, behavioral, and cognitive components of attitudes. *Journal of Experimental Social Psychology, 5,* 12–30.

Pennebaker, J. W. (1982). *The psychology of physical symptoms.* New York: Springer-Verlag.

Petty, R. E., & Cacioppo, J. T. (1977). Forewarning, cognitive responding and resistance to persuasion. *Journal of Personality and Social Psychology, 35,* 645–655.

Petty, R. E., & Cacioppo, J. T. (1981). *Attitudes and persuasion: Classic and contemporary approaches.* Dubuque, IA: Wm. C. Brown.

Petty, R. E., & Cacioppo, J. T. (1986). *Communication and persuasion: Central and peripheral routes to persuasion.* New York: Springer-Verlag.

Rajecki, D. W. (1983). *Attitudes: Themes and advances.* Sunderland, MA: Sinnaver Associates.

Rankin, R. E., & Campbell, D. T. (1955). Galvanic skin response to Negro and white experimenters. *Journal of Abnormal and Social Psychology, 51,* 30–33.

Rosenberg, M. J., & Hovland, C. I. (1960). Cognitive, affective, and behavioral components of attitude. In M. H. Rosenberg, C. I. Hovland, W. J. McGuire, R. P. Abelson, & J. W. Brehm (Eds.), *Attitude organization and change: An analysis of consistency among attitude components.* (pp. 1–14). New Haven, CT: Yale University Press.

Runes, D. D. (1961). *Dictionary of Philosophy.* Paterson, NJ: Littlefield, Adams, & Co.

Schwartz, G. E. (1975). Biofeedback, self-regulation, and the patterning of physiological processes. *American Scientist, 63,* 314–324.

Seligman, M. E. P. (1970). On the generality of the laws of learning. *Psychological Review, 77,* 400–418.

Seyle, H. (1956). *The stress of life.* New York: McGraw-Hill.

Shapiro, D., & Crider, A. (1969). Psychophysiological approaches to social psychology. In G. Lindzey & E. Aronson (Eds.), *The handbook of social psychology* (2nd ed., Vol. 3). Reading, MA: Addison-Wesley.

Smith, C. E. (1936). A study of the autonomic excitation resulting from the interaction of the individual opinion and group opinion. *Journal of Abnormal and Social Psychology, 30,* 138–164.

Smith, M. B. (1947). The personal setting of public opinions: A study of attitudes toward Russia. *Public Opinion Quarterly, 11,* 507–523.

Summers, G. F. (1970). *Attitude measurement.* Chicago: Rand McNally.

Thurstone, L. L. (1928). Attitudes can be measured. *American Journal of Sociology, 33,* 529–544.

Tomkins, S. S. (1981). The quest for primary motives: Biography and autobiography of an idea. *Journal of Personality and Social Psychology, 41,* 306–329.

Triandis, H. C. (1971). *Attitude and attitude change.* New York: Wiley.

Turpin, G. (1986). Effects of stimulus intensity on autonomic responding: The problem of differentiating orienting and defense reflexes. *Psychophysiology, 23,* 1–14.

Tursky, B., Schwartz, G. E., & Crider, A. (1970). Differential patterns of heart rate and skin resistance during the digit-transformation task. *Journal of Experimental Psychology, 83,* 451–457.

Weiskrantz, L. (1977). Trying to bridge some neurological gaps between monkey and man. *British Journal of Psychology, 68,* 441–445.

Wilson, W. R. (1979). Feeling more than we can know: Exposure effects without learning. *Journal of Personality and Social Psychology, 37,* 811–821.

Zajonc, R. B. (1980). Feeling and thinking: Preferences need no inferences. *American Psychologist, 25,* 151–175.

Zillmann, D. (1984). *Connections between sex and aggression.* Hillsdale, NJ: Lawrence Erlbaum Associates.

Zimbardo, P. G., Ebbesen, E. B., & Maslach, C. (1977). *Influencing attitudes and changing behavior* (2nd ed.). Reading, MA: Addison-Wesley.

Zola-Morgan, S., & Squire, L. R. (1986). Memory impairment in monkeys following lesions limited to the hippocampus. *Behavioral Neuroscience, 6,* 2950–2967.

12

Operationalizing Functional Theories of Attitude

Sharon Shavitt
University of Illinois at Urbana-Champaign

In the quarter century or more since functional theories of attitudes were first proposed (Katz, 1960; Katz & Stotland, 1959; Kelman, 1958, 1961; Sarnoff & Katz, 1954; Smith, Bruner, & White, 1956), they have become a popular set of theories to cite, if not to test. Although treated as an important set of theories in the domain of attitudes and persuasion (virtually every social psychology text that discusses attitudes presents a summary of the functional approach), until recently, they have almost completely eluded empirical scrutiny. Why have there been so few attempts to test functional theories?

Functional theories did not frame their hypotheses in readily testable terms, proposing no comprehensive methodology for identifying or manipulating the functions of an attitude. It has been suggested that this lack of operationalizations of attitude functions was the most critical deficiency of the functional approach (Eagly & Himmelfarb, 1974; Insko, 1967; Kiesler, Collins & Miller, 1969). Without adequate methods for determining the various functions of an attitude, empirical progress was stalled, and few experimental data were collected specifically to test functional theories.

Now, with a growing interest in the motivational underpinnings of cognitive constructs, researchers are turning again to the issue of the psychological needs served by attitudes. And the question of how to investigate attitude functions is being raised once more. In this chapter, some early and recent efforts to operationalize functional theories are described. Then, new directions for operationalizing functional theories are proposed and evaluated, focusing on methods for identifying as well as manipulating the functions of attitudes. We turn first to a summary of the various functions that attitudes have been proposed to serve.

FUNCTIONS OF ATTITUDES

Functional theories of attitudes (Katz, 1960; Katz & Stotland, 1959; Kelman, 1958, 1961; Sarnoff & Katz, 1954; Smith, Bruner, & White, 1956), although developed independently, shared some important features: They assumed that attitudes could be classified according to the psychological needs they met, and they proposed lists of functions that attitudes serve. In particular, Katz (1960) and Smith, Bruner, and White (1956) proposed similar sets of functions.

Katz proposed that attitudes serve a *knowledge* function, helping to organize and structure one's environment and provide consistency in one's frame of reference. This may be the most fundamental function attitudes serve, and all attitudes serve this function to some extent (see Fazio, chap. 7 in this volume). In addition, an attitude may serve any of a number of other functions that have been proposed: Attitudes can maximize rewards and minimize punishments obtained from objects in one's environment, summarizing the outcomes intrinsically associated with objects and guiding behavior that obtains the rewards associated with them. Katz labelled this the *utilitarian* (or *instrumental* or *adjustive*) function of attitudes. Smith, Bruner, and White proposed an *object-appraisal* function, which is similar to aspects of the knowledge and utilitarian functions in that it focuses on an attitude's role in classifying objects and structuring the environment to make responses available that maximize one's own interests. As an example, one's attitude toward ice cream may serve a utilitarian or object-appraisal function because it is likely to be based on the rewards (e.g., good taste) and punishments (e.g., weight gain) associated with ice cream and to guide behavior that maximizes the rewards and minimizes the punishments (e.g., eating one's favorite flavor, avoiding overeating).

Attitudes can also play an important role in facilitating self-expression and social interaction. Smith, Bruner, and White labelled this the *social adjustment* function, proposing that attitudes mediate self–other relationships through their judicious expression. (Kelman's [1958, 1961] *compliance* process of social influence also focused on the social effect of accepting influence.) Furthermore, simply holding particular attitudes can function to establish one's identity by fostering identification with various reference groups (see also Kelman's *identification* process of social influence). Similarly, Katz proposed that attitudes serve to express one's central values and self-concept, labelling this the *value-expressive* function. (Aspects of Kelman's *internalization* process are also relevant here.) The social adjustment and value-expressive functions imply that, through the attitudes we hold and discuss, we express our central values, establish our identity, and gain social approval. For example, one's attitude toward a controversial political issue may be held because it is seen as symbolic of the self. And it may be publicly expressed in contexts in which it is likely to gain social approval. This general social role of attitudes is referred to here as the *social identity* function.[1]

Finally, attitudes can play a major role in maintaining self-esteem. Functional theorists, guided primarily by psychodynamic principles, suggested that attitudes can help an individual cope with anxieties generated by internal conflicts, a function that Smith, Bruner, and White termed *externalization* and Katz labelled *ego-defense*. They assumed that attitudes can protect the ego from intrapsychic conflict through defense mechanisms, such as projection, distancing the self from disliked or threatening objects by projecting one's own unacceptable impulses onto them. For example, one's attitudes toward racial or ethnic outgroups, or toward such groups as homosexuals (Herek, 1983, 1987), may reflect attempts to protect the ego from the threats these outgroups are perceived to pose. Analyses of the maintenance of prejudiced attitudes focused on such ego-defensive notions (Adorno, Frenkel-Brunswik, Levinson, & Sanford, 1950). Recent research, although not taking a psychodynamic perspective, has also focused on the derogation of outgroups as a strategy used to protect self-esteem in response to threat (e.g., Crocker, Thompson, McGraw, & Ingerman, 1987; Wills, 1981).

Attitudes serve to maintain self-esteem in other ways, as well: One's attitudes toward the self and features of the self affect self-esteem directly (more precisely, they define self-esteem). Also, attitudes that support self-esteem by distancing the self from disliked or threatening objects may be complemented by a process of "basking in reflected glory" (Cialdini, Borden, Thorne, Walker, Freeman, & Sloan, 1976), through which attitudes that associate the self with positively regarded objects (e.g., becoming a fan of a winning sports team) also bolster self-esteem. The various ways that attitudes can support self-esteem are referred to here as the *self-esteem maintenance* function of attitudes. (Greenwald, chap. 17 in this volume, also proposes a broad "appraisal of self" function category encompassing multiple strategies for maintaining self-regard.)

The functions outlined here are not necessarily the only functions that attitudes can serve. Other functions, or delineations of functions, can be proposed (see footnote 1; see also research by Batra & Ahtola, 1987,

---

[1]Public and private identity motives could be considered as separate and distinct aspects of this general social identity function of attitudes, and much has been learned from a focus on this distinction (see chapter 13 by Snyder & DeBono in this volume for a review of their research on these differing aspects of the social identity function). For the purposes of the present discussion, we shall consider these aspects together because they comprise what has often been referred to more generally as a *symbolic* category of attitudes (e.g., Abelson, 1982; Herek, 1983, 1987; Sears & McConahay, 1973). Symbolic attitudes are based on what the attitude objects represent for one's identity and values. In a variety of attitude domains, this category of motives has been found to contrast sharply with the self-interested attitudes based on utilitarian or instrumental concerns.

suggesting that utilitarian and hedonic functions of attitudes are distinct and should be considered separately). Regardless of which functions are proposed, however, distinguishing between attitude functions suggests some interesting implications, One of the most intriguing concerns persuasion, and is a major hypothesis of the functional approach: In order to change an attitude, one must first know what psychological function(s) that attitude serves. This implies that eliciting attitude change requires targeting persuasive appeals to the function(s) of the attitude. Unfortunately, until recently, such functional hypotheses elicited little research largely because of the lack of functional operations.

Person Variations

Much of the functional research that was initially done built upon the focus on individual differences that characterized most of the functional formulations (Katz, 1960; Katz & Stotland, 1959; Sarnoff & Katz, 1954; Smith, Bruner, & White, 1956). It was assumed that the dominant psychological needs met by attitudes vary between individuals.[2] Smith, Bruner, and White's (1956) introduction of their functional model illustrated that approach with its focus on case studies of 10 men's attitudes toward Russia. In their book, *Opinions and Personality,* they argued: "An individual's opinions are but one of a number of consistent and regular forms of behavior which characterize him. From these consistencies in his behavior we infer the individual's personality . . . Opinions, like all behavior, both constitute part of the data from which personality is inferred and are in turn a function of personality" (p. 29). As tests of functional theories, some of the initial data were interesting but inconclusive. For example, Smith, Bruner, and White's detailed investigation of 10 men's attitudes toward Russia was the only evidence offered in support of their functional model. Insko (1967) noted that Smith, Bruner, and White's case history material, although extremely interesting, "is not a test of the theory's adequacy. In order to test the theory it would be necessary, first to establish operational

---

[2]An important exception in this regard is Kelman's (1958, 1961) model of compliance, identification, and internalization processes. Although Kelman's model is not strictly a theory of attitudes, but of social influence more broadly defined, his theory also implies that knowledge of how and why an attitude was formed is a prerequisite to knowing how to change that attitude. Although this is similar to the other functional models in its focus on the motives underlying acceptance of social influence, Kelman's emphasis on the antecedent social conditions associated with social influence makes this a more situation-based than personality-based approach. The operations associated with it will be discussed in the section on situation variations.

procedures for distinguishing between attitudes supported by different functional bases and, second, to establish whether or not these different attitudes respond in the expected manner to the appropriate change procedures" (p. 333).

Attempts to test aspects of Katz's (1960) formulation (e.g., Katz, Sarnoff, & McClintock, 1956; Katz, McClintock, & Sarnoff, 1957; McClintock, 1958; Stotland, Katz, & Patchen, 1959) provided evidence more relevant to the theory's adequacy. The operational approach in this research involved classifying individuals for the degree to which their attitudes were expected to serve an ego-defensive function. Unfortunately, these studies suffered from important interpretational ambiguities that limited the conclusions one could draw from their results.

Research by Katz, Sarnoff, and McClintock (1956) illustrated the difficulties associated with these studies. The authors attempted to use individuals' level of ego-defensiveness to predict the relative effectiveness of two appeals in reducing prejudice against Blacks. One appeal was termed *interpretational,* and was designed to give recipients insight into the dynamics and motivations underlying scapegoating and prejudice. The other appeal was *informational,* containing favorable information about Black people, presented in the context of cultural relativism. Katz and his colleagues predicted that moderately defensive subjects would manifest more attitude change in response to the interpretational appeal than low ego-defensive subjects (with highly defensive subjects likely to reject any attack on their opinions).

However, independent and dependent variable assessments were confounded in this research: Classifying subjects by their level of ego-defensiveness was based on a measure related to prejudice (a specially-designed TAT card). Other studies (e.g., McClintock, 1958; Stotland, Katz, & Patchen, 1959) made the same mistake, assessing ego-defensiveness with the F-scale, which was *designed* to correlate with prejudiced attitudes. Thus, with personality scores confounded with prejudice scores, it was difficult to know exactly what the data meant (see Kiesler, Collins, & Miller, 1969). To add to the interpretational ambiguities, Katz and his colleagues' (as well as McClintock's) results were presented in terms of the percent of subjects showing positive attitude change, rather than the mean change per subject. Thus, the degree of meaningful change elicited by the persuasive appeals was not clear.

Despite such methodological problems, which may have biased the data in favor of the hypotheses, the results of these investigations provided neither strong nor consistent support for functional predictions about ego-defensiveness and prejudice. The relationship between low, moderate, and high defensive subjects and attitude change in response to an interpretational appeal varied among the studies. In fact, at least two of the studies (Katz, Sarnoff, & McClintock, 1956; Stotland, Katz, & Patchen, 1959) yielded patterns that were opposite to initial functional predictions.

It should also be mentioned that, in addition to these studies on the role of the ego-defensive function in prejudice, researchers investigated a number of other ego-defense hypotheses that were closely linked to Freudian psychodynamic principles: Research by Sarnoff and his colleagues (e.g., Bishop, 1967; Sarnoff & Corwin, 1959) addressed such topics as the relationship between castration anxiety and the fear of death, and the role of anal personality characteristics in responses to cognitive dissonance (see Kiesler, Collins & Miller, 1969, for a detailed review and critique of these and other studies on ego-defensiveness; and see Clary & Tesser, 1985, for evidence contrary to Sarnoff & Corwin's conclusions).

Apart from the methodological problems described, an unfortunate limitation of the studies by Katz, Sarnoff, and colleagues was their sole focus on the ego-defensive function of attitudes. Their research did not address the broad array of motivational bases of attitudes posited by Katz, which did little to facilitate or encourage further functional research. The types of hypotheses associated with psychodynamic notions of ego-defense apparently did not attract many social psychologists to investigate functional theories of attitude. After the cluster of ego-defense studies in the 1950s by Katz, Sarnoff, and colleagues, interest in testing functional predictions waned. (See Herek, 1987, and Snyder & DeBono, chap. 13 in this volume, for a discussion of this and other factors affecting the popularity of functional theories.)

To arrive at the next significant set of studies on attitude functions, one has to "fast-forward" nearly three decades. It was not until the 1980s that a resurgence of interest in testing functional theories developed (e.g., DeBono, 1987; Herek, 1983, 1987; Shavitt, 1985; Shavitt & Fazio, 1988; Snyder & DeBono, 1985, 1987). Many of these studies also used an individual differences approach for operationalizing their predictions. However, they employed a variety of individual difference variables to investigate a broad range of attitude functions.

Research by Gregory Herek (1983, 1987) employed individual difference measures to validate new methods of measuring various attitude functions. Herek argued the need for methods of directly identifying the functions of individuals' attitudes toward a given object, rather than assessments of individuals' overall functional (personality) orientations. He chose homosexual persons as his primary attitude object because he expected they would engage opinions that not only vary widely in their favorability, but also in the functions they serve.

Herek performed exhaustive content analyses on over 100 students' attitude essays toward homosexuals, developing a detailed coding scheme consisting of 28 content themes. In another large sample of essays, patterns of these themes were identified that represented three types of functions for attitudes toward homosexuals: experiential-schematic, defensive, and self-expressive. According to Herek, the experiential-schematic function synthesized object-appraisal (Smith, Bruner, & White, 1956), with utilitarian and knowledge functions (Katz, 1960). The self-expressive function label corresponded with the social identity function. The essays were coded according to a series of decision rules for identifying the presence or absence of thematic patterns that represented these functions.

Validation of this coding scheme was based on an individual differences approach that employed traditional assessment techniques (e.g., for ego-defensiveness) as well as recently developed measures. Functional categorizations derived from the coding of subjects' attitude essays were compared with their responses on a variety of personality scales (e.g., need for approval scales, TAT stories scored for anxiety and hostility, an inventory of defense mechanisms, etc.) and other individual difference measures (e.g., assessments of religious ideology, density of one's social networks, degree of past experience with homosexuals, etc.). Several of the construct validity hypotheses about the relations between individual differences and the functional content of attitude essays were supported, suggesting the coding scheme reflects individual differences in the functions of attitudes toward homosexuals.

However, the coding procedure, based on identifying patterns made up of 28 content themes, is quite complex and time consuming. Thus, Herek (1987) also developed an *Attitude Functions Inventory* (AFI), employing similar content themes in a Likert-type structured format (e.g., "My opinions about ___ mainly are based on my concerns that we safeguard the civil liberties of all people in our society"). The AFI was then used to assess the functions of individuals' attitudes toward homosexuals and toward persons with stigmatizing illnesses (AIDS, cancer, and mental illness). Personality data and factor analyses of responses provided some preliminary evidence for the validity of the AFI. However, both the AFI and the coding scheme are fairly specific to homosexuals and stigmatized groups. Researchers interested in capitalizing on these procedures to investigate attitude functions for other objects would need to adapt (or, in the case of the coding scheme, substantially modify) the items or coding categories, and conduct further research to establish their construct validity. Nevertheless, Herek's research has provided rich and informative data on the variety of functions served by attitudes toward homosexuals and stigmatized groups, as well as useful methods for further study of these attitudes.

Like Herek's research, studies by Snyder and DeBono (DeBono, 1987; DeBono & Harnish, in press; Snyder & DeBono, 1985, 1987) capitalized on personality assessments to operationalize attitude functions (see Snyder & DeBono, chap. 13 in this volume, for a review). These studies employed assessments of the personality dimension of self-monitoring (Snyder, 1974) to identify the social functions individuals' attitudes were assumed to serve, focusing on contrasting aspects of the social identity function. Snyder and DeBono argued that high self-monitoring individuals, who strive to fit into various social situations, should tend to form atitudes that guide behavior appropriate to the relevant reference groups in each situation. This, they argued, implies that high self-monitoring individuals should tend to form attitudes that serve the function Smith, Bruner, and White (1956) labelled *social adjustment.* In contrast, low self-monitoring individuals, who strive to remain true to their inner values and attributes, should tend to form attitudes designed to reflect and express their true selves, regardless of the stituation. Thus, Snyder and DeBono suggested that low self-monitoring individuals should tend to form attitudes that serve the function Katz (1960) labelled *value-expression.*

Guided by these assumptions about the differing attitude functions of high versus low self-monitoring individuals, Snyder and DeBono's research focused on testing one of the key hypotheses of the functional approach: Attitudes serving different functions will respond to different types of persuasive techniques. Their studies provided consistent evidence that persuasive appeals are accepted to the extent that they address the function assumed to correspond with an individual's level of self-monitoring.

This self-monitoring methodology is likely to be more effective in encouraging further functional research than other methods proposed to date. For one thing, a reliable and easily administered measure of self-monitoring already exists (Snyder, 1974). Furthermore, as an operation of attitude functions, the self-monitoring approach has yielded impressively consistent results across a variety of studies (see Snyder & DeBono, chap. 13 in this volume, for a review). Thus, other investigators have been attracted to the self-monitoring approach as a vehicle for testing functional hypotheses (see Jamieson & Zanna, chap. 15 in this volume, for some examples).

In terms of translating the self-monitoring approach into functional terms, however, "social adjustment" versus "value-expression" may not fully convey the functional differences associated with high versus low levels of self-monitoring. The original definitions of these functional labels overlapped in meaning. Smith, Bruner, and White (1956) included motives relevant to the expression of one's inner values and the establishment of one's own identity when they proposed the social adjustment function: "The function of social adjustment served by holding an opinion is at once more subtle and more complex. For it is by holding certain views that one identifies with, or, indeed, differentiates oneself from various 'reference groups' . . . those groups in terms of whose standards the individual judges himself and with which he identifies or feels kinship" (p. 42).

Also, using the social adjustment versus value-expressive labels may obscure other types of differences that might exist in the attitude functions associated with high versus low self-monitoring individuals. For example, in addition to data suggesting that low self-monitoring people tend to form value-expressive attitudes, there are indications that the attitudes of low self-monitoring individuals are more likely to serve a utilitarian function than are the attitudes of high self-monitoring people. Snyder and DeBono (1985) found that, in the domain of consumer products, low self-monitoring people were particularly responsive to messages about the quality and features of particular brands, apparently reflecting a greater interest in the utilitarian dimension of the rewards or punishments associated with objects. Similarly, Shavitt, Han, Kim, and Tillman (1988) found that, for certain categories of products, low self-monitoring individuals were more likely to describe their attitudes in utilitarian terms than were high self-monitoring people. Thus, the functional underpinnings of low self-monitoring individuals' attitudes may be more multifaceted than the concept of value-expression allows.

In sum, data emerging from the self-monitoring approach, in addition to providing a useful functional operation, have some novel implications for the delineation of functional categories. Further consideration of the linkages between existing functional concepts, the self-monitoring construct, and new functional distinctions is worthwhile. As more is learned about the nature of attitude functions associated with low versus high levels of self-monitoring, the self-monitoring approach will continue to contribute to important modification and refinement of functional theories.

Overview of Person Variations

The individual difference operations described here represent the most commonly used approach to studying attitude functions. This focus derives from traditional functional theorizing, but recent investigations have broadened the range of individual difference dimensions that can be employed to identify the functions of attitudes.

Although an individual differences approach to attitude functions provides certain advantages (see Snyder & DeBono, chap. 13 in this volume, for a discussion of these), it also has some limitations. One of the most important concerns difficulties in predicting, a priori, the direction of the relation between personality scores, attitude functions, and functional outcomes. For example, in the studies by Katz, Sarnoff, and colleagues previously reviewed, it was predicted that moderately ego-defensive subjects would be more persuaded by an interpretational appeal than would highly defensive subjects (presumably because highly defensive people would reject any attack on their opinions). Yet, the opposite prediction could also have been made without modifying the basic hypothesis about the role of ego-defensiveness in persuasion.

Similarly, a study on the value-expressive function of attitudes by Kristiansen and Zanna (in press) predicted that, because high self-monitors are less oriented than low self-monitors to considering the relevance of their values to their attitudes, high self-monitors' attitudes should be correlated with *all* positive values, whereas low self-monitors' attitudes should only be related to values regarded as relevant to the attitude issue. Although their findings were consistent with these predictions, the opposite pattern of results could also have been considered supportive of the role of self-monitoring in the value-expressive function of attitudes. Low self-monitoring people, who are oriented toward expressing their values through their attitudes, might tend to form attitudes that are affected by any and all positive values. However, high self-monitors, who are unaccustomed to considering their values in forming their attitudes, might be more selective in terms of the values that do influence their attitudes, and as a result be influenced by only the most relevant values.

Finally, just predicting which level of a personality factor will be associated with the greatest level of an attitude function can sometimes be difficult. Consider the relation between one's level of self-esteem and the tendency to hold attitudes that serve a self-esteem maintenance function (e.g., negative evaluations of outgroups): One might expect that this tendency will be greatest for individuals with high self-esteem, based on the assumption that holding attitudes that serve this function is an effective strategy for maintaining a favorable self-concept. On the other hand, one could also expect the opposite relation, based on the assumption that individuals with low self-esteem have the greatest *need* to pursue self-enhancing strategies. Resolving this issue is more complex than simply proposing one type of relation over the other and assuming that it reflects a self-enhancing strategy. In fact, research by Crocker, et al. (1987) suggested that, under certain conditions, both relations can obtain, depending on the outcome in question. Crocker et al. (1987) found that, in response to a threat to the self-concept, people with high self-esteem were more likely than people with low self-esteem to derogate outgroups relative to their ingroup. However, people low as opposed to high in self-esteem were more negative overall in their evaluations of outgroup members—as well as ingroup members. Thus, Crocker, et al. showed that the relation of self-esteem and negative attitudes toward outgroups is a complex one, and does not always necessarily reflect self-enhancing strategies. (The generalized negativity of people low in self-esteem appeared instead to reflect the effects of the negative mood associated with low self-esteem on the perception of oneself and one's social environment.)

In sum, the examples presented of plausible opposing predictions for the role of personality in ego-defensive, value-expressive, and self-esteem maintenance functions underscore a difficulty with individual difference approaches to attitude functions: The process by which a trait is thought to elicit attitude functions and functional outcomes is often not articulated sufficiently enough for deriving specific, disconfirmable hypotheses.

It is important to recognize, however, that attitude functions are not linked solely to individual differences. Functional theories as originally proposed focused primarily on personality differences in exploring the functions of attitudes. And the research reviewed clearly indicates that personality is one of the factors that influences attitude functions. However, the scope of functional investigations need not be limited to personality-based strategies. The effects of attitude functions on attitude-relevant outcomes can also be addressed with strategies involving social factors. The characteristics of objects and situations should affect the motives that attitudes serve, and focusing on these social factors provides new operations of functional theories.

NEW DIRECTIONS FOR OPERATIONALIZING FUNCTIONAL THEORIES

Operations that focus on the role of social factors in attitude functions not only supplement current knowledge about attitude functions and personality, they provide some methodological advantages: Such operations provide means of determining the function(s) of an attitude experimentally, varying aspects of the stimuli to which subjects are exposed so as to elicit different functional goals. They can proceed by manipulating situational characteristics to vary the functions served by the same attitude. Or they can vary the attitude object so as to invoke different attitudes that serve different functions. These operations provide the advantages associated with experimental investigation—e.g., the capacity for drawing causal inferences and for employing powerful within-subject designs.

Moreover, developing such operations requires articulating specific relations between attitude functions and aspects of the social environment, and manipulating the relevant aspects. The direction of the relation between levels of the independent variable and attitude functions is therefore specified a priori, allowing disconfirmable hypotheses to be derived.

Object Variations

One method of varying functions experimentally focuses on the attitude functions that are typically associated with particular attitude objects. Shavitt (1985, 1987) proposed that, by building on the assumption that objects have differing potentials to engage particular attitude functions, straightforward and effective methods of varying the functions of attitudes can be developed.

Shavitt argued that the purposes or functions that an object can serve should exert an important influence on the functions that attitudes toward that object will serve. The functions served by objects can stem from a number of sources. Characteristics of the object itself, including its physical features (e.g., its taste, its size) and other attributes (e.g., its durability, its cost) should play an important role in determining the functions an object can serve. The predominant cultural or societal definitions of an object (e.g., "elegant," "out of style") may also play an important role. The functions that objects serve should not be construed as predetermined or immutable. They can change as attributes of the object are modified or as societal definitions change over time.[3]

Some objects seem to primarily serve only a single function. For example, coffee serves a utilitarian function because of the rewards and punishments intrinsically associated with it (e.g., pleasant taste, alertness, and nervousness). But it typically does not serve, for example, a social identity function of impressing others or expressing one's values. That is, the predominant societal definition of coffee does not imbue it with social

---

[3]The notion that attitude functions can be associated with particular attitude objects has an interesting parallel in J. J. Gibson's (1966, 1979) concept of *affordances* of objects, which was incorporated into an "ecological approach" to social perception proposed by McArthur and Baron (1983). Gibson's stress on the potential outcomes associated with an object parallels Shavitt's focus on the purposes that attitude objects can serve for an individual. Nevertheless, an important distinction should be drawn between the present assumptions and Gibsonian ones: A Gibsonian analysis focuses on the direct perception of affordances, as revealed in such features as the shapes and colors of objects. However, Shavitt's analysis also incorporates cognitively constructed functions, acknowledging the importance of shared societal definitions in imparting a social identity function to objects. Moreover, research based on this analysis has employed verbally presented stimuli and measures that would not be part of a Gibsonian analysis.

significance.[4] Other objects seem to serve multiple functions. For example, a car serves both the utilitarian function of providing transportation and the social identity function of communicating status and identity. Thus, coffee should tend to elicit attitudes that serve a utilitarian function (e.g., by guiding its purchase and consumption), but not tend to elicit social identity attitudes (that guide behaviors in which the attitude is discussed or displayed to others). Meanwhile, cars may elicit attitudes that serve either a utilitarian or a social identity function or both.

As Greenwald, chapter 17 in this volume, points out, the functions served by an object and those served by attitudes toward the object are distinct. One implication of this is that object functions and attitude functions may sometimes be manifest in different behaviors. For example, the social identity function of an American flag is manifest in displaying it. However, the social identity function of one's *attitude* toward an American flag is manifest not only in this behavior, but also in actions that maintain and protect its social value—e.g., keeping the flag clean, not flying it during potentially damaging weather, and so forth. Still, although the behavioral manifestations of object functions and attitude functions may sometimes vary, the functions served by an object should be useful in predicting the functions likely to be served by attitudes toward the object.

Objects that are likely to engage only certain attitude functions, and are unlikely to engage others (e.g., coffee), can be capitalized on as a basis for operationalizing attitude functions. By presenting subjects with different types of these attitude objects to respond to, the functions of subjects' attitudes can be varied experimentally.

How can such attitude objects be selected for experimental use? Some general criteria can be applied in identifying a priori the attitude functions that objects are likely to engage.[5] For example, to the extent that an object is considered to symbolize other concepts, such as values, traits or group affiliations, that object should engage attitudes that serve a social identity function. This is particularly true to the extent that any behavior aimed at an attitude object is likely to be performed in public, or be subject to public

---

[4]This is not meant to imply that *under no circumstances* can coffee serve a social identity function. There are exceptions. For example, some children may consider drinking coffee a symbol of maturity and adulthood, and Mormons disapprove of coffee on religious grounds. However, for most individuals in most situations, coffee serves primarily a utilitarian function. Although exceptions can be identified, coffee's utilitarian functional tendency is nevertheless meaningful and operationally useful.

[5]In addition, Shavitt (1985) developed and validated a coding scheme for identifying the functions reflected in individuals' cognitive responses to attitude objects. This coding scheme can be employed to categorize responses to a variety of attitude objects. Objects that consistently elicit particular functional responses may be classified as engaging the corresponding attitude function(s).

scrutiny. On the other hand, to the extent that an object is intrinsically associated with rewards and/or punishments, and that any behavior toward the object is likely to be aimed at obtaining its rewards and avoiding its punishments, it should engage attitudes that serve a utilitarian function. Finally, to the extent that an object represents a major component of an individual's self-concept it should engage attitudes that serve a self-esteem maintenance function. Objects that people tend to derogate or distance themselves from psychologically can also engage this attitude function, either by providing a basis for self-enhancing strategies or by serving as targets for externalizing inner conflicts. (See Shavitt, 1987, for further discussion of criteria for identifying a priori the attitude functions engaged by objects.)

Consider the function of individuals' attitudes toward an object such as an air conditioner. An air conditioner could be considered an object that engages primarily a utilitarian attitude function because one's attitude toward it should be based largely on the rewards (e.g., comfort) and punishments (e.g., high energy bills) intrinsically associated with it. Also, one's attitude toward an air conditioner should guide behaviors that maintain the rewards and avoid the punishments associated with this object (e.g., using the air conditioner on a hot day, turning it off at times to conserve energy).

In contrast, consider the functions of one's attitude toward a wedding ring. A wedding ring could be considered an object that primarily engages a social identity attitude function because one's attitude toward it should be based largely on what it symbolizes. Furthermore, wedding rings are worn (in public) primarily to communicate information to others about the wearer, and one's attitude toward wedding rings and what they symbolize should guide this behavior.

Finally, consider the functions of one's attitude toward one's own appearance or one's own personality. These features constitute major components of most individuals' self-concepts and, thus, attitudes toward them should be directly linked to self-esteem. Objects that primarily serve a self-esteem maintenance function by motivating individuals to distance themselves psychologically from the object may be harder to identify a priori. The objects that elicit such externalizing motives likely differ from person to person. However, the objects that have been traditionally studied in functional research on ego-defense—outgroups—are perhaps the most likely to serve these types of self-esteem maintenance motives. Thus, for example, a group such as homosexuals, which may be perceived as ego-threatening and may elicit internal conflicts associated with externalization, should be particularly likely to engage ego-defensive attitudes (cf. Herek, 1987).

A number of studies have yielded support for the viability and construct validity of object-based operations derived from these selection criteria (Shavitt, 1985, 1987; Shavitt & Fazio, 1987, 1988; Shavitt, Han, Kim, & Tillman, 1988). In one study (Shavitt, 1985), 96 subjects' cognitive responses toward a variety of objects (e.g., air conditioners, coffee, the flu, wedding rings, American flags, the Republican party, one's appearance, one's personality, and homosexuals) were collected and coded to assess whether objects that primarily engage one attitude function could be identified. For most of the objects, the predominant attitude functions emerging in the coding of cognitive responses were consistent with a priori assumptions about the attitude functions engaged by the objects. These assumptions were further validated by independent manipulation checks, in which subjects rated the contribution of function-relevant factors to their attitudes. Thus, the results suggested that manipulation of objects is a viable basis for varying attitude functions. In addition, the coding of cognitive responses yielded a valid and reliable coding scheme for measuring the functions of attitudes toward a variety of objects, from appliances to social groups (see footnote 5).

Subsequent research employed object variations to investigate a number of functional hypotheses (Shavitt, 1985; Shavitt & Fazio, 1987, 1988; Shavitt, Han, Kim, & Tillman, 1988). For example, in research on the role of attitude functions in the persuasiveness of appeals (Shavitt, 1985), subjects read appeals (advertisements) about products assumed to engage primarily either a utilitarian or a social identity attitude function. The products assumed to engage primarily a utilitarian attitude function were air conditioners and coffee. The products assumed to engage primarily a social identity attitude function were greeting cards and perfumes. For each product, subjects read an appeal for a brand advertised with utilitarian arguments (e.g., "The delicious, hearty flavor and aroma of Sterling Blend coffee come from a blend of the freshest coffee beans") and an appeal for a brand advertised with social identity arguments (e.g., "The coffee you drink says something about the type of person you are. It can reveal your rare, discriminating taste").

Across two studies, manipulation checks largely supported the effectiveness of this object-based method in varying the functions of subjects' attitudes. Furthermore, results of this research provided consistent evidence that appeals that were relevant to an attitude's primary function were more persuasive than appeals that were relevant to another function. Functionally relevant ads elicited more favorable attitudes toward the brands they supported, a preference for purchase of those brands, and even a greater liking for the ads themselves. Thus, these studies provided evidence for a key hypothesis of the functional approach: Attitudes serving different functions respond to different types of persuasive appeals.

Overview of Object Variations

The results of a number of studies indicate that attitude objects are a promising basis for operationalizing attitude functions. The selection criteria briefly reviewed here were, as indicated by a variety of measures, effective in identifying objects that engage particular attitude functions. And the operations that emerged, employing a range of objects, were successful in varying a range of attitude functions. The data emerging from these operations also illustrated the utility of this operational approach in providing insights about the role of attitude functions in persuasion (Shavitt, 1985) and in the attitude-behavior relation (Shavitt & Fazio, 1987, 1988, described in the following section).

Operations based on object variations also have the potential to facilitate and encourage further research on an array of functional issues. They provide a straightforward method of varying attitude functions that can be easily employed to test a variety of functional hypotheses. With careful selection of attitude objects, reliable results should be obtained across investigations. We have already discussed some criteria for selecting objects a priori (also see footnote 5).

There are, however, some limitations on the questions that can be addressed with this methodology. Because this variation of attitude functions relies upon objects that primarily engage a single attitude function, investigation of attitudes toward multiple-function objects would require a different approach. The functions of individuals' attitudes toward these objects could not be identified a priori on the basis of object characteristics because each person's attitude could serve any or all of the multiple functions the object could engage. One operational strategy would be to measure the functions of subjects' attitudes toward such objects directly, either by coding cognitive responses (e.g., Shavitt, 1985) or with more structured measures (e.g., Herek, 1987; see also Lutz, 1981, for a set of proposed functional measures based on expectancy-value principles). Another approach would be to assess person variations (previously described), categorizing individuals for the functions their attitudes tend to serve. Still another method would involve manipulating situational factors to elicit particular functional goals. We turn now to this approach.

Situation Variations

Just as some objects can be classified according to the attitude functions they typically engage, situations can also be categorized according to the attitude functions they are likely to elicit. By modifying features of the situation in which attitude objects, or messages about them, are encountered, the presence of particular functional goals can be varied.

Perhaps the best-known examples of this operational approach are the studies designed to test Kelman's (1958, 1961) model of compliance, identification, and internalization processes in social influence (see footnote 2). Kelman's approach assumed that, by manipulating aspects of messages to which subjects were exposed, different motives could be induced for the acceptance of influence. These motives were expected to affect the conditions under which the newly adopted opinions would be expressed.

In one study (Kelman, 1958), messages about segregation at Negro colleges, presented to students at a Negro college, varied information about the source of the communicator's power. The communicator was either presented as an official with control over funding for the college (to induce compliance), a socially attractive student (to induce identification), or a professor with high credibility (to induce internalization). The messages in another study (Kelman, 1961), regarding a new science education program, discussed the implications of the espoused opinion either for one's relation to reference groups (identification) or for the maintenance of an important value (internalization). Results of the studies suggested that these message manipulations were effective in inducing different motives for accepting social influence. As Kelman predicted, the conditions under which subjects expressed their newly adopted attitudes depended on their motives for accepting influence.

Kelman's operational approach differs from studies in which message aspects were varied in order to study the effect of attitude functions (operationalized by person or object variations) on the persuasiveness of functionally relevant versus irrelevant messages (e.g., DeBono & Harnish, in press; Snyder & DeBono, 1985; Shavitt, 1985). For Kelman, the message content was by definition functionally relevant, because the message determined which motives were served by attitude change. To study the persuasiveness of messages in interaction with attitude functions, functional operations external to the message would be needed. What other situational factors could be used to operationalize certain functional goals?

Situations that involve having to make a judgment or decision regarding an attitude object should heighten knowledge function motives for attitudes. As discussed earlier, to some extent all attitudes serve this fundamental function. However, situations that create a *need* for an attitude as a guide in upcoming judgment or decision tasks, especially under conditions of time pressure or uncertainty, should heighten the knowledge function motive. And, as Fazio, Lenn, and Effrein (1983) showed, when these situations involve unfamiliar attitude objects, attitudes are formed spontaneously. In their studies, some subjects were given goals associated with a knowledge function by inducing subjects to expect future questioning about, or interaction with, new attitude objects (intellectual puzzles). Thus, these subjects were led to believe that it would be useful in the future to know whether they like the puzzles. When knowledge function goals were introduced, attitudes toward the puzzles were apparently formed spontaneously, but were not formed spontaneously when such goals were absent (see also Jamieson & Zanna, 1986, for evidence about the structure of attitudes formed under high levels of knowledge function motivation).

Several other studies have situationally heightened the knowledge function served by existing attitudes (e.g., Bechtold, Naccarato, & Zanna, 1986; Jamieson & Zanna, 1985; Kruglanski & Freund, 1983; see Jamieson & Zanna, chap. 15 in this volume, for a review). These studies employed time pressures in attitude-relevant judgment and decision-making tasks to heighten knowledge function motives for attitudes. In general, time pressured subjects relied more on their existing attitudes and less on careful consideration of available data when making their judgments and decisions. Overall, therefore, results across a variety of studies have supported the effectiveness of situational inductions of knowledge function motives.

In addition to heightening the knowledge function of attitudes, situational factors may elicit a variety of other functions. For instance, situations that involve using or affiliating with an attitude object, or expressing one's attitude toward the object, in public or in the presence of reference group members (e.g., signing a public petition, wearing a school sweatshirt to the big game, or introducing a boyfriend or girlfriend to one's family) should be especially likely to instigate social identity motives.

On the other hand, situations in which the outcomes intrinsically associated with an object are made salient should tend to elicit utilitarian motives for attitudes. One way to increase the salience of an object's outcomes is to deprive a person of them (e.g., food deprivation should heighten the utilitarian function served by one's attitudes toward a pastrami sandwich). However, this approach would also heighten the favorability of attitudes toward an object, confounding evaluation with attitude function. Another situation that should increase the salience of objects' outcomes involves expecting to make a decision that has implications for obtaining the object's rewards and punishments (e.g., having to make a purchase decision about an air conditioner). Such decision-making situations should heighten the utilitarian function served by attitudes (as well as the knowledge function). Manipulations of personal involvement (e.g., Petty, Cacioppo, & Goldman, 1981; Petty, Cacioppo, & Schumann, 1983), in which subjects expect to be affected by or make decisions about objects that have intrinsic rewards and punishments (e.g., razors), could be characterized as heightening the utilitarian function of attitudes.

Finally, situations that involve success or failure experiences with an object that represents an important component of one's self-concept (e.g., feedback on a test that reflects valued skills) should be especially likely to elicit self-esteem maintenance motives for attitudes (e.g., self-protective opinions about the importance of the skill and the validity of the test in measuring it, self-serving attributions for one's performance, self-enhancing evaluations of outgroups, etc.). Similarly, the successes or failures of people with whom one is associated (e.g., one's friends, one's school's football team) should elicit attitudes that serve a self-esteem maintenance function by associating the self with or distancing it from these people (e.g., through "basking," see Cialdini, et al., 1976) and from the domains in which their performance occurred (see Tesser & Campbell, 1983, for a discussion of self-evaluation maintenance responses to such situations).

By manipulating the situational characteristics likely to be associated with particular functional goals, such as the characteristics described, the functions of attitudes can be manipulated. This approach to operationalizing attitude functions can be employed in an attempt to either, (a) induce new functions for attitudes that do not already serve those functions, or (b) increase the salience of functions already served by attitudes.

Inducing New Functions

A situational induction of new functions is not likely to succeed unless a number of important requirements are met. First, such an induction must be both powerful and focused, for it can easily fail to induce the intended function, or unwittingly induce more than one. For example, attempting to induce a social identity function for attitudes by telling subjects their attitudes will be evaluated by others may be ineffective. Unless the subjects know these other individuals and care about obtaining their favorable evaluations, subjects are not likely to attach social significance to their attitudes. Also, an induction can affect more than the function it was intended to. For example, a utilitarian function induction may become contaminated if, for example, subjects become concerned about being evaluated by the experimenter. An unwitting instigation of impression management concerns may induce social identity motives for attitudes.

Second, a situational induction should take into account the attitude functions that are typically engaged by attitude objects. That is, situational factors are unlikely to induce attitude functions for objects that rarely engage those functions. For example, the expectation that one's attitudes will be evaluated by others is unlikely to induce a social identity function for attitudes toward a primarily utilitarian object, such as an air conditioner. This suggests that attempts to induce new functions for attitudes would be more successful if they employed attitude objects that are unfamiliar to subjects and capable of engaging a variety of attitude functions, rather than objects for which attitudes serving other functions already exist. Instead of attempting to overcome the functions of existing attitudes, the function(s) to be induced could guide the formation of attitudes toward an unfamiliar object. For example, Kelman's (1961) message-based induction of motives may have succeeded in part because the message topic was an unfamiliar one, advocating a novel educational program.

Increasing the Salience of Functions

Manipulation of situational characteristics can also be employed to affect the salience of functions already served by attitudes. For example, the social identity induction already described—in which subjects anticipate that their attitudes will be evaluated by others—could be used to increase the salience of the social identity function already served by one's attitude toward, say, the American flag. For objects that engage more than one attitude function (e.g., cars, clothes), situational manipulations can be employed to make different functions salient for different people. Recall that Kelman's (1958) successful manipulation of motives employed different communicators delivering a message on segregation policies—a topic likely to engage a variety of attitude functions.

Thus, manipulating the salience of existing attitude functions is likely to be more successful than attempting to induce new functions for attitudes. Issues relating to the power and focus of a manipulation are still relevant here, but increasing the salience of an existing attitude function may not require such strong manipulations.

Recent evidence suggests that even rather subtle manipulations can temporarily affect the salience of functions served by attitudes (Schmitt, 1988; Shavitt & Fazio, 1987, 1988). In research on the role of functional dimensions in the attitude-behavior relation, Shavitt and Fazio (1987) manipulated the functional dimension salient at attitude assessment with an initial priming questionnaire. Subjects rated either 20 food items for their taste (utilitarian prime) or 20 behaviors for the impression they make on others (society identity prime). This was immediately followed by an assessment of attitudes toward one of two brands of a beverage. The simple task of rating other items along a certain dimension was expected to make that dimension salient when expressing one's attitude toward the beverage.

After a delay, subjects predicted their behavior toward the beverage. The function that was salient at behavior prediction was manipulated by varying the attitude object (in this case, the brand of beverage) that subjects responded to. One brand (7-Up) was presumed to engage largely a utilitarian attitude function at the time of behavior prediction, whereas the other brand (Perrier mineral water) was presumed to engage largely a social identity attitude function (although these were not expected to be single-function brands).

Apparently, the situational (priming) manipulation and the object (brand) variation successfully varied the functional dimensions salient at attitude assessment and at behavior prediction. When the functional dimension that was salient at attitude assessment (the primed function) matched the functional dimension that was salient at behavior prediction (the attitude function engaged by the brand) the correlation between attitudes and behavior predictions was significantly higher than when the salient functions did not correspond (see also Shavitt & Fazio, 1988). This suggested that if the functional dimension that is salient at the time of attitudinal and of behavioral expression is not the same, the two expressions may be guided by different evaluations, reducing the attitude-behavior correspondence.

Overview of Situation Variations

The results of a number of studies suggest that situational variations can be effective in operationalizing attitude functions. Simple situational manipulations that increase the utility of attitudes (e.g., time pressures in judgment tasks) have proven effective in heightening the salience of the knowledge function (e.g., Jamieson & Zanna, 1985, 1986). Priming-type manipulations have also shown promise as a method of increasing the salience of various functions (Shavitt & Fazio, 1987, 1988; see also Schmitt, 1988). Finally, manipulations of message aspects have successfully induced a range of motives for accepting social influence (Kelman, 1958, 1961). Other situational characteristics, already described, may also induce particular functional goals (e.g., affiliating with an attitude object in public may induce a social identity attitude function). Their effects on attitude functions await further research.

The data generated by the situational inductions employed to date have yielded information about an array of attitude functions and hypotheses, dealing with a broad range of attitude objects. Furthermore, these operations derive from social psychology's dominant research paradigm, which focuses on situational manipulation of constructs. Thus, situational operations are likely to foster further research on attitude functions. Researchers who might otherwise be disinclined to study the motivational bases of attitudes may be attracted by this paradigmatic approach and the links it can highlight between their own lines of inquiry and functional hypotheses.

Nevertheless, a number of caveats are in order. As suggested, situational operations may be effective only under certain conditions. Relatively simple, "one-shot" laboratory treatments, often effective in manipulating other social psychological constructs, may be inadequate for inducing subjects to invest their attitudes with goal-oriented significance. If subjects are to perceive a link between the attitudes they express in the laboratory and their central goals, situational operations of attitude functions should be both powerful and focused, and should take into account the attitude functions engaged by objects. Moreover, even if they meet these criteria, the effects of situational operations may be short-lived. That is, the induced salience of new or existing attitude functions may dissipate unless the inductions are ongoing or reinstated. Thus, dependent measures need to be administered to coincide with the induced salience of functions.

FUTURE DIRECTIONS
IN FUNCTIONAL RESEARCH

Exploration of Interactive Hypotheses

So far, the operations discussed have been considered primarily in terms of their main effects on attitude functions. However, much of this discussion has been built upon assumptions regarding the interactive effects of objects, situations, and personality on attitude functions. For example, we have assumed that situational operations will vary in their effectiveness, depending on the functional constraints associated with attitude objects. In fact, this is a hypothesis regarding the interaction of two classes of factors: *situational* and *object-related*. Situational factors will have a stronger impact on the functions of attitudes toward objects that can readily engage the attitude functions to be elicited than for objects that cannot. For example, as suggested earlier, the expectation that one's attitudes will be evaluated by others is unlikely to induce a social identity function for attitudes toward a primarily utilitarian object, such as coffee. But it should be more effective as a social identity induction for attitudes toward, for example, clothing.

The same type of hypothesis could be put forth with regard to the interactive role of personality characteristics and attitude objects in attitude functions. For example, although individuals who are chronically concerned with obtaining social approval will be more likely overall to have attitudes that serve a social identity function than individuals who are not, this effect should be enhanced for objects that can engage a social identity attitude function and attenuated for those that cannot. Evidence for this interaction of personality and object variations was provided in a recent study by Shavitt, Han, Kim, and Tillman (1988). In this study, subjects' level of self-monitoring predicted the functions of their attitudes toward consumer products to the extent that those products were likely to serve the public image concerns of the high self-monitor. For products that could serve such a social identity function (e.g., university insignia decals, high school class rings), high self-monitors were more likely to hold social identity attitudes and low self-monitors were more likely to hold utilitarian attitudes. However, for products that were unlikely to serve a social identity function (e.g., air conditioners, aspirin), attitudes were consistently utilitarian, regardless of self-monitoring levels.

This interaction between personality and object variations has operational implications, as well. It suggests that the effectiveness of personality variations as variations of attitude functions may be limited to attitudes toward objects that can engage the functions relevant to the corresponding personality types. For attitudes toward other objects, personality assessments may be less effective as functional operations. A set of studies by Snyder and DeBono (1985) provided suggestive evidence for this point. Their studies yielded consistent results, across a variety of messages, about the persuasiveness of different types of appeals for high versus low self-monitoring individuals. Nevertheless, it is interesting to note that there was variation among attitude objects in the strength of the effects. In two of the studies, the appeals were ads for brands of whiskey, coffee, and cigarettes. Strong results were obtained for whiskey, a product whose brands would appear to have some potential for serving a variety of functions, including social identity. However, nonsignificant results were obtained in both studies for coffee and cigarettes, products whose brands may have fewer implications for social approval or self-presentation (particularly for coffee). Thus, it appears that person variations are effective in identifying the functions of attitudes toward objects to the extent that those objects can engage the corresponding attitude functions (Snyder & DeBono's discussion of person variations, chap. 13 in this volume, acknowledges this point).

Another way of conceptualizing the personality–object interaction in attitude functions is to consider individual differences that relate directly to object domains. Individual difference factors could be viewed not only in terms of personality traits that are expected to affect attitude functions globally. They could also be conceptualized in terms of domain-specific differences between individuals' goals. For example, differences in individuals' occupations may be associated with differences in the functions of their attitudes toward work-relevant objects.

To illustrate, a chef's attitudes toward objects associated with cooking (a gourmet cookbook, expensive cookware, etc.) should serve a utilitarian function. However, an attorney's attitude toward the same objects may serve a social identity function, reflecting his or her perception that these items connote sophistication. These individual differences in attitude functions may be fairly consistent between chefs and attorneys, but only for certain domains of objects (e.g., gourmet cooking supplies). For other domains, not associated with goal differences between chefs and attorneys (e.g., stereos), there is no reason to expect individual differences in occupation to be associated with differences in attitude functions. This type of approach to person variations, focusing on the interaction between object domains and domain-specific individual differences, deserves attention in future research on attitude functions.

Finally, personality factors can mediate the effectiveness of situational manipulations in varying attitude functions. Certain personality characteristics may predispose individuals to be influenced by the situations they are in. For instance, Shavitt and Fazio (1988) found evidence suggesting that situational variations designed to heighten the salience of functional dimensions were effective for high but not for low self-monitors. Apparently, high self-monitors, who are predisposed to be influenced by situational circumstances in their attitudinal and behavioral expressions, were more influenced by whatever functional dimensions were salient at the time, while low self-monitors' responses were more likely to be guided by strong, pre-existing attitudes. This was particularly true for a manipulation of the social identity dimension, which is especially relevant to the concerns of the high self-monitor.

Incorporation of New Dependent Measures

This chapter has focused on reviewing the development of a variety of new approaches to identifying or manipulating the functions served by attitudes. Fortunately, operational progress at the independent variable level has been accompanied by new developments at the dependent variable level, as well. Studies reported in a number of chapters in this volume have employed measures adopted from a social cognition approach in order to investigate processes and outcomes associated with attitude functions (see, for example, chap. 7, 13, and 15 by Fazio, Jamieson & Zanna, and Snyder & DeBono).

This is a promising new direction for functional research. Traditional functional theorizing was not particularly concerned with cognitive processes. However, capitalizing on measures that tap specific dimensions of cognitive processes and knowledge structures will allow investigators greater sophistication in the functional hypotheses they can test. For example, as several of the chapters in this book attest, social cognition measures have been used extensively and profitably to address the second theme of this volume—attitude structure. As these measures become further incorporated into functional investigations, they will foster research on the relation of attitude function to attitude structure.

Some studies have already begun to explore this relation. For instance, Jamieson and Zanna (1986) employed a measure of attitude ambivalence to explore the effect of knowledge function motives on the formation of simply as opposed to complexly structured attitudinal affect. Studies by Fazio (chapter 7 in this volume) capitalized on response latency measures to show that the accessibility of an attitude in memory predicts the extent to which it serves the knowledge function. And research by Shavitt (1985), analyzing cognitive response content, provided evidence that utilitarian, social identity, and self-esteem maintenance functions are related to different types of content in the cognitive representations of attitude objects (see also Herek, 1987).

More research is needed on the relation of attitude structure and function. Fortunately, the availability of new approaches to operationalizing functional theory—at both the independent and dependent variable levels—will facilitate movement in this direction. As a greater variety and complexity of functional hypotheses are addressed, the development of new operations is sure to pay off in theory development, as well.

ACKNOWLEDGMENTS

Gratitude is expressed to Mahzarin R. Banaji and to the editors for helpful comments on a previous draft.

REFERENCES

Abelson, R. P. (1982). Three modes of attitude-behavior consistency. In M. P. Zanna, E. T. Higgins, & C. P. Herman (Eds.), *Consistency in social behavior: The Ontario symposium,* (Vol. 2, pp. 131–146). Hillsdale, NJ: Lawrence Erlbaum Associates.

Adorno, T. W., Frenkel-Brunswik, E., Levinson, D. J., & Sanford, R. N. (1950). *The authoritarian personality.* New York: Harper & Row.

Batra, R., & Ahtola, O. T. (1987). *The measurement and role of utilitarian and hedonic attitudes.* Unpublished manuscript, Columbia University, New York.

Bechtold, A., Naccarato, M. E., & Zanna, M. P. (1986). *Need for structure and the prejudice-discrimination link.* Paper presented at the annual meeting of the Canadian Psychological Association, Toronto.

Bishop, F. (1967). The anal character: A rebel in the dissonance family. *Journal of Personality and Social Psychology, 6,* 23–36.

Cialdini, R. B., Borden, R. J., Thorne, A., Walker, M. R., Freeman, S., & Sloan, L. R. (1976). Basking in reflected glory: Three (football) field studies. *Journal of Personality and Social Psychology, 34,* 366–375.

Clary, E. G., & Tesser, A. (1985). Another look at castration anxiety and fear of death. *Journal of Social Psychology, 125* (3), 397–398.

Crocker, J., Thompson, L. L., McGraw, K. M., & Ingerman, C. (1987). Downward comparison, prejudice, and evaluations of others: Effects of self-esteem and threat. *Journal of Personality and Social Psychology, 52* (5), 907–916.

DeBono, K. G. (1987). Investigating the social-adjustive and value-expressive functions of attitudes: Implications for persuasion processes. *Journal of Personality and Social Psychology, 52* (2), 279–287.

DeBono, K. G., & Harnish, R. (in press). Source expertise, source attractiveness and the processing of persuasive information: A functional approach. *Journal of Personality and Social Psychology.*

Eagly, A. H., & Himmelfarb, S. (1974). Current trends in attitude theory and research. In S. Himmelfarb & A. H. Eagly (Eds.), *Readings in attitude change* (pp. 594–610). New York: Wiley.

Fazio, R. H., Lenn, T. M., & Effrein, E. A. (1983). Spontaneous attitude formation. *Social Cognition, 2* (3), 217–234.

Gibson, J. J. (1966). *The senses considered as perceptual systems.* Boston: Houghton Mifflin.

Gibson, J. J. (1979). *The ecological approach to visual perception.* Boston: Houghton Mifflin.

Herek, G. M. (1983). *Individual differences in attitudes toward lesbians and gay men: Social psychological components of sexual ideologies.* Paper presented at the meeting of the American Psychological Association, Los Angeles.

Herek, G. M. (1987). Can functions be measured? A new perspective on the functional approach to attitudes. *Social Psychology Quarterly, 50,* 285–303.

Insko, C. A. (1967). *Theories of attitude change.* New York: Appleton-Century-Crofts.

Jamieson, D. W., & Zanna, M. P. (1985). *Moderating the attitude-behavior relation: The joint effects of arousal and self-monitoring.* Paper presented at the annual meeting of the Canadian Psychological Association, Halifax.

Jamieson, D. W., & Zanna, M. P. (1986). *Attitude formation: Dispositional and situational determinants of affect strength and complexity.* Paper presented at the annual meeting of the Canadian Psychological Association, Toronto.

Katz, D. (1960). The functional approach to the study of attitudes. *Public Opinion Quarterly, 24,* 163–204.

Katz, D., McClintock, C., & Sarnoff, I. (1957). The measurement of ego defense as related to attitude change. *Journal of Personality, 25,* 465–474.

Katz, D., Sarnoff, I., & McClintock, C. (1956). Ego-defense and attitude change. *Human Relations, 9,* 27–46.

Katz, D., & Stotland, E. (1959). A preliminary statement to a theory of attitude structure and change. In S. Koch (Ed.), *Psychology: A study of a science* (Vol. 3, pp. 423–475). New York: McGraw-Hill.

Kelman, H. C. (1958). Compliance, identification, and internalization: Three processes of attitude change. *Journal of Conflict Resolution, 2,* 51–60.

Kelman, H. C. (1961). Processes of opinion change. *Public Opinion Quarterly, 25,* 57–78.

Kiesler, C. A., Collins, B. E., & Miller, N. (1969). *Attitude change: A critical analysis of theoretical approaches.* New York: Wiley.

Kristiansen, C. M., & Zanna, M. P. (in press). Justifying attitudes by appealing to values: A functional perspective. *British Journal of Social Psychology.*

Kruglanski, A. W., & Freund, T. (1983). The freezing and unfreezing of lay-inferences: Effects on impressional primacy, ethnic stereotyping, and numerical anchoring. *Journal of Experimental Social Psychology, 19,* 448–468.

Lutz, R. J. (1981). A reconceptualization of the functional approach to attitudes. *Research in Marketing, 5,* 165–210.

McArthur, L. Z., & Baron, R. M. (1983). Toward an ecological theory of social perception. *Psychological Review, 90,* 215–238.

McClintock, C. (1958). Personality syndromes and attitude change. *Journal of Personality, 26,* 479–493.

Petty, R. E., Cacioppo, J. T., & Goldman, R. (1981). Personal involvement as a determinant of argument-based persuasion. *Journal of Personality and Social Psychology, 41,* 847–855.

Petty, R. E., Cacioppo, J. T., & Schumann, D. (1983). Central and peripheral routes to advertising effectiveness: The moderating role of involvement. *Journal of Consumer Research, 10,* 134–148.

Sarnoff, I., & Corwin, S. M. (1959). Castration anxiety and the fear of death. *Journal of Personality, 27,* 374–385.

Sarnoff, I., & Katz, D. (1954). The motivational bases of attitude change. *Journal of Abnormal and Social Psychology, 49,* 115–124.

Schmitt, B. H. (1988). *Situational determinants of attitude functions: Effects on the perception and evaluation of advertisements.* Paper presented at the meeting of the Association for Consumer Research, Honolulu.

Sears, D. O., & McConahay, J. (1973). *The new urban Blacks and the Watts riot.* Boston: Houghton Mifflin.

Shavitt, S. (1985). Functional imperative theory of attitude formation and expression. Unpublished doctoral dissertation, Ohio State University, Columbus, OH.

Shavitt, S. (1987). *Operationalizing functional theory: Exploring the role of objects in attitude functions.* Unpublished manuscript, University of Illinois, Urbana, Illinois.

Shavitt, S., & Fazio, R. H. (1987). *Attitude functions in the attitude-behavior relationship.* Paper presented at the meeting of the Midwestern Psychological Association, Chicago.

Shavitt, S., & Fazio, R. H. (1988). *Attitude functions and self-monitoring in the attitude–behavior relation.* Paper presented at the meeting of the Midwestern Psychological Association, Chicago.

Shavitt, S., Han, S. P., Kim, Y. C., & Tillman, C. (1988). *Attitude objects and self-monitoring interactively affect attitude functions.* Paper presented at the meeting of the Midwestern Psychological Association, Chicago.

Smith, M. B., Bruner, J. S., & White, R. W. (1956). *Opinions and personality.* New York: Wiley.

Snyder, M. (1974). Self-monitoring of expressive behavior. *Journal of Personality and Social Psychology, 30,* 526–537.

Snyder, M., & DeBono, K. G. (1985). Appeals to image and claims about quality: Understanding the psychology of advertising. *Journal of Personality and Social Psychology, 49,* 586–597.

Snyder, M., & DeBono, K. G. (1987). A functional approach to attitudes and persuasion. In M. P. Zanna, J. M. Olson, & C. P. Herman (Eds.), *Social influence: The Ontario symposium,* (Vol. 5). Hillsdale, NJ: Lawrence Erlbaum Associates.

Stotland, E., Katz, D., & Patchen, M. (1959). The reduction of prejudice through the arousal of self-insight. *Journal of Personality, 27,* 507–531.

Tesser, A., & Campbell, J. (1983). Self-definition and self-evaluation maintenance. In J. Suls & A. G. Greenwald (Eds.), *Psychological perspectives on the self* (Vol. 2). Hillsdale, NJ: Lawrence Erlbaum Associates.

Wills, T. A. (1981). Downward comparison principles in social psychology. *Psychological Bulletin, 90,* 245–271.

13

Understanding the Functions of Attitudes:
Lessons From Personality and Social Behavior

Mark Snyder
University of Minnesota

Kenneth G. DeBono
Union College

Within the domain of social psychology, no concept has enjoyed more attention, at both a theoretical and an empirical level, than the attitude construct. Indeed, it has been referred to as "the most distinctive and indispensable concept" in social psychology (Allport, 1935, p. 798). The centrality of the attitude construct is reflected in the many and diverse theoretical statements it has spawned. In the past 50 years, researchers have developed theories of attitude formation (Bem, 1967, 1972; Staats & Staats, 1958), attitude structure (Bem, 1972; Fishbein & Ajzen, 1975; Heider, 1958; Kothandapani, 1971), attitude change (Festinger, 1957; Hovland, Janis, & Kelley, 1953; McGuire, 1969; Osgood & Tannenbaum, 1955; Petty & Cacioppo, 1981, 1986; Sherif & Hovland, 1961; Sherif & Sherif, 1967; Zajonc, 1968), and attitude-behavior relations (Bem, 1967; Fazio & Zanna, 1981; Norman, 1975; Snyder, 1982; Zanna, Olson, & Fazio, 1980).

FUNCTIONAL THEORIES

Perhaps the most intriguing set of theories concerning attitudes remain the most empirically impoverished (Kiesler, Collins, & Miller, 1969). These theories concern the motivational bases of attitudes and are referred to collectively as the functional theories of attitudes (Katz, 1960; Katz & Stotland, 1959; Sarnoff & Katz, 1954; Smith, Bruner, & White, 1956). They address the simple, yet important, issue of why people hold the attitudes they do.

Functional theories propose that people maintain their attitudes for specific reasons. In particular, they posit that certain individualistic needs are being met by attitudes; that is, attitudes allow people to successfully execute plans and achieve goals. The most intriguing proposal of functional theories is the notion that the same attitude may serve very different functions for different people. This possibility has tremendous implications, particularly in the domain of persuasion. It suggests that, although people may maintain similar attitudes, the persuasive conditions that must be satisfied to alter those attitudes may be quite different, because it is hypothesized that, to successfully change an attitude, one must specifically address the function that is being served by the attitude (e.g., Katz, 1960).

Theorists working within the functional tradition have typically suggested four distinct functions that attitudes can perform (Katz, 1960; Smith, Bruner, & White, 1956). Although the precise name and nature of the functions varies across theoretical statements, the general nature of the functions proposed is sufficiently similar to allow the following taxonomy to be used.

Ego-Defensive

At times, it is proposed, people need to protect themselves from accepting truths about themselves that are particularly undesirable or threatening. To do so, they may develop attitudes by means of the classic psychodynamic defense mechanisms, such as projection or reaction formation (Freud, 1946). For example, a particularly prejudiced person may wish to repress these feelings and may do so through the defense mechanism of reaction formation, by forming a favorable attitude toward a very liberal political candidate.

Knowledge

People cannot possibly take account of every detail they encounter in their social worlds. Thus, to give meaning to objects, they need to organize information in an efficient manner. One strategy is to categorize objects on the basis of limited information and use attributes associated with general categories to make judgments about specific objects. This is the essence of the knowledge function; attitudes so formed represent attempts to impose organization on an otherwise potentially chaotic world.

Value Expressive

Attitudes serving a value expressive function allow a person to express his or her own true self, that is, his or her underlying values, dispositions, or personality. For example, a voter may support a particular political candidate because that candidate stands for and believes in ideas that the voter holds dear. That is, by favoring this candidate, the voter is expressing his or her own values.

Social Adjustive

Attitudes may be formed on the basis of how well they help people behave in ways appropriate to the various reference groups that comprise their social networks. That is, people may maintain their attitudes because these attitudes allow them to fit into important social situations and allow them to interact smoothly with their peers. For example, a person may hold a positive attitude toward the candidate previously mentioned, not because doing so constitutes an expression of true inner values, but because adopting this attitude may make it easier to fit into and establish smooth interactions with friends and associates who favor this candidate.

The introduction of the functional approach to the study of attitudes initiated a flurry of research to test hypotheses derived from analyses of attitude functions. The majority of this activity focused on the ego-defensive function (e.g., Katz, McClintock, & Sarnoff, 1957; Katz, Sarnoff, & McClintock, 1956; McClintock, 1958; Stotland, Katz, & Patchen, 1959). In particular, Katz and his coworkers examined defensive motivations underlying negative attitudes towards Blacks and, in addition, attempted to change such prejudicial attitudes with experimental manipulations directed at their defensive functional bases.

In one study, Katz, McClintock, and Sarnoff (1957) assessed defensive orientations with a battery of devices, including projective tests (such as TAT cards and sentence completion tasks) and questionnaire measures (such as items selected from the MMPI and the F-scale). People classified as high, moderate, or low in defensiveness then read a communication that described the psychodynamic foundations of defense mechanisms, particularly as they related to prejudice. In accord with the researchers' expectation that this intervention would allow people to gain some insight into defensive motivations underlying their prejudicial attitudes, there were some indications that moderately defensive people did alter their views toward Black people after reading the message.

Although the initial investigations of the functional theories met with moderate success (for a review, see Kiesler, Collins, & Miller, 1969), interest in this approach to the study of attitudes waned as quickly as it had waxed. Indeed, the past 20 years has seen little empirical research associated with functional theories. This decline of interest in functional approaches is, we believe, attributable to several factors, some intrinsic to the functional theories themselves, others more a part of the intellectual climate of the times in psychology.

The first, and perhaps the most important source of disenchantment, is an empirical matter. A major stumbling block in the paths of functionally oriented researchers has been the ability of the functional theories themselves to be tested empirically (Kiesler, Collins, & Miller, 1969). The problem, quite simply, has been the persistent difficulty experienced by researchers when they have tried to identify, on an a priori basis, what functions are being served by people's attitudes. After all, in an experimental setting, to adequately address hypotheses derived from functional theories, researchers need to know the functions being served by individuals' attitudes before any manipulations are attempted. The a priori identification of the functional bases of individuals' attitudes, however, has proved to be a difficult hurdle to leap. Uncertainties and ambiguities concerning the reliabilities and validities of some of the assessment devices used to identify functions (e.g., the specific applications of the TAT cards and sentence completion tasks) may have added height to this hurdle.

For example, among the early indicators of attitude function was the F-scale, used to classify people in terms of defensiveness. Unfortunately, in studies where it was used, this measure was often confounded with the attitudes of concern, namely racial prejudice. That is, high scorers on the F-scale tend to be highly prejudiced people and low scorers tend to be relatively unprejudiced people. As a consequence, people classified by researchers as high in defensiveness often were highly prejudiced and those classified as low in defensiveness were less prejudiced (Keisler, Collins, & Miller, 1969). Therefore any successes associated with this measure are not unambiguously supportive of functional speculations. After all, a central tenet of the functional approach is that the same attitude may serve different functions. Because, in the case of defensiveness and prejudicial attitudes, defensive and nondefensive people may differ in their degree of prejudice, it can hardly be said that they are holding the same attitudes for different functional reasons.

The limits of such research paradigms became apparent in the context of larger concerns about the study of attitudes and persuasion. The late 1960s and early 1970s were marked by a general dissatisfaction with persuasion and persuasion related phenomena as areas of psychological study (Eagly, 1987; McGuire, 1985). Reliable persuasion findings were increasingly difficult to obtain, and findings that did seem robust were often subject to numerous competing interpretations. Moreover, no general framework or theory appeared to be able to incorporate and make sense of these findings. As a result, researchers turned their efforts to more fruitful ventures and interest in persuasion declined; and, in something akin to guilt by association, interest in the functional theories also declined.

The waning of interest in functional theories of attitudes was further exacerbated by the emergence of the cognitive perspective in social psychology. Although some (e.g., Zajonc, 1980) have argued that social psychology has always been cognitive, the introduction in the 1960s of the attributional approaches to social psychological phenomena vaulted the cognitive perspective to a position of prominence in the field (Jones, 1985). Researchers began focusing their efforts on proposing, developing, and testing primarily cognitive explanations for social psychological events. As a consequence of this cognitive revolution in social psychology, attention to and interest in motivational explanations in social psychology declined precipitously (see also, Fiske & Taylor, 1984). As if tarred by the unfashionable motivational brush, so too did the decidedly motivational flavor of the functional approaches to attitudes and persuasion lose its appeal.

If this chapter were written early in the 1980s, one would be tempted to play umpire, call "three strikes—you're out!", and send the functional theories on their way. Fortunately, however, we are nearing the end of the 1980s, the times have changed, and an umpire would now have good reason to think again before calling those strikes against the functional batter. Interest in motivational processes is on the rise, partially due to recent concerns with motivated strategies in social cognition (e.g., Showers & Cantor, 1985). Concern for persuasion and attitude change is also on the rise, largely due to the emergence of global theoretical frameworks for conceptualizing attitude change (e.g., Petty & Cacioppo, 1986) and the relations between attitudes and behavior (e.g., Zanna, Higgins, & Herman, 1982). With the changing climate of the times removing the second and third strikes, it remains to consider how to remove the first strike called against the functional theories—how to identify the functions served by attitudes and hence systematically evaluate the utility of the functional approach to attitudes and persuasion. That task has been the ultimate goal of our program of theoretical and empirical explorations of attitudes and persuasion, and, hence, provides the central theme of this chapter.

A STRATEGY FOR INVESTIGATING FUNCTIONS

Given the potential importance of the motivational underpinnings of people's attitudes, how can we overcome the difficulties that historically have plagued the functional theories? One strategy to overcome these difficulties is to identify categories of people for whom attitudes may be serving different functions. Such a strategy reflects a larger, global strategy for the study of links between personality and social behavior. According to this strategy, one seeks to identify contrasting categories of people who typically manifest contrasting behavioral orientations in social situations, with the members of these contrasting categories then serving as subjects for investigation of the processes that account for these contrasting orientations. (For elaboration, see Snyder & Ickes, 1985).

Thus, by identifying people who typically manifest the phenomenon or process of concern, one gains access to candidates for investigating the psychology of that phenomenon or process. That is, identifying those people is undertaken, not as an end in itself, but rather as a means toward the end of understanding the phenomenon or process. Viewed from the perspective of this investigative strategy, to study the functional underpinnings of attitudes one would attempt to identify contrasting categories of people for whom attitudes might be serving different functions. Once identified, members of these categories could then serve as candidates for investigating the functional underpinnings of attitudes, particularly if their differing functional bases are part of a larger, more generalized syndrome of differing orientations to social situations and interpersonal events.

Are there, then, types of people for whom attitudes may be serving different functions? Consider the implications of empirical studies and theoretical formulations of the psychological construct of self-monitoring (Snyder, 1974, 1979, 1987), which suggest that it may be one construct that can be used to study attitudinal functions. High self-monitors (identified by their relatively high scores on the Self-Monitoring Scale) typically strive to be the type of person called for by each situation in which they find themselves. They are concerned about, and are adept at, tailoring their behavior to fit social and interpersonal considerations of situational appropriateness. To the extent that the characteristic interpersonal orientation of high self-monitors is one of fitting themselves to their social circumstances, this interpersonal orientation may also include social attitudes that are formed on the basis of how well they serve the ends of behaving in ways appropriate to the various reference groups that make up their social circumstances. As such, the attitudes of high self-monitors may, in the language of the functional theories, be serving a *social adjustive* function.

By contrast, low self-monitors (identified by their relatively low scores on the Self-Monitoring Scale) typically do not attempt to mold their behavior to fit situational and interpersonal considerations of appropriateness. Rather, these people tend to guide their behavioral choices on the basis of relevant inner sources (such as values, feelings, and dispositions) and are concerned that their behavior in social contexts be accurate reflections of underlying values, feelings, and dispositions. To the extent that the characteristic interpersonal orientation of low self-monitors is one of choosing behaviors to accurately reflect and meaningfully communicate their own personal attributes, that interpersonal orientation may also include attitudes formed on the basis of how well they reflect, express, and communicate more fundamental underlying values. As such, the attitudes of low self-monitors may, once again in the language of the functional theories, be serving a *value expressive* function.

This strategy, borrowed from the study of personality and social behavior, has generated a series of empirical investigations of the functional bases of attitude and persuasion. It also has stimulated theoretical inquiry, designed to place the findings of these investigations in the context of a larger, more global conceptual framework for understanding the interplay of features of persons, situations, and attitudes in the reemergence of the functional perspective. Let us examine, first, this research and, then, the theoretical analysis.

EMPIRICAL INVESTIGATIONS: DIFFERENT
FUNCTIONS FOR DIFFERENT PEOPLE

In our earliest research guided by this investigative strategy, we examined attitudinal functions in the context of the psychology of advertising and consumer behavior. Two prevalent approaches to advertising (the *soft sell* and the *hard sell*; Fox, 1984) provided a vehicle for investigating the functional bases of attitudes and persuasion. Members of the soft sell school typically create ads that appeal to the *images* that consumers may gain and project by using the product. One prominent instance of image-oriented advertising is the Marlboro man, who projects the rugged masculine image of the man who smokes Marlboro cigarettes. Members of the hard sell school typically create rather different ads, based on claims about the inherent *quality,* the intrinsic merit, and the functional value of the product. The long-running series of "Pepsi challenge" taste test ads (which dramatize the supposedly superior taste of Pepsi) are clearly examples of advertising based on claims about product quality.

As we contemplated the psychological mechanisms that render each of these advertising strategies successful, we were intrigued by the possibility that the different advertising strategies are appealing to different *functional* bases of attitudes. In particular, the soft sell approach, with its appeals to images, may be primarily influencing people for whom attitudes serve a social adjustive function, as its image appeals may allow such people to perceive that a product has the potential to create images appropriate to various social circumstances. By contrast, the hard sell approach may be particularly influential with people for whom attitudes serve a value expressive function. Information about product quality may be readily interpreted by those people in terms of underlying values and other evaluative reactions.

Appeals to Image, Claims About Quality

If these conjectures are correct, then people high and low in self-monitoring should be differentially responsive to ads that promise images and to those that feature product quality. To investigate these possibilities, we created ads that, in pictures and words, represented image-based and product-quality messages to consumers. We have advertised products as diverse as coffee and cars, whiskies and shampoos, and cigarettes. In some studies (Snyder & DeBono, 1985), we used sets of magazine advertisements, each containing two ads for a particular product that were identical in all respects save one—the written message associated with the picture. One message highlighted the *image* associated with the product; the other stressed the product's *quality.* For example, in a set of advertisements for Canadian Club whisky, the picture prominently displayed a bottle of Canadian Club resting on a set of house blueprints. The written copy for the image-oriented ad stated, "You're not just moving in, you're moving up." The product-quality-oriented ad claimed "When it comes to great taste, everyone draws the same conclusion."

Reactions to these advertisements revealed that high self-monitors thought the image-oriented ads were better, more appealing, and more effective. Moreover, they were willing to pay more for a product if its advertising appealed to considerations of image, and they were more likely to try a product if it was marketed with an image orientation. By contrast, low self-monitors reacted more favorably to product–quality-oriented ads. They were willing to pay more for a product if its advertising stressed the product's quality, and were likely to try a product if claims were made about its quality.

The differing kinds of persuasion involved in advertising are also revealed by people's reactions to ads involving endorsements and testimonials. For example, the race car driver who lends his expertise about things automotive to this or that brand of motor oil may be most influential with low self-monitoring consumers, who might weight his credibility highly in their judgments of the oil's quality. But the movie star who lends her aura to this or that brand of coffee may be most impressive to high self-monitoring consumers, who may be attracted to the image-fashioning potential of being identified with such an alluring figure.

Indeed, there is some support for these notions. In one study (Snyder & Miene, 1987), college undergraduates examined a profile of a fictitious person who would be giving a testimonial endorsement, either for a stereo headset or for a camera. Half read a profile of a person with a socially attractive personal image and the other half read a profile of a person possessing expertise with the product endorsed. These profiles contained no information or ad slogans about the product itself; the profile was simply paired with the name of the product. A content analysis of free responses to these profiles revealed that low self-monitors demonstrated a clear preference for an endorser with expertise, whereas high self-monitors showed a clear preference for an attractive endorser. Within a functional framework, the preference for expertise may be interpreted in terms of a value expressive function of attitudes toward consumer products, and the preference for an attractive image may be seen as consistent with a social adjustive function underlying such attitudes (see also, DeBono & Harnish, in press).

In our attempts to interpret the findings about the effectiveness of advertising messages, we have relied on speculations about the functional underpinnings of consumer attitudes. Soft sell, image-oriented advertising campaigns may succeed in engaging and motivating the image-making and social adjustive concerns of high self-monitoring consumers. Hard sell, claim-oriented advertising campaigns may be effective in engaging and motivating the product-quality and value expressive concerns of low self-monitoring consumers. For a discussion of issues in the practical implementation of these findings, see Snyder and DeBono (1987).

Persusasion and Social Influence

Although they are certainly suggestive and highly informative, the results of studies of the psychology of advertising provide only indirect evidence that the attitudes of high and low self-monitors may be serving different functions. The messages associated with the various advertisements focus on implications or consequences of holding value expressive or social adjustive attitudes, but not on the actual functions themselves. More direct evidence that attitudes may be serving different functions for different people would be provided by studies involving interventions designed to directly engage particular functions. For instance, what would happen if people learned that their present attitudes did not accurately reflect important values or, in other words, that they did not serve a value expressive function? What would happen if people learned that their attitudes were not shared by their friends or by members of important peer reference groups, that is, that their attitudes did not serve a social adjustive function? Are high and low self-monitors differentially responsive to such interventions?

Such questions of inquiry represent, perhaps, the most compelling way to experimentally test a functional theory. Such a test operates on the assumption that a message directed at the particular function an attitude is serving should be maximally effective in producing attitude change. Therefore, to provide the strongest test that attitudes are indeed serving different functions for different people, one would attempt to change an attitude by persuading a person that the attitude in question no longer serves its function. A study by DeBono (1987) employed precisely this approach, and provided relatively direct evidence of the role of attitude functions in persuasion and social influence.

In DeBono's study, college students listened to a tape of a professor speaking on various aspects of mental illness. Typically, students in this study were generally favorable toward the deinstitutionalization of the mentally ill before they heard the professor's message. Students randomly assigned to the *social adjustive* experimental condition heard the professor describe a survey revealing that 70% of college students favored treating the mentally ill in state hospitals and institutions, that 23% favored treatment at the community level in half-way houses, and that 7% had no opinion. That is, these students learned their support of deinstitutionalization was out of step with the majority of their peers. Those assigned to the *value expressive* condition heard him present the results of research suggesting that the values of loving and responsibility (values that *all* participants in the study rated as relatively important to them) underlie favorable attitudes toward the institutionalization of the mentally ill, and that the values of imaginativeness and courageousness (values they all rated relatively unimportant) underlie favorable attitudes toward the deinstitutionalization of the mentally ill. Thus, these students learned that their stance on deinstitutionalization was at odds with values they considered important as guides to behavior.

After listening to the professor, all students reported their personal attitudes toward the care, housing, and treatment of the mentally ill. In accord with the hypothesized social adjustive function of their attitudes, *high* self-monitoring students were particularly influenced by the message that played upon *social adjustive* concerns, reporting attitudes more favorable toward the institutionalization of the mentally ill than after hearing the value expressive message. And, in keeping with the hypothesized value expressive function of their attitudes, *low* self-monitoring students were more influenced by the message that addressed itself to *value expressive* concerns, stating more favorable attitudes toward institutionalization than after hearing the social adjustive message.

These results highlight the utility of adopting a functional approach to the study of persuasion and social influence. They suggest that the persuasion settings necessary for successful social influence may indeed need to be very different for different people. That is, people may have different motivational bases for maintaining their attitudes. In particular, these results strongly suggest that the attitudes of high and low self-monitoring individuals toward the care of the mentally ill are serving social adjustive and value expressive functions, respectively. Moreover, for a persuasive message to have its maximal impact, these motivations must be identified and addressed. In this context, in addition to establishing the discriminant validity for attitude functions as they relate to the self-monitoring construct, DeBono's (1987) study suggests that the most compelling persuasive communications will be those directed at the functional underpinnings of relevant attitudes.

The Question of Process

In addition to having implications for the persuasiveness of attitudinally relevant communications, DeBono's (1987) study and subsequent research suggest that depending on their functional relevance, people may process communications differently (DeBono & Harnish, in press; DeBono & Packer, 1988; DeBono & Snyder, in press). That is, when a communication is placed in a functionally relevant context, the strategies people use to evaluate the information presented appear to be markedly different from those used when a similar message is placed in a nonfunctionally relevant context. For example, DeBono (1987) found that, although presentation of a functional cue (e.g., your peers disagree) with no opportunity to elaborate on or systematically process the issue relevant arguments was sufficient to precipitate attitude change, this type of cue can have effects unlike most persuasion cues (e.g., source attractiveness) previously studied; to the extent that issue relevant arguments are present and individuals have the opportunity to carefully process them, people do not simply use the cue and disregard the arguments supporting the new attitude position. Rather, they tend to process the arguments in a careful, systematic, and critical manner. This state of affairs suggests that, to the extent they are able to do so, people pay close attention to, and are motivated to spend considerable cognitive effort on all aspects of messages perceived as functionally relevant.

Additional evidence in support of this notion is provided by DeBono and Harnish (in press). In their study, in addition to manipulating the functional relevance of a message, they varied the quality of the arguments supporting the new attitude position. Their results suggest that people may indeed be sensitive to the quality of the message arguments supporting a functionally relevant position, because participants in this experiment demonstrated more agreement if the position was buttressed by strong and compelling arguments than if by weak and specious ones. Moreover, there was evidence that individuals were more likely to think about and systematically process the message arguments when they were presented in a functionally relevant context than when presented in a nonfunctionally relevant context. Thus, although the specific conditions differentiating these possibilities have yet to be delineated, the results from the DeBono (1987) and DeBono and Harnish (in press) studies suggest that a functional approach to persuasion appears to represent (in contemporary parlance) a peripheral route to persuasion (DeBono, 1987), but at other times, a more central route (DeBono & Harnish, in press).

Differences in the ways people evaluate functionally relevant information are apparent not only for messages directly addressing attitude functions, but also for more indirect appeals. In particular, differences appear when people are presented with information in the form of advertisements. Just as Snyder and DeBono's (1985) advertising research indicates that people for whom attitudes serve different functions are differentially responsive to different advertising appeals, recent studies suggest that the inferences people make concerning a product's quality also may be dependent on the manner in which it is advertised. For example, DeBono and Snyder (in press) found that high self-monitoring individuals perceived an attractive car to be of a higher quality than an unattractive car, whereas low self-monitoring individuals judged the unattractive car to be of higher quality, even though the objective evidence concerning the cars' quality (here, ratings from *Consumer's Report*) was identical. In addition, DeBono and Packer (1988) demonstrated that high self-monitoring individuals perceived a product (e.g., a cassette tape) to be of higher quality if it was advertised with an image appeal as opposed to a product quality appeal; by contrast, low self-monitoring individuals perceived the quality of a product to be higher if it was marketed with a product-quality orientation. Taken together, these studies suggest that advertising appeals directed at the functional bases of people's attitudes are not only likely to engender attitude change, but also to affect their interpretation of information regarding the products' quality. In particular, it appears that, to the extent that a product is advertised in a manner congruent with the functional bases of individuals' attitudes, they tend to perceive that product as having high quality. Furthermore, they tend to interpret any subsequent information in line with their perceptions.

Studies such as these represent first steps toward understanding the mechanisms and processes by which the functional bases of people's attitudes are implicated in their judgments, evaluations, and actions. They suggest that the manifestations of these functional underpinnings are pervasive, and touch the cognitive, affective, and behavioral domains.

THEORETICAL CONSIDERATIONS: BUILDING
AN INTEGRATIVE CONCEPTUAL FRAMEWORK

At the outset, we characterized our strategy of inquiry as one borrowed from the domain of personality and social behavior. In this strategy, researchers try to identify categories of people who typically manifest the phenomena of concern to them. That is, this strategy dictates that many of the phenomena of personality and social behavior can be understood by focusing on people who typically display those phenomena. After first identifying categories of people who typically manifest the phenomenon under consideration, researchers can then use these people to investigate the psychology of that phenomenon. In our case, we used this strategy to identify categories of people whose attitudes typically serve social adjustive and value expressive functions.

At this point, we should recognize that much remains to be accomplished to fully realize this strategy. So far, only one vehicle for identifying the attitudinal functions typical of particular categories of people (i.e., self-monitoring) has been documented, and only two functions of attitudes (i.e., value expressive and social adjustive) have been examined using this vehicle. yet, evidence is accumulating of the generality of these functional orientations across attitude domains (e.g., Herek, in press; Jamieson & Zanna, chap. 15 in this volume; Kristiansen & Zanna, 1986a, 1986b). Nevertheless, we recognize the need for empirical evidence of the generality of this approach across functions and across personality domains. Elsewhere (see Snyder & DeBono, 1987), we have speculated about vehicles to identify types of people for whom other functions are characteristically served by their attitudes. This suggests that people high in need for cognition (Cacioppo & Petty, 1982) may be particularly likely to hold attitudes that serve a knowledge function and that the attitudes of people with authoritarian personalities (Adorno, Frenkel-Brunswik, Levinson, & Sanford, 1950) may typically serve ego defensive functions (although research on this hypothesis may need to take account of some of the problems, associated with assessing defensiveness, noted earlier). Moreover, we recognize that theoretical and empirical considerations may suggest other candidates, in addition to the four traditionally associated with functional approaches, for inclusion in analyses of attitude functions; assuming of course that it can be demonstrated that any newly proposed functions do capture truly distinct motivational underpinnings of attitudes.

Elsewhere, too, we have acknowledged that the strategy we have practiced has relied on relatively *indirect* indicators of function (Snyder & DeBono, 1987). We recognize the need for direct indicators of attitude functions such as those developed by Herek (1986) as well. Yet, we wish to underscore the virtues of indirect indicators. Consider the example of our own research. Because the psychological construct of self-monitoring was not developed specifically to characterize attitudinal functions, it is of necessity an indirect indicator. Self-monitoring is concerned, at its theoretical core, with attentiveness and responsiveness to situational and dispositional guides to action. However, the evidence does suggest that one of the many features of the generalized psychological orientations tapped by self-monitoring is attitudinal functions. Therefore, we are dealing with an indirect indicator that does allow differences in attitude function to be placed in the larger psychological context of these generalized orientations and in the larger conceptual network of self-monitoring theory (Snyder, 1987). More generally, it is such larger interpretive contexts that may be the chief benefit of working with relatively indirect indicators.

It is perhaps the grounding of the present research in the larger theoretical and interpretive context provided by the self-monitoring construct that may account for why our approach to studying attitude functions has worked as reliably as it has. Students of the literature on personality and persuasion are well aware of the conflicting sets of results and nonresults in this domain (cf. McGuire, 1968), in the context of which our converging findings may seem to be a refreshing change of pace. Generalizing from the case of our research (recognizing the potential hazards of generalizing from lone instances), we would expect that studies of personality and persuasion will work to the extent that they engage generalized psychological orientations whose networks of theoretical propositions permit clear derivations about attitudes and persuasion. Because "generalized psychological orientations," are, by definition, broader and more extensive than the domain of attitudes and persuasion (as vast as those domains may be), it is highly likely that the strategy of relatively indirect indicators will frequently provide linkages between personality processes and attitudes, persuasion, and social influence.

The particular personality and social behavior strategy we have worked with in our research, because it relies on the explanatory power of stable and enduring psychological orientations, is often referred to as the *dispositional* strategy (Snyder & Ickes, 1985). It is, however, but one of a family of strategies for studying personality and social behavior, the other members of that family being the *interactional* and the *situational strategies* (Snyder & Ickes, 1985). The interactional strategy, guided by the assumption that much of the variation in social behavior is attributable to interactions between personal dispositions and situational factors, seeks to identify moderating variables to specify instances in which dispositions will or will not influence behavior. The situational strategy, designed to cope with the dynamic interplay between individuals and situations, focuses on the processes by which properties of individuals guide their choices of social situations and their subsequent behavior in these chosen situations. For elaborations of these characterizations, see Snyder and Ickes (1985).

Often, in studies of personality and social behavior, there occurs (what amounts to) a sequential progression through the strategies. Inquiry often begins with the dispositional strategy, then proceeds to the interactional strategy, and then moves on to the situational strategy—with the net effect being an increasingly precise and sophisticated understanding of personality and social behavior. Thus far, we have approached questions about the functional bases of attitudes and persuasion from the vantage point of the dispositional strategy. As well as this strategy has served us, we can nevertheless readily imagine an evolutionary progression of strategies leading to a more elaborated and better articulated theoretical perspective on the functions of attitudes.

The Moderating Influences of Attitudes and Situations

Consider the functions of attitudes viewed from the vantage point of the interactional strategy for studying personality and social behavior. A (if not *the*) fundamental proposition of the functional theories is that the same attitude may serve different functions. Applying the interactional strategy, one would seek moderating variables that define the limiting conditions of this proposition—when it holds and when it does not. At least two kinds of moderating variables can, in principle at least, be specified: those dealing with the *attitudes* whose functions are of concern to investigators, and those dealing with the *situations* in which these attitudes are to be investigated.

Some attitudes may be capable of serving a wide variety of functions. For different types of people, racial prejudice, for example, may serve ego-defensive functions (allowing them to cope with their fears of inferiority by denigrating others), knowledge functions (turning a complex world into a simple one in which they think they can "know" people by knowing their race), value expressive functions (supporting a value system that dictates inequality and inequity of opportunity), and social adjustive functions (helping them get along and get ahead with others who harbor such prejudices). Other attitudes, by contrast, may be capable of serving a somewhat narrower range of functions. Some attitudes may even serve one and only one function. For example, although it is almost self-evident that favorable attitudes toward aspirin serve a knowledge function (it is, after all, a drug with a wide range of indicated uses, and attitudes toward its medicinal value may summarize those uses), it is hard to see how (at least for the typical person) attitudes toward aspirin could serve ego-defensive, value expressive, or social adjustive functions.

Only to the extent that attitudes are capable of serving multiple functions will it be possible to verify the fundamental tenet of functional theories. Only then will it be possible to identify classes of people whose attitudes typically serve one or another function. In other words, properly speaking, the functional theories (at least their fundamental tenet that the same attitude may serve different functions) apply only to attitudes that are capable of serving multiple functions. For this reason, we have heeded this prescription in our research. Thus, for instance, in studies of the psychology of advertising, we specifically chose products that could be advertised equally well with appeals to social adjustive and value expressive considerations (Snyder & DeBono, 1985). It remains, of course, to identify the moderating variables that specify the range of functions potentially served by particular attitudes. In this regard, Shavitt's theory (chap. 12 in this volume) of the functional "imperatives" inherent in attitude objects may prove useful in the quest for moderator variables.

Just as attitudes may vary in the functions they potentially can serve, so too can the situations in which attitudes operate vary in the functions they can engage. In situations with strong pressures for social comparison and/or social conformity, the attitudes people communicate (if not the ones they actually hold) may reflect social adjustive considerations. But, in situations that prompt a reflective, analytical, and introspective orientation, people may be particularly likely to display attitudes of a value expressive nature. Similarly, one can imagine situations (perhaps ones of great threat) particularly conducive to attitudes serving ego-defensive functions, and other situations (perhaps ones of uncertainty and need for informational clarity) highly supportive of knowledge-based attitudes.

To the extent that situations of each of these types are psychologically strong, they should permit little variability in the functional bases of attitudes displayed in them. Other situations, whose demands are less compelling, should be more conducive to multiple functions. It does, we recognize, remain to specify the precise moderating variables that define situations as ones limited to the operation of one particular function or those with the potential to engage multiple functions. Needless to say, it is this latter type of situation that has been of interest to us in our research. We have intentionally worked with situations in which it would be possible to observe some people responding as if motivated by social adjustive considerations and other people acting as if motivated by value expressive concerns. However, as we shall see, situations that tend to mandate particular functions do not fall outside the scope of our theoretical analysis of attitude functions. On the contrary, their importance is highlighted when the functions of attitudes are considered from the perspective of the situational strategy for studying personality and social behavior.

The Dynamic Interplay of Persons, Attitudes, and Situations

In its efforts to understand the dynamic interplay between individuals and situations, the situational strategy for studying personality and social behavior is particularly concerned with how people choose and influence situations (Snyder & Ickes, 1985). Central to the situational strategy is the premise that people typically have considerable freedom to choose where to be, when to be there, and with whom to be there. That is, the situations in which people operate are partially of their own choosing. A substantial body of research indicates that these choices of settings can and do reflect conceptions of self, beliefs, attitudes, values, traits, and dispositions, and other features of personal identity (Snyder, 1981; Snyder & Ickes, 1985).

How would investigators use the situational strategy to study attitude functions? First, they would identify types of situations that tend to engage specific functions. Next, they would identify categories of people who typically are found in these situations. Consider a more concrete example that is based on our own research on attitude functions. Theoretical and empirical considerations suggest that the attitudes of high self-monitors serve social adjustive functions and those of low self-monitors serve value expressive functions. We have already suggested features of situations that may define them as particularly likely to engage either social adjustive or value expressive functions. Working wth the situational strategy, researchers would seek evidence that people gravitate toward situations that are particularly conducive to holding and acting on attitudes reflecting their typical functions. That is, they would find out if high self-monitors choose situations that engage social adjustive functions, and low self-monitors choose situations that engage value expressive functions. If so, high and low self-monitors may find themselves operating in situations that support, maintain, and perpetuate their propensities to hold attitudes serving social adjustive and value expressive functions.

More generally, though, if we are now speaking of person factors, attitude factors, and situation factors, which—if any—of these determinants of attitude functions should be given primacy in our theoretical analysis? To be sure, we first examined the role of stable and enduring differences between people in their characteristic interpersonal orientations (as captured by the self-monitoring construct). Moreover, we have characterized features of attitudes and of situations as moderating influences that would determine when these differences in interpersonal orientation would be most likely to be manifested in the domain of attitude functions.

But, are we prepared to take the giant leap, to explicitly describe theoretical primacy to the role of these characteristic interpersonal orientations? Not quite yet. There is something we would like to know before committing ourselves on this issue. Recall our suggestion that people may gravitate toward situations conducive to their own typical attitude functions. Is it so? There is, of course, the well-documented propensity of individuals to choose situations supportive of their interpersonal orientations (Snyder & Ickes, 1985). Therefore, we *suspect* that people preferentially seek situations that promote attitudes that serve their own typical functions (or, at least, those situations that support attitudes serving multiple functions, including their own preferred function). But we do not yet *know* for sure that they do. If, however, people's characteristic interpersonal orientations do guide their choices of situations in this fashion, then these chosen situations will influence, in turn, the attitudes they hold. People who operate in environments that support attitudes serving a particular function will, it follows, tend to have repertoires of attitudes in which attitudes serving that function are particularly well-represented.

Thus, according to this line of argument, people's characteristic interpersonal orientations influence their choices of situations which then influence their repertoires of attitudes. That is, such an argument does suggest that properties of individuals be granted theoretical primacy in our analysis of the role of features of individuals, attitudes, and situations in understanding the functional underpinnings of attitudes and persuasion. But, until empirical evidence in support of this (no doubt controversial) argument is forthcoming, this conclusion should remain in the realm of speculation and conjecture.

CONCLUSION

At the outset of this chapter, we noted that interest in the functional approaches has waxed and waned over the years. That they initially rose to prominence, and that they are once again attracting attention, reflects the enduring importance of their central goal, that of discovering and understanding the psychological functions served by attitudes. That they lay dormant for so many years is due, we have suggested, to the difficulty of fulfilling their basic prerequisite—that of identifying a priori the functions served by specific attitudes of particular individuals. In our empirical and theoretical activities, we have worked to fulfill this prerequisite.

We began our inquiries into the functions of attitudes by identifying categories of people for whom we had theoretical reasons to believe that attitudes are serving different functions. We then used these people as vehicles for studying the dynamics of the functional bases of attitudes, persuasion, and social influence. However, as our attempt to place our research in the larger context provided by considerations of strategies for studying personality and social behavior reveals, our concerns are not limited to the role of differences between people in the functions typically served by their attitudes. On the contrary, in our theoretical analysis, we have pointed to the important moderating influences of types of attitudes (some attitudes may have greater potential than others to serve different functions for different people) and of kinds of situations (some situations may have greater potential than others to engage different functions in different people).

From our theoretical perspective, it should only be for these types of attitudes and in these kinds of situations that differences between individuals in their typical attitude functions can and will be observed. Admittedly, some of what we have had to say has a tentative tone to it, as it should have, as many of the propositions of our theoretical analysis await investigative scrutiny. In closing, let us underscore the fundamental lesson we believe personality and social behavior can and often does offer: Taking into account the dynamic interplay of features of individuals, of attitudes, and of situations may permit more precise specifications of the functional bases of attitudes, persuasion, and social influence. The functional approaches, long out of fashion, may once again be ready to claim the allegiances of new generations of basic and applied researchers.

ACKNOWLEDGMENTS

Some of the research discussed in this chapter was conducted with the support of the National Science Foundation, the Graduate School of the University of Minnesota, and the Internal Educational Fund of Union College.

REFERENCES

Adorno, T. W., Frenkel-Brunswik, E., Levinson, D. J., & Sanford, R. N. (1950). *The authoritarian personality.* New York: Harper & Row.

Allport, G. W. (1935). Attitudes. In C. A. Murchison (Ed.), *A handbook of social psychology* (Vol. 2). New York: Russell & Russell.

Bem, D. J. (1967). Self perception: An alternative interpretation of cognitive dissonance phenomena. *Psychological Review, 74,* 183–200.

Bem, D. J. (1972). Self-perception theory. In L. Berkowitz (Ed.), *Advances in experimental social psychology* (Vol. 6). New York: Academic Press.

Cacioppo, J. T., & Petty, R. E. (1982). The need for cognition. *Journal of Personality and Social Psychology, 42,* 116–131.

DeBono, K. G. (1987). Investigating the social-adjustive and value-expressive functions of attitudes: Implications for persuasion processes. *Journal of Personality and Social Psychology, 52,* 279–287.

DeBono, K. G., & Harnish, R. (in press). Source expertise, source attractiveness, and the processing of persuasive information: A functional approach. *Journal of Personality and Social Psychology.*

DeBono, K. G., & Packer, M. (1988). *The effects of image and quality based advertising on perceptions of product quality.* Unpublished manuscript, Union College, Schenectady, NY.

DeBono, K. G., & Snyder, M. (in press). Understanding consumer decision-making processes: The role of form and function in product evaluation. *Journal of Applied Social Psychology.*

Eagly, A. H. (1987). Social influence research: New approaches to enduring issues. In M. P. Zanna, J. M. Olson, & C. P. Herman (Eds.), *Social influence: The Ontario symposium* (Vol. 5). Hillsdale, NJ:Lawrence Erlbaum Associates.

Fazio, R. H., & Zanna, M. P. (1981). Direct experience and attitude-behavior consistency. In L. Berkowitz (Ed.), *Advances in experimental social psychology* (Vol. 14). New York: Academic Press.

Festinger, L. (1957). *A theory of cognitive dissonance.* Stanford: Stanford University Press.

Fishbein, M., & Ajzen, I. (1975). *Belief, attitude, intention, and behavior: An introduction to theory and research.* Reading, MA: Addison-Wesley.

Fiske, S. T., & Taylor, S. E. (1984). *Social cognition.* Reading, MA: Addison-Wesley.

Fox, S. (1984). *The mirror makers.* New York: Morrow.

Freud, A. (1946). *The ego and mechanisms of defense.* New York: International University Press.

Heider, F. (1958). *The psychology of interpersonal relations.* New York: Wiley.

Herek, G. M. (1986). The instrumentality of attitudes: Toward a neofunctional theory. *Journal of Social Issues, 42,* 99–114.

Herek, G. M. (in press). Can functions be measured: A new perspective on the functional approach to attitudes. *Social Psychology Quarterly.*

Hovland, C. I., Janis, I. L., & Kelley, J. J. (1953). *Communication and persuasion.* New Haven, CT: Yale University Press.

Jones, E. E. (1985). Major developments in social psychology during the past five decades. In G. Lindzey & E. Aronson (Eds.), *The handbook of social psychology* (3rd ed., pp. 47–107). New York: Random House.

Katz, D. (1960). The functional approach to the study of attitudes. *Public Opinion Quarterly, 24,* 163–204.

Katz, D., McClintock, C., & Sarnoff, D. (1957). The measurement of ego-defense as related to attitude change. *Journal of Personality, 25,* 465–474.

Katz, D., Sarnoff, D., & McClintock, C. (1956). Ego-defense and attitude change. *Human Relations, 9,* 27–45.

Katz, D., & Stotland, E. (1959). A preliminary statement to a theory of attitude structure and change. In S. Koch (Ed.), *Psychology: A study of a science* (Vol. 3, pp. 423–475). New York: McGraw-Hill.

Kiesler, C. A., Collins, B. E., & Miller, N. (1969). *Attitude change: A critical analysis of theoretical approaches.* New York: Wiley.

Kothandapani, V. (1971). Validation of feeling, belief, and intention to act as three components of attitude and their contribution to prediction of contraceptive behavior. *Journal of Personality and Social Psychology, 19,* 321–333.

Kristiansen, C. M., & Zanna, M. P. (1986a). *Justifying attitudes by appealing to values: A functional perspective.* Unpublished manuscript, University of Waterloo, Waterloo, Ontario.

Kristiansen, C. M., & Zanna, M. P. (1986b). *The value-expressive function of attitudes.* Unpublished manuscript, University of Waterloo, Waterloo, Ontario.

McClintock, C. G. (1958). Personality syndromes and attitude change. *Journal of Personality, 26,* 479–593.

McGuire, W. J. (1968). Personality and susceptibility to social influence. In E. F. Borgatta & W. W. Lambert (Eds.), *Handbook of personality and theory and research.* (pp. 1130–1187). Chicago: Rand McNally.

McGuire, W. J. (1969). Nature of attitudes and attitude change. In G. Lindzey & E. Aronson (Eds.), *The handbook of social psychology* (2nd ed., Vol. 3), Reading, MA: Addison-Wesley.

McGuire, W. J. (1985). Attitude and attitude changes. In G. Lindzey & E. Aronson (Eds.), *The handbook of social psychology* (3rd ed., pp. 223–346). New York: Random House.

Norman, R. (1975). Affective cognitive consistency, attitudes, conformity, and behavior. *Journal of Personality and Social Psychology, 32,* 83–91.

Osgood, C. E., & Tannenbaum, P. H. (1955). The principle of congruity in the prediction of attitude change. *Psychological Review, 62,* 42–55.

Petty, R. E., & Cacioppo, J. T. (1981). *Attitudes and persuasion: Classic and contemporary approaches.* Dubuque, IA: Wm. C. Brown.

Petty, R. E., & Cacioppo, J. T. (1986). The elaboration likelihood model of persuasion. In L. Berkowitz (Ed.), *Advances in experimental social psychology* (Vol. 19, pp. 123–205). New York: Academic Press.

Sarnoff, D., & Katz, D. (1954). The motivational bases of attitude change. *Journal of Abnormal and Social Psychology, 49,* 115–124.

Sherif, M., & Hovland, C. I. (1961). *Social judgment: Assimilation and contrast effects in communication and attitude change.* New Haven, CT: Yale University Press.

Sherif, M., & Sherif, C. W. (1967). Attitudes as the individual's own categories: The social judgment-involvement approach to attitude and attitude change. In C. W. Sherif & M. Sherif (Eds.), *Attitude, ego-involvement, and change.* New York: Wiley.

Showers, C., & Cantor, N. (1985). Social cognition: A look at motivated strategies. *Annual Review of Psychology, 36,* 275–305.

Smith, M. B., Bruner, J. S., & White, R. W. (1956). *Opinions and personality.* New York: Wiley.

Snyder, M. (1974). The self-monitoring of expressive behavior. *Journal of Personality and Social Psychology, 30,* 526–537.

Snyder, M. (1979). Self-monitoring processes. In L. Berkowitz (Ed.), Advances in experimental social psychology (Vol. 12). New York: Academic Press.

Snyder, M. (1981). On the influence of individuals on situations. In N. Cantor & J. F. Kihlstrom (Eds.), *Personality, cognition, and social interaction.* Hillsdale, NJ: Lawrence Erlbaum Associates.

Snyder, M. (1982). When believing means doing: Creating the links between attitudes and behaviors. In M. P. Zanna, E. T. Higgins, & C. P. Herman (Eds.), *Consistency in social behavior: The Ontario symposium* (Vol. 2). Hillsdale, NJ: Lawrence Erlbaum Associates.

Snyder, M. (1987). *Public appearances/Private realities: The psychology of self-monitoring.* New York: W. H. Freeman and Company.

Snyder, M., & DeBono, K. G. (1985). Appeals to images and claims about quality: Understanding the psychology of advertising. *Journal of Personality and Social Psychology, 49,* 586–597.

Snyder, M., & DeBono, K. G. (1987). A functional approach to attitudes and persuasion. In M. P. Zanna, J. M. Olson, & C. P. Herman (Eds.), *Social influence: The Ontario symposium* (Vol. 5). Hillsdale, NJ: Lawrence Erlbaum Associates.

Snyder, M., & Ickes, W. (1985). Personality and social behavior. In G. Lindzey & E. Aronson (Eds.), *The handbook of social psychology* (3rd ed.). New York: Random House.

Snyder, M., & Miene, P. (1987, May). *Evaluating the source of a persuasive message: Applying a functional approach to the study of attitudes.* Paper presented at the annual meetings of the Midwestern Psychological Association, Chicago, IL.

Staats, A. W., & Staats, C. K. (1958). Attitudes established by classical conditioning. *Journal of Abnormal and Social Psychology, 57,* 37–40.

Stotland, E., Katz, D., & Patchen, M. (1959). The reduction of prejudice through the arousal of self-insight. *Journal of Personality, 27,* 507–531.

Zajonc, R. B. (1968). Attitudinal effects of mere exposure. *Journal of Personality and Social Psychology Monograph Supplement, 9,* 1–27.

Zajonc, R. B. (1980). Cognition and social cognition: A historical perspective. In L. Festinger (Ed.), *Five decades of social psychology* (pp. 180–204). New York: Oxford University Press.

Zanna, M. P., Higgins, E. T., & Herman, C. P. (Eds.). (1982). *Consistency in social behavior: The Ontario symposium* (Vol. 2). Hillsdale, NJ: Lawrence Erlbaum Associates.

Zanna, M. P., Olson, J. M., & Fazio, R. H. (1980). Attitude-behavior consistency: An individual difference perspective. *Journal of Personality and Social Behavior, 38,* 432–440.

14

Beliefs as Possessions:
A Functional Perspective

Robert P. Abelson
Yale University

Deborah A. Prentice
Yale University

Lately there have been strong hints of a rebirth of interest in functional theories of attitudes. This class of theories, initiated long ago by Brewster Smith and Daniel Katz (Katz, 1960, 1968; Smith, 1947; Smith, Bruner, & White, 1956), posits that people hold and express certain attitudes and beliefs because doing so meets psychological needs, which vary from one individual to another. This interesting motivational view has been in long eclipse in the literature, partly because it flies in the face of the dominant information processing paradigm of social cognition (Hastie, 1983; McGuire, 1986; Wyer & Srull, 1984), partly because there have been no clear methods for measuring the several functions that attitudes might serve, and perhaps partly due to theoretical confusion as to what particular functions to distinguish.

Lately the pendulum is swinging away from the "cognitive imperialism" (Tomkins, 1981) of the last 20 years and toward an interest in motivation and emotion (e.g., Abelson, 1983; Isen, 1984; Zajonc, 1980). Social psychologists may be ready to seriously consider the functional properties of attitudes. Fortunately , recent suggestions may have changed the measurement picture. Both Herek (1986) and Shavitt (chap. 12 in this volume) demonstrated that reliable and valid coding schemes exist for identifying attitude functions from subjects' protocols concerning attitude objects, and Herek (1986) and Abelson (1988) formulated direct questions of respondents for the same function identification purpose.

As for the theoretical confusion, it cannot yet be said that clarity is upon us, but there is the hopeful sign that all function theorists seem to agree on at least one major functional dichotomy. On the one hand, there is an experiential or instrumental function, based on the direct benefits actually or potentially provided by the attitude object, and on the other hand, an expressive or symbolic function, by which attitudes toward the object are used as a means for expressing self-identity. This distinction is similar to the one made by Kinder and Sears (1981, 1985), who distinguish *self-interest* politics from *symbolic* politics in their analysis of the bases of public opinion.

Several theorists elaborate these two broad categories variously. On the instrumental side, Katz (1960) distinguished a *knowledge* function from an instrumental function, whereas Smith, Bruner, and White (1956) listed only an *object-appraisal* function. The Katz distinction has not endured, and we consider only a single instrumental function in this chapter. Within the symbolic category, however, two subfunctions can be usefully separated: a *social adjustment* function and a *value expressive* function. These symbolic subfunctions are discussed further later in the chapter.

Shavitt (chap. 12 in this volume) notes that the two major functions do not reside only in individuals; attitude objects can also be distinguished according to whether they are typically used instrumentally or symbolically. Thus, attitudes toward air conditioners presumably are based upon their benefits and costs, whereas attitudes toward the flag spring from patriotic feelings.

Many individuals develop passionate beliefs about matters that are remote from their personal experience, such as whether sanctions should be used against South Africa, or whether UFOs are real, or whether life begins at conception. Often such beliefs are tenaciously held, and seem impervious to persuasive argumentation. Because the common sense function of beliefs is to orient the individual to real world contingencies so as to guide everyday behavior, cases of deep personal involvement with distant causes or conjectures present something of a theoretical puzzle.

Of course, the functional theories of attitudes have long taken this phenomenon for granted. The garden variety, instrumental purpose of beliefs and attitudes is regarded to be what Smith, Bruner, & White (1956) called *object appraisal.* But symbolic purposes can also be served by beliefs and attitudes, requiring only a tenuous connection with reality factors. Personality needs and family experiences, for example, can be inappropriately projected into the drama of politics, as in the case of Smith, Bruner, and White's (1956) respondent who had many thoughts and feelings about the Soviet Union comparable to those he had about his grandmother. Such projections have been discussed by Lasswell (1930), Hoffer (1951), McClosky (1967), Roseman (1986), Tomkins (1963), and many others.

The purpose of this chapter is to take a fresh look at the symbolic versus instrumental distinction, by regarding people's orientations toward belief and attitude objects as consistent with their orientations toward their *possessions.* The starting point for our analysis comes from Abelson's (1986) position paper entititled, "Beliefs are like possessions." We first present that theoretical position, and then show how it illuminates the functional aspects of beliefs and attitudes.[1]

BELIEFS ARE LIKE POSSESSIONS

People express their identities through transactions with objects in their environments. The objects and transactions can be physical, as in people's uses of material possessions, or they can be verbal, as in the contemplation and expression of ideas and beliefs. Physical and mental transactions are both aspects of self, and it is our working supposition that these two aspects are connected. In other words, people tend to behave similarly (in senses to be defined) toward their possessions and toward their beliefs. As Abelson (1986) observed, various common linguistic expressions suggest posses-sionlike aspects of belief: we inherit or adopt opinions, we cherish or cling to our beliefs, and under duress we may surrender our principles or lose our beliefs. Like possessions, beliefs can be acquired in various ways, and are often displayed to sympathetic audiences. Their possessors frequently be-come highly attached to them, and resist giving them up.

Developmentally, children build up a representation of themselves based partly on people and things (parents, siblings, house, clothes, toys, school, etc.) in their daily experience, and partly on verbal and nonverbal symbols connected to those people and things: family name, photographs, jokes, stories, school banners, report cards, pictures tacked on the refrigerator, slogans on the bedroom wall, and so on. The self is captured both by mental and physical objects, often in combination. (See McGuire & Padawer-Singer, 1976).

We further speculate that the possession orientation tends to be primary, the belief orientation secondary. Children learn a great deal about posses-sions and possessing before they learn about beliefs. They learn early about things being "mine," and how that permits one to store them, use them, and possibly embellish them. It is only later that children are able to appreciate what it means for something to be "my belief," and what that implies for using it and embellishing it. It is our hypothesis that children and teenagers learn many of the properties of believing by generalizing from the proper-

---

[1]The terms *belief* and *attitude* are used more or less interchangeably in this chapter. Sidestepping the definitional quagmire surrounding these two concepts, we simply take an attitude to be an evaluative belief, a belief that some social object or policy is good or bad, right or wrong. Attitudes are typically accompanied with affect, and possibly also with action tendencies, but so are nonevaluative beliefs (e.g., belief that psychic phenomena exist), so that the distinction between the two terms is not one we care to emphasize.

ties of possessing. This is especially apt to be true for beliefs about remote sociopolitical objects, not amenable to reality testing.

Of course, different people have different developmental experiences, which could differentially affect the ways in which they learn about beliefs from their possessions. From an individual differences perspective, it is tempting to hypothesize that, in adult life, personal style of interacting with physical objects tends to be similar to style vis-a-vis mental objects. For example, a person who clings tenaciously to old possessions might also cling tenaciously to old beliefs; an individual who easily gets bored with possessions, forever trading them in for new ones, could well also be very inconstant in his or her beliefs; a person who cherished possessions with sentimental value might also cherish beliefs with symbolic significance; and so on.

The last of these hypothesized connections has recently been explored in our research, and we turn now to the relevant evidence.

Evidence for Consistent Individual Differences

Results from several studies have provided support for the notion of individual consistency in the functions served by mental and physical objects (Prentice, 1987a, 1987b). As a first result we were interested in identifying the psychological functions served by people's material possessions, taking as a point of departure the symbolic-instrumental distinction found in the attitude literature. Previous research by Csikszentmihalyi and Rochberg-Halton (1981) provided evidence that a similar distinction can be made in the possessions domain. These authors interviewed people about their favorite possessions and found that respondents' cherished objects fell into two categories: possessions that facilitate enjoyment (including televisions and stereos), and possessions that provide meaning and continuity in one's life and family (including family heirlooms and gifts). In addition to their own empirical work, Csikszentmihalyi and Rochberg-Halton cited sociological and anthropological evidence for the importance of instrumental and symbolic functions of possessions across societies and cultures. On the basis of these findings, our first study was designed to verify the significance of this particular dichotomy, and also to identify any other important sources of psychological benefit that people derive from their possessions.

We compiled a list of 70 valued possessions by asking college students to describe their five favorite possessions. Another group of students sorted these possessions into piles of objects "similar in their source of value." The resulting matrix of dissimilarity judgments summed across subjects was analyzed using multidimensional scaling. Our hypothesis was that the symbolic and instrumental functions would appear as one or two dimensions of the scaling solution. We interpreted the four-dimensional scaling solution by inspection of the objects loading at the ends of each polarity. We then collected ratings of each possession on bipolar scales representing the hypothesized dimension labels and regressed mean scale ratings of objects over the scaling solution. These regression results validated our subjective interpretations. (See Prentice, 1987b, for a more complete description of the scaling and interpretation procedures.)

Table 14.1 shows the possessions loading at the poles of each of the four dimensions. The first and most important dimension distinguished symbolic or self-expressive possessions, like a diary and family heirlooms, from instrumental possessions, like a stereo and a computer. These results replicate the primary distinction between types of possessions found by Csikszentmihalyi and Rochberg-Halton (1981) and provide a parallel to the symbolic and instrumental functions found in the attitude domain. The self-expressive polarity contains objects that give individuals a sense of continuity as well as objects that provide meaning and self-expression. The instrumental polarity contains possessions that have direct benefits, both for enjoyment and for improved functioning in the environment.

The remaining three dimensions contain elements of self-expression, but also suggest additional functions that possessions can serve. The second dimension contrasted recreational possessions, including toys and other objects from childhood, from practical possessions, such as a coat or contact lenses. The third dimension distinguished cultured possessions, like musical instruments and a script of *Hamlet,* from everyday possessions, like cooking utensils and a bed. Finally, the fourth dimension contrasted prestigious possessions, including golf clubs and formal clothes, from common possessions, like a coffee maker and a camera. These recreational, cultured, and prestigious dimensions may represent additional functions of material possessions, a conjecture supported by the work of Csikszentmihalyi and Rochberg-Halton (1981). Whether they correspond to analogous functions of belief objects, as the belief-possession metaphor would predict, remains untested.

With this evidence that the symbolic and instrumental functions are important to the way people organize their experience with physical objects, our next study was designed to examine individual consistency in functional orientation across mental and physical objects. Individuals who had listed their favorite possessions in the scaling study were classified into symbolic and instrumental possession groups by averaging the first dimension weights for each subject's five favorite possessions; those subjects with an average above zero were considered symbolic possessors, whereas those with an average below zero were considered instrumental possessors. All individuals received persuasive communications on six unfamiliar issues, including fetal alcohol syndrome, education for disabled children, statehood for Puerto Rico, and the pros and cons of state taxation. Each appeal

TABLE 14.1
Multidimensional Scaling Solutions for Possessions

Scaling Solutions	Weight
Dimension 1	
"Positive" polarity[a]: Self-expressive possessions	
Family heirlooms	1.88
Diary	1.84
Locket	1.81
Souvenirs	1.75
Photographs	1.68
Bible	1.65
Gifts from family members	1.57
Old letters	1.54
"Negative" polarity[a]: Instrumental possessions	
Stereo	−1.87
Walkman	−1.80
Computer	−1.72
Television	−1.60
Meal Card	−1.47
Boots	−1.46
Bicycle	−1.44
Sweatshirt	−1.40
Dimension 2	
"Positive" polarity: Recreational possessions	
Star Wars toys collection	2.14
Comic book collection	2.08
Model airplanes	1.99
Major league baseball bat	1.98
Eagle Scout award	1.89
Sports awards	1.84
Stuffed animals	1.48
"Negative" polarity: Practical possessions	
Futon	−1.47
Umbrella	−1.45
Credit cards	−1.42
Wallet	−1.33
Coat	−1.22
Contact lenses	−1.20
Watch	−1.19

TABLE 14.1
(Continued)

Scaling Solutions	Weight
Dimension 3	
"Positive" polarity: Cultured possessions	
Script of Hamlet	2.04
Art books	1.93
Musical instruments	1.92
Poetry books	1.87
Complete works of Shakespeare	1.84
Ballet clothes	1.78
Yale academic papers	1.68
Paintings	1.61
"Negative" polarity: Everyday possessions	
Cooking utensils	−1.48
Refrigerator	−1.45
Bed	−1.43
Telephone	−1.37
Quilt	−1.24
Family pets	−1.22
Family house	−1.20
Dimension 4	
"Positive" polarity: Prestigious possessions	
Golf clubs	1.64
Formal clothes	1.62
Collection of jewelry	1.56
Sailboat	1.49
Pearls	1.42
Exeter chair	1.31
Credit cards	1.12
"Negative" polarity: Common possessions	
Coffee maker	−1.34
Camera	−1.33
Electric typewriter	−1.31
Fireplace	−1.28
Own artwork	−1.23
Meal Card	−1.10
Popcorn popper	−1.02

[a]The labels of positive and negative to describe the polarities of each of the four dimensions have no substantive meaning regarding the nature of the possessions themselves. They correspond to the sign of the dimension weights and simply indicate that the listed possessions were located at opposite poles of the dimension.

presented a description of the issue, a proposed course of action, and four arguments supporting that course of action. Two sets of materials for each issue were created: one proposed a symbolically toned resolution, with arguments expressing widely shared and symbolic values (such as freedom of choice) the resolution would uphold; the other proposed an instrumentally toned course of action, with arguments expressing outcomes from the plan that would be directly and instrumentally beneficial. After reading the appeal for each issue, subjects rated how favorable they felt toward the proposal. Each participant received three instrumental and three symbolic communications. (For a more detailed description of these materials, see Prentice, 1987b.) We predicted a Possession Group X Appeal Type interaction, with people who valued symbolic possessions favoring symbolic appeals over instrumental appeals, and people who valued instrumental possessions favoring instrumental appeals over symbolic appeals.

The mean favorability of participants in each possession group toward each type of appeal is shown in Table 14.2. The predicted Possession Group X Appeal Type interaction was significant; individuals who favored symbolic possessions were more favorable toward symbolic appeals and less favorable toward instrumental appeals than instrumental possessors. It is important to note, however, that consistency in orientation across domains was limited to the symbolic group. Individuals who valued instrumental possessions did not respond differently to instrumental and symbolic appeals. This asymmetry may result from the very nature of instrumentality. Although any object, mental or physcial, could be used as a symbol or means of self-expression, instrumentality implies a more direct link between the object and its beneficial outcomes. The distal, unfamiliar issues used in the present study may not have been sufficiently based in immediate personal realities to engage this instrumental function.

In our final study, a priming manipulation was introduced to require people to focus on either their instrumental or their symbolic possessions.

TABLE 14.2
Group Means for Symbolic and Instrumental Attitude Measures

Possession Group	Type of Proposal	
	Symbolic	Instrumental
Symbolic	5.21	4.22
Instrumental	4.53	4.57

Note. 1 = Not at all favorable; 7 = Very favorable.

Of particular interest was the effect of priming people who favored instrumental possessions to focus on their symbolic possessions. We predicted that people primed symbolically would demonstrate the differential favorability toward symbolic appeals shown in Study 2, regardless of their initial orientation. Priming people instrumentally was expected to have little or no effect on initial possession orientation; this condition was expected to replicate the interaction in the previous study.

The materials and procedure were the same as in the previous study with three exceptions. First, two issues were added to the attitude materials, so that each subject read four instrumental and four symbolic appeals. Second, their favorite possessions were assessed using a questionnaire that presented them with the list of 70 objects collected in the first study and asked them to select their five favorites. Third, the priming manipulation was introduced before the attitude materials. After participants had completed the possession questionnaire, the experimenter told each person to describe either "the possessions that you have that represent important things in your life or that express who you are" or "the possessions that you have that are very useful to you, either for enjoyment or for getting things done." Half of the participants received each prime, and they spent about 5 minutes talking about their possessions before going on to complete the attitude measures. (For more details, see Prentice, 1987a.)

The top panel of Table 14.3 shows the mean favorability of participants who were primed instrumentally, by possession group, toward each type of appeal. This condition replicated the previous study, with individuals in the symbolic possession group responding more favorably toward symbolic appeals and less favorably toward instrumental appeals than the instrumental possessors. On the other hand, the results for participants who were primed symbolically, illustrated in the bottom panel of Table 14.3, did not show the Possession Group X Appeal Type interaction. Regardless of their general functional orientation toward possessions, people who were induced to think about their self-expressive physical objects favored symbolic appeals over instrumental appeals. These results strongly suggest that priming individuals to think about their symbolic possessions influences their general orientation across the domains of possessions and attitudes.

In summary, these studies have provided evidence for the importance of the symbolic-instrumental distinction in the functions served by material possessions and for systematic differences in the receptiveness toward different styles of argument by people who favor symbolic versus instrumental objects. The results have also underscored the remarkable consistency of the symbolic orientation: Whether subjects were inclined to favor their self-expressive possessions when they entered the experiment or

TABLE 14.3
Group Means for Symbolic and Instrumental Attitude Measures

Possession Group	Type of Proposal	
	Symbolic	Instrumental
Instrumental Prime Condition		
Symbolic	5.21	3.68
Instrumental	4.42	3.94
Symbolic Prime Condition		
Symbolic	5.21	3.90
Instrumental	4.83	3.45

Note. 1 = Not at all favorable; 7 = Very favorable.

were told to focus on their self-expressive possessions as part of an experimental manipulation, they consistently favored symbolic appeals over
instrumental appeals. Our future work on individual differences in possession and attitude functions will focus on three areas: developing a better
understanding of the instrumental function; relating our particular interpretations of these functional oreintations to such constructs as self-
monitoring (Snyder, 1974; Snyder & DeBono, 1985, chap. 13 in this
volume) and self-consciousness (Fenigstein, Scheier, & Buss, 1975); and
exploring individual consistency across domains in the functions suggested
by the second, third and fourth dimensions of the possession scaling solution.

THE BENEFITS AND COSTS OF BELIEFS

In the second half of this chapter, we return to the beliefs/possessions
metaphor from a perspective going beyond individual differences in functional orientation. In this broader perspective, we consider what features of
beliefs make them valuable to their holders. What are the benefits and costs
of a belief as a possession?

Possessions can be bought and sold, and can therefore be characterized
with economic concepts such as supply and demand, fair price, and so
on.Beliefs, on the other hand, seem to be free for the taking: When person A
gets a belief from person B, person B still has it. Having suffered no loss, B
exacts no charge for the transaction (and, in fact, may be pleased by A's

acquisition of the belief because this represents a "spreading of the word"). Accordingly, any potential model of a "belief market" would seem to be unlike models of usual economic markets. Beliefs vary in value, and therefore there would be variations in demand for a given belief; supply, however would be unlimited for people exposed to the belief. Therefore there is no market mechanism for establishing a price for a belief.

Although beliefs do not follow the market economics of value in relation to supply and demand, we argue that they do follow the personal economics of purchase (i.e., adoption) in relation to cost and benefit. In the next section we consider the psychological costs and benefits accruing to beliefs. These costs and benefits are not always identical to those from possessions, but the metaphor helps structure our analysis.

Sources of Belief Cost

There would seem to be costs associated with *changing* a belief, and costs associated with *expressing* a particular belief. In changing a belief, we should distinguish between adopting a belief and abandoning one.

There could be an "opportunity cost" for belief adoption; that is, other potential beliefs might have to be forsworn in order to take on a particular belief. Such a case is discussed by Batson & Ventis (1982), wherein recruits to a cult are more or less aware that in adopting the cult's beliefs they must relinquish any potential future beliefs incompatible with the cult's lifestyle. The type of cost implicated in belief abandonment is *sunk cost:* If an individual has spent energy or shown commitment on behalf of a set of beliefs, it may be quite difficult to abandon some of them in favor of new beliefs inconsistent with the rest of them.

Indeed, there is a general mechanism operating to produce opportunity costs and sunk costs for beliefs, quite apart from the question of interbelief consistency, namely, a need for identity maintenance. Individuals are aware that if they publicly endorse a controversial view at one moment, they will appear somewhat foolish if they renounce it (without some widely acknowledged reason) at a later moment. Other people become nervous about us if we change parts of our identities too often, and beliefs express parts of our identities (which in large measure is why they are "like possessions"). Identity change, besides unsettling other people, causes anxiety in ourselves. As Minsky (1986) said, "One function of the Self is to keep us from changing too rapidly" (p. 42). Thus, people may in general be cautious about adopting new beliefs, but once they adopt them (or even appear to adopt them, as in dissonance theory experiments in the Festinger & Carlsmith (1959) tradition), they are especially loathe to abandon them.

There is an interesting parallel phenomenon involving the gain or loss of possessions—the so-called "reluctance to trade" (Knetsch, Thaler, & Kahneman, 1987), or "endowment effect." With personal goods, the price at which people are generally willing to sell exceeds by far the price at which they are willing to buy the same article. This phenomenon is apparently well-known and somewhat vexing to classical microeconomic theorists (who wouldn't predict it).

In the basic paradigm used by Knetsch and his colleagues (1987), in a recent experimental demonstration, some subjects in a group setting were randomly designated as owners and potential sellers of a Cornell coffee mug, and some as potential buyers. Sellers far overpriced their mugs relative to what the buyers were offering, or what uninvolved subjects regarded as a fair price. From the fact that this tendency did not change on repeated trials, the experimenters inferred that the sellers were not misrepresenting for bargaining purposes. Rather, they appeared genuinely reluctant to part with their possession, probably because they were somewhat uncertain of its true value to them, and feared that if they parted with it, it might turn out to have had its maximum rather than minimum value. (This theoretical account calls to mind Langer's (1975) finding that, under appropriate conditions, subjects demand two to four times the price they paid for a lottery ticket before they will sell it.) Knetsch and his colleagues (1987) based this explanation on the "loss aversion" phenomenon (Tversky & Kahneman, 1981) specified in Kahneman and Tversky's (1977) prospect theory. This parallel with a possessions effect lends additional credence to our interpretation that it is anticipated regret—the fear of looking and feeling foolish—that restrains people from too frequent belief change.

Anticipated regret might be blunted and change made easier, if it were simple to *undo* the change. However, the undoing of belief change is not gracefully done—especially a double undoing. In adopting a belief, one might occasionally take comfort in the thought that one could conceivably backtrack later ("If I don't like Scientology, I'll give it up."). But if one is contemplating abandoning a belief, an anticipated undoing of the abandonment would be extremely tortured ("I've tried Scientology already, but if I give it up I can always try it again."). From this point of view, belief abandonment is more aversive than belief adoption—an asymmetry that also applies to the possessions case, where it is the seller rather than the buyer who balks at the deal.

Apart from the costs of changing a belief, there may be costs associated with expressing (or even simply holding) a belief. A major type of cost arises from potential damage to one's social acceptance. Deviant beliefs of many kinds can bring on ridicule; unacceptable beliefs can give rise to feelings of shame in the holder. Overly extreme beliefs, although they may have certain benefits discussed in the next section, may convey naivete, overzealousness, or other unadmired traits. At this point, little is known about the circumstances determining the resolution of the dilemma of holding a costly belief, whether it be abandoning the belief, keeping it "in the closet," or strengthening it because of reactance, dissonance reduction, or an assertive attempt to transcend suffering (Tomkins, 1965).

Sources of Belief Benefit

Belief costs seem to be general in nature, but the situation with benefits is different. As with physical possessions, sources of benefit of beliefs and attitudes are tied to their functions. We have already considered the crucial distinction between instrumental and symbolic functions, but actually there are *three* major functions addressed by various functional theories of attitudes (Herek, 1986; Katz, 1960; Smith, Bruner, & White, 1956). Beyond the instrumental function of providing tangible prospective rewards to the individual, the symbolic functions of social identification and value expression may be distinguished. Of these two symbolic functions, the first defines the social group anchorage of the individual, and the second, the nature of the individual's values. Symbolically, one's attitudes and beliefs, like one's possessions, signal who one is and what one stands for. These two symbolic functions, although conceptually separable, might often be simultaneously served by a given belief—or by a particular possession—because social groups tend to form around shared values. The social identity and value expression functions were apparently conflated in our possession scaling solution of Table 14.1. For example, a Bible could be valued because one finds personal inspiration from it, and/or because it marks one's membership in a valued church group. Similarly, a family heirloom might remind one of a cherished grandmother and/or of the ancestral continuity of the Smythe-Joneses.

The functional theories, although emphasizing that attitudes serve the individual's purposes, do not articulate the implication that different attitudes and beliefs could serve these purposes in greater or lesser degree. This is the implication we stress in belief possession theory. For each of the major functions, different properties of beliefs govern the degree to which the function is satisfied. We discuss what these properties might be for the respective functions of social identification, value expression, and instrumental reward. This discussion is speculative and exploratory.

Benefits from the Social Identification Function

Let us first consider the social identification function of beliefs, and the degree to which a belief might acquire benefit by serving that function. Maximum value would be achieved if a belief were highly and stably characteristic and important for a group of people with whom the individual was identified. We call this property *badge value.* Intrinsically, badge value is socially shared. To the extent that my friend (or churchmate, etc.) is known to have true conviction on an issue, it motivates me to adopt the same conviction. If I do, that reinforces his or her belief. A similar social reinforcement loop obtains for those physical possessions that people want to show off to earn approval (or envy) from friends and neighbors. Keeping up with the Joneses implies that the Joneses will keep up with you (status being equal). Adoption of aerobies or VCRs tends to occur in social clusters, as does support for capital punishment or for a particular political party, and so forth. In the case where the social group in question is a major part of the individual's permanent identity, such as an ethnic group, a whole cluster of interrelated beliefs may have high badge value. Prominent among such beliefs might be stereotypic conceptions of outgroup members, as emphasized in the social identity theory (Tajfel, 1981) of prejudice.

The concept of badge value requires amplification. In an earlier article on beliefs as possessions (Abelson, 1986), the property of "sharedness" was intended to capture the effect of social consensus on belief benefit. This does not seem to be quite apt. As part of an unpublished study by Abelson, Brown, and Ewing, respondents were asked to estimate what proportion of their friends agreed with their views on divestment in South Africa, nuclear energy, and the existence of God. These estimates were then correlated with their own strengths of conviction on the three respective issues. The results did not support the simple hypothesis that belief would be stronger when social consensus is seen as higher. For divestment, the correlation between perceived sharedness and strength was .48; for nuclear power, however, only .12; for belief in God, .00. A plausible conjecture about this pattern of correlations is that only when an issue is "hot" (as divestment was in New Haven at the time of the survey) does strength of conviction correlate with sharedness. Thus, it is not necessary to feel strongly to impute sharedness to one's beliefs. Indeed, there is a general tendency to perceive probable social agreement with even the most trivial of one's opinions—the "false consensus effect" (Ross, Greene, & House, 1977). What is needed for badge value is the perception that the people one cares about not only agree with a belief, but consider it central and important— and are even concerned with whether or not *you* agree with it. Thus the terminology of the "badge." The badge value of a belief will increase if it is displayed forcefully (perhaps in an extreme version) to members of one's group.

A second clarification has to do with steady states versus trends in belief. Compare the impact for an individual of knowing that 60% of her friends hold a given view, with the case where only 40% do now, but converts are being added at a rate of 5% a month. Research strongly suggests that, although steady state information on the opinions of others typically has very little impact, (especially on old, familiar issues) opinion trend information is quite powerful. Marsh (1985) used (bogus) reports of general public opinion poll data for this demonstration, but there is every reason to suppose that it would apply even more to information about the views in one's close social circle.[2]

The rationale is twofold. First, belief *change* information is newsworthy and attention-getting, whereas information about the status quo is usually less interesting. Second, the information that people are changing their beliefs diminishes the costs inherent in belief change. If my friends are adopting a new belief, it conveys the message that they are not concerned about the risk that they might later have to recant—the belief must really be worth more than the opportunity costs of self-commitment. In a related vein, if my friends are giving up an old belief we used to share, I can be reassured that despite the sunk costs, I need not feel foolish abandoning it.

Benefit from the Self-expressive Function

For the self-expressive function of beliefs, several properties, applicable also to the self-expressive functions of possessions, are relevant to belief benefit.

In some contrast to the group identification function, self-expressive functions may be served without social involvement. One may hold a belief because, privately, it makes one feel hopeful, or because it accords with one's sense of what is right, or for other personal reasons, without necessarily ever discussing the issue with others. Typically, however, we would expect that expressive values would be amplified through social interaction. As with the kick many individuals get from showing off prize possessions, many people are quick to sound off about their pet notions.

Value-centrality concerns the degree to which a given belief expresses deeper, more fundamental beliefs. An isolated belief is less personally satisfying, and easier to give up, than one linked into a network of other beliefs, particularly more generic, higher-order values. (This is akin to the comparison between a knick-knack and the centerpiece in furnishing a room). This point seems more or less obvious in principle, but in practice, knowing whether a given belief were central for an individual would require knowing not only his or her values but the relationship, if any, between the belief and those values. Thus, for example, although it is not clear whether artists

---

[2]In an observation years ago on the dramatic last-week trends in presidential primaries, Abelson (1968) noted in his "Triple Trend Law" that trends tend to snowball in a bandwagon effect. More recently, in an unpublished study of Stanford students on the issue of divestment of stock in South Africa, Jeremy Cohen found that estimates of percent of campus support for one's position did not correlate significantly with willingness to sign a petition, but that estimates of campus *trend* did correlate significantly with such willingness.

in general would find any special benefit from believing in psychic phenomena, a particular artist who associated telepathic powers with the necessary summoning of creative juices might well find such beliefs appealing.

By *emotional force* we mean the power of the belief to evoke strong feelings in the individual. Those feelings may be hope or pride or anger or fear. In other words, they need not necessarily be positive; but the stronger the feeling, the more the belief has expressive benefit to the individual. As the research of Roseman, Abelson, and Ewing (1986) suggests, some individuals may be especially prone to adopt and maintain beliefs expressive of sympathy, whereas others may be prone toward angry beliefs, and so on. (In this respect, beliefs seem to allow a greater range of possibilities than do valued possessions, which primarily evoke pride.) The match between temperament and expressive beliefs is what Tomkins (1965) called *ideo-affective resonance*. As with centrality, the conception here is clearer than the methodology with which to track it, because the particular emotional relevance of different beliefs is heavily an individual matter.

A third property controlling the degree of expressive benefit of beliefs is *self-enhancement*. To the extent that the belief makes the individual look good to self and others, benefit will be derived from holding it. Enhancement could derive from the apparent nobility, or rectitude, or ingenuity of the belief. The distinction between value-centrality and self-enhancement is that the grounds for the latter could be extrinsic, and unrelated to the individual's values. As with possessions, an individual might self-consciously manage a favorable impression in the eyes of others by adopting beliefs that in themselves seemed original, (Maslach, Stapp, & Santee, 1985) or chic, or profound, without any necessary connection to the individual's other beliefs. Nor need there be correspondence with the beliefs of the social audience, as obtains for beliefs serving a social identity function.

Benefits from the Instrumental Function

An instrumental belief concerns the consequences of some action, policy, or state of affairs. It specifies the likelihood that certain valued or disvalued end states will come about or be prevented (Rosenberg, 1956; Fishbein, 1963). Like a useful possession, a useful belief is one that guarantees well-being when the time for its application arrives. In other words, for the possessor of an instrumental belief, the most appealing situation would be one of subjective certainty that a highly desirable outcome would ensue (if the appropriate steps were taken).

However, in at least two respects, instrumental beliefs are not quite like toasters or stereos. For one thing, the ideas to which beliefs refer may not be applicable as often or be as controllable as possessions. An unemployed electronics worker may believe that tariffs against Japanese imports would restore many opportunities for his or her own employment, but both the tariffs and the jobs are spread out unpredictably in time, are incompletely communicated, and have an indirect relationship with one another. Secondly, beliefs, unlike physical objects could be unwarranted; their very existences are insecure, because they could turn out to be wrong. The effect of both of these types of uncertainty surrounding beliefs is to enhance the role of argumentation in the maintenance of belief benefit. The holder of the instrumental belief would like to be able to persuade others (and have others reassure him or her) that its promised rewards are indeed forthcoming and valuable.

The features relevant to this purpose we call *defensibility* and *wishfulness*. Defensibility refers to the ease with which it can be argued that the recommended means will lead to the promised end. Sometimes supporting arguments can be checked against a reasonably accessible reality. For example, whether taking vitamin C inhibits catching colds in winter is testable on a personal basis (albeit such tests may be subject to illusory correlation and other biases). Thus a fan of vitamin C might say, "It prevents colds. I know this for sure because I've been taking it for five years, and I haven't had a cold in all that time."

On many issues, however, reality is rather remote. The supporter of capital punishment may argue that it has a deterrent effect on crime, without being able to recount relevant statistical evidence. Instead, the argument may adopt the presumed causal reasoning that criminals contemplating deadly assault will think twice under threat of the death penalty. Subjectively, rhetorical supports are valuable not in terms of any necessary connection with canons of evidence, but in terms of their acceptability among people with whom the individual is likely to discuss the issue.

Wishfulness is an obvious source of benefit for instrumental beliefs, and indeed, some of the most popular beliefs are highly wishful. A national survey taken in 1983 indicated that 68% of the American public believe in an afterlife (General Social Surveys, 1983, p. 97). In a 1985 CBS/*New York Times* poll, 62% of the public endorsed the proposition that a "Star Wars" missile defense system could work (Graham & Kramer, 1986). Of course, there are constraints on the acceptance of wishful beliefs. The chief problem is that the promised outcomes may simply not be credible in the eyes of the general public. In other words, wishfulness can trade off against credibility. Over 70% of the American public, for example, believe that their chances of surviving a nuclear war are poor (Gallup, 1983). Why one belief should invite skepticism and another uncritical acceptance is a challenging question. One plausible speculation (though not the whole story) is that mystically mediated positive outcomes that cannot be refuted (such as the afterlife and Star Wars) are defensible on grounds of faith, whereas con-

cretely mediated negative outcomes with a well-publicized basis in reality
are harder to deny.

Summary and Discussion of Variables Determining Belief Benefit

We have outlined a preliminary list of six properties related to belief
benefit: badge value, serving the social identity function; value centrality,
emotional force, and self-enhancement, relevant to the self-expression function; and defensibility and wishfulness, pertaining to the instrumental function.

The first of these properties, badge value, arises differentially for different
population subgroups. A belief with badge value for one subgroup generally
lacks badge value for other subgroups—indeed, bundles of uniquely endorsed major beliefs are a large part of what generates and sustains subgroups. Political or social messages advancing beliefs with high badge value
for a given subgroup are therefore likely to be double-edged, appealing
greatly to individuals within that subgroup, while alienating or leaving
indifferent those in other subgroups.

Meanwhile, properties serving the self-expressive function are potentially variable from individual to individual in two distinct ways. First, different
individuals may have different values, so that a belief that is consonant with
the values of one person may be antagonistic to the values of another.
Second, even when particular values—such as freedom, peace, brother-
hood, and so forth—are widely shared, some individuals may be much more
sensitive than others to appeals to those values. Indeed, that was essentially
the conclusion of our study summarized in Table 14.2. The "symbolic
possessors"—but not the "instrumental possessors"—were significantly
more susceptible to idealistic appeals than to instrumental appeals. In terms
of the present discussion, it is as though some individuals (the symbolic
possessors) more readily search for the central value implications of persuasive appeals, or are more sensitive to emotional evocation, or are more
prone to self-enhancement through the endorsement of popular values.
Which of these possibilities, if any, pertains to symbolic possessors, is a
question awaiting further research.

The situation with the belief properties serving the instrumental function
is somewhat different. The attractiveness of an instrumental belief is relatively less likely to vary from one individual to the next than is the
attractiveness of a symbolic belief. People who differ extremely on ideological grounds can sometimes—though not always—converge on pragmatic
considerations. An instrumental belief position that is highly defensible for
one individual in general tends to be defensible for other individuals. But
defensibility varies considerably from one belief to another, and for the
same belief from one time period to another depending on circumstances.

The same can be said about wishfulness as about defensibility. Various federal policies—for example, social security, or welfare supports, or foreign aid—are at one time viewed by a majority to be worthy and practical, and at another time as wasteful and unworkable.

Thus, much as is the case with benefits from possessions, belief benefits sometimes act like "main effects," with some beliefs being generally of more benefit than others, and sometimes are interactive with characteristics of individuals or of historical periods. These complexities seem to be a necessary accompaniment of the rich possibilities of a functional analysis.

REFERENCES

Abelson, R. P. (1968). Computers, polls, and public opinion—some puzzles and paradoxes. *Transaction, 5,* 20–27.

Abelson, R. P. (1983). Whatever became of consistency theory? *Personality and Social Psychology Bulletin, 9,* 37–54.

Abelson, R. P. (1986). Beliefs are like possessions. *Journal for the Theory of Social Behavior, 16* (3), 223–250.

Abelson, R. P. (1988). Conviction. *American Psychologist, 43,* 267–275.

Batson, C. D., & Ventis, W. L. (1982). *The religious experience: A social-psychological perspective.* New York: Oxford University Press.

Csikszentmihalyi, M., & Rochberg-Halton, E. (1981). *The meaning of things: Domestic symbols and the self.* New York: Cambridge University Press.

Fenigstein, A., Scheier, M. F., & Buss, A. H. (1975). Public and private self-consciousness: Assessment and theory. *Journal of Consulting and Clinical Psychology, 43,* 522–527.

Festinger, L., & Carlsmith, J. M. (1959). Cognitive consequences of forced compliance. *Journal of Abnormal and Social Psychology, 58,* 203–210.

Fishbein, M. (1963). An investigation of the relationship between beliefs about an object and the attitude toward that object. *Human Relations, 16,* 223–240.

Gallup Poll (1983). *Gallup Poll 1983.* Wilmington, DE: Scholarly Resources.

General Social Surveys (1983). *General social surveys, 1972–1983: Cumulative codebook.* Chicago: National Opinion Research Center.

Graham, T. W., & Kramer, B. M. (1986). The polls: ABM and Star Wars. *Public Opinion Quarterly, 50,* 125–134.

Hastie, R. (1983). Social inference. *Annual Review of Psychology, 34,* 511–542.

Herek, G. (1986). *Can functions be measured? A new perspective on the functional approach to attitudes.* Unpublished manuscript, Yale University, New Haven, CT.

Hoffer, E. (1951). *The true believer.* New York: Harper.

Isen, A. M. (1984). Toward understanding the role of affect in cognition. In R. S. Wyer Jr. & T. K. Srull (Eds.), *Handbook of social cognition.* Hillsdale, NJ: Lawrence Erlbaum Associates.

Kahneman, D., & Tversky, A. (1977). Prospect theory: An analysis of decisions under risk. *Econometrica, 47,* 263–291.

Katz, D. (1960). The functional approach to the study of attitudes. *Public Opinion Quarterly, 24,* 163–204.

Katz, D. (1968). Consistency for what? The functional approach. In R. P. Abelson, E. Aronson, W. J. McGuire, T. M. Newcomb, M. J. Rosenberg, & P. H. Tannenbaum (Eds.), *Theories of cognitive consistency: A sourcebook.* Chicago: Rand McNally.

Kinder, D. R., & Sears, D. O. (1981). Prejudice and politics: Symbolic racism versus racial threats to the good life. *Journal of Personality and Social Psychology, 40,* 414–431.

Kinder, D. R., & Sears, D. O. (1985). Public opinion and political action. In G. Lindzey & E. Aronson (Eds.), *Handbook of social psychology* (Vol. 2, 3rd ed.). New York: Random House.

Knetsch, J., Thaler, R., & Kahneman, D. (1987). *Reluctance to trade: An experimental refutation of the Coase Theorem.* Paper presented at the Public Choice, Economic Science meetings, Tucson, Arizona.

Langer, E. J. (1975). The illusion of control. *Journal of Personality and Social Psychology, 32,* 311–328.

Lasswell, H. (1930). *Psychopathology and politics.* Chicago: University of Chicago Press.

Marsh, C. (1985). *Back onto the bandwagon: The effect of opinion polls on public opinion.* Unpublished manuscript, University of Cambridge, Cambridge, England.

Maslach, C., Stapp, J., & Santee, R. T. (1985). Individuation: Conceptual analysis and assessment. *Journal of Personality and Social Psychology, 49,* 729–738.

McClosky, H. (1967). Personality and attitude correlates of foreign policy orientation. In J. M. Rossenau (Ed.), *Domestic sources of foreign policy.* New York: Free Press.

McGuire, W. J. (1986). The vicissitudes of attitudes and similar representational constructs in twentieth century psychology. *European Journal of Social Psychology, 16,* 89–130

McGuire, W. J., & Padawer-Singer, A. (1976). Trait salience in the spontaneous self-concept. *Journal of Personality and Social Psychology, 33,* 743–754.

Minsky, M. (1986). *The society of mind.* New York: Simon & Schuster.

Prentice, D. A. (1987a). *The effects of priming possessions on attitude functions.* Paper presented at the annual meeting of the Eastern Psychological Association, Arlington, VA.

Prentice, D. A. (1987b). Psychological correspondence of possessions, attitudes, and values. *Journal of Personality and Social Psychology, 53,* 993–1003.

Roseman, I. (1986). *Psychology and ideology: Structures of belief about disarmament and defense.* Unpublished manuscript, New School for Social Research, New York.

Roseman, I., Abelson, R. P., & Ewing, M. (1986). Pity appeals and anger appeals in political persuasion. In R. R. Lau & D. O. Sears (Eds.), *Cognition and political behavior.* 19th Annual Symposium on Cognition. Hillsdale, NJ: Lawrence Erlbaum Associates.

Rosenberg, M. J. (1956). Cognitive structure and attitudinal affect. *Journal of Abnormal and Social Psychology, 53,* 367–372.

Ross, L., Greene, D., & House, P. (1977). The "false consensus effect": An egocentric bias in social perception and attribution processes. *Journal of Experimental Social Psychology, 13,* 279–301.

Smith, M. B. (1947). The personal setting of public opinions: A study of attitudes toward Russia. *Public Opinion Quarterly,* 507–523.

Smith, M. B., Bruner, J. S., & White, R. W. (1956). *Opinions and personality.* New York: Wiley.

Snyder, M. (1974). The self-monitoring of expressive behavior. *Journal of Personality and Social Psychology, 30,* 526–537.

Snyder, M., & DeBono, K. G. (1985). Appeals to image and claims about quality: Understanding the psychology of advertising. *Journal of Personality and Social Psychology, 49,* 586–597.

Tajfel, H. (1981). *Human groups and social categories.* Cambridge, England: Cambridge University Press.

Tomkins, S. S. (1963). Left and right: A basic dimension in ideology and personality. In R. W. White (Ed.), *The study of lives.* New York: Atherton.

Tomkins, S. S. (1965). The psychology of commitment. In S. Tomkins & C. Izard (Eds.), *Affect, cognition, and personality.* New York: Springer-Verlag.

Tomkins, S. S. (1981). The quest for primary motives. Biography and autobiography of an idea. *Journal of Personality and Social Psychology, 41,* 306–329.

Tversky, A., & Kahneman, D. (1981). The framing of decisions and the rationality of choice. *Science, 211,* 453–458.

Wyer, R. S., Jr., & Srull, T. K. (1984). *Handbook of social cognition.* Hillsdale, NJ: Lawrence Erlbaum Associates.

Zajonc, R. B. (1980). Feeling and thinking: Preferences need no inferences. *American Psychologist, 39,* 151–175.

15

Need for Structure in Attitude Formation and Expression

David W. Jamieson
University of Manitoba

Mark P. Zanna
University of Waterloo

Researching attitudes is a challenging endeavor because attitudes and attitude-related phenomena are highly complex. A functional approach to the study of attitudes is capable of capturing some of this complexity because it recognizes that the variety of psychological needs and goals served by various attitude processes (such as attitude formation, maintenance, change and expression) are constrained by properties inherent in the attitude objects under scrutiny, by the dispositional tendencies of persons holding the attitudes, and by the situational contingencies and demands of differing contexts. In brief, different attitude processes can serve different functions for different objects, and all this may be true for different people in different situations.

Faced with such a diverse array of possibilities, it is not surprising that research tends to tackle narrowly defined aspects of the problem. For example, researchers have variously focused their attention upon the great variety of needs served by attitudes (Herek, 1986), upon the functional inherences of attitude objects that specify the needs they may potentially reduce (Shavitt, 1985/1986, chap. 12 in this volume), and upon the chronic motivational differences in personality that identify functions that attitude processes typically fulfill for certain individuals (DeBono, 1985; Snyder & DeBono, 1985, chap. 13 in this volume). The present research is similar in the specificity of its approach. This chapter reports some attempts to induce, situationally, one need that attitude-related processes may satisfy. In particular, several studies are described in which people's motivation for cognitive clarity and structure was heightened by an induction of time pressure, and the manner in which the processes of attitude formation and expression functioned to meet this need were examined. We begin with a brief explanation of the motivation or need for structure.

THE NEED FOR STRUCTURE CONSTRUCT

The need for structure has been articulated recently by Arie Kruglanski as a basic motivation governing the process of knowledge acquisition (Kruglanski, 1980, in press). His theory of lay epistemology characterizes the motivation for structure generally, as a cognitive need, and defines it specifically as the desire for clear, certain, or unambiguous knowledge that will guide perception and action in preference to the undesirable alternative of ambiguity and confusion. A heightened need for structure is thought to "freeze" the process of knowledge acquisition; that is, to motivate a condition of rigidity in which a person is less likely to generate new alternate hypotheses about the world or to engage in extensive validation of the correctness of his or her current knowledge. Knowledge (i.e., structure) is broadly defined in the theory as any information to which a person may have access (norms, emotions, beliefs, etc.).

Evidence has now been generated to support this general conceptualization of epistemic motivations. Kruglanski and his coworkers have shown that conditions of heightened need for structure cause freezing on a wide variety of cognitive tasks, inducing effects such as heightened primacy in impression formation and increased numerical anchoring in probability estimation (Freund, Kruglanski, & Shpitzajzen, 1985; Kruglanski & Freund, 1983). High need for structure has been operationalized in these studies either by the manipulation of time pressures or by demands for unidimensional (vs. multidimensional) judgments, methods thought to induce the desire for clear and unambiguous knowledge.

The need for structure has been conceived as a content-free construct, and so should be distinguished from content-bound instantiations of other similar motivations such as authoritarianism (Adorno, Frenkel-Brunswick, Levinson, & Sanford, 1950). Instead, it has as its clearest intellectual forebearers notions such as intolerance of ambiguity (Frenkel-Brunswick, 1949), reduction of uncertainty (Lanzetta & Driscoll, 1968), and to a lesser extent the need for cognition (Cacioppo & Petty, 1982; Cohen, Stotland, & Wolfe, 1955). Additionally, it shares significant overlap with, and can even be seen as an important component of, other constructs. Convergent support for the need for structure may thus be found in the research literatures on arousal, stress, and threat, if these variables can be reconceptualized as motivating the desire for clarity and lack of ambiguity.

For example, in naturalistic studies, stress and threat have been shown to promote the adoption of highly structured religious ideologies (Sales, 1972) and the use of simpler political rhetoric (Suedfeld & Tetlock, 1977; Tetlock, 1985). Experimental manipulations of such variables also often result in a preference for perceptual, cognitive or behavioral simplicity, causing, for example, a primitization of attention and perceptual processing

(Postman & Bruner, 1948; Smock, 1955a, 1955b), an increased use of personal needs and values in structuring perception (Bruner & Goodman, 1947; Bruner & Postman, 1947a, 1947b, 1948; Postman, Bruner, & McGinnies, 1948), an over-reliance on attributional heuristics in causal inference (Ellis & Zanna, 1986; Strack, Erber, & Wicklund, 1982), and a retreat to dominant behavioral responses (Dollard, Doob, Miller, Mower, & Sears, 1939).

Another study that provides converging support for the effects of need for structure on attentional, perceptual, and judgmental processes was conducted by Holmes, Zanna, and Whitehead (1986). They hypothesized that in an impression formation context, heightened need for structure (induced by arousal) would exacerbate the tendency for subjects to use primed expectancies about a target person's personality in guiding their perceptions of him or her. Subjects with or without prior expectations about a female interviewer's personality were asked, under conditions of high or low arousal, to monitor a videotaped job interview and to record the interviewer's positive and negative nonverbal behaviors on an event recorder. Expectations that the interviewer was warm and friendly, versus no particular expectations, were manipulated by allowing subjects to read previous subjects' ostensible impressions of her. The level of arousal was varied by leading subjects to believe they would receive either a series of electric shocks (to be experienced as "pure stress or anxiety") or a series of electric pulses (to be experienced as a "mild tingling") during the task. (No shocks were ever delivered; they were only anticipated!)

As predicted, the cognitive structure provided by the "warm and friendly" expectation influenced the subjects' overall impressions of the interviewer, but only when they experienced some additional arousal. Subjects formed positive attitudes toward the female interviewer, perceiving her as especially warm and judging her to be especially friendly, only when they were both primed to expect a warm interviewer *and* were aroused; neither the expectation nor the arousal alone made a difference. Moreover, the behavioral tracking data suggested that the differential impressions may have been due, at least in part, to differential attention and encoding processes. Subjects had been asked to record two positive nonverbal behaviors (smiles and nods) and two negative nonverbal behaviors (averted gazes and movements away) while they were observing the interviewer. These measures showed that aroused subjects who were tuned for warm behavior were less able to detect the cold nonverbal behaviors of the interviewer, and made fewer errors of commission on those cues. The overall pattern of results suggested that when stressed or aroused, subjects' attentional style was marked by an inability to deal with information inconsistent with their expectations.

To the extent that manipulations of stress or arousal such as that described can be conceived of as inducing a heightened need for structure, past studies that have employed them may be viewed as providing evidence consistent with the formulation of epistemic motivations here adopted. The general point to be made from this brief review is that when the need for structure is aroused, processing restrictions are likely to occur as people retreat to overlearned, or recently activated, orientations and categories of knowledge. Under such conditions they may be described as processing information or acting on the basis of some guiding knowledge structure. The question an attitude theorist must ask is whether an individual's *evaluation* of some stimulus object is the kind of knowledge structure that a person would find functional to rely upon in structure-motivating conditions.

WHAT'S SO FUNCTIONALLY SPECIAL ABOUT ATTITUDES?

Although the guiding knowledge that people adopt under heightened need for structure circumstances may derive from a variety of sources (e.g., their beliefs, remembrances, feelings, emotions or other forms of information to which they have access), one of the most useful kinds of informational content that people use to organize the social world is their evaluative knowledge; that is, their attitudes. Attitudes may provide particularly efficient aids for sizing up the world and for guiding information processing and behavior because they order all objects along a common evaluative metric. What better way to know how to react to an object than to know how one feels about it?

Conceptual support for our assertion that attitudes serve basic needs for clarity and structure may be found in the theorizing of the early attitude functionalists. Katz's (1960) *knowledge* function and Smith, Bruner, and White's (1956) *object-appraisal* function bear a striking similarity to the present need for structure formulation. According to these workers, one of the primary functions of attitudes is to impart structure, consistency, and understanding to the world; clarity can be achieved in the ordering of objects along the evaluative dimension. Osgood, Suci, and Tannenbaum's (1957) analysis of meaning structures showed that the evaluative component of meaning far exceeds activity and potency in importance, and may come to totally dominate under conditions of high stress (need for structure?) or emotionality (Osgood, 1953). In other words, attitudes, one's evaluative summaries of the world, would seem to be prime candidates as structures of wide utility to individuals.

Theoretical precedents therefore exist for the view that attitudes may be just the kind of structured knowledge that may be formed or used when circumstances motivate a need for clarity and structure. But what empirical evidence is there for the idea that the use of a person's attitudes may function to well serve that person's need for guiding organization in situations demanding clarity of judgment? We now describe the results of several tests of this hypothesis.

NEED FOR STRUCTURE
AND ATTITUDE-BEHAVIOR CONSISTENCY

All studies of attitude-behavior consistency create some need for structure in so far as they require subjects to make a judgment or engage in a behavior potentially relevant to their attitudes. Few studies, however, have expressly manipulated the *degree* of structure motivation inherent in the situation and then examined its impact on the attitude-behavior relation. One that has done so is Kruglanski and Freund's (1983) study of epistemic motivations in stereotyping.

Moderating the Racial Stereotypes-Discrimination Relation

Kruglanski and Freund (1983) examined the influence of subjects' prior stereotypes about two racial groups on their judgments of the quality of writing produced by target members of each group. Time pressures were used to induce heightened needs for structure in some subjects in this experiment and these individuals were compared with control subjects unpressured by time. The results showed that, when asked to judge the quality of essays produced by children of the two ethnic backgrounds, subjects' ratings more closely corresponded with their stereotypes about the groups when they made their judgments in high need for structure circumstances than when they did not.

It is important to note that although attitudes may be just the kind of ready aids most useful to harassed decision makers, they are not the only kind of structure available, nor may they have been the only kind of heuristic processing strategy employed by subjects in this paradigm (cf. Wright, 1974, 1976). Nevertheless, the data indicated that stereotype-based categories of knowledge organized perceptions and biased judgments when subjects were situationally motivated to come to rapid decisions. To the extent that time pressures stimulated a psychological need for guiding structured knowledge, these data provide support for the notion that attitudes might be such a functional basis for perception and judgment.

Moderating the Gender
Attitudes-Discrimination Relation

One potential weakness of the Kruglanski and Freund study was that stereotypes were not assessed individually, but simply assumed on the basis of the racial origins of the perceivers. An experiment by Bechtold, Naccarato, and Zanna (1986) assessed individual attitudes while extending these findings to the gender domain. The study examined the influence of male and female subjects' attitudes toward women in management (Peters, Terborg, & Taynor, 1974) on their subsequent assessments of male and female job candidates. A personnel selection task required subjects to review a set of eight MBA job applicants whose resumes had been submitted for a marketing position. Four pairs of resumes had been constructed to represent four levels of quality (as assessed by independent judges) and a male and female name had been randomly assigned to the resumes within each matched pair. The subjects' task was to rank order the applicants from best to worst. It was expected that the implicit norm of nondiscrimination in hiring would be operative under low need for structure conditions and that relatively little evidence of discrimination against females would be evidenced by either male or female subject raters. More within-gender favoritism was predicted under high need for structure conditions because attitudes might be more likely to bias subjects' ratings when called forth by a context typified by demands for cognitive clarity. As in the Kruglanski studies, time pressures were used to induce a heightened need for structure.

Table 15.1 presents the subjects' mean discrimination scores as a function of conditions. These scores are the difference between subjects' rankings of the males and females, where zero represents nondiscriminatory behavior and positive numbers indicate pro-male bias. The data show that the male raters, despite their relatively more negative attitudes toward women in management, were not significantly more likely than their female counterparts to discriminate against the female applicants when needs for structure were low. Both gender groups were, in fact, somewhat discriminatory. When high needs for structure were induced, however, male subjects clearly favored the male applicants and thereby discriminated against the female applicants.

Among female subjects the result was somewhat more complicated but no less compelling. Little discrimination was evident in either experimental condition until the female subjects were dichotomized into groups on the basis of whether their attitudes toward women in management were liberal or traditional (i.e., conservative). The attitudes of the latter group were equivalent to those of the males in the study. It is apparent from the right half of Table 15.1 that although these women with traditional (more negative) attitudes toward women in management tended to discriminate some-

TABLE 15.1

Mean Discrimination Scores for All Males, All Females, and Females Dichotomized with Respect to Traditional versus Liberal Attitudes Toward Women in Management

| | Subject Group | | | |
Condition	All Males	All Females	Traditional Females	Liberal Females
No time pressure	+2.62	+0.85	+2.83	−0.86
	(13)	(26)	(12)	(14)
Time pressure	+7.33	+1.22	+6.25	−2.80
	(13)	(27)	(12)	(15)

Note. Cell *ns* appear in parentheses. Scores represent the mean difference in rankings between male and female job applicants. Zero indicates nonprejudicial rankings; positive scores represent pro-male bias; negative scores, pro-female bias.

what against their sister applicants under control conditions, they did so strongly only when they were asked to make their ratings under the press of time limits. In complementary fashion, liberal female subjects somewhat favored the female applicants under time unrestricted conditions, but did so significantly only under time restricted circumstances.

We believe these results show that attitudes may exert powerful influences in structuring perception and judgment when the situation surrounding people's ratings prompts them to come to speedy decisions. It appears that unbiased consideration of the facts contained in the resumes was hindered by strong needs for structure. As a result, the information seems to have been considered through the filter of people's preexisting knowledge structures regarding women at work. In this study, the efficiency (if not the wisdom or accuracy) of decision-making may have been particularly improved because one of the preemptory theories seized upon in processing were people's *evaluative* knowledge structures—their attitudes.

Moderating the Social Attitudes-Judgment Relation

An experiment conducted by Jamieson and Zanna (1985) extends this conceptualization into the domain of social attitudes, again with individualized attitude measurement. Subjects participated in a decision-making simulation in which they were placed in the role of jurors and asked to render individual verdicts on a series of court cases. The cases were crafted to be fairly ambiguous and to potentially implicate subjects' attitudes about controversial social topics such as affirmative action and capital punishment. We hypothesized that when people found themselves in a situation that aroused a need for cognitive structure, they would rely increasingly on their evaluations of the relevant general issues to structure their perceptions of the specific cases, and to guide their judgments and decision-making. Attitudes were not expected to relate to perceptions and judgments when the situation aroused these needs to a lesser degree.

In addition to the situational manipulation of need for structure, we also included a personality measure to assess individuals' predisposition to self-monitor in this study. We reasoned that an increased reliance on attitudes to structure perception and guide judgments when the need to do so is great might be a process especially characteristic of those individuals for whom attitudes normally serve important functions in the organization of their social worlds. Low self-monitors have been conceived as individuals whose perception, judgment, and behavior are influenced by internal referents such as attitudes (Snyder, 1974, 1979; Snyder & Tanke, 1976). High self-monitors, in contrast, tend to rely on situational cues of behavioral appropriateness in the guidance of their interactions with the world (Ajzen, Timko, & White, 1982). Recent evidence provided by Fazio and his colleagues demonstrates that the attitudes of low self-monitors are sometimes more accessible from memory than are the attitudes of their high self-monitoring counterparts (Kardes, Sanbonmatsu, Voss, & Fazio, 1986), and that attitudes that are, in general, more accessible, may better serve knowledge function needs than those evaluations that are less accessible (Fazio, Sanbonmatsu, Powell, & Kardes, 1986). We therefore expected that situational conditions demanding structure and dispositional tendencies to self-monitor might interactively moderate attitude-judgment consistency in this study, with attitudes exerting their greatest influence on case judgments among low self-monitors in high need for structure circumstances.

Subjects reported for a study of decision making in which they were told that their role was to deliver fair and objective decisions on a series of court cases. They were instructed to be "involved but impartial decision makers." These normative prescriptions for impartiality were reiterated several times throughout the procedure to insure that attitudes and judgments were generally uncoupled (Salancik, 1982). Need for structure was again manipulated in this study, as in others, by an inducement of time pressure. Subjects in the time pressure condition were provided little rationale for the constraints of time, save that "sometimes decisions have to be made quickly." They were given an average of just 3 minutes to read each case and answer its associated questions. No time pressure participants completed the cases without time restrictions.

The first case involved an affirmative action lawsuit modelled after materials used by Snyder and Swann (1976). Subjects read about a female biologist who had applied for an academic job at the University of Toronto but who had been passed over in favor of a slightly less qualified male applicant. Prosecution and defence arguments were presented and read

TABLE 15.2
Correlation of Affirmative Action Attitudes with Lawsuit
Judgments on a Case of Prejudicial Hiring

	Self-monitoring	
Condition	Low	High
No time pressure	.28	.27
	(26)	(20)
Time pressure	.42*	−.21
	(22)	(23)

Note. Cell *n*s appear in parentheses.
*p < .05.

before subjects recorded their perceptions and judgments of the matter on a series of measures that followed.

The pattern of correlations evident in Table 15.2 provides preliminary support for our hypothesis that high need for structure circumstances, here operationalized by time pressure, would effect a greater correspondence of attitudes with judgments than would low need for structure conditions, and that this effect would be particularly strong among persons low in self-monitoring. Subjects' attitudes toward affirmative action, collected in a prior context, were correlated with an index of their judgments about the case. Attitude scores were computed by summing subjects' responses to the issue of "affirmative action programs in the workplace." The four 9-point semantic differential scales used to assess their feelings were anchored by the adjectives *good-bad, desirable-undesirable, acceptable-unacceptable,* and *just-unjust.* The index of case judgments comprised subjects' perceptions of the unfairness of the University's decision regarding the plaintiff, averaged with their reported likelihood of deciding the case in her favor. The results showed that only the judgments of time pressured low self-monitors were significantly influenced by their personal attitudes, and that this was true despite situational demands for objectivity and impartiality given repeatedly throughout the procedure.[1]

A second case replicated this pattern more strongly on a capital murder offence. Subjects read about a putative premeditated murder that was largely based on circumstantial evidence. Once again they were asked to record their perceptions of the case and the likelihood that they would vote the defendant guilty of first degree murder. (Subjects were asked to imagine themselves at a time in the future when capital punishment had been

---

[1]Although the negative correlation between attitudes and judgments among time pressured high self-monitors may suggest a boomerang effect reflecting the concern of these individuals with the norm of objectivity, this correlation was not significant and did not consistently replicate across studies.

returned as law in Canada.) An index of subjects' capital judgments (their judged likelihood of conviction combined with their actual verdict decisions) was correlated with their attitudes toward the general social policy issue of the "reinstatement of capital punishment" (assessed by the same semantic differentials used for the affirmative action attitude). It is clear from Table 15.3 that although both high and low self-monitors were able to make attitude-independent judgments when unpressured by time, only high self-monitors were able to do so when time was limited. Attitudes again strongly influenced the decisions of time pressured low self-monitors, explaining some 49% of the variance in their case judgments.

Overall, these results show that the heightened need for structure, presumed to have been induced by time pressure, caused an increasing tendency for low self-monitors' general evaluations about the social issues implicated in the cases to color their specific decisions on related case materials. Although this is not to say that members of the other three groups in the study were completely free from any bias in their decision-making, the involvement of their attitudes as a particular source of bias appears to have been unlikely. The pattern of correlation coefficients obtained was not explainable by condition mean differences on the measures correlated. Neither were the results attributable to variance differences in the measures, nor to their reliability. In addition, other variables collected immediately after the cases were read that might have been expected to powerfully influence case decisions (e.g., subjects' affective reactions such as their felt anger), failed to predict case judgments at all. Thus, low self-monitors, those individuals characterized by a chronic motivation to rely on attitudinal knowledge in their transactions with the world, were the very persons who seized upon their evaluations as a way of structuring their perceptions and judgments when the need to do so was strong.

Additional analysis of this study suggested that divorcing attitudes from case decisions may have come with some effort for our low self-monitors.

TABLE 15.3

Correlation of Capital Punishment Attitudes with Capital Judgments on a Case of Premeditated Murder

| | Self-monitoring | |
Condition	Low	High
No time pressure	.03	−.02
	(28)	(20)
Time pressure	.69*	.14
	(23)	(23)

Note. Cell ns appear in parentheses.
*$p < .001$.

Under time unlimited conditions, low self-monitors took longer to render their verdicts than did the high self-monitors. Time pressure may have prevented the kind of controlled, careful cognition that low self-monitors need to be nonprejudicial (Posner & Snyder, 1975; Schneider & Shiffrin, 1977; Shiffrin & Schneider, 1977; Wilson, Dunn, Bybee, Hyman, & Rotondo, 1984). Instead, as a result of the high need for structure manipulation employed here, low self-monitors probably engaged in relatively automatic processing strategies to arrive at their judgments (as compared with the results of Snyder & Kendzierski, 1982, where low self-monitoring subjects who evidenced greater attitude-behavior consistency were first given time to carefully consider the implications of their attitudes). Two possible mediators seemed plausible in accounting for the increased involvement of low self-monitors' feelings in their judgments in this study.

Possible Mediators: Attitude and Norm Accessibility

First, attitudes may have become *more accessible* (Fazio, 1986) in the condition demanding structure than in the condition not presenting such demands. The arousing press of time limits may have caused the attitudes of the low self-monitors to come to mind more spontaneously than was the case for the highs. Eysenck (1976) argued that situational arousal leads to the retrieval of functional, dominant, or relevant information from memory. For low self-monitors, the internal referent of evaluative knowledge may be the kind of structure most easily called forth in pressing circumstances.

The second possibility is that low self-monitors evidenced greater attitude-judgment correspondence under time constraints because under these circumstances restraining situational norms became *less accessible* to them. The jury context is one in which attitudes are explicitly defined as inappropriate guides to judgment and action. However, to the extent that a heightened need for structure makes these competing norms less salient, people may begin to default to their attitudes as preemptory structures used to fulfill their need to organize case perceptions and judgments.

We tested these two ideas in a computerized version of our decision-making study (Jamieson, 1985/1987). The case materials were presented on a microcomputer to allow for reaction time recording, a presumed measure of the accessibility of attitudes and norms (Fazio, Chen, McDonel, & Sherman, 1982). Time pressure cues included a digital clock display in the lower part of the screen, which counted down the passage of time in decrements of 10 seconds, a warning message to inform subjects of the passage of one half of the 3-minute case display interval, and a flashing notification of the expiration of their time.

Attitude-judgment correlations for the affirmative action lawsuit replicated the previous results. Meanwhile, the correlations for the second case of premeditated murder did not because even the time unlimited groups evidenced strong attitude-dependent judgments. Despite this failure to replicate the results of the capital punishment case,[2] an examination of the first case still proved highly informative. As before, time pressured low self-monitors' case judgments were highly related to their attitudes, $r(22)$ = .68, whereas time unlimited low self-monitors' judgments were not, $r(23) = -.01$. High self-monitors' decisions were relatively independent of their evaluations of affirmative action in both conditions: time pressure, $r(17)$ = .33; no time pressure, $r(17)$ = .14. In addition, a measure of subjects' awards of damages to the plaintiff followed, significantly, the same interaction pattern.

In order to test the alternative accessibility hypotheses in this pattern of attitude-judgment consistency, subjects were asked to respond to dichotomous attitude and norm assessments immediately following completion of the case adjudications. For the attitude topics, subjects indicated as quickly and as accurately as they could if they favored (or felt good about) an issue by pressing the "y" key on the terminal keypad; if they opposed (or felt bad about) an issue they pressed the "n" key. A series of filler items was created in which the critical topics of affirmative action and capital punishment were embedded.

Reaction time analyses of these reports revealed that the affirmative action attitudes of time pressured low self-monitors became no more accessible than the attitudes of any of the other three groups. The possibility of a ceiling effect on the accessibility of our critical attitude items was raised by the fact that, relative to the accessibility of the filler attitude items in the set, subjects' attitudes toward affirmative action and capital punishment were among the most accessible attitudes assessed. This may not be surprising because it is probable that such controversial social topics represent symbolic domains (Ellsworth & Ross, 1983) for which, with or without time pressures, both low and high self-monitoring subjects have readily available feelings. Alternately, it is also possible that our reaction time methodology did not provide a sensitive test of the hypothesis and would have been employed more appropriately only as an indicator of chronic or

---

[2]Methodological differences between our paper-and-pencil and our computerized versions of the procedure may have accounted for this lack of replication across studies (for a fuller discussion see Jamieson, 1985/1987). However, combining results from the first two studies presented here with an additional replication we have recently completed revealed strong overall effects. Attitudes and judgments were significantly related for time pressured low self-monitors: affirmative action case $r(65)$ = .42, $p < .01$; capital punishment case $r(61)$ = .50, $p < .01$. All other correlations were nonsignificant and ranged between .02 and .21.

manipulated attitude accessibility and not as a trace measure of residual priming (Taylor & Fiske, 1981). In any event, we failed to obtain evidence for the notion that *differential* attitude accessibility was the mechanism explaining why high need for structure conditions potentiated a link between the general evaluations and the specific decisions of low but not high self-monitors.

The accessibility of norms, meanwhile, provided more interesting data. Norm accessibility was measured following a procedure based on the work of Price and Bouffard (1974). Subjects were asked to report, as quickly and as accurately as they could, the appropriateness of various decision-making strategies in different contexts where judgments are required. A matrix of decision-making strategies (e.g., being idealistic, being pragmatic) crossed with decision contexts (e.g., voting in a political election, helping a friend with a problem) was generated and presented to subjects. One of the critical items we embedded in this set of questions asked subjects to respond, yes ("y") or no ("n"), to whether "being subjective" was an appropriate way to approach decision-making when "serving as a juror in a courtroom." Although reaction time analysis again revealed no differences in subject response times to this question as a function of conditions, subjects' actual answers to this query were informative.

Under *rapid response conditions,* about three quarters of both the time pressure (71%) and the no time pressure (76%) high self-monitors reported that subjectivity was inappropriate in jury decision-making. No time pressure low self-monitors also recognized that the norm of impartiality should entail a suspension of subjectivity in jurisprudence with most (87%) correctly reporting this norm. Under time pressure conditions, however, only half (50%) of the low self-monitors in this study endorsed the belief that subjectivity was an impropriety in courtroom deliberations; the other half accepted the standard of nonobjectivity as appropriate.

We believe that these data illustrate an alternate mode by which attitudes may influence perceptions and judgments besides their heightened accessibility when called to action by pressing circumstances. Attitudes may sometimes function to organize perception and behavior through an automatic process in which individuals fail to heed otherwise restraining situational norms. Attitude-judgment congruence may have resulted among low self-monitors because salient normative prescriptions that otherwise would have defined their attitudes as inappropriate, were unattended or perhaps even consciously ignored under high need for structure conditions. Thus, those institutions in society seeking unbiased judgment would be well-advised to guard against creating contexts for decision-making that promote the expression of private values when what is really desired is an adherence to public principles.

Discussion

The latter two studies illustrate that even in the face of salient countervailing norms, attitudes can function to provide clarity in situations that motivate a need for structure, and that this may be particularly true among people for whom attitudes normally serve important organizing functions, low self-monitors. This is not necessarily to say, however, that in expressing their attitude-dependent judgments these people were capitalizing exclusively on the structuring function of attitudes. As an added benefit of reducing their needs for structure, the time pressured low self-monitors also may have been reducing other needs made salient in the situation. For example, high demands for value expression were probably created through our choice of experimental cases in the jury simulations. As previously suggested, many of the attitudes implicated in these cases were symbolic in character, being based less on behavioral experience than on affect or belief (Zanna & Rempel, in press). Katz (1960) proposed that the expression of such symbolic attitudes is likely to function to assert values. Therefore, low self-monitors, a group of individuals who tend to hold their attitudes for value-expressive reasons (Snyder & DeBono, 1985), may have demonstrated such strong correlations of attitudes with judgments because the use of their attitudes satisfied, for them, motivations for value expression above and beyond the needs for structure called forth by time pressure.

What this analysis suggests is that in addition to its direct structure-inducing effects, time pressure may also serve to potentiate the fulfillment of other needs (reducible by attitude processes) that are endemic to the situations where it is employed. Thus, to the extent that needs for social adjustment (Smith, Bruner, & White, 1956) may have been aroused in the studies of both racial (Kruglanski & Freund, 1983) and gender bias (Bechtold, Naccarato, & Zanna, 1986), in-group favoritism may have fulfilled subjects' needs for group connectedness and social identity engendered by the experimental tasks used there, in addition to satisfying their motivation for clarity and structure induced by time pressure. Still other motives, such as the need for ego defence, will be aroused in other contexts and time pressures may prove to be a catalyst for their satisfaction as well. What is needed to begin to explore the moderating influences of time pressure on need fulfillment are studies that systematically isolate and control the levels of various needs theoretically relevant to attitude functioning. What is needed to complete such an inquiry will be the development of a long-sought method for identifying, a priori, the functional inherences carried by specific attitude objects to the mix of chronic and situationally induced needs.

There is one more potential complication in the use of time pressures to create heightened needs for structure. Although it has been argued that time pressure is plausibly related to an increased need for perceptual and judgmental clarity, it has yet to be demonstrated that it does not directly stimulate needs other than those for structure. One way around this problem is to employ converging operations for the construct that are conceptually independent of the domain of attitudes and that appear to be more related to the need for structure than to the various other motivations with which attitude processes have been associated (for one attempt, see Freund et al., 1985). Although we have not yet done this by manipulation, we have completed a preliminary replication of our findings using a similar approach. On the basis of a scale recently developed by Naccarato, Thompson, and Parker (1986) to assess chronic individual differences in the need for structure, we preselected individuals low or high in structure motivation and exposed them to our jury simulation under no time pressure conditions (Jamieson, Naccarato, & Zanna, 1986). (Individuals scoring high on the scale endorsed such items as "I enjoy having a clear and structured mode of life," "It bothers me when something unexpected disrupts my daily routine," and "I become quite uneasy when put into an unpredictable situation.") Because the two-way classification of subjects conceptually replicated our previous studies, we made the following prediction: Those low self-monitors who were also high in chronic need for structure would evidence a stronger attitude-judgment relation than any of the other three groups.[3]

The pattern of results, although preliminary and based on low cell ns, are encouraging. Low self-monitoring/high need for structure subjects' attitudes correlated with their case judgments at $r(22) = .31$ on the affirmative action case and at $r(21) = .28$ on the capital punishment case. The other six correlations across the two cases ranged in absolute magnitude between .02 and .06 (with the exception of $r = .30$ on the capital punishment case among 13 high self-monitors who were low in need for structure). Further research is needed to examine the stability of these correlations. However, they provide tentative converging support for our findings.

In sum, what we believe is relatively clear from the investigations reported is that whatever other needs we may have imparted to subjects in these studies, the need for cognitive structure was also aroused. As a result, attitudes were employed by people in high need for structure circumstances to aid in guiding perception and judgment, even though other

---

[3] The correlation of self-monitoring with need for structure was $-.22$ in this sample, indicating a minor tendency for low self-monitors to be high in the need for structure.

possible structures and knowledge could well have been employed instead. A slightly different way to test the role of need for structure and self-monitoring in influencing attitude processes is to examine these variables in circumstances where the focus is not on whether preexisting attitudes are exercised, but is instead on the nature of the attitudes that may be formed as a functional response to situational demands for structure. It is to a description of such an approach that we now turn.

NEED FOR STRUCTURE
IN ATTITUDE FORMATION

We reasoned that to the extent that the need for structure is aroused in a situation in which a person has no prior knowledge, then the most functional kind of knowledge to evolve would be *simple* knowledge. Simple structure would seem to better serve a pressing need for clarity than would more complex structure. Thus, we predicted that the formation of an attitude could be a functional response to structure-arousing contexts, but that the attitudes so evolved would *best* fulfill needs for clarity if they were simple and univalent as opposed to complex and bivalent. Recent attitude theory speculates that people may form and hold multiple attitudes toward the same object, and that the evaluation called forth at any time may be a function of which informational bases of attitudes are currently salient (Zanna & Rempel, in press). We expected that the best kind of an attitude that could be formed by people under high need for structure conditions would be a clear and nonambivalent one because it would better enable knowledge and action.

It is also possible that this simplicity will be associated with more extremity in overall evaluations. Other workers have shown that if the multidimensionality of thought underlying evaluation is reduced, or if those cognitive dimensions are strongly interrelated, then the extremity of evaluations is increased (e.g., Judd & Lusk 1984; Linville, 1982). But, although cognitively simplifying circumstances have been shown to have this effect in some cases, in other research no consistent relation between evaluations and complexity has been found (e.g., Press, Crockett, & Delia, 1975). Thus, whereas extremity and complexity of evaluations may sometimes be related, they are, in principle, separable aspects of attitudes, and we predicted that the primary effect of need for structure would be in causing the formation of structurally simple attitudes.

To test these ideas we conducted an impression formation experiment in which we presented subjects with biographical summaries of two stimulus persons (Jamieson & Zanna, 1986). Positive, negative, and neutral information about each person's lifestyle habits, interests and personality were read under a communicator cognitive set (Zajonc, 1960). Despite the fact that such instructions to "learn enough about the person to be able to communicate the information to someone else" have been associated with a retention of information at a fine-grain level in memory, we were confident that our subjects would be able, at least potentially, to form overall attitudes about the two persons. Lingle and Ostrom (1981) argued that people sometimes form two memory traces when forming impressions of others, one for the denotative details of a person and the other to summarize their overall attitude about the target individual. We were relatively certain that our subjects would form overall on-line impressions, as well as remember specific information about the stimulus persons.

To examine the effects of high need for structure on attitude formation in this paradigm we again manipulated the press of time. Subjects given just 2 minutes to read biographies of stimulus persons "Bob" and "Jim" were compared with subjects allowed as much time as they required to read the personal summaries. After they had finished perusing the information, individuals were unexpectedly asked to state, on seven-point scales, the degree to which they liked, would like to work with, and would respect each person (Byrne, 1971). The sum of these three ratings constituted a traditional bipolar index assessing subjects' attitudes toward Bob and Jim.

Next, subjects provided separate reports of the degree of liking and of disliking that each stimulus person elicited in them. These measures of attraction and repulsion were made by having subjects consider separately first the positive and then the negative aspects of each person. They recorded their responses on separate four-point scales created by splitting the seven-point bipolar scale of liking-disliking with the neutral point retained in each. The degree of simplicity versus complexity of subjects' attitudes was assessed by computing from the two unipolar scales an index of ambivalence. This procedure was based on Kaplan's (1972) formula, which defines ambivalence as the total amount of affect experienced less the degree to which the summary evaluation is polarized. For example, $+2$ units of liking felt at the same time as -3 units of disliking produces 5 units of total affect ($|+2|+|-3|$), which can be decomposed into 1 unit of absolute polarization ($\|+2]+[-3]\|$), in this case slight disliking, and 4 units of ambivalence ($5-1$). Ambivalence is thus determined by the amount of the lessor effect, all of which overlaps with an equivalent amount of the stronger competing affect. If both liking and disliking are equal, all the affect present is considered to be ambivalent. In this research more ambivalence was deemed to represent greater complexity of evaluation, that is, more mixed affect.

The results of the study suggest that attitude formation, in addition to attitude utilization, is a process that can proceed in such a manner as to provide needed structure in pressing circumstances. The bipolar attitude index was not significantly related to the measure of ambivalence for either stimulus person; extremity of evaluation and complexity of attitudinal structure were largely independent overall. There were no significant differences in the attraction index as a function of conditions, suggesting that time pressure did not polarize evaluations. However, the measure directly testing our hypothesis, attitude ambivalence, did confirm our prediction and is presented in Table 15.4. For both stimulus persons, high need for structure, as operationalized by time pressure, engendered the formation of more simply structured attitudes than those evolved under lower levels of this motivation. Whether this occurred because subjects selectively encoded only consistent information, or discounted existing inconsistencies (Anderson & Jacobson, 1965), we again have evidence that attitude processes may provide ready responses to situations characterized by heightened needs for organization and clarity. What is more, the form that attitudes will take when derived in such contexts may follow the functional requirements aroused by those situations: The need for structural simplicity prompted the formation of simple attitudinal affect.

Interestingly, we again included a self-monitoring measure in this study to determine if these effects were more characteristic of low self-monitors than of high self-monitors. No main effect of self-monitoring or interaction with time pressure was obtained on our measure of complexity, a finding consistent with other work in which we have examined the structural ambivalence of the preexisting attitudes of high and low self-monitors

TABLE 15.4

Mean Ambivalence in Attitudes Formed Toward Two Stimulus Persons

Condition	Stimulus Person	
	Bob	Jim
No time pressure	3.66	4.55
	(29)	(29)
Time pressure	2.87	3.40
	(30)	(30)

Note. Cell *n*s appear in parentheses. Ambivalence scores are computed from a formula provided by Kaplan (1972), where higher numbers indicate greater ambivalence and complexity of affect. $p < .03$ for Bob. $p < .01$ for Jim.

(Jamieson & Zanna, 1984). However, there was some evidence that low self-monitors formed more extreme overall evaluations than did the highs independent of need for structure conditions. Low self-monitors were more favorably disposed to both Bob and Jim as evidenced on the attraction index. In addition, they also recorded more evaluationally congruent intrusions in a later free recall of information about one of the two persons (Bob) than did the highs. These findings may indicate that, in addition to being more willing to apply their preexisting attitudes, low self-monitors may more readily form evaluations from the start. Even under conditions where information processing is generally taxing, low self-monitors may be able to form more confident and extreme attitudes because for them the chronically accessible categories used in interpersonal perception are evaluative ones (cf. Bargh & Thein, 1985; Higgins, King, & Mavin, 1982). Although more research is obviously needed, these data could indicate that, whereas need for structure may represent an acute need for structuring social knowledge in general terms, self-monitoring may represent a chronic need for structuring social knowledge along specific, evaluative lines.

GENERAL DISCUSSION

The experiments reported in this chapter illustrate that the formation or expression of attitudes can be a highly functional response to situations motivating the need for cognitive structure. In circumstances where clarity of decision-making was a pressing concern, attitude processes proved to be efficient heuristics for perception and judgment. Time pressure caused subjects in the attitude-judgment experiments to rely less on careful cognition and more on basic attitudinal orientations when making their decisions. And when subjects formed their attitudes in situations high in need for structure they evolved simply, as opposed to complexly, structured attitudes; the form of the derived evaluations followed the functional demands of the situation. In sum, we conclude that the retreat to overlearned contents of evaluative knowledge and a reliance on more automatic forms of evaluative information processing can be highly adaptive responses to each of these circumstances. What better way exists to organize perception than by ordering the world along evaluative lines which specify the basic desirability or undesirability of objects?

Of course, some may still dispute our conclusion because of the manner in which we manipulated high need for structure in each of these experiments. It has been mentioned that time pressure may have psychological and physiological consequences other than simply heightening subjects' needs for cognitive clarity, and that these may be the critical mediators of the effects described herein. For instance, time pressures might arouse or stress people. Recalling Easterbrook's (1959) arousal–cue–utilization hypothesis, arousal may focus people's attention on central, dominant, or relevant information in the external stimulus field. It is important to note, therefore, that in our studies of the attitude-judgment relation *internal* referents served to color perception more than did *external* stimulus properties, and that in our study of attitude formation information other than the evaluative could have been, at least potentially, the object of subjects' narrowed attention. Nevertheless, the operation of attitude processes were evident in both cases. Moreover, subjects' self-reports of activation (Thayer, 1967) taken in several of these studies revealed that individuals were not overly stressed by our time pressure procedure and were only moderately aroused by it. Thus, we do not believe that physiological activation provides a compelling alternate explanation for our various findings, although it may further exacerbate needs for structure already present in the situation (A. W. Kruglanski, personal communication, March, 1985). Although it will be important to replicate these data with other manipulations of the need for structure construct, we believe both that the desire for structure is an important need state that attitude processes may satisfy, and that there is great empirical and ecological appeal in time pressure as a method for instantiating this situated motivation.

Despite our faith in the usefulness of time pressure conditions, the problems alluded to previously remain: How do we know what needs *any* situational manipulation has induced? Furthermore, how can we tell which needs various attitude processes have reduced in any context? Beyond the a priori identification of objects' functional inherences and of people's chronic motivations, we suggest that another approach to this problem is to develop measures that will identify the functional fulfilments of various attitude processes *after* they have occurred. Such measures could index the degree of need reduction achieved through, for example, attitude expression. High need for structure circumstances that prompt people to use their attitudes in providing clarity may result in lessened uncertainty and heightened confidence among those exercising their attitudes in the service of this function. Situations that motivate needs for value expression should cause heightened self-identity and feelings of personal adequacy when people react to them by exercising their attitudes and values. And situations creating needs for social adjustment should be associated with a stronger sense of group identity and feelings of social acceptance when attitudes are used to express reference group concerns. This approach has the potential to improve the study of the attitude-behavior relation beyond providing correlation information at the level of the group, for it can provide process information at the level of the individual as well (cf. Davidson & Morrison, 1983). Moreover, it may provide direction for the much needed development of measures of attitude-behavior consistency taken on individual subjects; that is, measures of the extent to which each individual has behaved in accordance with his or her private feelings and attitudes in a particular situation.

In conclusion, this chapter has addressed the functionality of two attitude processes (attitude formation and expression) to serve a specific need that was aroused as a result of situational demands. Other chapters in this book remind us that attitude formation and expression processes may serve different needs in different attitude domains for different people. Thus, the need for structure and its satisfaction are likely to be more associated with certain attitude processes than with others, to be more prevalent in certain situations than in others, to be more inherent in certain attitude domains and objects than in others, and to be of more chronic concern to certain individuals than to others. The complex interplay of such factors challenges future research.

ACKNOWLEDGMENTS

This research was supported, in part, by a Social Sciences and Humanities Research Council of Canada (SSHRCC) Doctoral Fellowship to David Jamieson and by a SSHRCC Research Grant to Mark Zanna. The chapter was prepared while the first author was a Canadian Government Laboratory Visiting Fellow resident at the Defence and Civil Institute of Environment Medicine in Downsview, Ontario. Special thanks go to Russ Fazio, Arie Kruglanski, and each of the editors for their helpful comments on earlier versions of the manuscript.

REFERENCES

Adorno, T. W., Frenkel-Brunswick, E., Levinson, D. J., & Sanford, R. N. (1950). *The authoritarian personality.* New York: Harper & Row.

Ajzen, I., Timko, C., & White, J. B. (1982). Self-monitoring and the attitude-behavior relation. *Journal of Personality and Social Psychology, 42,* 426–435.

Anderson, N. H., & Jacobson, A. (1965). Effects of stimulus inconsistency and discounting instructions in personality impression formation. *Journal of Personality and Social Psychology, 2,* 531–539.

Bargh, J. A., & Thein, R. D. (1985). Individual construct accessibility, person memory, and the recall-judgment link: The case for information overload. *Journal of Personality and Social Psychology, 49,* 1129–1146.

Bechtold, A., Naccarato, M. E., & Zanna, M. P. (1986, June). *Need for structure and the prejudice-discrimination link.* Paper presented at the annual meeting of the Canadian Psychological Association, Toronto.

Bruner, J. S., & Goodman, C. C. (1947). Value and need as organizing factors in perception. *Journal of Abnormal and Social Psychology, 42,* 33–44.

Bruner, J. S., & Postman, L. (1947a). Emotional selectivity in perception and reaction. *Journal of Personality, 16,* 69–77.

Bruner, J. S., & Postman, L. (1947b). Tension and tension-release as organizing factors in perception. *Journal of Personality, 15,* 300–308.

Bruner, J. S., & Postman, L. (1948). Symbolic value as an organizing factor in perception. *Journal of Social Psychology, 27,* 203–208.

Byrne, D. (1971). *The attraction paradigm.* New York: Academic Press.

Cacioppo, J. T., & Petty, R. E. (1982). Need for cognition. *Journal of Personality and Social Psychology, 42,* 116–131.

Cohen, A. R., Stotland, E., & Wolfe, D. M. (1955). An experimental investigation of need for cognition. *Journal of Abnormal and Social Psychology, 51,* 291–294.

Davidson, A. R., & Morrison, D. M. (1983). Predicting contraceptive behavior from attitudes: A comparison of within- versus across-subjects procedures. *Journal of Personality and Social Psychology, 45,* 997–1009.

DeBono, K. G. (1985). *On the systematic processing of persuasive messages: Functional theories revisited.* Unpublished manuscript, University of Minnesota, Minneapolis.

Dollard, J., Doob, L. W., Miller, N. E., Mower, O. H., & Sears, R. R. (1939). *Frustration and aggression.* New Haven, CT: Yale University Press.

Easterbrook, J. A. (1959). The effect of emotion on cue utilization and the organization of behavior. *Psychological Review, 66,* 183–201.

Ellis, R. J., & Zanna, M. P. (1986). *Arousal and causal attribution.* Unpublished manuscript, Wilfrid Laurier University, Waterloo, Ontario.

Ellsworth, P. C., & Ross, L. (1983). Public opinion and captial punishment: A close examination of the views of abolitionists and retentionists. *Crime and Delinquency, 29,* 116–169.

Eysenck, M. W. (1976). Arousal, learning, and memory. *Psychological Bulletin, 83,* 389–404.

Fazio, R. H. (1986). How do attitudes guide behavior? In R. M. Sorrentino & E. T. Higgins (Eds.), *Handbook of motivation and cognition: Foundations of social behavior* (pp. 204–243). New York: Guilford Press.

Fazio, R. H., Chen, J., McDonel, E. C., & Sherman, S. J. (1982). Attitude accessibility, attitude-behavior consistency, and the strength of the object-evaluation association. *Journal of Experimental Social Psychology, 18,* 339–357.

Fazio, R. H., Sanbonmatsu, D. M., Powell, M. C., & Kardes, F. R. (1986). On the automatic activation of attitudes. *Journal of Personality and Social Psychology, 50,* 229–238.

Frenkel-Brunswick, E. (1949). Intolerance of ambiguity as emotional and perceptual personality variable. *Journal of Personality, 18,* 108–143.

Freund, T., Kruglanski, A. W., & Shpitzajzen, A. (1985). The freezing and unfreezing of impressional primacy: Effects of need for structure and the fear of invalidity. *Personality and Social Psychology Bulletin, 11,* 479–487.

Herek, G. M. (1986). *Can functions be measured? A new perspective on the functional approach to attitudes.* Unpublished manuscript, Graduate Center, City University of New York, New York.

Higgins, E. T., King, G. A., & Mavin, G. H. (1982). Individual construct accessibility and subjective impressions and recall. *Journal of Personality and Social Psychology, 43,* 35–47.

Holmes, J. G., Zanna, M. P., & Whitehead, L. A. (1986). *Stress and social perception.* Unpublished manuscript, University of Waterloo, Waterloo, Ontario.

Jamieson, D. W. (1987). Going with gut feelings: The impact of arousal and self-monitoring on attitude utilization and formation (Doctoral dissertation, University of Waterloo, 1985). *Dissertation Abstracts International, 47,* 3161B–3162B.

Jamieson, D. W., Naccarato, M. E., & Zanna, M. P. (1986). [Self-monitoring, need for structure and attitude-judgment consistency]. Unpublished raw data.

Jamieson, D. W., & Zanna, M. P. (1984). [Assessing attitude ambivalence]. Unpublished raw data.

Jamieson, D. W., & Zanna, M. P. (1985, June). *Moderating the attitude-behavior relation: The joint effects of arousal and self-monitoring.* Paper presented at the annual meeting of the Canadian Psychological Association, Halifax.

Jamieson, D. W., & Zanna, M. P. (1986, June). *Attitude formation: Dispositional and situational determinants of affect strength and complexity.* Paper presented at the annual meeting of the Canadian Psychological Association, Toronto.

Judd, C. M., & Lusk, C. M. (1984). Knowledge structures and evaluative judgments: Effects of structural variables on judgmental extremity. *Journal of Personality and Social Psychology, 46,* 1193–1207.

Kaplan, K. J. (1972). On the ambivalence-indifference problem in attitude theory and measurement: A suggested modification of the semantic differential technique. *Psychological Bulletin, 77,* 361–372.

Kardes, F. R., Sanbonmatsu, D. M., Voss, R. T., & Fazio, R. H. (1986). Self-monitoring and attitude accessibility. *Personality and Social Psychology Bulletin, 12,* 468–474.

Katz, D. (1960). The functional approach to the study of attitudes. *Public Opinion Quarterly, 24,* 163–204.

Kruglanski, A. W. (1980). Lay epistemo-logic-process and contents: Another look at attribution theory. *Psychological Review, 87,* 70–87.

Kruglanski, A. W. (in press). *Basic processes in social cognition: A theory of lay epistemology.* New York: Plenum.

Kruglanski, A. W., & Freund, T. (1983). The freezing and unfreezing of lay-inferences: Effects on impressional primacy, ethnic stereotyping, and numerical anchoring. *Journal of Experimental Social Psychology, 19,* 448–468.

Lanzetta, J. T., & Driscoll, J. M. (1968). Effects of uncertainty and importance on information search in decision making. *Journal of Personality and Social Psychology, 10,* 479–486.

Lingle, J. H., & Ostrom, T. M. (1981). Principles of memory and cognition in attitude formation. In R. E. Petty, T. M. Ostrom, & T. C. Brock (Eds.), *Cognitive responses in persuasion* (pp. 399–420). Hillsdale, NJ: Lawrence Erlbaum Associates.

Linville, P. W. (1982). The complexity-extremity effect in age-based stereotyping. *Journal of Personality and Social Psychology, 42,* 193–211.

Naccarato, M. E., Thomspon, M. M., & Parker, K. C. H. (1986). *The development of two scales: The need for structure and fear of invalidity.* Unpublished manuscript, University of Waterloo, Waterloo, Ontario.

Osgood, C. E. (1953). *Report on development and application of the semantic differential.* Unpublished manuscript, Institute of Communications Research, University of Illinois, Urbana.

Osgood, C. E., Suci, G. J., & Tannenbaum, P. H. (1957). *The measurement of meaning.* Urbana, IL: University of Illinois Press.

Peters, L. H., Terborg, J. R., & Taynor, J. (1974). Women as managers scale (WAMS): A measure of attitudes toward women in management positions. *Catalogue of Selected Documents in Psychology, 4,* 27.

Posner, M. I., & Snyder, C. R. R. (1975). Attention and cognitive control. In R. L. Solso (Ed.), *Information processing and cognition.* Hillsdale, NJ: Lawrence Erlbaum Associates.

Postman, L., & Bruner, J. S. (1948). Perception under stress. *Psychological Review, 55,* 314–323.

Postman, L., Bruner, J. S., & McGinnies, E. (1948). Personal values as selective factors in perception. *Journal of Abnormal and Social Psychology, 43,* 142–154.

Press, A. N., Crockett, W. H., & Delia, J. G. (1975). Effects of cognitive complexity and of perceiver's set upon the organization of impressions. *Journal of Personality and Social Psychology, 32,* 865–872.

Price, R. H., & Bouffard, D. L. (1974). Behavioral appropriateness and situational constraint as dimensions of social behavior. *Journal of Personality and Social Psychology, 30,* 579–586.

Salancik, G. R. (1982). Attitude-behavior consistencies as social logics. In M. P. Zanna, E. T. Higgins, & C. P. Herman (Eds.), *Consistency in social behavior: The Ontario symposium* (Vol. 2, pp. 51–74). Hillsdale, NJ: Lawrence Erlbaum Associates.

Sales, S. M. (1972). Economic threat as a determinant of conversion rates in authoritarian and nonauthoritarian churches. *Journal of Personality and Social Psychology, 23,* 420–428.

Schneider, W., & Shiffrin, R. M. (1977). Controlled and automatic human information processing: I. Detection, search, and attention. *Psychological Review, 84,* 1–66.

Shavitt, S. (1986). Functional imperative theory of attitude formation and expression (Doctoral dissertation, Ohio State University, 1985). *Dissertation Abstracts International, 47,* 854B.

Shiffrin, R. M., & Schneider, W. (1977). Controlled and automatic human information processing: II. Perceptual learning, automatic attending and a general theory. *Psychological Review, 84,* 127–190.

Smith, M. B., Bruner, J. S., & White, R. W. (1956). *Opinions and personality.* New York: Wiley.

Smock, C. D. (1955a). The influence of psychological stress on the "intolerance of ambiguity." *Journal of Abnormal and Social Psychology, 50,* 177–182.

Smock, C. D. (1955b). The influence of stress on the perception of incongruity. *Journal of Abnormal and Social Psychology, 50,* 354–356.

Snyder, M. (1974). The monitoring of expressive behavior. *Journal of Personality and Social Psychology, 30,* 526–537.

Snyder, M. (1979). Self-monitoring processes. In L. Berkowitz (Ed.), *Advances in Experimental Social Psychology* (Vol. 12, pp. 85–128). New York: Academic Press.

Snyder, M., & DeBono, K. G. (1985). Appeals to image and claims about quality: Understanding the psychology of advertising. *Journal of Personality and Social Psychology, 49,* 586–597.

Snyder, M., & Kendzierski, D. (1982). Acting on one's attitudes: Procedures for linking attitude and behavior. *Journal of Experimental Social Psychology, 18,* 165–183.

Snyder, M., & Swann, W. B. (1976). When actions reflect attitudes: The politics of impression management. *Journal of Personality and Social Psychology, 34,* 1034–1042.

Snyder, M., & Tanke, E. D. (1976). Behavior and attitude: Some people are more consistent than others. *Journal of Personality, 44,* 501–517.

Strack, F., Erber, R., & Wicklund, R. A. (1982). Effects of salience and time pressure on ratings of social causality. *Journal of Experimental Social Psychology, 18,* 581–594.

Suedfeld, P., & Tetlock, P. E. (1977). Integrative complexity of communication in international crises. *Journal of Conflict Resolution, 21,* 169–184.

Taylor, S. E., & Fiske, S. T. (1981). Getting inside the head: Methodologies for process analysis. In J. H. Harvey, W. J. Ickes, & R. F. Kidd (Eds.), *New directions in attribution research* (Vol. 3). New York: Academic Press.

Tetlock, P. E. (1985). Integrative complexity of American and Soviet foreign policy rhetoric: A time series analysis. *Journal of Personality and Social Psychology, 49,* 1565–1585.

Thayer, R. E. (1967). Measurement of activation through self-report. *Psychological Reports, 20,* 663–678.

Wilson, T. D., Dunn, D. S., Bybee, J. A., Hyman, D. B., & Rotondo, J. A. (1984). Effects of analyzing reasons on attitude-behavior consistency. *Journal of Personality and Social Psychology, 47,* 5–16.

Wright, P. L. (1974). The harassed decision maker: Time pressures, distractions, and the use of evidence. *Journal of Applied Psychology, 59,* 555–561.

Wright, P. L. (1976). An adaptive consumer's view of attitudes and other choice mechanisms as viewed by an equally adaptive advertiser. In D. Johnson & W. P. Wells (Eds.), *Attitude research at bay.* Chicago: American Marketing Association.

Zajonc, R. B. (1960). The process of cognitive tuning in communication. *Journal of Abnormal and Social Psychology, 61,* 159–167.

Zanna, M. P., & Rempel J. K. (in press). Attitudes: A new look at an old concept. In D. Bar-Tal & A. W. Kruglanski (Eds.), *The social psychology of knowledge.* New York: Cambridge University Press.

16

On Defining Attitude and Attitude Theory:
Once More with Feeling

Steven J. Breckler
Johns Hopkins University

Elizabeth C. Wiggins
Barnard College of Columbia University

Attitude research is enjoying a renaissance. The perennial problems of attitude change and the attitude-behavior relationship continue to demand research attention (Chaiken & Stangor, 1987; McGuire, 1985). At the same time, new efforts are being made to understand the neglected problems of attitude structure and function. The renewed excitement and interest is well-represented by the chapters in this volume. Yet, as theory is refined and research proceeds apace, the emerging concept of attitude is decidedly narrow. Our goal in this chapter is to offer broader perspective on attitudes and attitude theory.

We focus specifically on how attitudes are respresented within a person. Representations provide a means for previous experience to influence later behavior (Roitblat, 1982). Although representations can take many forms (Palmer, 1978), contemporary attitude theory and research is premised in the assumption that attitudes are represented in propositional forms. This narrow interpretation is a departure from both historical and theoretical conceptions. Although the affective or emotional nature of attitudes has been traditionally emphasized, emotional experience is only partially represented by propositions.

THE ATTITUDE CONCEPT

Historical Overview

The concept of attitude has a rich history (Fleming, 1967). Once used to describe the spatial orientation of physical objects such as statues, the concept has evolved to refer to a person's mental and neural state of readiness (Allport, 1935). Historical perspective reveals the multifaceted nature of the attitude concept. Attitudes have been variously associated with strong emotional displays used by animals for purposes of social communication as well as emotional states free from behavioral manifestations, to describe the chronic motor activity with which animals are able to resist the forces of gravity, and in reference to mental and perceptual biases *(aufgabe)*. Thus, at different points in its history, the attitude concept has been associated with emotional, behavioral, and cognitive processes.

The multifaceted nature of attitudes is also reflected in contemporary research (cf. Hilgard, 1980). The behavioral component of attitude was the primary focus of behaviorist and learning analyses (Bem, 1968, 1972; Doob, 1947; Lott & Lott, 1968; Staats, 1968). More recently, research has been centering on the cognitive component of attitude (Fazio, chap. 7 in this volume; Greenwald, chap. 17 in this volume; McGuire, 1985; Petty, Ostrom, & Brock, 1981; Pratkanis, chap. 4 in this volume). Although affective and emotional processes have heretofore received very little direct attention in attitude research, interest in this important component of attitude appears to be increasing (Chaiken & Stangor, 1987; Millar & Tesser, 1986; Roseman, Abelson, & Ewing, 1986; Zanna & Rempel, in press).

Attitude Definitions

Two recent textbooks indicate the current theoretical status of the attitude concept. According to Fishbein and Ajzen (1975) an attitude is, "a learned predisposition to respond in a consistently favorable or unfavorable manner with respect to a given object" (p.6). Petty and Cacioppo (1981) define attitude as, "a general and enduring positive or negative feeling about some person, object, or issue" (p. 7). These definitions emphasize three important characteristics of attitudes: they are learned, they predispose action, and they imply evaluation (favorable–unfavorable, positive–negative, good–bad). The second definition also clearly ascribes an affective or emotional component to attitude.

Theoretical definitions of this sort are readily available and widely quoted. Nevertheless, these definitions appear to have had a minor influence on the way attitude research is actually done. If the operations used in empirical studies are used to define the concept, attitudes are best defined as: "Responses that locate objects of thought on dimensions of judgment" (McGuire, 1985, p. 239).

Evaluation, size, weight, expectancy, duration, and complexity are among the many dimensions of judgment (or "axes of meaning"), although evaluation is clearly most prominent in attitude research. This operational definition is important because it reflects a narrowing of the attitude concept to primarily semantic and propositional terms, especially in comparison to Allport's (1935) classic definition: "An attitude is a mental and neural *state of readiness* [italics added], organized through experience, exerting a directive or dynamic influence upon the individual's response to all objects and situations with which it is related" (p. 810).

Our own definition is offered in the spirit of Allport's earlier conceptualization: Attitudes are mental and neural *representations,* organized through experience, exerting a directive or dynamic influence on behavior. The concept of *representation* is used in place of *state of readiness,* primarily because *representation* has more precise psychological meaning. Formal treatments of representation (e.g., Paivio, 1986; Palmer, 1978; Roitblat, 1982) can be fruitfully applied in understanding the structure and function of attitudes. Our definition is fully consistent with the rich historical interpretation of the attitude concept, especially by allowing for an emotional component.

ATTITUDES AND EMOTION

Affect has been described as the central aspect of an attitude (Katz & Stotland, 1959). Indeed, attitude theory has traditionally emphasized the affective nature of attitudes. This is evident in the myriad attitude definitions that make reference to affect, emotions, and feelings (e.g., Insko & Schopler, 1967; Petty & Cacioppo, 1981; Rosenberg, 1956; Smith, 1947). Although affect is assigned a central role in definitions of attitude, the treatment of affective and emotional processes has been relatively narrow and largely neglected in attitude research. This becomes readily apparent in reviewing the current literature on emotion.

The Nature of Emotion

Early theories of emotion fall into three general categories (cf. Leventhal, 1984). *Bodily reaction theories* suggest that visceral and somatic feedback defines subjective emotional experience (James, 1890; Lange, 1885/1922). In contrast, *central neural theories* specify that emotions are produced by activity in the central nervous system, and that visceral arousal is irrelevant for emotion (Cannon, 1927). And according to *cognition-arousal theories,* emotion is the product of (undifferentiated) physiological arousal plus attributions about the source of arousal (an early statement of this position was given by Russell, 1927, and later restated and elaborated by Schachter, 1964 and Schachter & Singer, 1962). Each approach has its merits, but each has also been the target of severe criticism.

Contemporary theories of emotion draw from each of the early approaches. We focus specifically on differential emotions theory (Izard, 1977), perceptual-motor theory (Leventhal, 1984) and prime theory (Buck,

1985). Although differing in emphasis and assumptions, each theory accords some status to central neural, visceral, and somatic activity, and to cognition in the emotion process.

Differential emotions theory defines emotion as consisting of central and somatic neural activity, sensory feedback from the facial musculature, and subjective experience (Izard, 1977). The principle of differential emotions postulates, "a number of discrete emotions that can be differentiated in terms of their neurophysiological underpinnings, their facial patterns, and their experiential/motivational characteristics" (p. 101). Among the 10 fundamental (discrete) emotions are interest, joy, anger, and disgust. Affect is a more general concept that refers to the fundamental emotions, patterns of emotions, and drive states. Most importantly, differential emotions theory stresses that an emotion can occur independently of any semantic encoding of it.

Perceptual-motor theory postulates that *innate expressive-motor programs* each produce a different emotional experience and expressive-motor reaction in response to specific stimulation (Leventhal, 1984). Emotional experience is represented in two distinct memory systems. The *schematic system* "makes an analog record of the eliciting conditions, the expressive-motor and autonomic response accompanying them, and the subjective emotion itself" (p. 127). The *conceptual system* is "a set of abstract propositions or rules about emotional episodes and a set of rules for voluntary response to emotional situations and to emotions themselves" (p. 128). Innate motor programs, schematic memory, and conceptual memory form three levels of a central neural processing (CNS) hierarchy. The CNS hierarchy interacts with the visceral system in producing emotional responses. However, peripheral feedback is not viewed as a necessary component of emotion.

According to *prime theory* (Buck, 1985), emotions are based on primary motivational systems or *primes* that have evolved for purposes of bodily adaptation and homeostatic maintenance. Primes are based on innate central neural mechanisms that are hierarchically organized according to the particular brain structures involved and the extent to which they are modified by experience. Reflexes and instincts are at the lowest levels, and primary affects and effectance motivation are at the highest levels. Emotions carry information about the state of the primes, and take three basic forms:

> Emotion I is particularly associated with interoceptive feedback from autonomic and endocrine responses. Emotion II is particularly associated with proprioceptive feedback from the skeletal muscles involved in the external expression of the prime state, and Emotion III is associated with a direct *syncretic cognitive* [italics added] registration of emotion experience that is relatively distinct for each prime state. (Buck, 1985, p. 399)

Syncretic cognition is a representation of sensory information; it is a form of *knowledge by acquaintance,* as described by William James (1890):

> I know the color blue when I see it, and the flavor of a pear when I taste it . . . but *about* the inner nature of these facts or what makes them what they are, I can say nothing at all. I cannot impart acquaintance with them to any one who has not already made it himself . . . At most, I can say to my friends, "Go to certain places and act in certain ways, and these objects will probably come." (p. 221)

A variety of terms have been used in reference to knowledge by acquaintance (cf. Ryle, 1949), including prime theory's *syncretic cognition* (Buck, 1985) and perceptual motor theory's *schematic memory* (Leventhal, 1984). Both theories assign a central role to knowledge by acquaintance in the experience of emotion.

In contrast, *knowledge by description* "involves the interpretation of sense data, requires inference, and is propositional in that knowledge by decription can be false" (Buck, 1985, p. 401). Knowledge by description is identified as *analytic cognition* in prime theory, and as *conceptual memory* in perceptual motor theory. All three theories of emotion reviewed suggest that "emotional experience may occur in the absence of verbalizable (i.e., analytic) cognitions associated with that emotion" (Buck, 1985, p. 401).

The Measurement of Emotion

Emotion includes neurophysiological, expressive, and experiential components (Izard, 1977). The methods and techniques used to study emotion differ substantially for each component. At the neurophysiological level, common procedures include the use of surgical ablations and lesions, microelectrode implantations, and psychophysiological measures (heart-rate, skin conductance, etc.). Studies of the expressive component have used measures of overt facial expression (Ekman & Friesen, 1978), covert facial expression (Schwartz, Fair, Salt, Mandel, & Klerman, 1976), and vocal affect expression (Scherer, 1986). Self-reports and adjective check-lists are typically used to measure emotion at the experiential level.

The Mood Adjective Check-List (Nowlis, 1965) and the Differential Emotions Scale (Izard, 1972) are two well-validated measures of subjective emotional experience. Nevertheless, these and similar scales consist entirely of verbal items, and they require rather extensive linguistic capability. Emotion theorists have been the first to recognize the limitations associated with verbally based measures:

Such tests can measure emotion variables or emotion-determined functioning only insofar as these can be expressed symbolically via words, language, and the attendant higher-order cognitive processes. It is reasonable that these conditions or restrictions limit the degree to which verbal items measure emotion processes or emotion-determined functioning. (Izard, 1971, p. 374)

Substantial progress has been made in the development of nonverbal measures of emotion expression (cf. Scherer & Ekman, 1982). The Facial Action Coding System (FACS; Ekman & Friesen, 1978) offers a systematic method for coding all visible changes in the facial musculature. FACS can be used to reliably distinguish among hundreds of facial expressions, and specific patterns have been associated with each of the primary emotions (cf. Hager & Ekman, 1983). However, FACS can only be used to detect *outwardly visible* facial expressions. Contractions of the facial musculature are often too small to be visibly detected, but nevertheless participate in emotional episodes (Fridlund & Izard, 1983). Facial electromyographic measures of such covert facial expressions can reveal both the direction and intensity of affective responses (Cacioppo, Petty, Losch, & Kim, 1986).

Application of Emotion Theory to the Study of Attitudes

A rich vocabulary has clearly developed for describing emotions and emotion-related functioning. Included in this vocabulary is the concept of attitude. For example, differential emotions theory defines attitude as an *affective-cognitive structure,* which refers to "a bond, tie, or strong association of one of the affects . . . with images, words, thoughts, or ideas" (Izard, 1977, p. 65). This is very similar to a definition of attitude as *the affect associated with a mental object* (cf. Greenwald, chap. 17 in this volume).

Despite the obvious parallel in definitions between attitude and emotion theory, the two literatures rarely make contact. Thus, each has developed its own set of assumptions, research problems, measurement devices, and to a large extent, terminology. Nevertheless, emotion theory can offer significant insight into attitude structure and function. One way to facilitate an interaction between the two literatures is to develop a common framework for discussing attitudes and emotion. The concept of representation offers one such framework.

THE REPRESENTATION OF ATTITUDES AND EMOTION

Attitudes are learned. Learning means that the effects of experience are somehow maintained or represented by the organism. In his treatment of acquired behavioral dispositions (which include attitudes), Campbell (1963) noted: "It is a commonplace observation that for human and other organisms, *behavior is modified as a result of experience,* that somehow a person *retains residues of experience of such a nature as to guide, bias, or otherwise influence later behavior"* (p. 97). Representations are "residues of experiene." To understand the nature of attitudes, we must first understand the concept of representation. To do so, we draw heavily from Palmer's (1978) treatment of representational systems.

The Nature of Representation

A representation is something that stands for something else. More precisely, a representation requires "a correspondence (mapping) from objects in the represented world to objects in the representing world such that at least some relations in the represented world are structurally preserved in the representing world" (Palmer, 1978, pp. 266–267). A representational system can be described in terms of its domain, contents, code, medium, and dynamics (Roitblat, 1982). The class of objects or situations to which the representation applies is its *domain.* The elements in the represented world that are preserved by the representation are its *contents.* The transformational rule that maps features in the represented world to corresponding features in the representation is its *code.* The physical form of a representation is its *medium.* The *dynamics* of a representation refers to the manner in which it changes over time.

Experience with an object, person, or issue can produce multiple representations. Two representations are *informationally equivalent* if they preserve the same information (contents); otherwise, they are *nonequivalent* (Palmer, 1978). When two representations preserve the same information (contents) in the same way (code), they are *completely equivalent.* However, even two completely equivalent representations can still differ in medium and dynamics. Although the medium is not the message (Roitblat, 1982), the medium can determine empirical operations that will permit access to the message.

The Code of Cognitive Representations

A current debate in the study of human cognition concerns the code of mental representations. One view is that a propositional code is sufficient for the representation of knowledge (e.g., Anderson & Bower, 1973; Pylyshyn, 1973). Propositions are descriptions, usually expressed in language, that are either true or false. A propositional code preserves truth information about the represented world. Any structure that exists in a propositional representation is due to the truth-preserving quality of the transformation rule, and is extrinisic to the representation itself (Palmer, 1978).

Another view is that a propositional code is not sufficient, or even necessary, in accounting for some forms of mental representation. For example, representations of visual images are claimed to preserve spatial information, at least in part, in a spatial medium (Kosslyn, 1980). Thus, the code for representing visual images can be *non*propositional, and any structure that exists in such a representation will be intrinsic to the representation itself (Palmer, 1978).

A general perspective on mental representation is offered by *dual coding theory* (Paivio, 1986), according to which cognition is served by two distinct symbolic systems. One system is specialized for the representation and processing of language, the other for nonverbal objects and events. Both systems can represent information from the visual, auditory, and haptic sensorimotor systems. However, the nonverbal system is unique in its ability to represent information about taste and smell. Indeed, olfactory perception and memory appears to make very little contact with verbal knowledge (cf. Engen, 1982).

Representations from the two systems are never *completely equivalent* because they preserve information about real world experiences in different codes and media. Nevertheless, the two forms of representations can be *informationally equivalent,* and therefore indistinguishable in the information they preserve about the real world. However, representations from the two systems can also be *nonequivalent,* preserving different information about the same real world experience. In these cases, different forms of measurement can reveal *unique* information about a single experience.

Representations and Measurement

Measurement can be interpreted as the construction of a representation (cf. Michell, 1986; Townshend & Ashby, 1984). A scale of measurement is a rule for assigning a representing value (usually a number) to some property of an object (Hays, 1981). The rule for assigning numbers to true values is the representational code, and it establishes the level of measurement (i.e., ordinal, interval, or ratio). For example, values on an ordinal scale preserve information only about the true *ordering* of objects, whereas values on an interval scale are some *linear function* of the true values.

Psychological measurement is a special case in which a representing value is used to preserve information about some aspect of a mental representation. Thus, the purpose of psychological measurement is to construct a representation of a representation. We refer to such measures as *higher-order representations,* in order to distinguish them from the *primary representation.*

Different measures are often used to represent aspects of the same primary representation. Two measures will be informationally equivalent if the general form of the assignment rule (code) is the same. Fahrenheit and Centigrade scales are informationally equivalent because they are both linear transformations of true temperature. However, it is more often the case that two measures will produce nonequivalent higher-order representations. For example, a person's body temperature can be measured using a thermometer marked in Fahrenheit units or by requesting an introspective self-report in Fahrenheit units. The resulting higher-order representations will clearly differ in the information they preserve about body temperature.

The Representation of Emotion

Contemporary theories of emotion allow for both propositional and nonpropositional representations of emotional experience. This is clearly evident in the distinctions made between analytic versus syncretic knowledge (Buck, 1985), and conceptual versus schematic memory systems (Leventhal, 1984). However, it is useful to make a further distinction between *soft* and *hard* representations of emotion (Zajonc & Markus, 1984). Soft representations refer to the various forms of knowledge representation, including syncretic, schematic, conceptual, and analytic. In contrast, hard representations refer to the actual motor responses associated with an emotion, and do not require verbal or propositional mediation. Emotion can then be described in terms of three components:

> One is the *arousal* of autonomic and visceral activity. The second is the *expression* of emotion, which is mainly its motor manifestation. These two forms of discharge—the internal arousal processes and the manifest expression—constitute the basis of the *hard representation* of emotion. The third component is the *experience* of emotion, which is the basis of its *soft representation.* (Zajonc & Markus, 1984, p. 79)

In addition to motor responses, hard representations include autonomic, glandular, and visceral activity. Information about an emotional experience is partially preserved by soft representations and partially preserved by hard representations. No representational form alone can be expected to preserve all of the information about an emotional episode.

The Representation of Attitudes

We defined attitudes as mental and neural representations to emphasize the idea that attitudes can be supported in many different media and by multiple codes. Nevertheless, higher-order representations of attitude typically take the form of propositions, scale values, or signs:

Propositions	Scale Values	Signs
I dislike the smell of sour milk.	2	−
I am neutral about the color blue.	4	0
I like the taste of pears.	7	+

With rare exception, the empirical operations used to obtain these higher-order representations are based on verbal self-reports. Thus, it is assumed that verbal knowledge is capable of representing most (if not all) of the information associated with an attitude. Although verbal knowledge may contain information *about* nonverbal representations, some transformation of the primary representation is required to place it in verbal form. Information may be lost in such transformations, as when body temperature is measured by introspective self-report.

From this perspective, it is evident that the focus of attitude research has been on the soft representation of attitude, and more specifically on analytic forms of cognitive representation. Placing attitudes in the context of a representational framework helps to identify important aspects of attitude that have not yet received attention in attitude research.

CONTEMPORARY ATTITUDE RESEARCH

Attitude Measurement

A recent textbook divides attitude measurement techniques into two major categories: direct and indirect (Petty & Cacioppo, 1981). *Direct procedures* refer to the traditional verbal report techniques (cf. Edwards, 1957), and include equal-appearing interval (Thurstone & Chave, 1929), semantic differential (Osgood, Suci, & Tannenbaum, 1958), summated rating (Likert, 1932), and single-item self-rating scales. *Indirect procedures* include various disguised techniques (e.g., Hammond, 1948; Sigall & Page, 1971), behavioral indicators (e.g., Milgram, 1972), and physiological measures (e.g., Cacioppo & Petty, 1981).

The indirect procedures are rarely used in attitude research; most studies use verbal self-report techniques. Verbal report scales are attractive because they are easy to administer and generally have good reliability. Indeed, verbal measures are often used as the criterion against which other measures are evaluated. Thus, when a physiological measure fails to correlate with a verbal criterion, suspicion is cast upon the physiological rather than the verbal technique.

The distinction between direct versus indirect procedures creates a false dichotomy. A measure derived from physiological response patterns is no less direct than one derived from verbal self-report scales. Both approaches rely on transformations of a primary representation, and they may or may not preserve the same information. Thus, *all* attitude measurement techniques are indirect because they all share the common goal of constructing a higher-order representation. A more profitable way to classify measurement procedures is in terms of the information they preserve about attitudes. Two different higher-order representations can each preserve important but different information, and it may not be possible to establish one as the criterion against which others are evaluated (see Ajzen, chap. 10 in this volume for a similar view).

As one illustration, subtle changes in the instructions that accompany attitude scales can produce substantially different higher-order representations of attitude. For example, semantic differential scales are often assumed to represent the affective component of attitude. However, instructions that emphasize attributes of an object (Blood donation is good/bad) produce distinctly different ratings than do instructions that emphasize the affect-arousing properties of an object (Blood donation makes me feel good/bad) (Breckler & Wiggins, 1987). The first instructional format involves propositional ratings of an object, whereas the second involves a judgment about the affect associated with an object.

Verbal measures are certainly capable of representing many distinct aspects of attitude. However, an exclusive reliance on verbally based measures implies that people have accurate and complete access to their own attitudes. Clearly, this assumption is not supported by research (Nisbett & Wilson, 1977). Indeed, self-reports are often incongruent with independently obtained measures of affective responses (Wilson, 1985). Even when people do have good verbal access to attitudes, they may be motivated to misrepresent themselves (e.g., Crosby, Bromley, & Saxe, 1980). It is partly for this reason that elaborate unobtrusive measures of attitude have been developed (Webb, Campbell, Schwartz, & Sechrest, 1966).

Nonverbal measures of emotion expression (described in a previous section) offer great potential for representing attitudinal properties that are not captured by verbal measures (cf. Cacioppo, Petty, & Geen, chap. 11 in this volume). For example, facial electromyographic measures can reveal differences in affective reactions that are independent of verbal measures of arousal (Cacioppo, Petty, Losch, & Kim, 1986). The level of technical and data-analytic sophistication required by such methods is demanding, but the methods are becoming increasingly available to the research community (e.g., Cacioppo & Dorfman, 1987; Ekman, 1982; Scherer, 1982).

Attitude Structure

Three basic approaches have been taken to the study of attitude structure (cf. McGuire, 1985). One focus has been on the organization of individual attitudes, with research examining the structural properties of cognition (e.g., Scott, Osgood, & Peterson, 1979) and interrelationships among attitude components (e.g., Breckler, 1984). A second concern has been the organization of a person's many attitudes and belief systems (e.g., Kerlinger, 1984). A third approach places attitudes in the context of personality processes and behavior (e.g., Snyder & DeBono, chap. 13 in this volume).

The present approach is to recognize that attitudes are *complex* representations. A complex representation is composed of many simple representations, each of which can preserve information about a different aspect of the represented world. It is therefore possible for different aspects of the represented world to have qualitatively different representations (Palmer, 1978). Attitude structure refers to differences and interactions among the simple representations that comprise a complex representational system.

The complex representation that develops through experience with an odor illustrates this approach. Olfactory perception is mediated by areas of the brain that make very little contact with those that mediate language. Indeed, people are quite poor at learning associations between verbal labels and odorants, although recognition memory for the same odorants is superior. In contrast to the visual and auditory modalities, perception of an odor usually requires a distal stimulus. The spatial organization of olfactory receptors is preserved in the olfactory bulb, and several theories of odor perception assume a spatial and temporal coding of olfactory stimulation (cf. Engen, 1982).

Now consider the representation of a person's attitude toward the smell of sour milk. The evaluative words and labels associated with sour milk must be represented in different *media* than the olfactory stimulation caused by sour milk itself. Self-reports may reveal information about one's verbal knowledge of responses to sour milk, but they are unlikely to preserve much information about the olfactory stimulation itself. In response to the smell of sour milk physiological and motor activity must also be mediated by different primary representations than responses that occur without the olfactory stimulation. This indicates that each representation can have its own *domain* of application. For example, substantial differences in covariation among attitude components are observed when attitudes are measured in the presence of an attitude object than when they are measured in its absence (Breckler, 1984).

Attitude Function

Attitudes are said to serve four basic functions (Katz, 1960; Smith, Bruner, & White, 1956). First, attitudes guide behavior toward valued goals and away from aversive events (the *adaptive* or *utilitarian* function). Second, attitudes help to manage and simplify information processing tasks (the *knowl-*

edge or *economy* function). Third, attitudes allow people to communicate information about their personality and values (the *expressive* or *self-realizing* function). And fourth, attitudes protect people from unacceptable or threatening thoughts, urges, and impulses (the *ego-defensive* function).

These four functions are not mutually exclusive, nor do they form an exhaustive set. Research on attitude functions has shown that individual objects can be associated with a specific function (Shavitt, chap. 12 in this volume), and that situational demands can make one function more salient than another (Jamieson & Zanna, chap. 15 in this volume). However, functional theories do not distinguish among the functions in terms of their relative importance (but see Greenwald, chap. 17 of this volume).

In contrast, the definition of attitude as representation suggests that the primary function of attitude is to guide behavior. That is, attitudes serve an adaptive function by providing a mechanism for previous experience to influence later behavior. This is precisely the function of representation. "By virtue of their ability to model environmental phenomena, [representations] provide a level of internal, structural complexity not admitted by exclusively reflex-based systems" (Roitblat, 1982, p. 370).

The other hypothesized attitudinal functions are also adaptive, each implying a class of responses in relation to an attitude object. Thus, the adaptive function is viewed as primary, with the other functions serving more specialized roles.

Attitude-Behavior Relationship

Attitudes are defined as having a directive influence on behavior. Despite early pessimistic conclusions (e.g., Wicker, 1969), it now appears that attitudes and actions do covary *under certain conditions.* Progress in this area has been achieved in several ways (cf. Greenwald, chap. 1 in this volume). Methodological criteria have been proposed (Fishbein & Ajzen, 1974), formal models have been developed (Ajzen & Fishbein, 1977), and other variables have been found to strengthen or weaken the attitude-behavior relationship (e.g., Davidson, Yantis, Norwood, & Montano, 1985; Fazio & Zanna, 1981; Wicker, 1971).

Studies of the attitude-behavior relationship typically use verbal measures of attitude. Thus, attitude-behavior correlations reflect an association between a verbal representation of attitude and behavior. The model of reasoned action (Ajzen & Fishbein, 1977), which has stimulated a tremendous amount of research, specifies that the immediate determinant of behavior is one's intention (always verbally assessed) to engage in the action. Although this model has been revised (see Ajzen, chap. 10 in this volume), it continues to view behavior as being rationally determined.

Each representation has its own domain of application, and can therefore have a different influence on behavior in different situations (cf. Campbell, 1963). Studies that use verbal measures of attitude may not reveal the potentially important influence of nonverbal representations of attitude on overt action. Behaviors that occur in the presence of an attitude object may be guided by different representations than behaviors that occur in the absence of that object (Breckler, 1984). Attitudes that develop through direct experience with an object may have a greater influence on behavior than do attitudes that develop through indirect experience (Fazio & Zanna, 1981).

Attitude Change

Most persuasion research derives from the message learning approach (Hovland, Janis, & Kelly, 1953), according to which a persuasive communication is most effective when its recipient *attends* to and *comprehends* the message, *yields* to the advocated position, and *remembers* the conclusion. The recipient is assumed to generate message-related *cognitive responses* as an intermediate output step between comprehension and yielding (cf. McGuire, 1985). In a later development, cognitive response theory (Greenwald, 1968) suggested that recipient-generated thoughts were the critical determinant of attitude change, and that such thoughts need not be related to message contents. Cognitive response theory has since dominated attitude change research (Petty, Ostrom, & Brock, 1981).

Other approaches have been taken to the study of attitude change (see Petty & Cacioppo, 1981). Nevertheless, the majority of them are based on theories that emphasize some aspect of information processing (Eagly & Chaiken, 1984). The learning approaches (e.g., Doob, 1947; Staats, 1968) are one exception, but they have had a relatively minor impact on persuasion research. An important exception, however, is the *mere exposure hypothesis* (Zajonc, 1968), according to which repeated mere exposure to a stimulus is sufficient for enhancing attitudes toward it. Mere exposure can even produce attitude change outside of the observer's awareness (W. R. Wilson, 1979; Zajonc, 1980)—an effect that is not easily explained by most information processing theories of persuasion.

Several theorists have recently suggested that persuasion occurs in two distinct ways (e.g., Chaiken, 1980; Petty & Cacioppo, 1986). For example, the elaboration likelihood model (Petty & Cacioppo, 1986) postulates two *routes* to persuasion. The *central route* is followed when the recipient of a persuasive communication is motivated and able to engage in extensive processing of message content. Any resulting attitude change is assumed to be relatively enduring and to predict behavior. The *peripheral route* is followed when the motivation or ability to process a message is absent or weak, yet attitude change occurs because of a simple cue in the persuasion setting. Peripheral cues include positive or negative affect, source characteristics such as expertise or attractiveness, number of arguments, and so on. Attitude change via the peripheral route is assumed to be "relatively temporary, susceptible, and unpredictive of behavior" (Petty & Cacioppo, 1986, p. 126).

Most attitude change experiments use persuasive communications that are expressed in words, and presented either orally or in writing. The effectiveness of the persuasive communication is typically measured by a verbal rating scale. Participants in cognitive response experiments are additionally asked to verbalize or list their thoughts in response to the message. Thus, the majority of attitude change experiments examine the impact of propositions on verbally expressed attitudes, implicitly assuming that the dynamics of verbal representations are of greatest concern. This may be a faulty assumption, as T. D. Wilson (1985) noted:

> Processes are triggered which lead to changes in attitudes, yet people are unable to report either the cognitive processes or the resulting internal states. When asked to report these states, people rely on the conscious, verbal system to do so . . . When there is limited access, however, the verbal system makes *inferences* [italics added] about what these processes and states might be. (p. 16)

All representations can change, and the dynamic processes can differ according to domain, contents, code, or medium. A persuasive communication can successfully change some representations, and yet leave others unchanged. From this perspective, the central route to persuasion is found to be effective because it involves propositional communications that cause a change in verbal representations. In contrast, observations that the peripheral route is ineffective may be explained, in part, by the reliance on verbal methods to assess the influence of nonverbal attitude change processes. Attitude measures that preserve more information about nonverbal representations may indicate more substantial attitude change via the peripheral route. Indeed, verbal communications are often the least effective way to produce an enduring change in attitude (cf. Cook & Flay, 1978).

Very little research has investigated emotional determinants of attitude change (e.g., Roseman, Abelson, & Ewing, 1986). The only substantial literature on the topic concerns the impact of fear-arousing communications. Although a large number of studies indicate that the use of fear in a persuasive communication can effectively change intentions and behaviors in the advocated direction (Sutton, 1982), the mechanisms underlying such change are poorly understood.

Summary of Attitude Research

Contemporary attitude research is premised in the assumption that propositions are the primary code for attitude representations. The methods commonly used to measure attitudes rely heavily on a well-developed verbal capability, and they assume introspective access to the information preserved by attitude representations. Attitude-behavior studies focus on the relationship between verbally expressed attitudes and overt actions, and they rarely consider the influence of nonpropositional representations on behavior. Persuasion research has been dominated by the message learning approach, with its clear emphasis on the dynamics of propositional representations. The affective nature of attitude has been neglected in contemporary research. Attitudes have been narrowly interpreted as the location of a check mark on a verbally anchored continuum.

CONCLUSIONS

We defined attitudes as mental and neural representations that have a directive influence on behavior. Although contemporary theories of emotion suggest the importance of nonpropositional representations of attitude, a review of the attitude literature shows a primary emphasis on propositional and verbal forms of attitude representation. Perhaps the greatest value of this review is in identifying directions for future attitude research.

Attitude measurement technology can be improved if methods that have been developed for measuring emotion expression (overt and covert facial expression, vocal affect expression) are used in addition to verbal rating scales. Nonverbal methods might be especially valuable in measuring the attitudes of infants and young children (cf. Izard, 1982).

Past studies of the attitude-behavior relationship have focused primarily on propositional controls of behavior (e.g., Ajzen & Fishbein, 1977). Better behavioral prediction might be achieved if more emphasis is placed on nonrational and emotional determinants of behavior (cf. Millar & Tesser, 1986; Zanna & Rempel, in press).

Persuasion research has been preoccupied with the effects of rational appeals on verbally expressed attitudes. Affective processes are assigned a relatively minor role in theories of the persuasion process (e.g., Petty & Cacioppo, 1986). This is surprising given the heavy use of emotional appeals in politics and advertising (cf. Roseman, Abelson, & Ewing, 1986). Perhaps a greater consideration of affective processes will help to explain why experimentally induced attitude change rarely lasts longer than the experimental session (Cook & Flay, 1978; Zajonc & Markus, 1984).

Finally, the formation and development of attitudes has not received much attention in attitude research (cf. Zanna & Rempel, in press). Studies of attitude development can reveal the manner in which attitude representations initially form and then change with increasing experience. Developmental analyses may also indicate the origin and nature of nonequivalent attitude representations.

In commenting on the role of affect in attribution processes, Jones (1985) noted:

> The 1970s have been characterized as a period in which cognitive aproaches to the understanding of interpersonal relations have become ascendant . . . There are more than a few signs that the cognitive revolution will be at least moderated by an increasing interest in affect and arousal. (p. 93)

As attitude theory and research enters a new era (McGuire, 1985), we only hope that it too is done with feeling.

ACKNOWLEDGMENT

Preparation of this chapter was facilitated by a National Science Foundation Presidential Young Investigator Award (BNS-86-57093). We wish to thank Samantha Butler, Tony Greenwald, Paula Niedenthal, and Anthony Pratkanis for kindly commenting on earlier drafts of this chapter.

REFERENCES

Ajzen, I., & Fishbein, M. (1977). Attitude-behavior relations: A theoretical analysis and review of empirical research. *Psychological Bulletin, 84,* 888–918.

Allport, G. W. (1935). Attitudes. In C. Murchison (Ed.), *Handbook of social psychology* (pp. 798–844). Worcester, MA: Clark University Press.

Anderson, J. R., & Bower, G. H. (1973). *Human associative memory.* New York: V. H. Winston.

Bem, D. J. (1968). Attitudes as self-descriptions: Another look at the attitude-behavior link. In A. G. Greenwald, T. C. Brock, & T. M. Ostrom (Eds.), *Psychological foundations of attitudes* (pp. 197–215). New York: Academic Press.

Bem, D. J. (1972). Self-perception theory. In L. Berkowitz (Ed.), *Advances in experimental social psychology* (Vol. 6, pp. 1–62). New York: Academic Press.

Breckler, S. J. (1984). Empirical validation of affect, behavior, and cognition as distinct components of attitude. *Journal of Personality and Social Psychology, 47,* 1191–1205.

Breckler, S. J., & Wiggins, E. C. (1987). *Affect versus evaluation in the scructure of attitudes.* Manuscript submitted for publication.

Buck, R. (1985). Prime theory: An integrated view of motivation and emotion. *Psychological Review, 92,* 389–413.

Cacioppo, J. T., & Dorfman, D. D. (1987) Waveform moment analysis in psychophysiological research. *Psychological Bulletin, 102,* 421–438.

Cacioppo, J. T., & Petty, R. E. (1981). Electromyograms as measures of extent and affectivity of information processing. *American Psychologist, 36,* 441–456.

Cacioppo, J. T., Petty, R. E., Losch, M. E., & Kim, H. S. (1986). Electromyographic activity over facial muscle regions can differentiate the valence and intensity of affective reactions. *Journal of Personality and Social Psychology, 50,* 260–268.

Campbell, D. T. (1963). Social attitudes and other acquired behavioral dispositions. In S. Koch (Ed.), *Psychology: A study of a science* (Vol. 6, pp. 94–172). New York: McGraw-Hill.

Cannon, W. B. (1927). The James-Lange theory of emotions: A critical examination and an alternative theory. *American Journal of Psychology, 39,* 106–124.

Chaiken, S. (1980). Heuristic versus systematic information processing and the use of source versus message cues in persuasion. *Journal of Personality and Social Psychology, 39,* 752–766.

Chaiken, S., & Stangor, C. (1987). Attitudes and attitude change. *Annual Review of Psychology, 38,* 575–630.

Cook, T. D., & Flay, B. R. (1978). The persistence of experimentally induced attitude change. In L. Berkowitz (Ed.), *Advances in Experimental Social Psychology* (Vol. 11, pp. 1–57). New York: Academic Press.

Crosby, F., Bromley, S., & Saxe, L. (1980). Recent unobtrusive studies of black and white discrimination and prejudice: A literature review. *Psychological Bulletin, 87,* 546–563.

Davidson, A. R., Yantis, S., Norwood, M., & Montano, D. E. (1985). Amount of information about the attitude object and attitude-behavior consistency. *Journal of Personality and Social Psychology, 49,* 1184–1198.

Doob, L. W. (1947). The behavior of attitudes. *Psychological Review, 54,* 135–156.

Eagly, A. H., & Chaiken, S. (1984). Cognitive theories of persuasion. In L. Berkowitz (Ed.), *Advances in Experimental Social Psychology* (Vol. 17, pp. 267–359). New York: Academic Press.

Edwards, A. L. (1957). *Techniques of attitude scale construction.* New York: Appleton-Century-Crofts.

Ekman, P. (1982). Methods for measuring facial action. In K. R. Scherer & P. Ekman (Eds.), *Handbook of methods in nonverbal behavior research* (pp. 45–90). Cambridge, England: Cambridge University Press.

Ekman, P., & Friesen, W. V. (1978). *Facial action coding system.* Palo Alto, CA: Consulting Psychologists Press.

Engen, T. (1982). *The perception of odors.* New York: Academic Press.

Fazio, R. H., & Zanna, M. P. (1981). Direct experience and attitude behavior consistency. In L. Berkowitz (Ed.), *Advances in experimental social psychology* (Vol. 14, pp. 161–202). New York: Academic Press.

Fishbein, M., & Ajzen, I. (1974). Attitudes toward objects as predictors of single and multiple behavioral criteria. *Psychological Review, 81,* 59–74.

Fishbein, M., & Ajzen, I. (1975). *Belief, attitude, intention, and behavior: An introduction to theory and research.* Reading, MA: Addison-Wesley.

Fleming, D. (1967). Attitude: The history of a concept. *Perspectives in American History, 1,* 287–365.

Fridlund, A. J., & Izard, C. E. (1983). Electromyographic studies of facial expressions of emotions and patterns of emotions. In J. T. Cacioppo & R. E. Petty (Eds.), *Social psychophysiology: A sourcebook* (p. 243–286). New York: Guilford Press.

Greenwald, A. G. (1968). Cognitive learning, cognitive response to persuasion, and attitude change. In A. G. Greenwald, T. C. Brock, & T. M. Ostrom (Eds.), *Psychological foundations of attitudes* (pp. 147–170). New York: Academic Press.

Hager, J. C., & Ekman, P. (1983). The inner and outer meanings of facial expressions. In J. T. Cacioppo & R. E. Petty (Eds.), *Social psychophysiology: A sourcebook* (pp. 287–306). New York: Guilford.

Hammond, K. R. (1948). Measuring attitudes by error-choice: An indirect method. *Journal of Abnormal and Social Psychlogy, 43,* 38–48.

Hays, W. L. (1981). *Statistics* (3rd ed.). New York: Holt, Rinehart & Winston.

Hilgard, E. R. (1980). The trilogy of mind: Cognition, affection, and conation. *Journal of the History of the Behavioral Sciences, 16,* 107–117.

Hovland, C. I., Janis, I. L., & Kelley, J. J. (1953). *Communication and persuasion.* New Haven, CT: Yale University Press.

Insko, C. A. & Schopler, J. (1967). Triadic consistency: A statement of affective-cognitive-conative consistency. *Psychological Review, 74,* 361–376.

Izard, C. E. (1971). *The face of emotion.* New York: Appleton-Century-Crofts.

Izard, C. E. (1972). *Patterns of emotions: A new analysis of anxiety and depression.* New York: Academic Press.

Izard, C. E. (177). *Human emotions.* New York: Plenum.

Izard, C. E. (Ed.). (1982). *Measuring emotions in infants and children.* Cambridge, England: Cambridge University Press.

James, W. (1890). *The principles of psychology* (Vol. 1). New York: Dover.

Jones, E. E. (1985). Major developments in social psychology during the past five decades. In G. Lindzey & E. Aronson (Eds.), *Handbook of social psychology* (3rd ed., Vol 1, pp. 47–107). New York: Random House.

Katz, D. (1960). The functional approach to the study of attitudes. *Public Opinion Quarterly, 24,* 163–204.

Katz, D., & Stotland, E. (1959). A preliminary statement to a theory of attitude structure and change. In S. Koch (Ed.), *Psychology: A study of a science* (Vol. 3, pp. 423–475). New York: McGraw-Hill.

Kerlinger, F. N. (1984). *Liberalism and conservatism: The nature and structure of social attitudes.* Hillsdale, NJ: Lawrence Erlbaum Associates.

Kosslyn, S. M. (1980). *Image and mind.* Cambridge, MA: Harvard University Press.

Lange, C. G. (1922). *The emotions: A psychophysiological study.* (I. A. Haupt, Trans.). Baltimore, MD: Williams & Wilkins. (Original work published 1885)

Leventhal, H. (1984). A perceptual-motor theory of emotion. In L. Berkowitz (Ed.), *Advances in Experimental Social Psychology* (Vol. 17, pp. 117–182). New York: Academic Press.

Likert, R. (1932). A technique for the measurement of attitudes [Special issue]. *Archives of Psychology, 140,* 1–55.

Lott, A. J., & Lott, B. E. (1968). A learning theory approach to interpersonal attitudes. In A. G. Greenwald, T. C. Brock, & T. M. Ostrom (Eds.), *Psychological foundations of attitudes* (pp. 67–88). New York: Academic Press.

McGuire, W. J. (1985). Attitudes and attitude change. In G. Lindzey & E. Aronson (Eds.), *Handbook of social psychology* (3rd ed., Vol. 2, pp. 233–346). New York: Random House.

Michell, J. (1986). Measurement scales and statistics: A clash of paradigms. *Psychological Bulletin, 100,* 398–407.

Milgram, S. (1972). The lost-letter technique. In L. Bickman & T. Henchy (Eds.), *Beyond the laboratory: Field research in social psychology* (pp. 245–250). New York: McGraw-Hill.

Millar, M. G., & Tesser, A. (1986). Effects of affective and cognitive focus on the attitude-behavior relation. *Journal of Personality and Social Psychology, 51,* 270–276.

Nisbett, R. E., & Wilson, T. D. (1977). Telling more than we can know: Verbal reports on mental processes. *Psychological Review, 84,* 231–259.

Nowlis, V. (1965). Research with the Mood Adjective Check List. In S. S. Tomkins & C. E. Izard (Eds.), *Affect, cognition, and personality* (pp. 352–389). New York: Springer-Verlag.

Osgood, C. E., Suci, G. J., & Tannenbaum, P. H. (1957). *The measurement of meaning.* Urbana, IL: University of Illinois Press.

Paivio, A. (1986). *Mental representations: A dual coding approach.* New York: Oxford University Press.

Palmer, S. E. (1978). Fundamental aspects of cognitive representation. In E. Rosch & B. B. Lloyd (Eds.), *Cognition and categorization* (pp. 259–303). Hillsdale, NJ: Lawrence Erlbaum Associates.

Petty, R. E., & Cacioppo, J. T. (1981). *Attitudes and persuasion: Classic and contemporary approaches.* Dubuque, IA: Wm. C. Brown.

Petty, R. E., & Cacioppo, J. T. (1986). The elaboration likelihood model of persuasion. In L. Berkowitz (Ed.), *Advances in Experimental Social Psychology* (Vol. 19, pp. 123–205). New York: Academic Press.

Petty, R. E., Ostrom, T. M. & Brock, T. C. (Eds.). (1981). *Cognitive responses in persuasion.* Hillsdale, NJ: Lawrence Erlbaum Associates.

Pylyshyn, Z. W. (1973). What the mind's eye tells the mind's brain: A critique of mental imagery. *Psychological Bulletin, 80,* 1–24.

Roitblat, H. L. (1982). The meaning of representation in animal memory. *The Behavioral and Brain Sciences, 5,* 353–406.

Roseman, I., Abelson, R. P., & Ewing, M. F. (1986). Emotion and political cognition: Emotional appeals in political communication. In R. R. Lau & D. O. Sears (Eds.), *Political cognition* (pp. 279–294). Hillsdale, NJ: Lawrence Erlbaum Associates.

Rosenberg, M. J. (1956). Cognitive structure and attitudinal affect. *Journal of Abnormal and Social Psychology, 53,* 367–372.

Russell, B. (1927). *Philosophy.* New York: W. W. Norton.

Ryle, G. (1949). *The concept of mind.* New York: Barnes & Noble.

Schachter, S. (1964). The interaction of cognitive and physiological determinants of emotional state. In L. Berkowitz (Ed.), *Advances in experimental social psychology* (Vol. 1, pp. 49–80). New York: Academic Press.

Schachter, S., & Singer, J. E. (1962). Cognitive, social, and physiological determinants of emotional state. *Psychological Review, 69,* 379–399.

Scherer, K. R. (1982). Methods of research on vocal communication: Paradigms and parameters. In K. R. Scherer & P. Ekman (Eds.), *Handbook of methods in nonverbal behavior research* (pp. 136–198). Cambridge, England: Cambridge University Press.

Scherer, K. R. (1986). Vocal affect expression: A review and a model for future research. *Psychological Bulletin, 99,* 143–165.

Scherer, K. R., & Ekman, P. (Eds.) (1982). *Handbook of methods in nonverbal behavior research.* Cambridge, England: Cambridge University Press.

Schwartz, G. E., Fair, P. L., Salt, P., Mandel, M. R., & Klerman, G. L. (1976). Facial muscle patterning to affective imagery in depressed and nondepressed subjects. *Science, 192,* 489–491.

Scott, W. A., Osgood, D. W., & Peterson, C. (1979). *Cognitive structure: Theory and measurement of individual differences.* Washington, DC: V. H. Winston.

Sigall, H., & Page, R. (1971). Current stereotypes: A little fading, a little faking. *Journal of Personality and Social Psychology, 18,* 247–255.

Smith, M. B. (1947). The personal setting of public opinions: A study of attitudes toward Russia. *Public Opinion Quarterly, 11,* 507–523.

Smith, M. B., Bruner, J. S., & White, R. W. (1956). *Opinions and personality.* New York: Wiley.

Staats, A. W. (1968). Social behaviorism and human motivation: Principles of the attitude-reinforcer-discriminative system. In A. G. Greenwald, T. C. Brock, & T. M. Ostrom (Eds.), *Psychological foundations of attitudes* (pp. 33–66). New York: Academic Press.

Sutton, S. R. (1982). Fear-arousing communications: A critical examination of theory and research. In J. R. Eiser (Ed.), *Social psychology and behavioral medicine.* London: Wiley.

Thurstone, L. L., & Chave, E. J. (1929). *The measurement of attitude.* Chicago: University of Chicago Press.

Townshend, J. T., & Ashby, F. G. (1984). Measurement scales and statistics: The misconception misconceived. *Psychological Bulletin, 96,* 394–401.

Webb, E. J., Campbell, D. T., Schwartz, R. D., & Sechrest, L. (1966). *Unobtrusive measures: Nonreactive research in the social sciences.* Chicago: Rand McNally.

Wicker. A. W. (1969). Attitudes versus actions: The relationship of verbal and overt behavioral responses to attitude objects. *Journal of Social Issues, 25,* 41–78.

Wicker, A. W. (1971). An examination of the "other variables" explanation of attitude-behavior inconsistency. *Journal of Personality and Social Psychology, 19,* 18–30.

Wilson, T. D. (1985). Strangers to ourselves: The origins and accuracy of beliefs about one's own mental state. In J. H. Harvey & G. Weary (Eds.), *Attribution: Basic issues and applications* (pp. 9–36). New York: Academic Press.

Wilson, W. R. (1979). Feeling more than we can know: Exposure effects without learning. *Journal of Personality and Social Psychology, 37,* 811–821.

Zajonc, R. B. (1968). Attitudinal effects of mere exposure. *Journal of Personality and Social Psychology Monograph Supplement, 9,* (2, part 2), 1–27.

Zajonc, R. B. (1980). Feeling and thinking: Preferences need no inferences. *American Psychologist, 35,* 151–175.

Zajonc, R. B., & Markus, H. (1984). Affect and cognition: The hard interface. In C. E. Izard, J. Kagan, & R. B. Zajonc (Eds.), *Emotions, cognition, and behavior* (pp. 73–102). Cambridge, England: Cambridge University Press.

Zanna, M. P., & Rempel, J. K. (in press). Attitudes: A new look at an old concept. In D. Bar-Tal & A. Kruglanski (Eds.), *The social psychology of knowledge.* New York: Cambridge University Press.

17

Why Attitudes are Important: *Defining Attitude and Attitude Theory 20 Years Later*

Anthony G. Greenwald
University of Washington

> In all honesty we must confess that we do not think the time is ripe to be theoretically solemn about the definition of an attitude. Definitions are matters of convenience, and they attain high status only in the advanced stages of a science. In time, greater precision will come. (Smith, Bruner, & White, 1956, p. 34)

Chapter 1 argued that the importance of attitudes has been obscured in recent years by an insufficiently focused definition, and by flawed implicit assumptions about attitude-behavior relations. The present chapter seeks a solution to these problems by defining attitude in complementary relation to other major motivational constructs and by integrating existing analyses of attitude functions in terms of a single major function.

ATTITUDE STRUCTURE: LEVELS OF REPRESENTATION/MOTIVATION

A partial listing of psychology's motivational concepts includes (alphabetically) *affect, attitude, drive, emotion, incentive, need, secondary reinforcement,* and *value.* For the most part, these (and other) motivational terms stand in poorly defined relation to one another, and are free to occupy relatively unbounded domains. The present analysis of attitude structure starts by attempting to define the position of attitude more precisely in relation to the broader set of motivational constructs.

Just as in its motivational domain, in psychology's cognitive domain there exists a diverse array of theoretical constructs, among which relationships have not been well described. The author has recently proposed that relations among these cognitive (mental representation) concepts can be interpreted in terms of *levels of representation* (Greenwald, 1987). In a levels-of-representation (LOR) system, representational units of each of several systems (levels) are constructed from units of an immediately subordinate, but qualitatively distinct, system of representations. Each level succeeds in representing properties of the environment that are not captured by lower levels (i.e., these are emergent properties of the multilevel system).

A specific LOR theory on which Greenwald (1987) focused described five representational levels: features, objects, categories, propositions, and schemata. (This theory was identified as LOR_{h5}—"h" for human and "5" for its number of levels.) In LOR_{h5} the most elementary level, *features,* consists of primitive sensory qualities such as brightness, loudness, warmth, and sharpness. Combinations of features that are capable of becoming figural constitute *objects,* the second level. A class membership relation permits objects to be grouped into units of the third level, *categories.* Syntactic relations among abstract category types (such as action, actor, instrument, and target) produce units of the fourth level, *propositions.* The units of the fifth and highest level, *schemata,* are rule-governed groupings of propositions, such as narrative sequences or logical proofs. The present approach to defining attitude starts by associating motivational terms with each of these five levels of representation. These associations are discoverable by first noting variations in motivational properties of the units at each level.

At the level of sensory *features,* one can distinguish pleasant features (warm temperature, soft texture, quiet sound, moderate illumination) from painful ones (cold temperature, shrill sound, rough texture, glaring light). At the level of *objects* one can identify liked objects (an ice cream cone, a 20-dollar bill) and disliked ones (a rotten apple, a hand grenade). People recognize both evaluatively positive *categories* (such as food or money) and evaluatively negative ones (such as garbage or weapons). *Propositions* describe actions and states that range from desirable to undesirable. The units of LOR_{h5}'s highest level, *schemata,* include (among other subtypes) stories, persuasive arguments, mathematical proofs, and scientific theories; for each of these types of schemata, there are readily noticeable evaluative variations, identified by terms such as aesthetic quality of prose, rhetorical excellence of persuasion, parsimony of proofs, and validity of theories. Table 17.1 suggests relationships of motivational terms to LOR_{h5}'s levels.[1]

TABLE 17.1
Relations Among Levels of Representation
and Motivational Constructs

Level	Motivational Terms
Feature	affect, appetite, drive, feeling
Object	*attitude, emotion,* incentive
Category	*attitude, value*
Proposition	*attitude,* belief, intention, opinion, *value*
Schema	*attitude, emotion,* ideology, justification (moral reasoning), motive, plan, script

Note: Italicized terms appear at two or more levels.

The breadth of the current concept of attitude is indicated by its placement at four of Table 17.1's five levels. The problems with such broad usage can be illustrated with an example in which these multiple interpretations are applied simultaneously. Consider a professor's motivational orientation toward a new graduate student. Should *attitude* refer to the professor's (a) (object-level) liking response to the particular student, (b) (category-level) evaluations that relate to the student (e.g., students, women, Chinese persons, etc.), (c) (proposition-level) intentions that relate to students (e.g., *Don't judge a book by its cover, Be encouraging but reserved),* or to women or to Chinese persons, or (d) (schema-level) complexes of beliefs, policies, and evaluation that relate to students, etc.?

By permitting several interpretations simultaneously, the current broad conception of attitude precludes precise reference; it obliges attitude to serve only as a general motivational term. Two possible solutions to this problem are: (a) to adopt a more restrictive use of attitude, or (b) to develop new labels for level-of-motivation distinctions that are not ade-

---

[1]Previous hierarchical conceptions of relations among motivational constructs have rarely sought to encompass more than two of Table 17.1's five levels. Examples include the primary-secondary process distinction in psychoanalytic theory (Freud, 1900/1953), the distinction between innate (primary) and acquired (secondary) drives in learning-behavior theory (e.g., Miller, 1951), the distinction between first and second signaling systems by Pavlov (1955), and the relation between evaluation of subject-verb-object propositions and evaluations of their category-level components (e.g., Gollob, 1974; Insko, 1981; Osgood & Tannebaum, 1955; Wyer, 1974). The social behaviorist treatment of motivation by Staats (1968) is unusually differentiated in encompassing three levels (which approximate the first three of Table 17.1's five levels). Vallacher and Wegner's (1985; 1987) recent analysis of *action identification* describes variations in the perceived control of behavior, ranging from abstract, high levels (e.g., in terms of long-term goals) to lower, more concrete levels (e.g., in terms of specific movements). However, their theory does not commit itself to specific identities of levels, nor does it take a position on the number of distinct levels.

quately captured by existing terms. However, even if it is clear that one of these solutions is desirable, either would be strongly opposed by the inertia of long-established usages. Accordingly, the present treatment attempts a compromise that is in part a narrowing of the usage of attitude and in part a proposal to make distinctions (among types of attitudes) that can permit increased precision of usage while preserving much of the term's present breadth.

In the present treatment, attitude is defined as the *affect associated with a mental object.* This is both (a) a substantial retreat to the past (the definition is virtually identical to Thurstone's [1931], "Attitude is the affect for or against a psychological object") and (b) a narrowing relative to recently popular definitions that have permitted attitudes to be proposition- or schema-level entities. (In particular, this definition excludes the 3-component interpretation of attitude, which is a schema-level conception.)

The present definition's reference to the object of attitude as a *mental object* requires clarification to avoid confusion with the more restricted notion of object as one of LOR_{h5}'s five levels of representation. A mental object is a representation at any of LOR_{h5}'s four highest levels (object, category, proposition, or schema). In contrast, object (*qua* level) in LOR_{h5} designates an entity that is conceived as being located in physical space and time. These two uses of "object" will be kept distinct by referring to *mental object* or *attitude object* for the broader conception, and *ordinary object* or *spatiotemporal object* or *object* (without qualifier) for the narrower one. Table 17.2 gives examples of attitude objects at each of LOR_{h5}'s four highest representational levels.

TABLE 17.2
Examples of Mental (Attitude) Objects at LOR_{h5}'s Object,
Category, Proposition, and Schema Levels of Representation

Level	Examples
Object[a]	a friend, an automobile, an insect, a poison ivy plant
Category	Eskimos, paintings, snakes, Christmas trees
Proposition	Terrorists hijacking airplanes, citizens paying income tax, drinking to become intoxicated, using contraceptive devices
Schema	Psychoanalytic theory, the game of baseball, The 10 Commandments, a career in medicine

[a]The listed objects should be interpreted as specific individuals (e.g., the poison ivy plant on which one is about to sit).

The distinctions among levels of attitude objects in Table 17.2 can be used to avoid confusions of the sort that were noted in chapter 1's discussion of LaPiere's (1934) research. The young couple who accompanied LaPiere can be construed as attitute objects (a) in their identities as individual persons, or (b) as the intersection of several categories, or (c) as constituents of various propositions, and so forth. Confusion results if it is not clear that just one of these levels of mental object is intended in any context.

This analysis has used the theory of levels of representation in two ways. First, LOR_{h5} was used in noting that attitude has sometimes been defined as having the structure of a high-level representation such as a proposition or schema. (The three-component definition, for example, is a schema structure.) The presently preferred definition interprets attitude as an affective associate of a mental representation, a compound structure that links a mental object at one of the four higher levels with lowest (feature-)level affective qualities. Second, LOR_{h5} was used to make distinctions within the broad class of mental representations that can be attitude objects. Attitude objects can be representations at any of the four highest levels of LOR_{h5}.

Implications for Attitude Research

If the author were reading rather than writing this chapter, his reaction to the proposal just made would be: Why bother? Why not maintain the present broad conception of *attitude* as is? What is to be gained by introducing distinctions that others haven't seen fit to make previously? or (borrowing from the chapter-opening quote from Smith, Bruner, & White, 1956) Why is it now the time to become "theoretically solemn" by introducing "greater precision"? The answer can equally be taken from the Smith, Bruner, and White quote—from their observation that "Definitions are matters of convenience." The broad definition of attitude appears to have become inconvenient, as reflected in the difficulty of both (a) producing a satisfying account of the relationship of attitudes to behavior and (b) reaching consensus on the functions of attitudes. (See the introductory discussions of these points in chap. 1.)

The major research-procedural recommendation of the present analysis concerns the necessity for care in specifying the attitude object in attitude measurement; the attitude object should be presented so as to target the single representational level (i.e.,[ordinary] object, category, proposition, or schema) that is most appropriate for the research objectives. For example, in measuring an attitude toward snakes as a category, one should present the respondent with a photograph of a prototypical snake, or with the category name "snake" rather than presenting a live (ordinary object) snake. (Breckler, 1984, found that these variations in presenting the attitude object produced substantial variations in correlations of attitudes with behavioral intentions and with other conceptually linked measures.)

ATTITUDE FUNCTION: MOTIVATIONAL ORIENTATION TO MENTAL OBJECTS

In the two most definitive treatments of attitude functions, Smith et al. (1956) named three attitude functions (*object appraisal, social adjustment,* and *externalization)* and Katz (1960) described four (*adjustive,*[2] *ego-defensive, value-expressive* and *knowledge*). In contrast with those treatments, the present analysis interprets attitudes as having one major function, which is to set an evaluative level with which one's behavior in relation to the attitude object should be consistent—an *object appraisal* function.

The Object Appraisal Function

Smith et al. (1956) described the object appraisal function as follows: "The holding of an attitude provides a ready aid in 'sizing up' objects and events in the environment from the point of view of one's major interests and going concerns. . . . [T]he person is saved the energy-consuming and sometimes painful process of figuring out *de novo* how he shall relate himself to it" (p. 41). These two sentences manage to incorporate the major features of two of Katz's (1960) four functions: the adjustive function (one "develops favorable attitudes toward the objects . . . associated with satisfactions of . . . needs" [p. 171]) and the knowledge function (providing "standards or frames of reference for understanding [the] world" [p. 175]).

The present conception of the object appraisal function is thus a synthesis of Smith, Bruner, and White's function of that name with Katz's adjustive and knowledge functions. The object appraisal function is of great importance in part because many of the objects in our environments are potentially *instrumental* to our adjustment. For the infant, the nipple that delivers milk may be the first instrumental object, and also the object of the first positive attitude. (The mother who delivers the nipple may become a positive attitude object only somewhat later.)

Quite apart from the instrumentality of objects, there is a noticeable pressure to "take sides" in many situations by favoring one object over others. This pressure to express preference is apparently strong enough so that happenstance spectators may find themselves preferring unknown Team A over unknown Team B when observing an athletic competition, and

---

[2]Katz used *utilitarian* and *instrumental* as alternative designations for the adjustive function.

drama audience members routinely find themselves liking some characters and disliking others. (Perhaps a significant attraction of drama and literature is the opportunity to practice forming attitudes that will be tested only vicariously, in terms of target characters' successes and failures as the drama unfolds.) Attitudes formed toward novel objects when one is a passive spectator obviously do not depend on pressures to act. Their formation suggests that the value of being ready with appraisals of objects is sufficient that we form attitudes even when their usefulness is not directly apparent (cf. Jones & Gerard's [1967] discussion of the value of an "unequivocal behavioral orientation"). Furthermore, we appear to be sufficiently skilled at producing attitudes toward novel objects that the process is mentally effortless.

Functions of Attitudes Versus Functions of Their Objects

It is useful to maintain a distinction between functions of the object and those of the attitude. The usefulness of this distinction is obvious only in the case of objects that are harmful. Such an object (for example, a stinging insect) has *negative* instrumental value, but the negative attitude toward the object has *positive* instrumental value (protecting the person from getting stung). It is tempting to use the *instrumental* or *utilitarian* label for this major function of attitudes, as suggested by Katz (1960). However, these labels are too easily confused with the object's instrumental or utilitarian function, a problem avoided by using instead Smith, Bruner, & White's *object appraisal* label.

Appraisal of the Self

As already noted, the object appraisal function encompasses three of the total of seven functions that were named in Smith, Bruner, and White's (1956) and Katz's (1960) analyses of attitude functions (Smith et al.'s object appraisal function and Katz's adjustment and knowledge functions). The remaining four functions can also be interpreted in terms of object appraisal in that they depend on the importance of the appraisal of a single mental object, the self (cf. discussions of the self as an attitude object by Greenwald & Pratkanis, 1984; Rosenberg, 1965; Sherif & Cantril, 1947). Katz's *ego-defensive* function ("Many of our attitudes have the function of defending our self-image") and Smith, Bruner, and White's similarly conceived *externalization* function directly acknowledge the importance of the self as an object of appraisal. The remaining two functions, Smith, Bruner, and White's *social adjustment* function and Katz's *value-expressive* function can be interpreted as reflecting strategies for establishing or maintaining a favorable attitude toward the self.

Three Facets of the Self

In a recent analysis, Greenwald and Breckler (1985; see also Breckler & Greenwald, 1986; Greenwald, 1982) identified three classes of strategies for establishing and maintaining self-esteem, which they labeled *ego tasks* of public, private, and collective facets of the self. The public self's strategy is to establish self-worth by earning favorable evaluations from important others (a public audience); the private self achieves self-worth by meeting or exceeding internalized evaluative standards (the approval of an internal, private audience); and the collective self establishes self-worth by seeking to attain the goals of reference groups (a collective audience). Attitudes toward objects other than the self readily participate in these strategies for establishing and maintaining self regard.

When the *public facet* is emphasized, the person should display attitudes that are agreeable to significant others; these attitudes can be instrumental in earning the approval of significant others and, via this public-self strategy, self-regard. This strategy of the public self corresponds to Smith, Bruner, and White's *social adjustment* function ("[O]ne will more readily and forthrightly express acceptable attitudes while inhibiting or modulating the expression of less approved ones" [pp. 41–42]).

The *private facet* of the self earns self-regard by meeting or exceeding internalized criteria of success. Consistency within one's repertory of object appraisals is such a criterion, and consistency-maintenance is a private-self strategy. By this analysis, Katz's (1960) *value-expressive* function ("the individual derives satisfactions from expressing attitudes appropriate to his personal values" [p. 170]) is a manifestation of the private facet of the self.

The *collective facet* of the self establishes self-worth by helping to achieve the goals of important reference groups (family, church, profession, etc.). An obvious strategy toward that end is to value objects that are identified with one's reference groups. Attitudes that are shaped by this strategy may be said to serve a *group solidarity* or *social identification* function. (This last is not one that appears in the Smith, Bruner, and White or Katz lists; in chap. 12 in this volume, however, Shavitt describes such a social identification function.)

Self-appraisal, Attitude Functions, and Social Influence Processes

Insko (1967) rightly identified Kelman's (1961) analysis of the influence processes of compliance, internalization, and identification as an original analysis of attitude functions. The Greenwald-Breckler three-strategy ego-task analysis converges with Kelman's analysis. As described by Kelman, *compliance* is yielding to influence in the presence of powerful others, which corresponds to the public self's strategy for earning approval; *internalization* is the acceptance of influence that is consistent with established values, corresponding to the private self's cognitive consistency strategy; and *identification,* the acceptance of influence that comes from admired others, corresponds to the collective self's strategy of adopting reference-group attitudes.

WHY ATTITUDES ARE IMPORTANT

Chapter 1 raised the question of the attitude concept's importance in social psychology, and stated a criterion for establishing that attitudes are important. There must be some important social behaviors that cannot be explained without appealing to attitudes. It remains to determine whether the present treatment of attitude structure and function has provided a basis for making the importance of attitudes compellingly apparent.

Summary

The preliminary analysis given in Chapter 1 identified three correctible sources of interference with many previous attempts to describe relationships of attitudes to social behavior. These are:

1. *The attitude object may be inappropriately identified.* Studies of behavior directed at objects (such as a specific person) have often attempted to predict the object-directed behavior from measures of attitude toward just one of several categories into which the object falls (e.g., a racial group). This problem is related to one described in previous analyses as a difference between attitude and behavior measures in their *level of specificity* (e.g., Fishbein & Ajzen, 1975).

2. *Behavior may be under the control of attitudes toward objects other than that on which the research is focused.* Attitude objects can be arrayed in a hierarchy of importance, with the self and persons on whom one is dependent often being at or near the top. In a research setting that focuses on attitude and behavior toward an unimportant object, the attempt to demonstrate attitude-behavior relations is likely to be undermined by the relevance of some more important object. As an example, the subject may find it more important to act on the self-attitude (e.g., by doing what would earn the experimenter's approval) than to act on the attitude toward some less important object that is the ostensible focus of study.

3. *The conception of the attitude-behavior relation is intrinsically confused by the widely advocated three-component definition of attitude.* When the three-component definition is used, a set of data that includes measures of attitude and behavior can be interpreted interchangeably as assessing (a) the attitude-behavior relationship, (b) relations of the be-

havioral (conative) attitude component to other attitude components, or (c) the relation between behavior and the conative attitude component. Such theoretical ambiguity undermines the achievement of consensus on conceptual analysis.

The present chapter sought to overcome these recurrent difficulties through its formulations of attitude structure and function. Attitude was defined as the association of a mental representation (i.e., an object, category, proposition, or schema) with affect, and attitude function was analyzed in terms of a single major function, object appraisal (a synthesis of Smith, Bruner, & White's [1956] function of that name and Katz's [1960] adjustive and knowledge functions). The implications of this analysis can be summarized as a set of three propositions that specify conditions under which attitudes play a powerful role in determining social behavior.

1. *Attitude toward the self (self-esteem) is a powerful determinant of social behavior.* The self is for many people the most important attitude object. Behavior that is interpreted in terms of evaluation apprehension and impression management is esteem-related, and self-esteem has sometimes been credited as the effective basis for the broad range of phenomena studied in investigations of cognitive dissonance (see Aronson, 1969; Greenwald & Ronis, 1978). Additionally, the powerful phenomena of attraction to similar others (Byrne, 1969) or repulsion from dissimilar others (Rosenbaum, 1986) can be understood in terms of the self-esteem implications of these responses.

2. *Attitude is a powerful determinant of evaluative responses to the source and content of influence attempts.* The person with a favorable attitude toward some mental object can be counted on to respond favorably to statements that place that object in a favorable light, or to oppose communications that evaluate the object negatively. The sources of such communications will be evaluated in correspondingly positive or negative fashion.

3. *Attitude is a powerful determinant of behavior in relation to novel (ordinary) objects with which the person has had direct experience.* Fazio and Zanna (1981) demonstrated that direct experience increases the strength of prediction of behavior from measures of attitude toward an object. As noted in discussing the object appraisal function, people are adept at rapidly forming attitudes toward unfamiliar objects. However, it is rare for attitude researchers to confront subjects with novel objects. (The subject in the typical attitude investigation inhabits a largely abstract world.) Consequently, the rapid development and attachment of attitudes to novel (ordinary) objects may be the most understudied aspect of attitudes.

Attitude Theory: Past, Present, and Future

Twenty years ago, there was a broad acceptance of a definition of attitude that was stated in terms of the venerable partition of mental activity into affection, conation, and cognition. Presently, this three-component definition of attitude is being abandoned. Twenty years ago, attitude theory was strongly dominated by cognitive consistency principles that were associated with the concepts of balance, congruity, and dissonance. Presently, the influence of consistency theories has been replaced with analyses of the role of the self in cognition and behavior. Twenty years ago, it was regarded as evident that attitude was social psychology's most important theoretical construct. Presently, the importance of attitudes is questioned.

These observations could suggest that the attitude construct is in its twilight. However, a decidedly optimistic view of the attitude construct comes from considering its position in the evolution of psychological theory of motivation. In the behaviorist and learning theory years of psychology (from the 1920s to the 1960s), theories of human motivation focused on the role of *physical stimuli* (such as electric shock, sexual contact, hunger contractions, intracranial electrical stimulation, and food taste) in directing and energizing behavior. During those same years, social psychologists were gradually evolving the construct of attitude as a conception of motivation in relation to *mental objects*.

The physical stimuli studied by learning-behavior theorists correspond to the lowest (feature) level of a representational system such as the five-level system (LOR_{h5}) used in the present analysis. In contrast, the motivational functioning of attitudes depends on the representational ability needed to cognize mental objects and to comprehend such objects' instrumentality in achieving desired goals. Attitude is thus the central theoretical construct for describing the motivational significance of mental objects.

REFERENCES

Aronson, E. (1968). Dissonance theory: Progress and problems. In R. P. Abelson, E. Aronson, W. J. McGuire, T. M. Newcomb, M. J. Rosenberg, & P. H. Tannebaum (Eds.), *Theories of cognitive consistency: A sourcebook* (pp. 5–27). Chicago: Rand McNally.

Aronson, E. (1969). The theory of cognitive dissonance: A current perspective. In L. Berkowitz (Ed.), *Advances in experimental social psychology* (Vol. 4, pp. 1–34). New York: Academic Press.

Breckler, S. J. (1984). Empirical validation of affect, behavior, and cognition as distinct components of attitude. *Journal of Personality and Social Psychology, 47,* 1191–1205.

Breckler, S. J., & Greenwald, A. G. (1986). Motivational facets of the self. In R. M. Sorrentino & E. T. Higgins (Eds.), *Handbook of motivation and cognition* (pp. 145–164). New York: Guilford Press.

Byrne, D. (1969). Attitudes and attraction. In L. Berkowitz (Ed.), *Advances in experimental social psychology* (Vol. 4, pp. 36–89). New York: Academic Press.

Fazio, R. H., & Zanna, M. P. (1981). Direct experience and attitude-behavior consistency. In L. Berkowitz (Ed.), *Advances in experimental social psychology* (Vol. 14, pp. 161–202). New York: Academic Press.

Fishbein, M., & Ajzen, I. (1975). *Belief, attitude, intention and behavior: An introduction to theory and research.* Reading, MA: Addison-Wesley.

Freud, S. (1953). *The interpretation of dreams.* In Standard Edition (Vols. 4–5). London: Hogarth. (Original work published 1900).

Gollob, H. F. (1974). The subject-verb-object approach to social cognition. *Psychological Review, 81,* 286–321.

Greenwald, A. G. (1982). Ego-task analysis: In A. H. Hastorf & A. M. Isen (Eds.), *Cognitive social psychology* (pp. 109–147). New York: Elsevier/North Holland.

Greenwald, A. G. (1987). *Levels of representation.* Manuscript submitted for publication.

Greenwald, A. G., & Breckler, S. J. (1985). To whom is the self presented? In B. R. Schlenker (Ed.), *The self and social life* (pp. 126–145). New York: McGraw-Hill.

Greenwald, A. G., & Pratkanis, A. R. (1984). The self. In R. S. Wyer & T. K. Srull (Eds.), *Handbook of social cognition* (Vol. 3, pp. 129–178). Hillsdale, NJ: Lawrence Erlbaum Associates.

Greenwald, A. G., & Ronis, D. L. (1978). Twenty years of cognitive dissonance: Case study of the evolution of a theory. *Psychological Review, 85,* 53–57.

Insko, C. A. (1967). *Theories of attitude and attitude change.* New York: Appleton-Century-Crofts.

Insko, C. A. (1981). Balance theory and phenomenology. In R. E. Petty, T. M. Ostrom, & T. C. Brock (Eds.), *Cognitive responses in persuasion* (pp. 309–338). Hillsdale, NJ: Lawrence Erlbaum Associates.

Jones, E. E., & Gerard, H. B. (1967). *Foundations of social psychology.* New York: Wiley.

Katz, D. (1960). The functional approach to the study of attitudes. *Public Opinion Quarterly, 24,* 163–204.

Kelman, H. C. (1961). Processes of opinion change. *Public Opinion Quarterly, 25,* 57–78.

LaPiere, R. T. (1934). Attitudes versus actions. *Social Forces, 13,* 230–237.

Miller, N. E. (1951). Learnable drives and rewards. In S. S. Stevens (Ed.), *Handbook of Experimental Psychology* (pp. 435–472). New York: Wiley.

Osgood, C. E., & Tannenbaum, P. H. (1955). The principle of congruity in the prediction of attitude change. *Psychological Review, 62,* 42–55.

Pavlov, I. P. (1955). *Selected works* (S. Belsky, Trans.; J. Gibbons, Ed.). Moscow: Foreign Languages Publishing House.

Rosenbaum, M. E. (1986). The repulsion hypothesis: On the nondevelopment of relationships. *Journal of Personality and Social Psychology, 51,* 1156–1166.

Rosenberg, M. (1965). *Society and the adolescent self-image.* Princeton, NJ: Princeton University Press.

Sherif, M., & Cantril, H. (1947). *The psychology of ego-involvements.* New York: Wiley.

Smith, M. B., Bruner, J. S., & White, R. W. (1956). *Opinions and personality.* New York: Wiley.

Staats, A. W. (1968). Social behaviorism and human motivation: Principles of the attitude-reinforcer-discriminative system. In A. G. Greenwald, T. C. Brock, & T. M. Ostrom (Eds.), *Psychological foundations of attitudes* (pp. 33–66). New York: Academic Press.

Thurstone, L. L. (1931). The measurement of social attitudes. *Journal of Abnormal and Social Psychology, 26,* 249–269.

Vallacher, R. R., & Wegner, D. M. (1985). *A theory of action identification.* Hillsdale, NJ: Lawrence Erlbaum Associates.

Vallacher, R. R., & Wegner, D. M. (1987). What do people think they're doing? Action identification and human behavior. *Psychological Review, 94,* 3–15.

Wyer, R. S., Jr. (1974). *Cognitive organization and change: An information processing approach.* Hillsdale, NJ: Lawrence Erlbaum Associates.

Author Index

Freud, S., 431*n*, *440*
Freund, T., 328, *336*. 384, 387, 396, 397, *404, 405*
Frick, F., 77, *95*
Fridlund, A. J., 291, 301, *307,* 412, *424*
Friesen, W. V., 284, 301, 302, *306,* 411, 412, *424*
Froming, W. J., 190, 191, 204, *208, 209*
Funk, S., 44, *63*

G

Gaertner, S. L., 181, 184,196, 198, 199, 200, 204, *209*
Galanis, C. M. B., 82, *94*
Galanter, E. 51, *66*
Gallant, J. L., 142, 144, *151*
Gallup, G. H., 80, *94*
Gallup Poll, 377, *379*
Gamble, E., 88, *96*
Ganellin, R. J., 190, 191, *208*
Gazzaniga, M. S., 299, *307*
Geen, T. R., 294, *307*
Gehring, W. J., 276, 283*n, 306*
General Social Surveys, 377, *379*
Gentner, D., 51, 60, *63*
Gentry, W. D., 234, *237*
Gerard, H. B., 435, *440*
Gibbs, B. L., 221, *239*
Gibson, J. J., 322*n, 336*
Gilson, C., 40, *63*
Glass, D. C., 199, 200, *210*
Goethals, G. R., 79, *94*
Goffman, E., 51, *63*
Goldberg, L., 45, *69*
Goldberg, P. A., 91, *94*
Goldman, R., 224, *238,* 328, *336*
Goldwater, B. C., 282, *307*
Gollob, H. F., 39, *63, 67,* 431*n, 440*
Goodman, C. C., 385, *403*
Gordon, J. R., 234, 235, *238*
Gordon, P. C., 52, *64*
Gordon, R. L., 77, *94*
Gottesdiener, M., 91, *94*
Graber, D., 50, *63*
Graham, T. W., 377, *379*
Granberg, D., 49, *63,* 78, 80, 81, *94*
Gratton, G., 276, 283*n,* 299, *306*
Greaves, G., 82, *94*
Greeley, A. M., 181, 210, *212*
Green, B. F., 242, *271*
Green, D. E., 219, 220, *237*
Green, L. W., 227, *237*
Greene, D., 78, *97,* 374, *380*
Greenslade, L., 40, *67*

Greenwald, A. G., 3, 6, 7, *9,* 24, 25, *34,* 54, *67,* 78, 82, 83, 88, *94,* 192, 193, *210,* 420, *424,* 430, 435, 436, 438, *439, 440*
Griffitt, W., 103, *125*
Gross, P., 82, *93*
Grube, J. W., 46, *62*
Gustafson, L., 88, *94*
Guttman, L., 18, 20, *34,* 250, *271*
Guyton, A. C., 286*n, 307*

H

Hager, J. C., 412, *424*
Hagner, P. R., 103, 105, *126, 127*
Halcomb, C. G., 222, *237*
Hamilton, D. L., 103, *125*
Hammond, K. B., 79, *94,* 416, *425*
Han, S. P., 325, *332*
Hannum, K., 144, *151*
Harary, F., 112, *125, 126*
Hardee, B. B., 191, 191*n,* 198, *211*
Harding, J., 185, *210*
Harnish, R., 317, 327, *335,* 347, 349, 350, *357*
Harrison, A. A., 222, 229, *237*
Hartman, H., 227, *236*
Hartman, K. A., 60, *65*
Harvey, O. J., 44, *63,* 159, *177*
Hass, R. G., 43, *64,* 199, *210*
Hastie, R., 44, 51, 54, *64, 67,* 91, *93, 94,* 361, *379*
Hastorf, A. H., 76, *94*
Hatfield, E., 77, *94*
Hays, W. L., 414, *425*
Healy, A. F., 40, *64*
Heider, F., 40, *64,* 75, *94,* 99, 101, 107, 109, 111, *126,* 339, *358*
Heise, D. R., 122, *126*
Helmholtz, H. L. F. von, 51, *64*
Henninger, M., 47, *64*
Herek, G. M., 313, 313*n,* 316, 317, 324, 326, 335, *336,* 351, 358, 361, 373, *379,* 383, *404*
Herman, C. P., 43, *62,* 343, *359*
Herr, P. M., 108, *126,* 160, 161, 162, 171, *177,* 192, *209*
Herzlich, C., 60, *64*
Hess, E. H., 282, *307*
Hiebel, G., 281, *304*
Higgins, E. T., 161, *177,* 189, 190, 194, *210,* 343, *359,* 401, *404*
Hilgard, E. R., 40, *64,* 242, *271,* 408, *425*
Hill, R. J., 241, 250, *271*
Himmelfarb, S., 311, *335*
Hinckley, E. D., 20, *35*
Hintzman, D. L., 52, *64*

Subject Index

representation of, 415–16
research on
    characteristics of, 71
    implications for, 433–34
    precautions in, 135n
    summary of, 422
schematic conception of, 278
schematic function of, 84–89
self-esteem maintenance function of, 313
single expression of, 166–67
social cognition and, 30–32
social identity function of, 312–13, 313n
specifying a property of, 21–24
strength variables of, 73
structural concerns of, 21–22
structural view of, 230–31
structure of, 241–47
syllogistic reasoning and, 77
three-component definition of, 6–7
tripartite model of, 277–300
    reasons for questioning of, 279–84
    schematic conception of , 278
utilitarian function of, 312
    among habitual behaviors, 220–22
value-expressive function of, 312–13,
    320
verbal expressions of, 303
versus behaviors, 244–45
voting behavior and, 168
Attitude-behavior
approaches to, 214–15
consistency, measurement of, 214
correlations, 5
process, 170
structure, need for, 387–98
    attitude accessibility as mediator, 393–
        95
    discussion on, 396–98
    gender attitudes-discrimination rela-
        tion, 388–89
    norm accessibility as mediator, 393–95
    racial stereotypes-discrimination rela-
        tion, 387
    social attitudes-judgment relation, 389–
        93
relationship, 419–20
    affective-cognitive consistency and,
        261–63
    affective-conative consistency and,
        263–65
    amount of information and, 258
    conclusions on, 260–61, 267–69
    direct experience and, 258–59
    involvement and, 264
    reflection and, 259–60
    self-perception and, 264–65
    summary on, 267–69
Attitude Functions Inventory (AFI), 317

Attitude-guided information processing, 3
Attitude-nonattitude continuum, 159–61
Attitude object(s)
    conception of, 5
    examples of, 432t
    identification of, 4
    multiple, 4–5
    variations of, 322–26
Attitude structure, 37–61, 417–18
    attributes × evaluation models of, 41–42
    basal-peripheral models of, 43
    and behavior, 241–69
    behavioral approach to, 73–74
    between-component, 261
    bipolar, 84–85
    cognitive, 258
    cognitive-affective-conative models of,
        40–41
    cognitive differentiation in, 257
    cognitive approach to, 74–75
    conceptualizations of, 72–75
    conclusion on, 204–07
    definitional approach to, 72
    dimensional models of, 43–44
    expectancy-value approach to, 74
    and function, 275–304
    functions of, 91
    indications for future work on, 57–61
    motivation in, 429–33
    multicomponent view of, 242–44
    in political beliefs systems, 129–48
    and prediction of behavior, 253–67
    representation in, 429–33
    serial sufficing-selections models of, 42–
        43
    sociocognitive model of, 89–92
    subjects-on-dimensions models of, 39
    subject-verb-object models of, 39–40
    tripartite model of, 73
    unipolar, 86–89
    within-component, 256–57
Attitude system(s)
    action system and, 54–56
    informational system and, 52–54
    miniature, 51
    multiple topics projected on multiple di-
        mensions, 49–51
    multiple topics projected on single di-
        mension, 45–47
    needed work on structure of, 59–60
    and other systems, 60–61
    in relation to other systems within, 51–
        57
    single topics projected on multiple di-
        mensions, 47–49
    structure of, 44–51
Attitude theory(ies), 24, 439
    measurement and, 11–16